# Enterprise Information Systems and Implementing IT Infrastructures:
## Challenges and Issues

S. Parthasarathy
*Thiagarajar College of Engineering, India*

**BUSINESS SCIENCE REFERENCE**

Hershey · New York

| | |
|---|---|
| Director of Editorial Content: | Kristin Klinger |
| Director of Book Publications: | Julia Mosemann |
| Acquisitions Editor: | Lindsay Johnson |
| Development Editor: | Elizabeth Arder |
| Typesetter: | Greg Snader |
| Production Editor: | Jamie Snavely |
| Cover Design: | Lisa Tosheff |
| Printed at: | Yurchak Printing Inc. |

Published in the United States of America by
Business Science Reference (an imprint of IGI Global)
701 E. Chocolate Avenue
Hershey PA 17033
Tel: 717-533-8845
Fax: 717-533-8661
E-mail: cust@igi-global.com
Web site: http://www.igi-global.com/reference

Copyright © 2010 by IGI Global. All rights reserved. No part of this publication may be reproduced, stored or distributed in any form or by any means, electronic or mechanical, including photocopying, without written permission from the publisher.

Product or company names used in this set are for identification purposes only. Inclusion of the names of the products or companies does not indicate a claim of ownership by IGI Global of the trademark or registered trademark.

Library of Congress Cataloging-in-Publication Data

Enterprise information systems and implementing IT infrastructures : challenges and issues / S. Parthasarathy, editor.
     p. cm.
  Includes bibliographical references and index.
  Summary: "This book aims at identifying potential research problems and issues in the EIS such as Enterprise Resource Planning (ERP), Supply Chain Management (SCM), and Customer Relationship Management (CRM)"--Provided by publisher.
  ISBN 978-1-61520-625-4 (hbk.) -- ISBN 978-1-61520-626-1 (ebook)  1. Management information systems. 2. Information technology--Management. 3. Business logistics--Data processing. I. Parthasarathy, S., 1979-
  T58.6.E5785 2010
  658.4'038011--dc22
                                        2009036872

British Cataloguing in Publication Data
A Cataloguing in Publication record for this book is available from the British Library.

All work contributed to this book is new, previously-unpublished material. The views expressed in this book are those of the authors, but not necessarily of the publisher.

# Editorial Advisory Board

Vicky Manthou, *University of Macedonia, Greece*
Rogerio Atem De Carvalho, *Instituto Federal Fluminense, Brazil*
Veena Bansal, *Indian Institute of Technology Kanpur, India*
B. Ramdoss, *National Institute of Technology (NIT), India*
V. Mohan, *Thiagarajar College of Engineering, India*
G. Arivarignan, *Madurai Kamaraj University, India*
S. P. Natchiappan, *Thiagarajar College of Engineering, India*
N. Anbazhagan, *Alagappa University, India*
Muthu Ramachandran, *Leeds Metropolitan University, UK*
Prabin Panigrahi, *Indian Institute of Management (IIM), India*
K. Vivekanandan, *Pondicherry Engineering College, India*

# List of Reviewers

Rogerio Atem De Carvalho, *Instituto Federal Fluminense, Brazil*
Veena Bansal, *Indian Institute of Technology Kanpur, India*
B. Ramdoss, *National Institute of Technology (NIT), India*
S. P. Natchiappan, *Thiagarajar College of Engineering, India*
N. Anbazhagan, *Alagappa University, India*
Muthu Ramachandran, *Leeds Metropolitan University, UK*
Prabin Panigrahi, *Indian Institute of Management (IIM), India*
B. S. Girish, *National Institute of Technology (NIT), India*
Maya Daneva, *University of Twente, Netherlands*
Yadavalli, *University of Pretoria, South Africa*
K. Ganesh, *Tata Consultancy Services Limited, India*
Dragana Bečejski-Vujaklija, *University of Belgrade, Serbia*

# Table of Contents

### Section 1
### Challenges and Issues in Enterprise Information Systems

**Section 2**
**Supply Chain Management (SCM) System using**
**Information Technology (IT) and Mathematical Modeling**

# Detailed Table of Contents

## Section 1
## Challenges and Issues in Enterprise Information Systems

**Chapter 1**

*Maya Daneva, University of Twente, the Netherlands*

There is yet little knowledge about cross-organizational Enterprise Resource Planning (ERP) implementation projects when it comes to determining requirements and achieving alignment between IT and businesses. Consequently, the requirements engineering (RE) processes are often more expensive and less effective as they could be. In this chapter, we view a cross-organization ERP implementation as a coordination problem, and introduce a coordination complexity model based on an organization's level of participation in a business network. We show how the external coordination characteristics of an organization can be mapped to ERP-supported mechanisms for cross-organizational coordination. To incorporate this activity in the state-of-the-art ERP RE processes, we propose a set of good practices that counterpart certain coordination issues at different complexity levels. Our paper is based on empirical data gathered from secondary sources. We also carried out an early validation assessment based on an online focus group composed of ERP solution architects.

**Chapter 2**

*Rogério Atem de Carvalho, Fluminense Federal Institute, Brazil*
*Björn Johansson, Copenhagen Business School, Denmark*
*Rodrigo Soares Manhães, State University of North Fluminense, Brazil*

Customization of ERP systems is a complex task, and great part of this complexity is directly related to requirements management. In this context, a well-known problem is the misfit between the ERP functionalities and the business requirements. This problem comprises communication bottlenecks and difficulties on responding to changes. The proposals for minimizing these misfits are mostly focused on traditional, heavyweight waterfall-like approaches for software development. On the other side, the last decade has witnessed the rise and growth of agile methods, which have both close communication and fast response to changes among their main values. This chapter maps some of the main agile practices to ERP customization processes, using, where applicable, practices from a real-world ERP project. Moreover, some limitations on the agile approach to ERP customization are presented and discussed.

*Muthu Ramachandran, Leeds Metropolitan University, UK*
*S. Parthasarathy, Thiagarajar College of Engineering, India*

The demand for ERP systems grows rapidly along with complexity and integration of enterprise systems. ERP is an enterprise oriented information system for resource planning which integrates various departments and systems. This chapter identifies a set of key characteristics of ERP system and then map onto a software component model which has been customised for ERP characteristics. A component based software process model for ERP projects is proposed and its significance during the ERP implementation is indicated.

*S. Parthasarathy, Thiagarajar College of Engineering, India*

Business information system is an area of the greatest significance in any business enterprise today. Enterprise Resource Planning (ERP) projects are a growing segment of this vital area. Software engineering metrics are units of measurement used to characterize the software engineering products and processes. The research about the software process has acquired great importance in the last few years due to the growing interest of software companies in the improvement of their quality. Enterprise Resource Planning (ERP) projects are very complex products, and this fact is directly linked to their development and maintenance. One of the major reasons found in the literature for the failure of ERP projects is the poor management of software processes. In this chapter, we propose a Software Metrics Plan (SMP) containing different software metrics to manage software processes during ERP implementation. Two hypotheses have been formulated and tested using statistical techniques to validate the SMP. The statistical analysis of the collected data from an ERP project supports the two hypotheses, leading to the conclusion that the software metrics are momentous in ERP projects.

*Sanjay Kumar, MDI Gurgaon, India*
*Anurag Keshan, IBM, India*
*Souvik Mazumdar, TISS, India*

The case describes an ERP implementation in a steel major in India. The various factors which impact ERP implementation as identified in literature are discussed. The implementation of ERP systems in the organization has been described at each stage of the implementation. The activities at each stage and also the issues arising at each stage of the implementation have been discussed. The benefits identified by the managers have also been included.

**Chapter 6**

*Manoj Jha, SAP Consultant, India*
*Sanjay Kumar, MDI Gurgaon, India*

The model discusses the implementation of ERP systems. The article discusses the process based implementation approach and also the critical success factors approach for the implementation. A gap identified in literature is that critical success factors and ERP implementation has not been studied from the viewpoint of other stakeholders. This chapter tries to address this gap by proposing a seven stage model of ERP implementation and adoption from the viewpoint of the ERP implementation consultant. The model also addresses subsequent stages such a data exploitation stage where organizations learn to use data for decision making and process management. The model also addresses the subsequent stages of extension of ERP to partners like suppliers and dealers, and the innovation stage when the organizations starts to experiment with newer solutions based on ERP systems.

**Chapter 7**

*Lidia Ogiela, AGH University of Science and Technology, Poland*
*Ryszard Tadeusiewicz, AGH University of Science and Technology, Poland*
*Marek R. Ogiela, AGH University of Science and Technology, Poland*

This publication presents cognitive systems designed for analyzing economic data. Such systems have been created as the next step in the development of classical DSS systems (Decision Support Systems), which are currently the most widespread tools providing computer support for economic decision-making. The increasing complexity of decision-making processes in business combined with increasing demands that managers put on IT tools supporting management cause DSS systems to evolve into intelligent information systems. This publication defines a new category of systems - UBMSS (Understanding Based Management Support Systems) which conduct in-depth analyses of data using on an apparatus for linguistic and meaning-based interpretation and reasoning. This type of interpretation and reasoning is inherent in the human way of perceiving the world. This is why the authors of this publication have striven to perfect the scope and depth of computer interpretation of economic information based on human processes of cognitive data analysis. As a result, they have created UBMSS systems for the automatic analysis and interpretation of economic data. The essence of the proposed approach to the cognitive analysis of economic data is the use of the apparatus for the linguistic description of data and for semantic analysis. This type of analysis is based on expectations generated automatically by a system which collects resources of expert knowledge, taking into account the information which can significantly characterize the analyzed data. In this publication, the processes of classical data description and analysis are extended to include cognitive processes as well as reasoning and forecasting mechanisms.

As a result of the analyses shown, we will present a new class of UBMSS cognitive economic information systems which automatically perform a semantic analysis of business data.

**Chapter 8**

*Juan Ignacio Guerrero Alonso, University of Seville, Spain*
*Carlos León de Mora, University of Seville, Spain*
*Félix Biscarri Triviño, University of Seville, Spain*
*Iñigo Monedero Goicoechea, University of Seville, Spain*
*Jesús Biscarri Triviño, University of Seville, Spain*
*Rocío Millán, University of Seville, Spain*

The increasing of the storage system capacity and the reduction of the access time has allowed the development of new technologies which have afforded solutions for the automatic treatment of great databases. In this paper a methodology to create Enterprise Information Systems which are capable of using all information available about customers is proposed. As example of utilization of this methodology, an Enterprise Information System for classification of customer problems is proposed. This EIS implements several technologies. Data Warehousing and Data Mining are two technologies which can analyze automatically corporative databases. Integration of these two technologies is proposed by the present work together with a rule based expert system to classify the utility consumption through the information stored in corporative databases.

**Chapter 9**

*M. Vignesh, The American College, India*

According to the Moore's law, the number of transistors per microprocessor will double in every two years. In no doubt, this exponential increase in the processing speeds would be flanked by the increasing amount of data that corporates contend on a daily basis. Hence all corporates are literally drowning in data. But definitely there exists a hiatus between the data storage and the information retrieval. One can ask an enigmatic question, how effectively a stored data can be utilised for the decision making in the long-term perspective. The answer is not yet arrived out. Hence the "Organizations are data rich, but information poor!". If capturing and storing the relevant data is a hectic task, then analyzing and translating this data into the actionable information is the other corner stone in any information systems of a concern. This gap can be bridged or overruled by the concept of business intelligence. Business Intelligence (BI) can be simply defined in terms of data –driven approach rather than information driven which includes methods as decision support systems, online analytical processing (OLAP), statistical analysis, query and reporting, forecasting which can be primarily done by data mining. BI along with customer relationship management (CRM) software forms the second tier of a firm's IT infrastructure. This chapter holds a bird's eye view of the usage of datawarehousing approaches for a systematic business intelligence approach and its varied applications in view of electronic customer relationship management.

## Chapter 10

*Petraq Papajorgji, Center for Applied Optimization, University of Florida, USA*
*Panos M. Pardalos, Center for Applied Optimization, University of Florida, USA*

This chapter aims to present a new modeling paradigm that promises to significantly increase the efficiency of developing enterprise information systems. Currently, the software industry faces considerable challenges as it tries to build larger, more complex, software systems with fewer resources. Although modern programming languages such as C++ and Java have in general improved the software development process, they have failed to significantly increase developer's productivity. Thus, developers are considering other paths to address this issue. One of the potential paths is designing, developing and deploying enterprise information systems using the Model Driven Architecture (MDA).MDA is a model-centric approach that allows for modeling the overall business of an enterprise and capturing requirements to developing, deploying, integrating, and managing different kinds of software components without considering any particular implementation technology. At the center of this approach are models; the software development process is driven by constructing models representing the software under development. Code that expresses the implementation of the model in a certain underlying technology is obtained as a result of model transformation. Thus, the intellectual investment spent in developing the business model of an enterprise is not jeopardized by the continuous changes of the implementation technologies. Currently there are two main approaches trying to implement MDA-based tools. One of the approaches is based on the Object Constraint Language and the other on Action Language. An example of designing, developing and deploying an application using this new modeling paradigm is presented. The MDA approach to software development is considered as the biggest shift since the move from Assembler to the first high level languages.

## Chapter 11

*Salem Al-Marri, Leeds Metropolitan University, UK*
*Muthu Ramachandran, Leeds Metropolitan University, UK*

Emergency needs occur naturally, manually (error and terror) and accidentally in addition to worldwide death by hunger and poverty. These situations can arise anytime, anyplace and thus globally, people are in need of any emergency help by every second. This paper proposes a model for Disaster Classification system of Natural Disasters and Catastrophic Failures activity. This model also proposes the use of emerging technologies such as ubiquitous computing and wireless communications systems that are used by people in recent years to communicate in event of any disaster. The use of emerging technologies also depends on the role of the people and their culture and global support. Furthermore, the paper will propose the deployment of Global Information Systems (GIS) as an aid to emergency management by identifying the related areas pertaining to disaster and thus to help the personnel involved to analyze disasters more accurately by developing a tool. The aim of this tool is to determine potential and affected disaster areas using the GIS technology and to provide support for decision makers during emergencies. Due to the significant development of computerization, networking and mobile systems, reporting a disaster, nowadays, is only a matter of seconds whereas, in the past it would take days or even weeks for the news to reach the people.

The rapidly changing nature of business environments requires organizations to be more flexible to gain competitive advantages. Organizations are turning into a new generation of software called Enterprise Application Integration (EAI) to fully integrate business processes. It is an activity that integrates and harmonizes an enterprise's isolated business applications, processes and functions. EAI is a complex task involving both technological and business challenges. Developing quality EAI projects is quite a big challenge. Even though success of EAI projects depends on so many parameters, 'testing' is the most significant phase that can ensure the quality as well as the success of EAI projects. Modern enterprises heavily rely on integrations linking systems and business processes using real time data. Components integrated without testing in EAI systems may affect the enterprise system as a whole. This in turn may result in revenue loss and status degradation in the competitive edge. This chapter focuses on the testing aspects related to EAI applications. Especially the significance of testing for various types of "Integrations" is discussed in detail.

In this chapter we focus on the iterative process that occurs within the implementation phase of an ERP which we depict as a series of learning cycles: managers make decisions, identify mistakes, and accumulate experience (lessons learned). We examine these "learning cycles" through the lens of absorptive capacity and we use a case study and a qualitative perspective. We identify a number of tradeoffs that represent the learning paths of Alpha Co. and we find that such learning process is path dependent, organizational memory plays a fundamental role, and double loop cycles contribute in the development of absorptive capacity seen as a dynamic capability.

Enterprise Information Systems are the most integrated information systems that cut across various organizations as well as various functional areas. Small and medium enterprises, competitor's behavior, business partner requirement are the identified and established dimensions that affect these systems. Further it has been observed that such enterprise wide software systems prove to be a failure either in the design or its implementation. A number of reasons contribute in the success or failure of such systems. Enterprise information systems inherently present unique risks due to tightly linked interdependencies of business processes, relational databases, and process reengineering, etc. Knowledge of such risks is important in design of system and program management as they contribute to success of overall system. In this chapter an attempt has been made to study the design and implementation risks factors for ERP systems in large scale manufacturing organizations. Based on the model used to study ERP risks and thus the findings, various recommendations have been put forward to suggest a strategy so as to mitigate and manage such risks.

## Section 2
### Supply Chain Management (SCM) System using Information Technology (IT) and Mathematical Modeling

*S.P. Anbuudayasankar, Amrita School of Engineering, India*
*K. Ganesh, Global Business Services – Global Delivery, IBM India Private Limited, India*
*K.Mohandas, Amrita School of Engineering, India*
*Tzong-Ru Lee, National Chung Hsing University Taiwan, ROC*

This chapter presents the development of simulated annealing (SA) for a health care application which is modeled as Single Depot Vehicle routing problem called Mixed Vehicle Routing Problem with Backhauls (MVRPB), an extension of Vehicle Routing Problem with Backhauls (VRPB). This variant involves both delivery and pick-up customers and sequence of visiting the customers is mixed. The entire pick-up load should take back to depot. The latest rapid advancement of meta-heuristics has shown that it can be applied in practice if they are personified in packaged information technology (IT) solutions along with the combination of a supply chain management (SCM) application integrated with an enterprise resource planning (ERP) resulted to this decision support tool. This chapter provides empirical proof in sustain of the hypothesis, that a population extension of SA with supportive transitions leads to a major increase of efficiency and solution quality for MVRPB if and only if the globally optimal solution is located close to the center of all locally optimal solution.

*Subramanian Nachiappan, Thiagarajar College of Engineering, Madurai, India*
*Natarajan Jawahar, Thiagarajar College of Engineering Madurai, India*

Supply chain is a network of firms interacting in a linear fashion to produce, sell and deliver a product or service to a predetermined market segment. The soft issues of supply chain models can be dealt through proper information sharing, communication and coordination between the stages of supply chain. Vendor managed inventory is a proven concept for successful collaborative and cooperative agreements in supply chain. This chapter reviews some of the soft issues in two-echelon supply chain models and proposes a classification schema. This chapter surveys the theoretical background and application of vendor managed inventory systems based on environment, operational issues and solution approaches. Hence it is concluded that the framework presented in this chapter would aid supply chain managers and researchers to further look into the soft issues while modelling supply chain with information technology enabled vendor managed inventory systems.

This article presents a two commodity stochastic inventory system under continuous review. The maximum storage capacity for the -th item is fixed as    It is assumed that demand for the -th commodity is of unit size and demand time points form Poisson distribution with parameter    The reorder level is fixed as   for the -th commodity  and the ordering policy is to place order for  items for the -th commodity (i = 1, 2) when both the inventory levels are less than or equal to their respective reorder levels. The lead time is assumed to be exponential. The two commodities are assumed to be substitutable. That is, if the inventory level of one commodity reaches zero, then any demand for this commodity will be satisfied by the item of the other commodity. If no substitute is available, then this demand is backlogged up to a certain level ,  for the -th commodity. Whenever the inventory level reaches , , an order for  items is replenished instantaneously. For this model, the limiting probability distribution for the joint inventory levels is computed. Various operational characteristics and expression for long run total expected cost rate are derived.

Selection of service providers in the global supply chains of today has been recognized as having a very important effect on the competitiveness of the entire supply chain. It results in achieving high quality end results (products and/or services), at reasonable cost coupled with high customer satisfaction. This article discusses the use of Fuzzy Analytic Hierarchy Process (FAHP) to effectively manage the qualitative and quantitative decision factors which are involved in the selection of providers of 3PL services under Lead Logistics Provider (LLP) environments of today. Lead logistics providers (LLP) are increasingly being banked upon to integrate the best of 3PL service providers and allow for synchronized and optimized operations. In the asset free environments of today, many a times, the LLP uses the services of the 3PL and hence the issue of reliably choosing them assumes increasingly greater significance. The fuzzy-AHP has been adequately demonstrated in literature to be an effective tool which can be used to factor-in the fuzziness of data. Triangular Fuzzy Numbers (TFN) has been deployed to make over the linguistic comparisons of criteria, sub-criteria and the alternatives. The FAHP based model formulated in this paper is applied to a case study in the Indian context using data from three leading LSPs with significant operating leverages in the province of Uttrakhand (India). The proposed model can provide the guidelines and directions for the decision makers to effectively select their global service providers in the present day competitive logistics markets.

## Chapter 19

*Rajeshwar S. Kadadevaramath, Siddaganga Institute of Technology, India*
*Jason C.H. Chen, Gonzaga University, USA*
*Mohanasundaram K.M, Karpagam College of Engineering, India*

During the past decade, great studies have been made in the development of standardized tools for supply chain modeling and network optimization Network optimization is the most basic type of modeling that can be performed with tools which helps to identity optimum paths or flow of goods in supply chain network. In this case, the network is defined by the flow of finished goods from origin to destination. Network modeling becomes more complex as the dimensions and scope of the supply chain expand Uncertainties in the supply chain usually increase the variance of profit or cost to the company, increasing the likely hood of decreased profit i.e. increase in total supply chain cost. Demand uncertainty and constraints posed by the every echelon are important factors to be considered in the supply chain design operations. This paper specifically deals with the modeling and optimization of a three echelon supply chain network architecture using new Particle Swarm Optimization algorithm.

## Chapter 20

*Ashutosh Mohan, Banaras Hindu University (BHU), India*
*Shikha Lal, Banaras Hindu University (BHU), India*

Information and communication technology infrastructure has changed modern business practice. The ever-changing information and communication technology infrastructure of organizations' is opening new vista, which has not only bundles of opportunities to encash but also tremendous obstacles as survival threats. The concern about organizational competitiveness and development is closely linked to notions of the information sensitive society and global knowledge based economies. The business organizations under global knowledge economy can emerge and grow rapidly by formulating and adopting the innovative business practices. Information's impact is easily seen—it substitutes for inventory, speeds product design and delivery, drives process reengineering, and acts as a coordinating mechanism, helping different members of the supply chain work together effectively. While the potential of information sharing is widely promoted, relatively few companies have fully harnessed its capability to enhance competitive performance. The chapter tries to provide insight into how information and communication technology can be leveraged for supply chain value creation and make it possible to achieve synergy with customer relationship management.

The usage of Information Technology (IT) in organizations across the supply chain has become a determinant of competitive advantage for many corporations. This chapter focuses on the usage of IT tools for Supply Chain Management (SCM). It also highlights the contribution of IT in helping restructure the entire distribution set-up to achieve higher service levels, lower inventory, and lower supply chain costs. An overview and tangible benefits of the existing IT tools, which are widely deployed, is provided with focus on existing configuration considerations, available applications, and deployments in India. The role of existing communication technologies in making IT an enabler of SCM, is highlighted by addressing a range of different point and enterprise solutions in a variety of supply chain settings. Critical IT demonstrations and implementations in SCM are discussed. Fundamental changes have occurred in today's global economy. These changes alter the relationship that we have with our customers, our suppliers, our business partners, and our colleagues. Reflection on the evolving and emerging IT trends like software agents, RFID, web services, virtual supply chains, electronic commerce, and decision support systems, further highlights the importance of IT in the context of increasingly global competition. The rapid adoption of the Internet for communication with all stakeholders seems to reflect the potential of the new-age communication media. It has also been observed that several progressive Indian companies are extensively using emerging tools like virtual supply chains, web services, RFID, and electronic commerce to shore up their supply chain operations. However, adoption of tools like software agents and decision support systems for supply chain integration by Indian companies is limited.

Supply Chain Management (SCM) is the practice of coordinating the flow of goods, services, information and finances as they move from raw materials to parts supplier to manufacturer to wholesaler to retailer to consumer. Different supply chains have been designed for a variety of firms and this chapter discusses some issues in this regard. This chapter attempts to find why we require different supply chain for different companies. This chapter discusses the role of stochastic models in supply chian management system. This chapter also discusses other mathematical models for SCM.

flow and storage of goods, services, and related information from the point-of-origin to the point-of-consumption in order to meet customers' requirements. Supply Chain Management (SCM) is the practice of coordinating the flow of goods, services, information and finances as they move from raw materials to parts supplier to manufacturer to wholesaler to retailer to consumer. This chapter introduces the concept of Supply Chain Management System(SCMS). Two stochastic modelling problems are discussed in this chapter. Poisson demand process with (s,S) installation policy at retailer nodes are assumed to simplify the study . The system performance measures are computed with reference to specific cost structure. The total average annual variable cost is taken as optimization criterion. Numerical examples are provided to illustrate the problem.

# Foreword

Enterprise information systems (EIS) comprises of information systems such as enterprise resource planning (ERP), supply chain management (SCM), customer relationship management (CRM) and e-commerce. The ERP package aims to integrate all key business activities through improved relationships at all levels to achieve a competitive advantage. ERP systems can be considered as an information technology (IT) infrastructure to facilitate the flow of information between all business processes in an organization. SCM is the practice of coordinating the flow of goods, services, information and finances as they move from raw materials to parts supplier to manufacturer to wholesaler to retailer to consumer. The fundamental theory behind CRM is to identify profitable customers, attract and retain them, and maximize their useful life span and the profits from them by establishing and fostering good relationships with them.

The primary objective of this edited book is to provide comprehensive coverage and understanding of various enterprise information systems (EIS) such as ERP, SCM and CRM. Design, development and implementation issues of EIS have been discussed. These include organizational, technological and managerial issues of EIS. The secondary objective of this edited book is to expand the knowledge on EIS and in turn help researchers and practitioners to develop suitable strategies, tactics, and operational policies for EIS and for improving communication in organizations. I believe, that this book would enable the young research scholars to kick off their research in the EIS effortlessly and provide them the channels required to do research in the EIS meticulously to help the enterprises improve their performance through the successful implementation of an information system. Discussing the design and implementation issues of EIS from different perspectives will help the practitioners to get themselves adapted to the information system in a smooth way and reap its benefits. This book intends to be a forum for exchanging new ideas and developments in the field of EIS. It also acts as a medium of communication among EIS researchers and practitioners.

This edited book comprises of two sections namely '*Challenges and Issues in Enterprise Information Systems*' and '*Supply Chain Management (SCM) System using Information Technology (IT) and Mathematical Modeling*'. Section 1 consists of fourteen chapters and Section 2 consists of nine chapters. Section 1 addresses the software engineering approaches and methods for information systems. Specifically, requirements in cross-organizational ERP projects requirements management, agile software development for customizing ERPs, software metrics and processes for ERP projects, success stories and lessons learned from ERP projects, future of information systems, designing a CRM, designing test cases for enterprise application integration are very well discussed in this edited book. Section 2 deals with the application of mathematical modeling in SCM, designing an information technology enabled SCM system and applying fuzzy concepts to logistics.

Business information system is an area of greatest significance in any business enterprise today. This edited book "*Enterprise Information Systems and Implementing IT Infrastructures: Challenges and Is-*

*sues*" aims at identifying potential research problems and issues in the Enterprise Information Systems. The editor of this book has done an outstanding job by identifying the most demanding chapters for this book. I am confident that this book will definitely contribute to the information systems community and would be widely referred by the faculty members, researchers and practitioners in information systems across the globe.

*Dr. Angappa Gunasekaran*

**Dr. Angappa Gunasekaran** *is a Professor of Operations Management and the Chairperson of the Department of Decision and Information Sciences at the Charlton College of Business, University of Massachusetts Dartmouth (USA). He has a PhD in Industrial Engineering and Operations Research from the Indian Institute of Technology (Bombay). Dr. Gunasekaran has held academic positions at Brunel University (UK), Monash University (Australia), the University of Vaasa (Finland), the University of Madras (India) and the University of Toronto, Laval University, and Concordia University (Canada). He is teaching undergraduate and graduate courses in operations management and management science. Dr. Gunasekaran has received Thomas J. Higginson Award for Excellence in Teaching (2001-2002) within the Charlton College of Business. He has over 200 articles published/forthcoming in 40 different peer-reviewed journals. Dr. Gunasekaran is on the Editorial Board of over 20 peer-reviewed journals which include some prestigious journals such as Journal of Operations Management, International Journal of Production Economics, International Journal of Computer-Integrated Manufacturing, International Journal of Production Planning and Control, International Journal of Operations & Production Management, Technovation, and Computers in Industry: An International Journal. Dr. Gunasekaran is involved with several national and international collaborative projects that are funded by both private and government agencies. Dr. Gunasekaran has edited a couple of books that include Knowledge and Information Technology Management: Human and Social Perspectives, (Idea Group Publishing) and Agile Manufacturing: The 21st Century Competitive Strategy (Elsevier). Dr. Gunasekaran is the Editor of Benchmarking: An International Journal and the North-American Editor of the International Journal of Enterprise Network Management. He has edited special issues for a number of highly reputed journals. Dr. Gunasekaran is currently interested in researching benchmarking, agile manufacturing, management information systems, e-procurement, and competitiveness of SMEs, information technology/systems evaluation, performance measures and metrics in new economy, technology management, logistics, and supply chain management. He actively serves on several university committees. He is the Editor-In-Chief of several international journals in the areas of Operations Management and Information Systems. Dr. Gunasekaran is also the Director of Business Innovation Research Center (BIRC).*

# Preface

The success of an enterprise today is funded by its information system. Enterprise information systems (EIS) comprise of information systems such as enterprise resource planning (ERP), supply chain management (SCM) and customer relationship management (CRM). The information system of an enterprise is composed of both software and hardware, and information can be represented in both the human cognitive system and in the digital device system. Disruption of information systems even for a short period of time would cause big problems for business operations.

This edited book "Enterprise Information Systems and Implementing IT Infrastructures: Challenges and Issues" aims at identifying potential research problems and issues in the EIS such as enterprise resource planning (ERP), supply chain management (SCM), and customer relationship management (CRM). It seeks to guide the research scholars and members of faculty working in this area to get a quick glimpse of the current research issues in EIS and the channel to manage those issues. Most of the research works in EIS expresses concern over the managerial factors only and very few research works deal with the technical factors. This book addresses both the managerial and the technical factors.

This book consists of two sections. Section 01 deals with the challenges and issues in enterprise information systems. Section 02 deals with the supply chain management (SCM) system using information technology (IT) and mathematical modeling. An overview of the chapters is presented hereunder.

Chapter 1, "*Engineering the Coordination Requirements in Cross-Organizational ERP Projects: A Package of Good Practices*" by Maya Daneva considers a cross-organization ERP implementation as a coordination problem, and introduce a coordination complexity model based on an organization's level of participation in a business network. It also shows how the external coordination characteristics of an organization can be mapped to ERP-supported mechanisms for cross-organizational coordination. To incorporate this activity in the state-of-the-art ERP RE processes, we propose a set of good practices that counterpart certain coordination issues at different complexity levels. This chapter is based on empirical data gathered from secondary sources. An early validation assessment based on an online focus group composed of ERP solution architects has been carried out.

Chapter 2, "*Agile Software Development for Customizing ERPs*" by Rogério Atem de Carvalho, Björn Johansson, and Rodrigo Soares Manhães maps some of the main agile practices to ERP customization processes. Customization of ERP systems is a complex task, and great part of this complexity is directly related to requirements management. In this context, a well-known problem is the misfit between the ERP functionalities and the business requirements. This problem comprises communication bottlenecks and difficulties in responding to changes. Limitations on the agile approach to ERP customization have been discussed and well illustrated in this chapter.

Chapter 3, "*Software Components for ERP Applications*" by Muthu Ramachandran and S. Parthasarathy identifies a set of key characteristics of ERP system and then map onto a software component model which has been customised for ERP characteristics. A component based software process model for ERP projects is proposed and its significance during the ERP implementation is indicated.

Chapter 4, "*Application of Software Metrics in ERP Projects*" by S. Parthasarathy proposes a Software Metrics Plan (SMP) containing different software metrics to manage software processes during ERP implementation. Two hypotheses are formulated and tested using statistical techniques to validate the SMP. The statistical analysis of the collected data from an ERP project supports the two hypotheses, leading to the conclusion that software metrics are momentous in ERP projects. This chapter presents the literature to emphasize the fact that the failure of ERP projects is because of the poor management of software processes during ERP implementation.

Chapter 5, "*ERP Implementation in a Steel Major in India*" by Sanjay Kumar, Anurag Keshan, and Souvik Mazumdar presents a case study of an ERP implementation in a steel major in India. The implementation of ERP systems in the organization has been described at each stage of the implementation. The activities at each stage and also the issues arising at each stage of the implementation have been discussed. The benefits identified by the managers have also been highlighted.

Chapter 6, "*Implementation of ERP Systems: A Seven Stage Adoption Model*" by Manoj Jha and Sanjay Kumar gives us a new model for effective ERP implementation. This chapter proposes a seven stage model of ERP implementation and adoption from the viewpoint of the ERP implementation consultant. The model also addresses subsequent stages such a data exploitation stage where organizations learn to use data for decision making and process management. The model also addresses the subsequent stages of extension of ERP to partners like suppliers and dealers, and the innovation stage when the organizations starts to experiment with newer solutions based on ERP systems.

Chapter 7, "*Understanding Based Managing Support Systems: The Future of Information Systems*" by Lidia Ogiela, Ryszard Tadeusiewicz and Marek R. Ogiela presents cognitive systems designed for analyzing economic data. Such systems have been created as the next step in the development of classical DSS systems (Decision Support Systems), which are currently the most widespread tools providing computer support for economic decision-making. This chapter defines a new category of systems - UBMSS (Understanding Based Management Support Systems) which conduct in-depth analyses of data using on an apparatus for linguistic and meaning-based interpretation and reasoning. This type of interpretation and reasoning is inherent in the human way of perceiving the world. In this chapter, a new class of UBMSS cognitive economic information systems has been designed. This will automatically perform a semantic analysis of business data.

Chapter 8, "*EIS for Consumers Classification and Support Decision Making in a Power Utility Database*" by Juan Ignacio Guerrero Alonso, Carlos León de Mora, Félix Biscarri Triviño, Iñigo Monedero Goicoechea, Jesús Biscarri Triviño and Rocío Millán presents a new methodology to create Enterprise Information Systems which are capable of using the customers' information completely. As example of utilization of this methodology, an Enterprise Information System for classification of customer problems is proposed. This EIS implements several technologies. Data Warehousing and Data Mining are two technologies which can analyze automatically corporative databases. Integration of these two technologies is proposed by the present work together with a rule based expert system to classify the utility consumption through the information stored in corporative databases.

Chapter 9, "*Enhancing the Electronic Customer Relationship Management through Data Mining: A Business Intelligence Approach*" by M. Vignesh holds a bird's eye view of the usage of datawarehousing approaches for a systematic business intelligence approach and its varied applications in view of electronic customer relationship management. There exists a hiatus between the data storage and the information retrieval. If capturing and storing the relevant data is a hectic task, then analyzing and translating this data into the actionable information is the other corner stone in any information systems of a concern. This chapter attempts to bridge this gap by the concept of business intelligence.

Chapter 10, *"Towards a Model-Centric Approach for Developing Enterprise Information Systems"* by Petraq Papajorgji and Panos M. Pardalos aims to present a new modeling paradigm that promises to significantly increase the efficiency of developing enterprise information systems. Currently, the software industry faces considerable challenges as it tries to build larger, more complex, software systems with fewer resources. MDA is a model-centric approach that allows for modeling the overall business of an enterprise and capturing requirements to developing, deploying, integrating, and managing different kinds of software components without considering any particular implementation technology. Currently there are two main approaches trying to implement MDA-based tools. One of the approaches is based on the Object Constraint Language and the other on Action Language. An example of designing, developing and deploying an application using this new modeling paradigm is presented. The MDA approach to software development is considered as the biggest shift since the move from Assembler to the high level languages.

Chapter 11, *"Global Emergency-Response System Using GIS"* by Salem Al-Marri and Muthu Ramachandran proposes a model for Disaster Classification System of Natural Disasters and Catastrophic Failures activity. This model also considers the emerging technologies such as ubiquitous computing and wireless communications systems. Furthermore, this chapter proposes the deployment of Global Information Systems (GIS) as an aid to emergency management by identifying the related areas pertaining to disaster and thus to help the personnel involved to analyze disasters more accurately by developing a tool. The aim of this tool is to determine potential and affected disaster areas using the GIS technology and to provide support for decision makers during emergencies. Due to the significant development of computerization, networking and mobile systems, reporting a disaster, nowadays, is only a matter of seconds whereas, in the past it would take days or even weeks for the news to reach the people.

Chapter 12, *"Testing Guidelines for Developing Quality EAI Projects"* by S. R. Balasundaram and B. Ramadoss focuses on the testing aspects related to EAI applications. Especially the significance of testing for various types of "Integrations" is discussed elaborately. Organizations are turning into a new generation of software called Enterprise Application Integration (EAI) to fully integrate business processes. It is an activity that integrates and harmonizes an enterprise's isolated business applications, processes and functions. EAI is a complex task involving both technological and business challenges. This chapter frames the guidelines for a developing quality EAI projects.

Chapter 13, *"The Post Implementation Phase of a Large-Scale Integrative IT Project"* by Marco Marabelli and Sue Newell focuses on the iterative process that occurs within the implementation phase of an ERP which is depicted as a series of learning cycles: managers make decisions, identify mistakes, and accumulate experience (lessons learned). The author examines these "learning cycles" through the lens of absorptive capacity and illustrates using a case study. It is observed that the learning process is path dependent, organizational memory plays a fundamental role, and double loop cycles contribute in the development of absorptive capacity seen as a dynamic capability.

Chapter 14, *"Challenges in Enterprise Information Systems Implementation: An Empirical Study"* by Ashim Raj Singla identifies the critical success factors for the implementation of enterprise information systems. Enterprise information systems inherently present unique risks due to tightly linked interdependencies of business processes, relational databases, and process reengineering, etc. Knowledge of such risks is important in design of system and program management as they contribute to success of overall system. In this chapter an attempt has been made to study the design and implementation risks factors for ERP systems in large scale manufacturing organizations. Guidelines are presented to mitigate and manage such risks.

Chapter 15, *"Meta-Heuristic Approach to Solve Mixed Vehicle Routing Problem with Backhauls in Enterprise Information System of Service Industry"* by S. P. Anbuudayasankar, K. Ganesh and K. Mohandas presents the development of simulated annealing (SA) for a health care application which is modeled as Single Depot Vehicle routing problem called Mixed Vehicle Routing Problem with Backhauls (MVRPB), an extension of Vehicle Routing Problem with Backhauls (VRPB). This chapter provides empirical proof in sustain of the hypothesis, that a population extension of SA with supportive transitions leads to a major increase of efficiency and solution quality for MVRPB if and only if the globally optimal solution is located close to the center of all locally optimal solution.

Chapter 16, "*Information Technology enabled Vendor Managed Inventory in modeling Supply Chain Issues: A Review*" by Subramanian Nachiappan and Natarajan Jawahar reviews some of the soft issues in two-echelon supply chain models and proposes a classification schema. This chapter surveys the theoretical background and application of vendor managed inventory systems based on environment, operational issues and solution approaches. Hence it is concluded that the framework presented in this chapter would aid supply chain managers and researchers to further look into the soft issues while modelling supply chain with information technology enabled vendor managed inventory systems.

Chapter 17, "*Two-way Substitutable Inventory System with N–Policy*" by N. Anbazhagan presents a two commodity stochastic inventory system under continuous review. The maximum storage capacity for the $i$-th item is fixed as $S_i$ ($i = 1, 2$)   It is assumed that demand for the $i$-th commodity is of unit size and demand time points form Poisson distribution with parameter $\lambda_i$, $i = 1, 2$ The reorder level is fixed as $S_i$ for the $i$-th commodity (i = 1, 2) and the ordering policy is to place order for $Q_i$ ($= S_i - s_i$) items for the $i$-th commodity (i = 1, 2) when both the inventory levels are less than or equal to their respective reorder levels. The lead time is assumed to be exponential. The two commodities are assumed to be substitutable. That is, if the inventory level of one commodity reaches zero, then any demand for this commodity will be satisfied by the item of the other commodity. If no substitute is available, then this demand is backlogged up to a certain level $N_i$, ($i = 1, 2$) for the $i$-th commodity. Whenever the inventory level reaches $N_i$, ($i - 1, 2$), an order for $N_i$ items is replenished instantaneously. For this model, the limiting probability distribution for the joint inventory levels is computed. In this chapter, various operational characteristics and expression for long run total expected cost rate are derived.

Chapter 18, "*A Fuzzy AHP model for 3PL Selection in Lead Logistics Provider Scenarios*" by Rajbir Singh Bhatti, Pradeep Kumar and Dinesh Kumar discusses the use of Fuzzy Analytic Hierarchy Process (FAHP) to effectively manage the qualitative and quantitative decision factors which are involved in the selection of providers of 3PL services under Lead Logistics Provider (LLP) environments of today. The fuzzy-AHP has been adequately demonstrated in literature to be an effective tool which can be used to factor-in the fuzziness of data. Triangular Fuzzy Numbers (TFN) has been deployed to make over the linguistic comparisons of criteria, sub-criteria and the alternatives. The FAHP based model formulated in this chapter is applied to a case study in the Indian context using data from three leading LSPs with significant operating leverages in the province of Uttrakhand (India). The proposed model can provide the guidelines and directions for the decision makers to effectively select their global service providers in the present day competitive logistics markets.

Chapter 19, "*Achieving Alignment in Production and Logistics Operations in Three Echelon Supply Chain Network through New Heuristic Optimizer*" by Rajeshwar. S. Kadadevaramath, Jason. C. H. Chen and Mohanasundaram deals with the modeling and optimization of a three echelon supply chain network architecture using new Particle Swarm Optimization algorithm. Network optimization is the most basic type of modeling that can be performed with tools which helps to identity optimum paths or flow of goods in supply chain network. It is observed that the demand uncertainty and constraints posed by the every echelon are important factors to be considered during the supply chain design operations.

Chapter 20, "*Achieving Supply Chain Management (SCM): Customer Relationship Management (CRM) Synergy through Information and Communication Technology (ICT) Infrastructure in Knowledge Economy*" by Ashutosh Mohan and Shikha Lal tries to provide insight into how information and communication technology can be leveraged for supply chain value creation and make it possible to achieve synergy with customer relationship management. The concern about organizational competitiveness and development is closely linked to notions of the information sensitive society and global knowledge based economies. The business organizations under global knowledge economy can emerge and grow rapidly by formulating and adopting the innovative business practices. Information's impact is easily seen—it substitutes for inventory, speeds product design and delivery, drives process reengineering, and acts as a coordinating mechanism, helping different members of the supply chain work together effectively.

Chapter 21, *"Benefits of Information Technology Implementations for Supply Chain Management: An Explorative Study of Progressive Indian Companies"* by Prashant R. Nair focuses on the usage of IT tools for Supply Chain Management (SCM). It also highlights the contribution of IT in helping restructure the entire distribution set-up to achieve higher service levels, lower inventory, and lower supply chain costs. An overview and tangible benefits of the existing IT tools, which are widely deployed, is provided with focus on existing configuration considerations, available applications, and deployments in India. The rapid adoption of the Internet for communication with all stakeholders seems to reflect the potential of the new-age communication media. It has also been observed that several progressive Indian companies are extensively using emerging tools like virtual supply chains, web services, Radio Frequency Identification (RFID), and electronic commerce to shore up their supply chain operations. However, adoption of tools like software agents and decision support systems for supply chain integration by Indian companies is limited.

Chapter 22, *"Mathematical Modeling of Supply Chain Management Systems"* by C. Elango and N. Anbazhagan attempts to find why we require different supply chain for different companies. This chapter discusses the role of stochastic models in supply chian management system. This chapter also discusses other mathematical models for SCM.

Chapter 23, *"Stochastic Modeling in Supply Chain Management Systems"* by C. Elango introduces the concept of Supply Chain Management System (SCMS). Two stochastic modelling problems are discussed in this chapter. Poisson demand process with $(s,S)$ installation policy at retailer nodes are assumed to simplify the study . The system performance measures are computed with reference to specific cost structure. The total average annual variable cost is taken as optimization criterion. Numerical examples are provided to illustrate the problem.

The objective of this book is to expand the knowledge on enterprise information systems (EIS) and in turn help researchers and practitioners to develop suitable strategies, tactics, and operational policies for EIS and for improving communication in organizations. The book tries to enable the young research scholars to kick off their research in EIS effortlessly and provide them the channels required to do research in EIS meticulously to help the enterprises improve their performance through the successful implementation of an information system. Discussing the design and implementation issues of EIS from different perspectives will help the practitioners to get adapted to the information system in a smooth way and reap its benefits. This book intends to be a forum for exchanging new ideas and developments in the field of EIS. It also acts as a medium of communication among EIS researchers and practitioners.

# Acknowledgment

Each chapter in this book has been prepared by eminent professors and research scholars involved information systems' research. Many thanks for their contribution. I thank Ms. Jan Travers, Vice President, IGI Global, Ms. Kristin Klinger, Director of Editorial Content, Ms. Erika Carter, Assistant Acquisitions Editor, and Ms. Christine Bufton, Assistant Development Editor, for their support and guidance. I am thankful to Dr. (Mrs.) Radha Thiagarajan, Chairman Emeritus, Shri. Karumuttu T. Kannan, Chairman & Correspondent, Dr. V. Abhai Kumar, Principal of the Thiagarajar College of Engineering, Madurai, India for their encouragement. I thank Professor V. Sankarasubramanian, Department of English, Madura College, Madurai, India, for his valuable suggestions to fine tune the book.

Coming to my family, I am ever grateful to my mother Mrs. Ambujam Sudhaman, whose dream has made me take up this book project. Without the support of my father Mr. S. Sudhaman, I would never have been able to reach this page. I am also grateful to my brother Mr. S. Manivannan, sisters-in-law and all other relatives and friends for their support. Finally, many thanks to my wife Mrs. Rekha Parthasarathy, the first person to comment on my work candidly and who has extended support in the course of this book project.

*Dr. S. Parthasarathy*
*Editor-in-Chief*

# Section 1
# Challenges and Issues in Enterprise Information Systems

# Chapter 1

# Engineering the Coordination Requirements in Cross-Organizational ERP Projects:
## A Package of Good Practices

**Maya Daneva**
*University of Twente, the Netherlands*

## ABSTRACT

*There is yet little knowledge about cross-organizational Enterprise Resource Planning (ERP) implementation projects when it comes to determining requirements and achieving alignment between IT and businesses. Consequently, the requirements engineering (RE) processes are often more expensive and less effective as they could be. In this chapter, the authors view a cross-organization ERP implementation as a coordination problem, and introduce a coordination complexity model based on an organization's level of participation in a business network. They show how the external coordination characteristics of an organization can be mapped to ERP-supported mechanisms for cross-organizational coordination. To incorporate this activity in the state-of-the-art ERP RE processes, the authors propose a set of good practices that counterpart certain coordination issues at different complexity levels. Their chapter is based on empirical data gathered from secondary sources. They also carried out an early validation assessment based on an online focus group composed of ERP solution architects*

## INTRODUCTION

Conceptualizing the requirements and developing the architecture design of ERP applications, mostly takes place in an inter-organizational context. Cross-organizational ERP solutions are the preferred vehicles that profit-and-loss responsible business actors use to achieve cooperation in a value web

(Davenport, 2000; Holland, Shaw & Kawalek, 2005; Nicolaou, 2008). An example of ERP-enabled value web is the business network of WalMart Stores Inc. who collaborates - by means of a global ERP coordination support system, with a large number of non-U.S. companies and gives them direct access to the American market (Champy, 2002).

This chapter defines cross-organizational ERP systems as multi-module application packages supporting cross-organizational coordination. This

DOI: 10.4018/978-1-61520-625-4.ch001

Copyright © 2010, IGI Global. Copying or distributing in print or electronic forms without written permission of IGI Global is prohibited.

definition means those information systems that consist of standard ERP software packages and automate cross-organizational process work flows and data control flows, composed of flow fragments owned by or shared among multiple companies. The packages in a cross-organizational ERP system may or may not all be shared by the participating companies; and they may each be provided by the same vendor or by different vendors, each having its own application logic, data formats, and data semantics. Transforming ERP into cross-organizational coordination support systems poses to ERP adopters a number of complicated coordination issues. For example, partner companies may well vary in terms of levels of trust, needs for cooperation, decision making processes pushed out into other organizations, business processes, semantics of data, authorization hierarchies, enterprise systems, and infrastructure (Daneva & Wieringa, 2006). When a company ventures out to partner in a value web for a particular purpose, all these differences still exist. No participating party is prepared either to change its infrastructure, business processes, and data semantics just for this particular cooperation, or to reveal the confidential business rules embedded in its processes and applications. Yet, to build a profitable ERP-supported network, each business must be able to decide which processes it will carry out itself and which ones it will perform for or with other actors (Champy, 2002). These decisions need to be explicit part of the requirements engineering (RE) stage in any cross-organizational ERP project. Though, existing approaches to cross-organizational ERP RE, by and large, ignore these issues.

This chapter addresses the cross-organizational coordination issues and proposes to augment the state-of-the art ERP RE processes by using a set of 'good' practices that counterpart these issues. These practices are derived from the author's own project experience (Daneva, 2004) and from secondary sources. The chapter makes the claim that for each company, there are different complexity levels of coordination in a value network, and that if a company aims to be involved in cross-organizational coordination at a certain level, then certain RE techniques are relevant and others are not. The author draws on previously published results (Daneva & Wieringa, 2006) from applying a coordination theory perspective to cross-organizational RE problems. The earlier research by the author and R.J. Wieringa (Daneva & Wieringa, 2006) yielded (i) a model of undocumented assumptions about coordination built into modern ERP systems, and (ii) a library of ERP-supported coordination mechanisms that the requirements engineer can match to the coordination needs of the businesses participating in a network. The present chapter refines the earlier work by introducing an organization's coordination complexity levels and by linking these to appropriate RE practices. The specific technique we used to identify and characterize these practices is compliant with the approach which Sommerville and Sawer, 1998, deployed to define the practices in their RE Good Practice Guide.

The chapter is organized as follows: Section 2 provides the background for this research and presents related work. Section 3 reports on the method we used to design our solution proposal. Section 4 describes the solution. Therein, we discuss how companies differ in terms of who they participate with in business networks. We also map their scope of participation in a network to levels of coordination complexity that companies face. For each complexity level, we summarize the typical sets of cross-organizational coordination requirements that companies will have at this level. Based on this, we derive RE practices that address four types of ERP-supported coordination. All results are based on empirical data gathered from secondary sources. Section 5 presents the first validation study we carried out to evaluate whether the practices make sense to practicing ERP professionals. The section presents an online asynchronous focus group study and discussed its results and its limitations. Section 6 discussed the implications of our results for practice and research, and it concludes the chapter.

## BACKGROUND AND RELATED WORK

### Coordination Requirements in ERP Projects

For the purpose of our research, we call 'coordination requirements' those requirements concerned with the inter-organizational relationships in ERP projects. These requirements address: (1) what partner companies in a value network share and (2) how they share it. The coordination requirements in a cross-organizational ERP project are derived from the overall business goal of the value network. For example, a goal may well be to raise productivity by transforming the supply chain (Champy, 2002; Saliola & Zanfei, 2009; Simatupang, Wright & Sridharan, 2002; Simatupang, Sandroto & Lubis, 2004; Xu & Beamon, 2005). Engineering cross-organizational coordination requirements means getting stakeholders from the partner companies arrive at a consensus about (1) and (2).

Eliciting, documenting and validating these requirements is important because they are deemed critical (Champy, 2002; Marcotte, Grabot & Affonso, 2008) to the successful implementation of the multi-enterprise business model (e.g. value collaboration model, customer-centric network) that coordinates all players in a business network. In our earlier study (Daneva & Wieringa, 2006), we found that for the project stakeholders to be able to achieve this, an analysis of four ERP-enabled forms of coordination should to be performed: utility-oriented, semantics-oriented, process-oriented, and communication-oriented coordination. Each form of coordination is realized through specific coordination mechanisms. In this chapter, we define a coordination mechanism as the set of activities enacted by people

and ERP transactions that are composed into the cross-organizational collaborative processes (Daneva & Wieringa, 2006). Different coordination mechanisms are supported to various extents in modern ERP packaged systems. Companies may decide to use these mechanisms in isolation or in combination. The choice for ERP adopters is to arrange the available coordination mechanisms in a way that makes it possible to achieve the execution of the cross-organizational collaborative processes. Our earlier publication (Daneva & Wieringa, 2006) presented a library of the coordination mechanisms which modern ERP systems make available to ERP-adopters. We also provided a set of high level guidelines about how to use it. In this chapter, we move a step further towards how to incorporate the use of this library in the state-of-the-art ERP RE processes.

### Insights from Related Work on (Cross-)Organizational Coordination in Information Systems Research and in Requirements Engineering

The issue of how to treat coordination in cross-organizational ERP-supported partnerships has been approached by practitioners and researchers in a variety of fields: human-computer interaction, social sciences, organizational semiotics. In this chapter, we chose to limit our discussion to how cross-organizational coordination has been approached in two particular disciplines: the one of information systems and of requirements engineering. We chose these two fields because of their relevance to the task of designing an approach to engineering the requirements for cross-organizational coordination. We collected insights from the following streams of information systems literature: organization network research, (cross-organizational) coordination and cooperation, and ERP misalignment. The studies in organization network research (Alstyne, 1997; Babiak, 2009; Brass, Galaskiewicz, Greve & Wenpin, 2004; Cäker, 2008; Daniel & White,

2005; Gulati, Nohria & Zaheer, 2000; Lorenzoni & Lipparini, 1999; Nassambeni, 1998; Smith-Doerr & Powell, 2005) gave us the cues of why and how companies participate in networks. Publications on coordination (Alexander, 1995; Alsène, 2007; Alstyne, 1997; Christiansen, Kotzab & Mikkola, 2007; Gosain, Zoonky & Kim, 2003; Kawalek, Warboys & Greenwood, 1999; Malone & Crowston, 1994; Saliola & Zanfei, 2009; Simatupang, Wright & Sridharan, 2002; Simatupang, Sandroto & Lubis, 2004; Xu & Beamon, 2005) and on cooperation (Dunne, 2008; Marcotte, Grabot & Affonso, 2008) elucidated how companies manage what they share in a network. Studies on ERP misalignments (Clemmons & Simon, 2001; Daneva & Wieringa, 2006; Davenport, 2000; Gefen, 2004; Kelly & Holland, 2002; Soh, Sia, Boh & Tang, 2003) brought us to understand the dimensions of the trade-offs to be made in cross-organizational ERP implementations. In the RE field, we drew on our own previously published research ERP RE (Daneva, 2004; Daneva & Wieringa, 2006) as well as on results by other RE authors (Rolland & Prakash, 2000) which helped us think holistically about the implication of our coordination theory perspective for RE professionals.

In our observation from reviewing these sources, the IS and RE communities seem to converge on that coordination misalignments represents a considerable challenge in ERP projects and should be approached at the level of requirements. Both communities studied the phenomenon of ERP misalignment (or misfit) from a variety of perspectives. For example, Morton and Hu, 2008, investigated the misfit between ERP and ERP-adopters' organizational structures by taking as a lens the structural contingency theory, Rose and Kraemmergaard, 2006, apply a discourse transformation perspective to study aspects of ERP-misfits in Danish companies, Gattiker, 2007, investigates coordination and interdependency aspects by using the view of information processing theory, and Soh, Sia, Boh and Tang, 2003, structure their experiences in ERP misalignments by applying

a dialectic perspective. We noticed that most publications focus on the misalignment discussion primarily in intra-organizational context and relatively few authors - for example (Babiak, 2009; Clemmons & Simon, 2001; Gefen, 2004), shed light into coordination issues and solutions to them in cross-organizational settings. Very few authors explicitly explored how to prevent cross-organizational ERP misalignments (Clemmons & Simon, 2001; Daneva & Wieringa, 2006; Holland, Shaw & Kawalek, 2005). Notwithstanding the extensive body of contributions, the literature fails to provide an ERP approach able to capture the multiplicity of inter-company coordination and architectures that fall under the term network. In the next sections, we will see how the insights from the literature sources mentioned in this section were used to devise an approach to engineering the coordination requirements in cross-organizational ERP projects.

## The Approach to Designing a Solution to Coordination Requirements

The objective of the solution approach we propose in this chapter is twofold: first, to facilitate the use of our library of ERP-supported coordination mechanisms (Daneva & Wieringa, 2006), and second, to build a foundation for good cross-organizational RE practice. The approach to designing our solution was informed by inter-organizational relationship (Babiak, 2009; Cäker, 2008), coordination (Alsène, 2007; Clemmons & Simon, 2001; Christiansen, Kotzab & Mikkola, 2007; Saliola & Zanfei, 2009; Simatupang, Wright & Sridharan, 2002; Simatupang, Sandroto & Lubis, 2004), cooperation (Dunne, 2008; Marcotte, Grabot & Affonso, 2008) models that were based on ERP or on inter-organizational systems which include ERP as an essential part. These models emphasize - from a variety of angles, how companies may have different preferences for coordinating their actions via ERP, which may shape their choices when making trade-offs in cross-organizational ERP implementations.

Furthermore, these models point out the industry's current trend to build value networks by using three key participation forms (Alexander, 1995; Brass, Galaskiewicz, Greve & Wenpin, 2004; Champy, 2002, Nassambeni, 1998; Smith-Doerr & Powell, 2005; Xu & Beamon, 2005), namely, participation on the buying side, on the sales side, and in intermediation. We consider this trend and include it as a starting point in our process of designing a solution for engineering the cross-organizational coordination requirements. As Champy, 2002, states, each form offers to a partner company opportunities for and constraints on business behavior. As per business scholars studying inter-organizational relationships (Babiak, 2009; Cäker, 2008), the scope of these opportunities and constrains is determined by (i) the goal of coordination set up by the company, (ii) the functional area of sharing, and (iii) the vehicle for sharing. For example, a supply chain network (i) has the goal to realize operations synergy, (ii) has the operating core of the partners as its area of sharing, and (iii) uses as a vehicle for sharing the material flow that intersects the partners.

In our previously published research (Daneva & Wieringa, 2006), we identified the major ERP-supported coordination mechanisms operating on these participation forms. We also found that companies select different ERP-supported coordination mechanisms (Daneva & Wieringa, 2006) to support the different participation forms. That is, a company who shares processes with both its suppliers and corporate clients and a company who lets its individual consumers participate in its sales processes will have different requirements for coordination and alignment. The ERP coordination mechanisms that are likely to best support the cross-organizational alignment needs of the first company are different from the mechanisms that the second company would implement. This in turn has implications for cross-organizational RE.

To design a solution which lays out the foundation for the systematic, incremental adoption of good ERP RE practice in cross-organizational projects, we applied the following two-stage design approach: we first developed a coordination complexity model and, then, we linked it to an existing RE improvement framework (Sommerville & Sawyer, 1998). Our coordination model reflects our conviction that, although many unsolved problems exist in ERP RE due to misalignments in the coordination requirements, many of them can be solved by using a well-established good practice. We support the common sense notion that even where cross-organizational coordination requirements problems are inadequately understood, the consequences for individual projects can usually be contained if adequate support exists within the cross-organizational ERP RE process. Below, we describe the two stages of development of our solution.

## Deriving a Coordination Complexity Model

To model coordination complexity, we adapted Champy's levels of participation (Champy, 2002) to the context of implementing cross-organizational ERP coordination support systems. Our coordination complexity model was also inspired by the framework of Christiansen, Kotzab and Mikkola, 2007, which classifies different ERP solutions based on (1) the level of IOS sophistication and (2) the types of logistics information sharing.

We defined four levels of coordination complexity, each reflecting how extensively a company crosses organizational boundaries. Each level is characterized by types of partner companies involved, unique cross-organizational coordination goals, areas of sharing, and coordination mechanisms used. We adopt two underlying assumptions: First, we assume that the complexity of coupling different types of companies within a network combines with the complexity arising from how within-company elements (e.g. departments) are linked together (Daneva & Wieringa,

2006). Second, we assume that the more diverse the business actors are and the larger their number, the greater their coordination challenge (Champy, 2002, Gosain, Zoonky & Kim, 2004; Smith-Doerr & Powell, 2005; Xu & Beamon, 2005).

In our model, Level 1 represents the least challenging coordination scenarios and the least complex alignment requirements. Levels 2, 3, and 4 successively progress to more challenging coordination processes and more complex alignment requirements. The levels are defined as follows:

- At Level 1, a company aligns its own processes. An ERP-adopter at Level 1 has the goal to improve internal coordination among departments. There are no cross-organizational challenges and cross-organizational coordination requirements addressed at this level.
- At Level 2 an organization aligns its processes along with the processes of one other type of organization. A Level 2 ERP-adopter's goal is to improve coordination with this type of organization, namely either a client, or a supplier (Champy, 2002).
- At Level 3, a company aligns its processes along with the processes of two other types of organizations. A Level 3 ERP-adopter's goal is to improve coordination with two more company types, e.g. suppliers as well as clients.
- At Level 4, a company aligns its processes with the processes of organizations of three other types. A Level 4 ERP-adopter works to improve coordination with three other types of organizations. At this level, it is not uncommon for these networks to change the coordination mechanisms in an entire business sector (Babiak, 2009; Holland, Shaw & Kawalek, 2005).

Our choice of these levels and of their definitions is motivated by the published results obtained by other researchers (Christiansen, Kotzab & Mikkola, 2007; Dunne, 2008; Marcotte, Grabot & Affonso, 2008; Saliola & Zanfei, 2009). Dunne (Dunne, 2008) indicates that for firms to successfully engage supply chain partners, they first have to develop their own collaborative capabilities. This finding motivates the inclusion of Level 1 in the complexity model.

Furthermore, Christiansen Kotzab & Mikkola, 2007, state that "there are different types of logistics information that should match different types of collaboration levels shared amongst the partners in a supply chain". Sanders (SAN08] found that each pattern of IT-use by a supplier in a business network, directly promotes a specific type of coordination activities with this supplier's buyers. Marcotte, Grabot & Affonso, 2008, claim that the type of "collaboration situation influences information processing all along the supply network". The collective experience of these authors let us believe that adopting a four-level complexity model makes sense and converges with common sense notions of ERP-enabled inter-organizational relationships.

We also observe that the choice of ERP-enabled coordination mechanisms that companies use as vehicles for sharing depends on the coordination complexity level the companies decide to target. This observation came out of a study done as part of preparing this chapter. Therein, we screened the 2008 list of Fortune 500 public companies (http://money.cnn.com/magazines/fortune) to identify those using ERP coordination technology. For each company, we determined its coordination complexity level and the forms of ERP-supported coordination it activated to align its network partners' contributions to the entire cross-organizational processes. A detailed list of the sources in this study is available from the author. Due to space limitations, we use in this chapter a subset only which refers to circa 50 companies (Champy, 2002; Danese, Romano & Vinelli, 2004; Davenport, 2000; Davenport, 2005; Holland, Shaw & Kawalek, 2005; Knolmayer,

*Table 1. Use of utility-oriented cross-organizational coordination mechanisms at four coordination complexity levels*

| Coordination mechanisms | What does it mean to ERP adopters? | Level 1 | Level 2 | Level 3 | Level 4 |
|---|---|---|---|---|---|
| C1 Shared vision of the overall benefits for the networked organization | Presenting one face to clients and sharing corporate identity. | | x | x | x |
| C2 Shared view of services offered by network to clients | Motivating dependencies between services of different businesses. | | x | x | |
| C3 Shared organizational control mechanisms | Ensuring that behaviors originating in partner companies are compatible and support common organizational goals. | | x | x | x |
| C4 Common framework for empowering staff | Keeping employees up to date and prepared to actively participate in decision making and problem solving. | | x | x | |
| C5 Dual focus on local and overall performance | Connecting local partner operations to process mission by balancing local (partner) performance with the overall (network process) performance. | | x | x | x |
| C6 Shared agreement on how the capabilities of different partners are utilized in joint processes | Assigning and accepting responsibility for each facet of the network business relationship. | | x | x | x |

Mertens & Zeier, 2001; Narayanan & Ananth, 2004; Peppard & Ward, 2005; Xu & Beamon, 2005). Tables 1, 2, 3, and 4 report on our observations from reviewing these literature sources. In the tables, the x-sign means that a coordination mechanism is actually used to facilitate coordination at organizations of coordination complexity Level 1, 2, 3 or 4. We make the note that when a coordination mechanism is required at a certain coordination complexity level, the tables show that it is not necessarily required for every higher level. For example, in Table 1, the mechanism C1 (Shared vision of the overall benefits for the networked organization), is used to facilitate coordination at Level 2 organizations, Level 3 and level 4 organizations.

## Augmenting the State-of-the-Art Requirements Engineering Practice

Our coordination complexity model served as input to the process of augmenting the state-of-the-art ERP RE practice. Because the author's expertise lies in SAP package implementation, we chose to extend the Accelerated SAP (ASAP) RE framework (Daneva, 2004) with guidelines that

directly address the cross-organizational coordination requirements problem. The extension work was done by following the REAIMS approach (Sommerville & Sawyer, 1998) to formulation and qualitative assessment of RE practices. This approach suggests a researcher abstract a practice from observations he/she makes in specific project settings of interest and evaluate these observations in four respects: (i) a way to introduce the practice in an organization, (ii) cost of introducing and using the practice, (iii) immediate benefits of using the practice and (iv) long-term benefits (Sawer, Sommerville & Viller, 1998). We applied the REAIMS approach iteratively, whereby we abstracted 13 good practices from ERP experience reports on coordination, standards, and the first author's experience (Daneva, 2004) and related these to coordination goals at each coordination complexity level. When formulating each practice, we considered how it can be introduced to an RE team, how it can be implemented, what benefits it would bring to the project and what are the costs to incur due to the practice (Sommerville & Sawyer, 1998). We, then, added the newly formulated practices to the existing ASAP RE framework. We have recognized that, while agreement is likely

*Table 2. Use of process-oriented cross-organizational coordination mechanisms at four coordination complexity levels*

| Coordination mechanisms | What does it mean to ERP adopters? | Level 1 | Level 2 | Level 3 | Level 4 |
|---|---|---|---|---|---|
| C7 Common agreement about business process environment | Standardized operational procedures, access permissions, and control patterns. | x | x | x | x |
| C8 Agreement about process-orientation | Reducing organizational operations to a large series of procedural steps tied together to sequences, sub-functional categories, modules and cross-modular operations. | x | x | x | x |
| C9 Common agreement on management policies | Sharing enforceable business rules that are explicit and consistent. | x | x | x | x |
| C10 Solution maps | Descriptions of the most important business processes within an industry sector, the technologies (ERP elements, add-ons) & services needed to support the processes. | | | | x |
| C11 Common secure or non-secure customer "self-serve" practices | Opening up segments of the process logic that customers and suppliers can execute on their own. | x | x | | |
| C12 Shared transaction processing engines | Shared understanding of the position of ERP in the cross-organizational architecture. | | | x | x |
| C13 Common agreement on market-making mechanisms (matching and aggregation) | Sharing a base of potential suppliers and customers and using the potential for lower-cost purchasing through aggregation. | | | x | |

on the utility of some practices, the benefits of others are dependent on the position of the ERP adopter in the value network. To reflect this, we classified the practices according to whether they seem mostly applicable to organizations with coordination complexity level 2, 3, and 4. Table 5 formulates each practice as a RE guideline (see the first column). The second column in Table 5 explains what form of cross-organizational coordination the guideline addresses. The third

*Table 3. Use of semantics-oriented cross-organizational coordination mechanisms at four coordination complexity levels*

| Coordination mechanisms | What does it mean to ERP adopters? | Level 1 | Level 2 | Level 3 | Level 4 |
|---|---|---|---|---|---|
| C14 Shared data dictionary | Common definitions of information entities. | x | x | x | |
| C15 Shared reporting formats and semantics | Standard presentation formats and information content of output. | x | x | x | |
| C16 Delegation about data access permission | Distributed access to data and distributed application logic. | x | x | x | |
| C17 Shared access to information across the firewall | Standard methods for producing a global, enterprise-wide view of business operations. | | x | x | x |
| C18 Common principles of cross-org. data management | Data consistency and alignment with businesses. | | x | x | |
| C19 Reference models | Representing practices embedded in the package in the form of reusable process and data models. | x | x | x | |
| C20 Shared product models | Industry-specific solution aspects of the ERP package. | | | | x |

*Table 4. Use of communication-oriented coordination mechanisms at four coordination complexity levels*

| Coordination mechanisms | What does it mean to ERP adopters? | Level 1 | Level 2 | Level 3 | Level 4 |
|---|---|---|---|---|---|
| C21 Agreements about communication channels and a common language | Shared understanding about transmission and interpretation of complete and legally valid business documents. | | | | x |
| C22 Sharing of knowledge | Bringing employees to the required level of understanding to get their job done. | x | x | | |
| C23 Shared understanding on conformance on messaging services | Automating the sending and receiving of business documents between partners. | | x | | |
| C24 Shared learning | Using what each partner learns in interaction with customers both to respond to immediate needs and to determine what future markets will require. | | | x | x |

column indicates the benefits expected to happen when the guideline is implemented. The rightmost column suggests the coordination complexity level of those organizations most likely to use and benefit from the guideline. The data in this column is not derived empirically. Instead, it is concluded from the author's experience in cross-organizational projects (while being employed by TELUS (Daneva, 2004) and from case study reports about 12 ERP adopters, namely IBM, Intel, Hewlet Packard, Lear Automotive, 3COM, Moen, Unilever, Shell, British Petroleum, and DHL, who developed and managed SAP global roll-outs (Rohde, 2005). We make the note that they are therefore hypotheses that must be tested in further research.

Table 5 suggests that ERP adopters at Level 2 and Level 3 share seven out of 13 practices. In addition, 3 out of 13 practices seem unique to coordination complexity Level 4. Clearly, we share the view of Sawer, Sommerville & Viller, 1998, that the value of each practice to an organization depends great deal on the project, the other organizations in the network and, ultimately, on the RE team members involved.

## Early Evaluation of the Practices

We planned and executed a focus group study for the purpose of validating the 13 practices and their association to specific complexity levels. Below, we present it along with our findings and their evaluation. The latter means evaluating our focus group experiences to understand the limitations of this early validation study itself.

Our focus group study represents an early assessment exercise in which we set out to analyze two questions:

i.    whether what we think to be a good cross-organizational ERP RE practice is what ERP architects see in their project realities, and

ii.   if architects do observe a practice, then which complexity level would they put it at?

We researched these questions by using an asynchronous online focus group (Gaiser, 1997; Kivits, 2005; Orgad, 2005). Generally, a focus group is a group discussion on a given topic, which is monitored, facilitated (if needed) and recorded by a researcher. It is a way to better understand how people think about an issue, a practice, a product or a service. In essence, the researcher provides the focus of the discussion, and the data comes from the group interaction.

As a qualitative research technique, it can serve the purpose of both exploration and confirmation studies (Morgan, 1997). An online focus group is a focus group organized by using internet resources. We selected the focus group research method, because of the following reasons: (1) it is suitable technique for an inquiry like ours, e.g.

focus groups are well-know to help clarify findings resulting from using another method, and (2) in this first validity evaluation we needed to collect a concentrated set of observations in a short time span. More specifically, we selected the online asynchronous form of focus group because (i) it is known for its cost-effectiveness (Kivits, 2005),

*Table 5. Cross-organizational ERP RE practices*

| RE Practice | Explanation | Key Expected Benefits | Relevant Complexity Level for Organizations to use the practice |
|---|---|---|---|
| P1. Define how work gets divided between partner companies. P1 supports utility-oriented coordination (C2, C3, C4, C5, C6). | For a cross-organizational ERP project to be successful, it must start with clarity on the network vision that partners share and the shared services that operationalize their common goals (Davenport, 2000). | 1. A statements about shared vision and services is an input to feasibility analysis to assess whether or not ERP coordination technology can be effectively integrated in the network's envisioned way of working. 2. Understanding which process fragment are executed by whom in a collaborative process model makes clear who the process owners are to be consulted in selecting coordination mechanisms and validating the coordination requirements. | 2, 3, 4 |
| P2. For each network partner, document data, processes, and communication channels to be shared and with whom. P2 supports process, data, communication-oriented coordination (C7-C23). | A list of what is shared eliminates uncertainties and makes explicit the mapping between the partners' expectations about coordination and the hidden build-in assumptions in the ERP package (Daneva & Wieringa, 2006). | 1. Creating common awareness of what data, processes, and communication channels will be shared keeps RE team focused on those aspects in cross-organizational coordination. 2. A list of the shared elements offers support to the process of validating the coordination requirements. | 2, 3 |
| P3. Document values and goals to be shared and with whom. P3 supports coordination mechanism C1. | This increases one's sensitivity to cross-organizational factors which are potential sources of misalignments and which may conceal the real coordination requirements from requirements engineers. | 1. Documenting shared values and goals is what will drive the cross-organizational ERP RE process and will keep partners with conflicting interests focused on what counts. 2. In requirements validation, each process or data requirement can be validated against how it supports the shared goals and values. | 4 |
| P4. Collect enough knowledge about the ERP supported internal processes before starting for cooperating ERP scenarios. P5 supports process-oriented coordination (C7, C8, C9). | For a company to be able to participate in cross-organizational cooperation, it needs first to make its internal coordination processes work efficiently (Champy, 2002). | 1. Knowledge of internal ERP processes helps making sure that what external coordination processes require can be integrated with the past, current, and future solution development plans of each partner company. 2. It helps understand which requirements of each partner are rigid and which are flexible and why. | 3 |
| P5. Document what data the separately-kept applications of partners' companies will share via interfaces to a common ERP system. P6 supports semantic-oriented coordination (C14, C15, C16, C17, C18). | This adds clarity to business owners who need to adapt their data management styles to the new ERP coordination model shared by the network. | 1. Fewer requirements for unnecessary customization. Leaving the question of how applications would share data unanswered may mean calls for complex and expensive customization in the later project stages because business owners may find themselves unprepared to change their process designs late [DAN04b]. 2. Conforming to some company-specific interfaces may be an important interoperability requirement for the cross-organizational system. | 4 |

(ii) it provides ready-to-use transcribed data, (iii) it is flexible so that our group members sitting in various time zones could contribute at their most convenient time, (iv) it encourages candid interchanges and reduces issues of interviewer's effect as focus group members can not "see" each other, and (v) it allows responses that are usually lengthier and more measured than in a synchronous mode (Orgad; 2005).

## Focus Group Planning

The planning steps in our focus group study followed the guidelines proposed by the methodologists (Gaiser, 1997; Kivits, 2005; Krueger & Casey, 2008; Morgan, 1997; Orgad, 2005). Our questions (stated in the previous paragraphs) drove our choices in composing the focus group. Our focus group plan included 18 ERP solution architects from four telecommunications services providers, two financial service companies, two retail businesses, and one real estate corporation. The focus group members were selected because (i) they had a characteristic in common, which pertains to the topic of the focus group and (ii) they had the potential to offer information-rich experiences. We make the note that focus groups do not gather to vote or to reach consensus (see Morgan, 1997; p. 4). The intent is to promote self-disclosure and that is what we were after in this study. According to Morgan, 1997, we planed to implement a research procedure, known as 'a participatory focus group'. It collects data through group interaction of people with various backgrounds but with common professional values and common roles in which they execute their professional duties.

All 18 ERP architects had the following characteristics:

- They all were in charge of cross-organizational projects that had stakeholders and users at locations distributed in at least four Canadian provinces, namely Quebec, Ontario, Alberta and British Columbia.

- Each architect (i) had at least 6 years of experience in cross-organizational ERP RE, (ii) has been familiar with cross-organizational coordination issues, and (iii) has done proposals to improve his/her company's ERP RE process.

- 13 architects had experience with SAP only. One architect had experience in Oracle only. Two architects had experience with SAP and Peoplesoft, and other two – with SAP and Oracle.

- Five architects were working in Level 2 organizations, eleven architects were employed at Level 3 ERP adopters, and two architects were working for Level 4 ERP adopters.

All architects were known to the first author, as she had worked with them on a professional basis between 1995 and 2004. As Krueger and Casey, 2008, recommend, the moderator (in this case, the researcher) "should be similar to the respondents", meaning he/she comes from the same population. The focus group members were selected to participate using purposive sampling, based on the first author's knowledge and their typicality. The author chose them among a large group of colleagues based on her judgment whether they meet the requirement to be the professionals who have "the greatest amount of insights on the topic" (as Krueger and Casey, 2008, say).

The focus group members were contacted on a personal basis by the author using e-mail. Before opening the discussion, the first author provided the background of this research study and presented the 13 practices as a checklist. The focus group members, then, worked in two stages, dealing with one research question at each stage. This was to ensure that the group members are not overwhelmed with a long list of inquiries at the start of the process.

*Table 6. Cross-organizational ERP RE practices observed by 18 ERP architects*

| RE Practice | Number of architects who observed it |
|---|---|
| P1. Define how work gets divided between partner companies | 18 |
| P2. For each network partner, document data, processes, and communication channels to be shared and with whom | 17 |
| P3. Document values and goals to be shared and with whom | 11 |
| P4. Collect enough knowledge about the ERP supported internal processes before starting for cooperating ERP scenarios | 8 |
| P5. Document what data separately kept applications of partners' companies will share via interfaces to a common ERP system | 18 |
| P6. Align what is shared to what is kept separate | 18 |
| P7. Discover and document the market-making mechanisms and common learning models for partners to share | 0 |
| P8. Understand how ERP-supported coordination mechanisms will be used | 18 |
| P9. Assess compatibility of partner companies' values and beliefs | 9 |
| P10. Make a business coordination model | 12 |
| P11. Map the business coordination model into a set of ERP-supported coordination mechanisms | 6 |
| P12. Use the reference architecture for the package provided by the ERP vendor | 18 |
| P13. Validate coordination models and their execution | 10 |

## Results from the Two Stages of Focus Group interaction

In the first stage, the architects were asked to review the checklists and mark those practices which they either personally used or witnessed someone else on their RE team using it in the early stage of their ERP projects. Their responses are summarized in Table 6. For each practice, we report the number of architects who observed it at least once in real-life settings. Table 6 indicates that 12 out of 13 practices make sense for practicing requirement engineers and were actually observed in real-life projects. One practice was not observed at all but the architects attributed this to the fact that this practice referred to coordination with intermediaries and that no focus group member worked on a project with intermediation businesses.

In the second stage, we excluded the practice which no one observed. We sorted randomly the list of 12 remaining practices and asked the ar-

chitects to position them in the four complexity levels. We, then, compared how the architects associated the practices to the levels and how we did it (Table 7). For each practice, we assessed its mapping to a complexity level by using the percentage occurrences of those architects' rankings which coincide with ours. We adopted a cutoff of 75% as an acceptable matching level, as recommended in previous validation studies of software engineering practices (Krishnan & Kellner, 1999; Ramasubbu, Kompalli & Krishnan, 2005). The data in Table 7 suggests our mappings matched well with the architects'. Though, we observe four pairs of practices and associated levels, which do not meet the 75% cutoff level. These are the practices labeled P2, P6, P10, and P12. These practices all refer to the role of modeling in cross-organizational ERP RE. They were subjected to a second review by the architects.

The focus group accepted practices P2 and P6 for all complexity levels. This lets us conclude that we need a deeper analysis of these practices

*Table 7. Cross-organizational ERP RE associated to complexity levels by 18 ERP architects*

| RE Practice | Complexity level in Table 5 | Architects' rankings for Level 2 match | Architects' rankings for Level 3 match | Architects' rankings for Level 4 match | Architects' rankings for Level 2 and 3 match | Architects' rankings for Level 3 and 4 match | Architects' rankings for Level 2,3, and 4 match | Correct (%) |
|---|---|---|---|---|---|---|---|---|
| P1. Define how work gets divided between partner companies | 2,3,4 | - | - | - | - | - | 18 | 100.00 |
| P2. For each network partner, document data, processes, and communication channels to be shared and with whom | 2,3 | 1 | 1 | 1 | - | - | 15 | 5.55 |
| P3. Document values and goals to be shared and with whom | 4 | - | - | 15 | - | 3 | - | 83.33 |
| P4. Collect enough knowledge about the ERP supported internal processes before starting for cooperating ERP scenarios | 4 | - | - | 14 | - | 4 | - | 77.77 |
| P5. Document what data separately kept applications of partners' companies will share via interfaces to a common ERP system | 3 | 2 | 14 | - | 2 | - | - | 77.77 |
| P6. Align what is shared to what is kept separate | 4 | - | 1 | 1 | - | 1 | - | 5.55 |
| P8. Understand how ERP-supported coordination mechanisms will be used | 3 | - | 15 | - | 3 | - | - | 83.33 |
| P9. Assess compatibility of partner companies' values and beliefs | 2,3,4 | - | - | 1 | - | 3 | 15 | 83.33 |
| P10. Make a business coordination model | 2,3,4 | - | - | 9 | 5 | - | - | 50.00 |
| P11. Map the business coordination model into a set of ERP-supported coordination mechanisms | 2,3,4 | - | - | - | - | 1 | 17 | 94.44 |
| P12. Use the reference architecture for the package provided by the ERP vendor | 2,3,4 | - | - | 6 | - | 10 | 2 | 11.11 |
| P13. Validate coordination models and their execution | 2,3,4 | 1 | 1 | - | - | - | 16 | 88.88 |

at a finer granularity level. We think that these practices are interdependent and may also depend on the choice of other practices. So, we decided to analyze the possible combinations scenarios so that we can clearly get incremental complexity stratification.

The focus group was divided according to three standpoints on positioning practice P10. Nine architects thought that documenting cross-organizational coordination processes should be done by Level 4 ERP adopters because this is a very expensive effort and its pay-offs are much less tangible for Level 2 or 3 organizations. These architects witnessed organizations at lower levels of complexity modeling cross-organizational processes only when the costs for this are split up among the partner companies in the network. When there is no consensus on the costs, each partner models its own part of the process by using its own preferred modeling technique. Special attention is paid, then, on the inter-companies' process interface points. This is where a process changes its owners and one company hands over the process execution to another. Furthermore, five experts associated practice P10 to Level 2 and 3 and argued that modeling prior to architecture design is critical (i) to the remaining implementation stages and (ii) to the architects' ability to connect the cross-organizational solution built now with the one to be built in the future. Four architects stood on the point that modeling is a Level 1 organization's business and claimed that unless an organization does not have an established modeling culture, coordination process modeling would not make much sense, as it may well be perceived as sunk costs from high-level management perspective. We acknowledge that studies in ERP modeling (Davenport, 2000; Daneva, 2004) indicated that whenever modeling was done, it turned out to be useful. Modeling the current coordination requirements has key implications in terms of handling requirements for ERP upgrades, system consolidation, and maintenance projects.

So, we decided to leave the practice mapped to Levels 2, 3, and 4.

The fourth practice below the 75% cutoff level was P12. Sixteen architects found P12 as the most controversial activity in ERP project implementation. Six architects associated it to Level 4 ERP adopters and motivated it by stating that reference models are truly beneficial in networks among competitors. Ten architects argued that reference models do not capture shared data control flows and this is a key roadblock in using them efficiently at organizations with a complexity level higher than 2. The author's experience was that reference models were indispensable but the focus group member's knew that the author worked at Level 4 organization. Therefore, the focus group was not convinced at the end of the discussion on where to place this practice. So, we decided to research this question in the future.

## Limitations of the Focus Group Study

We considered the possible threats to validity (Krueger & Casey, 2008; Morgan, 1997; Orgad, 2005) of our results. The major limitation of our focus group setup is that it is centered on a single focus group, which restricts the extent to which generalizations can be drawn from its outcomes. This limitation is off-set by the opportunity to gain a deeper understanding of the association between coordination requirements engineering practices and coordination complexity levels. As Morgan states, generalizations are likely appropriate only to professionals in settings similar to the setting of our focus group members. In this respect, we consider the data as "incompletely collected" (Morgan, 1997), meaning that what is collected is the experience of the architects. Furthermore, we acknowledge that a plan of at least three-four focus groups, as methodologists suggest (Krueger & Casey, 2008; Morgan, 1997), would have brought much richer results. However, we could not complete this because of resource constraints. We consider this as our most important issue and, therefore, it tops our agenda for immediate future research. We plan to replicate the focus group in two other countries, the United State and the Netherlands, until we reach saturation, that is, the point when we have collected the range of ideas feedback to us and we are not getting new information (Krueger & Casey, 2008; Morgan, 1997). (We make the note that we did not consider tracking inter-rater agreements because Krueger and Casey, 2008, indicate that focus group members do not gather to come to consensus).

We also acknowledge the inherent weakness of focus group techniques that they are driven by the researcher, meaning that there is always a residual threat to the accuracy of what focus group members say. However, we believe that in our study, this threat was reduced, because the online focus group was completely transcribed and every single email exchange in the focus group was available for reference purposes.

Furthermore, a validity concern in focus group studies is that the researcher influences the group interaction. However, a study by Morgan, 1997, indicates that "in reality, there is no hard evidence that the focus groups moderator's impact on the data is any greater than researcher's impact in participant observation or individual interviewing". We also were conscious that the focus group members can influence the data they produce, for example, by means of imbalanced level of participation by the focus group members. We made sure that the focus group was not dominated by a small number of very active participants and that everyone gets a chance to write. This was achieved: (i) by establishing a 'one-message-at-a-time' policy, which states that a participant may write only one answer to a message in which there was no pointed question, and (ii) by researcher's approaching individual focus group members any time when she felt participants did not elaborate enough on pointed questions.

## CONCLUSION

Cross-organizational ERP RE addresses three business questions: (i) how a company needs to change, (ii) for what benefits, and (iii) with whose collaboration. The RE framework presented in our earlier publication (Daneva & Wieringa, 2006) responds to the first two questions, while the present chapter is about addressing the third question. In cross-organizational ERP RE, the coordination goals for a system are the partner companies' shared goals to do things together. The reality, however, indicates that many ERP misalignments (Daneva & Wieringa, 2006) are due to unmet external coordination requirements. Our position is that while coordination requirements are not traditionally distinguished in the ERP vendors' standard RE processes, they can be incorporated simply by using the list of practices we suggest in this chapter. We presented a coordination complexity model that, we believe, can serve as an instrument for determining and translating the goals and the needs of an ERP adopter for cross-organizational coordination into RE practices that offer practical solutions to certain challenges. Our model reflects who a company participates with in the creation and delivery of their value proposition and how complex it goes in integration. Early focus group results showed that the analysis of coordination mechanisms at the RE stage of a cross-organizational ERP project is what architects observe in ERP projects. The key benefit of our effort was that it made knowledge about engineering cross-organizational ERP coordination requirements available to both researchers and practitioners for further evaluation or adoption. The list of practices resulting from this research could be considered as a vehicle which practitioners can consider using in a number of situations. For example, we believe that the list of practices could be used to guide the establishment and improvement of ERP RE processes in cross-organizational settings, compare different requirement process solutions qualitatively, develop methods for evaluating benefits from RE process improvements, and structure the application of knowledge about cross-organizational RE. To researchers, the list of practices forms a theoretical basis on which future research could justify theoretical models and present theoretically-sound arguments for the examination of the use of standard ERP-vendor or consulting company-provided methodologies for ERP implementation.

A limitation of our model is that we did not determine it based on context attributes of how a coordination mechanism should be implemented for a given network constellation. More research is needed to detail characteristics of the specific implementation of a particular type of mechanism. For example, suppose the complexity model suggests for a Level 3 ERP adopter to implement a common agreement on market-making mechanisms. There are four ways to implement it and each implementation is unique in terms of costs and benefits. Our future work will include investigating these aspects. We also envision carrying out in-depth case studies in the specific business sectors to validate the applicability of the cross-organizational ERP RE practices.

## REFERENCES

Alexander, E. (1995). *How Organizations Act Together: Interorganizational Coordination*. Amsterdam: Gordon & Breach.

Alsène, É. (2007). ERP systems and the coordination of the enterprise. *Business Process Management Journal*, *13*(3), 417–432. doi:10.1108/14637150710752326

Alstyne, M. (1997). The state of network organizations: A survey in three frameworks. *Journal of Organizational Computing*, *7*(3), 83–151. doi:10.1207/s15327744joce0702&3_2

Babiak, K. M. (2009). Criteria of Effectiveness in Multiple Cross-sectoral Interorganizational Relationships. *Evaluation and Program Planning*, *32*(1), 1–12. doi:10.1016/j.evalprogplan.2008.09.004

Bendoly, E., & Jacobs, F. R. (2004). ERP architectural/operational alignment for order-processing performance. *International Journal of Operations & Production Management*, *24*(1), 99–117. doi:10.1108/01443570410511013

Brass, D. J., Galaskiewicz, J., Greve, H. R., & Wenpin, T. (2004). Taking stock of networks and organizations: a multilevel perspective. *Academy of Management Journal*, *47*(6), 795–817.

Cäker, M. (2008). Intertwined coordination mechanisms in interorganizational relationships with dominated suppliers. *Management Accounting Research*, *19*(3), 231–251. doi:10.1016/j.mar.2008.06.003

Champy, J. (2008). *X-Engineering the Corporation: the Next Frontier of Business Performance*. New York: Warner Books.

Christiansen, P. E., Kotzab, H., & Mikkola, J. H. (2007). Coordination and sharing logistics information in league supply chains . *International Journal of Procurement Management*, *1*(1-2), 79–96. doi:10.1504/IJPM.2007.015356

Clemmons, S., & Simon, S. J. (2001). Control and coordination in global ERP configuration. *Business Process Management Journal*, *7*(3), 205–215. doi:10.1108/14637150110392665

Danese, P., Romano, P., & Vinelli, A. (2004). Managing business processes across supply chain networks: the role of coordination mechanisms. *Journal of Purchasing and Supply Management*, *10*, 165–177. doi:10.1016/j.pursup.2004.11.002

Daneva, M. (2004). ERP requirements engineering practice: lessons learnt. *IEEE Software*, *21*(2), 26–33. doi:10.1109/MS.2004.1270758

Daneva, M., & Wieringa, R. J. (2006). A requirements engineering framework for cross-organizational ERP systems. *Springer Requirement Engineering Journal, 11*(3), 194–204.

Daniel, E. M., & White, A. (2005). The future of inter-organizational system linkages: findings of an international delphi study. *European Journal of Information Systems, 14*(2), 188–203. doi:10.1057/palgrave.ejis.3000529

Davenport, T. (2000). *Mission Critical: Realizing the Promise of Enterprise Systems*. Boston: HBS Press.

Davenport, T. (2005). The Coming Commodization of PROCESSES. *Harvard Business Review, 83*(6), 100–108.

Dunne, A. J. (2008). The impact of an organization's collaborative capacity on its ability to engage its supply chain partners. *British Food Journal, 11*(4-5), 361–375. doi:10.1108/00070700810868906

Gaiser, T. (1997). Conducting online focus groups: A methodological discussion. *Social Science Computer Review, 15*(2), 135–144. doi:10.1177/089443939701500202

Gattiker, T. F. (2007). Enterprise resource planning systems and the manufacturing-marketing interface: an information-processing theory view. *International Journal of Production Research, 45*(13), 2895–2917. doi:10.1080/00207540600690511

Gefen, D. (2004). What makes an ERP implementation relationship worthwhile: Linking trust mechanisms and ERP usefulness. *Journal of Management Information Systems, 21*(1), 263–288.

Gosain, S., Zoonky, L., & Yongbeom, K. (2005). The nanagement of cross-functional inter-dependencies in ERP implementations: Emergent coordination patterns. *European Journal of Information Systems, 14*(4), 371–387. doi:10.1057/palgrave.ejis.3000549

Gulati, R., Nohria, N., & Zaheer, A. (2000). Strategic networks. *American Journal of Sociology, 104*(5), 203–215.

Holland, C. P. (2003). Introduction to international examples of large scale systems: Theory and practice. *Communications of the Association for Information Systems, 11*(19).

Holland, C. P., Shaw, D. R., & Kawalek, P. (2005). BP's multi-enterprise asset management system. *Information and Software Technology, 47*(15), 999–1007. doi:10.1016/j.infsof.2005.09.006

Kawalek, P., Warboys, B. C., & Greenwood, R. M. (1999). The case for an explicit coordination layer in modern business information systems architectures. *IEE Software, 146*(3), 160–166. doi:10.1049/ip-sen:19990615

Kelly, S., & Holland, C. P. (2002). The ERP systems development approach to achieving an adaptive enterprise: the impact of enterprise process modelling tools . In Henderson, P. (Ed.), *Systems engineering for business process change* (pp. 241–252). London: Springer.

Kivits, J. (2005). Online interviewing and the research relationship . In Hine, C. (Ed.), *Virtual methods: issues in social research on the internet* (pp. 35–49). Oxford, UK: Berg Publishers.

Knolmayer, G., Mertens, P., & Zeier, A. (2001). *Supply chain management based on SAP systems*. Berlin: Springer.

Krishnan, M. S., & Kellner, M. I. (1999). Measuring process consistency: Implications for reducing software defects. *IEEE Transactions on Software Engineering, 25*(6), 800–815. doi:10.1109/32.824401

Krueger, R. A., & Casey, M. A. (2008). *Focus groups: A practical guide for applied research*. Thousand Oaks, CA: Sage.

Lorenzoni, G., & Lipparini, A. (1999). The leveraging of interfirm relationships as a distinctive organizational capability: a longitudinal study. *Strategic Management Journal, 20*(4), 317–338. doi:10.1002/(SICI)1097-0266(199904)20:4<317::AID-SMJ28>3.0.CO;2-3

Malone, T., & Crowston, K. (1994). The interdisciplinary study of coordination. *ACM Computing Surveys, 26*(1), 87–119. doi:10.1145/174666.174668

Marcotte, F., Grabot, B., & Affonso, R. (2008). Cooperation models for supply chain management. *International Journal of Logistics Systems and Management, 5*(1-2), 123–153.

Morgan, D. L. (1997). Focus Group as Qualitative Research Method, (2nd Ed., Qualitative Research Method Series, Vol. 16). Thousand Oaks, CA: Sage.

Morton, N. A., & Hu, Q. (2008). Implications of the fit between organizational structure and ERP: A structural contingency theory perspective. *International Journal of Information Management, 28*(5), 391–402. doi:10.1016/j.ijinfomgt.2008.01.008

Narayanan, V. G., & Ananth, R. (2004). Aligning incentives in supply chains. *Harvard Business Review, 82*(11), 94–102.

Nassambeni, G. (1998). Network structures and coordination mechanisms: A taxonomy. *International Journal of Operations & Production Management, 18*(6), 538–554. doi:10.1108/01443579810209539

Nicolaou, A. I. (2008). Research issues on the use of ERP in inter-organizational relationships. *International Journal of Accounting Information Systems, 9*(4), 216–226. doi:10.1016/j.accinf.2008.09.003

Orgad, S. (2005). From online to offline and back: Moving from online to offline relationships with research informants . In Hine, C. (Ed.), *Virtual methods: Issues in social research on the internet* (pp. 51–65). Oxford, UK: Berg Publishers.

Peppard, J., & Ward, J. (2005). Unlocking sustained business value from IT investments. *California Management Review, 48*(1), 52–70.

Ramasubbu, N., Kompalli, P., & Krishnan, M. S. (2005). Leveraging global resources: A process maturity model for managing distributed development. *IEEE Software, 22*(3), 80–86. doi:10.1109/MS.2005.69

Rohde, J. (2005). *Conquering the challenge of global SAP implementations: SAP roll-out strategy & best practices*. Greenwood Village, CO: CIBER Inc.

Rolland, C., & Prakash, N. (2000). Bridging the gap between organizatonal needs and ERP functionality . *Requirements Engineering, 5*, 180–193. doi:10.1007/PL00010350

Rose, J., & Kraemmergaard, P. (2006). ERP systems and technological discourse shift: Managing the implementation journey. *International Journal of Accounting Information Systems, 7*(3), 217–237. doi:10.1016/j.accinf.2006.06.003

Saliola, F., & Zanfei, A. (2009). Multinational firms, global value chains and the organization of knowledge transfer. *Research Policy, 38*(2), 369–381. doi:10.1016/j.respol.2008.11.003

Sawer, P., Sommerville, I., & Viller, S. (1999). Capturing the benefits of requirements engineering. *IEEE Software, 16*(2), 78–85. doi:10.1109/52.754057

Simatupang, T. M., Sandroto, I. V., & Lubis, S. B. H. (2004). Supply chain coordination in a fashion firm. *International Journal of Supply Chain Management, 9*(3), 256–268. doi:10.1108/13598540410544953

Simatupang, T. M., Wright, A. C., & Sridharan, R. (2002). The knowledge of coordination for supply chain integration. *Business Process Management Journal, 8*(3), 289–308. doi:10.1108/14637150210428989

Smith-Doerr, L., & Powell, W. W. (2005). Networl and economic life . In Smelser, N., & Swedberg, R. (Eds.), *The Handbook of Economic Sociology* (pp. 379–402). Princeton, NJ: Princeton University Press.

Soh, C., Sia, S. K., Boh, W. F., & Tang, M. (2003). Misalignments in ERP implementations: A dialectic perspective. *International Journal of Human-Computer Interaction, 16*(1), 81–100. doi:10.1207/S15327590IJHC1601_6

Sommerville, I., & Sawyer, P. (1998). *Requirements engineering: A good practice guide*. London: Wiley.

Xu, L., & Beamon, B. (2006). Supply chain coordination and cooperation mechanisms: An attribute-based approach. *Journal of Supply Chain Management, 42*(1), 4–12. doi:10.1111/j.1745-493X.2006.04201002.x

## ADDITIONAL READING

Cropper, S., Ebers, M., Huxham, C., & Smith Ring, P. (Eds.). (2008). *The Oxford Handbook of Inter-Organizational Relations*. Oxford: Oxford University Press. doi:10.1093/oxford-hb/9780199282944.001.0001

Davenport, T. (2000). *Mission Critical: Realizing the Promise of Enterprise Systems*. Boston: HBS Press.

Hagemann Snabe, J., Rosenberg A., Mueller, C. & Scvillo, M. (2008), Business process management: The SAP roadmap, Walldorf: SAP Press.

Keller, G., & Teufel, T. (1998). *SAP R/3 Process Oriented Implementation: Iterative Process Prototyping*. Harlow: Addison-Wesley Professional.

# Chapter 2
# Agile Software Development for Customizing ERPs

**Rogério Atem de Carvalho**
*Fluminense Federal Institute, Brazil*

**Björn Johansson**
*Copenhagen Business School, Denmark*

**Rodrigo Soares Manhães**
*State University of North Fluminense, Brazil*

## ABSTRACT

*Customization of ERP systems is a complex task, and great part of this complexity is directly related to requirements management. In this context, a well-known problem is the misfit between the ERP functionalities and the business requirements. This problem comprises communication bottlenecks and difficulties on responding to changes. The proposals for minimizing these misfits are mostly focused on traditional, heavyweight waterfall-like approaches for software development. On the other side, the last decade has witnessed the rise and growth of Agile methods, which have both close communication and fast response to changes among their main values. This chapter maps some of the main agile practices to ERP customization processes, using, where applicable, practices from a real-world ERP project. Moreover, some limitations on the agile approach to ERP customization are presented and discussed.*

## INTRODUCTION

The last decades have witnessed two movements in industrial companies, namely Enterprise Resource Planning systems (ERPs) and Lean Manufacturing techniques. Lean techniques first appeared in the automobile industry within the so-called Toyota Production System, and afterwards were adapted and extended for application in practically all industry segments, forming the basis of what is now called Lean Manufacturing. Lean techniques are based on the principle that activities not delivering value to the final product should be eliminated from the production process. The lean techniques also, instead of just trying to anticipate demand fluctuations, try to follow fluctuations, by the use of the "pull" effect, where instantaneous demand is propagated from clients to suppliers, not the opposite, as was the usual approach some decades ago.

DOI: 10.4018/978-1-61520-625-4.ch002

Copyright © 2010, IGI Global. Copying or distributing in print or electronic forms without written permission of IGI Global is prohibited.

The term ERP was coined in the early 1990s by the Gartner Group (Wylie, 1990), and gained momentum in the years before the Y2K, considered the single event that signaled both the maturing of the ERP industry and the consolidation of large and small vendors (Jacobs & Weston, 2007). Blackstone and Cox (2005) define ERP as a "framework for organizing, defining, and standardizing the business processes necessary to effectively plan and control an organization so the organization can use its internal knowledge to seek external advantage." ERP systems aim to realize integrated management, through the integration of business processes and the data they manipulate (Wier et al., 2007).

As was to be expected, some ERP vendors support Lean production planning and control techniques too, although some problems of this combination can be considered as still opened – since according to lean philosophy, some ERP features are too heavy (Seradex, 2009).

Development of ERP systems is an endeavor with a high level of complexity, and a great deal of this complexity is directly related to requirements management – being the misfit between ERP functionality and business requirements a "classical" problem (So, Kien & Tay-Yap, 2000). The problem of misfit means that there is a gap between functionality offered by the package and functionality required from the adopting organization. Askenäs & Westelius (2000) describe this in the following way: "Many people feel that the current ERP system has taken (or been given) a role that hinders or does not support the business processes to the extent desire". Another way of describing this is as said by Bill Swanton, vice president at AMR research, that only 35 per cent of the organizations are satisfied with the ERP system they use at the moment, and the reason for this dissatisfaction is that the software does not map well with the business goals (Sleeper, 2004). It can be argued that the misfit results from deficiency in the requirement management process, in which business analysts and developers are supposed to agree on what functionality the ERP system should support (Johansson & Carvalho, 2009).

Johansson & Carvalho (2009) suggest that the misfit problem is related to the requirements management process used in ERP development. In fact, the communication between business people and the development teams to a high extent occurs in a waterfall-based software process, which creates a bureaucratic environment where communication is done by documents and not directly between people. Besides that, the ever-changing globalized business environment makes requirement changes could be seen as "natural" events. Therefore, it's necessary to define a customization (and maintenance) process that simultaneously enhances communication between ERP stakeholders and copes with change. Another angle of this problem is that information systems, such as ERPs, deliver too much functionality, which overload users with information. The information overload results in that even if the system contains needed functionality, user may not know about it and have a hard time to find as well as understand how to use the specific functionality. This indicates that instead of talking about misfit or misalignment a better way of describing what is needed could be synchronization between stakeholders, or more specifically, business synchronization. From this it can be said that a focus on business synchronization in the form of describing how ERPs as well as organizations could be developed in tandem would be fruitful. This implies that a focus on how to achieve efficient communication between developers and users, and fast response to change is needed.

A way of both achieving an efficient communication and fast response to change is to deliver software in small and frequent increments, as advocated by Agile software development methods. Agile methods are a reflection of Lean Manufacturing techniques in the Software Engineering realm. Sutton (1996) pointed out that Lean can be a good middle ground between craft development and "software factories", analyzing a real project in which use of lean techniques lead to both quality improvement and cost reduction. Later, Raman (1998) argued that Lean Software Development is a feasible methodology for software development[1].

These methods are well accepted in the general software development community, however, there is no evidence that they are in use in the ERP development community. Additionally, Shehab et al. (2004), Esteves & Bohorquez (2007), and Botta-Genoulaz et al. (2005), show that there exists great extent of ERP research, however the major part is on deployment of ERP systems, being processes for customization a very poorly approached subject.

Therefore, the aim of this chapter is to propose a mapping of agile practices to ERP customization processes, using, where applicable, real world practices from the ERP5 project (Smets-Solanes & Carvalho, 2003). The authors believe that since Lean Manufacturing has proved itself as a way of providing a better production system to enterprises, there is an indication that Lean principles applied to software development can provide better ERP customization, by reducing the misfit problem and thereby increasing synchronization between business processes and process support in the ERP system, while reducing the waste of resources, such as time and money, in ERP customization. It is important to note that customization goes from parameterization to code change (adaptation or creation of new modules), being this second situation – that involves coding, is the one on which this chapter focuses. It is important to note that this work takes as a premise that the decision to modify the ERP code was already taken by the adopting organization.

## AGILE SOFTWARE DEVELOPMENT

Agile development is a generic label for all methodologies based on Agile Manifesto values (Beck et al., 2001). This manifest is a document recognizing four values and twelve principles that basically points out: close collaboration and proximity between the development team and the stakeholders; recognizing requirement changes as results of learning and opportunities to achieve competitive advantage for the organization; the search for simplicity and elimination of unnecessary documentation and processes; emphasizing people rather than processes; and establishment of delivering business value to the stakeholders as the ultimate goal and the ultimate measure of progress. Most of these ideas are not new, but the innovation from Agile Manifesto's proponents was to add all this into a cohesive whole.

Fowler (2005) lists two fundamental differences on agile and traditional approaches to software development. First, agile approaches are adaptive rather than predictive. While predictive approaches see change as a problem to be avoided and an undesirable and costly deviation from the plan, adaptive methods embrace change as an opportunity for improvement. Second, agile approaches are people-oriented, not process-oriented. In the agile view, processes are intended to support people's work rather than to be strictly followed. This leads to recognizing software developers as self-organizing "responsible professionals" and not as disposable and interchangeable "plug compatible programming units".

Unlike traditional approaches, agile methods do not make comprehensive up-front planning. From an agile point of view, planning is a "constant process of reevaluation and course-correction throughout the lifecycle of the project" (Beck & Fowler, 2000). Development is a learning process, an exercise in discovery (Poppendieck & Poppendieck, 2003), and constant planning is the key point for achieving a process that accommodates learning. However, it is impossible to improve learning if the development team has few or no contact with stakeholders, which are the ultimate specification producers. In fact, agile methods recognize that developers and stakeholders must have close cooperation, so development activities are based on concrete feedback rather than speculation.

Brooks (1995) said it is impossible for customers to specify, in a complete and precise way, exact requirements of a relatively complex software project before effectively use some versions of that software. This means that working software is a valuable tool for requirements elicitation, what goes against the phased lifecycle of traditional, waterfall-based approaches, in which programming is a later activity. For achieving an effective learning, the software delivered should be a production-quality, full-featured release rather than a prototype.

Agile methods solve this question with the use of short iterations. In short periods of time, working software is released so that the stakeholders can check if the implemented software is exactly what they need. For each iteration is allocated a small number of features, which are implemented by the team within the iteration. The iterations must be as short as possible. This means that the software is delivered into frequent and small increments. This technique is common to all iterative and incremental lifecycles, and is used to cope with not well established or instable requirements. In that way, it is possible for both developers and users to explore incrementally the requirements and the way the software is built, allowing a better adherence to the users' demands. Furthermore, smaller increments and shorter iterations, faster feedback cycles, leads to a very fine granularity project control and allows rapid correction of deviations from business needs (Martin, 1999).

In the same way, the requirements elicitation process could also be incremental. The features are not detailed at the beginning of the project, but only a list of features is initially extracted. In this context, each item from this list is not a requirement, but a record of its existence, a commitment for future conversation (Jeffries et al., 2000). The details about a feature are only analyzed in deep within the iteration which the feature is allocated.

During a project, the feature list can be changed several times reflecting its learning about the software being created and about the needs of the software. Agile methods is therefore a powerful tool for minimizing waste and promoting simplicity in the software development process, because decisions of what will be the scope is not made once in the beginning of the project, but iteratively in the project. Thus, only really needed features are implemented.

Currently, the most widely adopted agile-based methods are Scrum (Schwaber, 2004) and Extreme Programming (Beck, 1999; Beck & Andres, 2004). Scrum is a management-centered approach characterized by time-boxed iterations called sprints, project tracking by feature lists called backlogs, diary meetings and iteration periodic retrospectives for continuous improvement. Scrum do not prescribe engineering practices, the team must choose the techniques that best adapt to its environment. Extreme Programming (XP) is an approach that strongly supports the development team at the engineering point of view. XP is built around a set of values, principles and practices. The values are the philosophical background, the practices are the concrete expressions of the values and principles are guidelines to translate the values into practices. XP's practices focus on very small iterations (1-2 weeks), all-time peer review, test-first programming, refactoring, emergent design and continuous integration. In the real world, several teams use both Scrum for project management and XP for engineering issues (Kniberg, 2007), though XP itself also covers management, planning and so on.

In the next sections the main agile-related practices are discussed. It is important to note that some of them are directly related to agile practices, while others where embraced by these methods. Since the distinction of techniques' origins is not in the scope of this chapter, they are treated equally in this text.

## Ubiquitous Language

The concept of *ubiquitous language* is very important for communication, feedback and close collaboration between customers and developers (Evans, 2004). When communication between customer and the development team uses less documents and textual specifications and goes more to face-to-face dialogue and learning, there is a need for an effective shared language between those groups. The ubiquitous language is a common language for the whole project, covering the entire communication chain from customer and business analysis to the team's internal conversations and coding. The ubiquitous language reflects and feedbacks the knowledge about the domain and must be exercised all the time in all communication tasks. This language does not necessarily uses the exact customer jargon, but an unambiguous and contradiction-free version of the domain knowledge. An ubiquitous language is not built in a single step, but it is iteratively refined and improved. According to Evans (2004), the model has to be used "as a backbone of a language", so "a change in the ubiquitous language is a change to the model".

## Test-Driven Development

Test-Driven Development (TDD) is a technique that consists of writing test cases for any programming (new or feature adaptation, improvements, bug corrections etc.), before these implementations are performed. TDD is also known as test-first programming, which is the label when TDD is included as XP practices. Koskela (2007) said TDD is intended for "solving the right problem right", meaning to achieve the correct solution that exactly matches the business problem.

For obtaining the correct solution, TDD prescribes automated unit tests, pieces of code that excite the code that has to be implemented. Thus, automated unit tests written before implementation lead the programmer to think and

work in terms of contracts and collaborations between objects.

For matching business problems, TDD brings automated acceptance tests, which see the system as a black box. Thus, a full suite of acceptance tests fulfills, for most projects, any need for requirements documentation, having the advantage to be verifiable at any time. Furthermore, the collaboration between customers and developers provided by TDD is a tool for the improvement of the ubiquitous language (Crispin, 2006).

There are also integration tests, that tests collaboration of the units with the outside world (network, persistence, operating system and so on) and the collaboration of the units between themselves. There are several techniques and tools for supporting both unit, integration and acceptance tests, available for most programming languages and platforms.

TDD is not only a set of testing tools, but, primarily, a design technique, and in TDD design are made all the time (Beck & Andres, 2004), having no place for a "design phase". In fact, in an agile environment, up-front design is considered an anti-pattern (Ambler, 2002). In the TDD approach, the current design is only suitable in the current iteration, being the design improved for accommodating new requirements in every iteration. With good programming and design techniques, the design of a system can be continuously improved without to fall into the famous Boehm's cost of change curve (Boehm, 1981), which established that the cost of change in a software project increases exponentially through the time. Modern programming techniques, powerful development tools, more expressive and simple languages, more powerful computing and other advances make the cost of change increase very slowly through the time for the most features. Poppendieck & Poppendieck (2003) pointed out that there are a few "high-stake constraints" such as the choice of programming language and architectural layering decisions which could have a high cost of change later on. All other, largely the most follow a horizontally asymptotic cost of change curve.

For supporting this kind of evolving design, the unit tests are written in very small increments called baby steps. Baby steps, when applied to TDD, minimizes the time between an error and its discovering and keeps the complexity low (Beck, 1999). In this context, each baby step could be seen as one iteration in the TDD lifecycle.

## Continuous Integration

In several projects, integration brings up a bunch of problems that needs to be taken into account: incompatibility between modules, broken dependencies, out of date modules, low test coverage, lack of compliance to coding standards etc. This is the so-called "integration hell" which implies that the greater the amount of code to integrate is, the more complex is the integration process, as described by Fowler (2006).

Continuous integration (CI) is a software development practice proposed to solve the integration problems by providing both agility and fast feedback, consisting of making (at least) daily project builds (Fowler, 2006). The concept of build used here is the whole process comprising: get the latest source code from the main repository, build the application and the database, perform both testing, inspection and deploying, run software in a production similar environment and give automatic and real-time feedback to developers, ensuring that the integrated parts act as a cohesive whole and that there is always a working version of the software available in the repository.

The environment needed for CI to work can be from a simple script to complex, full-featured continuous integration servers. Though CI seems to be an infrastructural topic, it is primarily a "shared agreement by the team" so that they keep the source code always passing on all tests and inspections and running the build process every few hours (Shore, 2005). A CI environment must also have a single source code repository, usually

managed by a version control system. Besides the source code, everything that is not automatically generated should be in the repository.

CI plays an important role on providing information just-in-time to projects. A CI environment provides a means to anyone get the latest executable and run it on his machine. Furthermore, most CI environments have a website, automatically updated by the build process, which gives useful information such as hosting status about the builds, test coverage rates and code inspection reports.

The main goals of continuous integration are improving quality and reducing risk (Duvall et al., 2007). Quality improvement comes from the execution of all tests, code inspections and deployments for each build. This assures that overall software is always on a valid state and prevents the system to be inadvertently broken by a developer's code commit. The risk reduction is provided by the high frequency of builds and the fast feedback mechanisms. CI servers immediately warn the developers if something goes wrong, usually by e-mail, but even by SMS messages, visual warnings in light globes or big monitors, sound flags and so on, depending on project specificities.

## Emergent Design

In an iterative and incremental, agile-style life-cycle, design is not performed up-front, but is incrementally evolved. At each iteration, the design is only that enough to match the current requirements. Any feature that can be useful to future iterations must be designed in the future iterations. This avoids both speculation and resource wasting and keeps the team focused on designing the features prioritized by the stakeholders.

Bain (2008) defines emergent design as "a process of evolving systems in response to changing requirements, better understanding of existing requirements, and in response to new opportunities that arise from new technology, better ideas, and a changing world". For a safe application of this principle, some technical disciplines must be applied, as TDD, refactoring, expressive code and a heavy use of patterns.

## Expressive Code

Applications are intended to be maintained for a long time, so it is safe to conclude that a program, in its whole lifetime, will be much more read than written, making code expressiveness a must. The key point to analyze code expressivity is that simple, clean and readable code matters (Beck, 2007). In fact, if the codebase is not good, programmers will face a number of problems: excessive code complexity, bad design decisions obfuscated by confusing codification, excess of comments due to unreadable code - polluting the source file, difficulties on applying improvements or corrections and, consequently, rapid degeneration towards legacy code.

Accepting that source code is the ultimate software design (Reeves, 1992) and its tendency is to be as complex as the domain in which it is applied, makes code expressivity a quest to minimize the complexity of source code. Therefore code expressivity means choosing the simplest effective solution; avoiding over-engineering by using iterative and incremental approaches; applying both meaningful, plain English, pronounceable, non-abbreviated, domain-related, ubiquitous language-compliant and unambiguous names for all identifiers; avoiding any kind of duplication; applying optimization only where demonstrably necessary and so on. Expressive code is the code that reveals the programmer's intention with absolute clarity. Excellent fonts on coding best-practices and how to write expressive code are Beck (2007) and Martin (2008).

## Agile and ERP

Others authors have already proposed the use of Agile methods in ERP customization. One of the first was Alleman (2002), who states that manag-

ing an ERP project is not the same of managing a large IT project. The ERP environment faces constant changes and reassessment of organizational processes and technology, therefore the project management method used with ERP deployment must provide adaptability and agility to support this evolutionary environment. Alleman (op. cit.) and Meszaros & Aston (2007) agree that the application of scientific management – here represented by "high-ceremony" or document-driven processes – is understandable in many ERP deployment cases since many target companies has a tradition in engineering and business that make them think in terms of waterfall development processes. However, Alleman (op. cit.) alerts that "the use of predictive strategies in this [ERP deployment] environment is inappropriate as well as ineffective since they do not address the emergent and sometimes chaotic behaviors of the market place, the stakeholders, and the vendors' offerings." Alleman (op. cit.) goes forward proposing a different decision method in ERP project management, using an options approach to decision making, given that ERP projects has the flexibility to make changes to investments when new information is obtained, by treating this flexibility as an option allows decisions to be made in presence of uncertainty.

Meszaros & Aston (2007) present the specific case of the customization of a SAP/R3 module using agile principles and techniques. In this case study, major cultural and technical problems were identified:

It is most accepted in the SAP community [and in every ERP community in general] that most companies should change their business processes to match SAP's. This "product works this way" goes against "whatever the customer wants" mindset of the agile philosophy.

Developers' roles in SAP are quite separated, for instance ABAP programmers (who actually write the code) need to be helped by "Basis" specialists to install software. As well as "Functional" analysts are needed to configure components. This specialization of roles, besides going against the agile principle that a developer must be a generalist, also difficult effort estimation. Traditional SAP development is a document driven process, while agile philosophy emphasizes on person-to-person collaboration. ABAP development in SAP is server based. Without the capacity of creating individual development environments for running unit tests, a strategy of pessimist locks in code had to be assumed, creating a serious impediment for Continuous Integration.

Frequent deployment, even in the ERP development environment, needed to go through strict governance processes, which forced discussions to identify the integration points and "pre test" the integration. Moreover, it uses typical waterfall Quality Assurance processes, focused on "could this possibly work" way of thinking, instead of the "does this line up with how the company wants to do things" agile way. There was the necessity of aligning the customization schedule to the release of SAP's service packs, so that important new features wouldn't be overlapped.

Seeking to overcome the cultural problems the development team, composed by programmers and the other necessary SAP's roles, was stimulated to work in a closer fashion, for instance sitting side-by-side to implement both coding and configuration. Regarding the technical problems, an "Agile Zone", consisted of one dedicated developer workspace for each pair of developers, was created to address the server-based development issues. Although these measures had the expected effect, the costly SAP specialized personnel altogether with less-than-state-of-the-art development tools caused the final project cost hit more than the double of the estimated allocated costs for off-the-shelf tools and generalist professionals.

This chapter aims to contribute to this discussion by providing a mapping between the specific techniques used by Agile methods and ERP customization, being these techniques necessary to make the agile practices work. This proposal complements Meszaros & Aston (2007), who

describe the creation of a development environment and the cultural changes needed for agile development for a specific ERP product, and Alleman (2002), who describes the decision process involved in customizing and deploying an ERP using agile principles.

The next topic will discuss the mapping of the Agile practices described previously to ERP customization, focusing on programming and integration techniques, since the "higher" level techniques and philosophy were already described by other authors.

## MAPPING AGILE AND LD TO ERP CUSTOMIZATION

When mapping Agile and Lean Development to the efforts of customizing an ERP system, it is important to clearly state what customization means. In the paper we define customization as the changes that are made to the system that are deployed in the using organization. This means that there is a need to distinguish between different ways of deployment. The basic difference needed to distinguish between is if the using organizations buy the software which they then host by themselves or if they buy the hosting of the ERP as a service. The difference between these is that changes made in the software as customization is done at different places and by different actors. In the external hosting case it can be said that customization is done closer to the vendor and that means that they have a "better" chance of learning from the changes but also to more easily implement the changes for other users. However, independent on who does the customization, customization means to a high extent to adjust the specific software to the business processes it should support. The basic thinking about customization is that it should be done for one specific instance of the software, which means that for the development of commercial off the shelf (COTS) products, such as ERP systems, could be seen as a paradox since the basic assumption is that the software should be so general that it could be sold as a product attracting a broad customer base. However, customization exists and in some cases in a high extent.

Another question is if the kind of business model used to deliver the ERP system - open source ERP, in-house development (based on open source or not), external hosting ERP, direct sale ERP (the ERP vendor sales directly to its customer) or indirect sale ERP (the vendor use a partner channel as distributor of the ERP), can influence how customization is done and, therefore, on how Agile practices can be applied. An answer to that question is that, as a general rule, the influence is more related to the customization level than to the business model. If customization is limited to parameterization then Agile techniques do not apply, while if customization goes beyond parameter adjustments there are code changes, Agile techniques can be applied; being the in-house development the extreme case of customization, where all Agile techniques can be applied.

## Iterative and Incremental Development

Customizing an ERP incrementally conflicts with the common sense in the Enterprise Information Systems community of the necessity of modeling the organization's processes, manufacturing resources and structure, as suggested by Vernadat (2002) and Shen et al (2004), in advance to the system development. In fact, modeling beforehand is necessary to, among other things, to identify possible process improvements and integration points, however, this creates a waterfall development process, bringing all the well known problems related to this kind of process.

Therefore, one question to be solved when using Agile methods, or any iterative incremental lifecycle in general for customizing ERPs, is how to both achieve (a) incremental requirements elicitation and (b) light rework due to late

process integration identification? This second situation, which occurs when, during the system development, a given business process is implemented into the software without identifying all its connections with other process, or even as it was a standalone process – a natural situation in a process where the requirements are identified incrementally. Thus, what happens if in later iterations, when requirements are better understood, it is realized that this process needs to be integrated to other processes, leading to changes in code and consequent rework?

This situation is here labeled as the "Late Integration Problem", and will occur every time that the whole Business Process Modeling is not done before the actual customization of the system takes place. Moreover, this problem can be generalized to how to cope with constant changes in business processes, without incurring in excessive rework.

The answer to this problem is that the ERP framework must provide fast and flexible process integration – preferably through configuration instead of coding, so that integration points identified lately during the requirements detail will not demand heavy rework. In that way it is possible to rapidly reconfigurate and integrate business processes so that both incremental requirements elicitation and fast changing is achieved. For achieving this, the framework must provide ways to rapidly connect business process while keeping louse coupling, enabling the automatic – or configurable - creation of proper calling chains, GUI navigation, and information passing between processes. With these features it is possible to identify lately integration points and rapidly provide integration among the process.

To exemplify how this can be done in practice, ERP5's framework is briefly presented in the Annex. ERP5 shows how proper programming techniques can make a system highly flexible, helping the adoption of Agile principles and thereby treating changes in the software as natural – and low cost - events.

## Ubiquitous Language

Creating a ubiquitous language is, as described earlier, extremely important for making communication between developers and users more effective. How this can be done in the ERP system case to a high extent depends on the ERP business model. Grudin (1991) describes this problem by identifying when and how the users are identified in the development process. He distinguishes between three different development situations: competitively bid/contract development, product development, and in-house/custom development. The difference between these three is that, when it comes to when users are identified, the product development situation first identifies the users when the system is delivered. To deal with this problem, proprietary ERP vendors use different methods. Microsoft, for instance, in the development of their Dynamics products uses "Personas". The basic thinking about Personas is that they are fictive users that are developed from interviews with a small sub-set of potential users, used to provide the developer with a better view over for whom they develop a specific system. To be able to do so the Personas are rich descriptions which should give the developer an understanding on who the users are, what they do and the context in which they do their work. However, even if Personas is one substitute for having a direct communication with the users it could be questioned if that is enough to higher customization levels. In those cases, the direct relation with real users is more efficient.

## Test-Driven Development

TDD is directly applicable to ERP customization, in special when dealing with high-level (black-box) testing. Given that an ERP will either substitute an exiting system (or collection of systems) or will automate business processes, plenty of test cases will be available.

However, the presence of testing data is not enough. Since ERP is both an integrated software and an adaptable framework, regression testing is a must. Regression testing occurs, for instance, when a given module is altered to meet a given customer's specific needs. After proceeding with the unit tests, it is necessary to run integration tests to assure that modifications do not create side effects on related parts of the system. Although this seems to be obvious, one of TDD tenets is that automated test are built in a incremental way, so when the system becomes more complex, testing also becomes more complex, but if the tests follow this complexity growing (as they are designed even before the actual coding), they will cope with heavy testing jobs. Therefore, a possible difference between current ERP customization and this technique is that besides supplying the necessary information for changing the system code – including the code itself or proper APIs, it is necessary also to supply all the test scripts, so that integration also can be tested.

Moreover, when new updates are provided to all users, customers that have implemented exclusive features must (a) re-implement these features on the upgraded version and (b) run all the tests against the new version of the system. Although this can be seen as an extra customization job, thorough testing is necessary for obtaining quality software and it is an important benefit. If all testing is automated, it is possible, even before actually implementing a customization (initial or upgrade related) to test if the customization will work, by the use of mocks, objects that are injected into the unit under test and act in place of the real objects for testing purposes. Moreover, by verifying side effects and errors identified during the tests using mocks, it is possible to enhance estimates for re-implementing customizations in the newly upgraded module.

Therefore, automated testing and mocking can reduce substantially the customization effort, even helping detecting integration problems between standard code and customized code before the second is totally implemented or re-inserted into upgraded modules.

## Continuous Integration

This technique can bring a series of benefits for ERP customization involving code changes. First, CI can help on continuously provide working versions of a customized module, which can be checked by users as modifications and new features are introduced, in a incremental way, reducing the risks of occurring misfits. Of course, to achieve such benefit, it is necessary that key users stay near the development team, testing the increments and providing constant feedback. In fact, using CI automated tests and expressive code – that provides direct mapping between requirements and code can automate part of the validation tasks, reducing the effort of key users, and providing very fast feedback.

An ERP provider and/or its partner network must keep not only a CI environment but also all configuration and test cases, both the ones used for standardized deployments, and also the customized ones. This environment can be recovered at the time of any future upgrade, and will help when a new upgrade comes and the modifications of specific customizations must be re-inserted into the upgraded module.

## Emergent Design

When it comes to ED and ERP customization it can be stated that this technique is limited, given that in any ERP environment[3] in general, ED has limitations in refactoring deepness, since the core framework cannot be changed ad hoc. One restriction could be access to the ERP source code which is directly related to the basic architecture of the ERP. For instance, in the SAP case we have the use of ABAP (Advanced Business Application Programming) which probably restricts the possibilities to implement an ED approach. From that it could said maybe ED is more applicable to the creation of entire new ERP modules, when programmers have access to all design decisions in this particular piece of the system. Also, it is

highly applicable in in-house and open source ERP development, but also in some proprietary ERP systems such as Microsoft Dynamics Navision that provides its end-user with total accessibility to the source code.

## Limitations to the Agile Approach in ERP

A series of limitations to the use of Agile methods in the current ERP realm can be identified, some of them, mainly the cultural ones, also happens with other types of systems, other are very specific to ERP customization and life cycles.

## Cultural Limitations

Scientific Management and its predictive planning approach are well disseminated and work well in other types of projects, making it hard to high management to accept following a reactive way of managing the ERP customization and deployment project.

Many ERP, such as SAP, uses document-driven processes to make clear separated roles communicate. This type of process not only makes communication slower, but also stimulates the creation of modeling and communication artifacts that do not aggregate value to final users. Besides that, stimulates the high specialization of the workforce, making people less flexible in skills, going against one of the modern production principles of flexible production resources. Flexible resources makes adaptation to fluctuations (such as in specific skills during the project) easier and cheaper, reducing resource bottlenecks and allowing higher degrees of product customization.

## Technical Limitations

Pioneer ERPs pay the price of legacy technologies and their limitations, which sometimes becomes a burden for the use of fully object oriented techniques, in which Agile methods rely. Moreover, built-in tools, such as SAP's ABAP, on one hand simplify some development tasks, but on the other, make the whole ERP development community depend on a single supplier to evolve these tools - while ERPs based on open languages and standards take advantage of all language and tool evolution, independently of the ERP supplier.

The database-centric ERP configuration task brings all the limitations of using RDBMS, including the difficult of using Agile techniques such as Refactoring and Emergent Design (Ambler, 2008)[4].

## Language Limitations

A limitation to Agile-based ERP customization can be in the ubiquitous language, if the ERP, because of eventual architectural idiosyncrasies, does not allow a one-to-one mapping between business domain and domain model. In some cases, uncoupling techniques as façades (Gamma et. al, 1995) or even an anticorruption layer (Evans, 2004) can be useful. These techniques, however, does not eliminate the duplicity of languages (non-compliant to UL in the ERP itself and compliant in the customization).

## CONCLUSION AND RESEARCH DIRECTIONS

This chapter starts on the premise that the adopter have already chosen a specific ERP and already decided to change part of its code to make it fit better to the adopter's business needs. Although this situation seems to be somehow a paradox for the ERP world, it is more common than it should be. Additionally, considering new ways of providing and developing ERPs, such as open source ERPs, it can be stated that the role that end-users have in development have changed, indicating that they are more involved the development and in that way it could be a change towards agile methods (and their Lean principles). Moreover, the statistics on

unsuccessful ERP implementations urges for new ways of facing the customization problem.

It can be concluded that agile methods in development of ERPs builds on the premises that efficient communication between developers and ERP end-users can be achieved. One way that agile development advocates how this could be achieved is by delivering software in small and frequent increments. However, interesting research questions is then how efficient communication can be gained in different kinds of business models used to deliver the ERP system - open source ERP, in-house development (based on open source or not), external hosting ERP, direct sale ERP (the vendor sales directly to the customer) or indirect sale ERP (the vendor uses a partner channel as distributor), since these models differs a lot on how to deliver the software.

It can also be concluded that a potential benefit in agile development of ERPs, which is especially relevant for ERP customization, is the fact that agile development approaches are adaptive rather than predictive. This means that if it is possible to implement them in ERP customization, it can be stated that it is more likely that the ERP and the organizations' business processes will develop in tandem and thereby fulfill the goals of business synchronization. The main conclusion is that agile software development for customizing ERPs have a great potential but it demands a close cooperation between different ERP stakeholders, so that customization is based on concrete feedback and not speculation.

A future outcome of this work is to identify the Agile and Lean practices adoption level in ERP customization, differentiating the proprietary, free/open source, and in-house solutions. Also, investigating how ERP frameworks technologies have evolved to accompany the new demands for flexible solutions would help understanding the technological hindrances to better ERP deployment. In that way, it would be possible to identify the process and product related problems that have been making ERP deployment sometimes failure.

# REFERENCES

Alleman, G. B. (2002). Agile Project Management Methods for ERP: How to Apply Agile Processes to Complex COTS Projects and Live to Tell About It. In Extreme Programming and Agile Methods: XP/Agile Universe 2002 (LNCS 2418, pp. 70–88). Berlin: Springer Verlag.

Ambler, S. (2002). *Agile Modeling: Effective Practices for Extreme Programming and the Unified Process*. New York: Wiley.

Ambler, S. (2008). When IT Gets Cultural: Data Management and Agile Development. *IEEE IT Professional*, *10*(6), 11–14. doi:10.1109/MITP.2008.135

Askenäs, L., & Westelius, A. (2000). Five roles of an information system: a social constructionist approach to analyzing the use of ERP systems. In *Proceedings of 21st International Conference on Information Systems*. Brisbane, Australia: Association for Information Systems.

Bain, S. (2008). *Emergent Design: The Evolutionary Nature of Professional Software Development*. Reading, MA: Addison-Wesley.

Beck, K. (1999). *Extreme Programming Explained: Embrace Change*. Reading, MA: Addison-Wesley.

Beck, K. (2007). *Implementation Patterns*. Reading, MA: Addison-Wesley.

Beck, K., et al. (2001). *Manifesto for Agile Software Development*. Retrieved February 10, 2009, from http://agilemanifesto.org

Beck, K., & Andres, C. (2004). *Extreme Programming Explained: Embrace Change* (2nd ed.). Reading, MA: Addison-Wesley.

Beck, K., & Fowler, M. (2000). *Planning Extreme Programming*. Reading, MA: Addison-Wesley.

Blackstone, J. H., Jr., & Cox, J. F. (2005). APICS Dictionary, (11th ed., pp. 38). Chicago: APICS: The Association for Operations Management.

Boehm, B. (1981). *Software Engineering Economics*. Upper Saddle River, NJ: Prentice-Hall.

Botta-Genoulaz, V., Millet, P. A., & Grabot, B. (2006). A survey on the recent research literature on ERP systems. *Computers in Industry*, *56*(6), 510–522. doi:10.1016/j.compind.2005.02.004

Brooks, F. P. (1995). *The Mythical Man-Month*. Reading, MA: Addison-Wesley.

Bulka, A. (2001). *Relationship Manager Pattern*. Retrieved January 31, 2009 from http://www.atug.com/andypatterns/rm.htm

Carvalho, R. A., Campos, R., & Monnerat, R. M. (2009). ERP System Implementation from the Ground up: The ERP5 Development Process and Tools . In Ramachandran, M., & Carvalho, R. A. (Eds.), *Org.), Handbook of Research on Software Engineering and Productivity Technologies: Implications of Globalisation*. Hershey, PA: IGI Global.

Carvalho, R. A., & Monnerat, R. M. (2007). ERP5: Designing for Maximum Adaptability. In G. Wilson & A. Oram, (Org.), Beautiful Code: Leading Programmers Explain How They Think, (pp. 339-351). Sebastopol, CA: O'Reilly Media.

Carvalho, R. A., & Monnerat, R. M. (2008). Development Support Tools for Enterprise Resource Planning. *IT Professional*, *10*, 39–45. doi:10.1109/MITP.2008.100

Crispin, L. (2006). Driving Software Quality: How Test-Driven Impacts Software Quality. *IEEE Software*, *23*(6), 70–71. doi:10.1109/MS.2006.157

Duvall, P. (2007). *Continuous Integration: Improving Software Quality and Reducing Risk*. Reading, MA: Addison-Wesley.

Esteves, J., & Bohorquez, V. (2007). An updated ERP systems annotated bibliography: 2001-2005. *Communications of AIS, 19*, 386–446.

Evans, E. (2004). *Domain-Driven Design: Tackling Complexity in the Heart of Software*. Reading, MA: Addison-Wesley.

Fowler, M. (2005). *The New Methodology*. Retrieved January 28, 2009 from http://martinfowler. com/ articles/newMethodology.html

Fowler, M. (2006). *Continuous Integration*. Retrieved February 8, 2009 from http://martinfowler. com/ articles/continuousIntegration.html

Fowler, M. (2008). *Agile Versus Lean*. 2008. Retrieved January 12, 2009 from http://martinfowler. com/bliki/AgileVersusLean.html

Gamma, E. (1995). *Design Patterns: Elements of Reusable Object-Oriented Software*. Reading, MA: Addison-Wesley.

Grudin, J. (1991). Interactive Systems: Bridging the Gaps Between Developers and Users. *Computer, 24*(4), 59–69. doi:10.1109/2.76263

Jacobs, F. R., & Weston, F. C. (2007). Enterprise resource planning (ERP): A Brief History. *Journal of Operations Management, 25*(2), 357–363. doi:10.1016/j.jom.2006.11.005

Jeffries, R. (2000). *Extreme Programming Installed*. Reading, MA: Addison-Wesley.

Johansson, B., & Carvalho, R. A. (2009). Management of Requirements in ERP development: A Comparison between Proprietary and Open Source ERP. In SAC conference 2009, Hawaii.

Johnson, J. (2002). *ROI, It's Your Job*. Published Keynote on the 3rd International Conference on Extreme Programming, Alghero, Italy.

Kniberg, H. (2007). *Scrum and XP from the Trenches: How We Do Scrum*. Retrieved December 28, 2008 from http://www.crisp.se/henrik.kniberg/ ScrumAndXpFromTheTrenches.pdf

Koskela, L. (2007). *Test-Driven: TDD and Acceptance TDD for Java Developers*. Manning.

Martin, R. (1999). *Iterative and Incremental Development*. Retrieved February 1, 2009 from http://www.objectmentor.com/resources/ articles/ IIDII.pdf

Martin, R. (2008). *Clean Code: A Handbook of Agile Software Craftsmanship*. Upper Saddle River, NJ: Prentice-Hall.

Meszaros, G., & Aston, J. (2007). Agile ERP: "You don't know what you've got 'till it's gone!" In *Proceedings of the Agile 2007 Conference* (pp. 143-149). Washington, DC.

Monnerat, R. M., Carvalho, R. A., & Campos, R. (2008). Enterprise Systems Modeling: the ERP5 Development Process. In *Proceedings of the XXIII ACM Simposium on Applied Computing*. v. II. (pp. 1062-1068). New York: ACM.

Poppendieck, M., & Poppendieck, T. (2003). *Lean Software Development: An Agile Toolkit*. Addison-Wesley.

Raman, S. (1998). Lean Software Development: Is It Feasible? In *Proceedings of the 17th Digital Avionics Systems Conference* (pp 13-18). Washington, DC: IEEE.

Reeves, J. (1992). What Is Software Design? In *C++ Journal, Fall 1992*. Retrieved January 10, 2009 from http://www.developerdotstar.com/mag/ articles/reeves_design.html

Schwaber, K. (2004). *Agile Project Management with Scrum*. Redmond, WA: Microsoft Press.

Seradex. (2009). *Lean Manufacturing: Seradex ERP Solutions*. Retrieved February 5, 2009 from http://www.seradex.com/ERP/Lean_Manufacturing_ERP.php

Shehab, E. M., Sharp, M. W., Supramaniam, L., & Spedding, T. A. (2004). Enterprise resource planning: An integrative review. *Business Process Management Journal*, *10*(4), 359–386. doi:10.1108/14637150410548056

Shen, H., Wall, B., Zaremba, M., Chen, Y., & Browne, J. (2004). Integration of Business Modeling Methods for Enterprise Information System Analysis and User Requirements Gathering. *Computers in Industry*, *54*(3), 307–323. doi:10.1016/j.compind.2003.07.009

Shore, J. (2005). *Continuous Integration is an Attitude, Not a Tool*. Retrieved December 30, 2008 from http://jamesshore.com/Blog/Continuous-Integration-is-an-Attitude.html

Sleeper, S. Z. (2004). *AMR Analysts Discuss Role-Based ERP Interfaces - The User-Friendly Enterprise*. Retrieved December 20, 2008 from http://www.sapdesignguild.org/editions/edition8/print_amr.asp

Smets-Solanes, J., & Carvalho, R. A. (2002). An Abstract Model for An Open Source ERP System: The ERP5 Proposal. In *Proceedings of the VIII International Conference on Industrial Engineering and Operations Management*, Curitiba, Brazil.

Smets-Solanes, J.-P., & Carvalho, R. A. (2003). ERP5: A Next-Generation, Open-Source ERP Architecture. *IEEE IT Professional*, *5*(4), 38–44. doi:10.1109/MITP.2003.1216231

Soh, C., Kien, S. S., & Tay-Yap, J. (2000). Cultural fits and misfits: Is ERP a universal solution? *Communications of the ACM*, *43*(4), 47–51. doi:10.1145/332051.332070

Sutton, J. M. (1996). Lean Software for the Lean Aircraft. In *Proceedings of the 15th Digital Avionics Systems Conference* (pp. 49-54). Washington, DC: IEEE.

Vernadat, F. B. (2002). Enterprise Modeling and Integration (EMI): Current Status and Research Perspectives. *Annual Reviews in Control*, *26*, 15–25. doi:10.1016/S1367-5788(02)80006-2

Wier, B., Hunton, J., & Hassab-Elnaby, H. R. (2007). Enterprise Resource Planning Systems and Non-Financial Performance Incentives: The Joint Impact on Corporate Performance. *International Journal of Accounting Information Systems*, *8*, 165–190. doi:10.1016/j.accinf.2007.05.001

Wylie, L. (1990). A Vision of the Next-Generation MRP II. *Scenario*, S-300-339.

## KEY TERMS AND DEFINITIONS

**ERP:** Enterprise Resource Planning system, a kind of software which main goal is to integrate all data and processes of an organization into a unified system.

**ERP Customization:** In the paper ERP customization is defined as code changes that are made either with the aim of adaptation or creation of new modules, which means that ERP customization from the adopters point of view already are decided upon beforehand. ERP customization is thereby not something that is done on already deployed code.

**ERP Customization Life Cycle:** The set of activities accomplished to customize and keep the customization code up-to-date with new system upgrades and new requirements, during the whole ERP particular instance lifecycle.

**Late Integration Problem:** Occurs when during the system development, a given business process is implemented into the software without identifying all its connections with other process, or even as it was a standalone process – a natural situation in a process where the requirements are identified incrementally. When in later iterations, as requirements are better understood, it is realized that this process needs to be integrated to other ones, changes in the code will be necessary, incurring in rework. This situation will always occur when the entire Business Modeling is not done before the actual development or customization of the system.

**Business Synchronization:** Synchronization means that the organization's business processes and the supporting technology evolves in tandem so that when either of these parts changes the other part adjust to the change. Business synchronization then means that there exists organization-technology synchronization.

**Agile Methods:** Agile methods are a generic label for development and/or project management methodologies that view software development as a learning process, and prescribe close collaboration with the customers; working, production-quality software released at short iterations; code-centric development; fast feedback chain; simplicity; and the elimination of processes that do not aggregate value to the product. Agile methods emphasize people rather than processes and have delivering business value as the ultimate measure of progress.

**Lean Development:** Lean Development is a mapping of Lean concepts to the software development domain. It is based on Lean principles as waste elimination, team empowerment, built-in quality, late irreversible decisions and so on. In recent years, Lean Development has gained mo-

mentum within the Agile community, since many of its propositions match agile views.

## ENDNOTES

[1]   It is important to note that the term "Lean Development" (LD) is becoming more used nowadays, however the authors understand, in concordance to Fowler (2008), that Agile methods are conceptually aligned to Lean Manufacturing and adopt a series of its concepts.

[2]   The complete code can be found at http://svn.erp5.org/erp5/trunk/products/ ERP5/tests/testTradeCondition.py and http://svn.erp5.org/erp5/trunk/bt5/erp5_ trade/SkinTemplateItem/portal_skins/ erp5_trade/Order_applyTradeCondition. xml?revision=24616&view=markup

[3]   In fact in any framework based environment.

[4]   In fact that's a half cultural and half technical limitation.

## APPENDIX – ERP5 BASIC PRINCIPLES

*Figure 1. Simple example of expressive coding in ERP5[2]: A requirement generates a test and a method, all keeping very close, directly related names.*

Requirement: "For a given order, apply to it a trade condition
negotiated between buyer and seller"

Test Class  TestApplyTradeCondition()

Business Class Method Order_applyTradeCondition()

This annex briefly presents the ERP5 framework, showing how it can support the use of Agile and Lean Development techniques in ERP customization. A Model Driven approach for developing enterprise systems on top of ERP5 can be found at Carvalho, Campos & Monnerat (2009).

## ERP5

The ERP5 project (Smets-Solanes & Carvalho, 2002; Smets-Solanes & Carvalho, 2003) is a Free and Open Source (FOS-ERP) that aims at offering an integrated management solution based on the open source Zope platform, written in the Python scripting language. This platform delivers an object database (ZODB), a workflow engine (DCWorkflow), and rapid GUI scripting based on XML. Additionally, ERP5 incorporates data synchronization among different object databases and a object-relational mapping scheme that stores indexing attributes of each object in a relational database, allowing much faster object search and retrieval, in comparison to ZODB, and also analytical processing and reporting. This project was initiated in 2001 by two French companies, Nexedi – its main developer, and Coramy – its first user, and since then is in development and use by a growing community from France, Brazil, Germany, Poland, Senegal, Japan, and India, among others. ERP5 is named after the five core business entities that define its Unified Business Model (UBM, Figure 1

*Resource:* describes an abstract resource in a given business process (such as individual skills, products, machines etc). Material lists, as well as prototypes are defined by the relationship between nodes.

*Node*: a business entity that receives and sends resources. They can be related to physical entities (such as industrial facilities) or abstract ones (such as a bank account). Metanodes are nodes containing other nodes, such as companies.

*Path*: describes how a node accesses needed resources.

*Movement*: describes a movement of resources among nodes, in a given moment and for a given period of time. For example, such movement can be the shipping of raw material from the warehouse to the factory.

*Item*: a physical instance of a resource.

The structure of an ERP5 instance is defined through mappings of the particular instance concepts to the five core concepts and supportive classes or, in very rare cases, through the extension of the UBM.

*Figure 2. ERP5 Unified Business Model*

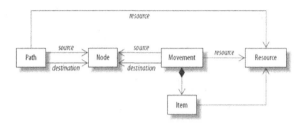

This mapping is documented by a proper instance's lexicon. For example, debit and credit values can be mapped to the Quantity property of the Item class. Its behavior is implemented through workflows, which implement the business processes, and consider the concept of Causalities (chains of related events). Very flexible and extensible modules, called Business Templates, are also provided for Accounting, Production Planning, Payroll, Finance, MRP, CRM, Trading, Electronic Commerce, Reporting, and others. Additionally, a project management toolset is provided to support both the customization and development processes (Carvalho & Monnerat, 2008).

## Using ERP5 Framework to Support Agile Development

Among the various features in the ERP5 framework, that make it flexible, some of these can be directly mapped as supportive to an Agile development process, in special, three of its design patterns, providing rapid customization, which makes the framework very adaptive to changes in business requirements.

The prototype pattern is the most obvious design pattern in ERP5, a thoroughly explanation on its use within this framework can be found in Carvalho & Monnerat (2007). ERP5 Modules work as Clients; asking concrete prototypes to get instantiated (clone themselves). In that way, business processes can be implemented on top of the UBM with few programming, using template structures and algorithms. Concrete prototypes provide masked names for abstracts terms – for instance, attributes like "movement source" and "movement destination", when used in an implementation of a money transfer transaction, are translated into "source account" and "destination account". ERP5 core provides a template method called newContent, which creates concrete prototype objects according to a concrete class' name parameter. Concrete subclasses use the GUI to mask elements in accordance to specific business terms,

*Figure 3. Prototype pattern implementation. The Trade module calls the template method newContent, provided by ERP5 core to create new concrete prototype instances. The _init_() constructor is the equivalent to the pattern's Clone() operation.*

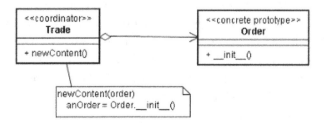

*Figure 4. Mediator pattern for intra- and inter-module integration*

which are stored on a documentation tool called Lexicon, responsible for keeping track of these mappings (Carvalho & Monnerat, 2008).

The use of prototype objects makes it easy to reuse and compose UBM elements. However, it is still necessary to solve the Late Integration Problem. For achieving this, two other design patterns are deployed, namely Mediator (Gamma et al., 1996) and Relationship Manager (Bulka, 2001). In ERP5, mediators are called Builder objects, and are used to integrate the behavior of both UBM elements and system modules, or, in other words, mediators are responsible for inter and intra-module integration. These objects are Singletons that reduce coupling among business entities' workflows, like Delivery and Order; and among modules' workflows, such as Trade and Accounting. When integrating UBM elements behavior, they form macro-processes, which in turn describe the behavior of the modules. Figure 4 left shows the Mediator pattern for intra-module integration. The delivery builder object mediates the communication between order and delivery, reducing behavior coupling between both classes. For instance, in an implementation for a logistics company, after confirmed, an order object's workflow signals to the builder that it can start the creation of a new delivery and start its workflow. In an implementation for a manufacturing company, an order would signal to a production order builder object, with no need to change the workflow configured for Order objects. On Figure 4 right, the same pattern is used for inter-module integration. The invoice builder integrates trading and accounting. Even if the Accounting module is installed long after the Trade module, it is possible to generate invoices for all trading transactions executed in the past.

While Builder objects are used to integrate workflows by creating appropriate calling chains, it is still necessary to connect the objects that are used to represent the business entities that collaborate to realize these processes, providing navigation facilities among them. Coding relationship logic into each business class is often a tedious and error-prone task. Also, traditional relationship code means to spread out code (back–pointers, deletion notifications, etc) amongst many classes, which is more difficult to track, maintain and keep in synch than mediated approaches (Bulka, 2001). Therefore, while mediators are used to integrate behavior, Relationship Managers are used to integrate structure. Actually, in ERP5 a central relationship manager, called Portal Categories, is used to maintain all the one-to-one, one-to-many and many-to-many relationships between groups of related objects. Query methods and relationship code are provided. The Portal Categories is a Singleton object that generates code for receivers and senders automatically, and contains Base Category objects, which in turn are responsible to connect classes that collaborate in a given business (macro) process. Figure 5 presents an example use of Portal Categories, which offers a complete relationship management service to objects by using configurable rules that creates the necessary getters, setters, and references.

*Figure 5. Relationship Manager Pattern implementation*

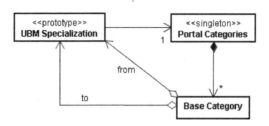

Given that both Builders and Base Categories objects provide all code necessary to integrate business entities, they are configurable structures, therefore when new business processes integration points are identified, it is just a question of configuring the proper relationships to provide integration. By providing ways of rapidly and cheaply integrating structure and behavior, ERP5 framework allows late business integration during the customization process, allowing an incremental process with its late discovery of integration points. In that way, it is possible to improve the sometimes dynamic and cross organizational requirements for management of collaborative processes.

# Chapter 3
# Software Components for ERP Applications

**Muthu Ramachandran**
*Leeds Metropolitan University, UK*

**S. Parthasarathy**
*Thiagarajar College of Engineering, India*

## ABSTRACT

*The demand for ERP systems grows rapidly along with complexity and integration of enterprise systems. ERP is an enterprise oriented information system for resource planning which integrates various departments and systems. This chapter identifies a set of key characteristics of ERP system and then map onto a software component model which has been customised for ERP characteristics. A component based software process model for ERP projects is proposed and its significance during the ERP implementation is indicated.*

## INTRODUCTION

Enterprise systems are complex and expensive to create a dynamic organizational change. There are common issues across all IT related projects such as cost, time, and people, are well known. A modern definition of Enterprise Resource Planning (ERP) is the computer-based and an integrated software package (composed of various self-executable sub-components that are working together) which has been designed to process organisational transactions and to facilitate integrated and distributed real-time planning, production, manufacturing, and customer responses. The current trend in business sectors require continuous change in business requirements hence requires system to adapt changes quickly. According to a report by Advanced Manufacturing Research (AMR), we find that the entire enterprise applications market which includes Knowledge Management (KM), Customer Relationship Management (CRM) and Supply Chain Management (SCM) software will top $70 billion by 2007. Many researchers and practitioners have suggested that it is easier and less costly to mould business processes to ERP systems rather than vice versa (Davenport 1998, Holland and Light 1999).

DOI: 10.4018/978-1-61520-625-4.ch003

Copyright © 2010, IGI Global. Copying or distributing in print or electronic forms without written permission of IGI Global is prohibited.

## PROBLEM OF CURRENT ERP DESIGN

In the traditional software projects, the software is developed by the software engineering after collecting the requirements from the customer and they are the end users for the developed software system. But in the ERP projects, the software is developed for once considering the basic requirements of the customers and the best practices adopted in the industry for a particular domain, say, finance, banking and so no. During the actual implementation of the ERP software, it is customized to meet the specific requirements of the customer. In simple, we can say, the ERP product is developed once to suit many customers. Current ERP designs in industry lack reusability and interchangeability of domain application components. To develop a successful and dominant company in the ERP market, a strategic move to a component based-based ERP design and marketing will be required. ERP vendors should be in a business of specifying the ERP components as well as building them. Once the design of specifications for ERP components is produced, developing each component can be outsourced to third-party developers thereby compressing the duration of an ERP implementation.

## CBSE AND ERP SYSTEM CHARACTERISTICS

ERP provides new business opportunities as it integrates several business processes together to provide a unique business contact. Appuswamy (2000) predicts the holistic integrated business transactions and analysis has provided the synergy to keep business processes dynamic and to deal with customer needs in real-time. ERP system is an integrated business software system and its characteristics that allow an organisation to:

- Automate and integrate various business processes hence we need a component to support business process modeling and integration strategies
- Enterprise wide support for sharing common data and practices across the enterprise systems
- Able to share access product services and information in real-time
- Seamless integration
- System configuration

In summary, characteristics of ERP systems are to provide:

- Seamless integration
- Packaging
- Vendor management
- Change management

Figure 1 (Christiansson and Jacobsson 1999) shows the composition of component based information systems. The development of component-based systems is different from the development of traditional systems. A component-based information system can be viewed as a three-layer system. The innermost level is the component infrastructure i.e. the components themselves and the necessary glue-code to make them interoperational. The middle layer is the software application, i.e. the grouping of cooperating components into software applications. The outer layer is the information system infrastructure i.e. the information systems that the different applications supports or consists of. These layers are described in Figure 1.

Software reuse has emerged supporting software quality as well as an important factor for productivity. Software component has been identified as a self-contained unit of abstraction which can be independently used to compose systems. Computer hardware systems and other industrial applications are mostly composed and assembled rather than being built where as soft-

*Figure 1. Composition of component based information systems (Christiansson and Jacobsson, 1999)*

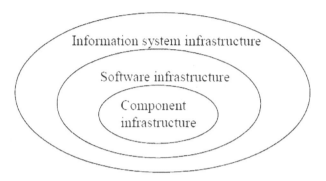

ware systems remains being crafted from scratch rather than being assembled. There have been a number of works on reuse and component based product development and product-line approach to software development (D'Souza and Wills (1999), Szyperski (1998), Cheesman and Daniels (2000)). In general systems are composed of components (software and hardware inclusively) some of which are tightly integrated and/or embedded. For now let us take the definition provided by Brown and Wallnau (1998) that a component is "a self-contained entity with interfaces and provides an independently deliverable set of reusable services."

Components has been applied successfully to a range of applications starting from embedded systems, creative technologies such as games, mobile, robotics, entertainment, and music technologies, to a very high end and large scale systems such as aerospace, commercial, missiles, space vehicles, large scale telecomm and networking, internet and distributed systems. Therefore, component-based systems are comprised of multiple software components that:

- are ready *'off-the-shelf'*, whether from a commercial source (COTS) or re-used from another system,

*Table 1.*

| Enterprise system requirements | Component characteristics | ERP system characteristics |
|---|---|---|
| Flexibility to meet changes in business requirements | √ | √ |
| Interoperability | √ | √ |
| Web services | √ | √ |
| Data sharing | √ | √ |
| Business integration | √ | √ |
| Process integration | √ | √ |
| Common user interface | √ | √ |
| Open architecture | √ | √ |
| Reconfigurable systems | √ | √ |
| Availability | √ | √ |
| Real-time | √ | √ |

- have significant aggregate functionality and complexity,
- are self-contained and possibly execute independently,
- preferably used 'as-is' rather than modified,
- must be integrated with other components to achieve required system functionality,
- use software component architectures to build resilient architectures

Examples of components based systems can be drawn from many domains, including computer-aided software engineering (CASE), engineering design and manufacturing (CAD/CAM), office automation, workflow management, command and control, and many others. The benefits of component-based systems and its best practice guidelines for designing and implementing software components are discussed in Ramachandran (2008).

Current work on CBSE for ERP systems by Kim and Lockwood (2001), Malm (2001), and Christiansson and Jacobsson (1999) have reported the benefits of CBSE approach to ERP systems. They have reported current ERP systems have the low reusability and inter-changeability of various modules among different vender's packages and this is mainly due to the following reasons:

- There are a tight coupling of domain knowledge with the particular implementation tools
- Lack of establishing specification standards for ERP applications
- Lack of applying abstraction at the module specification level which can extract implementation details
- Lack of software engineering expertise for ERP systems
- Lack of abstracting and componentising domain knowledge from embedding them onto a particular implementation tools

such as SAP, Baan, PeopleSoft, Oracle, OneWorld (J. D. Edwards), Microsoft Dynamics NAV, and others.

Therefore, the main motivation for this research is to address a life-cycle support for developing ERP applications systematically. In a simple term we can describe a component based software development process as a set of planned activities consist of identifying product requirements, matching those onto existing components, parts, glues, frameworks, and architectures to a fully functional system. This is illustrated in Figure 2.

As shown in the diagram product requirements are gathered from business needs which are then analysed, negotiated, conflicts are identified, negotiated and resolved by requirements engineers and development group. The clearer requirements are then mapped on to existing component library, if there are any mismatches, new code could be developed or requirements can also be re-negotiated depending on the budget and implementation constraints. This is also known as software development with reuse and COTs (commercial-off-the-shelf components). Whatever model we may use to develop components and products based on components, the important point here is to continuously assess and identify improvement over the years. This will maximise the benefits of CBSE based development. Established component standards such as Sun's JavaBean/EJB, Microsoft COM/DCOM/.NET, and OMG's CORBA have been popular which meets one of the ERP stated problem earlier. Therefore the following section provides a model for ERP requirements method and continuous improvement.

## Requirements Engineering Method and Erp Maturity Model

ERP projects integrate three major areas of Information Technology (IT) projects such as knowledge management (KM), customer relationship

*Figure 2. CBSE based system assembly process*

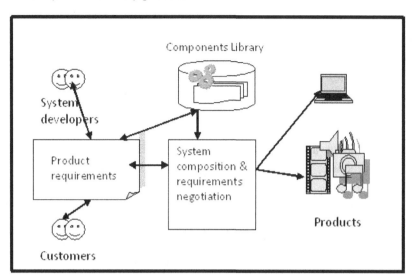

management (CRM), and supply chain management systems (SCM) as predicted by Holland and Light (1999). This is illustrated in Figure 3 shown as ERP systems integration.

Knowledge Management (KM) comprises a range of practices used by organizations to identify, create, represent, and distribute knowledge for reuse, awareness and learning. Therefore the issues of identifying requirements for an ERP project become much more complicated than traditional software projects. The growing number of horror stories found in the literature about the failed ERP projects clearly indicates that the existing requirements capturing methods are inadequate. We propose a matrix driven model for capturing requirements as shown in Figure 4. As shown in Figure 4, Requirements Engineering Method for ERP (REM-ERP) has multi-user perspective than usual software projects which integrates requirements from ERP end users, supply chain systems users, CRM users, and KM users. The captured requirements are recorded using our ERP requirements matrix (ERP-RM) shown in table 2. The process database is a repository of process performance data from successful projects, which can be used for project planning, estimation, analysis of

productivity and quality and other purpose (Grady and Caswell 1999). The process database consists of data from successfully completed projects and forms the quantitative knowledge about experience in project execution. As can be imagined, to populate the process database, data is collected in projects, analyzed and then organized for entry into the process database (Humphrey 1989).

The data captured in the process database can be classified into the following categories: Project characteristics, Project schedule, Project effort, Size and Defects (Applegate et al. 1999; Strong et al. 2004). The Capability Maturity Model (CMM) requires that the organization have a process database which is used for planning, though the CMM does not specify what this process database contains. ERP-RM considers the RE based performance measures such as customization, Business Process Reengineering (BPR) and the metrics and the process database for data and system integration. This matrix will be validated by various stakeholders. This process will be useful to highlight the various expected performance indicators for ERP projects thereby making the ERP systems implementation, integration, and testing much faster and reliable.

*Figure 3. ERP systems integration*

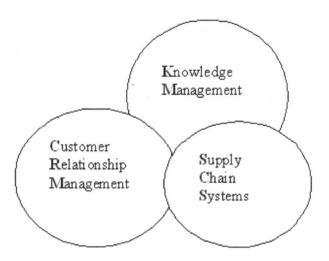

Our earlier work on applying REM-ERP and EMM to real projects has revealed some interesting results in improving the customer satisfaction index (CSI). The ERP requirements matrix and the ERP maturity model have been applied to the ABC Company to study their problems and details have been reported by Parthasarathy and Ramachandran (2008).

## COMPONENT MODEL AND COMPONENT BASED DEVELOPMENT PROCESS FOR ERP PROJECTS

Software components provide interfaces that support integration of services at various business levels and at implementation level. Components can also support horizontal as well as vertical integration. The software component model shown in Figure 5 shows a generic model for

*Figure 4. Requirements engineering method for ERP projects (REM-ERP)*

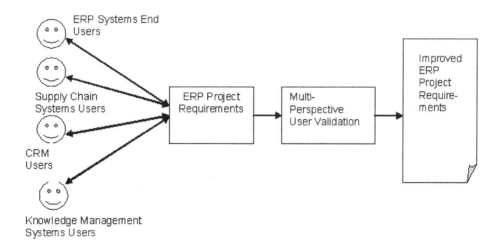

*Table 2. ERP requirements matrix (ERP-RM)*

| | Performance based requirements engineering | Customization | Process database | Organizational structure | Business goals | BPR & Improved resource utilization | Data & System integration |
|---|---|---|---|---|---|---|---|
| **ERP users** | | | | | | | |
| **CRM users** | | | | | | | |
| **KM us-ers** | | | | | | | |
| **SCM users** | | | | | | | |

ERP applications. The requires interface services such as:

- IdataShare allows access to receive real-time data from different subsystems and business levels
- ISubsystems allows integration with other subsystem which can be enabled and disabled depending on the nature of services and integration required.

The set of provider interface services are:

- Iwebservice provides a set of services to web service functions
- Itime-constrained Services provides a set of time constrained services
- IbusinessIntegrationServices provides a set of integration services
- IprocessIntegrationService provides a set of services for business process integration

The component model presented here addresses the needs for ERP implementation and to keep components as generic as possible. This allows us to develop a set of reusable software components

*Figure 5. Component model for ERP applications*

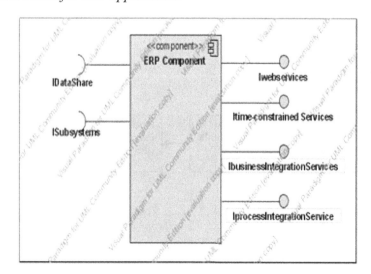

*Figure 6. Component based development process model for ERP projects (E-CBSE)*

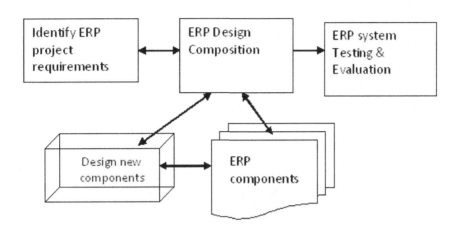

for ERP applications across business domains thus reducing cost, time, and effort but at the same time improving functional qualities and reliabilities.

CBSE process provides a step-wise approach to assembling systems from a set of reusable components that have been developed and includes a new set of components that might be emerged by changing and adding functionalities of the existing components, and therefore we should be able to maintaining those components. Figure 6 shows a component based development process model for ERP applications (E-CBSE).

The E-CBSE process shows a set of steps starting from identifying requirements for ERP systems using our REM-ERP method, secondly to develop design based on assembling existing software components and also identifying new components (which may involve allowing a set of new requirements), conducting system level testing and evaluation, and finally deliver or install the ERP system.

## CASE STUDY: DISTRIBUTED PROCESSING SYSTEM FOR A MANUFACTURING COMPANY

The case study chosen is a distributed process for a manufacturing system as shown in Figure

7. The Engineering computer control system consists of a number of CAD/CAM workstations and all relevant data are stored in an engineering database system. This is connected to a corporate mainframe. The Engineering site may be located geographically across the globe to access any relevant and similar data about any specific manufactured item to save time to redraw sketches again. The corporate mainframe is then connected to a corporate database and a manufacturing computer control system. The manufacturing computer consists of a number of geographically distributed gateways and a manufacturing database. A gateway consists of a locally networked PCs and a database server which is also connected to a local database. This aim is to design component-based development for the distributed manufacturing system. We can also use the specialised component model which has been presented in Figure 5 to model the distributed manufacturing system.

## Component-Oriented Design

Components based design will make an impact on the design of a distributed manufacturing system. Figure 8 shows a simple set of software components which include CAD/CAM component providing interface to Engineering Design Centre

*Figure 7. Distributed processing architecture for a manufacturing system*

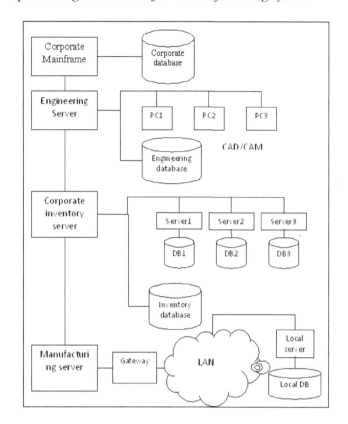

component which then connects to Corporate Manufacturing Centre.

Other components include EngineeringDatabase, CorporateGateway, CorporateDatabase, EngineeringKnowledgeBase, and Manufacturing-KnowledgeBase. Figure 9 shows the number of components identified for this system against their percentage of ERP characteristics suitability. The four components shown for illustration are CAD/CAM workstation, EngineeringDatabaseDesign-Center (EngDB), Corporate Manfacturing (Corp-Man), and CorporateDesignDatabase (CorpDB). The data representation suggest us high percentage on reuse, interchangeability, re-configurability, and real-time.

*Figure 8. Component design for distributed processing for a manufacturing system*

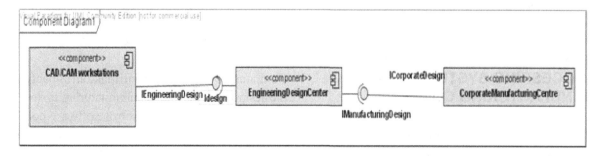

*Figure 9. Components versus ERP characteristics*

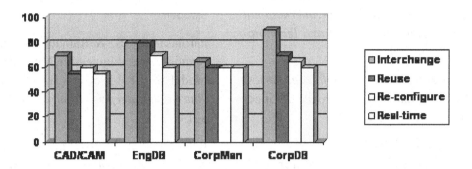

## CONCLUSION

The demand for ERP applications grow rapidly and strive for reuse and dynamic integration. Component based development approach provides support for reuse and dynamic integration. This chapter has introduced life-cycle support for developing ERP applications systematically with customised process and methods for CBSE. Another key feature of component-based technology is that developers should have the ability to use components developed by others. One key feature of component-based technology and a rapid software development process is the ability to reuse components. This study shows that it takes time to develop components that can be reused and if components can't be reused then many of the advantages of using a component based approach disappear. The component-based technology can help system developers, in an easier way, build more custom-made ERP systems. Another positive aspect that increases the customers' chances to achieve a more tailor-made system is the ability to develop applications step by step. This will involve allowing customers to choose, to a much greater extent, what functionality they want. For instance when one type of functionality is implemented, then customers can, if they are satisfied with that implementation, add functionality without affecting that already implemented functionality too much.

## REFERENCES

Alleman, G. B. (2002). *Architecture–Centered ERP Systems in the Manufacturing Domain.* USA: Nivot.

Applegate, L. M., McFarlan, F. W., & McKenney, J. L. (1999). *Corporate Information Systems Management: Text and Cases* (5th ed.). New York: McGraw-Hill.

Appuswamy, R. (2000). Implementation issues in ERP. In *1st Intl. Conference on Systems Thinking in Management.*

Brown, A. W. & Wallnau, K. C. (1998). *The Current state of CBSE.*

Cheesman, J., & Daniels, J. (2000). *UML Components.* Reading, MA: Addison Wesley.

Christiansson, B., & Jacobsson, L. (1999). Component-Based Software Development Life Cycles. Karlstad University, Institution for Information technology, Sweden.

D'Souza & Wills. (1999). *Objects, components and frameworks with UML.* Reading, MA: Addison Wesley.

Davenport, T. H. (1998, July-August). Putting the enterprise into the enterprise system. *Harvard Business Review*, 1998, 121–131.

Dumbrava, S., Panescu, D., & Costin, M. (2005). A Three-tier Software Architecture for Manufacturing Activity Control in ERP Concept. *International Conference on Computer Systems and Technologies - CompSysTech'05.*

Grady, R., & Caswell, D. (1999). *Software Metrics: Establishing a Company-wide program.* Upper Saddle River, NJ: Prentice Hall.

Holland, C. P., & Light, B. (1999, May/June). A Critical success factor model for ERP implementation. *IEEE Software*, 1999, 30–36. doi:10.1109/52.765784

Humphrey, W. (1989). *Managing the software process.* Reading, MA: Addison-Wesley.

Kim, B.-O., & Lockwood, D. (2001). A component-based design approach to ERP design in a distributed object environment. In IACIS 01.

Malm, B. (2001). Component-based ERP systems. Master thesis, Mid Sweden University, Sundsvall, Sweden.

Parthasarathy, S., & Ramachandran, M. (2008). Requirements Engineering Method and Maturity Model for ERP Projects. [IJEIS]. *International Journal of Enterprise Information Systems*, *4*(1), 1–14.

Ramachandran, M. (2008). *Software components: guidelines and applications.* New York: Nova Publishers.

Strong, D. M., & Volkoff, O. (2004). *A Roadmap for Enterprise System Implementation.* Washington, DC: IEEE Computer Society.

Szyperski, C. (1998). *Component Software.* Reading, MA: Addison Wesley.

# Chapter 4
# Application of Software Metrics in ERP Projects

**S. Parthasarathy**
*Thiagarajar College of Engineering, India*

## ABSTRACT

*Business information system is an area of the greatest significance in any business enterprise today. Enterprise Resource Planning (ERP) projects are a growing segment of this vital area. Software engineering metrics are units of measurement used to characterize the software engineering products and processes. The research about the software process has acquired great importance in the last few years due to the growing interest of software companies in the improvement of their quality. Enterprise Resource Planning (ERP) projects are very complex products, and this fact is directly linked to their development and maintenance. One of the major reasons found in the literature for the failure of ERP projects is the poor management of software processes. In this chapter, the authors propose a Software Metrics Plan (SMP) containing different software metrics to manage software processes during ERP implementation. Two hypotheses have been formulated and tested using statistical techniques to validate the SMP. The statistical analysis of the collected data from an ERP project supports the two hypotheses, leading to the conclusion that the software metrics are momentous in ERP projects.*

## INTRODUCTION

Software process improvement often receives little orderly attention. If it is important enough to do, however, someone must be assigned the responsibility and given the resources to make it happen. Until this is done, it will remain a nice thing to do

DOI: 10.4018/978-1-61520-625-4.ch004

someday, but never today. Software engineering process is the total set of software engineering activities needed to transform a user's requirement into software (Humphrey 2005). In other words, software process is a set of software engineering activities necessary to develop and maintain software products. The reason for defining the software process is to improve the way the work is done. By thinking about the process in an orderly way, it is

Copyright © 2010, IGI Global. Copying or distributing in print or electronic forms without written permission of IGI Global is prohibited.

possible to anticipate problems and to devise ways to either prevent or to resolve them.

The software processes that are of great concern during the ERP implementation are requirements instability, scheduling and software maintenance (Parthasarathy and Anbazhagan, 2006). Here, we use software metrics to manage and improve these software processes during the ERP implementation. It explains specifically how the software processes can be quantified, plotted, and analyzed so that the performance of ERP software development activities can be predicted, controlled, and guided to achieve both business and technical goals. As mentioned by Parthasarathy & Anbazhagan (2006), though there are a handful of software processes for ERP projects, the processes such as requirements stability, schedule slippage and monitoring the software maintenance tasks are considered more important and account for the performance enhancement of ERP projects. Hence, only these software processes are dealt with using software metrics in the proposed Software Metrics Plan (SMP) developed in this chapter.

Many project managers acknowledge that measurement helps them understand and guide the development of their projects (Fenton et al 2003). They want to select particular metrics, perhaps as part of an overall development plan, but they do not know how to begin. The answers to a manager's metrics questions should appear in the project's metrics plan, so that managers and developers know what to collect, when to collect it and how the data relate to management decisions. The plan enables managers to establish a flexible and comprehensive metrics program as part of a larger process or product improvement program. The research about the software process has acquired great importance in the last few years due to the growing interest of software companies in the improvement of their quality. ERP projects are very complex products, and this fact is directly linked to their development and maintenance.

The total quality management (TQM) notion of prevention rather than correction can be applied successfully in software engineering. The project schedule slippage and tracking problems during maintenance are not uncommon. A key issue in ERP implementation is how to find a match between the ERP system and an organization's business processes by appropriately customizing both the system and the organization (Arthur 1997). This is badly affected due to the instability in the requirements proposed by the customer and the poor capability of the ERP vendor.

The phase "Gap Analysis" in ERP implementation is a step of negotiation between the company's requirements and the functions an ERP package possesses (Carmel et al 1998). Poor requirements specification and its instability badly affects the gap analysis phase of an ERP project which in turn leads to schedule slippage and bubbles of problems during the maintenance phase of the software project. The requirements instability is probably the most important single software process issue for many organizations. The failure of many software projects can be directly linked to the requirements instability (Davenport 1998). Customization, the biggest technology headache is considered as the critical success factor for ERP implementation (Parthasarathy and Anbazhagan, 2007).

Even for those companies that have successfully implemented large-scale information systems projects in the past, ERP implementation still presents a challenge, because it is not simply a large-scale software deployment exercise. Also as ERP implementation is often accompanied by large-scale organizational changes, agile software processes could not create much impact on the ERP projects (Glass 1998). One of the major reasons found in the literature for the failure of ERP projects is the poor software process management. Hence a Software Metrics Plan (SMP) has been developed to deal with the software processes discussed in the literature review and found to be more important for successful ERP implementation. The software processes dealt with in the SMP for effective software process management during the ERP implementation are:

i. Requirements Stability Index (RSI)
ii. Schedule Slippage (SS)
iii. Arrival Rate of Problems (ARP)
iv. Closure Rate of Problems (CRP)
v. Age of Open Problems (AOP)
vi. Age of Closed Problems (ACP)

The SMP contains a set of software metrics to manage these software processes during ERP implementation. Two hypotheses have been formulated and tested using statistical techniques to validate the SMP. The statistical analysis of the collected data from an ERP project supports these two hypotheses, leading to the conclusion that the software metrics are momentous in ERP projects. The results give fruitful information to the ERP team to identify the influence of one process on another.

## SOFTWARE METRICS PLAN (SMP)

A metrics plan is much like a newspaper article: it must describe the who, what, where, when, how and why of the metrics. With answers to all of these questions, whoever reads the plan knows exactly why metrics are being collected, how they are used, and how metrics fit into the larger picture of software development of maintenance. The plan usually begins with the "why". It is in this introductory section that the plan lays down the goals or objectives of the project, describing what questions need to be answered by project members and software process management. For example, if reliability is a major concern to the developers, then the plan discusses how reliability will be defined and what reporting requirements are imposed on the project; later sections of the plan can then discuss how reliability will be measured and tracked.

Next, the plan addresses "what" will be measured. In many cases, the measures are grouped or related in some way. For instance, productivity may be measured in terms of two component pieces, size and effort. So the plan will explain how size and effort are defined and then how they are combined to compute productivity. At the same time, the plan must spell out "where" and "when" during the process the measurements will be made. Some measurements are taken once, while others are made repeatedly and tracked over time. The time and frequency of collection are related to the goals and needs of the project, and those relationships should be made explicit in the plan.

"How" and "Who" address the identification of tools, techniques, and staff available for metrics collection and analysis. It is important that the plan discusses not only what measures are needed but also what tools are to be used for data capture and storage, and who is responsible for those activities. Often, metrics plans ignore these crucial issues, and project members assume that someone else is taking care of the metrics business; the result is that everyone agrees that the metrics are important, but no one is actually assigned to get the data. Likewise, responsibility for analysis often slips though the project cracks on and data pile up but are never used in decision making.

The plan must state clearly what types of analysis will be created with the data, who will do the analysis, how the results will be conveyed to the decision makers, and how they will support decisions. Thus, the metrics plan prints a comprehensive picture of the measurement process, from the initial definition of need to analysis and application of the results. Software processes have an important influence on the quality of the final software product, and for this reason companies are becoming more and more concerned with software process improvement.

Successful management of the software process is necessary in order to satisfy the final quality, cost and time of the marketing of the software

*Table 1. Metric-01 in the software metrics plan (SMP)*

| Metric | Schedule Slippage |
|---|---|
| Formulae | {(Actual number of days – Estimated number of days) / Estimated number of days} * 100 |
| Measure (Indirect Metric) | Actual number of days is the difference between the date when a particular activity (phase) or project got completed and the date when a particular activity/phase or project started. Estimated number of days is the difference between the planned start date of a particular activity/phase or project based on the latest plan and the planned end date of a particular activity/phase or project based on the latest plan. |
| Source of Data | Actual End Date: Project Schedule<br>Expected Start Date: Project Schedule<br>Expected End Date: Project Schedule |
| Collection Responsibility | Project Manager |
| Frequency of Analysis | Weekly Progress Review, Phase End (Milestone), Event Driven Analysis can be done using the Schedule Tracking Sheet |
| Significance to ERP Project | Used to control the project activities and ensure on-time delivery. Can be used for better estimation for future ERP projects leading to effective software process management. |

products (Kitchenham et al 2002). To improve the software processes (Pressman 2006), a great variety of initiatives have arisen like the Capability Maturity Model (CMM), etc. All these initiatives focus on software processes for developing, implementing or improving a quality management system. An ERP project involves software processes that will exist even after the implementation of the ERP system. In fact, the actual processes start only when the going alive is fixed during implementation. Traditional software projects have requirements collected from the customers for whom the software is developed. But in ERP projects, the software is made available to the customers readymade after fine tuning its functionality to match the exact requirements of the customers. The purpose of the SMP is to enhance the performance of ERP projects by improving their software processes. The SMP will have a set of well-defined metrics that will deal with measuring the requirements stability, project schedule slippage and tracking the problems arising during the maintenance phase. The SMP can also be further extended involving other aspects like effort distribution, productivity, etc if desired. The SMP will contain the following:

*Table 2. Metric-02 in the software metrics plan (SMP)*

| Metric | Requirements Stability Index (RSI) |
|---|---|
| Formulae | Number of Requirements Changed (Added/Deleted/Modified)/Total Number of Initial Requirements |
| Measure (Indirect Metric) | Number of requirements changed is the sum of the requirements that were either added/modified/deleted from the initial set of requirements approved by the client. Initial requirements are the number of requirements initially approved by the client. |
| Source of Data | Initial requirement: Initial set of approved requirements from the client. Number of changes in the requirement can be found from Client Request Form (CRF) and Client Complaint Form (CCF) |
| Collection Responsibility | Project Manager |
| Frequency of Analysis | At the end of every phase of ERP implementation using the RSI tracking sheet |
| Significance to ERP Project | RSI is used to monitor the magnitude of change in requirements it gives a picture of clarity of the requirements in the customers mind. RSI is useful for fine software process management. |

*Table 3. Metric-03 in the software metrics plan (SMP)*

| Metric | Arrival Rate of Problem (ARP) |
|---|---|
| Formulae | Number of problems arrived (reported by the client) every month |
| Measure (Direct Metric) | Number of problems reported by the client in a particular month |
| Source of Data | Modification Request Form |
| Collection Responsibility | Project Manager |
| Frequency of Analysis | The problem arrival rate when compared with the problem closure rate gives an indication of the amount of work still pending and helps to anticipate the work for the next month |
| Significance to ERP Project | Used for effective software maintenance |

1. Source of data and how it will be captured
2. Periodicity of data capture
3. Formulae to measure the software process
4. Team member responsible for data collection
5. Nature of Measurement
6. Significance of the proposed metric to the ERP Project.

The following tables (From Table 1 to Table 6) collectively form the Software Metrics Plan (SMP). In this SMP, six software metrics have been defined, each one dealing with a specific software process leading to successful software process management.

The goal of this study is to establish the significance of software metrics in ERP projects. We use correlation and multiple correlations (Levine et al 1999) to test the two hypotheses formulated below to investigate the impact of one metric over another. The relationship between two variables is such that a change in one variable result in a positive or negative change in the other and also greater change in one variable results in a corresponding greater change in the other. This is known as correlation. Positive or negative values of coefficient of correlation 'R' between two variables indicate positive or negative correlation. We have used Karl Pearson's Coefficient of correlation which is defined below. Note that R has no units and is a mere number. If there is some relationship between two variables, their scatter diagram will have points clustering near about some curve.

$$R = \frac{\frac{1}{N}\left(\sum X_i * Y_i - \bar{X} * \bar{Y}\right)}{\left(\frac{1}{N}\sum X_i^2 - \bar{X}^2\right)^{1/2}\left(\frac{1}{N}\sum Y_i^2 - \bar{Y}^2\right)^{1/2}} \quad (1)$$

*Table 4. Metric-04 in the software metrics plan (SMP)*

| Metric | Closure Rate of Problems (CRP) |
|---|---|
| Formulae | Number of problems closed each month based on severity |
| Measure (Direct Metric) | Number of problems closed in a particular month |
| Source of Data | Modification Request Form |
| Collection Responsibility | Project Manager |
| Frequency of Analysis | The problem closure rate when compared with the problem arrival rate gives an indication of the amount of work still pending and helps to anticipate amount of work which can be completed next month |
| Significance to ERP Project | Used for effective software maintenance |

*Table 5. Metric-05 in the software metrics plan (SMP)*

| Metric | Age of Open Problems (AOP) |
|---|---|
| Formulae | Sum of time (days per month) that problems have been open/No. of open problems per month |
| Measure (Direct Metric) | Number of problems open in a particular month of each severity |
| Source of Data | Modification request form |
| Collection Responsibility | Project Manager |
| Frequency of Analysis | The age of open problem gives the time for which a problem of a particular severity remains open and helps in setting realistic schedule estimates. |
| Significance to ERP Project | Used for effective software maintenance |

Equation (1) is used to compute the correlation coefficient R. Multiple correlations are used to find the degree of inter-relationship among three or more variables. The objective of using multiple correlations is to find how far the dependent variable is influenced by the independent variables. We denote the multiple correlations between $x_1$, the dependent variable and $x_2, x_3, \ldots x_n$, independent variables, by $R_{1.234\ldots n}$. The multiple correlation coefficient of $x_1$ on $x_2$ and $x_3$ is the simple correlation coefficient between the observed value of $x_1$ and its estimated value $b_{12.3} x_2 + b_{13.2} x_3$ denoted by $\epsilon_{1.23}$. We denote the multiple correlation of $x_1$ on $x_2$ by $R_{1(23)}$. Equation (2) gives the value of $R_{1(23)}$.

$$R_{1(23)} = Cov(x_1, \epsilon_{1.23})/(\sqrt{[Var(x_1)]} * \sqrt{[Var(\epsilon_{1.23})]}) \quad (2)$$

The following two hypotheses are formulated to focus our study on the usage of the software metrics defined in the SMP for effective software process management during the ERP implementation and to facilitate statistical analysis.

**Hypothesis 1:** The metric RSI influences the metric schedule slippage (SS)

**Hypothesis 2:** The metrics AOP, ACP determine maintenance efforts (ME) (i.e) person-hours.

In the traditional software projects, from the view point of software engineering, there are five phases in the software development life cycle (SDLC). They are: Requirements Analysis, Design, Coding, Testing and Implementation. ERP is a packaged software and its implementation in an enterprise involves six phases called the ERP implementation lifecycle (Alexis Leon 2005). They are: Requirements Analysis, Gap Analysis, Reengineering, Configuration Management, Testing and Maintenance. The RSI value and the SS

*Table 6. Metric-06 in the software metrics plan (SMP)*

| Metric | Age of Closed Problems (ACP) |
|---|---|
| Formulae | Sum of time (days per month) that problems have been closed/No. of closed problems per month |
| Measure (Direct Metric) | Number of problems closed in a particular month of each severity |
| Source of Data | Modification Request Form |
| Collection Responsibility | Project Manager |
| Frequency of Analysis | The age of closed problems gives the time taken to close a problem of a particular severity and helps in setting realistic schedule estimates. |
| Significance to ERP Project | Used for effective software maintenance |

*Table 7. RSI and SS values for an ERP Project Á*

| Phases in ERP implementation | Requirements Analysis | Gap Analysis | Re-engineering | Configuration Management | Testing | Main-tenance |
|---|---|---|---|---|---|---|
| Requirements Stability Index (RSI) | 0.27 | 0.15 | 0.076 | 0.63 | 0.59 | 0.7 |
| Schedule Slippage (SS) | 0.11 | 0.059 | 0.072 | 0.29 | 0.36 | 0.51 |

value for these phases for the ERP project A are shown in the Table 7. The requirements of the customers are collected and analyzed during the requirements analysis phase. The gap analysis phase is the step of negotiation between the customer's requirements and the functions the ERP package possesses (Alexis Leon 2005).

Reengineering is defined as the fundamental rethinking and radical redesign of business processes to achieve dramatic improvements in critical, contemporary measures of performance, such as cost, quality, service and speed (Alexis Leon 2005). Table 7 provides the RSI and SS values computed based on the data from ERP Project A. This Project A was done by a medium scale software company involved in the development of the ERP software for a manufacturing industry at a lower cost with standard configurations. It is not a large scale information system project like the one being done by the leading ERP vendors SAP, Oracle, etc., But from the research perspective, these data sets are found to be useful to validate the hypotheses. The coefficient of correlation 'R' between RSI and SS is calculated as 0.9406.

The value of R, being greater than zero, indicates a positive correlation between the two variables RSI and SS. This indicates that the requirements stability index has an impact over the schedule slippage of the phases during the ERP implementation. Hence, a Metric-02 (shown in Table 2) has been defined to monitor the RSI. Data obtained from the same project A were used to compute the simple correlations between the metrics ME $(x_1)$, AOP $(x_2)$ and AOC $(x_3)$ as $r_{12} = 0.863$, $r_{13} = 0.648$ and $r_{23} = 0.709$ respectively. The multiple correlation $R_{1(23)}$ computed using the Equation (1) gives 0.864. Since $R_{1(23)}$ is very large, it follows that the variables $x_2$ and $x_3$ have considerable influence on the variable $x_1$. In other words, regression equation of $x_1$ on $x_2$ and $x_3$ will be excellent.

This data analysis gives a great deal of support to the two hypotheses formulated in this study. The clearest result observed from the value of R and $R_{1(23)}$ is: (i) The strong relationship between RSI and SS; (ii) The influence of the Age of Open Problems (AOC) and the Age of Closed Problems (ACP) over the Maintenance efforts (ME). The most reasonable inference that can be drawn from this study is the considerable influence of the software processes in boosting the performance of the ERP projects, because it helps the ERP team to effectively monitor the important software processes during the ERP implementation.

## DISCUSSION

Measurement enables us to gain insight into the process and the project by providing a mechanism for objective evaluation. Measurement can be applied to the software process with the intent of improving it on a continuous basis. Measurement can be used throughout a software project to assist in estimation, quality control, productivity assessment and project control. Measurement is a management tool. If conducted properly, it provides a project manager with insight. And as a result, it assists the project manager and the software team in making decisions that will lead to a successful project. The intent of the SMP is to provide a set of process indicators that lead to long-term software process improvement. The only rational way to improve any process is to measure specific attributes of the process, develop a set of meaningful metrics based on these attributes, and then use the metrics to provide indicators that will lead to a strategy for improvement. SMP enables the software engineering team to take a strategic view by providing insight into the effectiveness of a software process.

Many organizations jump into the implementation without defining the project in "bite-sized chunks" that can be accomplished in a reasonable period of time. As schedules drag on and requirements are heaped on the initial phase, the customer loses faith in the initiative and organizational inertia can take hold. If requirements are managed scrupulously and reflected in the form of clearly articulated scope elements, the entire project is more likely to succeed, and chances are better for its ultimate adoption and survival.

Two kinds of observation are noted in this research study on using the software metrics for managing the software processes of the ERP projects. One observation is based on the statistical analysis and another observation is related to the usefulness of software metrics in ERP projects. Statistical analysis shows that the SMP proposed in this study plays a significant role in the successful ERP implementation. There is sufficient evidence from the literature review that the ERP projects are smashed heavily by poor software process management, especially the varying requirements due to organizational changes and customization. These varying requirements lead to schedule slippage.

It is apparent that large maintenance efforts are required for ERP projects as the real software processes get life only after ERP implementation. It is evident that the proposed software metrics in the SMP is a pragmatic, useful method for improving the software processes in ERP projects, because it enables the ERP team to resolve the important issues such as requirements instability, schedule slippage and efforts required for maintenance.

Furthermore, the SMP determines decisions for the ERP team and provides against the possibilities of various defects that might arise during or after the implementation. In simple, the SMP helps the ERP team to keep track of their project and pilot it in the right path as and when there is a deviation. The results obtained here underscore the importance of effective software process management during the ERP implementation.

A number of software processes are involved in the software development and its maintenance. The six processes that require monitoring and effective management are considered in this study and a SMP has been developed consisting of a set of software metrics to quantitatively measure the software processes. A software process is the collection of processes for the various tasks involved in executing projects for building software systems. As a result of changes in technology, knowledge, and people's skill, the processes for performing different tasks change. In other words, processes evolve with time. With knowledge and experience, processes can, and should, be "fine tuned" to give better performance.

Software process management is concerned with this tuning of the software process. There are many published reports showing the benefits the software process management can bring to quality, productivity, and cycle time of ERP projects. Currently, most organizations that embark upon a software process management program tend to use a framework like the quality models for their process improvement. From the application of the SMP to an ERP project A, it can be seen that it is a straight forward approach to manage the crucial software processes and help the ERP implementation team to improve it.

A future research study could compare the performance of various ERP projects using this SMP with those not using the SMP and the application of other statistical techniques like multiple linear regressions, etc. If the software metrics are linked with some software quality factors, then the performance of the project can be further improved (Mohammad Aishayeb 2003). Hence generating suitable metrics to consider quality aspects of software processes will strengthen the developed software product. It is also proposed to develop a software tool to execute SMP. In the future, we plan to generate a project database to make the results of SMP from each ERP project publicly available for the ERP team.

# REFERENCES

Aishayeb, M., & Li, W. (2003). An empirical validation of object-oriented metrics in two different iterative processes. *IEEE Transactions on Software Engineering, 29*(11).

Alexis, L. (2005). *Enterprise resource planning.* New Delhi, India: Tata McGraw-Hill.

Ambler, S. W. (2002). *Agile Modeling: Effective Practices for Extreme Programming and the Unified Process.* New York: Wiley.

Arthur, L. J. (1997). Quantum improvement in software system quality. *Communications of the ACM, 40*(6), 47–52.

Beck, K. (1999). Embracing changes with extreme programming. *Computer,*Embracing change with extreme programming, 70–77. doi:10.1109/2.796139

Carmel, E., & Sawyer, S. (1998). Packaged software development teams: what makes them different? *Information Technology & People, 11*(1), 7–19. doi:10.1108/09593849810204503

Chidamber, S. R., & Kemerer, C. F. (1994). A metrics suite for object-oriented design. *IEEE Transactions on Software Engineering, 20*(6). doi:10.1109/32.295895

Davenport, T. H. (1998). Putting the enterprise into the enterprise system. *Harvard Business Review,* 76(4), 121–131.

Dunsmore, H. E. (1984). Software metrics: an overview of an evolving methodology. *Information Processing & Management, 20,* 183–192. doi:10.1016/0306-4573(84)90048-7

Fenton, N. E., & Pfleeger, S. L. (2003). *Software Metrics-A rigorous and Practical approach.* New York: Thomson Publisher.

Glass, R. L. (1998). Enterprise Resource Planning—Breakthrough and/or term problems. *The Data Base for Advances in Information Systems, 29*(2), 14–16.

Holland, C. P., & Light, B. (1999). A critical success factors model for ERP implementation. *IEEE Software, 16*(3), 30–36. doi:10.1109/52.765784

Humphrey, W. (2005). *Managing the software process.* Reading, MA: Addison-Wesley.

Kitchenham, B. A., Huges, R. T., & Linkman, S. G. (2002). Modeling software measurement data. *IEEE Transactions on Software Engineering, 27*(9), 788–804. doi:10.1109/32.950316

Levine, D. M., Berenson, M., & Stephan, D. (1999). *Statistics for managers.* Upper Saddle River, NJ: Prentice Hall.

Lucus, H. C. (n.d.). Implementation: The Key to Successful Information Systems. *Columbia Management, 11*(4), 191–198.

Luo, W., & Strong, D. M. (2004, August). A framework for evaluating ERP implementation choices. *IEEE Transactions on Engineering Management, 51*(3). doi:10.1109/TEM.2004.830862

Parthasarathy, S., & Anbazhagan, N. (2007). Evaluating ERP Implementation Choices using AHP. *International Journal of Enterprise Information Systems, 3*(3), 52–65.

Pressman, S. (2001). *Software engineering-A practioner's approach.* New Dehli, India: Tata McGraw-Hill.

Robey, D., Ross, J. W., & Boudreau, M. C. (2002). Learning to implement enterprise systems: An exploratory study of the dialectics of change. *Journal of Management Information Systems, 19*(1).

Sambamurthy, V., & Kirsch, L. J. (2000). An integrative framework of the information systems development process. *Decision Sciences, 31*(2), 391–411. doi:10.1111/j.1540-5915.2000. tb01628.x

Sharma & Goyal. (1994). *Mathematical statistics.* Meerut, India: Krishna Prakashan Mandir.

Stensurd, E., & Myrtveit, I. (2003, May). Identifying high performance ERP projects. *IEEE Transactions on Software Engineering, 29*(5).

# Chapter 5
# ERP Implementation in a Steel Major in India

**Sanjay Kumar**
*MDI Gurgaon, India*

**Anurag Keshan**
*IBM, India*

**Souvik Mazumdar**
*TISS, India*

## ABSTRACT

*The case describes an ERP implementation in a steel major in India. The various factors which impact ERP implementation as identified in literature are discussed. The implementation of ERP systems in the organization has been described at each stage of the implementation. The activities at each stage and also the issues arising at each stage of the implementation have been discussed. The benefits identified by the managers have also been included.*

## INTRODUCTION

This case study was conducted to study the various phases in the implementation of an ERP system in a vertically integrated steel plant. The implementation occurred primarily in two phases. In the first phase ERP systems were implemented in the sales and distribution side of operations. Fairly positive results were achieved in the first phase, and this led to an expanded implementation across the company in the subsequent phases. The company seemed to follow the normally recommended practices for

ERP implementation, till they decided to retain their mainframe based legacy systems for production planning and shop floor control. (Parr & Shanks, 2000; Nah et al., 2001; Markus et al., 2000; Markus & Tanis, 2000; O'Leary, 2000; Prasad et al., 1999; Sumner, 2000; Wallace & Kremzer, 2001; Huang & Palvia, 2001). The company was not satisfied with the functionality for production planning and execution as provided by the vendor (SAP). The company felt that its production planning and execution functionality was much better defined in the mainframe based IT legacy systems, which were being used at the time of SAP implementa-

DOI: 10.4018/978-1-61520-625-4.ch005

Copyright © 2010, IGI Global. Copying or distributing in print or electronic forms without written permission of IGI Global is prohibited.

tion. These were integrated into the company's IT architecture through the use of about 45 complex interfaces. (Wei et al., 2005; Markus & Tanis, 2000; Sumner, 2000; Sumner, 2004; Kim et al., 2005) These interfaces were created using SAP provided tools like BAPIs which enabled a seamless flow of information across the enterprise.

The emerging architecture is given in Appendix 2. The seamless working of the data and information flow and the benefits achieved by the company after the implementation, as a result of the ERP implementation have been brought out in the case. Also project management of the complex task of creation of interfaces with the legacy systems has been successfully handled. (Nah et al., 2001; Adam & O'Doherty, 2000; Markus et al., 2000; Markus & Tanis, 2000; Prasad et al., 1999; Sumner, 2000; Sumner, 2004; Umble & Umble, 2002; Huang & Palvia, 2001) From an implementation perspective the case is an example of a very large implementation and the execution has been handled well and without any major delays or slip ups in schedule.

Company Background: The Steel Company (TSC) under consideration is one of the few select steel companies in the world that is EVA positive (Economic Value Addition). TSC annually produces 9 million tonnes of steel[1]. In the fiscal year 2005-06 the company's turnover was Rs 22,518 crores and it produced a record-breaking 5.0 million tonnes of salable steel in its Jamshedpur plant. In the year 2000, TSC was recognized as the 'world's lowest-cost producer of steel'. The company has also been recognized as the 'world's best steel producer' by World Steel Dynamics, three years in a row through 2005-07.

## CHALLENGES TOWARDS THE GOAL

In the period 1997-98 to 2002-03, global steel prices were close to their 10-year lows and in many markets, prices were hovering close to the cash cost levels of major producers. However, owing to continued overcapacity in the industry and persistent financial support (by lenders and governments) to inefficient producers, prices were not expected to recover in the near term. The managing board of the company took a strategic decision to concentrate on three areas:

1. Achieve world class operational excellence and to be amongst the world's lowest cost producers
2. Become a learning organization
3. To be the supplier of choice for the customer through world class products and services.

To maintain profitability and to remain competitive, the company decided to focus relentlessly on the on cost cutting and upgradation of the plant' and machinery. To meet the objective of cost competitiveness and operational excellence, company knew that it needed to improve its processes. It also needed better business-process support, particularly in the area of sales, purchasing and financial costing and accounting. The company was wasting a lot of effort in gathering information for fulfilling customer requirements, due lack of visibility of finished goods inventory. The company had high levels of overdue debt due to low control over customer credit. In purchasing there was lack of integrated planning and procurement for items related to maintenance, repair and operations.

The company had to provide unnecessary efforts for calculating net realization values used for profitability analysis at product and product-group levels for deciding better product mixes and identifying areas which required thrust. The legacy systems could not account for cost variances and cost buildup at different stages of production, required for analyzing inefficiencies in the operations. With the absence of an integrated costing, the company's costing department had to address a lot of effort towards the reconciliation of cost and financial figures which delayed the publishing of monthly accounts. The company thus chose to implement ERP systems as they supported two of the three strategic objectives enunciated by the company's board- namely cost visibility and improvement in operations and for providing world class products and services to it's customers.

Thus the following measures needed pertinent implementation:

- Improve revenue through improved gross margins.
- Resolving issues related to the fragmented, geographically dispersed IT systems.
- Improve business process for sales, order fulfillment, purchasing, maintenance and financial accounting.

## Moving Toward Enterprise Resource Planning

The company appointed IBM Global Services (Business Process Reengineering consultants) to help in streamlining the processes of 'Order Generation and Fulfillment', and 'marketing development'. TSC had multiple geographically dispersed business locations. The present IT structure of the company was supported by a number of independent stand alone systems which resulted in a large number of databases. There was little visibility of information through the company which was critical to the decision making process.

Various in-house systems had been developed in the company to support the steel making processes at the shop floor. These in house legacy systems had been developed in the late Nineties and were based on mainframe based technology. These systems supported the data capture and use at the technical level, for a particular shop or steel making phase, but were not fully integrated with each other, thus resulting in a situation where the business processes were broken into islands. The employees and management at TSC faced a cumbersome task exchanging and retrieving

information from these different systems. There was no built-in integrity check for data from various data sources, and often the information against certain items was found missing. These fragmented processes made it impossible to get updated information about the business processes, so that decisions could be taken to manage and improve these processes.

Around 1997, TSC recognized that its business processes needed to be more customer-centric. In an effort towards this goal, the company decided to reengineer two of its core processes – Order Generation and Fulfillment & Marketing development.

In 1998-99 a small cross-functional in-house team along with consultants from Arthur D. Little (Strategy Consultants) and IBM Global Services (BPR Consultants) re-designed the two-core business processes; Order Generation & Fulfillment and the Marketing Development processes, to improve customer focus, facilitating better credit control and reduction of stocks. Realizing the need to further support the re-engineered core business processes with an IT based solution, which would also seamlessly integrate with its existing systems, the company developed a business case for supporting the need to go in for Enterprise Resource Planning (ERP). Process and gap analysis was done, as the company was aiming for its transition from a production-driven company to a customer-driven one. Various alternative systems (including in-house development) were explored before zeroing in on ERP systems, as a solution to the current problems being faced, such as fragmented systems and lack of information support to business processes. TSC also wanted the software to result in quick decision-making, transparency and credibility of data and improve responsiveness to customers, apart from solving the issues of fragmented IT systems and Y2K. This would enable TSC to achieve a world-class status for its products and services and strengthen its leadership position in the industry.

## Project Preparation and Vendor Selection

The company evaluated the various ERP packages available at that time. Finding an ERP package which was tailor made for a steel industry was difficult, and the company found large gaps in functionality required and that available in the packages evaluated. After an in-depth study of factors such as available functionality, cost, time, compatibility, esteem, inter-operability, service support and future organizational requirements, SAP was selected. . The company first chose to implement the package for supporting the Order Generation and Fulfillment process, and also as a pilot implementation. Later it was decided to also implement SAP R/3 to support the functionality related to Financial Accounting, Costing, Procurement and materials management etc. This led to the second phase implementation of SAP named 'Rupanter'

1. **Project OG&F:** Improvement of Order Generation and Fulfillment processes. Implementation of SD[2] and related FI module of SAP R/3.
2. **Project SAP Extension:** Better revenue management through improved gross margins. Implementation of Procurement, Financial Accounting, Material Management, Costing, Asset Accounting, and Plant Maintenance modules of SAP R/3.

TSC wanted to do a pilot launch of the modules in ERP related to in the OG&F process and then depending on whether it succeeded or not, it would decide on the future course of action. Two additional **benefits** of first implementing SAP in OG&F function were that (i)The consultants and their expertise could be evaluated, and (ii) The officers in the marketing function were the most educated, hence the acceptability was expected to be high, and the resistance to the system to be low.

## OG&F: 1998-2001

The process reengineering effort at the marketing division –namely in the order generation and fulfillment process, was started under a team of officials led by the Chief of Marketing. The team was having considerable problem as there was no information visibility. Some of the problems faced by the company were:

- Lack of comprehensive inventory visibility
- Lack of information about ready to sell products and receivables
- Lack of visibility in material sales and prices charged by P/Q/S at different locations
- Price **realization** patterns of products across regions not known
- No metrics available to benchmark the performance of the processes

With such pertinent needs for ERP systems, the marketing team was just ready for an ERP implementation.

In February 1999, TSC launched the Order Generation and Fulfillment process (OG&F) program. The company hoped to reduce working capital by decreasing overdue debt and finished goods inventory. The main objectives of the OG&F project were outlined as:

- Identify the value of finished-goods inventory and reduce the inventory by improving visibility in multiple stockyards and reconciling inventory in transit.
- On-line credit check for better receivable management.
- Implement a credit-control policy that would help reduce overall customer debt, especially overdue accounts.
- Enable profitability analysis that would include calculations for net **realization** of value.
- Integrate online sales processes with financial-accounting systems.

A project manager from the sales and marketing department of TSC was chosen. Approval of budget and schedule was finalized. A core team consisting of 18 people was decided and christened 'TEAMASSET' an acronym for 'Achieve Success through SAP Enabled Transformation'.

The core team was vigorously trained in SAP by the best available external faculties from mostly the consultation partner, PWC. SAP overview programs were conducted for even the top management including the Deputy Managing Director, as the concept of SAP was totally new for the company. The End Users training was also complemented with Online Training Material for ready reference which was banked on a dedicated training server.

The management knew from the very beginning that an **ERP implementation** had intense inherent risks involved and a possible collapse of its entire business processes in the event that the SAP implementation did not succeed. Another of its biggest challenges was to convince its employees with regard to the need for a SAP system and conveying the broader picture and potential advantages that the management was seeing that this system could bring about. The prime objective of 'Change Management' was to reach out to people involved non-directly in the project to apprise them of the developments taking place.

## The Implementation

TSC decided not to do any customization to the source codes follow the Accelerated SAP (ASAP) methodology, which provided proper templates and guidelines to help define business processes, dramatically reducing implementation time.

The key stages of SAP implementation along with the key activities in each phase are:

## Project Preparation Phase

The ASAP tools have replaced the formerly common implementation practice of defining 'as-is'

and 'to-be' by streamlining process definitions by integrating them with system configuration actions. In simple words, process templates from the ERP software are used to map the organization's processes, and then the forms and interface screens are generated as per the mapped process. This cuts down on the time taken for process mapping and then configuring the process in the ERP software.

## Business Blueprint 'Design'

This phase mapped the areas defined in the scoping process (*Scoping involves detailed documentation to map the tasks to be taken up in the project. Specifically the tasks which are not included in the project are also mentioned, This allows all parties more clarity on what tasks comprise the project*) to a detailed project plan that accounted for every individual transaction which was to be configured in SAP. Team responsibilities, translation tasks and rollover requirement were set. The task was major since all the branch offices of the firm, all over India were to be covered by the implementation, along with the main marketing office at Kolkata.

## Realization 'Build'

This is the longest phase involved the actual baseline and client configuration. Final integration tests were performed and end user training material was also prepared. An organization and job impact analysis was conducted to develop the organization **transition** plan.

## Final Preparation 'Transition'

This phase involved preparation of data for migration and the final configuration just before **transition**. Integration testing, end-user training and data conversion were also a part of the final preparation phase.

The process of developing KPIs (Key Performance Indicators) to measure the success of the implementation had started well in advance, during the blueprint design stage, and been fine-tuned over the subsequent phases.

On 1st November, TSC went live with its SD and related FI module in a span of approximately nine months. All the sales and distribution branches, which had huge number of transactions and complexity, were identified as a Hub while the smaller branches along with the consignment agents were defined as Spokes which were attached to these branches. Different Teams who were trained in SAP were sent to these Hubs, who addressed the issues of the respective branches. These teams were stationed in the Hubs till the stabilization period of about three months after Go-Live to provide immediate support to the people throughout the country.

## The Results of OG&F

The choice of Marketing and Sales department and the launching of the SD Module and related FI Module paid off as the implementation was a great success. It was a boon to the salespersons as now they did not have to undergo the cumbersome process of background research as to which product to push given the company's annual product mix plan. Due to the related FI module at his disposal the salesperson knew exactly which high Net Realizable (revenue minus costs) grades needed to be pushed in the market.

The project improved visibility and management of the company's finished-goods inventory – both in stockyards and in transit. The company also improved its process for sales-order handling, pricing and conditions, availability checks, sales reporting and profitability analysis.

## Improved Information Visibility and Customer Service

With SAP's solution TSC could now update their customers on a daily basis and provide seamless services across the country, thus improving cus-

tomer management. The sales team could provide information on orders received, on stock, and on dispatches. With respect to sales orders, the software now provided support for credit limits, rebate arrangements, sales returns and debit and credit memos. All stock positions at all the company's stockyards, customer outstanding and realizations, and all the company's earnings from each product were available to everyone. The company could, therefore, make decisions related to customer service and management with every possible bit of customer information available to it.

Furthermore, sales orders could now be processed through TSC's sales offices in addition to the head office. The system could handle deliveries from the steel production unit in Jamshedpur (for direct dispatch to customers, stock transfers and transfer to export, profit center and production facilities) and from stockyards and external processing agents through external logons (for dispatches to customers and inter-stockyard transfers).

## Moving Ahead

After the OG&F project, legacy systems continued to support functions for buying, manufacturing and financial accounting and costing, whereas the sell operations were now on SAP (Figure 1).

After the OG&F implementation went live for sales and marketing, the front end of the company's activities became completely transparent, but the iron and steel-making activities and refinery operations continued to be shrouded. The top management realized that unless costs were visible from the moment raw materials enter the plant to when the finished product leaves, TSC would not be able to optimize the use of its resources and achieve better levels of profitability. The company was unable to accurately capture manufacturing costs, taxes, freight costs and other related costs necessary for the calculation of net realization value gross margins at product level.

*Figure 1. IT architecture after OG & F Implementation*

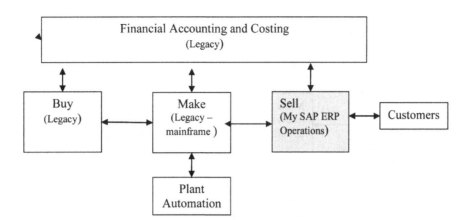

Soon it also became evident that the SD module and related FI Module were not sufficient to enable a smooth sales and distribution function. The Branch Managers started feeling the need to have the cost figures so as to decide on the margins for each product. Need for inventory (un-finished) visibility started to be felt as without it they were not in a position to commit to the orders of the customers. This necessitated the implementation of other related modules so as to enable the Branch Managers to take margin based product-mix decisions and inventory visibility of un-finished goods for better inventory management and order promising.

## SAP EXTENSION: 2000- 2005

In line with the strategic objectives spelt out by the Board members of TSC (page 3), the focus on cost measurement and cutting was maintained. Fresh from the success from the perceived success of the first phase of ERP implementation in the Order Generation and Fulfillment process, the company decided to study the further implementation and possible **benefits** from implementing SAP R/3 in other functional areas in the organization. A project team decided to conduct a survey of the managers in various functional areas to ascertain what the

goals of the project should be. The main points which emerged from the survey were:

1. There was no uniform consolidation of accounts across various divisions and subsidiaries across the company. This was urgently required for a fast closing cycle.

2. The product wise costs were not easy to measure and the data was often not available to various stakeholders in the organization. Without proper measures of product wise costs, the efforts at cost cutting were always in doubt. Also deciding a product mix could only be done with the availability of product wise costs, and price realization.

3. Inventory across the plant, especially of the MRO items (Maintenance, Repair and Operational items) was a priority since it was an area where some major cost cutting was possible.

4. Procurement was an area where major procedural and other cost savings could be achieved, so procurement should be covered in the ERP implementation.

5. In any process plant maintenance was a major activity which would determine the uptime of the plant.

*Figure 2. IT architechture after SAP extension implementation*

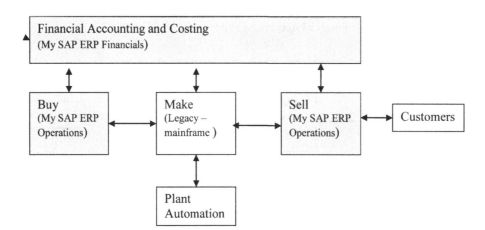

Thus phase two of the ERP implementation was undertaken, with the above specific objectives. The team also did an exhaustive evaluation of the functionality available in the SAP R/3 software, with the help of the implementation partners and came to the conclusion that the software did not support the manufacturing of steel, and that it would not be wise to replace the newly developed mainframe based systems with SAP R/3. Thus the architecture of implementation of SAP (as shown in figure 2) was that the overall finance and accounting (including costing) functions were supported by SAP, along with the 'buy' and 'sell' functions. But 'make' or manufacturing function was supported by the mainframe based systems.

Phase II was appropriately named *'SAP Extension '*. The management faced a bigger challenge of implementing SAP in Jamshedpur works wherein a majority of TSC's (approximately 45,000 employees) employees and would be users of the software were based. This phase included the implementation of Procurement, Financial Accounting, Material Management, Costing, Asset Accounting, and Plant Maintenance modules of SAP R/3 with the intention of improving its internal processes. This phase started in November (See Figure 2).

The functions addressed in this phase were:

- Financial Accounting
- Costing
- Materials Management
- Inventory Management
- Raw Materials Accounting
- Asset Accounting
- Maintenance Management (Pilot Project)
- Production Recording
- & Upgrade OG&F

## Project Management / Organization Structure

This time the core team consisted of 60 people as against 18 people in the earlier phase.

## Top Executives

- Vice President (Finance) -Sponsor
- Deputy Managing Director (Steel) -Co-Sponsor
- Chief Information Officer

## Working Teams

- Project Manager (TSC)

- Project Manager (PWC)
- Module Leaders
- Group Leader (IT)
- Members (11 from ITS Department and 45 functional experts/end users)
- 60 Consultants

## Supporting Teams *Steering Committee*

- (Project Charter, Guidelines/Principals and Monitor Resource, Validation of project scope, Constant monitor of risk and its mitigation)
- Executive Committee
- (Business rules validation, cross- departmental issues)

## IT Support Groups

- (Technological and faculty support from the best available resource)

## Change Management

This phase was even more challenging as apart from the technical and business considerations it also had an added and important element of Change Management. The management followed the 'Top-Down' approach with a clear directive from the Sponsor to the employees that it was 'his project'. Identification of all major change initiatives was done at the beginning of the project and the same was shared with key members of the management and the stakeholders. A number of workshops and analysis were carried out including Stakeholder Analysis, Project Visioning, Change History Analysis and Team Building. A detail scrutiny of requisite competencies was performed prior to project staffing. The necessary information about the implementation and its success was communicated to the company employees with the help of newsletters.

## Training and Knowledge Transfer

**SAP Knowledge to core team:** A composite training about the over all SAP system was provided to all team members. Module level comprehensive training was conducted for all 61 team members who in turn got expertise in their concerned module. A number of training rooms were facilitated with SAP India as the training partner. The training was complemented with a large database of online training material for the team members.

## Specialization Competency

Three BASIS experts were developed after a comprehensive training in Sapient College. Whereas other domain experts; ABAP(15), BW(15), LSMW (20) were developed in-house. Faculties from leading organization and experts were involved in providing competency to these experts in the specially equipped training rooms. A special training website was also launched on the company Intranet.

## End User Training

Three equipped training rooms were developed for conducting training sessions. A lot of interest and resources were allocated to train around 41 Site Champions, 2200 End Users along with 350 Refreshers. The training sessions were also complemented with Online Training Material for ready reference which was banked on a dedicated training server.

## Hand Holding

Hand holding training at all end user sites were provided. The training server was frequently updated and real data was made available to all the users.

## Implementation

TSC followed the Accelerated SAP (ASAP) roadmap for the implementation. The key stages of SAP implementation along with the key activities in each phase are:

## Noticeable Changes and Obstacles

Suddenly, the people found that the new system had made the transactions more disciplined and there was a loss of flexibility. The users had to enter a lot of data into the system without which the system would not carry out the transaction, which was not the case earlier. All required fields had to be filled for every single process. There was no surpassing to it. This change was creating problems throughout the organization as it was a mass change incorporating as much as 2000 widespread end-users. TSC addressed this problem by the creation of site champions who helped the users after Go-Live. They acted as local helpdesks in their department and areas of work.

There were a lot changes in roles and responsibilities of individuals and changes in work practice. TSC provided training regarding the new roles and adequate information and knowledge to the affected individuals and groups facilitating faster and easier adjustment. The management also had to address the problems of workforce becoming redundant in some areas of the organization after the implementation. For, example the group of around 35 account clerks in the bill passing department were suddenly doing nothing. Their job of manually matching the purchased orders, certified challans and invoices was now done automatically in SAP. The management had to re-deploy these employees into other divisions.

The core team received a lot of suggestions/complaints regarding the new system. The management decided to establish a Change Control Board, headed by a very senior person to look into the incoming suggestion or changes from all over the organization. The board evaluated the various suggestions in detail along with their interlinked effects with other processes every week. The changes approved were then implemented to the system by the core team

## Technical Challenge

### Need to Build Complex Interfaces

As mentioned before, at the time TSC decided to go in for **ERP implementation** there weren't any tailor made packages addressing all the business processes involved in the steel industry. The company decided not to do away with certain mainframe based systems such as the FPCIS (Flat Product Complex -Information System) and CRM-IS (Cold Rolling Mill -Information System) as they were effective and complied well to the requirements of the production processes in the Flat Product Complex. The objective was to build system integration by exploiting the standard features of implemented hardware and software as far as practicable.

The Technical feasibilities were tried out by developing prototype system interfaces (Appendix 2). The prototype systems developed were evaluated by the implementation partner and the technology group and rated as one of the best available technical solutions for integrating the custom-build systems with SAP. About 45 such interfaces were built to integrate the SAP system to the mainframe based systems, and formed a major part of the implementation initiative.

## Incorporation of mySAP.com

In August, 2000 TSC incorporated mySAP.com, the collaborative Internet business model, to strengthen customer relationships. This enabled the customers to access information, any time and from any place, on the order status to delivery status, invoices to credit notes, payment dues to credit status and a host of other customer-desired reports. It also included Internet sales or placement of order, in which the customers were able to place, orders online.

## Results of 'SAP Extension'

Project SAP Extension helped TSC expand the integration of business processes and systems and achieve its goal of better revenue management. Profitability analysis enabled by new processes and software helped the company make better decisions about its product mix – including decisions about the discontinuation of unprofitable products – which helped in improving gross margins. Integrated materials-requirement planning and an inventory-aging overview for maintenance repair, and operations items have helped the company reduce inventory. Cost visibility at the product-group level has helped to lower production costs and enable margin-based decision making. The processes have been automated and drudgery has been removed, leading to better utilization of managerial time. Other **benefits** include:

- A reduction in lead time for spending approvals, now 18–20 days from 65–70 days.
- Faster closing of accounts.
- Support for a customer-optimization model for increasing profit from individual customers.
- Reduced effort for complying with statutory requirements.
- Improved availability of production assets due to improved maintenance.
- Cost-conscious decision making with respect to material and contract services, which has improved budgetary compliance for maintenance functions.

The SAP Extension project has helped reduce inventory for maintenance, repairs, and operations to 12% of total spending in this area, down from 36%. Downtime caused by breakdowns in Hot Strip Mill has decreased by 2.8% due to better maintenance planning. Account closing dates have moved to the fifth of the month from the tenth, and the lead time for approval of purchases has been cut to 18 days from an average of 65 to 70

days. In addition, the number of purchase orders decreased by 2,000 per year, due to an increased number of contracts.

## SAP Competence Centre

With the implementation of SAP to support major business functions, creation of SAP Competence Centre as common support structure was necessitated in 2002. The competence centre would provide ongoing support and improve business processes so as to leverage the SAP system for maximizing business **benefits** to the organization.

The main functions of SAP Competence Centre were:

1. Provide ongoing support in functional and technical areas of SAP for projects implemented.
2. Identify and implement roll outs, upgrades and new functionalities of SAP for optimizing and improving business processes.
3. Manage interfaces with other systems and support agencies.

## The Benefits from SAP Implementation

Taken together, the OG&F and SAP Extension projects provide better system integration – ensuring end-to-end, on-time information visibility. With this information, TSC can adapt to business and market changes more quickly. The company benefits from unified processes across its business units. In addition, TSC has gained better control of its business policies. This is particularly helpful in the area of credit-limit control, where software checks help TSC's sales force comply with company policy.

Overall the implementation had freed the top management team from routine functions, allowed them to devote greater time to strategic thinking, and let us make production and procurement decisions that are more informed and focused on higher-margin product lines.

The major benefits attained by TSC post implementation are:

- Levels of data aggregation and iteration are eliminated by the single entry of transactions into the database.
- Access to the system is according to the authorization provided to the user. No unauthorized person can have access to the company data.
- There is complete visibility of information throughout the enterprise.
- Managerial time is freed up for job enrichment and qualitative enhancements.
- Better product mix decision by profitability analysis.
- Inventory reduction through integrated planning for MRO items.
- Lower product cost through cost visibility.

## Overdue-Debt Reduction

Overdue debt was reduced from 17 days (of sales) in FY2000 to less than one day in FY2005. The analysis found that the SAP implementation contributed 50% of the overall debt reduction. The analysis estimated the total cumulative benefit over five years from improved debt control to be Rs1.14 billion, of which Rs568 million is believed to be the contribution from SAP implementations.

## Finished-Goods-Inventory Reduction

Finished-goods inventory was reduced from 29 days (of sales) in FY2000 to 23 days in FY2005. The analysis found that improved visibility across stockyards and in-transit inventory enabled by the SAP software implementation contributed 10% to the overall reduction in finished-goods inventory. The analysis estimated the total cumulative benefit over five years from a reduction in finished-goods inventory to be Rs980 million, of which Rs98 million is believed to be the contribution from SAP implementation.

## Improved Gross Margins

Availability of costs at the product level has helped TSC make more informed decisions about pricing and product mix. There have been several instances following the SAP Extension implementation, for example, where the price of a product was changed to match the margin requirements. Products have also been discontinued because of lower margins. This has contributed to improved margins in both the flat and long products divisions of TATA STEEL.

## Working Capital Reduction

Working capital was reduced through a decrease in inventory for maintenance, repair, and operations – including inventory for spare parts – from 36% of total spending for this area in FY2002 to 12% in FY2005. The total cumulative benefit over five years achieved due to such inventory reduction is estimated to be Rs2.305 billion, out of which Rs230 million is believed to be the contribution from SAP solutions.

## Improved Maintenance– Reduction in Breakdowns

SAP software for plant maintenance was implemented during Project SAP Extension in two mills: LD2 and Hot Strip Mill. In Hot Strip Mill, the implementation helped reduce downtime due to breakdowns from 1,224 hours in FY2002 to 456 hours in FY2005. This reduced production losses from Rs141 million in FY2002 to Rs81 million in FY2005. As mentioned earlier, TSC has been the lowest-cost producer of steel since 2000. (Table 1 in Appendix 1a).

## CONCLUSION

The implementation of ERP in the company was carried out successfully in terms of time and

*Table 1.*

| Stage | Duration/Time Frame | Activities |
|---|---|---|
| **Project Preparation** | Feb Year 1-March Yr 1 | Detail Project Scoping<br>Project Kickoff<br>Sizing Assessment<br>Project Team Training |
| **Business Blueprint** | March Yr 1-May Yr 1 | Define Organization Hierarchy<br>Define Business Blueprint<br>Develop and Implement Communications Plan<br>Project Checkpoint |
| **Realization** | May Yr1-SepYr 1 | Baseline Configuration<br>Final Configuration<br>Final Integration Test<br>Create End User Training Material<br>Conduct Org/Job Impact Analysis<br>Develop Org Transition Plan<br>Develop Custom Code<br>Project Checkpoint |
| **Final Preparation** | Sep Yr 1-Nov Yr 1 | Train End Users<br>Implement Org Transition Plan<br>Assess Change Readiness<br>Site Support Planning<br>Cut-over<br>Project Checkpoint |
| **Go-Live & Support** | Nov Yr 1-Dec Yr 1 | Go Live<br>Production Support<br>Conduct Hand-over<br>Project Checkpoint |
| **Stabilization and Benefits Accrual** | Jan Yr 2 – Jan Yr 5 | Stabilization<br>Learning and usage<br>Benefits accrual |

budget. As discussed in the case, the involvement of a large ERP implementation team and the involvement and leadership of the top management was a crucial factor in the implementation. The company avoided many potential traps or failure factors which would potentially slow down the implementation (Parr & Shanks, 2000; Adam & O'Doherty, 2001; Markus et al., 2000; Markus & Tanis, 2000; Prasad et al., 1999; Sumner, 2000; Sumner, 2004; Umble & Umble, 2002; Kim et al., 2005) also the additional work of integrating the legacy systems using 45 interfaces was also managed such that the overall project schedule was not affected.

Various benefits were reported by the manager's and are given in the preceding section. These were in line with the benefits reported from successful ERP implementations. (Markus et al., 2000; Shang & Seddon, 2002; Stein, 1999; Sumner, 2004) Later an audit was undertaken by a third party agency for the entire ERP implementation, and the ERP implementation was found to have been successful, and the benefits reported were supported in the audit report.

# REFERENCES

Adam, F., & O'Doherty, P. (2000). Lessons from enterprise resource planning implementations in Ireland – towards smaller and shorter ERP projects. *Journal of Information Technology, 15*(4), 305–317. doi:10.1080/02683960010008953

Huang, Z., & Palvia, P. (2001). ERP implementation issues in advanced and developing countries. *Business Process Management Journal, 7*(3), 276–285. doi:10.1108/14637150110392773

Kim, Y., Lee, Z., & Gosain, S. (2005). Impediments to successful ERP implementation process. *Business Process Management Journal, 11*(2), 158–170. doi:10.1108/14637150510591156

Markus, M. L., Axline, S., Petrie, D., & Tanis, S. C. (2000). Learning from adopters' experiences with ERP: problems encountered and success achieved. *Journal of Information Technology, 15*(4), 245–265. doi:10.1080/02683960010008944

Markus, M. L., & Tanis, C. (2000). The enterprise systems experience: from adoption to success . In Zmud, R. W. (Ed.), *Framing the domains of IT research: Glimpsing the future through the past* (pp. 173–207). Cincinnati, OH: Pinnaflex Educational Resources Inc.

Nah, F. F., Lau, J. L., & Kuang, J. (2001). Critical factors for successful implementation of enterprise systems. *Business Process Management Journal, 7*(3), 285–296. doi:10.1108/14637150110392782

O'Leary, D. (2000). *Enterprise Resource Planning Systems: Systems, Life Cycle, Electronic Commerce, and Risk* (1st ed.). Cambridge, UK: Cambridge University Press.

Parr, A., & Shanks, G. (2000). A model of ERP project implementation. *Journal of Information Technology, 15*(4), 289. doi:10.1080/02683960010009051

Prasad, B., Sharma, M. K., & Godla, J. K. (1999). Critical issues affecting an ERP implementation. *Information Systems Management, 16*(3).

Shang, S., & Seddon, P. B. (2002). Assessing and managing the benefits of enterprise systems: the business manager's perspective. *Information Systems Journal, 12*, 271–299. doi:10.1046/j.1365-2575.2002.00132.x

Stein, T. (1999, May 24). Making ERP add up. *Information Week*, 59.

Sumner, M. (2000). Risk factors in enterprise-wide/ERP projects. *Journal of Information Technology, 15*(4), 317–327. doi:10.1080/02683960010009079

Sumner, M. (2004). *Enterprise Resource Planning*. Upper Saddle River, NJ: Prentice Hall.

Umble, E. J., & Umble, M. M. (2002). Avoiding ERP Implementation Failure. *Industrial Management (Des Plaines), 44*(1), 25–34.

Wallace, T. F., & Kremzar, M. H. (2001). *ERP: Making It Happen: The Implementers' Guide to Success with Enterprise Resource Planning* (3rd ed.). New York: Wiley.

Wei, H., Wang, E.T.G., & Ju, P. (2005). Understanding misalignment and cascading change of ERP implementation: a stage view of process analysis. *European Journal of Information Systems, 14*(01 Dec 2005), 324-334.

## ENDNOTES

[1] TSC in 2007 acquired a large international competitor and raised its total output to 27 million Tonnes of steel annually and a turnover of $25 Billion approximately.

[2] SAP modules (www.sap.com)

## APPENDIX

IT Architecture of TSC

*Figure 3.*

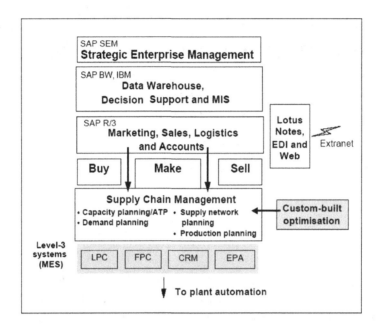

*Figure 4. Integration architecture of SAP R/3 and custombuilt systems in TSC*

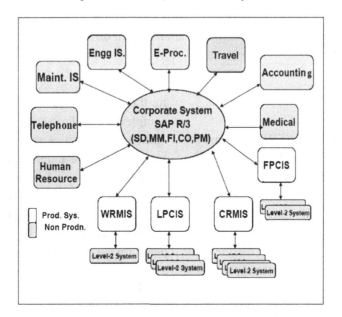

# Chapter 6

# Implementation of ERP Systems:
## A Seven Stage Adoption Model

**Manoj Jha**
*SAP Consultant, India*

**Sanjay Kumar**
*MDI Gurgaon, India*

## ABSTRACT:

*The model discusses the implementation of ERP systems. The article discusses the process based implementation approach and also the critical success factors approach for the implementation. A gap identified in literature is that critical success factors and ERP implementation has not been studied from the viewpoint of other stakeholders. This chapter tries to address this gap by proposing a seven stage model of ERP implementation and adoption from the viewpoint of the ERP implementation consultant. The model also addresses subsequent stages such a data exploitation stage where organizations learn to use data for decision making and process management. The model also addresses the subsequent stages of extension of ERP to partners like suppliers and dealers, and the innovation stage when the organizations starts to experiment with newer solutions based on ERP systems.*

## INTRODUCTION

Enterprise Resource Planning (ERP) systems are commercial software packages that enable the integration of transaction oriented data and business processes throughout an organization (Markus & Tanis, 2000). As more and more organizations around the world have chosen to build their IT infrastructure around this class of off-the-shelf applications, there has been a greater appreciation

DOI: 10.4018/978-1-61520-625-4.ch006

for the challenges involved in implementing these complex technologies (Youngbeom et al., 2005). Although companies spend millions of dollars on both the package and the implementation process, the overall success rate is low. Business and popular press is full of horror stories describing major problems in ERP implementation projects and project failures, even leading to liquidation. More common place are the problems reported in academic press, such budget and time over runs, failure to realize full functionality, process mis-specification, organizational resistance or inertia, improper conversion

Copyright © 2010, IGI Global. Copying or distributing in print or electronic forms without written permission of IGI Global is prohibited.

and uploading of legacy data, problems related to training and use etc. (Stedman, 1999) In response there has been a developing body of academic literature which addresses the difficulties of ERP implementation by proposing critical success factors required for a successful ERP implementation (Frederic & O'Doherty, 2000; Sumner, 2000; Youngbeom et al., 2005; Huang & Palvia,2001; Gargeya & Brady, 2005; Umble & Umble, 2002; Nah et al., 2001; Babu & Dalal, 2006; Yu, 2005; Grossman & Walsh, 2004; Yokovlev & Anderson, 2001; Prasad et al., 1999) and a parallel stream of literature which proposes process models of the implementation process(Wei et al., 2005; Markus et al., 2000; Kraemmerand et al., 2003; Markus & Tanis, 2000). The effort of both approaches is to better understand the implementation process and the factors which affect it, and hence to provide guidelines so that the ERP implementation process can be better managed.

## What are ERP Systems

ERP systems are transaction oriented software packages, at the heart of which lies a central database, that draws data from and feeds data into a series of applications supporting a wide range of company functions such as accounting, warehousing, human resource management, sales, distribution and production planning (Kraemmerand et al., 2003). They differ from other packages as they encapsulate a range of pre-configured standard processes based on industry best practices. Alternative process routes and supporting database transactions are engineered into the software package and can be accessed through various customizing screens (Kirchmer, 1999; Brehm, 2001). Once a 'process route' is chosen, the transactions and the supporting data flow as per the defined route. The software vendors also release 'business process reference models' which are basically maps of the standard processes built into the system, and which can be used as an aid to choosing the best-fit process. (Kirchmer, 1999)

Best fit here refers to the fit with the operational process followed by the organization. The job of implementing an ERP system thus involves mapping the as-is processes of an enterprise, deciding the selected processes to be used in the future and mapping these processes into the software, using the configuration screens available in the system. Certain processes which are desired by the organizations cannot be mapped into the ERP system, as a pre-configured path is not available in the product. These processes need customization of the software i.e. the program code to be modified for supporting the desired functionality (Markus & Tanis, 2000; Kirchmer, 1999; Brehm et al., 2001)

## LITERATURE REVIEW

ERP systems are integrated systems with mechanisms based on planning and forecasting, which support the management of the entire enterprise and integrate all of its activity. The effective implementation of such a system can bring about many benefits, such as enterprise management and information flow enhancement. Consequently, improvement of economic indicators is achievable, which finally leads to an increase in enterprise profitability.

However, the achievement of these above-mentioned benefits depends upon the effective implementation of the full functionality of the ERP system, which is quite difficult. There are a great many implementation projects that do not bring about the planned effects, or even end up in project abandonment. The duration and budget of the implementation projects significantly exceed initial estimates, and the planned scope of the implementation is limited (Parr & Shanks, 2000). Therefore, conducting research seems crucial in order to explore the conditions having an influence on the project outcome.

*Figure 1. Enterprise system implementation cycle (source: Marcus and Tanis, 2000)*

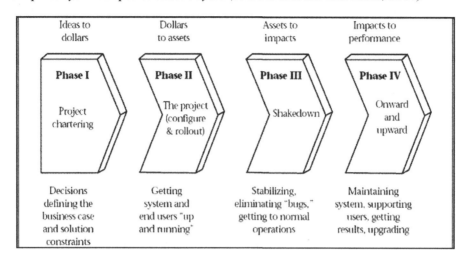

## ERP Implementation Models

On one hand researchers and practitioners have proposed various implementation models such as Wallace & Kremzer (2001), Parr & Shanks (2000) and Markus & Tanis (2000).Majority of these models include the technical activities involved in the implementation, as well as change management and organizational factors (a good description of these technical activities is given in Markus & Tanis (2000) and Miller (1998) (Accelerated SAP implementation) etc). The models proposed by practitioners tend to be prescriptive in nature, and the model proposed by Kremzer and Wallace is also prescriptive. The normal implementation is proposed in 18 months time, while an accelerated implementation model is proposed in 18 weeks.

The model proposed by Parr & Shanks (2000) also uses the project management phases for the implementation such as planning, project management and enhancement. The authors also recommend that the model be merged with the process model of ERP implementation by Markus and Tanis. The design phase is broken up into sub phases of set up, reengineer, design, configuration and testing and installation phase. Each of these phases has a set of critical success factors

for guiding the practitioner as to the desired and undesired activities.

The process model of Markus & Tanis (2000) has a process based approach to ERP implementation. Earlier work of the author has identified the three phases to value of any IT project – namely the "IT conversion process", the "IT Use process" and the "Competitive process". Markus argues that all three phases are important to the 'success' of any IT implementation.

Based on the above phases, the model then proposes four phases as shown in 1, namely Project Chartering comprising the activities of developing the business case and the solution constraints in terms of manpower, timeline and budgets, Project Rollout involving the activities of configuring the system, getting the system and users up and running (training), Shakedown in which the concentration is on elimination of bugs, legacy data transfer and cleaning and getting to normal operations, and Onwards and Upwards in which system maintenance, user support, getting results and upgrading are the main activities.

Bajwa et al. (2000) propose an ERP implementation model incorporating Business constructs such as external and internal stakeholders, technology constructs, business integration and technical efficiency constructs and show how they become effective in the main steps of ERP implementation such as- specific package selection, as – is and to- be states in process mapping, implementation and going live steps.

Metaxiotis et al. (2005) suggest a goal directed project management methodology for ERP implementation where the project goals drive the selection of the activities of planning, organization and control. The authors claim that this methodology helps to focus the activities of the project and thus reduce the time for the implementation and also conserve the resources being used in the project.

Karakanian (1999) suggests the use of nine factors such as drivers of ERP implementation, resources, package functionality fits, the modules to be implemented, existing technology platforms and budgets etc to suggest an ERP implementation strategy. This strategy would help in choosing the minimum resources in terms of personnel and the time phasing strategy of the ERP implementation project to match with the other constraints of the implementation, so that the overall ERP implementation is in sync with the available actors.

## The Identification of ERP Implementation Success Factors

Researchers and practitioners have used the critical factors approach to draw up a implementation plan for successful implementation of ERP systems. ERP system implementation is a process of great complexity, with a great many conditions and factors potentially influencing the implementation. These conditions could have a positive effect on the outcome of ERP project, while their absence could generate problems during implementation.

A Critical Success Factor (CSF) approach has been a used by a number of researchers, to identify various factors of importance to the success of the implementation process, at each stage of the implementation process(Sun et al., 2005; Al-Mashari et al., 2006; Huang & Palvia, 2001;

Sumner, 2000; Markus & Tanis, 2000; Lan et al., 2005; Markus et al., 2000; Parr & Shanks, 2000; Frederic & O'Deherty, 2000; Youngbeom et al., 2005; Hillman et al., 2002; Umble & Umble, 2002; Ilya et al., 2001; Prasad et al., 1999)

Nah et al. (2007) in an empirical assessment of CSFs have identified that some factors such as change management, enterprise wide communication and project management are perceived to be more important. Ehie & Madsen (2005) have tried to develop ERP implementation theory to help in identifying the critical issues in ERP implementation, while Plant & Willcocks (2007) have used a case study of an international ERP implementation to identify some CSFs for ERP implementation.

Some main factors identified by these researchers are

1. Change Management
2. Project Charter and Project Management
3. BPR and ERP customization
4. Software development, testing and troubleshooting
5. IT knowledge and appropriate business & legacy systems
6. ERP systems training and use

Most of these factors can be further broken down into multiple sub-factors, for example change management may be taken to include top management support, and communication of need for change, building a supporting coalition for change and the need for small successes during the implementation of the change. Similarly Project management may be taken to include assignment of adequate project resources, break down of project work structure, and proper project phasing etc.

Burns et al. (1991) researching critical success factors in MRP implementation, suggested dividing potential factors into environmental and methodological. Environmental factors include, apart from those describing enterprise activity, the product technology level and the organisation's willingness to change. The methodological factors are connected with the implementation approach incorporated. On the basis of 504 survey responses, most of the methodological factors were identified as being associated with MRP II success, while only two of the environmental factors were found to be connected with implementation success – product technology and organisation willingness to change.

In other research, Parr et al. (1999) turned to experts participating in many implementation projects. The research sample consisted of ten experts who had participated in a total of 42 ERP implementation projects, mainly as project managers. Based on interviews with the experts, ten candidate factors necessary for successful implementation of ERP systems are identified. These factors were divided into groups related with management, personnel, software and project. Of these ten candidate factors, three are of paramount importance. They are management support of the project team and of the implementation process, a project team that has the appropriate balance of business and technical skills, and commitment to change by all the stakeholders.

Holland & Light (1999) and Holland et al. (1999) presented a number of potential success factors in ERP implementation and suggested their division into strategic and tactical factors. The model was illustrated on a sample of two ERP implementation projects. Among 12 factors, the authors highlighted the critical impact of legacy systems upon the implementation process and the importance of selecting an appropriate ERP strategy. However, they did not formulate conclusions regarding factors' ranking.

Esteves & Pastor (2000) suggested a unified ERP implementation critical success factors model. This model is based on the analysis of considerable research regarding implementation success factors. The authors indicated that factors should be categorised into strategic and tactical factors from organisational and technological perspectives.

Similarly, the research of Nah et al. (2000) was based on literature review and yielded a model of 11 critical success factors. These models were fitted into the four stages of ERP implementation identified by Markus & Tanis (2000). This model was next verified on the basis of the opinions of 54 CIOs implementing ERP into their organizations (Nah et al., 2001) The five most critical factors identified by the CIOs were: top management support, project champion, ERP teamwork and composition, project management, and change management program and culture.

Somers & Nelson (2001) described the importance of critical success factors across the stages of ERP implementations using the responses from 86 organisations implementing ERP. From their broad list of 22 critical success factors for ERP implementation, in overall ranking, the most important are: top management support; project team competence; interdepartmental cooperation; clear goals and objectives; project management; and interdepartmental communication.

Al-Mashari et al. (2003) presented taxonomy of ERP critical factors where 12 factors were divided into three dimensions related to the stages of ERP project, which are: setting-up, deployment and evaluation. The taxonomy presented emphasizes that a clear vision and business director is fundamental for the success of ERP system implementation. It also highlights the importance of business process management and suggests that the evaluation and performance monitoring of ERP system's implementation can lead to the achievement of all desired business goals and objectives. Finally, the authors conclude that the most essential element of success and the pre-requisite for successful and effective ERP implementation is leadership and commitment.

Brown & Vessey (2003) on the basis of their research concluded that there are five success factors for ERP projects and illustrated their significance with the use of three successful ERP implementations case studies. The resulting factors are: top management is engaged in the project, not just involved; project leaders are veterans, and team members are decision makers; third parties fill gaps in expertise and transfer their knowledge; change management goes hand-in-hand with project planning; and a "satisficing" mindset prevails.

Sun et al. (2005) and Nah et al. (2007) have studied the effect of some major factors which may influence the perception of ERP systems success. Other researchers have used the list of CSFs to create a scale for measuring ERP implementation success. Snider et al. (2009) have compared 5 cases of ERP implementation in Small and Medium Enterprises and have identified the factors associated with successful and unsuccessful ERP implementations. Ehie & Madsen (2005) have identified CSFs which correlate with the success of ERP implementation, while Plant & Willcocks (2007) have studied international ERP implementation to identify the perception of critical success factors at each stage of implementation in two longitudinal studies. Hsu et al have used innovation diffusion theory to assess the impact of CSFs on ERP implementation success. Hsu et al. (2008) and Furomo & Melcher (2006) have used adaptive structuration theory to study the importance of social structure on ERP implementation success.

Finney & Corbett (2007) have compiled and analyzed critical success factors from about 45 research papers. Their analysis showed that at an aggregated level, the main critical success factors [CSFs] identified were largely similar, but at the sub factor level there was a wide variation in the sub factors which comprised each factor. Also there was a gap in identification of critical success factors from the view point of the stake holders in the ERP implementation.

The results of the above-mentioned research on ERP implementation success factors illustrate the problem complexity and the variety of approaches. It is also clear from the study by Finney & Corbett (2007) that there exists a gap in the fact that stakeholder perceptions on critical success factors have not been researched. This chapter brings a view from one of the stakeholders in the ERP implementation process – the implementation consultants.

## NEED FOR THE SEVEN STAGE ADOPTION MODEL

The successful adoption process of an Enterprise System has been of significant importance for the successful progress made by Enterprise Systems over last few decades.

A number of research have been carried out since early 1990s till date to analyse the process of adoption of Enterprise System by organizations of different sizes and across different industries and identify and enlist critical success factors of the adoption process.

Enterprise Resource System vendors have gone through the process of incorporating technological advances and business process enhancements into their software. The organizations adopting these solutions and the consulting companies helping them in the adoption process have also modified and optimized the processes over these years.

The advantage of this model is that the development and focus of this model is from a consultant view point and is based on the experiences of consultants over a period of time.

The author has presented a new Enterprise Systems Adoption Model called the "Seven Stage Enterprise Systems Adoption Model". The seven stages, the significance, characteristics and interrelationship among various stages have been explained in a very simple style (Figure 2). The model is an extended ERP implementation model since the consultants have to plan not only for the implementation of the ERP system but also for it's adoption and use by the managers in the organization. Thus the ERP implementation model consists of seven stages. The stages known as determining project charter and change management

*Figure 2. Seven stage ERP adoption model*

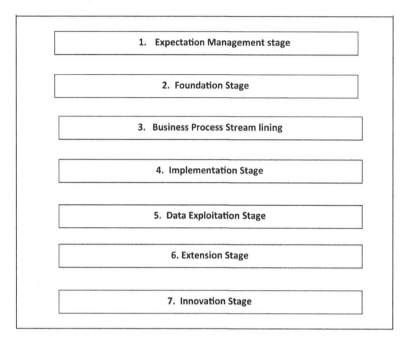

are subsumed into the new stages called Expectation management where the scope of the project is decided and the objectives of the project are decided. In the foundation stage, the act of team formulation, starting formal communication with the whole organization, other change management activities are undertaken.

The Business Process streamlining stage incorporates the work of mapping business processes and streamlining them through process improvement. The implementation stage involves all the other activities of configuring the processes into the ERP software, testing, data migration, going live with ERP. Then the system is stabilized by removing bugs and re training managers to work on these systems.

After ERP stabilization, the next stage is that the organization gains sufficient confidence and expertise to then start using the ERP system better. This is called the Data Exploitation stage. Here the managers use data for supporting their decisions and for managing their key processes based on real time information. Thus process management using data is the key focus of this stage.

Then the organization is ready to extend the ERP system to its suppliers and customers through add on products or modules such as supplier relationship management (SRM), customer relationship management (CRM) and supply chain management (SCM).

While the new model brings in the practical experience of working with Enterprise Resource Systems in various roles and from different perspectives, the last segment brings in the richness of understanding of ERP landscape from an academic perspective while reviewing the relevance of the proposed model.

## ENTERPRISE SYSTEMS (ES) ADOPTION MODEL

A detailed scan and analysis of Enterprise Solution stories across over two decades indicate the common thread among all successful ERP adoptions. The following Seven Stage model could be effectively used to understand the maturity and development of Enterprise Solution in an organization.

The overall success of Enterprise Solution is greatly dependent on successful management of each of these stages by various stakeholders.

## Expectation Management Stage

This is the initial stage of ERP adoption. This stage is either driven by Management Consultants who have been engaged to prescribe changes for overall improvements in an organization or by a task force who are entrusted with remarkable changes in the way the organization functions. In this stage, group of people start making suggestions about Enterprise Solutions and its advantages and limitations, what is needed for successful implementation and who need to drive the changes? 'Build vs. Buy' debate also gets initiated at this stage.

A realistic expectation needs to be set at this stage. Some consultants or even employees oversell Enterprise Solutions that give rise to disappointments at a later stage.

The best managed Expectation Setting Stage will set realistic goals and improve awareness about the kind of commitment that would be required both by senior management and people involved in the adoption process. It also carries out awareness sessions for those who may not directly be involved but would be impacted by the new ways of managing processes.

## Foundation Stage

Foundation stage also aims at preparing an organization for the challenges ahead in the process of Enterprise Solution adoption process. Sometimes it may run concurrent with the Expectation Management Stage as the fundamental goals of the two stages are similar. At the end of these two preparatory stages the organization by and large is ready for the long journey of ERP adoption.

The result is generally a formal requirement or expectation document or a near consensus understanding of what is required. A list of pos-sible Enterprise Solutions to look at and type and names of vendors to engage also gets into play at this stage of adoption. Some organizations make the decision on Enterprise Solution and Implementation Consulting vendors at this stage itself.

## Business Process Streamlining Stage

Business Process Streamlining Stage ensures current business processes are reviewed and revised to enable better functioning of the organization. It is done by a team of process engineers. They are from a consulting organization, an internal team of high performers or a combination. They work as a task force coming up with new process model for the organization.

The degree of changes suggested at this stage depends upon the current stage of automation, organizational maturity and the industry. A highly matured automation will invariably mean less dramatic business process changes. The changes will invariably be related to process integration. Similar is the case of a matured organization.

In some cases Business Process streamlining stage runs concurrently with Implementation stage and is managed as part of change management initiative. In this model of ES adoption, the organizations use ES as an enabler of change and as the process changes are required for smooth implementation of ES, the Change Management team is entrusted with the task of streamlining the processes.

## Implementation Stage

This stage is the most crucial one. Depending upon the decisions made during the previous stages, the functional fit of the selected Enterprise Solution and the overall management of this stage, the duration of implementation stage varies from a few quarters to a few years.

*Table 1.*

| Area | High/Low | Probability of Success |
|---|---|---|
| Degree of Readiness | | |
| Top Management Support | | |
| Product Functionality | | |
| Degree of Customization | | |
| Consultant capabilities | | |
| Strength of Business Case | | |
| Team Commitment | | |
| Organizational Awareness | | |
| Swiftness of Decision Making | | |
| Organizational Maturity on Project Management | | |
| Change Management Capabilities | | |
| | | |

Some of the key success factors of this stage as identified in literature (referred in section 1.2) are provided in Table 1.

The success of implementation stage is impacted by the following key stakeholders:

- Implementation Consultants
- Internal Contributing Team
- Senior Management
- ES Vendor
- Key User Group
- Change Management Team

One of the key differentiator is presence of experienced members in the above team. This means having members who have been previously involved in successful ES adoption process. Such members are generally provided by the Implementation Partner organization. Therefore, selection of right vendor partner is extremely important.

High degree of commitment of Internal Team is also extremely critical. The commitment comes from usual high profile associated with such an implementation. Organizations are advised to pick up the best for this kind of transformational projects.

Since Implementation is a transformational project, Senior Management commitment at various stages contribute towards the success of the adoption process.

## Data Exploitation Stage

Once Enterprise Solution is successfully implemented, organizations start experiencing the benefits of integrated processes and single database. Invariably the problems associated with inconsistent reporting vanish and there is general feeling of data richness. However, the Enterprise Solutions usually fail to live up to expectations from end users in terms of providing useful decision support information. They often come up with 'We have Data; please provide us reports' type of requests. Inability of ERP to provide all sorts of information can lead to frustration. However, good Enterprise Resource adapting organizations start building BI environment, Data Warehousing solutions around the ERP database integrating their Custom data and ERP data for meaningful analytical reporting leading to more efficient decision-making processes.

## Extension Stage

In this stage, the organizations have gained confidence on Enterprise Systems and have built data analytics around their different data sources. This leads to efficient processes and decision making. At this stage, the organizations start building applications using web technologies and integrating non-core processes with the enterprise. They start looking beyond the information within the organizations and start exploring possibilities of providing their customers and suppliers/ partners the ways to integrate with them.

The ES vendors also have built different extensions to their offerings that enable organizations to integrate supply chains. ERP II solutions are part of this stage of adoption. Depending upon the maturity and strength of their internal IT Teams, organizations either develop their own extensions or buy extensions to these ERPs.

The Data Exploitation and Extension stages give real competitive advantages to organizations in realizing the ROI and Business Cases.

The time taken by organizations to reach this stage depends upon decisions made and quality of handling of earlier stages.

Since, competitive advantage comes from continuous improvements of the whole 'Supply Chain Process', many organizations permanently stay in this stage. They will have an in-house Enterprise Solutions group who work on building/ buying, implementing and maintaining these extensions and improving the core Enterprise Solution. But in the stable industry verticals, where technical innovations as against business process improvements give competitive edge, the organizations are able to reach this a stable extension stage.

## Innovation Stage

After organizations have built extension around both sides of 'Supply Chain', integrated well with their suppliers and customers, they start using these capabilities to improve efficiencies across the supply chain. They supply chain partners use technology to outsmart their competitor supply chains. They start using new age technologies like Mobile Technology, Satellite Imaging to keep their user groups informed while on the move.

They start aiming for technology leadership positions in their industry verticals and even provide non-competing Extended Enterprise Solutions to other customers. The expertise they have built over the years of successful adoption process of Enterprise Solution gets appreciation from the Enterprise user world and they are able to influence the innovations in the technology exploitation in their verticals.

Very few organizations are able to successfully reach this stage. But whoever reaches this stage starts realizing the competitive advantages of successful Enterprise Solution adoption that become of the important critical success factors taking them to leadership position.

## CONCLUSION

The current paper reviews the vast literature based on ERP implementation and also the models for implementation proposed by various researchers. The literature on critical success factors has also been reviewed. The gap in literature which has been identified Finney & Corbett (2007) is that there are very few studies from the viewpoint of the other stakeholders in the ERP implementation process such as the consultants or managers.

The current article addresses this gap in literature by proposing a seven stage ERP adoption model from the view point of the implementation consultant. This seven stage model covers the stages of ERP implementation and then extends this to the usage of the ERP system in stage 5 called the data exploitation stage. In this stage the organization tries to use the data generated by the ERP system for supporting managerial decisions and also in managing critical businesses processes. In stage six, the extension stage the organization extends the ERP implementation to its partners i.e. the suppliers through the supplier relationship management portal and the customer relationship management portal. Finally in stage seven, the organization develops the maturity to start innovating with these enterprise systems and starts using these systems in novel ways to gain competitive advantage.

## REFERENCES

Al-Mashari, M., Al-Mudimigh, A., & Zairi, M. (2003). Enterprise resource planning: a taxonomy of critical factors. *European Journal of Operational Research, 146*, 352–364. doi:10.1016/S0377-2217(02)00554-4

Al-Mashari, M., Ghani, S. K., & Al-Rashid, W. (2006). A study of the Critical Success Factors of ERP implementation in developing countries. *International Journal of Internet & Enterprise Management, 4*(1), 1–1.

Aladwani, A. M. (2001). Change management strategies for successful ERP implementation. *Business Process Management Journal, 7*(3), 266–275. doi:10.1108/14637150110392764

Babu, T. K. S., & Dalal, S. S. (2006). ERP Implementation Issues in SMEs: 'Microsoft Great Plains' Implementation in a BPO Organization. *South Asian Journal of Management, 13*(1, Jan.-Mar.), 61-75.

Bajwa, D. S., Garcia, J. E., & Mooney, T. (2004). An integrative Framework for the Assimilation of Enterprise Resource Planning Systems: Phases, Antecedents and Outcomes. *Journal of Computer Information Systems, 44*(3), 81–90.

Baldwin, S. (1999). *ERPs Second Wave: Maximizing the Value of ERP-Enabled Processes*. Retrieved May 4, 2008 from http://www.ctiforum.com/technology/CRM/wp01/download/erp2w.pdf

Bancroft, N., Seip, H., & Sprengel, A. (1998). *Implementing SAP R/3: How to introduce a large system into a large organization*. Greenwich, CT: Manning Publishing Company.

Bock, G. W., Kwan, S. K., Flores, E., Latumahina, D., Cheng, H., & Lam, C. V. (2009). Integrating ERP Systems in a Decentralized Company: A Case Study. *Journal of Information Technology Cases and Research, 11*(1).

Brehm, L., Heinzl, A., & Markus, M. L. (2001). Tailoring ERP Systems: A Spectrum of Choices and their Implications. In *Proceedings of the 34th Hawaii International Conference on System Sciences*.

Brown, C. V., & Vessey, I. (2003). Managing the next wave of enterprise systems – leveraging lessons from ERP. *MIS Quarterly Executive, 2*(1), 65–77.

Brynjolfsson, E., & Hitt, L. (1996). Paradox lost? Firm-level evidence on the returns to information systems. *Management Science, 42*(4), 541–558. doi:10.1287/mnsc.42.4.541

Brynjolfsson, E., & Hitt, L. (2000). Beyond computation: Information technology, organizational transformation and business performance. *The Journal of Economic Perspectives, 14*(4), 23–48.

Burns, O. M., Turnipseed, D., & Riggs, W. E. (1991). Critical success factors in manufacturing resource planning implementation. *International Journal of Operations & Production Management, 11*(4), 5–19. doi:10.1108/01443579110136221

Chen, C. C., Chuck, C. H., & Yang, S. C. (2009, February). Managing ERP Implementation Failure: A Project Management Perspective. *IEEE Transactions on Engineering Management, 98*(2), 189–203.

Dawson, J., & Jonathan, O. (2008). Critical success factors in the chartering phase: a case study of an ERP implementation. *International Journal of Enterprise Information, 14*(3).

de Seán, B., Fynes, B., & Marshall, D. (2005). Strategic technology adoption: extending ERP across the supply chain. *Journal of Enterprise Information Management, 18*(4), 427–440. doi:10.1108/17410390510609581

Ehie, I. C., & Madsen, M. (2005). Identifying critical issues in enterprise resource planning (ERP) implementation. *Computers in Industry, 56*(6), 545–557. doi:10.1016/j.compind.2005.02.006

Esteves, J., & Pastor, J. (2000). *Towards the unification of critical success factors for ERP implementations.* Paper presented at 10th Annual BIT Conference.

Finney, S., & Corbett, M. (2007). ERP implementation: a compilation and analysis of critical success factors. *Business Process Management Journal, 13*(3), 329–347. doi:10.1108/14637150710752272

Frédéric, A., & O'Doherty, P. (2000). Lessons from enterprise resource planning implementations in Ireland – towards smaller and shorter ERP projects. *Journal of Information Technology - Regular Paper, 15*(4), 305-317.

Furomo, K., & Melcher, A. (2006). The importance of social structure in implementing ERP systems: A case study using adaptive structuration theory. *Journal of Information Technology Cases and Research, 8*(2), 39–39.

Gable, G. G., Sedera, D., & Chan, T. (2003). Enterprise Systems Success: A measurement model. In *Proceedings of the 24th International Conference on Information Systems,* (pp.576-576).

Gargeya, V. B., & Brady, C. (2005). Success and failure factors of adopting SAP in ERP system implementation. *Business Process Management Journal, Research paper, 11*(5), 501-516.

Grossman, T., & Walsh, J. (2004). Avoiding the pitfalls of ERP system Implementation. *Information Systems Management, 21*(2, Spring), 38-42.

Hawking, P., Stein, A., & Foster, S. (2004). Revisiting ERP Systems: Benefit Realization. In *Proceedings of the 37th Hawaii International Conference on System Sciences.* Edwards, H.M. & Humphries, L. P. (2005). Change Management of People & Technology in an ERP Implementation. *Journal of Cases on Information Technology, 7*(4, Oct-Dec), 144-160.

Hillman, T. W., Hillary, A., & Brown, W. (2002). Extending the value of ERP. *Industrial Management & Data Systems, 102*(1).

Hitt, L. M., Wu, D. J., & Zhou, X. (2002). Investment in Enterprise Resource Planning: Business Impact and Productivity Measures. *Journal of Management Information Systems, 19*(1), 71–98.

Holland, C., & Light, B. (1999). A critical success factors model for ERP implementation. *IEEE Software,* (May/June): 30–35. doi:10.1109/52.765784

Holland, C., Light, B., & Gibson, N. (1999). *A critical success factors model for enterprise resource planning implementation.* Paper presented at 7th European Conference on Information Systems ECIS.

Hsu, L. L., Robert, S. Q., & Weng, Y. (2008). Understanding the critical factors effect user satisfaction and impact of *ERP* through innovation of diffusion theory. *International Journal of Technology Management, 43*(1-3), 30–47. doi:10.1504/IJTM.2008.019405

Huang, S., Hung, Y. H., Chen, H., & Ku, C. (2004). Transplanting the best practice for implementation of an ERP System: A structured inductive study of an international company. *The Journal of Computer Information Systems, 44*(4, Summer), 101-110.

Huang, Z., & Palvia, P. (2001). ERP implementation issues in advanced and developing countries. *Business Process Management Journal, 7*(3), 276–285. doi:10.1108/14637150110392773

Ioannou, G., & Papadoyiannis, C. (2004). Theory of constraints-based methodology for effective ERP implementations. *International Journal of Production Research, 42*(23), 4927–4954. doi:1 0.1080/00207540410001721718

Karakanian, M. (1999). Choosing an ERP implementation strategy Year 2000. *The Practitioner, 2*(7), 1–6.

Kirchmer, M. (1999). *Business Process Oriented Implementation of Standard Software: How to Achieve Competitive Advantage Efficiently and Effectively* (2nd ed.). Berlin: Springer.

Koh, C., Soh, C., & Markus, M. L. (2000). A Process Theory Approach to Analyzing ERP Implementation and Impacts: The Case of Revel Asia. *Journal of Information Technology Cases and Research, 2*(1).

Kotter, J. P. (2005). Leading Change: Why transformation efforts fail. *Harvard Business Review,* (March-April): 59.

Kraemmerand, P., Møller, C., & Boer, H. (2003). ERP Implementation: an integrated process of radical change and continuous learning. *Production Planning and Control, 14*(4), 338–349. doi:10.1080/0953728031000117959

Lan, W. H., Eric, T. G. W., & Hung, J. P. (2005). Understanding misalignment and cascading change of ERP implementation: a stage view of process analysis. *European Journal of Information Systems, 14*(01 Dec), 324-334

Loh, T. C., & Koh, S. C. L. (2004). Critical elements for a successful enterprise resource planning implementation in small-and medium-sized enterprises. *International Journal of Production Research, 42*(17), 3433–3455. doi:10.1080/0020 7540410001671679

Markus, M.L., Axline, S., Petrie,D., & Tanis.C, (2000). Learning from adopters' experiences with ERP: problems encountered and success achieved. *Journal of Information Technology - Regular Paper,* 15(4), 245-265

Markus, M.L., Axline, S., Petrie, D., & Tanis,S. C.(2000). Learning from adopters' experiences with ERP: problems encountered and success achieved. *Journal of Information Technology - Regular Paper, 15*(4),245-265.

Markus, M. L., & Tanis, C. (2000).The enterprise systems experience: from adoption to success. Zmud, R. W. (Ed), Framing the domains of IT research: Glimpsing the future through the past, (pp. 173-207). Cincinnati, OH: Pinnaflex Educational Resources Inc.

Metaxiotis, K., Zafeiropoulos, I., Nikolinakou, K., & Psarras, J. (2005). *Goal directed project management methodology for the support of ERP implementation and optimal adaptation.*

Miller, S. (1998). *ASAP Implementation at the Speed of Business: Implementation at the Speed of Business Computing.* New York: Mcgraw-Hill.

Molla, A., & Bhalla, A. (2006). Business transformation through ERP: Case of an Asian company. *Journal of Information Technology Cases and Research, 8*(1), 34–34.

Nah, F. F., Islam, Z., & Tan, M. (2007). Empirical Assessment of Factors Influencing Success of Enterprise Resource Planning Implementations. *Journal of Database Management, 18*(4), 26–50.

Nah, F. F., Lau, J. L., & Kuang, J. (2001). Critical factors for successful implementation of enterprise systems. *Business Process Management Journal Literature review, 7*(3), 285-296.

Nah, F. F., Zuckweiler, K. M., & Lau, J. L. (2000). ERP Implementation - CIOs Perceptions of CSFs. *International Journal of Human-Computer Interaction, 16*(1), 5–22.

Parr, A., & Shanks, G. (2000) .A model of ERP project implementation. *Journal of Information Technology, 15*(01 Dec), 289-303.

Parr, A., Shanks, G., & Darke, P. (1999). Identification of necessary factors for successful implementation of ERP systems. New Information Technologies in Organizational Processes – Field Studies and Theoretical Reflections on the Future of Work, (pp. 99-119). Kingston-upon-Thames, UK: Kluwer Academic Publishers.

Plant, R., & Willcocks, L. (2007).critical success factors in international ERP implementations: a case research approach. *Journal of Computer Information Systems, 47*(3, Spring), 60-70.

Prasad, B., Sharma, M. K., & Godla, J. K. (1999). Critical issues affecting an ERP implementation. *Information Systems Management, 16*(3).

Sankar, C. S., Raju, P. K., Nair, A., Patton, D., & Bleidung, N. (2005). Enterprise Information Systems and Engineering Design at Briggs & Stratton: K11 Engine Development. *Journal of Information Technology Cases and Research, 7*(1).

Sawah, S. E., Tharwat, A. A. E. F., & Rasmy M. H.(2008). A quantitative model to predict the Egyptian ERP *I*mplementation success index. *Business Process Management Journal, 14*(3, June), 288-306.

Shang, S., & Seddon, P. B. (2002). Assessing and managing the benefits of Enterprise systems: the business manager's perspective. *Information Systems Journal, 12*, 271–299. doi:10.1046/j.1365-2575.2002.00132.x

Shanks, G., Sheldon, P. B., & Wilcocks, L. P. (2003). *Effectiveness*. Cambridge, UK: Cambridge University Press.

Sharma, R., Palvia, P., & Salam, A. F. (2002). ERP Selection at Custom Fabrics. *Journal of Information Technology Cases and Research, 4*(2).

Siau, K. (2004). Enterprise resource planning (ERP) implementation methodologies. *Journal of Database Management, 15*(1, Jan-Mar).

Sieber, T., Keng, S., Fiona, N., & Sieber, M. (2000). SAP Implementation at the University of Nebraska. *Journal of Information Technology Cases and Research, 2*(1).

Snider, B., Silveira, G. J. C., & Balakrishnan, J. (2009). ERP implementation at SMEs: analysis of five Canadian cases. *International Journal of Operations & Production Management, 29*(1/2), 4–29. doi:10.1108/01443570910925343

Soh, C., Sia, S. K., Boh, W. F., & Tang, M. (2003). Misalignments in ERP Implementation: A Dialectic Perspective. *International Journal of Human-Computer Interaction, 16*(1, May), 81-100.

Somers, T., & Nelson, K. (2001).The impact of critical success factors across the stages of enterprise resource planning implementations, In *Proceedings of the 34th Hawaii International Conference on System Sciences HICSS*.

Stedman, C. (1999). Failed ERP Gamble haunts Hershey. *Computerworld, 1*(Nov).

Stein T. (1999). Making ERP add up. *Information Week*, May 24, 59-59.

Sumner, M. (2000). Risk factors in enterprise-wide/ERP projects. *Journal of Information Technology - Regular Paper, 15*(4), 317-327.

Sun, A.Y.T., Yazdani, A., & Overend, J. D. (2005). Achievement assessment for enterprise resource planning (ERP) system implementations based on critical success factors (CSFs). *International Journal of Production Economics, 98*(2, Nov), 189-203.

Umble, E. J., & Umble, M. M. (2002).Avoiding ERP Implementation Failure. *Industrial Management, 44*(1, Jan/Feb), 25-34.

mVerville, J., & Halingten, A. (2001). Decision Process for Acquiring Complex ERP Solutions: The Case of ITCom. *Journal of Information Technology Cases and Research, 3*(2).

Wallace, T. F., & Kremzer, M. H. (2001). *ERP: Making It Happen: The Implementers' Guide to Success with Enterprise Resource Planning* (3rd ed.). New York: Wiley.

Wei, H., Wang, E. T. G., & Ju, P. (2005). Understanding misalignment and cascading change of ERP implementation: a stage view of process analysis. *European Journal of Information Systems, 14*(01 Dec), 224-334.

Yakovlev, I. V., & Anderson, M. L. (2001). Lessons from an ERP Implementation. IT Professional Magazine, 3(4, Jul/Aug), 24-30.

Yongbeom, K., Lee, Z., & Gosain, S. (2005). Impediments to successful ERP implementation process. *Business Process Management Journal, 11*(2), 158–170. doi:10.1108/14637150510591156

Yu, C. (2005). Causes influencing the effectiveness of the post-implementation ERP system. *Industrial Management + Data Systems, 105*(1/2), 115-131.

# Chapter 7
# Understanding Based Managing Support Systems:
## The Future of Information Systems

**Lidia Ogiela**
*AGH University of Science and Technology, Poland*

**Ryszard Tadeusiewicz**
*AGH University of Science and Technology, Poland*

**Marek R. Ogiela**
*AGH University of Science and Technology, Poland*

## ABSTRACT

*This publication presents cognitive systems designed for analysing economic data. Such systems have been created as the next step in the development of classical DSS systems (Decision Support Systems), which are currently the most widespread tools providing computer support for economic decision-making. The increasing complexity of decision-making processes in business combined with increasing demands that managers put on IT tools supporting management cause DSS systems to evolve into intelligent information systems. This publication defines a new category of systems - UBMSS (Understanding Based Management Support Systems) which conduct in-depth analyses of data using on an apparatus for linguistic and meaning-based interpretation and reasoning. This type of interpretation and reasoning is inherent in the human way of perceiving the world. This is why the authors of this publication have striven to perfect the scope and depth of computer interpretation of economic information based on human processes of cognitive data analysis. As a result, they have created UBMSS systems for the automatic analysis and interpretation of economic data. The essence of the proposed approach to the cognitive analysis of economic data is the use of the apparatus for the linguistic description of data and for semantic analysis. This type of analysis is based on expectations generated automatically by a system which collects resources of expert knowledge, taking into account the information which can significantly characterise the analysed data. In this publication, the processes of classical data description and analysis are extended to include cognitive processes as well as reasoning and forecasting mechanisms. As a result of the analyses shown, we will present a new class of UBMSS cognitive economic information systems which automatically perform a semantic analysis of business data.*

DOI: 10.4018/978-1-61520-625-4.ch007

Copyright © 2010, IGI Global. Copying or distributing in print or electronic forms without written permission of IGI Global is prohibited.

## INTRODUCTION TO COGNITIVE DATA ANALYSIS

Processes taking place in the human brain have been the subject of theoretical analyses and empirical research for very many years. However, although we increasingly frequently feel we can explain almost everything that takes place in the human brain, a closer study always reveals something to undermine this certainty we have. Among all the processes taking place there, key ones include thinking, cognitive, interpretation and reasoning processes as well as processes for the varied, complex and in-depth analysis of information received from the senses or recalled from memory. These very types of human cognitive processes were used by the authors of this publication to attempt to combine human information analysis processes with automatic, computer data analysis. This combination has lead to creating a class of IT systems whose operation is founded on a meaning-based interpretation of data and a cognitive process of analysing it. The essence of this approach to building management-support systems is that by performing an in-depth analysis of data on the basis of its semantic contents and of knowledge possessed, such a system can understand the meaning of the analysed data, so it can classify and interpret it more precisely.

This type of detailed semantic analysis of data is possible because UBMSS IT systems use a linguistic description and a characterisation of data based on knowledge. In such systems, computer linguistics is employed to ensure the appropriate semantic representation of the layer of data (information), thanks to which automatic procedures, using the appropriate resources of expert knowledge collected in the system, can make the proper (content-related) classification and categorisation of this information and data.

The proposed semantic data analysis systems have been termed UBMSS (Understanding Based Managing Support Systems) to distinguish them from other classes of cognitive data analysis systems, described in the following publications (Ogiela 2007; Ogiela 2008; Reisberg 2001; Tadeusiewicz 2003; Tadeusiewicz 2008; Tanaka 1995; Wang 2003).

So what is the phenomenon of cognitive data analysis about? To answer this question, you have to realise what the phenomenon of the human cognitive process is about. Processes that the human mind uses for various purposes, e.g. for analysing a selected phenomenon or assessing the significance of specific information, are always based on cognitive processes. They form the foundations for the stages of describing, analysing, interpreting, reasoning and classifying. It must also be borne in mind that in data analysis processes there is an unwritten doctrine of the consistency of learning, behaviour and experience which says that in cognitive processes a close and perfect consistency is noticeable between what we know, how we behave and what we experience.

In cognitive data analysis systems this rule is of utmost importance for their correct operation. In data analysis, there must be absolute consistency between the knowledge (which is input into the system as a base of knowledge obtained from experts), the behaviour (in the system this comprises recommendations given to the user as a result of completing an in-depth analysis of the current socioeconomic situation, which is automatically assessed based on the semantic content of the analysed data) and the experience (in cognitive data analysis systems this means processes of collecting knowledge using observations of recommendations given earlier and their effects). It should be added that UBMSS systems are always learning systems, with more intense learning occurring when the phenomenon analysed is new or completely unknown to the system.

So cognitive data analysis systems use a kind of computer introspection, understood as the process of acquiring (gaining) knowledge or extracting it (by deduction or induction) from system memory. The approach presented shows that it is possible to initiate an automatic process of semantic reflection about the consequences of analysed data, which consists in using the human (expert) knowledge stored in the system to generate various expectations as to what should be detected during the analysis of input data conducted by the system. Every such automatically-generated set of expectations has some element of the meaning-based interpretation of the data currently analysed linked to it. If the data analysis confirms that the data is consistent with the expectations generated, this raises the probability of the hypothesis about the interpretation of the meaning of input data used to generate the expectations as to the features of input data. The hypotheses generated, which are based on the knowledge collected in the system, may concern either what we expect in this data or what we should not detect in it. So a semantic hypothesis which makes the meaning-based interpretation (i.e. understanding) of the analysed data possible shows both to what extent we can expect certain solutions of features of the analysed data, which we have no doubt will be present if the hypothesis is true, and the possible features which should not appear. The verification of this hypothesis in the process called the cognitive resonance consists in checking those generated expectations by confronting them with the actual features of the analysed data. This makes it possible to positively confirm true hypotheses and to negate wrong hypotheses based on the variance between the actual data and the patterns adopted and stored in the system.

Cognitive data analysis systems which make use of the consistency doctrine find the appropriate interpretation and diagnosis during the analysis conducted by the system. In addition, by using the semantic content of the analysed data, systems of this type can correctly understand it and reason based on it. However, such systems should not be put in a situation where there is some piece of information (some type of data) to which no knowledge corresponds in the system database, because then the system will get disoriented and will not make the correct interpretation (just as

a person put in a situation which is completely novel and without precedent in the past will be unable to make the correct assessment and interpretation). If such a novel situation occurs for the first time, the UBMSS system will not be able to interpret it correctly. However, this is exactly the reason why such a situation and all the circumstances related to it will be recorded and mapped in the system, thus extending and enhancing the knowledge base possessed. When a similar situation occurs in the future, the system will analyse the data associated with it again, but it will have a newly-developed knowledge base and so will be able to draw the correct conclusions from it. Thus the knowledge of the UBMSS system will be constantly enhanced during its operation as a result of the process of continuous learning from every previously unclassified case.

## SEMANTIC ANALYSIS IN THE COGNITIVE DATA ANALYSIS PROCESS

Cognitive data analysis processes based on the process of data interpretation, description, classification and reasoning use the stage of semantic analysis, during which features are defined and correctly identified for every unit of data for which the appropriate record existed previously or is created by learning in the knowledge base of the system. Every unit considered (units may be various types of data or information) is defined by a set of the appropriate semantic dimensions, every one of which is assigned a certain weight defining how important the dimension is and how significant it is in the analysis conducted. So every piece of information is characterised by the distribution of possible values along the appropriate dimension which corresponds to the classification of values obtained using expert knowledge about the significance and the semantic importance of the described feature.

The semantic analysis conducted in cognitive data analysis systems refers not only to the simple analysis, but very frequently it also takes place at the stage of information processing during which the features contained in the analysed data set are compared to the features stored in the knowledge base and in the form of defined patterns related to the analysed data, in order to quickly select data which contains information significant (from the semantic point of view) from the huge volume of data recorded and collected in every IT system. The need to define patterns is due to the fact that the data we analyse must be compared to some representative characteristic for the given data group, which will unambiguously exhibit its features, advantages and differences from other, related types of data. Features are compared and individual similarities and overlaps are found in three stages.

At the first stage, a list of features of the specimen and of the category identified for the analysed data is defined; this list contains all features of the information related to the dimensions characteristic for this information and features obtained from the defining dimensions for the given category. The list of features of characteristic dimensions and the list of features of defining dimensions are compared and the measures of total similarity, which means the complete consistency of the compared features, are determined at this stage.

The second stage supports establishing the full consistency (or inconsistency) of the knowledge collected in the system in the form of expert knowledge bases, which the system uses to generate certain expectations as to the data analysis conducted, with the features of this data identified during its acquisition, definition, interpretation and classification. At this stage, we define pairs of features characteristic for the analysed data, which pairs are made up of the features of characteristic dimensions and defining dimensions.

Total similarity features obtained as above are compared (at the third stage) to criterion levels of total similarity which determine a low or high consistency of the compared features. A high level means that the attempt to compare the features was successful, a low level means the opposite. The feature comparison stage is of great importance in the semantic analysis process, as it determines to what extent the pattern data contained in the system is consistent with models of features developed as a result of the data analysis conducted.

Processes of semantic, cognitive data analysis are characteristic for all classes of cognitive data analysis systems. Due to the nature of the subject discussed and elaborated, in this publication we will restrict ourselves to presenting and discussing only cognitive economic systems. It has been mentioned previously that such economic, cognitive information systems are called UBMSS systems. Lower down we will show how systems of this proposed class can be used for decision making within the scope of efficient information management and the in-depth understanding of the economic situation.

## ALGORITHMS FOR THE SEMANTIC REASONING, INTERPRETATION AND MEANING-BASED ANALYSIS OF DATA

The authors initially used semantic reasoning algorithms leading to an in-depth cognitive analysis of data to interpret image-type data (Ogiela 2006; Ogiela 2008). Like in the solutions described in the earlier work cited, in UBMSS cognitive data analysis systems we also make extensive use of syntactic analysis algorithms resulting from the linguistic representation of the information analysed. After mapping the analysed economic data to formulas of a specially constructed language, we analyse it using semantic parsing procedures employed during a syntactic analysis based on context-free grammars, for example.

The parser algorithm used in our work is based on the operating principle of stack automata. In this method, the parser first reads subsequent symbols of the structural description (called tokens) from the input. These symbols are placed at the top of the parser stack, where they are allocated corresponding values of semantic variables that play a significant role in the entire semantic (meaning) analysis of the reasoning conducted. This process is referred to as the action of shifting another token to the top of the stack (operation: shift). When a so-called handle (i.e. the right side of one of productions) is formed at the top of the stack from the group of several recently read terminal symbols, a reduction (operation: reduce) is made, and as a result all elements are grouped and at the same time replaced at the top of the stack with a single non-terminal symbol taken from the left side of that production.

The parsing principle outlined above is used for various purposes, e.g. when compiling programming languages. A new and very important element necessary from the perspective of the semantic reasoning and cognitive analysis in UBMSS systems is that during parsing, a semantic action defined for a given production must occur during the reduction operation. In that case, the operation of the parser aims at reducing the entire input sequence of individual symbols of the syntax analyser software implementation to just one non-terminal symbol - the start symbol of the grammar - by performing the shift and reduce operations. Parsers based on the above method of operation are called – bottom-up parsers. This type of parsers is represented, for example, by the class of parsers for LR(1) grammars or their subclass - LALR(1) grammars.

As semantic connotation can be more important when building UBMSS systems than the syntactic consistency of symbols on which operations are executed, a new element introduced by the authors is the action of "previewing" future analysis elements. As a result of this innovation, it often happens that the analysers discussed do not perform the reduction operation if the right side of one of the productions is at the top of the stack, as then it is necessary to take into account ("preview")

subsequent symbols appearing on the input of the analyser for the further analysis. In this situation, the next symbol on the input is analysed, and after this process is finished, further operations take place. This procedure is necessary to conduct a correct syntactic analysis and semantic reasoning e.g. for certain language sequences found in languages for describing economic systems and processes. This method was known before in the context of compiling some programming languages, but it has gained new significance in UBMSS systems. When the next symbol of the software interpretation of the syntax analysis appears on the input, the parser does not shift that symbol to the top of the stack, but leaves it for the so-called preview, as a result of which the parser can freely make the number of reductions at the top of the stack necessary to perform the shift of the aforementioned element.

This phenomenon is not a rule in the operation of the parser, but only an additional action provided for in it, executed depending on the type of token viewed and leading to a delay in the application of several rules. This will happen if a conflict arises between the shift and reduce actions, as a result of which the parser (depending on the situation) reduces the expression found at the top of the stack, or shifts the next token from the input to the top. Such a conflict is routinely resolved with priority given to the shift operation, unless the grammar author has used the appropriate precedence operators.

Another type of problems specific for grammars used in UBMSS systems is connected with the reduce/reduce conflict which occurs if there are no obstacles to using two or more productions of the grammar to reduce the expression found at that moment at the top of the stack and it is necessary to select this correct operation based on the analysis of semantic - and not syntactic - conditions.

The correct operation of semantic reasoning and cognitive analysis algorithms is largely due to the activity of the parser algorithm described above

*Figure 1. Cognitive information system UBMSS –type. (Source: Tadeusiewicz 2007)*

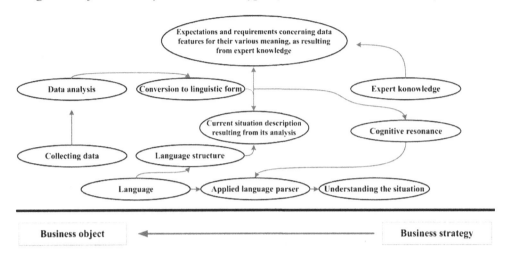

(obviously in a simplified way). Consequently, it seems important to ensure that the fewest conflicts possible occur (regardless of their type) and to indicate the right class of analysers used during the entire process of cognitive analysis. This is due to the selection of the form of the language used to describe the features of the analysed economic data, which features are important for assessing its significance.

## UBMSS SYSTEMS AS AN ELEMENT OF COGNITIVE DATA INTERPRETATION AND EFFECTIVE MANAGEMENT

We have mentioned above that UBMSS systems were developed from smart corporate management systems as well as economic information and decision-support systems. Such systems are designed to improve the operations of a company or its selected departments. The essence of the correct operation of UBMSS systems is the semantic analysis conducted by those systems on data which is analysed at all management levels of companies and which concerns every decision taken. The use of these systems may turn out to be particularly significant and beneficial when

taking strategic decisions, typical for the highest levels of decision-makers in the hierarchy.

UBMSS systems are to suggest to persons responsible for taking such (frequently final) decisions the possible optimum solutions presented based on the semantic analysis of data, which takes into account the (frequently hidden) meaning of the recorded facts, economic trends and tendencies. The operating concept of UBMSS systems stemming from the principles outlined above, is shown in Fig. 1.

The essence of our approach to the in-depth meaning-based analysis of economic data is such an interpretation of facts suggested by data, but requiring the correct content-based (and not just formal) interpretation, that makes it possible to adopt the strategy that is the best for the individual company. Such a strategy selection is always grounded in correctly understanding the analysed data, interpreting it as well as reasoning and forecasting from the data possessed (analysed), but in the systems currently used in practice, computers are limited to collecting, processing and presenting the data, while it falls to the people (the managers) to interpret it and draw conclusions.

UBMSS systems stand a chance of changing this stressful (for decision-makers) division of responsibilities for the better. This is because these systems take all the data collected and choose for the analysis process only that which can have a significant impact on the current or future situation of the company, and then they present this data with some suggested interpretation of its significance. It must be borne in mind that the information possessed by the company is not always useful for the decision that is to be taken, and this fact cannot be determined by a simple data analysis. This is because the majority of this data only represents information noise, based on which it is impossible to conduct the right reasoning process, and therefore also the decision-making process. So first the information that may be significant for the process aimed at indicating and taking the best strategic business decisions for the specific company must be extracted from huge knowledge bases. For this job, the semantic data analysis offered by UBMSS systems is indispensable, as no formal analysis, which supports any transformation of economic data, can show that this is simply not the kind of data that should be used as the basis in the present situation.

The initial selection stage is followed by a stage during which the analysed data is subjected to language conversion, yielding its linguistic representation in the correctly selected formal language. At this stage it is of the utmost importance to correctly select the language structures based on which the parser indicated for the selected language will make it possible to correctly transform the data into a linguistic representation. So UBMSS systems must be equipped with such methods of the linguistic representation of the economic reality assessed which will make it possible to analyse the data using the knowledge collected in the system.

The cognitive conceptual base of UBMSS systems means that the core element of the system is knowledge, which is input into them both in the form of the appropriate language rules (discussed above) and bases of interpretation knowledge formulated from the information and knowledge obtained from a group of experts. It has been mentioned

above that the system uses the expert knowledge collected in it to generate certain expectations as to the data analysed, which expectations are compared to the identified semantic features of the data currently being analysed. This stage brings about cognitive resonance, as a result of which certain comparisons turn out to be significant, and other ones insignificant. Significant comparisons become the basis for subsequent analysis, as a result of which the correctly defined language for describing the analysed data, the parser and the defined semantic dimensions (features) are employed to understand the analysed data. The application of UBMSS systems thus makes it possible to take the right strategic decision and to reason about the future based on the current situation.

## An Example Ubmss System Illustrating Cognitive Data Interpretation Methods for the Efficient Management of the Investment Process

UBMSS systems can be used for the cognitive analysis of economic ratios, particularly financial or macroeconomic ones. UBMSS systems can, for example, conduct analyses using the following ratios:

1. profitability ratios

- gross margin,
- profit margin,
- operating margin,
- net profitability ratio,
- gross profitability ratio,
- ROA (return on assets),
- ROE (return on equity),
- ROI (return on investment),
- ROIC (return on invested capital),
- ROS (return on sales),
- NPM (net profit margin),
- ROCE (return on capital employed),

- RONA (return on net assets),
- IRR (internal rate of return),
- WACC (weighted average cost of capital)

2. liquidity ratios

- COGS (cost of goods sold),
- EBIT (earnings before deducting interest and taxes),
- NPV (net present value),
- CR (current ratio),
- QR (quick ratio),
- cash ratio,
- inventory turnover,
- ACP (average collection period).

This publication is an attempt at defining a UBMSS system for the cognitive analysis of investments on the basis of five key financial indicators, which include: NPV – net present value (symbol: W1), r – discount rate (W2), IRR – internal rate of return (W3), EBIT – earnings before interest and tax (W4), and WACC – weighted average cost of capital (W5).

For the proposed UBMSS systems, a sequence grammar of the following form has been defined:

$$G_{INV} = (\Sigma_N, \Sigma_{T,} P, S)$$

where:

$\Sigma_N$ – the set of non-terminal symbols

$\Sigma_N = \{INVESTMENT, W1, W2, W3, W4, W5,$ *WEAK_ACCEPT, ACCEPT, STRONG_AC-CEPT, NO_ACCEPT, A, B, C, D, E*$\}$

$\Sigma_T$ – the set of terminal symbols

$\Sigma_T = \{'a', 'b', 'c', 'd', 'e'\}$, and the particular elements were defined as follows:

$a = \{0\%\}, b \in (0\%, 15\%], c \in (15\%, 45\%),$
$d \in [45\%, 100\%), e \in (-100\%, 0\%)$

$S$ – the start symbol, $S \in \Sigma_N,$

$S = INVESTMENT$

$P$ – the set of productions shown below:

1. INVESTMENT→ WEAK_ACCEPT | ACCEPT | STRONG_ACCEPT | NO_ACCEPT
2. WEAK_ACCEPT→ W1 W2 W3 W4 W5 *//if (w1 & w2 & w3 & w4 & w5= weak accept) final_decision:= weak accept*
3. ACCEPT→ W1 W2 W3 W4 W5 *//if (w1 & w2 & w3 & w4 & w5= accept) final_decision:= accept*
4. STRONG_ACCEPT → W1 W2 W3 W4 W5 *//if (w1 & w2 & w3 & w4 & w5= strong accept) final_decision:= strong accept*
5. NO_ACCEPT → W1 W2 W3 W4 W5 *//if (w1 & w2 & w3 & w4 & w5=not akcept) final_decision:= not accept*
6. W1 → A | B | C | D | E *// w1=decision*

*Figure 2. The set of terminal symbols (Source: own development)*

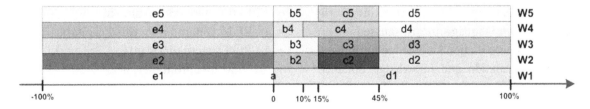

7.  $W2 \rightarrow A \mid B \mid C \mid D \mid E \; // \; w2 = decision$
8.  $W3 \rightarrow A \mid B \mid C \mid D \mid E \; // \; w3 = decision$
9.  $W4 \rightarrow A \mid B \mid C \mid D \mid E \; // \; w4 = decision$
10. $W5 \rightarrow A \mid B \mid C \mid D \mid E \; // \; w5 = decision$
11. $A \rightarrow a \; // \; decision := weak$
12. $B \rightarrow b \; // \; decision := weak$
13. $C \rightarrow c \; // \; decision := accept$
14. $D \rightarrow d \; // \; decision := strong$
15. $E \rightarrow e \; // \; decision := not\ accept$

The analysis of economic ratios conducted in UBMSS systems allows the semantic contents of the analysed data to be used to determine the nature of that data, its impact on the current situation of the company and the extent of changes they cause to the company and its environment taking into account the information currently possessed. Such an analysis is possible due to semantic information contained in the analysed data. Semantic information may relate to:

* The scale (value) of analysed economic ratios,
* The frequency of their changes,
* The manner of their changes,
* The regularity of repetition,
* The number of changes observed,
* The type of changes observed.

The example UBMSS system discussed here can conduct a cognitive analysis of selected financial and economic ratios, which will make it possible to take the best strategic decision for the selected (analysed) company. Figure 3 shows example results of the operation of the UBMSS system proposed for meaning-based analyses and interpretations stemming from understanding the analysed set of five financial ratios: the net present value, the discount rate, the internal rate of return, earnings before income and tax and the weighted average cost of capital.

The presented examples of the cognitive analysis of economic data and its meaning-based interpretation allow the right decision to

be taken as to the acceptability of an investment subjected to the decision-making analysis process. In this case, the UBMSS system performs a meaning-based analysis of the situation using the values of five selected ratios: NPV, $r_d$, IRR, EBIT, WACC.

Figure 4 presents three examples of semantic reasoning conducted by an UBMSS system for three companies: Mode, Sweet and Machine. The input data, namely values of economic ratios, was acquired during a computer simulation and used by the UBMSS system for a meaning-based data analysis by comparing the ratios with the definition values stored in the system database.

In addition, the system correctly interpreted the economic ratios and proposed a semantic reasoning which yielded a decision suggestion consisting in selecting the right strategic decision for the entire enterprise.

Based on the values of the selected economic/financial ratios, the UBMSS system shows what strategic decision is best when it takes the said ratios into the analysis process. This decision is taken by comparing the analysed values with the values, kept by the system in particular knowledge bases, which have been defined based on optimum ratio values assumed by experts.

The above semantic information associated with the analysed economic data presented in the form of financial ratios allows a detailed identification of the type of situation (whether it is pathological or is a phenomenon expected and accepted by the company management with regard to the considered investment) prevailing within the company.

It must be borne in mind that changes taking place inside companies are brought about by various types of situations, phenomena and determinants. These situations may be either external or internal. This is why defining the right patterns applied to UBMSS systems which will be taking strategic and business decisions is very difficult, as it requires analysing a whole range of various factors that can have a significant impact on the

*Figure 3. Example UBMSS system for analysing and assessing the acceptability of an investment based on selected economic ratios (Source: own development)*

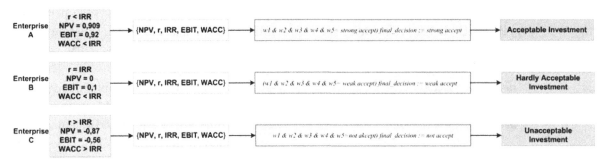

decision-making process. It is because of this fact that the UBMSS systems presented in this chapter for supporting the right decision whether to make (or forego) a given investment greatly help choose the best decision and determine whether the investment under consideration is acceptable or not; and if the decision is acceptable, then whether the acceptance is unconditional, or whether there is a certain danger (risk) inherent in implementing it (this situation is illustrated by the minimum permissible values of financial ratios selected for analysing).

UBMSS systems are of great help in understanding the analysed economic, financial and strategic situation with regard to the analysed company, investment and strategy. So they are systems which perform a very important type of analysis - a cognitive, interpretational, reasoning and forecasting analysis based on mechanisms of the linguistic and meaning-based description of data.

*Figure 4. Using a UBMSS system for an example of an analysis of economic ratios for three selected companies (Source: own development)*

## CONCLUSION

The presented cognitive data analysis systems developed to analyse data strategic to companies can perform in-depth analyses, interpretations and reasoning with regard to various economic data, in particular financial and economic ratios. UBMSS systems which carry out in-depth analyses of information presented in the form of various types of ratios are aimed at classifying them correctly by reference to the semantic content and meaning-based interpretation of that data. The meaning-based interpretation allows the complexity of the studied phenomenon to be determined and also allows the right strategic business decision to be taken. It also supports reasoning on the basis of the current situation (e.g. the value of the analysed economic ratio achieved at present depending on the situation inside the company and in its environment) and offers forecasting opportunities. This is because the values of analysed ratios form the foundation for decision-making and forecasting by reference to the current situation of the company.

Consequently, cognitive data analysis systems are designed for its in-depth analysis, interpretation and reasoning based on it, so they have a great future, as they justify the hope that the use of the semantic contents extracted by computer systems from analysed data sets, will make it become possible to conduct analysis and interpretation processes taking into account a broad spectrum of various (semantically consistent) information.

## ACKNOWLEDGMENT

This work has been supported by the Ministry of Science and Higher Education, Republic of Poland, under project number N N516 196537

## REFERENCES

Albus, J. S., & Meystel, A. M. (2001). *Engineering of Mind – An Introduction to the Science of Intelligent Systems*. New York: John Wiley & Sons Inc.

Branquinho, J. (Ed.). (2001). *The Foundations of Cognitive Science*. Oxford, UK: Clarendon Press.

Cohen, H., & Lefebvre, C. (Eds.). (2005). *Handbook of Categorization in Cognitive Science*. Amsterdam: Elsevier.

Ogiela, L. (2009). UBIAS Systems for the Cognitive Interpretation and Analysis of Medical Images. *Opto-Electronics Review*, 17(2), 17.

Ogiela, L., Tadeusiewicz, R., & Ogiela, M. R. (2007). Cognitive Informatics In Automatic Pattern Understanding. In D. Zhang, Y. Wang, & W. Kinsner, (eds.), *Proceedings of the Sixth IEEE International Conference on Cognitive Informatics, ICCI 2007*, Lake Tahoe, CA, (pp. 79-84).

Ogiela, L., Tadeusiewicz, R., & Ogiela, M. R. (2008). Cognitive techniques in medical information systems. *Computers in Biology and Medicine*, *38*, 502–507. doi:10.1016/j.compbiomed.2008.01.017

Ogiela, M. R., Tadeusiewicz, R., & Ogiela, L. (2006). Image languages in intelligent radiological palm diagnostics. *Pattern Recognition*, *39*, 2157–2165. doi:10.1016/j.patcog.2006.03.014

Reisberg, D. (2001). *Cognition, Exploring the science of the mind*. New York: W.W. Norton & Company, Inc.

Rutkowski, L. (2008). *Computational Intelligence, Methods and Techniques*. Berlin: Springer Verlag-Heidelberg.

Tadeusiewicz, R., & Ogiela, L. (2008). Selected Cognitive Categorization Systems. *LNAI, 5097*, 1127–1136.

Tadeusiewicz, R., Ogiela, L., & Ogiela, M. R. (2008). The automatic understanding approach to systems analysis and design. *International Journal of Information Management, 28,* 38–48. doi:10.1016/j.ijinfomgt.2007.03.005

Tadeusiewicz, R., Ogiela, M., & Ogiela, L. (2007). A New Approach to the Computer Support of Strategic Decision Making in Enterprises by Means of a New Class of Understanding Based Management Support Systems. In *IEEE Proceedings 6th International Conference CISIM'07 – Computer Information Systems and Industrial Management Applications,* Ełk, Poland, (pp. 9-13).

Tadeusiewicz, R., & Ogiela, M. R. (2003). Artificial intelligence techniques in retrieval of visual data semantic information. *LNAI, 2663,* 18–27.

Tanaka, E. (1995). Theoretical aspects of syntactic pattern recognition . *Pattern Recognition, 28,* 1053–1061. doi:10.1016/0031-3203(94)00182-L

Wang, Y. (2003). On Cognitive Informatics. *Brain and Mind: A Transdisciplinary Journal of Neuroscience and Neurophilosophy, 4*(2), 151-167.

Wang, Y. (2007). The Cognitive Processes of Formal Inferences. *International Journal of Cognitive Informatics and Natural Intelligence, 1*(4), 75–86.

# Chapter 8
# EIS for Consumers Classification and Support Decision Making in a Power Utility Database

**Juan Ignacio Guerrero Alonso**
*University of Seville, Spain*

**Carlos León de Mora**
*University of Seville, Spain*

**Félix Biscarri Triviño**
*University of Seville, Spain*

**Iñigo Monedero Goicoechea**
*University of Seville, Spain*

**Jesús Biscarri Triviño**
*University of Seville, Spain*

**Rocío Millán**
*University of Seville, Spain*

## ABSTRACT

*The increasing of the storage system capacity and the reduction of the access time have allowed the development of new technologies which have afforded solutions for the automatic treatment of great databases. In this chapter a methodology to create Enterprise Information Systems which are capable of using all information available about customers is proposed. As example of utilization of this methodology, an Enterprise Information System for classification of customer problems is proposed. This EIS implements several technologies. Data Warehousing and Data Mining are two technologies which can analyze automatically corporative databases. Integration of these two technologies is proposed by the present work together with a rule based expert system to classify the utility consumption through the information stored in corporative databases.*

DOI: 10.4018/978-1-61520-625-4.ch008

Copyright © 2010, IGI Global. Copying or distributing in print or electronic forms without written permission of IGI Global is prohibited.

# INTRODUCTION

Enterprise Information Systems (EIS) are applications that provide high quality services by means of a treatment of great volumes of information. Frequently, these processes include artificial intelligence methods or any knowledge-discovery technology.

Enterprise Information Systems can integrate any technology that helps in the information treatment, in this way turn into Integrated Systems consisting of several modules that work jointly to solve a certain problem.

The great quantity of methodologies and technologies that have appeared for EIS development, have allowed the proliferation in many markets. This situation has provoked the diversification of the EIS, depending on the goal that they search for and on how EIS comes close to it.

In this paper, an Enterprise Information System that integrates knowledge to help the human experts in the making decision, called Decision Support System (DSS) is proposed. This kind of systems is very useful for the utilities distribution companies. This kind of companies has several similar characteristics. For example, the consumption in water, power or gas utility is hardly controlled. The company installs measure equipments to register the client consumption and, in some case, it adds control equipments to avoid the overloads. Normally, these equipments are property of utility company and its manipulation without company authorization is illegal.

In order to show the proposed DSS generic methodology, an example of its application is showed in the case of a power utility. This DSS example try to help in the non-technical loss classification process.

Mainly, the utilities present two classes of incidents:

- Technical losses. These losses are produced in distribution stage. In the power distribution companies, they correspond with energy losses:

    ○ Wire warming (Joule Effect).
    ○ Distribution facility blemishes.
    ○ Natural reasons.
- Non-technical losses. This type of incidents represents, faults and/or manipulations on the installation that induce the total or partial absence or modification of the consumption on the company side. If the company cannot control the consumption correctly it is not possible to invoice the utility and, therefore, an economic loss is produced.

Nowadays, companies have predictive systems of technical losses that work with a very low mistake percentage; because normally they are based on physical and climatic calculations. On the contrary, the non technical losses are very difficult to detect and control. Normally, the more common non-technical are:

- Anomalies. They are characterized itself by breakdowns or mistakes by the company installation technical personnel or by deterioration of the client facilities.
- Frauds. They are inadequate manipulations realized by the clients in their installation, with the objective to modify for their own profit the energy that is registered on the meter.

In most of the references (see 'Overview and fraud detection' section), this detection type is realized treating the client's consumption and more characteristics, such the economic sector and the geographic location. Nevertheless, on the corporate databases there exists a lot of information that includes:

- Client information.
- Contract information.
- Client facilities technical specifications.
- Results and commentaries realized by the company inspectors and technicians.

According to the company, it is possible that more information exists.

The joint treatment of all this information allows the detection and classification procedures of non-technical losses. This treatment demands the utilization of diverse technologies to adapt the procedures to the information type that is used. At the same time, it is necessary to design integration methods to construct the Information System.

In the present chapter a general revision will be done about the Information System checking each of the following points:

- Objective of the present paper.
- The form in which companies realize the activities related with client consumption control.
- The methodology adopted by the Information System development.
- The information management methods that companies have.
- The Information System basic architecture joined with the integration limits that are established, followed by all module descriptions.
- Information System verification and validation methods.
- Presentation of experimental results obtained.

## OBJECTIVES

The EIS main objective consists of the accomplishment of an exhaustive client analysis, using the most available information. This EIS proposes a classification of the different clients analyzed, depending on the found incidents, in this way, it supports the inspector as a Decision Support System on using the knowledge acquired to realize a classification, depending on the obtained results.

To obtain this goal, the EIS must take advantage of all the client information available and apply the

inspector knowledge to this information, in search of any anomaly or fraud that could mask a problem in the client installation (non-technical loss).

Most of the studies realized till now use a lot of information related to the client consumption and the economic activity. The present paper raises the need to use all the available information about the client because the utility company distribution commercial systems have more information available, not only the information relating to consumption. Due to this need, it will be necessary to first perform an available information study and to use the inspector knowledge to determine what information is interesting. Once decided it is necessary to determine what technology is most adequate to extract the knowledge necessary for the analysis of each information type.

The company inspector and expert knowledge includes from the structure and information contained in the company commercial system, up to the procedures and devices of the different existing facilities.

The available information in utility distribution companies has similarity characteristics and it is possible to apply the same techniques to treat the available information.

## OVERVIEW ON FRAUD DETECTION

Normally, the existing references limit themselves to the information treatment about the consumption.

There exist three precedents directly related to the topic that is shown in this chapter:

- F. Biscarri et al. (Biscarri, 2008) proposed different artificial intelligence techniques and statistical methods for **non-technical losses** detection. These techniques apply various methods that allow the detection of anomalous **consumption** patterns.

- J.R. Galván et al. (Galván, 1998) proposed a technology based on radial basis neural networks, using only the consumption evolution in monthly periods. Also it uses the economic sector indirectly, since is the test only uses agricultural clients.

- José E. Cabral (Cabral, 2004; Cabral, 2006) proposed the application of rough sets to classify categorized attribute values. This one is the only found offer capable of taking advantage of a lot of information from the databases, this system works with dicretized information, therefore, it is necessary to design discretization processes in the information that possesses continuous values.

Another one of the technologies used often for the fraud detection is the forecasting using artificial neural networks (ANN) with different architectures combined with other methods like: data mining (Wheeler, 2000), fuzzy logic (Lau, 2008) and temporal series (Azadeh, 2007). This application has a wide representation nowadays since it is used both for energy and for finance (Hand, 2001; Kou, 2004) and telecommunications (Daskalaki, 2003).

The forecasting load subject is much more extensive since it includes short (Hobbs, 1998), medium (Gavrilas, 2001) and long (Padmakumari, 1999) forecasting methods, but it is used for client sets and not for detecting frauds in specific certain client. In other articles there appears the possibility of adding climatic parameters to increase the forecasting efficiency (Shakouri, 2007).

## UTILITY DISTRIBUTION COMPANIES

All utility distribution companies have measure equipment installation and information about client consumption. Concretely, in specific case of power utilities there are three types of samples. These samples depend on installed tension (low,

medium or high). Normally, the low tension client consumption is more difficult to control. Power utilities have million of clients with low tension contracts. To control the consumption of all clients there are mainly two methods:

- Telemeasuring. This type needs that in the client installation there be placed MODEMs that communicate the measuring of telematic form to the distribution company.
- Manual measuring. This type needs that a company employee must visit each and every of the registers to take the measure manually.

The telemeasuring equipment provides a more exhaustive control of the measurements. Nevertheless, the manual measuring is normally taken monthly or bi-monthly, which is what normally happens in clients of low tension. This complicates the client consumption analysis, because it reduces the consumption information and it is on this that the present paper has been tested.

An activity that the inspectors and technical staff realize of the distribution companies are defined by the companies by means of procedures. In these procedures there are defined actions that the inspector or technician must do according to the goal that they pursue.

When inspectors or technicians visit the client facilities they must perform the actions that are specified in a procedure, having ended it, must register it in the company commercial system and the results. Normally, the inspectors or technicians have the possibility of adding a commentary or some observation. This information provides a great advantage on the methods and technologies that only use the client consumption information, since they give very important information that normally would not be available in the numeric information on the company databases.

When an inspector finds a fraud or anomaly in the client installation this must be communicated to the company, which should create a process that stores all the information relating to the fraud or anomaly from its detection until it is corrected. These processes are very important in the research because of it can be used to determine the efficiency of the automatic methods.

All these characteristics are normally common in all existing utilities distribution companies who have a large number of clients.

## BUSINESS MANAGEMENT INFORMATION

All the utility distribution companies store great quantities of information about clients. Normally these type of companies need a great infrastructure to support and to manage all this information. At the same time, the infrastructure allows the company personnel to add, to modify or to eliminate information on the company database. These type of processes are the most common and are more numerous than realized on the company database.

The companies cannot interrupt these processes because it might provoke an economic loss. Nevertheless, it is necessary to do a series of processes that need a bigger load on the database, it is mainly performed during the night or at weekends, when client administrative activities are not necessary.

Another solution why they choose the companies is Datamarts creation. These represent small images of the original database so that it adapts to the needs of the activity that is going to be used. These Datamarts do not allow it to be employed with online information, but it is updated in short predefined or even incremental periods. Normally, the update processes also are realized during periods of inactivity.

In addition, also periodically, to perform massive reviews on a set of clients who satisfy series of conditions, so it is necessary to realize batch processes that are executed on nightly schedules and initiate the necessary procedures. This one

is the expedient main source for the companies, since normally they are created by inspectors who search a certain pattern.

## METHODOLOGY

The methodology used for this kind of EIS must consider the existence of two types of processes: research and development processes.

This methodology could be used for implementing generic EIS to analysis any kind of information. In this chapter, this methodology is used to make a system for treat available information of utility distribution companies in order to make a classification of losses.

In the figure 1 the evolutionary methodology type proposed is shown. Later, each of the phases is described briefly:

- Identification. In this phase, the familiarization by the vocabulary and aspects related to the problem subject is made.
- Knowledge extraction. This is a research phase. It consists of two stages, which can be realized in parallel:
  - Knowledge Acquisiton. The researchers obtain the necessary knowledge to perform the consumers' analysis using the meetings knowledge acquisitions with the experts. Also, one seeks to perform a design of the group of tests and the validation criteria for EIS.
  - Information Review. The researchers familiarize themselves with the available information on the databases, which determine the usable information for the solution.
- Information Preprocessing. In this stage the preprocessing of the available information in the database is realized in order to facilitate the adaptation of the same one and to allow the design and structure

*Figure 1. Methodology diagram*

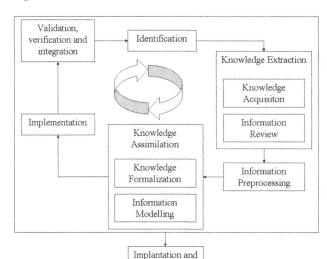

of the necessary databases. In addition, it establishes the design of preprocessing techniques that can be used to solve the problem.

- Knowledge Assimilation. It has two research stages:
  ◦ Knowledge Formalization. It establishes the design and structure of knowledge base.
  ◦ Information Modelling. Modelling algorithms to the preprocessed information are applied.
- Implementation. The development and codification process of the knowledge base and modeling process.
- Validation, Verification and Integration. The acquired knowledge validation is done in the extraction phase, by means of expert validation. The verification tests are designed in the knowledge extraction stage, establishing the evaluation criteria with the company. The different technology integration tests will allow the fitting the different technology processes of the different technologies, in agreement with the evaluation criteria established, it will be carried out at

the same time as the processes of verification, since the unification of the different technologies for the correct functioning of the EIS is necessary.

- Implantation and Maintenance. It is necessary to make a implantation and maintenance plans that allows to the company assimilate the new EIS.

This methodology has been created from the existing generic methodologies of each one of the most common technologies, trying to combine the different activities accomplishment of development and investigation. In this type of projects in which competitive companies have been involved, it is necessary to establish additional processes that allow a control investigation, establishing criteria that determines when a development is necessary and when an investigation phase has been satisfactorily completed.

The example that is shown in this paper presents the application of this methodology. EIS for classification losses in power utilities is made. This system could be applied to other utilities.

## INTEGRATION

In general, the integration of different modules is necessary to solve some questions:

- The output format of each module for integrating must verify a set of conditions to allow the utilization inside a solid integration. To solve this problem there are two options:
  - The design of translation intermediate processes is one of the most used options, since it allows supporting a modular design. The disadvantage of this module types is that in applications that use artificial intelligence, they provoke the need to modify the translation intermediate module to integrate a new module. Another disadvantage of this solution is the increase of the execution time.
  - The design of modules that obtain the results in the necessary format. This option has the main disadvantage of forcing design specific modules.
- Selecting how one is going to direct the Information System execution. Traditionally, two options existed: centralized or distributed. With the use of artificial intelligence technologies, modules that use the knowledge extracted by other modules to obtain new knowledge or as help in the decision taking can be designed. This raises a distributed control system at every module that is employed independently, but with the existence of an implicit relation, because it is the set of all modules that allows the decision making process.
- Determining the way in which the Information System will communicate with the user. In this sense it is necessary to define a series of questions:
  - How is one going to present the information to the user?

  - What information is one going to present to the user?
  - In what levels can the user interact?
- Determining the synchronization way of the different modules:
  - Synchronous modules. It is necessary to perform the coordination of the different modules according to execution times. In artificial intelligence problems this solution type is very complex, because if heuristic search processes (typical in artificial intelligence) are used it is very complicated to determine the execution time.
  - Asynchronous modules. In this case it would be necessary to establish a few minimal conditions of functioning for each of the modules, so that the taking of decisions could be done without needing the modules to be done completely. Logically, the results will be more efficient if the modules have performed their jobs.
  - Sequential modules. An execution order is established among the different modules. This is the most common, used in artificial intelligence processes.

These questions raise a series of limits that force taking certain decisions in the design and development of each module.

In some proposed sample aspects, combined solutions have been chosen, for example, only in certain occasions are they going to use intermediate processes (middleware) because normally the utilization of fixed modules will be more useful.

In the interaction with the user, it proposes the utilization of reports with graphs to present the information related to the client with a possible conclusion. This conclusion is designated by means of the client classifications in different categories that identify the problem related to the client. With this information the expert can determine if he/she agrees or not with the classification, performing the System fixing in case it is necessary.

In execution, initially the sequential way has been chosen, but thanks to the adopted structures and the used technologies it is possible with small modifications to realize a System capable of working in an asynchronous form and of allowing the work with incremental load.

In this kind of projects is necessary to use the best applications for each technology. But, in some case, it will be necessary to use only one application, that integrates all technologies. This application is oriented to information treatment of great volume. Normally, this condition is associated to a project that is limited to one or more applications

## BASIC ARCHITECTURE

The Information System basic architecture is based mainly on:

- The type of information that is going to treat. The nature of the information to treat will determine what type of technology is most adapted to analyze it, since the same methods for numerical and alphanumeric information directly cannot be used.
- The way the information is presented to the user. The activities that the employee develops, determines which is the most suitable information presenting form.
- The company infrastructure. The Information System must be measured correctly to allow the implantation in the company infrastructure.

These conditions are the same for all utilities distribution companies, because they use very similar information and have closed volume of clients.

To determine the influence of these three factors it is necessary to do a knowledge extraction phase, selecting information parts that can contribute something in the classification and detection process of **non-technical losses**.

In this database types there exists information of different natures: numerical, date and alphanumeric. For each of them, it is necessary to investigate the procedure or technology most adapted for the extraction and treatment. In this respect, the typical information in the utility distribution companies are:

- Client and contract data.
- Facility information.
- Consumption information.
- Inspector documentation and commentaries.

Once the necessary information is identified the procedures for the treatment and analysis could be designed.

So the different modules that compound this architecture are shown in Figure 2.

The process begins with the different source information existence, that in some cases, will be necessary to apply preprocessing methods, because of possible problems existing in the information getting.

Information System needs user interface to show the getting of results, this module is essential, due to DSS Enterprise Information System need some interaction form with the user. In the same form, the possibility in which an administrator can modify or update the system, in some exceptional times must exist. This interface gives access to each of the modules that make part of the EIS.

Each one of these modules (1, 2, 3, …) performs a treatment on the information that allows adding new data to the knowledge database. The goal of each one is to help on the fitting phase and on adaptation to different problems, decreasing the maximum possible interaction by the admin-

*Figure 2. Generic architecture*

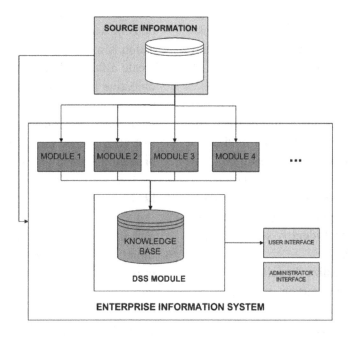

istrator. This information is treated by the DSS module in the decision process according to the stored information.

## INFORMATION PREPROCESSING

The System has to use the necessary information to perform the analysis. The different development and investigation phases are intended to determine what information is used in the analysis and what information has be made in order that the Information System uses it.

The realized studies on large amount of information sets are not useful, due to the long time process needed to get results. In addition, the companies need many resources for the information maintenance normal job and new client updates. All these reasons force the decrease of the study sample, allow the extraction in inactivity periods (night schedule) and the execution reduction time of the different studies. The previous information extraction is used creating offline databases with

all the necessary information, although it is not updated, it allows the acceleration of the investigation and depends on the commercial databases working locally.

## PROPOSED ARCHITECTURE

The proposed architecture for utility distribution company client analysis has the following modules:

- Data Warehousing for the treatment of great volume of information available in power utility companies databases. These techniques improve the state and quality of information, verify the coherence, the integrity and several kind of errors (format errors, incorrect values, etc.).
- Data Mining for making the power consumption studies; the trends and ranges of consumption are established by means of statistical techniques. The studies of

consumption ranges are carried out through the application of a statistic study which searches normal pattern behaviour, but taking into consideration a series of criterium which allow the distinction of one type of consumptions from the other.

- Text Mining for analyzing the documentation of inspections made in electrical installation clients. Initially, this module is made based on experience, using concept extraction processes on documentation and inspection commentaries of client facilities. These concepts are organized in several categories that identify several events in client facilities.
- Auxiliary tools realize the follow-up of the client who presents certain characteristics.

The Rule Based Expert System is used for coordinating the results of the different modules and to take the decision about the client's final classification. The expert system uses some rule sets classified in 7 different groups according to they function. The rules have a structure IF-THEN-ELSE.

These 7 rule groups allow implementing the integration between the modules and the decision system (in this case, the expert system). As is shown in Figure 3, the modules allow extracting knowledge, that it generates the antecedent of the rules in a dynamic way.

This EIS has 135 static rules. But client analysis may apply round 500 rules, adding the rules with dynamic antecedent.

## Rule Based Expert System

The Information System is mainly structured using as a basis a rule based expert system. Each one of the rules is used to analyze a selected aspect about the client; in this way there exists seven groups of rules that try to check all the available information aspect: consumption, contract, installation, etc.

To access quickly the information and to allow the analysis of large client volumes, Data Warehousing techniques are used. This system uses the Ralph Kimball (Kimball, 2002) point of view to create a fact table in which the analysis subject objective is sorted, from it, the client contracts who want to analyze it is extracted. Around this table work the expert system applies the rules that allow clustering the client according to the problem the client presents.

## Data Mining

The information system is used like an additional classification system, complementing the previous studies that are realized, using mainly the consumption anomalous pattern detection by means of statistical techniques, neural networks and artificial intelligence. The anomalous consumption patterns are varied in range. Due to this, it is necessary to establish additional criterions to allow the analysis of large quantity of information.

The Data Mining process in this EIS is limited to the implementation of a series of statistical techniques for combined rates and trends of normal consumption. This module proposes the idea of a study of normal consumption patterns of customers. This operation can not be performed directly. The methods applied in this EIS began with a pre-filter that tries to remove clients who have allegedly anomalous consumption. After the removal with the statistical study of the resulting sample, of customer begins.

It is necessary to do this study on the largest possible number of customers since the availability of more number of clients in the sample is statistically representative.

There is a problem applying this method on all clients. For example, a customer who has a pub with a capacity exceeding 15 kW on the coast, does not consume like a warehouse or another pub located in interior places. Thus arises the need for some kind of division that provides normal

*Figure 3. Integration method*

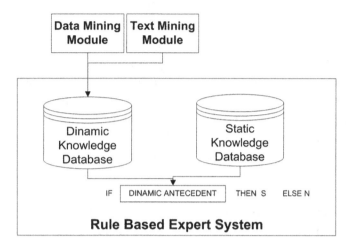

patterns of consumption for each of the desired characteristics.

During the various investigations and tests, it has been concluded that there are a number of key information fields for determining acceptable consumption standard patterns: geographical location, economic activity, billing frequency, time discrimination and contracted power. In addition, due to the different patterns that may be found necessary to establish a temporary division in the information for consumption patterns: total annual, seasonal and monthly. These groups provide us with divisions within which are defined normal conditioned patterns by the client characteristics. The customer consumption comparison who possess the relevant groups with the same features will provide us an idea of client normal consumption.

As can be inferred, the division of a sample can lead to groups that have no statistical significance. Because of this it is necessary to carry out two processes, not to solve the problem completely, but it does allow use of information in most of the groups:

1.  Discretized values of the powers to enable that within each group there is a greater representation.

2.  The study on the largest possible number of customers, it also may have increased statistical representation in each group, although it requires a higher processing capacity.

3.  Perform different groups, so that there are groups that contain only 4 of those specified characteristics, and others that use 5 or 6 of these features. This way, if the most stringent statistical entity is not sufficient, it can be compared with less restrictive for a rough estimation of client normal consumption.

This study also provides additional information about the behaviour of each of the groups studied, as it can be checked whether a certain group of customers presented a seasonal consumption or an irregular consumption.

Moreover, this study along with the text mining, which will be described in the next section, provides an inherent capability of automatic adaptation to the characteristics of the sample to be analyzed, because if you study as many customers as possible, this will provide information on all possible cases analysable.

Currently, this study must be made on virtually all existing customers in the company, and it has provided enough information to analyze different types of customers, except in some groups where there is not enough information.

## Text Mining

The purpose of the Text Mining process is to analyze the content of comments added by different inspectors or alphanumeric fields. These provide useful information in analyzing the consumption of the clients as they provide additional data on the status of the facility and the inspector observations.

The techniques used in this process are reduced to the extraction and classification of concepts. The concepts are a set of one or more words that represent an idea, event, action or real object. In this way, a concept can be anything from a simple word to a full term. The classification of these concepts has been done according to the experience of the inspectors and fuzzy techniques to detect similarities between different forms of spelling.

The classification of these terms is based on problems that you want to identify. Thus, this information is used to verify the conclusions of the analysis of customers.

Not all clients have this information. In such cases, the information system can provide all that is additional information on the client consumption and different incidents identified in the information.

As the implementation result of Text Mining techniques, this yields a dictionary of concepts to be added to the knowledge base information system. This EIS process was particularly complex because the initial classification was made according to the knowledge provided by experts and inspectors, and has been a large volume of work of classification and verification.

## VERIFICATION AND VALIDATION METHODOLOGY

The checking is whether the information system performs the analysis without losing information and without making mistakes in this process. This requires reviewing the results of each module separately and Information System as a whole. Using the EIS cyclically in cases pre-designed, we can fix the system so as not to lose information and calculations are performed correctly.

The loss of information is one of the most common problems in systems that are created by the merger of several modules. If not properly designed and constructed, to two modules may be missing if there is not a successful conversion of information.

Validation is a procedure for determining whether the information system does the work for which it was created in a robust and effective. You have to define, first, estimated limits of efficiency to be achieved and make different prototypes, refining the information system to equal or exceed the objectives.

The objectives for information systems are defined in terms of time cost, robustness and efficiency. In general, it is preferable to obtain systems with a temporary low-cost, high efficiency and ruggedness, looking for a good balance, because a very robust system is usually less efficient and temporary high cost.

In the sense of efficacy, validation of this information system and other systems in the utility distribution subject is quite complex. There are mainly two methods to validate the different prototypes that are created:

- Perform analysis of data from a closed set of customers and, through inspection, to determine whether there is a non-technical loss in the client facilities. This method is quite common in some references (Cabral, 2004; Cabral, 2006). It presents several problems:

○ The method is very inefficient, because the inspections need time, because he/she must visit them one by one and complete the related documentation.

○ The amount of clients that can be reviewed is quite small, since more clients will take longer to get results. This decreases the probability of finding a client with a non-technical loss reduction by decreasing the entire study.

• Using two samples of the same clients that are extracted in different moments of time. This way you can see which clients have a problem or if they are correct or have not been visited. The procedure is to analyze the information from the oldest sample and compare the results with the new sample. This comparison is an investigation process and we must determine whether the detected **non-technical losses** in the most recent match what the analysis concludes. Moreover, the possibility of refining the system using the client wrongly classified (as we have information on clients who have not confirmed a non-technical loss). However, this technique presents a problem: it is not possible to establish any conclusion on the remaining clients of which there is no information on the new sample.

In the case of this sample of Enterprise Information System the second option described has been proposed, choosing a closed set of customers in two separate moments of time.

This method has allowed the refinement of the Information System in order to achieve the correct margins classifications proposed.

There is an additional problem, which occurs in the two methods and problems in the information. For example, in some cases, companies have taken measurement of the client facilities, in such cases and where the problem is prolonged in time,

may cause a non-technical loss. In fact, this may mask a fraud.

The Enterprise Information System use within the complete project validation procedure used is the first method described.

## EXPERIMENTAL RESULTS

This system analyzes the information to potential clients identified with **non-technical losses** through statistical techniques, neural networks and artificial intelligence in a practical application in a particular company. Then you get all information about these clients and they are analyzed in the present Enterprise Information System. As a result of this analysis, reports and graphs for each client are obtained.

It has been found that this Enterprise Information System provides a complex filtering process to prevent clients who are inspected are not actually non-technical losses. In this sense, the Enterprise Information System provides a filter that removes usually between 20% and 70% of clients who otherwise would be a wasted expenditure, since in most cases they do not have non-technical losses.

The reports of the Enterprise Information System allow the inspectors and researchers more information about the client and on the problems presented, as are just and necessary information, using graphic information on a temporary basis (consumption, etc.). Moreover, in these reports, the reasons why the client has been included in a given category can be found.

## CONCLUSION

This paper explores the expert system investigation in the utility consumption subject, and its combination with other technologies to enable the design and construction of an Enterprise Information System.

Particularly, the research focuses on a very little exploited area: the automation of the available information analysis for anomalies or fraud classification on utility companies.

In the Enterprise Information System discussed in this paper, the main source of complexity was the huge amount of knowledge required and the variety of problems that may occur in the client analysis.

The main tasks of investigation, which made major contributions, focus on:

- Methodology design for classification systems with different type of available information.
- Identification and classification of knowledge necessary.
- Identification and classification of the analysis cases of utility distribution client.
- Use of different information types in the analysis of clients.
- Using different integration techniques.
- Implementation of the Enterprise Information System.
- Design and construction of an Enterprise Information System that automates their adaptation to the different test samples.
- Provides a Decision Support System (DSS) making through analysis of reports and graphs.

## REFERENCES

Azadeh, A., Ghaderi, S. F., & Sohrabkhani, S. (2007). Forecasting electrical consumption by integration of Neural Network, time series and ANOVA. *Applied Mathematics and Computation, 186*, 1753–1761. doi:10.1016/j.amc.2006.08.094

Biscarri, F., Monedero, I., León, C., Guerrero, J. I., Biscarri, J., & Millán, R. (2008, June). A data mining method base don the variability of the customer consumption: A special application on electric utility companies. In *Proceedings of the Tenth International Conference on Enterprise Information Systems, Volume Artificial Intelligence and Decision Support System (AIDSS)* (pp. 370-374). Barcelona, Spain.

Cabral, J., Pinto, J., Linares, K., & Pinto, A. (in press). Methodology for fraud detection using rough sets. *IEEE International Conference on Granular Computing.*

Cabral, J., Pinto, J. O. P., Gontijo, E., & Filho, J. Reis (2004, October). Fraud Detection In Electrical Energy Consumers Using Rough Sets. In *IEEE International Conference on System, Man and Cybernetics,* (Vol. 4, pp. 3625-3629).

Daskalaki, S., Kopanas, I., Goudara, M., & Avouris, N. (2003). Data Mining for decision support on customer insolvency in telecommunications business. *European Journal of Operational Research, 145*, 239–255. doi:10.1016/S0377-2217(02)00532-5

Galván, J. R., Elices, A., Muñoz, A., Czernichow, T., & Sanz-Bobi, M. A. (1998, November). System For Detection Of Abnormalities and Fraud In Customer Consumption. In *12th Conference on the Electric Power Supply Industry*, Pattaya, Thailand.

Gavrilas, M., Ciutea, I., & Tanasa, C. (2001, June). Medium-term load forecasting with artificial neural network models. *CIRED2001, Conference Publication No. 482.*

Hand, J. D. (2001). Prospecting for gems in credit card data. *IMA Journal of Management Mathematics, 12*, 172–200. doi:10.1093/imaman/12.2.173

Hobbs, B. F., Helman, U., Jitprapaikulsarn, S., Konda, S., & Maratukulam, D. (1998). Artificial neural networks for short-term energy forecasting: accuracy and economic value. *Neurocomputing, 23*, 71–84. doi:10.1016/S0925-2312(98)00072-1

Kimball, R., & Ross, M. (2002). *The Data Warehouse Toolkit: The Complete Guide to Dimensional Modeling* (2nd ed.). New York: John Wiley & Sons Computer Publishing.

Kou, Y., Lu, C., Sinvongwattana, S., & Huang, Y. (2004). Survey of Fraud Detection Techniques. In *Proceedings of the 2004 IEEE Intenational Conference on Networking, Sensing & Control,* (pp. 21-23), Taipei, Taiwan.

Lau, H. C. W., Cheng, E. N. M., Lee, C. K. M., & Ho, G. T. S. (2008). A fuzzy logic approach to forecast energy consumption change in a manufacturing system. *Expert Systems with Applications, 34*, 1813–1824. doi:10.1016/j.eswa.2007.02.015

Padmakumari, K., Mohandas, K. P., & Thiruvengadam, S. (1999). Long term distribution demand forecasting using neuro fuzzy computations. *Electrical Power and Energy Systems, 21*, 315–322. doi:10.1016/S0142-0615(98)00056-8

Shakouri, H., Nadimi, R., & Ghaderi, F. (2008). A hybrid TSK-FR model to study short-term variations of electricity demand versus the temperature changes. *Expert Systems with Applications*. doi:. doi:10.1016/j.eswa.2007.12.058

Szkuta, B. R., Sanabria, L. A., & Dillon, T. S. (1999, August). Electricity Price Short-Term Forecasting using artificial neural networks. *IEEE Transactions on Power Systems, 14*(3). doi:10.1109/59.780895

Wheeler, R., & Aitken, S. (2000). Multiple Algorithms for Fraud Detection. *Review Knowledge-Based Systems, 13*, 93–99. doi:10.1016/S0950-7051(00)00050-2

## KEY TERMS AND DEFINITIONS

**Client Facilities:** This represents from the finish of utility line distribution to client home. Normally, in this facilities, there are measure and control equipment for client consumption.

**Company Commercial System:** The company needs a database with the client information. This database has an interface for interaction with user.

**Data Mining:** It is a set of techniques based initially on statistical techniques. Actually, the present techniques are based on other investigations related to artificial intelligence. The main objective of data mining is the automatic pattern extraction from data.

**Data Warehouse:** This technology proposes another way to organize the information in databases. The information is specially oriented to the subject related with the problem. This idea includes information redundancy but accelerates the queries.

**Datamart:** It is small image of large database. This image is specially oriented for one specific objective. Normally, the datamart is made with data warehouse technology.

**Expert Systems:** The expert systems are programs that it is used for specific problem solution. These systems are made with the knowledge of experts implemented in knowledge base.

**Inspector:** Normally, he (she) represents a person that is in company staff. He (she) is a technician that visit the client facilities and is capable of manipulate the measure equipment and has the company authorization.

**Low Tension:** Normally it is the set of clients with tension less than 1000 Volts.

**MODEM:** MOdulator-DEModulator. This electronic device is used for transmission of information by means of modulation of signal.

**Rule Based Expert Systems:** Expert systems whose have the knowledge base implemented by a set of rules.

**Text Mining:** It is a technology born under Data Mining. Recently, this technology became a great investigation field. The main objective of text mining is the automatic patter extraction from unstructured information. The Text Mining techniques usually use natural language processing (NLP) for categorizing the information of unstructured information.

Chapter 9

# Enhancing the Electronic Customer Relationship Management through Data Mining:
## A Business Intelligence Approach

**M. Vignesh**
*The American College, India*

## ABSTRACT

*According to the Moore's law, the number of transistors per microprocessor will double in every two years. In no doubt, this exponential increase in the processing speeds would be flanked by the increasing amount of data that corporates contend on a daily basis. Hence all corporates are literally drowning in data. But definitely there exists a hiatus between the data storage and the information retrieval. One can ask an enigmatic question, how effectively a stored data can be utilised for the decision making in the long-term perspective. The answer is not yet arrived out. Hence the "Organizations are data rich, but information poor!". If capturing and storing the relevant data is a hectic task, then analyzing and translating this data into the actionable information is the other corner stone in any information systems of a concern. This gap can be bridged or overruled by the concept of business intelligence. Business Intelligence (BI) can be simply defined in terms of data –driven approach rather than information driven which includes methods as decision support systems, online analytical processing (OLAP), statistical analysis, query and reporting, forecasting which can be primarily done by data mining. BI along with customer relationship management (CRM) software forms the second tier of a firm's IT infrastructure. This chapter holds a bird's eye view of the usage of datawarehousing approaches for a systematic business intelligence approach and its varied applications in view of electronic customer relationship management.*

DOI: 10.4018/978-1-61520-625-4.ch009

Copyright © 2010, IGI Global. Copying or distributing in print or electronic forms without written permission of IGI Global is prohibited.

## INTRODUCTION

The very purpose of Customer Relationship Management (CRM) is to enable organizations to better serve its customers through the integration of reliable processes and procedures for interacting with those customers. The Customer Relationship Marketing revolves around the crux of relationship marketing wherein, the real concept of marketing plays a major role than that of selling a product. Hitherto, the relationship marketing is purely a strategy to bring and to nurture the relationships with the customers so as to maintain a long-term value. Selecting and acquiring customers based on their lifetime value results in higher profits than seeking out customers based on other criteria (Venkatesan and Kumar, 2004). Thanks to the concept of ebusiness and eSCM, where corporates played a major role in maintaining their relationship with their customers through the electronic means. Companies as Dell Computers, DHL services maintain such eCRM practices in terms of ordering, supply chain management, online tracking facilities and so on. In fact, relationship marketing, the underlying premise of CRM, cannot be effective without an appropriate use of information technology (IT) (Zineldin, 2000).

The crux of CRM is customer selectivity. The company must therefore be selective and tailor its campaign efforts by segmenting and selecting appropriate customers for individual marketing programs in terms of marketing automation or sales force automation (SFA), campaign management, internet personalization and email management . In extraordinary instances, it could even lead to "outsourcing of some customers" so that a company better utilize its resources on those customers. However, the motto of the concern is not to prune off its customer base but to identify appropriate customer programs and methods that would be profitable and create value for the firm and the customer. Also there is a saying that, it fetches ten times more cost to acquire a new customer than to retain a new customer. Hence

it is imminent to select and to retain the existing profitable customers in this competitive era.

## Missions and Learning Outcomes of the Chapter

With the advancement of IT, CRM can be redefined in terms of eCRM which allows aplenty of opportunities for organizations to reach their goals by the a clear cut way of setting up their mission and value propositions of the business through a better understanding of their customers and to serve them accordingly and to personalize online experiences and agent interaction in the ECRM environment.

From this chapter, learners will learn how to:

- The differences between CRM and eCRM
- How to build the knowledge infostructure to support decision making and marketing
- The advancements in business forecasting through the Knowledge Discovery (KD) rather than a decision support system.
- Trends in applying the CRM tools and techniques
- CRM-based business strategies
- Futurological aspects in Business Intelligence.

## What is an eCRM?

The stepping stone of a CRM programme is "customer selectivity". As several research promulgates not all customers are equally profitable (Infact in some cases 80% of the sales come through 20% of the customers). Therefore a concern must be selective and tailor its program and marketing efforts accordingly, by segmenting and selecting appropriate customers for a better relationship management.

With the advent of Information and Communication Technologies (ICT), the letter 'e' gained its significance elsewhere. Needless to say, that

CRM is also being prefixed with the same. ICT involves the information and communication channels as well as hardware and software used to generate, prepare, transmit, and store data. Hence, eCRM provides companies with means to conduct interactive, personalized and relevant communications with customer across both electronic and traditional channels. It utilizes a complete view of the customer to make decisions about messaging, offers and channel delivery. It synchronises communication across otherwise disjoint-customer facing systems. It adheres to permission based practices, respecting individual's preferences regarding how and whether they wish to communicate with you and it focuses on understanding how the economics of customer relationship affect the business.

This electronic channel does not replace the sales force, the call Centre, or even the fax. It is simply another extension, albeit a powerful new one, to the customer. The thrust of eCRM is not what the organisation is "doing on the web" but how fully the organisation ties its on-line channel back to its traditional channels, or Customer touch points.

To achieve their goal of providing a solution for the process of the customers, enterprises need to focus on three sorts of knowledge in CRM processes (Osterle 2001), which make up what we consider to be customer knowledge.

i.    They need to understand the requirements of customers in order to address them. This is referred to as *"Knowledge about customers"*.

ii.   Customers have information needs in their interaction with the enterprise. This is *"Knowledge for customers"*.

iii.  At last, customers have knowledge about the products and services they use as well as about how they perceive the offerings they purchased. This is *"Knowledge from customers"*.

As CRM revolves around the concept of relationship marketing, hitherto, the baseline for eCRM is can be classified into two different operational strategies viz., marketing process automation, which means, concentrating on the development of information pertaining to the customers with the aide of ICT and secondly, marketing intelligence which encompasses the knowledge discovery techniques, OLAP and data mining principles etc., which can be later used to derive out a new concept the customer intelligence.

## eCRM Architecture and Components

Even though the basic structure of the eCRM varies with the organisation and its implementational levels as strategic informational level or tactical or ites operational level, almost all the eCRM infrastructure are being supported by the facilities driven by ICT as Electronic Point of Sale(EPOS), an internet connection, dictaphone facilities etc., which are being governed by a Customer service helpdesk.

The primary inputs to this module are mainly from the eCRM Assessment and strategy alignment modules. During this stage the company will try and develop a Connected Enterprise Architecture (CEA) within the context of the company's own CRM strategy. The following is a set of technical eCRM capabilities and applications that collectively and ideally comprise a full eCRM solution:

- Customer Analytical Software
- Data mining software
- Campaign Management software
- Business Simulation
- A real time decision engine

## Key Components of eCRM

Even though eCRM is being flanked by the tools and techniques of ICT, some other parameters

*Figure 1.* Key Components of eCRM *Source: Cho et al., 2002*

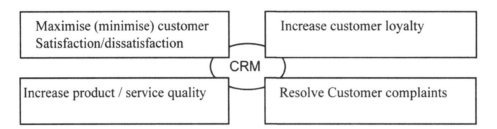

form the foundation of eCRM as suggested by Cho et al., 2002.

The role of ICT can be aptly applied for CRM as i) marketing process automation and ii) marketing intelligence. Marketing process automation involves the construction and usage of the database carrying the details of marketing information systems whereas, the marketing intelligence can be perceived as a separate system which includes the strategies of knowledge management of customer intelligence and that can be derived by special processing systems as online analytical processing (OLAP), applications of data mining etc.

## Customer Lifecycle (CLC)

A customer for any product can surpass distincive stages which referred to as the Customer life cycle (CLC). A knowledge in the life cycle is very much essential for a better relationship marketing as different strategies can be adopted in each stage. The stages can be categorically explained as:

i.    **Prospects**: These are the persons in the target market, but who all not yet the customers. By a strong influential marketing, they can be converted as potential customers.

ii.   **Responders**: are the turned-out persons from a fascinating marketing strategies. They are said to be the fresh customers or buddy persons to enter into a new market segment.

iii.  **Established customers**: persons who have been accustomed to a particular product and they are the regular users.

iv.   **Churn stage or declining stage**: Churn is the transition of a customer from one product towards a new product. In other words, this migration of the customer may cause loss to the previous concern. This is the ultimate stage where the product is set in a state of oblivion by a customer. This may be due many reasons as voluntary churn as well involuntary churn.

## Relating eCRM with CLC

As discussed earlier, CRM focuses on a long-term customer value. This long term relationship can be maintained by factors such as increase in their usage or purchases and through selling more or higher-margin products and thereby keeping them for a very longer period. Hence a valuable customer is not usually a static customer. Their relationship with the concern may be a fluctuating one and changes over time.

As the customer base of a concern increases with the increase in the burgeoning population, essential management practices must be necessary to retain their long term loyal customers. Some of such strategies that can be derived through the maintenance of an eCRM are – loyalty programmes, cross-selling, continuous replenishment, personalization, affinity partnering and strategic partnership etc.,

*Figure 2. CRISP model of data mining process*

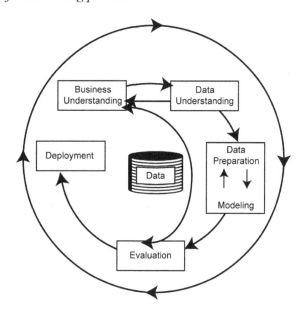

## DATA WAREHOUSE & DATA MINING

### Introduction

A *data warehouse* can be defined as a *subject-oriented, integrated, time-varying, non –volatile collection of data in support of the management's decision-making process.* (Inmon). A data warehouse differs from a database in the sense that, it carries the historical data rather than a operational data which is being stored by a database.

*Data mining* is a step in the retrieval of the historical data that utilizes a Knowledge Discovery in Databases (KDD) process and refers to mathematical modeling that are applied to get patterns from the data. The extracted information can then be used to form a prediction or a classification model, identify trends and associations, refine an existing model or provide a summary of the database being mined (Fayyad *et al.,* 1996a). Thus data mining utilizes the knowledge discovery, defined by William Frawley and Gregory Piatetsky-shapiro (MIT Press) as "… *the nontrivial extraction of implicit, previously*

*unknown, and potentially useful information from data…."*.

Even data mining can be applied in various streams as business, scientific data and mathematical modeling, Van der Putten (1999) explained a data mining process in relevant to business suite, which is often referred to as CRISP, the <u>CR</u>oss <u>I</u>ndustry <u>S</u>tandard <u>P</u>rocess

The quantum of data used in a data warehouse is in geometric progression in all corporates. However, only a limited portion of the data can be utilized for informative purposes. It is often referred to the data usage in a concern as a *garbage in and garbage out process*(GIGO) which means, all the data dumped in a database cannot be used for informative purpose, it simply remains as a junk data. The data usage in a data warehouse is characterized by its unique features as:- Separate DSS data base, Storage of data only and, no room for data entry or modification of existing data, use of historical data and Read only source only (no recasting of history).

*Table 1. Metamorphosis of Data analysis to data mining in era of business intelligence*

| Evolutionary Step | Business Question | Enabling Technologies | Vendors | Output System |
|---|---|---|---|---|
| Data Collection (1960s) | "What was my total profit in the past decade?" | Computers, tapes, disks | IBM, CDC | Retrospective, static data report delivery |
| Data Access (1980s) | "What were unit sales in southern zone in last May?" | Relational databases (RD-BMS), Structured Query Language (SQL), ODBC | Oracle, Sybase, Informix, IBM, Microsoft | Retrospective, dynamic data delivery |
| Data Warehousing & Decision Support (1990s) | "What were unit sales in Chennai last March? Drill down to Chennai." | On-line analytic processing (OLAP), multidimensional databases, data warehouses | Pilot, Hyperion, Arbor, Cognos, Microstrategy | Retrospective, dynamic data delivery at multiple levels |
| Data Mining (Today's technological ambit) | "What's likely to happen to my business in the next season? Why?" | Advanced algorithms, multi-processor computers, massive databases | Clementine, Pilot, Lockheed, IBM, SGI, | Prospective, proactive approach |

Types of Data in a Data warehouse

## i) Meta Data

Metadata can be defined as the data about the data and the overall processes that governs a data ware house.. It serves as a index for the data warehouse administrator to give instructions about the usage of the DWH and also serves to identify the contents and location of data in a data warehouse. It may contains the,

- attributes of the data set such as type, units, scales, etc.
- comments and other syntax operations to be performed in a DWH for a OLAP purpose.

However, when considering the data warehouse for a eCRM suite it may answers the following business-related questions.

- How the business definitions and trends were changed over time?
- How do product lines vary across organizations?
- What business inferences can i made?
- How do I find the data I need?
- What is the original source of the data?
- How was this summarization created?

- What queries are available to access the data?

## ii) Dormant Data

Any data that is hardly used in a data warehouse is called dormant data. The faster data warehouses grows the more data becomes dormant. Over a period of time the amount of dormant data in a data warehouse increases

## Online Analytical Processing (OLAP) in eCRM

Online Analytical processing (OLAP) uses the historical data in form of a data cube. *A data cube* can be defined as the multidimensional arrangement of the information of the database with a specified set of dimensions, say for example, name, style and month. A data cube can be viewed in a hyper cube format.

The normal OLAP operations for a customer database are:-

i. **Dicing:** The process involves a forming a subcube from the main cube . Say for example, the segmentation of profitable

*Figure 3. Data mining concepts linking the eCRM and business intelligence*

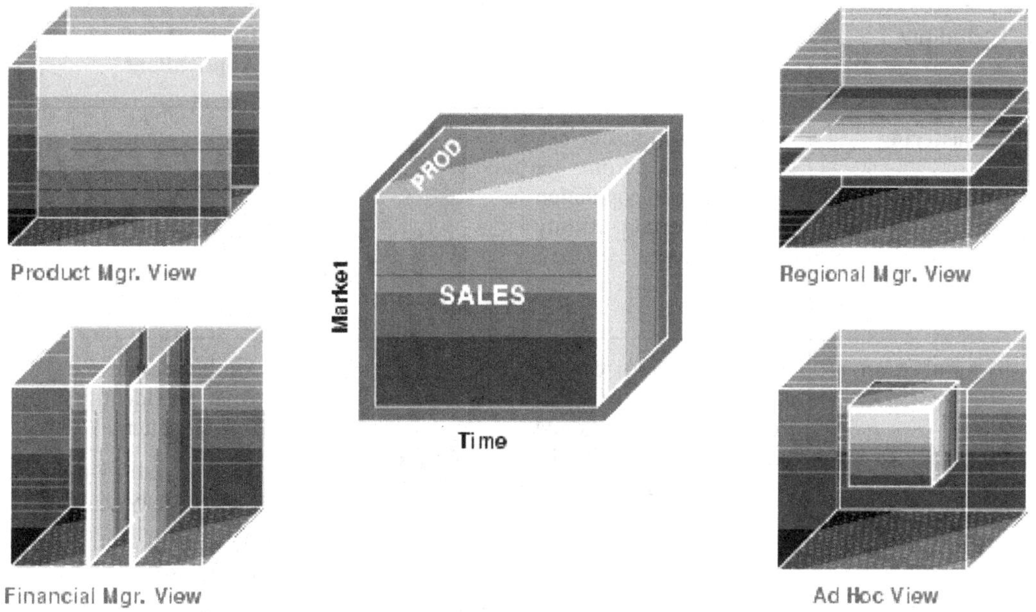

Product Mgr. View

Financial Mgr. View

SALES

Market

PROD

Time

Regional Mgr. View

Ad Hoc View

customers during a particular time period or data cube containing the loyal customers of a selected geographical locality. This can be done to select a target dimension of two or more from the data cube and thereby to prune off the unwanted areas of interest.

ii. **Slicing:** This method involves slicing out a particular zone for one dimension of the data cube, resulting in a sub cube. We can quote the cube slice for the zone 'tamilnadu' or slice for the sales during the month of 'January' etc.,

iii. **Drilling:** This type of OLAP operation is to drill-up(roll up)or drill-down along the classification sectors of a cube, based on some operational specificity. Say for example, analysis of total sales contributed by a person x, in zone a, during the time period January to December. In other words, it is a summative measure for a prediction.

However, one should know the differences between a OLAP operations and a data mining procedures. The differences can be defined as i) OLAP is a presentation tool to represent the reports

from the data and the operations are purely hypothesis driven whereas, data mining approaches are not a presentation tool and it is primarily meant to discover patterns in the data.

A cube considered in its 3-D parameters and each cell as a 'bucket' for a single customer.

The OLAP operations for the above figure can be discussed in terms of i) dicing – which answers who are the loyal customers? ii) slicing – provides the contribution done in terms of a single entity and iii) the drilling which enables to know the net profit generated by a customer over a time period say for month of November or December.

## DATA MINING TECHNIQUES

Witten & Frank (2000) marked a clear distinction between the desired output from the information sources and the tools used for this. The type of output information is the way in which the newly gained knowledge is represented. For instance: classification of data, clustering of data, association rules, decision trees are apt for the numeric

*Figure 4. Data mining techniques*

| Technique | Core concept | Report model | Business Applications |
|---|---|---|---|
| i) **Clustering** | A group or a cluster can be formed from a heterogeneous population based on certain affinity or homogeneity. | 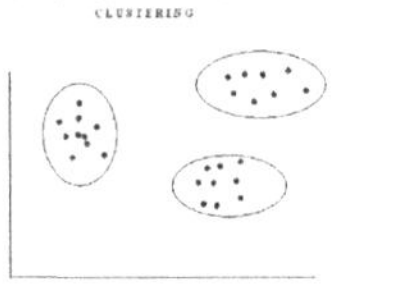 *Figure 4a. Clustering model* | Market segmentation. Defect analysis as reasons for customer attrition |
| ii) **Association** | dependency rules can be derived for desired items from a set of records and such rules can predict the possible occurrence. | 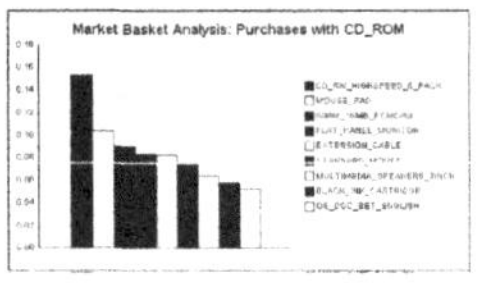 *Figure 4b. Association analysis* | Market Basket Analysis (Identify buying patterns) Sequence and Time Series Analysis Cross Selling & upselling Inventory Management |

predictions. All these types of output can be the result of one or more of a wide range of techniques called as the algorithms.

## ECRM IMPLEMENTATION

The skeleton elements of a typical eCRM remains the same, even if the entire tier varies from company to company. i) A customer-centric data and a computing architecture ii) Business rules to coordinate between customer communication and interaction using the infrastructure iii) a well-equipped system and process that facilitate the integration of analytical and operational CRM systems.

## Business Intelligence : The Next Step

**Business Intelligence (BI)** is a business term that dates to 1958. It refers to applications and technologies that are being used to gather, provide access to, and to analyze data about the concern's operations. Business Intelligence systems can help concerns to have a more integrated knowledge of the factors affecting their business, such as sales, production and internal operations, and which in turn help concerns to make better business decisions.

## Rationale for Using Business Intelligence

BI applications and technologies enable organizations to make more informed business decisions. In other words, they may afford a company competitive advantage. Say for instance, companies use business intelligence to define the indicators that enable to forecast the trends in their business. It aids the concerns in analyzing the changing trends in market share, customer behavior and spending patterns. Business Intelligence systems can help concerns develop consistent, "data-based" business decisions that produce better results than decisions based on a mere guess work. It enables to share selected strategic information with business partners as in case of sharing of information as inventory levels, performance metrics, supply chain management etc.

BI often uses key performance indicators (KPI) to assess the current status of business and to recommend a suitable course of action. As of now, this methodology of KPI was further modified and refined and expanded with the Chief Performance Officer which was integrated into a single methodology.

Data mining from a data warehouse is being supported by the Knowledge Discovery in databases (KDD) and as the concept defined as "the nontrivial extraction of implicit, previously unknown, and potentially useful information from data…."(William Frawley and Gregory Piatetsky Shapiro, 1991)

*Figure 5. Data mining*

| Technique | Core concept | Report model | Business applications |
|---|---|---|---|
| **Genetic algorithms** | Outcomes may be analysed in terms of mutation (sudden changes), crossing over ( combination of outputs) , duplication ( false occurrence of events ) etc., . All events are synchronized with the natural genetics. | 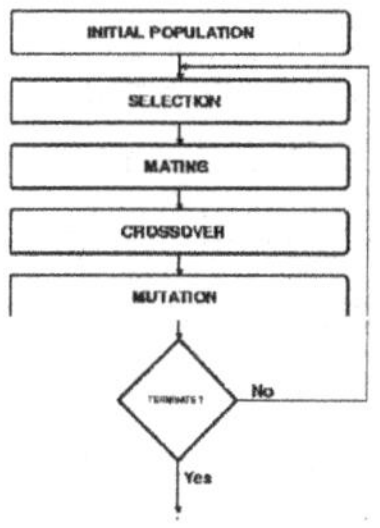 *Figure 5a. Model Genetic algorithms* | Training Neural Networks. Generating scoring functions for Memory Based Reasoning (MBR). |
| **Decision trees** | Decision Trees are tree shaped structures drawn from a parent node and many branches from that represent sets of decisions or outcomes. | 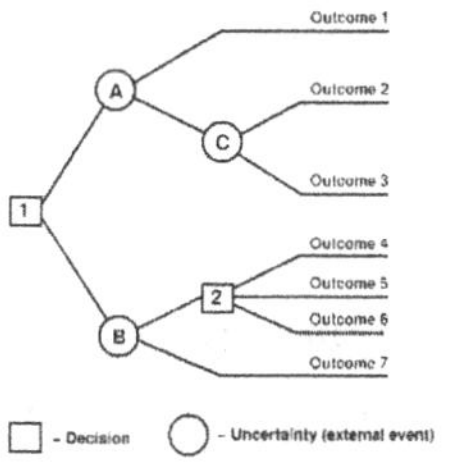 *Figure 5b. Decision tree* | Forecasting Fraud Detection in banking and financial sectors. |
| **Neural networks** | To analyse a set of outputs from the given layer of inputs with the hidden facts underlying for the causal relationship. | 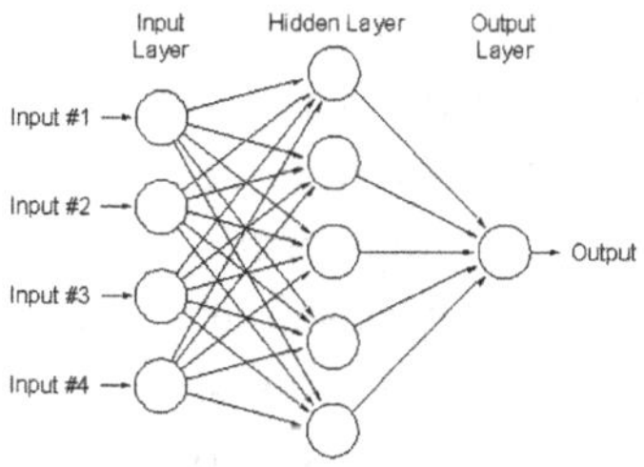 *Figure 5c. Neural network* | Optimization of marketing strategies and Trend Analysis ; Stock Forecasting Fraud Detection |

## BI Infrastructure

A typical BI infrastructure includes operational system elements, their associated databases and possible replications of their data, such as data warehouses or operational data stores. The data warehouse is being backboned by different data marts, which are tailored in a way to support specific analytical applications. The analyst uses an interface to access data from reporting and analytics engines. Warehouse data flows into these engines, which prepare forecasts, format reports, build optimization models and complete many similar tasks.

## BUSINESS INTELLIGENCE COMPETENCY CENTRE (BICC)

Many of the corporates they set up a Business Intelligence Competency Centre (BICC) where, the skills, knowledge and qualities of the man power can be integrated for a decision making. At an absolute minimum, the BICC should comprise a BICC manager, a business analyst, a chief data steward and a technical consultant. Larger BICCs can also include product mangers, internal communicators, application designers, warehouse consultants, license administrators, statisticians and training consultants.

The warehouse architect plans the overall architecture of the solution, including the performance considerations, storage repository selections, data schemas and his or her role will be in accordance with the BICC manager who promotes the value and the potential of BI, whereas the Business Analyst understands the business rules and processes of the organization and knows how the organization uses data, including any transformations applied to data and the analytical consultant understands the models and analytical reports, and applies the results of statistical analyses to business problems.

## Meta Data Management

Hence from the architecture point of view, irrespective of mode of implementation or the process involved, the components of the eCRM can be broadly classified as,

i.  **Operational CRM:** includes a horizontal integration of all the business processes with the front office systems operating in accordance with the available customers, data entry of their details, their purchasing habits inclusive of the customer touch points (CTP), the ways and means in which the CRM process is being channelised. It supports the employees in the execution of CRM processes, as designing a marketing campaign or in follow-up of a complaint. Operational part of CRM typically involves three general areas of business. They are (according to Gartner Group) a Enterprise marketing automation (EMA), Sales force automation (SFA) and a Customer service and support (CSS).

ii. **Analytical CRM:** The data accumulated from the front office side through the operational CRM may be of a heterogenous one and it must be homogenised for integrating with the warehouse and can be later utilised for the analysis purpose as OLAP for the information needs on the customer segmentation, their purchasing habits etc.,

iii. **Collaborative CRM:** It includes the process of integration and different communication channels and is often referred to as the multichannel management. This integration can be done with the usage of interactive voice response (IVR), the World Wide Web (WWW), or mobile communication means (m-commerce) to achieve an optimal channel mix (Senger et al. 2002). It also involves the facilitation of collaborative services such as e-mail, personalized publishing, e-communities and other channels to facilitate

*Figure 6. A typical data warehouse process in a business intelligence activity*

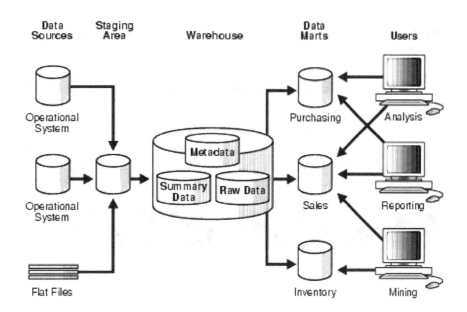

interactions between customers and the organisations, for example, online shops, and call centers (Keen et al, 2000).

## ECRM - BUSINESS APPROACHES

### Customer Identification and Segmentation Approaches

Market Basket Analysis by Association Rules

Association among the data from the data sets received a attention and thereby decisions can be drawn . Such deriving association problems was formulated by Agrawal et al.,(1993) and commonly known as market-basked problem. Here, a associative rules are drawn for a given set of items say, the consumer goods and the degree of transaction carried over by the different categories of customers, where the transactions or the purchases are assumed to be the subsets (baskets). This delivers an idea to the analyst

about the customers' spending habits on specified intervals and also to have an idea about what type of products can a customer purchase simultaneously with the purchase of a other product say for example, socks can be purchased during the purchase of shoes, ties with the coats and so on. An research in US evinced that there exists a association of purchase of diapers during the sales of beer in weekends.

Identification of Customer Loyalty – RFM and Segmentation Approach

Customer relationship management is considered to be a closed-loop marketing strategy because it encompasses all the stages in the life cycle of the customer such as identification of prospective customers, creating value for the customers, identification of loyalty as the baseline for a CRM approach and thereby for a post sales services. Customer loyalty in retails services as well as BFSI can be measured in quantitative terms of both frequency of visits and the quantum purchased which can be owed towards the profit of

*Figure 7. A screenshot of Oracle Discoverer illustrating the affinity rate in market basket analysis*

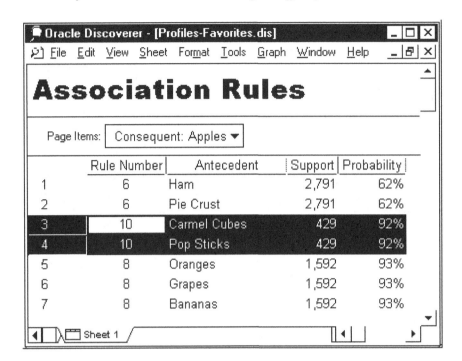

the concern. This can be studied through a RFM approach, which studies the Recency, frequency and monetary factors made by a customer. Aptly, the answers for the questions – How long has it been since the customer's most recent purchase?; How often has he / she has done a purchase in some specified time period? and finally how much does the customer spent for purchasing over the period.

Consider a retail outlet wants to segment its customer base based on the RFM factors, must feed the customers' RFM details as a data cube format and the cube can be divided into quintiles. The customers who fall in the top quintile may be given a value of **8**, the next lower level of people accordingly the least values. Customers who fall into the same RFM cell are said to be in the same bucket and the the marketing strategy to them can be given equally and those with high RFM value must be given top most priority for loyalty programmes, special offers and discount etc.,

## CUSTOMER RETENTION APPROACHES

### Churn

The transition or migration of customers from one product or a service provider to another product or a service provider either voluntarily or forced means is said to be the churn. This is crucial in case of domains such as telecom industry, financial service sectors etc.

### Churn Prediction

Today's service sectors as telecom, BFSI (banking, financial services and insurance) are being challenged not only by the competitors but also by volatility and change. Managing and responding quickly to challenges as convergence, deregulation, mergers and acquisitions, impact of technology, high customer attrition towards the other products viz., the churn rate, increasing pressures on band-

*Figure 8. Online application tool for a market basket analysis*

**TOP 20 Product Affinities**

| If Purchase Included | Then Purchase Included | Association % | of Baskets | Basket Count |
|---|---|---|---|---|
| 1 Coffee Tables | Chairs | 90.25% | 0.033% | 692 |
| 2 Chairs | Coffee Tables | 89.92% | 0.033% | 692 |
| 3 Compact Stereos | Blu-ray Disc Players | 87.55% | 0.025% | 528 |
| 4 Bracelets | Brooches & Pins | 87.22% | 0.024% | 501 |
| 5 Compact Stereos | DLP HDTVs | 87.19% | 0.048% | 1010 |
| 6 Brooches & Pins | Bracelets | 86.99% | 0.024% | 501 |
| 7 Blu-ray Disc Players | Compact Stereos | 86.91% | 0.025% | 528 |
| 8 DLP HDTVs | Compact Stereos | 86.82% | 0.048% | 1010 |
| 9 Bedspreads & Coverlets | Blankets & Throws | 85.61% | 0.021% | 437 |
| 10 Bedspreads & Coverlets | Decorative Pillows | 85.48% | 0.021% | 445 |
| 11 Blankets & Throws | Bedspreads & Coverlets | 85.45% | 0.021% | 437 |
| 12 Decorative Pillows | Bedspreads & Coverlets | 85.34% | 0.021% | 445 |
| 13 Body Jewelry | Bracelets | 81.86% | 0.045% | 950 |
| 14 Bracelets | Body Jewelry | 81.46% | 0.045% | 950 |

width, soaring costs, shrinking revenues because of the offers and privileges provided by the competitors is critical to business success. Also from the customers' side, the manifold increase in the dumping of customer data. This also adds the complexity to the customer relationship management.

In other words, churn is said to be a core CRM issue which may include:

a. Customer acquisition
b. Customer retention
c. Cross-sell / Up sell
d. Maximising the life time value (LTV) of customer

For analyzing a churn, a proper churn management application (CMA) is necessary. The construction of a CMA includes the following steps.

i.    **Collection of inventory data**: The data may include the customer details such as the name, age, gender, occupation and the details about their utilization history say for example, the scheme which the customer is utilizing, activation and renewal date etc., and details about the billing system, i.e., about the credit balance etc.,

ii.   **Building a churn model**: As churn is an ongoing business problem, building the models is not a onetime event, such as building a response model for a single marketing campaign. For any churn modeling, it is a good idea to experiment to determine which model provides a good fit to the data and to the business needs. Techniques such as decision trees and neural networks are apt for a churn model. However, decision trees are considered to be the best modeling theme as neural networks is slightly a complicated technique and it doesn't expose all the hidden factors of a customer.

iii.  **Scoring of the churn pattern**: This is the final set of rule in any churn estimation, where the previous period or month data can be considered as a model set input and taking latency into account a month i.e., skipping a month for estimating the score set input can be done.

Once the telecom subscribers can be identified either by churn trend analysis i.e., for sales analysis or customer churn profiling or chustomer segmentation, a suitable marketing or advertising campaign measures could be adopted accordingly without spending hefty amounts. Hence, the real customer relationship management starts with true **customer intelligence** i.e., understanding the potential of every customer. Thus the application

*Figure 9. RFM cells for different levels of customers*

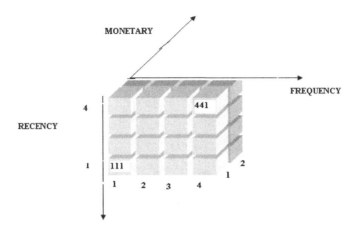

of BI in relevance to CRM enables to answer the enigmas such as, which customers are wasting the concern's time and marketing rupees?, which customers are prime for a cross-sell opportunity? And which ones can the concern bank on for profit-making potential?

Normally, churn is well predicted using the CART (Classification and Regression Trees) method developed by the Lightbridge, Inc.

## APPRAISAL OF ECRM TOOLS

### CRM Products and Services

Generally, vendors may supply CRM products in different categories as Customer service systems, Sales force automation systems, Call center systems, Billing systems, technology –based and enterprise wide CRM systems as Siebel, Oracle etc.

There are many commercial packages such as the SAS, PASW Modeler (Clementine) from SPSS, Cognos 4Thought, Cognos Scenario, Hyperion, DataMind (DataMind), Darwin (Oracle), Database Mining Workstation (HNC), Decision Series (NeoVista) and Intelligent Miner(IBM) find its applications in various datamining applications.

Some tools are being integrated with a separate CRM packages. Even some of the advanced versions are being integrated with ERP packages. The operating concept of such BI packages are based on the predictive analysis.

Among them, SAS (Statistical Analysis Systems) from the SAS Institute Inc., Cary, NC, USA was found to be a successful tool as it has its own SAS Enterprise Miner (EM) which streamlines the entire datamining process from data access to model deployment by supporting all necessary tasks within a single, integrated solution.

### SAS – Statistical Analysis Systems

SAS Institute, Cary, NC, USA (www.sas.com) is the largest of the software providers that provide a full range of the state-of-the-art statistical tools. SAS delivers a wide range of products such as SAS – enterprise guide, Enterprise Miner, Marketing Optimisation, SAS/STAT, SAS/Visual Data Discovery. SAS can be supported by a display manager as the main screen menu, the explorer or results window, a program editor to run the programmes and a log window for diagnosing the problems. Any data can be imported in to the SAS system through the SAS library. SAS provides a wide range of customer intelligence

*Figure 10. Graph model showing the churn pattern*

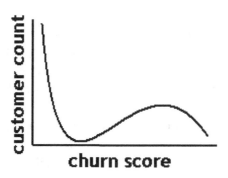

facilities as campaign management, email marketing, marketing mix analysis and marketing optimization etc.

## SAS Enterprise Miner (EM)

EM has been developed by the SAS Institute. It works on the principle of Sample, Explore, Modify, Model and Assess (SEMMA) methodology for a proper datamining system which supports different datamining models such as association, clustering, decision trees, neural networks and regression. Normally this SAS EM runs in a client-server model or as a stand-alone mode.SAS EM offers a GUI interface that enables an easy manipulation of data mining functionality.

## PASW Modeler Software

This data mining tool was developed by SPSS and erstwhile known as the Clementine . SPSS is a leading supplier of statistical tools. It launched its latest SPSS- Statistics 12. It enables arich source of data-access options and relational databases via ODBC(open database connectivity). The functionaries involves data access, manipulation and preprocessing etc.

## Oracle – Siebel CRM

Oracle's Siebel Customer Relationship Management (CRM) enables organizations to nourish their customer relationship managment by providing solutions in different modules as *Comprehensive*

*Table 2. A comparative analysis of different CRM products*

| CRM FUNCTIONARIES | VENDORS | USAGE PURPOSE |
|---|---|---|
| General Customer Service | Epiphany, BroadVision, Egain, ServiceSoft, Primus. | Increase cross-selling revenue and to decrease cost of sales Improve customer service |
| Sales Force Automation(SFA) | Goldmine, Saratoga, SalesLogix Firepond. | Increase the sales by mass customization . |
| Call Centers | Vantive, PeopleSoft, Onyx, Remedy | Decrease cost of customer retention. |
| Technology-enabled Lead generation | Broadbase, XChange | Based on the state-of-the-art technology . |
| Billing or customer service Integration | People Soft, MySAP, Oracle, | Increase the efficiency and effectiveness of customer service process. |
| Enterprise wide CRM | Siebel, Oracle | Enables the customers to go for modular selectivity. |

*CRM* which caters the needs of Strategic sales, service, call center, marketing, customer order management and customer mastering capabilities, *Industry –specific modules, On demand CRM* through which the CRM applications that are easily consumed by business users and *Pre-built integrations* which coordinates the business processes, business rules and the decision support systems.

## Cloud Computing in eCRM

*"Nearly 90& of the organisations expect to maintain or grow use of Saas in 2009 "* – says the Gartner Inc., user survey analysis, 2008.

The *Cloud* is a term which found its place in the history of telephony and internet based services and large ATM networks. As customers generally don't want to own and maintain a infrastructure for computing, they merely access or rent on ad hoc basis, so as to avoid capital expenditure and consume resources as a service.

*Cloud computing* is purely based upon the services delivered through the data centers and built on servers with different levels of virtualization technologies. These services are accessible from any node at any time . Hence the Cloud appears as a single point of access for all the computing needs of consumers.

Cloud computing is a paradigm that is interlinked by several strata of services as infrastructure, storage, platform and software as a service (SaaS). Different cloud providers have developed various access models to these services. The access to these services is based on internet protocols as HTTP, SOAP, REST, XML and the infrastructure is based on widely-used technologies as virtualisation etc.,

Some of the eCRM tools based on cloud computing are Sales Force CRM, Amazon S3 and Zoho CRM.

## Sales Force CRM

Salesforce CRM is a typical example that operates on the concept of Cloud computing. Salesforce.com was established by Marc Benioff and Parker Harris, The developed the CRM application suite on basis of "On demand" and "**SaaS**" (Software-as-a-Service) with their real business and successful customers. The key for SaaS is being customizable by customer alone or with a small amount of help. They provided the service as a **PaaS** *i.e.,* Platform as a Service

## SAGA OF SAS IN ECRM

## Role of Sas in Matching Quality Job Applicants

Monster Canada (www.monster.ca) is the Canada's leading career management portal which spread its tentacles even in India as www.monsterindia.com . It sells a variety of products and services to companies hiring the prospective employees, where the screening process includes the basic access to posted job openings, advanced screening, online resume mining services and career site hosting etc., The concern wanted to understand its clients better so it could offer the right mix of services, and it needed a better way to extract and organize its customer data, run its performance dashboards efficiently, analyze and segment its customers and job seekers, thereby providing fruitful results to its clients. SAS as a part of its customer intelligence done a RFM (recency, frequency and monetary value) segmentation of Monster's portal customer base, there by increase the customer retention and enhance the marketing efficiency.

*Figure 11. A screenshot of SAS – Enterprise Miner. Created with SAS(R) software. Copyright 2009, SAS Institute. All Rights Reserved, ©Inc, Cary, NC, USA. Reproduced with permission of SAS Institute Inc. Cary, NC.*

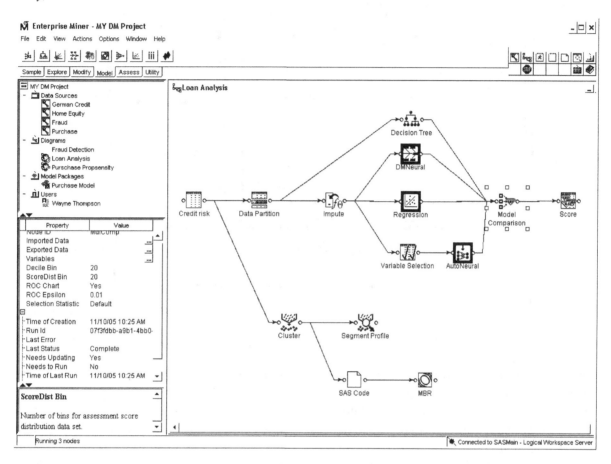

## SAS for a CRM in Harrah's Entertainment

Harrah's Entertainment, the world's largest gaming company has chosen to invest heavily in customer relationship management technologies. As a part of it, they included SAS for predictive analysis and business intelligence. Their prime emphasis was towards the relationship marketing which could be done by business intelligence derived from the profiling of the customers with highest potential to return.

## THRUST AREAS FOR FUTURE ENHANCEMENTS OF BI

Any organisation which is going to be or currently implementing BI has several questions such as – How can a BI assist a decision making on-the-fly? Can BI respond to an external event such as the swipe of a credit card or the arrival of a telephone call? Normally, when a concern customize their environment for a BI, it help employees for a on-the-spot decisions, more informed decisions.

In this scenario, the business process or operational application will need to "call out" to the BI infrastructure for help. This call will trigger the

*Figure 12. A screenshot of datamining software Clementine (PASW Modeler) from SPSS*

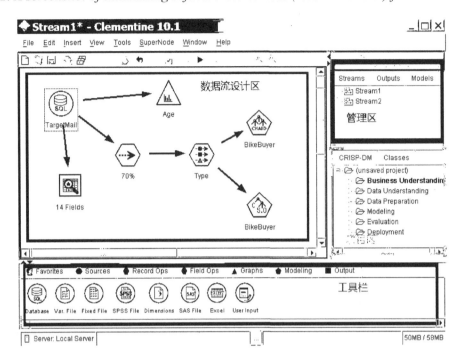

scoring or recommendation engine to execute very quickly and return a result in the form of a mere suggestion.. Say for instance, the result could be go / no go decision for a potentially fraudulent transaction, or it could be a "next offer" suggestion based on a customer rating. Under these circumstances, prescoring techniques are commonly used, but prebuilt models do not respond dynamically to changes in the customer situation

because the scores typically get calculated some time before the previous push cycle.

The steps of classic BI are still necessary to build the real-time models based on historical data. The first step to improving classic BI is to add steps for data quality, as traditional BI is based on data that exists in the databases of operational applications and not on real-time access and such data often voids in quality and modularity for

*Table 3. showing the comparison of prominent datamining tools providing eCRM facility based on the supporting algorithms*

| Algorithm Tool | Decision Tree | Nearest Neighbor | Bayes | Rule Induction | Association Rule for Market Basket analysis | Correlation |
|---|---|---|---|---|---|---|
| Clementine | √ | -- | -- | √ | √ | √ |
| Darwin | √ | √ | -- | -- | -- | -- |
| Enterprise Miner | √ | -- | -- | -- | √ | √ |
| Intelligent Miner | √ | -- | -- | -- | √ | -- |

the pursuit of analysis and requires a hectic task by usage of DML (data modification language) or manipulation of data.

According to the IDC, the premier global market intelligent firm's research (www.idc.com), the BI market moves in 15-year cycles. The first phase was from 1975-1990, which was characterized by production reposting on mainframes and some statistical software. The second phase was during 1990-2005 which was considered to be the "modern era" of BI which was enhanced by the client/server-based BI tools and later on by query, reporting and OLAP technology and web-based architecture. In hindsight, 2005 was viewed as another turning point in the BI market – where the spearheading of BI in all organizations where the focus would be on expanding the research of BI to users inside and outside the concern, as well as moving BI from its traditional focus on reporting to decision-centric process.

The conventional BI market has focused primarily on the analysts or the power users who represent only a small subset of any concern. Hence the usage of BI tools as complex report development, OLAP and advanced analytics solutions are not at all conducive for the decision makers. To rule out this hiccup, BI solutions need to become more broadly accessible to all range of users through enhance data visualization techniques, better GUI, enriched data and text mining methodologies. So the general thrust in this BI solution approach is to metamorphose the stand-alone BI software interface into something resembling an online media site, such as My Yahoo!

Another parallel approach is to infuse more BI into operational applications, where the concept termed as intelligent process automation (IPA) which is the convergence of BI tools and business process automation (BPA) deployment software was applied. IPA software automates repeatable, operational decisions within business process sets in response to events where analytics drive the workflow. As of now, no single, prepackaged

IPA software solution is available. Besides this, the other thrust area is the development is the move from information delivery (reporting) to collaborative, decision – centric BI (DCBI) .

Future enhancements may be focused an end-user enabled BI, simply termed as the version BI 2.0, which deals with the real time data on a Multi Source Simple Objects (MSSO) technology.

## CONCLUSION

The chapter clearly evinces that Information Technology plays a pivot role in CRM, but "getting closer to customer isn't only about an information technology system" (Gulati and Oldroyd, 2005, p. 101). And needless to say that eCRM goes beyond the web and implementing such infrastructure is a strategic investment. Many key players for CRM software such as Oracle, SAP, Siebel, SAS and PeopleSoft enhance their latest package versions with developed modules are vying to find a niche in the corporate market. On the other side, these application suites, either it is a product of in-house R&D or through off-the-shelf, primarily focuses on a stereotypic system. Hence the successful implementations of a CRM implementation generally require an incremental approach, yet with great attention paid to the data infrastructure and to the organizational change processes (Goodhue et al., 2002).

Even implementation of a datamining system for a business intelligence approach in a corporate is largely driven by huge investments and state-of-the-art tools, it has filed to cope up with the business managers' expectations. The reasons may be due to i)The architectures are quite cumbersome to build and are inflexible to change as business processes or needs change ii) the analytical applications are expensive to change and to maintain and also if change roll-back to the previous state is impossible and iii) the lack of technical knowledge and persons to work with and the success of implementating a eCRM concept purely doesn't depeneds on the ROI (Return on Investment) but only on the magnitude of the customer relationship maintained.

Business intelligence has witnessed its peak usage in the customer relationship management and organisational play because of its cost effectiveness and user friendliness and needless to say, its demand curve will grow in uptrend in near future.

However, when considering the bottlenecks in the implementations, 80% of concerns are unaware of BI and some of them opined that customization is a tough criteria.

To cater the needs of different sectors, the future BI systems must be real-time/near-real-time, proactive and pervasive. It is a supportive news that that Microsoft may incorporate some of BI capabilities into their next generation of office software, Office 12. Service-oriented architecture and open-source architectures will also help reduce the total ownership cost of a BI system. To quote some of the open source BI vendors, JasperSoft and Pentaho are already foraying in advertising promising products.

Also it has been inferred that a majority of BI packages were implemented only on a needy basis and at a departmental level and not at the strategic level .Definitely, there must be a wait-and-watch approach for the corporates to customize a proper BI application and to be used in a phased and successful manner.

# REFERENCES

Agrawal, R., Imielinski, T., & Swami, A. (1993). Mining associations between sets of items in massive databases. In *Proceedings of the ACM SIGMOID International Conference on Management of Data*, Washington D.C., (pp. 207-216).

Berson, A. smith, S. & Thearling, K. (2000). Building Data Mining Applications for CRM. New Dehli, India: Tata McGraw Hill.

Cho, Y., Im, I., Fjermestad, J., & Hiltz, R. (2002). An analysis of online customer complaints: Implications for Web complaint management. In *Proceedings of the 35ᵗʰ Hawaii International Conference on System Sciences*, Big Island, Hawaii.

Fayyad, U. M., Piatetsky-Shapiro, G., Smyth, P., & Uthurusamy, R. (1966). *Advances in Knowledge Discovery and Data mining*. Cambridge, UK: AAAI/MIT Press.

Fjermestad, J., & Romano, N. C. Jr. (2006). *Electronic Customer Relationship Management (Advances in Management Information Systems)*. New Dehli, India: Prentice-Hall.

Goodhue, D. L., Wixom, B. H., & Watson, H. J. (2002). Realizing business benefits through CRM: Hitting the right target the right way. *MIS Quarterly Executive, 1*(2), 79–94.

Gulati, R., & Oldroyd, J. (2005). The quest for customer focus. *Harvard Business Review, 83*(4), 92–101.

Inmon, W. H. (1996). *Building the Data Warehouse*. New York: John Wiley and Sons.

Keen, P. W., Ballance, C., Chan, S., & Schrump, S. (2000). *Electronic Commerce relationships: Trust by Design*. Upper Saddle River, NJ: Prentice Hall.

Lu, J. (n.d.). *Predicting Customer churn in the Telecommunications industry – An application of survival Analysis Modeling using SAS*. Overland Park, KS . *Sprint Communication*.

(2005)... *Marketing Intelligence & Planning, 18*, 19–23.

Michael, J. Berry, A. & Linoff, G. (2000). Mastering Data Mining- The Art and Science of Customer Relationship Management. India: Wiley Computer Publishing.

Osterle, H., Fleisch, E., & Alt, R. (2001). *Business Networking: Shaping Collaboration Between Enterprises* (pp. 7–54). Berlin: Springer.

Senger, E., Gronover, S., & Riempp, G. (2002). Customer Web interaction: Fundamentals and decision tree. In *Proceedings of the Eighth Americas Conference on Information Systems (AMCIS)*, (pp. 1966-76). Dallas: AmCIS. *SPSS for Windows, Rel. 15.0.0*. (2006). Chicago: SPSS Inc.

van der Putten, P. (1999). *Sentient Machine Research*. CMG Academy.

Venkatesan, R., & Kumar, V. (2004). A customer lifetime value framework for customer selection and resource allocations strategy. *Journal of Marketing*, 68(4), 106–125. doi:10.1509/jmkg.68.4.106.42728

Witten, I. H. & Eibe, F. (1999). *Data Mining: Practical Machine Learning Tools and Techniques with Java Implementations*.

Zineldin, M. (2000). Beyond relationship marketing: Technologicalship marketing.

140

# Chapter 10
# Towards a Model-Centric Approach for Developing Enterprise Information Systems

**Petraq Papajorgji**
*Center for Applied Optimization, University of Florida, USA*

**Panos M. Pardalos**
*Center for Applied Optimization, University of Florida, USA*

## ABSTRACT

*This chapter aims to present a new modeling paradigm that promises to significantly increase the efficiency of developing enterprise information systems. Currently, the software industry faces considerable challenges as it tries to build larger, more complex, software systems with fewer resources. Although modern programming languages such as C++ and Java have in general improved the software development process, they have failed to significantly increase developer's productivity. Thus, developers are considering other paths to address this issue. One of the potential paths is designing, developing and deploying enterprise information systems using the Model Driven Architecture (MDA). MDA is a model-centric approach that allows for modeling the overall business of an enterprise and capturing requirements to developing, deploying, integrating, and managing different kinds of software components without considering any particular implementation technology. At the center of this approach are models; the software development process is driven by constructing models representing the software under development. Code that expresses the implementation of the model in a certain underlying technology is obtained as a result of model transformation. Thus, the intellectual investment spent in developing the business model of an enterprise is not jeopardized by the continuous changes of the implementation technologies. Currently there are two main approaches trying to implement MDA-based tools. One of the approaches is based on the Object Constraint Language and the other on Action Language. An example of designing, developing and deploying an application using this new modeling paradigm is presented. The MDA approach to software development is considered as the biggest shift since the move from Assembler to the first high level languages.*

DOI: 10.4018/978-1-61520-625-4.ch010

Copyright © 2010, IGI Global. Copying or distributing in print or electronic forms without written permission of IGI Global is prohibited.

## INTRODUCTION

Business environment is very dynamic. On the one hand mergers and acquisitions impose changes in the business model and therefore changes in the information system. On the other hand, the introduction of new technologies forces constant change in the business environment. In this case the same business model has to be rewritten using a new implementation technology. In order to survive, businesses must have the ability to thrive in a continuously changing and difficult to predict environment. Therefore, it is important to know what aspects of the business are more likely to change and what are not when dealing with constant change.

An important part of the efforts in developing a new information system are spent in mastering the technological complexity of the solution (a particular implementation technology such as Java or .NET or other technology) rather than focusing on understanding the problem to be solved (Pastor & Juan Carlos Molina, 2007). Experience shows that most of the time it is the implementation technology that changes rather than the business model. Therefore, it is desirable to have a software engineering approach that separates the business knowledge from the implementation technology so they can continue to develop without necessitating a complete rework of existing systems (Papajorgji, Clark & Jallas, 2009; Pastor & Juan Carlos Molina, 2007).

The Model Driven Architecture (MDA) is a framework for software development defined by the Object Management Group (OMG) (Object management group [OMG], 2009; OMG Model driven architecture: How systems will be built). The OMG defines MDA as "*Fully-specified platform independent models can enable intellectual property to move away from technology-specific code, helping to insulate business applications from technology evolution and further enable interoperability*" (OMG Model driven architecture: How systems will be built). As presented by OMG,

models should be provided with behavior to be able to be executed and therefore tested. At the center of this approach are models; the software development process is driven by constructing models representing the software under development (Papajorgji, Clark & Jallas; Pastor & Juan Carlos Molina, 2007). Code that expresses the implementation of the model in a certain underlying technology is obtained as a result of model transformation.

The MDA approach is often referred to as a model-centric approach as it focuses on the business logic rather than on implementation technicalities of the system in a particular programming environment (MDA Guide V1.0.1, 2009). Thus, the focus of OMG is to take advantage of new technologies and make the application development process independent of the infrastructures they use. Once the model is constructed, it can be transformed into code in several languages (Pastor & Juan Carlos Molina, 2007). The MDA approach to software development is considered as the biggest shift since the move from Assembler to the first high level languages.

An information system is regarded in MDA from three different perspectives: computation independent, platform independent and a platform specific. The computation independent perspective focuses on expressing the business model (business processes, stakeholders, departments and the relationships amongst them) without any consideration about the information system that will be used during the implementation phase. Efforts to represent the business model independently of the computing platform are referred to as Computational Independent Model (CIM) (Gasevic, Djuric & Devedzic, 2006; Kleppe, Warmer & Blast, 2003; Object Management Group, 2009). A CIM represents a high level model that describes the relationships amongst principal elements of the business model. As an example, a simple model expressing relationships between the manufacturing sector and the sales department can be considered as a CIM. Usually

CIM's are designed by analysts. Parts of a CIM may be supported by software, but in general a CIM is software independent.

The platform independent perspective focuses on the functional capabilities of a system without considering any specific platform (or set of platforms) that will be used for its implementation. Such a model is referred to as PIM (**P**latform **I**ndependent **M**odel) (Object Management Group, 2009, OMG/MDA). PIM's are constructed using UML and they express the relationships amongst concepts of the domain under study without referring to any particular computing platform (Kleppe, Warmer & Blast, 2003; Papajorgji & Shatar, 2004).

A platform specific perspective enriches a platform independent perspective with details relating to the use of a specific computing platform. In this case, details of the technology used for the implementation of the PIM will be part of the model. A model that represents details of the underlying technology is referred to as a Platform Specific Model (PSM) (Object Management Group, 2000, OMG/MDA, 2009).

Currently the MDA market is evolving. Several vendors have implemented OMG guide lines using one or the other approach such as Kennedy Carter (Kennedy Carter Inc., 2009), Oliva Nova (Pastor & Juan Carlos Molina, 2007), ANDROMDA (http://www.andromda.org/), Virtual Enterprise (http://intelliun.com) (Visual Enterprise, 2009) to name a few.

After analyzing the current state of the MDA implementation, it is reasonable to say that there are two main responses to the OMG's definition: the *elaborationist* and the *translationist* approach.

## The Elaborationist Approach

The approach, referred to as the *elaborationist* approach, is embraced by the followers of the school of Meyer (Meyer, 1988). According to the *elaborationist* view, behavior can defined using pre-conditions and post-conditions for an operation. The pre- and post-conditions are specified using the Object Constraint Language (OCL), (Warmer & Kleppe, 1999) which is a formal language for specifying assertions (formally, an "expression language"). Although Meyer's work has been well implemented in several programming languages (one of these languages is his own language Eifel (Meyer, 1992)), it is not sufficient to completely generate code from the pre- and post-conditions of an operation. Even the most ardent defenders of this approach (Kleppe, Warmer & Blast, 2003) state that total code generation may not be possible and the corresponding code has to be added manually in later phases of the implementation.

## The Object Constraint Language (OCL)

OCL was first developed in 1995 by a group of researchers at IBM Europe with the goal of creating a formal language and yet simple to be used by software engineers (Warmer & Kleppe, 1999). Currently OCL is part of the UML standards and thus available to modelers to apply constraints to objects (Kleppe, Warmer & Blast, 2003; Papajorgji, Clark & Jallas, 2009; Warmer & Kleppe, 1999). Constraints are necessary as they provide software engineers with a set of well-defined rules in order to define and control the behavior of objects. Within UML, OCL is used to specify invariants, preconditions, postconditions, and other kinds of constraint (Warmer & Kleppe, 1999). OCL extends the power of UML as it allows software engineers to create more expressive and more precise models.

OCL is purely an expression language: it does not have side effects as it does not change the status of the model (Papajorgji, Clark & Jallas, 2009, Warmer & Kleppe, 1999). OCL is not a programming language and thus, it does not allow writing code. When an expression in OCL is evaluated, it simply delivers a value.

*Figure 1. Example of constraints and preconditions*

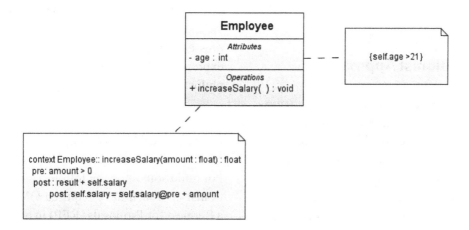

## Using OCL with UML

Initially, OCL has been used to specify constraints on objects while defining object's behavior. The behavior of an object can be expressed using preconditions and postconditions on its operations (Kleppe, Warmer & Blast, 2003; Meyer, 1988; Warmer & Kleppe, 1999). This approach was introduced and largely used by Meyer (Meyer, 1988) and it is the basis of his "Design by Contract" philosophy of software development. Only recently, has OCL been used to express other types of expressions such as specifying initial values for attributes, specifying derivation rules for attributes or associations, specifying guard conditions in state charts and etc (Kleppe, Warmer & Blast, 2003). OCL constraints are always connected to an object-oriented model be it a UML model or other type of object-oriented model. In UML, constraints can be used in different places.

## Invariants

An invariant is a constraint that can be associated to any UML modeling element. An invariant states that the result of the expression must be true for all instances of the UML modeling element any time. The context of an invariant is always a specific element of the UML model (Kleppe, Warmer & Blast, 2003) and the OCL expression expressing a certain constraint is always evaluated from the point of view of this particular context. UML provides a particular stereotype, noted <<*invariant*>> to indicate an invariant constraint. In a class diagram constraints are presented between brackets in a note as shown in Figure 1. This figure shows that the context of the constraint is *Employee*, a UML class, represented by *self*.

## PRECONDITIONS AND POSTCONDITIONS

Preconditions and postconditions are an effective way to express the semantics of operations and methods (Warmer & Kleppe, 1999). A precondition is a constraint that must be true at the start of the execution of the operation and a postcondition is a constraint that must be true at the end of the execution of the operation. UML provides the stereotypes <<*precondition*>> and <<*postcondition*>> for expressing these kinds of constraints. In a class diagram though, preconditions and postconditions can be presented using notes similarly as in the case of invariant as shown in Figure 1. The precondition in Figure 1 shows that the amount must be non negative and the postconditions shows that the salary after the increase is equal to the salary before plus the amount.

## The Translationist Approach

The second approach, referred to as the ***translationist*** approach, embraces the early efforts of Mellor's state machine for describing behavior (Mellor & Balcer, 2002). According to this approach, only a PIM is needed to represent the conceptual model and it is translated directly to code (McNeile & Simons, 2003). This second approach has mostly been used in the embedded system world, but lately has positioned itself as a viable approach to MDA under the name of "Executable UML". Executable UML combines an abstract program model with a platform-specific model compiler that outputs an executable application. Grady Booch in his talk *The Limits of Software* states:

*Today, we're at the beginning stages of the next level. Executable UML is the next logical, and perhaps inevitable, evolutionary step in the ever-rising level of abstraction at which programmers express software solutions. Rather than elaborate an analysis product into a design product and then write code, application developers of the future will use tools to translate abstract application constructs into executable entities. Someday soon, the idea of writing an application in Java or C++ will seem as absurd as writing an application in assembler does today. And the code generated from an Executable UML model will be as uninteresting and typically unexamined as the assembler pass of a third generation language compile is today.*

Recently, under the same umbrella of the ***translationist*** approach, it has appeared another slightly different method referred to as the ***event based*** approach. This approach considers ***events*** as the focus of the modeling effort (McNeile &

Simons, 2003; McNeile & Simons, 2004). In general, the ***translationist*** approach is based on the idea that the behavior of an object can be expressed using state machines. The main tool for expressing object's behavior in the translationist philosophy is the *Action Language*.

## ACTION LANGUAGE

For quite sometime the followers of the translationist approach have required OMG to launch a Request for Proposals (RFP) in order to define the standards for a language that is UML compatible, executable and complete, implementation independent at a level of abstraction above any implementation technology. In 2001 OMG adopted the Precise Action Semantics for the Unified Modeling Language specification. The standard was the result of a collaborative work of a large industry consortium comprising some of the best-known companies in the field of software engineering such as Rational Software (http://ibm.com), Kabira Technologies (http://www.kabira.com/), Mentor Graphics (http://www.mentor.com/), Kennedy-Carter (http://kc.com), Oliva Nova (http://www.care-t.com) and others.

The *Precise Action Semantics for the UML* standard provides a well-defined and an unambiguous semantic set of the operations needed to specify object's behavior in a UML model. The level of detail is such that a translation engine (or compiler) can completely generate an executable application from that model. The semantic set includes operations that support the so-called CRUD (create, read, write, delete) manipulation of objects, the generation and handling of asynchronous events (signals), and all the logical constructs to support the definition and the specification of algorithms. The modeler defines the behavior of objects using a text-based *action language*. The main characteristics of this language are:

*Figure 2. Producing code from a PIM model through transformations*

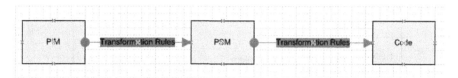

- The action language allows modelers to define behavioral specification at a higher level of abstraction.
- The language is independent of any specific implementation technology in the execution environment.

In order to illustrate the idea of defining object's behavior using the *Action Language* let us refer to an MDA tool named Virtual Enterprise (Visual Enterprise, 2009) that is used to develop the application presented in section **MDA and Application Development**. The model allows for searching for a job description using the following expression in *Action Language*:

```
Dialog.readln(first(TheJobBoard.
jobDescriptions[code == $code]))
```
As presented in the expression, *TheJobBoard.jobDescriptions* returns a collection of job descriptions present in the system. *first(TheJobBoard.jobDescriptions[code == $code])* returns the first job description whose code is equal to the value of the input parameter *$code*. The execution of the entire expression will display job descriptions details satisfying the criterion.
The following expression will display the item of a certain number selected from the collection of items related to an order; *$itemNumber* is the entry

parameter. In this example the association between **Order** and **Item** is **one to many**.
```
AllOrders.select ([:order | or-
der.items.detect([:item | item.
itemNumber == $itemNumber])
!=null ])
```

The final product of the MDA approach is generating code to be executed in a defined platform. How is code generated from models? This is the subject of the next section.

## MDA Transformations

The central idea in the MDA approach is to start first by developing a PIM. The PIM must represent the main concepts of the domain under the study and their relationships. The PIM may also include some general rules for model transformation. Note that the same PIM could be transformed in different PSM based on the specific computing platform. As an example, the same PIM could be transformed into an EJB (Enterprise Java Beans) or into a relational-based (SQL-based) platform. In this case the rules guiding the transformation process are different. Transformations in the MDA approach are presented in Figure 2.

The transformation rules are a set of unambiguous specifications that will guide the transformation process with the goal of obtaining a target model. The target model could be another model (presented in UML) or code in a specific programming language (Kleppe, Warmer & Blast, 2003; Sewal, 2003).

*Figure 3. Classes related with an association*

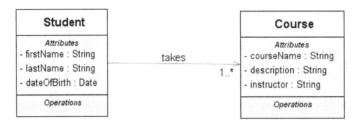

## PIM to Java transformation

Let us consider a simple example to illustrate this transformation process. Figure 3 shows a simple UML model with two classes related with an association and our goal is to describe the transformation of this simple model into code in Java. The model shows that classes *Student* and *Course* are linked with an association named *takes*, which models the fact that a student takes courses. Note that the association *takes* is one to one or many. Class *Student* contains three attributes: *firstName, lastName* and dateOfBirth and class *Course* contains attributes *courseName, description*, and *instructor.*

A UML class will be transformed into a Java class, thus classes in the model presented in Figure 2 will be transformed into Java code as presented in Figure 4. The transformation rules are:

- A UML class will be transformed into a Java class,
- An attribute in the UML model will be transformed into a private attribute in Java,
- For each attribute in the UML class two public methods (a get and a set method) are generated in the corresponding Java class.
- For each association end there is a private attribute of the same name in the opposite class of type equal to the type of the class in the case when the association is *one to one*. In the event the association is of type *one to many*, as it is our case, then the type of the private attribute is *Set*. In the case the association is navigable (directed association) then the private attribute will be added only to the class origin of the association (in our example, class *Student*).

*Figure 4. PIM to Java transformation*

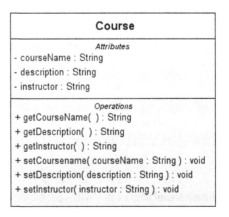

*Figure 5. PIM to relational transformation*

Note that the principle of encapsulation is respected during the transformation process; values of attributes are accessed only by the object itself. Therefore, both classes *Student* and *Course* attributes are declared private and the corresponding *get* and *set* methods are defined. In a similar way are defined the rules of transformation for obtaining a relational model from a PIM model expressed in UML.

## PIM to Relational Transformation

Let us consider the same model presented in Figure 4 and transform this PIM into a relational model. Before presenting the transformation of the model, let us introduce some rules that guide the transformation of attributes defined in classes *Student* and *Course*. Some of these rules are defined as follows (Kleppe, Warmer & Blast, 2003):

- A UML string will mapped onto a SQL VARCHAR.
- A UML integer will be mapped onto a SQL INTEGER.
- A UML date will be mapped onto a SQL DATE.

A class in UML will be transformed onto a table in the relational model. Thus, classes *Student* and *Course* will be transformed onto two tables named *student* and *course* as shown in Figure 5. Attributes of each class are transformed using the above-mentioned rules.

Associations in UML are transformed into foreign keys in the Entity-Relationship (ER) model.

The relationship *takes* of Figure 4 is transformed onto relationship *takes* as shown in Figure 5. Note that the association *takes* in Figure 5 is necessary only to visually show that tables *student* and *course* are linked using the foreign key *studentId*. It is important to note that non foreign keys attributes may contain the NULL value whereas attributes that are foreign keys, such as *studentId*, may not contain NULL values. This observation will be clear if the Entity-Relationship (ER) model obtained by the transformation process is viewed with an ER tool.

## MDA and Application Development

### Objects, Associations and Code Generation

Let us consider a simple example to demonstrate the power of this approach. Figure 6 shows a simple model where the relationship between the objects *Client* and *Address* is modeled as a simple one-to-one association.

The model execution causes the system to automatically generate the web page as shown in Figure 7. Note that there are two input fields for both attributes of object *Client* and a hyperlink named *Address*, that when used, it will display another page prompting to enter data for attributes of object *Address*. As it is shown in Figure 7, the life-cycle of objects *Client* and *Address* are completely independent: Instances of objects *Client* and *Address* can be created, modified and deleted independently.

*Figure 6. Client-address relationship modeled as a simple association*

*Figure 7. Web form representing the simple association*

Figure 8 shows the relationship between *Client* and *Address* modeled as a composition. A composition is a strong relationship where the whole *owns* the part (Booch, Rumbaugh & Jacobson, 1999; Papajorgji & Pardalos, 2006). The model execution will automatically generate the web form shown in Figure 9. In this case, data entry for objects *Client* and *Address* are presented in the same web form; data entry fields for the object *Address* (the part) are presented in a tab in the form where data entry fields for object *Client* are presented. When the form is submitted, the submitted data are used to populate objects *Client* and *Address* at the same time. The lifecycle of both objects are synchronized, they are created and deleted at the same time. Note that object *Client* (the whole) is responsible for creation, maintenance and destruction of object *Address*

(the part) (Booch, Rumbaugh & Jacobson, 1999; Papajorgji & Pardalos, 2006).

The above example shows the relevance of understanding the relationships amongst concepts in the domain under study; different models generate different views.

## Example of Application Development

In order to show issues that need to be addressed during the design and the implementation of a system using the MDA approach, let us consider as an example, the system managing job offers and job applications presented in (Visual Enterprise, 2009). The system should allow applicants to browse job offers, apply for a job, browse his/her application status, and so on. The system should provide the human resources with the capability

*Figure 8. Client- Address relationship modeled as a composition*

*Figure 9. Web form representing the composition association*

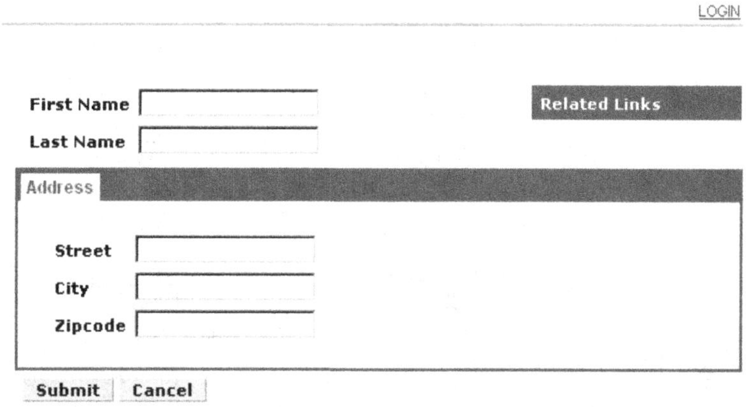

to update different job categories, job descriptions, to post openings, to view submitted applications, and other necessary functionalities for managing well the system. Three packages are created; each holding a well-determined part of the application is shown in Figure 10. Thus, package applicant contains classes and relationships among them for all objects necessary to cover functionalities dealing with applicants. These functionalities allow applicants to browse for jobs, apply for a job, and so on.

Each package contains a UML model representing only a subset of the entire model. The main reason for separating the entire domain in packages is that it helps reuse particular components of the system. Figure 11 shows classes with their attributes, methods and relationships of the core

*Figure 10. Packages representing parts of the application domain*

*applicants* package. The model shows that a job board contains many job openings; many applicants may apply for a job opening and an applicant may apply for many job openings. The job board contains information for many applicants.

Figure 12 shows classes with their attributes, methods and relationships necessary to model an applicant. An applicant has a profile expressing the work history of the applicant, his/her education and technical skills.

The UML model shown in Figure 13 shows classes with their attributes, methods and relationships contained in the package *jobs*. The black dot denotes the root object of the system; it serves as the starting point for navigating the system. Object *JobBoard* is linked to object *JobOpening* using the association *jobOpenings* of cardinality *0 to many*. Thus, *TheJobBoard.jobOpenings* provides a collection of all job openings in the system. In the event a particular posted job opening is needed it can be identified using the following instruction:

TheJobBoard.jobCategorie.select ([: j | j.status == "Posted" && j.jobDescription.jobCategory. >name == name])

The MDA-based tool used (Visual Enterprise, 2009) has an interesting feature that links the

*Figure 11. Classes, attributes and relationships for the job package*

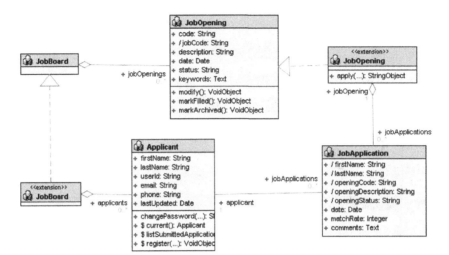

value of an attribute to a set of potential values. As shown in Figure 13, attribute *category* of class *JobDescription* is prefixed by the sign "/". This sign shows that the value of attribute *category* can be selected from a list of all instances of class *JobCategory* already created in the system. Figure 14 shows the formula for calculating the value of attribute *category* of class *JobCategory* using the association *jobCategory*. The list of potential values of job categories is created by constraining

the domain of association *jobCategory* to contain only the job categories created in the system. Thus, the values for this domain are defined by *TheJob-Board.jobCategories* that returns a collection of job categories created in the system.

Use cases are implemented as **processes**. Figure 15 show how processes can be ensemble to create a navigation model that will allow users to launch different functionalities provided by the system.

*Figure 12. The applicant model*

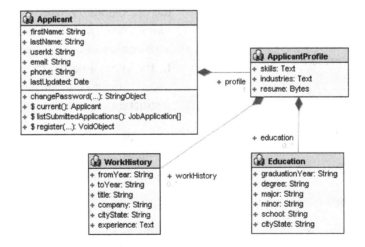

*Figure 13. UML model for the job package*

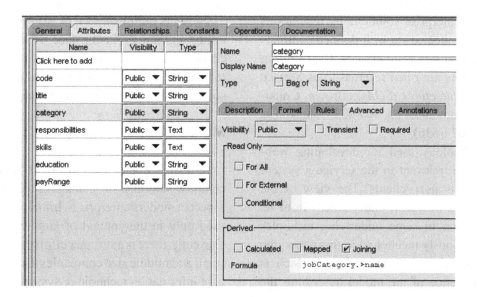

## Persistence in the MDA Approach

One of the advantages of using the MDA approach for developing complex enterprise systems is that the persistence of data is done automatically. As previously mentioned, MDA tools interpret the UML model and automatically generate the database schema for the corresponding model. Figure 16 shows the database schema generated by Virtual Enterprise tool (Visual Enterprise, 2009) for the UML model presented in Figures 11, 12 and 13. The user has only to define the name of

*Figure 14. Joining values of attributes*

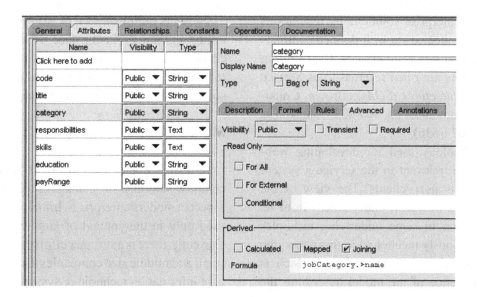

*Figure 15. The navigation model*

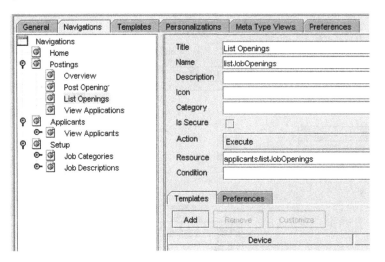

the database and some other parameters and the database and the functionalities for storing the data onto the database are generated by the MDA tool. Note that the MDA tool does not normalize the model; therefore it is the user's responsibility to design a UML model that does not require normalization.

## WEB SERVICES

A new approach that is currently gaining strong support in the software industry is based on considering enterprise solutions as federations of services connected via well-defined contracts that define their service interfaces. The resulting system designs are often referred to as *Service Oriented Architectures (SOAs)* (Brown, Conallen & Tropeano, 2005, pp. 403-432; Johnston & Brown, pp. 624-636).

The technology used for developing web-services is not relevant to the service a system provides to its users/clients. The view of the service should be totally independent from its implementation in some underlying technologies. As previously mentioned in this paper, the main characteristics of the MDA approach is the independence of the model describing the

business from its implementation in underlying technologies. Therefore, using the MDA approach to design and develop web-services will provide the same benefits; independence, flexibility and speed in software development.

MDA provides an environment to design Web services at a more abstract level than that of technology-specific implementations. The technologies implementing Web services depend on Port 80. The fact that developers of Web services program directly in these technologies makes software development vulnerable to rapid obsolescence and is also far too labor-intensive.

Systems built using MDA exhibit more flexibility and agility in the face of technological change—as well as a higher level of quality and robustness, due to the more formal and accurate specification of requirements and design.

### MDA and ERPs

Enterprise Resource Planning (ERP) systems are complex solutions for managing the multi-facet aspect of modern enterprises. Initially, ERPs were used only in the context of large corporations. Currently, there is a stronger effort to use ERPs by small and middle size companies to develop their core information technology systems (van Ever-

*Figure 16. Database schema generated from the UML model*

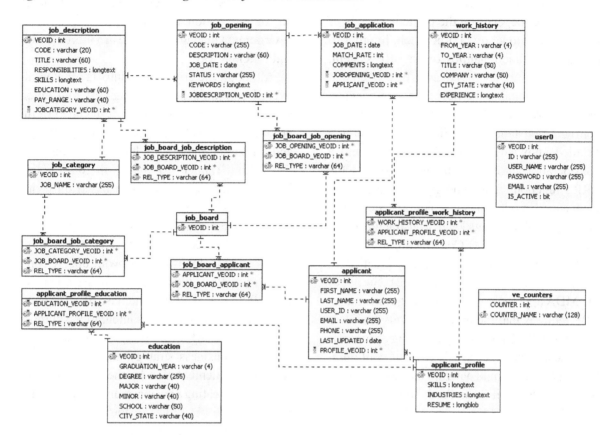

dingen Y., van Hillergersberg & Waarts, 2000). There is a wide spread opinion in the industry that ERPs can be seen as a viable alternative to custom application development for the standard management needs (Dugerdil & Gaillard, 2006). Besides numerous advantages of using ERPs as a basis for the IT needs, there are several major disadvantages that are a serious obstacle for using ERPs in a large scale by small and medium enterprises. One major issue is the inherent complexity of ERPs; often their implementation requires a large dependency on the ERP provider that most of the managers would like to avoid at any cost. Other consequence of the inherent complexity of ERPs is that most of the clients trying to implement them do not have a deep understanding of the ERP solution and therefore large amounts of money must be invested in consultancy for ERP providers.

A solution to these problems is the use of the MDA approach to configure functionalities provided by an ERP system. MDA provides enterpriser managers with a high level model, totally independent of ERP's target platform, at the level of business processes and expressed using visual tools. The UML extension proposed by (Ericsson & Penker, 2000) closely matches business modeling standards and complements the UML Business Modeling Profile published by IBM (Johnston, 2004).

One of the most relevant efforts to use the MDA approach in a context of an ERP implementation is presented by (Dugerdil & Gaillard, 2006). They have used Eriksson-Penker's UML profile (Ericsson & Penker, 2000) and implemented it using IBM's XDE modeling tool to create a business modeling environment in the context of an ERP implementation.

ERPs provide a large amount of functionalities and their use depends on the particular needs of the business model of a corporation. In order to activate the functionalities of an ERP system, some configuration tables need to be created that will make available the necessary components/modules. As previously mentioned producing configuration tables is difficult and requires a detailed knowledge of the ERP system and a considerable amount of manual labor. As the ERP's functionalities to be activated depend on the business model, then it is natural to develop a business model at a high level of abstraction using UML-based visual tools. Constructing a high level business model is also one of the best practices in ERP implementation (Thomas, 2002). The use of the MDA approach when the target system is an ERP requires that the transformations leading a PIM into a PSM, instead of generating code as it is the case in general, they will generate configuration tables that would activate the required ERP modules (Dugerdil & Gaillard, 2006).

## MODEL-DRIVEN BUSINESS INTEGRATION

Business process integration and management (BPIM) is an important element in the continuous efforts enterprises undertake to adjust and transform their business to respond to many challenges of the competition. BPIM solutions should be efficient, fast, reusable, robust and low-cost.

Initially integration solutions were focused on connecting systems. The approach used was to provide various Enterprise Application Integration (EAI) adapters that would establish an ad hoc point-to-point connection (Zhu, Tian, T., Li, Sun & al, 2004). Later, the same problem was addressed by creating a hub or a centralized integration engine hosting the integration logic. Such hubs are IBM WebSphere Business Integration (WBI), Microsoft BizTalk Server and BEA Weblogic Integrator to name a few. This solution facilitates the creation, maintenance, and changing of integration logic and provides a better environment managing change in a more flexible and efficient way.

Although the creation of hubs facilitated the overall communication among different enterprise modules, it did not address the heart of the problem: is how to design, develop, maintain, and utilize the integration hub for real business cases (Zhu, Tian, T., Li, Sun & al, 2004). Existing solutions were very much based on trying adjusting exiting IT systems to address change in enterprise business.

Currently, there is a widely-accepted opinion, (Frankel, 2003; Johnston & Brown, 2005; Kleppe, Warmer & Blast, 2003; Pastor & Juan Carlos Molina, 2007; Sewal, 2003; Thomas, 2002) to name a few, that today's business integration solutions must be elevated to the design and analysis of high-level business strategy and processes before any implementation by the IT department. Therefore, creating a business model representing the goals and objectives of the enterprise must come first and must determine the way in which IT systems can be refined or developed. An IT system that does not totally support the business model is inadequate. The creation of UML extension for business modeling (Ericsson & Penker, 2000) creates a homogenous environment where the business model and the supporting software model can be designed and developed using the same formalism. Therefore, there is hope this new environment will help eliminating discrepancies that could exist between the business model and the software model. Any change occurring in the business model will be propagated down to the IT system. We believe that the model-driven approach is the key to solving above-mentioned challenges.

### Industrial Use

MDA is making a constant progress in the software industry. Away from any hype, MDA gives

*Figure 17. Savings from using the MDA approach in industry*

| Activity | % of Savings |
|---|---|
| Business Requirements Gathering | 10% |
| Design and UML Modeling | -20% |
| Application Construction | 60% |
| Application Iterations | 70% |
| Testing | 80% |
| Documentation | 70% |
| Runtime Environment Tuning | 85% |
| Project Management | 60% |

companies a viable alternative to application development instead of corporate stagnation or offshore (Pastor & Juan Carlos Molina, 2007). Not only the number of MDA-compliant vendors is increasing over the time but most importantly, the number of companies that are using this approach for developing large scale enterprise information systems. Following are some examples of success in using the model driven architecture. A complete list of companies that have this approach successfully can be found in (Object Management Group, 2000).

Daimler-Chrysler has used the MDA approach for developing its information system. The results of this experience include (Object Management Group, 2000):

- 15% increase in development productivity in first year,
- ROI (Return Of Investment) in less than 12 months,
- Expected total productivity increase of 30% in second year compared to a non-MDA approach

Lockheed Martin Aeronautics has used the OMG's MDA to develop the F-16 Modular Mission Computer Application Software. Their goal was to achieve cross-platform compatibility and increased productivity and quality, all in the context of the demanding environment of avionics software development (Object Management Group, 2000).

Conquest, Inc., is a premier provider of advanced large-scale systems and software technology solutions to federal and commercial customers. MDA helped facilitate communication by graphically representing vast amounts of data into discrete views that could be reviewed and understood across different organizational groups and business areas. Modeling also encouraged collaboration between groups, helping them identify redundant and non-mission enhancing activities, and driving significant cost savings (Object Management Group, 2000). A more detailed study that provides reasons and advantages of using the MDA approach is presented in (Pastor & Juan Carlos Molina, 2007). Figure 17, borrowed from (Sewal, 2003), presents a convincing list of savings when using the MDA approach.

Currently, the use of the MDA approach is rather limited; there is a relatively small number of developers that master this technology at industrial level. Historically in the software industry, there is a well defined gap between developers and modelers/architects and they have very different tasks in the software development process. Modelers design the system and its architecture and developers translate models into a programming language. The use of MDA narrows the gap existing between developers and modelers and creates the need for a modeler/developer of high level. Modeling is a more abstract activity than coding and therefore, while the market is full of developers in all major technologies (Java, .NET, etc) there is great deficit in high level modelers proficient in UML and its various profiles. Training developers to become modelers is a necessity considering the important savings provided by the use of the MDA approach (Figure 17). The MDA approach offers automation of code generation that includes:

- Automatically generating complete programs from models (not just class/methods skeletons and fragments)
- Automatically verifying models at high level of abstraction (for example, by executing them)

History teaches us that automation is by far the most effective technological means for boosting productivity and reliability. It will take time and efforts for the MDA to widely be accepted and only the future will decide when the MDA will become a mainstream technology.

## CONCLUSION

This paper describes the concept and the feasibility of using MDA-based tools for designing, developing and implementing Enterprise Information Systems using the MDA approach. The center of the approach is a conceptual model that expresses concepts from the domain problem and their relationships. The conceptual model is built using UML, a standard in the software industry. The model is developed visually and the language used is simple and understandable to programmers and non-programmers alike and therefore it facilitates the dialog with stakeholders.

This modeling paradigm is specialist-centric, as it allows for a greater participation of specialist in model construction. The model is constructed conceptually, focusing on the business logic that is familiar to the specialists. Thus, the intellectual investment spent for the design of the business model is preserved as it is not affected by the changes of underlying technologies.

The conceptual model is constructed at a higher level of abstraction without considering any implementation or computing platform issues. Therefore, the model is platform independent; it can be implemented in different programming environments and computing platforms. A platform independent model can be transformed into several platform specific models that take into consideration different computing platforms.

Once the business logic of the problem is clarified and expressed in the model using a high level of abstraction, then implementation issues can be addressed. Implementation details are applied to the general model by a set of transformations. The model obtained considers a particular implementation environment and therefore is specific to the selected computing platform. A platform specific model contains all the necessary details so that code can be generated automatically. Code can be generated in a number of programming environments such as Java, C#, .NET etc.

MDA separates the business model form the implementation technologies and thus, it creates a better environment to implement the same business model in a newer underlying technology. As an example, the switch from a traditional networking environment into a wireless environment comes without the efforts and pains caused by the process of rewriting the business model using another computing platform. Important efforts are directed to use the MDA approach modeling the business model when the target platform is an ERP.

MDA allows for a better and faster update with the latest achievements in software engineering techniques, as once new design patterns are invented, they will be implemented in the MDA tools by venders and therefore the quality of the code obtained at the end of the process will be the same independently of the qualifications of team of developers.

As MDA is a relatively new modeling paradigm, it is not well-known in the community of software developers. There is a substantial lack of qualified modelers able to apply at large scale this new modeling paradigm.

Currently, there is a wide variety of commercial tools available pretending to apply MDA principles as they are defined by OMG. Some allow users to choose the implementation environment (Pastor & Juan Carlos Molina, 2007) and some have a defined implementation technology (Visual Enterprise, 2009). Different tools provide different level of code generation and vendors of these tools claim to be MDA-compliant. There is no any formalism for checking the compliance with OMG principles. Therefore, there is need to have better collaboration and better standards for what would be an MDA-compliant product.

## REFERENCES

Booch, G. (1999). *The unified modeling language user guide*. Reading, MA: Addison Wesley.

Booch, G., Rumbaugh, J., & Jacobson, I. (1999). *The unified modeling language user guide*. Reading, MA: Addison Wesley.

Brown, W. A., Conallen, J., & Tropeano, D. (2005). Practical insights into MDA: Lessons from the design and use of an MDA toolkit . In Beydeda, S., Book, M., & Gryhn, V. (Eds.), *Model-driven software development* (pp. 403–432). New York: Springer. doi:10.1007/3-540-28554-7_18

Dugerdil, P., & Gaillard, G. (2006). Model-driven ERP implementation. In *Proceedings of the 2nd international workshop on model-driven enterprise information systems*.

Ericsson, E. H., & Penker, M. (2000). Business modeling with UML business patterns at work. Needham, MA: OMGPress.

Frankel, D. S. (2003). *Model driven architecture applying MDA to enterprise computing*. New York: Wiley Publishing Inc. OMG Press.

Gasevic, D., Djuric, D., & Devedzic, D. (2006). *Model driven architecture and ontology development*. Berlin: Springer.

Guide, M. D. A. *V1.0.1*. (n.d.). Retrieved 2003, from Object Management Group Web site http://www.omg.org

*How systems will be built*. (n.d.). Retrieved 2009, from Object Management Group Web site http://omg.org

Johnston, J. K., & Brown, A. W. (2005). A model driven development approach to creating service-oriented solutions . In *Model-driven software development*. New York: Springer.

Johnston, J. K., & Brown, A. W. (2005). A model driven development approach to creating service-oriented solutions . In *Model-driven software development* (pp. 624–636). New York: Springer.

Johnston, J. K., & Brown, A. W. (2005). Model-driven development approach to creating service-oriented solutions . In Beydeda, S., Book, M., & Gyhn, V. (Eds.), *Model-driven software development*. New York: Springer.

Johnston, S. (2004). Rational UML profile for business modeling. *IBM developerworks*. Retrieved from http://www.ibm.com/developerworks/rational/library/5167.html.

Kennedy Carter Inc. (n.d.). Retrieved 2009, from Kennedy Carter Web site http://www.kc.com

Kleppe, A., Warmer, J., & Blast, W. (2003). *MDA explained the model driven architecture: Practice and promise*. Reading, MA: Addison Wesley.

McNeile, A., & Simons, N. (2003). MDA the vision with the hole. *White Paper, Metamaxim Ltd.* Retrieved from http://www.metamaxim.com.

McNeile, A., & Simons, N. (2004). Methods of behaviour modelling a comentary on behaviour modelling techniques for MDA. *White Paper, Metamaxim Ltd.* Retrieved from http://www.metamaxim.com

Mellor, S. J., & Balcer, M. J. (2002). *Executable UML, a foundation for model driven architecture*. Reading, MA: Addison Wesley.

Meyer, B. (1988). *Object-oriented software construction*. Englewood Cliffs, NJ: Prentice Hall.

Meyer, B. (1992). *Eiffel: The language*. Upper Saddle River, NJ: Prentice Hall.

(n.d.). Retrieved 2003, from MDA Guide V1.0.1 Web site: http://www.omg.org

*Object Management Group*. (n.d.). Retrieved 2009, from Object Management Group Web site: http://omg.org

*Object management group* [OMG]. (2009). Retrieved from http://omg.org

*OMG Model driven architecture: How systems will be built*. (2009). Retrieved from http://omg.org

OMG/MDA. (2009). *How systems will be built*. Retrieved 2009, from Object Management Group Web site http://omg.org

Oscar, P., & Juan Carlos Molina. (2007). *Model-driven architecture in practice*. Germany:

Papajorgji, P., Clark, R., & Jallas, E. (2009). The Model driven architecture approach: A framework for developing complex agricultural Systems. In P. Papajorgji & P. M. Pardalos (Eds.), Advances in modeling agricultural systems. New York: Springer. (Springer Optimization and Its Applications).

Papajorgji, P., & Pardalos, P. M. (2006). *Software engineering techniques applied to agricultural systems an object-oriented and UML approach*. New York: Springer.

Papajorgji, P., & Shatar, T. (2004). Using the unified modeling language to develop soil water-balance and irrigation-scheduling models. *Environmental Modelling & Software*, *19*, 451–459. doi:10.1016/S1364-8152(03)00160-9

Pastor, O., & Molina, J. C. (2007). *Model-driven architecture in practice*. Germany: Springer Verlag.

Sewal, S. J. (2003). *Executive justification for adopting model driven architecture*. Retrieved from http://omg.org/mda/presentations.html

Thomas, L. J. (2002). *ERP et progiciel de gestion integres*. Paris: Dunod.

van Everdingen, Y., van Hillergersberg, J., & Waarts, J. (2000). ERP adoption bu european midsize companies. *Communications of the ACM*, *43*(4), 27–31. doi:10.1145/332051.332064

*Visual Enterprise*. (2009). Retrieved 2009, from http://intelliun.com

Warmer, J., & Kleppe, A. (1999). *The object constraint language precise modeling with UML*. Reading, MA: Addison Wesley.

Zhu, J., Tian, Z., T., Li, Sun, W., & al, e. (2004). Model driven business process integration and management. A case study with bank sinoPac regional platform. *IBM Journal of Research and development*.

# Chapter 11
# Global Emergency–Response System Using GIS

**Salem Al-Marri**
*Leeds Metropolitan University, UK*

**Muthu Ramachandran**
*Leeds Metropolitan University, UK*

## ABSTRACT

*Emergency needs occur naturally, manually (error and terror) and accidentally in addition to worldwide death by hunger and poverty. These situations can arise anytime, any place and thus globally, people are in need of any emergency help by every second. This paper proposes a model for Disaster Classification system of Natural Disasters and Catastrophic Failures activity. This model also proposes the use of emerging technologies such as ubiquitous computing and wireless communications systems that are used by people in recent years to communicate in event of any disaster. The use of emerging technologies also depends on the role of the people and their culture and global support. Furthermore, the paper will propose the deployment of Global Information Systems (GIS) as an aid to emergency management by identifying the related areas pertaining to disaster and thus to help the personnel involved to analyze disasters more accurately by developing a tool. The aim of this tool is to determine potential and affected disaster areas using the GIS technology and to provide support for decision makers during emergencies. Due to the significant development of computerization, networking and mobile systems, reporting a disaster, nowadays, is only a matter of seconds whereas, in the past it would take days or even weeks for the news to reach the people.*

## INTRODUCTION

Disasters are the most destructive phenomena that can occur in natural or technological processes. It is defined as threats to life, well-being, material goods and environment. It is for sure that each type of a disaster has a different impact and each country and government has a different way to deal with such incidents. Therefore, it is essential to

DOI: 10.4018/978-1-61520-625-4.ch011

Copyright © 2010, IGI Global. Copying or distributing in print or electronic forms without written permission of IGI Global is prohibited.

design an appropriate policy and apply successful strategy that can minimize the threat of disasters. Developing a global emergency management information network that provides electronic access to emergency management knowledge would be crucial. Disasters are of a national interest however; dealing with disaster is the responsibility of emergency management in the organization. The emergency management is expected to be well prepared in order to decrease the impacts of disaster on human lives as well as properties and have to have effective policies for response and recovery. However, the emergency management suffers from very limited manpower resources as well as equipments. Therefore, they need help to successfully accomplish their mission (Auf der Heide 2004).

World economy faced destruction, people lives were taking by many natural disasters, other events happened in the last recent years such as Hurricane Katrina in USA during 2006, the Tsunami in Asia during 2004, the September 11 attacks, and other information technologies related failures. Such incidents showed that people lives along with both technical and constructed infrastructure can be easily damaged. It is observed that the increasing use of technology put more stress and uncertainties when disasters happen. According to a report by the secretariat of the International Strategy for Disaster Reduction (ISDR, 2004), over than 478,100 people were killed, more than 2.5 billion people were affected and about $ 690 billion losses in economy caused by natural and man-made disasters. In addition, in Asia tsunami earthquake during 2004, around three hundred thousand people were killed in eleven countries and a whole area and infrastructure was destroyed in the disaster (Aljazeera, 2005). Disasters triggered by hydro-meteorological hazards amounted for 97% of the total people affected by disasters, and 60% of the total economic losses (Shaw 2006). According to the International Federation of Red Cross and Red Crescent Societies (IFR-CRCS), World Disasters Report 2004; the number

of natural and technological disasters in the last decade has increased by 67 percent reaching 707 disasters each year (IFRCRCS 2004). Therefore, as Lavell (1999) said the risks and disasters are dynamic and changing rapidly. This risk differs from person to person regardless being in the same or different organization.

Moreover, the most advanced information systems and technologies did even contribute to relief the affected populations. The information technologies manager should be ready all times for such kind of disaster by taking on this consideration the provisions by pre-disaster planning which guarantee the business continuity and less damage (Christoplos et al 2001). These tools must have the capacity to facilitate the end users with geographical, geophysical, and socioeconomic information as well as the functionality to determine, visualize and analyse the likely extent of disasters. It is essential for emergency managers to be aware of the possible risks to contain the impacts of disasters. By using a geographic information system (GIS), such tools can be developed as a decision support aid to help decision makers at emergency management agencies. Disaster management consists of different phases: mitigation, preparedness, response, and recovery (Auf der Heide 2004). GIS is a significant tool in analysing each phase of disaster management.

The GIS technology has become more affordable. Emergency management personnel are able to enhance their efforts to understand and manage the magnitude of and mitigate the potential damage of natural and artificial disasters (Johnson, el al. 2007). The Emergency managers can achieve a variety of efficiencies and gains in productivity by employing GIS technology. Some of the major categories are

- Efficiencies gained from automating tasks previously done manually.
- Efficiencies realized through the reduction, elimination, and/or coordination of

tasks previously done that currently are duplicated by multiple individuals in different organization units.

- Efficiencies obtained when GIS performs tasks that are too time consuming and costly to be done manually or with current outmoded technologies.

- Enhancements provided by the deployment of GIS technology in productivity that other, more traditional technologies do not provide.

## Disaster Classification System

The Disaster Classification System included Natural Disasters such as earthquakes, oil overflow, famine, floods, hurricanes, landslide, tsunamis, volcanic eruptions, accidents, flight missing, etc. They have a significant impact on different resources like the natural, ecological and cultural resources. It has been known that some parts of the world are more likely to be affected by certain types of disasters such as earthquakes in southern California, Hurricane Hugo, Andrew, and Katrina in southern USA 2006 and floods in the southern coast of Asia 2004. Additional, Catastrophic Failures such as the bombing of Oklahoma City Government and 9/11 terrorist attacks. Furthermore, computer systems are prone to hackers, security violations and viruses that can corrupt valuable information and data.

We propose the Figure 1 given below, to explain the Classification of Natural Disasters and Catastrophic Failures, as shown the Disaster Classification System: consists of four phases: Prevention/Mitigation and Preparedness in the pre-disaster stage, and Response and recovery in post-disaster stage. According to Auf der Heide, E. (2004) The Federal Emergency Management Agency (FEMA) divides emergency management into four categories: mitigation, preparedness, response, and recovery. The area that deals with reduction of the degree of long-term risk to hu-

man life and property from natural and man-made hazards is called mitigation, (e.g. constructing appropriate dams or dikes to prevent flooding and building breakwaters in ports and low-lying coastal areas). While developing operational capabilities for responding to an emergency is called preparedness (e.g. emergency drills and public awareness, equipping and training specialized personnel). Response means the actions taken before, during or after a disaster that aim at saving lives, minimizing damage to properties and improving the recovery procedures (Shaluf 2007). The activities, which involve returning life to normal, is called recovery.

Very few countries and organizations commit sufficient resources to disaster management, regardless of past experience or future potential. Disaster management becomes a pressing concern only after the disaster has struck—a concern that may be short-lived, as other needs quickly resurface. While this is an obvious truth for poorer developing nations, it is also often the case in richer developed countries. In the developing and developed country's there are many higher-priority projects that need funding, and investment in disaster preparedness remains low around the world (Currion 2007). There are still substantial gaps in the information systems for large-scale disaster response. "the information technology revolution, the primary driving force in changes to disaster response, was well reflected in the overall response to the tsunami" (Tsunami 2006). Due to the significant development of computerized and mobile systems, reporting a disaster, nowadays, only takes seconds whereas, in the past it would take days or even weeks for the news to reach the people. Therefore, we need to use current technologies to prepare, communicate and locate people in case of such emergency / disaster situation. One of such technology, which has emerged serenity, is known as the Geographical Information Systems (GIS).

*Figure 1. Disaster classification system*

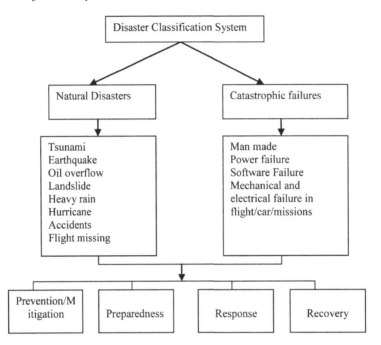

## Geographical Information Systems (GIS) Roles in Emergency Management

A GIS is a tool that has the ability to collect the data from digital imagery or aerial photography. It can be a very useful tool in emergency management. It can store, manipulate, form, analyse and visualize data. The GIS is a technology that allows the users to integrate, store, and process geographic information. It collects data from numerous sources and then displays the information graphically (Fulcher et al. 1995). Emergency management staff requires the information accurately, quickly, and in the right format in order to make appropriate decisions. They need to have a conjecture about future probabilities by analyzing the data about what has happened and where it happened and what resources are available to respond to emergency (Drabek, 2000). Therefore, we have proposed a model for using GIS in emergency management which is shown in Figure 2.

Our model offers that the Emergency management officers use GIS in the following situation:

- **Disaster forecast:** information concerning the possible extent of a particular disaster; to determine which areas included critical facilities that would be subject to the potential hazard.
- **Vulnerability analysis:** information on critical facilities (hospitals, shelters, police and fire facilities, dams, trauma centers, etc.) that can be used for mitigation efforts.
- **Resource inventory:** vital information concerning supplies, equipment, vehicles, or other material resources as well as mutual aid availability from neighboring companies
- **Infrastructure:** shows transportation networks (roads, railroads, bridges, traffic control points, and evacuation routes) as

*Figure 2. GIS in emergency management*

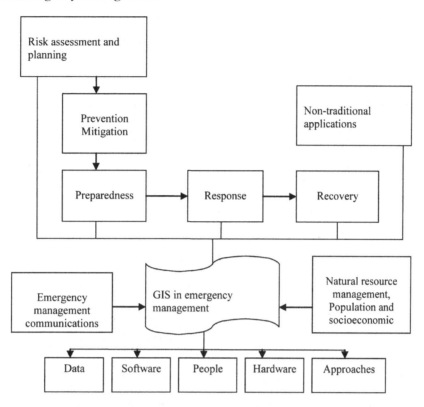

well as complete utility grids (electric, gas, water, and sewer)

## Geographical Information Systems (GIS) and Communications Problems in Disasters

As discussed before, the GIS is considered as an important tool for emergency management. It aids to face emergencies and disasters and predict future disasters and thus the personnel engaged can take precautionary measures to face the disaster situation in case it arises. The Geographical Information Systems (GIS) applications, emergency management is not secluded, and there are numerous related notional, management, application, and technical innovations that affect this application arena, as detailed GISEM model as summarised in Figure 2.

GIS in emergency management and related areas include three main databases: Disaster/ Emergency database, Facilities database and Resources database. The aim of introducing three main databases that it is to be used in different stages of emergency management. The first database, which is disaster/ emergency database, is designed to help emergency mangers getting a damage overlay in order to picture the extent of the emergency. Thus, in the case of flood, the visual or graphic data will be displayed to view the flood zone. This database is also used to have the grids on the map and to know the zones, which are on the same elevation on the map. Disasters have destructive impacts and effects on communications. Communications with all their different types usually are damaged as well as hampered. The types of communication can be commercial and public communication, infrastructure-telephone

*Figure 3. applications of GISEM model*

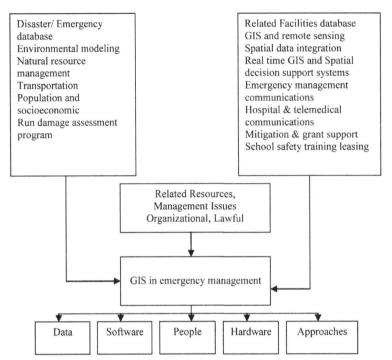

lines, radio towers, communication switches and network operation centers. In the wake of disaster the demand of communication will increase dramatically. This demand will also be acute and intense on mobile communication.

Establishing communication in the region of disaster is the first essential and critical starting step in the process of emergency response. Communication is very important in the event of disaster because it helps the emergency agencies to respond to disasters more effectively. Through communications, emergency agencies, for example, can inform the public for the need of evacuation. It is essential to develop the tools used for communications in event of disaster and improve the availability of systems. This can be done through hardening infrastructure, improving network resilience and adaptability, providing redundancy and diversity, improving component robustness, and optimizing recovery speed. It is a well-known fact that the communication problems arise during disasters is because, due

to communication, devices or lines are usually damaged; radio towers and other infrastructure loose power and mobile devices and handsets cannot be recharged.

The facilities database has an important role in identifying and evaluating the damaged public facilities. The needs of the emergency management agency will be taken into consideration when designing this database. This is listed as the most critical and most important facilities that should be preserved in case of disasters. These facilities are schools, medical facilities, day care facilities, industrial facilities, hotels/motels, recreational areas, mobile home parks, and government buildings. Each facility is assigned a spot in the database along with all the important information pertaining to that specific facility. This database will accessible directly from the base map.

Moreover, it is vital to include and update the current information about the most crucial facilities. As far as the resource database is concerned, it plays vital role in developing the response plan. This database will include construction and engineering resources for supporting the response operations during disasters. However, it is important to know that developing the three databases is a hard task because the information used in those databases are of constant changing nature. Although it would be nice to know where everything useful in disaster planning and response is located, it is not realistic (Kaplan, 2006). Therefore, the best thing to do is to track government assets only because they are more stable.

## CONCLUSION

There are many advantages of developing a system like the GIS in emergency and disaster management. It gives the emergency manager the chance to picture the potential problems. Moreover, the visual image helps the non-technical observers to understand the information without extensive training. Improving emergency management system and response can decrease the risk of loosing lives and properties. The implementation of this system is considered one of the main problems. This is because each site should be recognized, added to the appropriate database and located on the map. This requires time and manpower. Moreover, maintaining this system is not an easy task because it depends on the size of the area covered and the population density. Therefore, each county should have a cost-benefit analysis to determine the viability of maintaining the system. The success of such systems depends heavily on the support of the state. It is mentionable that a third database has been introduced in this model. The location and types of resources proposed are to be included in this database. Those resources are suppose to help the response operations during disasters. This research concentrated on flood management however, it can be used on other forms of disasters. The facilities database remains the same, whereas the hazard database can be adjusted to cope with different types of disasters.

## REFERENCES

Aljazeera. (2005). *Tsunami slowed time* [Online]. Retrieved April 2008, from http://english. aljazeera.net/NR/exeres/A46E0B05-1DC7-4852-83A1-5B6C1D9521E3.htm

Auf der Heide, E. (2004). *Disaster response: Principles of preparation and coordination.* Retrieved March 2008 from http://orgmail2.coe-dmha.org/dr/pdf/DisasterResponse.pdf

Christoplos, I., Mitchell, J. & Liljelund, A. (2001). Re-framing Risk: The Changing Context of Disaster Mitigation and Preparedness, September 2001. *Disasters journal, 25* (3) 185.

Currion, P., Chamindra, S., & Bartel, V. (2007). Open source software for disaster management evaluating how the Sahana disaster information system coordinates disparate institutional and technical resources in the wake of the Indian Ocean tsunami. *Communications of the ACM, 50*(3).

Drabek, T. (1990). *Emergency Management: Strategies for Maintaining Organizational Integrity.* New York: Springer-Verlag.

Fulcher, C., Prato, T., Vance, S., Zhou, Y., & Barnett, C. (1995). *Flood impact decision support system for St.* Retrieved March 2008 from http://gis.esri.com/library/userconf/proc95/to150/p118.html

IFRCRCS. (2004). International Federation of Red Cross and Red Crescent Societies. *World Disasters Report* [Online]. Available April 2008 from http://www.ifrc.org/publicat/wdr2004/chapter8.asp

Johnson, N., Uba, O. G., McGuire, M., Milheizler, J., Schneider, P., & Whitney, M. (1997). Fire flood, quake, wind! GIS to the rescue: how new mapping systems are being used to cope with natural disasters. *Planning, 63*(7).

Kaplan, L. G. (1996). *Emergency and Disaster Planning Manual. New York: McGraw-Hill, & Emergency Planning, Perspective on Britain.* London: James & James.

Lavell, A. (1999). *Natural and Technological Disasters, Capacity Building and Human Resource Development for Disaster Management,* [Online]. Retrieved April 2008 from http://www.desenredando.org/public/articulos/1999/ntd/ntd1999_mar-1-2002.pdf

Shaluf, I. M. (2007). Disaster types, University of Zawia, Libya. *Disaster Prevention and Management, 16*(5), 704–717. doi:10.1108/09653560710837019

Shaw, R. (2006). Indian Ocean tsunami and aftermath Need for environment-disaster synergy. *Disaster Prevention and Management, 15*(1), 5–20. doi:10.1108/09653560610654202

Tsunami Evaluation Coalition. (2006). *Joint Evaluation of the International Response to the Indian Ocean Tsunami.* Tsunami Evaluation Coalition.

# Chapter 12
# Testing Guidelines for Developing Quality EAI Projects

**S.R.Balasundaram**
*National Institute of Technology, Tiruchirappalli, India*

**B.Ramadoss**
*National Institute of Technology, Tiruchirappalli, India*

## ABSTRACT

*The rapidly changing nature of business environments requires organizations to be more flexible to gain competitive advantages. Organizations are turning into a new generation of software called Enterprise Application Integration (EAI) to fully integrate business processes. It is an activity that integrates and harmonizes an enterprise's isolated business applications, processes and functions involving real time data. Developing quality EAI projects is quite a big challenge. Even though success of EAI projects depends on so many parameters, 'testing' is the most significant phase that can ensure the quality as well as the success of EAI projects. Components integrated without testing in EAI systems may affect the enterprise system as a whole. This chapter focuses on the testing aspects related to EAI applications. Especially the significance of testing for various types of "Integrations" is discussed in detail.*

*"The greatest challenge to I/S in every large enterprises finding better and simpler ways of making application systems work together more effectively"*
*- Gartner Group*

## INTRODUCTION

Enterprises across the globe have come to the realization that within the increasingly complex environment of the business world, there is a fundamental need for many varied information platforms to be properly enabled and optimized. To possess the state

DOI: 10.4018/978-1-61520-625-4.ch012

Copyright © 2010, IGI Global. Copying or distributing in print or electronic forms without written permission of IGI Global is prohibited.

of the art business processes, enterprises need to go for devising newer approaches to benefit the maximum from the underlying Information Technology (IT) (Kumar & Mota, 2009) world. These approaches are strongly based on various types of integrations possible within as well as across the enterprises. Majority of the enterprise code deals with different types of integrations. Integration does not stop with linking various fragments of software products. Rather integration can be defined for databases, hardware, network, people, standards etc. This in turn will result in the following major benefits:

- Cost reduction towards expenses incurred in Technologies, Administrations and Operations.
- Improved customer satisfaction
- Better and faster business decisions.

Earlier information systems defined point-to-point interfaces from one application to all other applications to share information. Defining these interfaces and managing them were highly difficult as well as challenging. To overcome these problems the era of Enterprise Resource Planning (ERP) came into existence. In general, ERP has focused on the integration of various internal business functions to provide "one-system-fits-all" solution. The implementation of ERP requires a substantial amount of time and financial commitment (Inmon, 2000). As an alternate, Enterprise Application Integration (EAI) automates the integration process with less effort than that required with ERP. The strength of any EAI totally lies on the levels of integration and their supporting features. At each and every level of integration care must be taken to see whether the integration is possible, feasible and durable. Due to technological, physical and conceptual changes, these integrations may weaken the entire system.

Bringing harmony to the entire system by linking various entities of the system (entities -intra as well as inter) is quite a big challenge in any EAI development scenario. Also, developing successful EAI projects need lot of care to be taken related to the correctness of various entities, namely the individual components available in the integrated systems, the types of integrations and the environmental factors supporting these integrations.

Modern enterprises heavily rely on integrations linking systems and business processes using real time data. Components integrated without testing in EAI systems may affect the enterprise system as a whole. This in turn may result in revenue loss and status degradation in the competitive edge. To overcome this, testing becomes the mandatory process. Testing is an important activity in software development applications. It is the process of determining whether a system has any error or not. When testing is essential for simple applications, it becomes the most essential activity for enterprise applications.

This chapter focuses on the testing aspects related to EAI applications. Especially the significance of testing for various types of "Integrations" is discussed in detail.

## ERP AND EAI

Enterprise Resource Planning (ERP) systems are more popular software applications that have emerged to help business managers to implement their business activities. The aim of ERP systems is to integrate all data and processes of an organization into a unified system (Polson, 2009; Enterprise, 2009). Typical ERP system will use multiple components of computer software and hardware to achieve the integration. An ERP system may combine the functionalities of several subsystems of an enterprise such as Inventory Management System (IMS), Marketing Management System (MMS), Customer Management System (CMS), Financial Accounting System (FAS), Supply Chain Management (SCM) System, etc.

ERP systems have certain limitations in defining the complete business processes. Building effective ERP systems is complex and costly. While integrating ERP systems with legacy systems, building necessary interfaces is a critical task. At this point, various integration solutions were developed leading to Enterprise Application Integration (EAI). As enterprises need to streamline their processes to be competitive, there is a need for integrating different information systems to make information consistent and easily accessible (Hasselbring, 2000; Laudon & Laudon, 2003). As a better and highly extensible step, industries are moving towards the next generation integration system called EAI.

In the mid-1990s, EAI was introduced as an alternative or supplemental technique for ERP. EAI is a business computing term which refers to the plans, methods and tools aimed at modernizing, consolidating, and coordinating the computer applications in an enterprise (Lee et.al. 2003; EAI-Enterprise, 2009). Typically, an enterprise has existing legacy applications and databases and wants to continue to use them while adding or migrating to a new set of applications that exploit the internet, e-commerce and other new technologies. EAI is an emerging generation of integration software used to integrate and harmonize an enterprise's isolated business applications, processes and functions even other ERPs. It provides common, sharable business applications, functions and services within as well as across the enterprise. It is clear that industries are moving towards a new era of business computing from a system of point-to-point integration applications to a system of EAI applications (see Figure.1).

Software products such as SAP, Oracle ERP, PeopleSoft, JDEdwards, Siebel and Clarify would work well individually, but possibly would create "information islands". When changes in data occur, such changes have to be reflected manually in the related domains. This is not an efficient ap-

proach. To cater to long term scalability solutions, EAI paradigm came into existence (Enterprise Application, 2009). The following are some of the commonly used EAI example scenarios (see Figure.2):

i.  Figure 2.a, represents manufacturing systems which are linked with EAI that provides a way to communicate with external systems for sales tracking, demand forecasting, and maintaining pricing details.

ii. Figure 2.b, EAI Seebeyond eGate software is used to integrate the various individual legacy systems with the SAP-based purchase order system. In this scenario, the SAP-based purchase order system acts as a data hub for all the legacy systems such that all the procurement orders would be routed through that.

## Features of EAI Projects

EAI has always focused on integrating new software modules or applications with its existing systems. Over the past decade, EAI solutions provide the infrastructure and mechanisms for extending and integrating both old and new application systems. They also provide the facility for the internet access of an enterprise's applications and help enterprises to share the information and applications. On one hand, though EAI offers lot of advantages to the enterprise, on the other hand it poses technological and business challenges (UML, 2009; Gorton et al. 2003).

EAI solutions vary in their underlying approaches and adopt different terminologies and concepts. The diversity of the EAI approaches has made selection of an EAI solution difficult. Consequently, the more the EAI approaches, the more the EAI solutions, the harder it is for an enterprise to find the most suitable solution Mosawil et al. (2006). Lot of research activities are already in the streamline to improve the performance of

*Figure 1. Migration from simple integrated solution to the level of EAI*

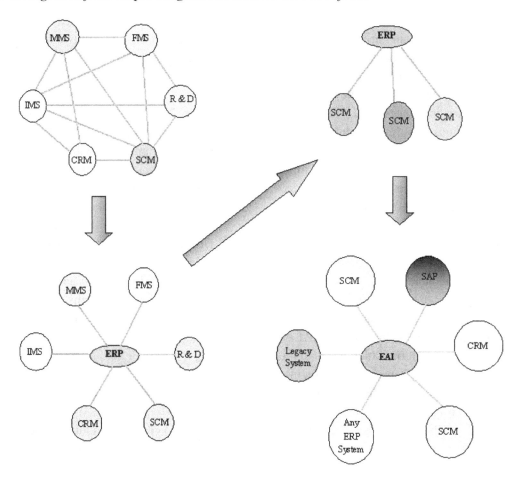

EAI projects. Much of the research is focused towards certain prime areas such as data mining and reverse engineering applicable to EAI systems [(Davis & Aiken, 2000; Stonebraker & Hellerstein, 2001). Also, sufficient literature is available on areas such as common messaging middleware (Medvidovic, 2002; Young et al. 2002). Sauer et al. (2003) have discussed more on activities related to encapsulation and wrapping of legacy systems in a component-based approach. But, there exists very little information about research activities on testing of EAI projects. In this regard, the concern of this work is to concentrate on levels of testing possible in EAI projects. Especially, the work highlights the identification of key areas where testing activities have to be involved

by the developers in EAI projects. More to say, testing concerned with 'integrations' is the focus of this chapter.

## TYPES OF INTEGRATIONS

An enterprise system is based on business processes and data (Kumar & Mota, 2009). The designer or developer of EAI systems must understand and define clearly the amount of work to be done, the duration required to complete the activity and the types of integrations available in EAI systems. Mainly, EAI projects are characterized by the availability of different types of integrations with them. Mosawi et al. (2006) have analyzed and

*Figure 2. Examples of EAI (b) scenario 2*

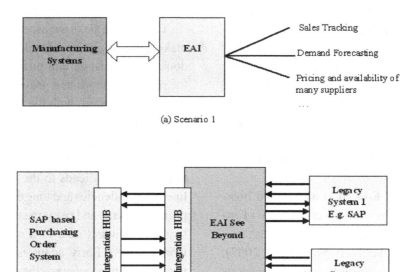

(a) Scenario 1

(b) Scenario 2

identified the following types of integrations in EAI. (see Figure.3):

- **Data-level EAI:** This is the most common integration approach to implement. At this level, backend data stores are integrated to enable the movement of data between them. This deals with the information extraction from one database, if needed, processing that information and updating the same in another database (Linthicum, 1999; Ruh et al. 2000). This approach provides access to a wide range of data and allows data to be reused across other applications (Mosawil et al. 2006; Vujasinovic et al. 2006).

- **Application Interface Level EAI:** This refers to defining interfaces contained within custom or packaged applications such as SAP, PeopleSoft or Baan. These interfaces are leveraged to provide access to business processes and information. Using these interfaces, developers are able to bring many applications together, allowing them

to share business logic and information (Mosawil et al. 2006; Linthicum, 1999).

- **User Interface-level EAI:** This approach is based on developing a user interface that imitates end user actions by using screen scraping or advanced terminal emulation (Linthicum, 1999). It is the most primitive form of EAI that integrates various applications through the user interfaces. Though not preferable, this approach is the only way of integrating tasks (Kumar & Mota, 2009; Mosawil et al. 2006).

- **Method level EAI:** This is a more complicated form of application-level integration and is used less frequently. It involves approaches to share the business logic available within the enterprise. Operations that are common to several applications are combined to form a single application (Linthicum, 1999; Ruh et al. 2000).

- **Object-level EAI:** It encapsulates the business logic and data within objects. This in turn allows the objects to be linked together in a plug and play manner to interoperate. This has the highest level of significance for the enterprise of heterogeneous systems and architectures. Legacy systems can be wrapped into objects so that they can form part of the integration Mosawil et al. (2006).

- **Presentation level EAI:** This approach allows creating new user interface by re-mapping the old presentations Mosawil et al. (2006).

- **Process level EAI:** It is also called business method as it involves the flow of information and automation of business systems (Mosawil et al. 2006; Gerrard, 2007). It enables the coordination of decisions and the management of the dependencies between enterprise processes.

- **Internal process level EAI:** This approach allows tracking the status of business process activities internally Mosawil et al. (2006).

- **Cross-enterprise process level EAI:** This approach allows sharing processes among multiple Business-2-Business (B2B) corporate entities. So it is suitable for B2B application integration Mosawil et al. (2006).

## Problems Related to EAI Projects

According to 2008 Gartner research, the global revenue for the application infrastructure and middleware software market totaled more than $14 billion in 2007, increasing nearly 13 percent from the previous year. Enterprise service buses and business process management suites contributed to this steadfast growth. Focus on EAI project development has considerably increased in various parts of the globe including North America, Western Europe, Japan and Latin America. On the other hand, this growth may be slowed down due to several issues such as B2B integration challenges and availability of varieties of tools

and technologies, complex human factors and other environmental factors.

Though the positive aspects of EAI projects make them to be acceptable by industries, no doubt there exist certain pitfalls or demerits. As the market changes and grows, enterprises often struggle to keep up with the fast pace of innovations (How the future, 2009). There exists a basic phenomenon that EAI projects need to wait for completion of the other streams of work in order to proceed. This leads to the elongation of time lines. Dependencies and long durations make EAI projects as large and risky, making them particular targets of budget cuts in a recession (Thought works, 2008). Early adapters of EAI struggled with new technologies and they lacked established processes to define the EAI architecture and manage project lifecycles and ongoing operations. Though solutions can be provided for the above said problems, the testing of EAI systems has not attained much significance.

EAI projects also involve integrations of ERP projects. The software vendors have their own methodologies for testing ERP products, but they focus on process flows through configured components. The behavior of ERP suites are typically controlled by configuration parameters. Software maintenance is not involved in them. As testing ERP systems is a time consuming and cost involving process, needless to say the same may be expected in EAI systems also. Data migration, the prime component of ERPs, may pose challenges in EAI also.

## SOFTWARE TESTING

Software testing is the most important phase in any software development projects, so that we know whether the project is going to be successful or it will fail before it goes live. So software testing is a process of verifying and validating that a software application works as expected and it meets the business and technical requirements that guided

*Figure 3. Types of integrations in EAI*

its design and development. The main purpose of testing is to find the presence of faults before the customer finds them. Even if testing does not reveal any fault it still provides confidence in the correctness of the program.

There are various forms of testing for discovering different types of faults and effects in software. Testing may be done by the end-user to evaluate the usability or human-interaction issues of the software. Performance testing is often done to assess the behavior of software under special usage scenarios such as when the system is under heavy stress of data loading. Ultimately, the software must be functionally correct in order for it to serve its designated purpose and be accepted by the user.

In software development phase, planning stage is applicable for development and testing activities. A software project test plan is a document that describes the objectives, scope, approach, and focus of a software testing effort. The process of preparing a test plan is a useful way to think through the efforts needed to validate the accept-

ability of a software product. The following are the elements of test plan:

- Establish objectives for each test phase
- Establish schedules for each test activity
- Determine the availability of tools and resources
- Establish the standards and procedures to be used for planning and conducting the tests
- Reporting test results
- Set the criteria for test completion
- Set the criteria for the success of each test

## Testing of EAI Projects

EAI methodologies are widely accepted in main stream market. But, testing which can define quality assurance is the most neglected component of EAI (EAI Quality, 2009). It is due to the fact that, EAI testing is often delayed until the end of the project. There is too little time available for the developers to focus on complete testing of systems before the delivery of the products. Moreover, defining testing strategies for EAI projects are challenging ones and also much expertise is needed to define such strategies. For the entire life span of EAI systems, not much testing tools are available. The major hurdle is that testing has to be focused on various levels of EAI to provide quality systems.

EAI systems are mainly characterized by their individual enterprises, external components and the integrations. To provide better deliverables, the testing scenario of EAI projects should focus on testing these components namely individual systems, integrations and the environment (see Figure.4). Here, $E_i$ represents the individual enterprise. $A_i$, $B_i$ and $C_i$ are individual subsystems of various enterprises. For example, $\{A_1, A_2, A_3\}$ may correspond to {MMS, FMS, CRM}. The colored lines indicate the integrations that are possible to link the entities within the enterprises, internal or external or other components of the systems. Within the enterprise, individual subsystems can be linked. Between enterprises, integrations can be defined. Business partners, consumers and service providers act as external components which can be integrated with EAI systems. The entire system is driven through numerous supporting parameters such as networks, devices, technologies, etc.

## Testing Individual Enterprises

Every enterprise is composed of various sub systems and in turn every sub system has numerous components related to data, procedures, user interfaces, objects etc. Testing must be performed at every stage of defining, building and assembling these individual components. Every component is tested as separate unit, in isolation, so that when it is integrated to the rest of the system, no faults are encountered. Same way, every enterprise system must be tested on the whole before it is integrated to any other part of the entire application.

## Testing on Integrations

Integrations are the key factors defined in EAI projects. Testing 'Complex Integration' involving many end systems is difficult but identifying faults at an early stage than at a later stage is less expensive. Various challenges and possibilities for designing testing methodologies for EAI projects related to integration levels are discussed as follows (Sauer et al. 2003; Linthicum, 1999; EAI Quality, 2009; Vengayil, 2009; Linthicum, 2001):

## Data Level

An EAI project allows data to be reused across various applications. This limits the 'real time' transactional capabilities. EAI solutions depend on asynchronous messages. This in turn poses new problems (concurrency problems and temporal conditions). The development/test team must have complete knowledge about messaging standards technologies such as XML, Middleware brokers, TCP/IP etc.

## Interface Level

Application Interface: An EAI solution may be expected across multiple languages and platforms. That is, EAI may exist in a heterogeneous environment. Not much standards available for creating API level integrations across applications with varying languages and protocols.

User Interface: This approach is synchronous in its communication style, and requires the original application to be online. It cannot be scaled, and thus cannot handle more than a few screen interfaces at a given time. It only takes place at the presentation, and not at the actual inter-connection between applications and data. Special attention has to be given for the verification of handshaking mechanisms to ensure the proper message delivery in asynchronous system to guarantee delivery of message at the presentation. Business requirements have to be thoroughly understood to

*Figure 4. Categories of testing EAI projects*

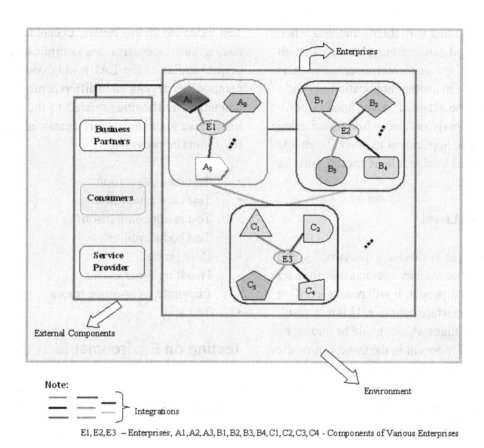

Note:
Integrations

E1, E2, E3 — Enterprises; A1, A2, A3, B1, B2, B3, B4, C1, C2, C3, C4 - Components of Various Enterprises

verify the transactions across the interface.

In general, interface integration requires a lot of co-ordination and follow ups to be done by the testers. To reduce the failure of EAI projects, application of interface testing is highly recommended.

## Method Level

Consider the 'Update Product Information' method. This method can be accessed from various applications and there is no need to rewrite each method within the respective application. Since all applications interact with the integrated applications through single front end application, method-level integration requires the integrated applications to support a Remote Procedure Call

(RPC). Testing must be focused on the integrated application API which will break the front application components and the applications that are coupled with them.

Verification of failover mechanisms and recovery mechanisms are of more important in case of integration projects. It is almost impossible in a large integration project to orchestrate end-to-end tests with application test tools. Performance tests defined earlier in the development phase may help to avoid the risks associated though this integrations.

## Object Level

This object level integration allows the legacy system to be wrapped into objects, and participate in the object integration. However, this approach is complex and the most difficult approach. Every object must be tested with their semantics when they are extended across enterprises. That is, an object intended for one enterprise, when it is extended for use in another application, its basic meaning must be retained. Also, interoperability must be properly defined while transferring objects from one application to other. To enable this, rules related to object level testing must be made available.

## Presentation Level

Presentation level is driven, especially by end user actions. When the user interacts with the user interface of a component, it will react according to its own user interface behavior. This may result in some state changes which should be known by the rest of the component in the same composite application. So that, they can update their user interfaces accordingly. Testing should be done to cope up with the state changes.

## Process Level

When the integration solutions streamline development and architecture of an existing solution the complexity, paths and permutations still remain and need to be tested. Testing has to be done for all of the complex business logic, which will be now under another layer of integration-ware after the streamlining process.

Inter process level: V-model testing may be suitable which explicitly specifies testing activities associated with each phase of the development cycle. This inter process level requires higher dependency on an availability of end applications to perform different levels of testing.

Cross-enterprise process level: A complete understanding of the business requirement is needed in order to verify all the transactions across the enterprise process.

## Miscellaneous

Test cases involving timers, events and re-producing such scenarios are complicated. Other major hurdles in the EAI testing could include components developed in different programming languages. Difficulties related to the following items have to be thoroughly examined and solutions must be provided:

- Test data generation
- Test case generation
- Test result comparisons
- Test bed identifier
- Base lining
- Handling timer events
- Elaborate error-prone traces
- Test stub

## Testing on Environments

As a complete product, the EAI projects rely on so many related factors in and around the project environment. These factors may be:

i.   Human Related: Various human related issues to be understood and managed while linking the enterprises.
ii.  Device Oriented: The applications may be activated through various devices such as PDAs, Mobiles, Handheld devices, etc. The applications should provide flexibility to take care of technological changes and upgradations.
iii. Connectivity/Networks: When applications across boundaries are connected, the entire system may be defined with heterogeneous network models. While integrating applications involving intranets, extranets, internet, proper testing guidelines have to be framed to smoothen the information flow.

## CONCLUSION

EAI is the ongoing process of putting an infrastructure in place. It is not something that we can buy nor is a product. It is something we build to increase the business value of the IT environment. Though several benefits can be attained through EAI projects, successful development and deployment depends on so many issues. To achieve quality as well as to define successful EAI projects, the designers must focus on testing aspects of the systems. In this regard, the chapter highlights the importance of testing in three broad areas of EAI systems, namely, Individual enterprise level, Integration level and Environmental level. Especially testing the integration levels of EAI projects is discussed in detail.

## REFERENCES

Davis, K. H., & Aiken, P. H. (2000). Data reverse engineering: A historical survey. In *Proceedings of the Seventh Working Conference on Reverse Engineering (WCRE'00)*, 1095-1350, IEEE.

EAI-Enterprise. (2009). *EAI-Enterprise Application Integration – Solutions from iWay software*. Retrieved April 2009, from http://www.iwaysoftware.com/eai-enterprise-application-integration.html

Enterprise. (2009). *Enterprise resource planning*. Retrieved March 2009, from http://moneyterms.co.uk/erp/

Enterprise Application. (2009). *Enterprise application integration techniques*. Retrieved April 2009, from http://www.cs.ucl.ac.uk/staff/ucacwxe/lectures/3C05-02-03/aswe21-essay.pdf

Gerrard, P. (2007). Test methods and tools for ERP implementations. *Testing: Academic and Industrial Conference Practice and Research Techniques – MUTATION*, 40-46.

Gorton, I., Thurman, D., & Thomson, J. (2003). Next generation application integration challenges and new approaches. In *Proceedings of 27th Annual International Computer Software and Applications Conference (COMPSAC)*, 585-590, IEEE.

Hasselbring, W. (2000). Information system integration. *Communications of the ACM, 43*(6), 33–38. doi:10.1145/336460.336472

How the future. (2009). *How the future of the EAI Market?* Retrieved March 2009, from http://toostep.com/idea/how-the-future-of-the-eai-market

Inmon, W. (2000). A brief history of integration. *eAI Journal*. Retrieved from www.eaijournal.com/applicationintegration/BriefHistory.asp

Kumar, S., & Mota, K. (2009). *Enterprise application integration*. Retrieved March 2009, from http://www.roseindia.net/eai/enterpriseapplicationintegration.shtml

Laudon, K. C., & Laudon, J. P. (2003). *Management information systems* (8th ed.). Upper Saddle River, NJ: Pearson Education Publications.

Lee, J., Siau, K., & Hong, S. (2003). Enterprise integration with ERP and EAI. *Communications of the ACM, 46*(2), 54–60. doi:10.1145/606272.606273

Linthicum, D. (1999). *Enterprise Application Integration*. Reading, MA: Addison-Wesley Publications.

Linthicum, D. (2001). *B2B application integration*. Reading, MA: Addison-Wesley Publication.

Medvidovic, N. (2002). On the role of middleware in architecture-based software development. In *Proceedings of the 14th International Conference on Software Engineering and Knowledge Engineering (SEKE)*, 299-306, New York, ACM Press.

Mosawi1, A. A., Zhao, L., & Macaulay, L. (2006). A model driven architecture for enterprise application integration. In *Proceedings of the 39th Hawaii International Conference on System sciences*.

Polson, J. (2008). *Why you should use SAP ERP System.* Retrieved December 2008, from www.planetarticle.net

Quality, E. A. I. (2003). *EAI quality assurance a service oriented architecture.* Zetta Works. Retrieved March 2009, from http://hosteddocs.ittoolbox.com/ER102904.pdf

Ruh, W., Maginnis, F., & Brown, W. (2000). *Enterprise Application Integration.* New York: John Wiley &Sons Inc., Publications.

Sauer, L. D., Clay, R. L., & Armstrong, R. (2000). Metacomponent architecture for software interoperability. In *Proceedings of International Conference on Software Methods and Tools (SMT)*, 75-84, IEEE.

Stonebraker, M., & Hellerstein, J. M. (2001). Content integration for E-Business. *SIGMOD Record, 30*(2), 552–560. doi:10.1145/376284.375739

Thought works. (2008). Thought works: *Recession news Cios can use, adding value in uncertain Times – the Agile and lean Advantage.* Retrieved June 2008.

UML. (2009). *UML™ for EAI.* Retrieved April 2009, from http://www.omg.org/docs/ad/01-09-17.pdf

Vengayil, P. (2009). *Quality assurance in EAI projects.* Wipro Technologies. Retrieved March 2009, from http://hosteddocs.ittoolbox.com/PV111805.pdf

Vujasinovic, M., Marjanovic, Z., & Bussler, C. (2006). Data level application integration. [*BPM workshops*, Springer Verlag Berlin Heidelberg.]. *LNCS, 3812*, 390–395.

Young, P., Chaki, N., & Berzins, V. & Luqi. (2003). Evaluation of middleware architectures in achieving system interoperability. In *Proceedings of 14th IEEE International Workshop on Rapid Systems Prototyping*, 108-116, IEEE.

## KEY TERMS AND DEFINITIONS

**API:** An Application Programming Interface is a set of functions, procedures, methods or classes that an operating system, library or service provides to support requests made by computer programs.

**Data Mining:** It is sorting through data to identify patterns and establish relationships.

**EAI:** Enterprise Application Integration is a process of data and application integration technologies which focuses on linking transactional applications together, typically in real time.

**Encapsulation:** It is the inclusion of one thing within another thing so that the included thing is not apparent.

**Enterprise:** An environment where more than one computer is used. These computers are joined by a network.

**Enterprise System:** A system that supports enterprise-wide or cross-functional requirements, rather than a single department or group within the organization.

**ERP:** Enterprise Resource Planning systems are more popular software applications that have emerged to help business managers to implement their business activities. The aim of ERP systems is to integrate all data and processes of an organization into a unified system

**Integration Testing:** Integration testing is the phase of software testing in which individual software modules are combined and tested as a group. It follows unit testing and precedes system testing.

**Legacy Systems:** A computer system that has been in operation for a long time, and whose functions are too essential to be disrupted by upgrading or integration with another system.

**Message-Oriented Middleware:** It is the term for software that connects separate systems in a network by carrying and distributing messages between them. The messages may contain data, software instructions, or both together.

**Metadata:** Metadata is Information about the data warehouse or data mart system. Metadata encompasses all aspects of the data warehouse or data mart system, including technical, human and data resources.

**QA:** Quality Assurance for short refers to planned and systematic production processes that provide confidence in a product's suitability for its intended purpose.

**Reverse Engineering:** Legally sanctioned method of copying a technology which begins with an existing product and works backward.

**RPC:** Remote Procedure Call is a programming interface that allows one program to use the services of another program in a remote machine. The calling program sends a message and data to the remote program, which is executed, and results are passed back to the calling program.

**SCM:** Supply Chain Management is the management of a network of interconnected businesses involved in the ultimate provision of product and service packages required by end customers.

**TCP/IP:** Transmission Control Protocol / Internet Protocol, a set of protocols (including TCP) developed to get data from one network device to another.

**Testing:** It is the process of determining whether a program has any error or not.

**Test Bed:** An execution environment configured for testing. May consist of specific hardware, operating system, network topology, configuration of the product under test, other application or system software, etc.

**Test Case:** The specification (usually formal) of a set of test inputs, execution conditions, and expected results, identified for the purpose of making an evaluation of some particular aspect of a Target Test Item.

**Test Data:** The definition (usually formal) of a collection of test input values that are consumed during the execution of a test, and expected results referenced for comparative purposes.

**Validation:** Validation is the process of ensuring that a product or a process conforms to defined user needs, requirements, and/or specifications under defined operating conditions.

**Verification:** In the context of hardware and software systems, formal verification is the act of proving or disproving the correctness of a system with respect to a certain formal specification or property, using formal methods.

**XML:** It stands for eXtensible Markup Language. XML is the World Wide Web Consortium's (W3C) recommended standard for creating formats and sharing data on the Web.

# Chapter 13
# The Post Implementation Phase of a Large–Scale Integrative IT Project

**Marco Marabelli**
*Cattolica University, Milan, Italy*

**Sue Newell**
*Bentley University, Waltham, MA, USA & University of Warwick, UK*

## ABSTRACT

*In this chapter the authors focus on the iterative process that occurs within the implementation phase of an ERP which they depict as a series of learning cycles: managers make decisions, identify mistakes, and accumulate experience (lessons learned). They examine these "learning cycles" through the lens of absorptive capacity and they use a case study and a qualitative perspective. The authors identify a number of tradeoffs that represent the learning paths of Alpha Co. and find that such learning process is path dependent, organizational memory plays a fundamental role, and double loop cycles contribute in the development of absorptive capacity seen as a dynamic capability.*

## INTRODUCTION

According to Markus, Tanis, and Fenema (2000) Enterprise Resource Planning (ERP) systems are based on developing a common IT infrastructure and common business processes that will support the integration of an entire business activity. Use of ERP has spread rapidly since the late 1990s –and especially in large organizations where the need for efficiency and effectiveness of processes is crucial.

Practically, ERP systems are packaged software that has been developed and licensed out to clients. ERP systems typically have built-in standardized functionalities that allow organizations to integrate disparate data (Davenport, 2000; Cortada, 1998). Examples of popular application packages and their developers are SAP, Oracle, PeopleSoft, and JD Edwards (Jacobs and Weston Jr., 2007).

The main reason for the popularity of ERP systems is that they are perceived to improve both productivity and speed (Davenport, 1998). Their successful incorporation potentially brings huge

DOI: 10.4018/978-1-61520-625-4.ch013

Copyright © 2010, IGI Global. Copying or distributing in print or electronic forms without written permission of IGI Global is prohibited.

economic benefits to firms, such as reduced cycle times, faster transactions, better financial management, and a foundation for the implementation of e-commerce, knowledge documentation, etc. (Davenport, 2000). While potentially ERP systems can help to improve organizational performance, many firms are unable to fully exploit this potential and realize all the benefits (Stein, 1998). In this chapter we focus on some of the problems that can arise in the implementation (for the first time) of an ERP system in a large organization.

Much of the research advocates ERP implementation as a sequence of linear phases, beginning with preparation and ending with actual deployment or "going -live". This linear view is based on traditional innovation diffusion theory (Cooper and Zmud, 1990) that sees ERP implementation as part of the organizational effort to diffuse ERP innovation throughout a user community. Markus et al. (2000) introduce a process view of ERP implementation, which includes a maintenance phase that captures the "onward and upwards" efforts of users as they learn to exploit the ERP system to support their work once the package is implemented. Our definition of the implementation phase is consistent with Markus et al. (2000) as is our adoption of a process perspective of the implementation phase, that is, as an iterative rather than a linear process (Elbanna, 2006). In highlighting some of the problems than can arise during this process, we use a case study (Alpha Co.) approach and focus on a particular ERP system, that is, Customer Relationship Management (CRM). CRM systems are defined as ERP modules that specialize in capturing, integrating, managing, and analyzing customer data, such as how and when a particular customer interacted with the organization –the "who, what, when and how" of this interaction (Gefen and Ridings, 2002). CRM systems integrate and synthesize a broad array of activities related to customer services, sales, and marketing (Mankoff, 2001). Combining these activities into a single seamless interaction gives organizations a strategic tool to maintain and improve their customer relationships through customized integrated services (Davids, 1999). Like other ERP systems, CRM systems often involve prolonged and difficult phases of system design, development, implementation, and post implementation.

In this chapter we focus on the iterative process that occurs within the implementation phase which we depict as a series of learning cycles: managers make decisions, identify mistakes, and accumulate experience (lessons learned). We argue that ERP development is a process of continuous evolution with no final design being possible or warranted. Moreover, we argue that ERP implementation is best viewed not as a one-time process but rather as a series of implementation and practical use cycles, each of which encompasses different degrees of reflection and learning such that the system becomes more embedded and better adapted to the context. We examine these "learning cycles" through the lens of absorptive capacity. We take from Cohen and Levinthal's (1990) original construct, the concept of "knowledge accumulation." From its further development we borrow concepts such as double loop learning and absorptive capacity (Dyer and Singh, 1998); relative absorptive capacity, that is what a firm can learn in terms of new knowledge acquired through consultancy (Lane and Lubatkin, 1998); how learning cycles can be seen as a dynamic capability (Todorova and Durisin, 2007); and the importance of framing the learning process within a multilevel perspective (Cohen and Levinthal, 1990; Lane, Koka, and Pathak, 2006; Quigley et al., 2007; Van de Bosch, Wijk, and Volberda, 2005)

Below we identify a number of themes that represent the learning paths in Alpha Co. as a result of its implementation of CRM software, which began in 2001 and is still ongoing at the time of writing (2009). The four themes have emerged from observations and interviews with persons from ALPHA CO. are the following:

1.  *customization vs. configuration*: this theme includes the process that allows management to understand the extent of customization required and the extent to which it is possible to work with the vanilla characteristics of the CRM package where modification is confined to what can be done using the configuration tools;

2.  *user acceptance vs. the business process that management wants*: we look at the importance of user commitment and highlight the problems experienced by Alpha Co. in involving all users, in all departments. We highlight areas where political problems can occur; noting how organizations with multiple departments and objectives are particularly vulnerable;

3.  *short vs. long term performance management focus*: we look at the extent to which Alpha Co. focused on the short term (financial) indicators, such as return on investment (ROI), rather than long term organizational performance –often represented by intangible assets and how this focus changed over time;

4.  *organizational insularity vs. capability to accumulate knowledge through inter-organizational learning*: in 2001 Alpha Co. hired a consultant company (Xcons) to assist management during the ERP system implementation phase but failed to adhere to its recommendations and suggestions. We argue that is not always straightforward for a firm to follow the lead of an external company even if it has been hired for its advice and has huge experience; rather an organization has to learn to trust the advice of an external party.

In this book chapter we aim to run an explorative research focusing on Alpha Co. case study. In so doing we develop these themes and investigate the learning process involved in the accumulation of new knowledge in organizations.

More specifically, our research question is: how do organizations learn to exploit the benefit from an ERP system over time? We argue that organization learning is a continuous process (that needs long term perspective) and we give importance to the accumulation of knowledge, borrowing theory from absorptive capacity (Cohen and Levinthal, 1990).

In Section 2 we introduce the case study which is further discussed in Section 3. We offer some suggestions for further research in Section 4.

## A CRM IMPLEMENTATION CASE ILLUSTRATION

Our case study is based on Alpha Co., an international company with its headquarters in the United States, which sells product development technologies to manufacturing firms. In 2001, for a number of reasons, Alpha Co. decided to purchase a CRM system in order to improve the efficiency of its sales, marketing, distribution, and service functions. The main reason was that the business side needed a forecast system; consequently the idea to integrate data from different departments seemed to be an effective solution in order to develop DSS (Decision Support Systems) for managers. Another reason is connected to the fact that in the early 2000s many large companies started buying CRMs. The third reason was that in 2000 the competitive environment of Alpha Co became more competitive –in terms of more competitors –and the management decided that it was better to focus on the customer in order to maintain a competitive advantage.

An interesting detail of our study is that in 2001 Alpha Co. had no experience of an ERP system. This is an important detail since our perspective, which includes the absorptive capacity framework, assumes that prior experience (and consequently knowledge) is fundamental for the ability to exploit such a system. However, in our case, Alpha Co. was embarking on its first experience of the implementation process and, as we will demonstrate, went on to experience an iterative learning process of knowledge accumulation.

This longitudinal analysis allows us to study the post implementation process as a dynamic capability development, which we assume contributes to competitive advantage (Leonard Burton, 1992; Teece, Pisano, and Shuen, 1997). Our case study focuses on the subsequent learning processes, that is, on what Alpha Co. learned from mistakes/failures and to what extent these have been exploited to refine its decision making.

We conducted a case study of Alpha Co drawing data from several sources (observation, interviews, and document analysis), and the longitudinal perspectives is from 2001 to today. Our research design has been developed as follows: firstly we obtained a number of slides and documentation from the pas steering committees (from 2001 to today). Then we started developing a narrative of the company to identify the key persons and the key events that have characterized the learning process that allowed Alpha Co. to implement ULTRA-CRM. We made observation while attending both steering committees (cross department-strategic meetings) and working committees (operative meetings that focus on the implementation and integration of ULTRA-CRM). The interviews were addressed to both persons that are still working at Alpha Co. and persons that have played important roles when key decisions were made (although not still at Alpha Co.). All interviews were managed trying to let the speaker tell us a story (his/her version of what happened on a certain occasion, e.g. when he or she was involved in a decision). Specific questions were asked only when needed to write the full story of the implementation of the CRM system, for instance we asked about specific dates or who made a decision, how long an implementation phase took etc. According to Yin (1993) we have tested the construct validity using multiple sources of evidence and having a draft case study report reviewed by key informants. We compared the interviews with the slides that we consider the official source of data. Moreover we have interviewed different persons on the same topic verifying that the details provided were the same. Finally we made interviewed with both persons that are still working on Alpha Co. and persons that are no longer working there in order to have data from ex-managers that are not still involved in the implementation of ULTRA-CRM and that are not conditioned from Alpha Co. management (e.g. there is the possibility that some employees prefer not to say the true they want to say something bad about the organization they are currently working), contacting persons that are no longer working at Alpha Co. was also useful in order to review our narrative of the case study.

## CUSTOMIZATION VS. CONFIGURATION OF ULTRA-CRM

The two main approaches to the implementation of an ERP are a) implementation of a standard package with minimum deviation from the standardized settings, or b) customization of a system, to suit the requirements of existing processes and activities (Brehm, Heinzl, and Markus, 2001; Holland and Light, 1999; Lee, Siau, and Hong, 2003; Luo and Strong, 2004).

According to Alshawi, Themistocleous, and Almadani (2004) organizations might seek to avoid customization because of the problems involved. For example, a highly customized system involves manual writing of code (programming) whenever a new release of the package is delivered by the vendor (Light, 1999). This is both expensive, because the company is required to pay programmers, and risky. It keeps the organization beholden to two suppliers: the software vendor and the programmers who maintain the system customization. However, despite these disadvantages of heavy customization it is common for organizations to customize certain parts of the software in order to achieve its hidden and unique capabilities (Bingi, Shama, and Godla, 2001; Wenhong and Strong, 2004).

During the first three years of implementation, Alpha Co.'s decision in relation to this trade-off (between customization to suit the organization and upgradability) was heavily weighted towards customization and they made very extensive modifications of the package purchased. The main reason for customizing was that the management wanted to exploit the new ERP in the short run and thought that hard customization should have been a good start. Moreover, managers started customizing without involving the user –to try building the system quicker. In doing so there was made the decision to focus on the needs of the management, incredibly overlooking themes such as the users acceptance (they didn't run any UAT –User Acceptance Tests),they didn't interview the employees and, moreover, they didn't make any marketing activity to promote the new system. However, it was soon clear that the customization was not being exploited because users found it too complicated –customizations had increased complexity rather than making it more suited to the needs of the company. As Paul, Vice Chief Information Officer in Alpha Co. told us in an early interview:

*We implemented this highly customized thing that these guys thought was fantastic, but nobody used it. [...] Because it's so customized, nobody is using it. You built it as a management tool. But [it was argued] don't give up yet. Hang in there."*

The system was found to be too complicated because it had been customized originally to the Sales Department's needs and "nobody [from any other departments] could use it because it was too complicated". The interfaces did not have the fields required by other departments and many users continued to use their spreadsheets with the obvious result that data were not consistent and there were multiple versions of data.

Alpha Co.'s main objective after two years of implementation, to have one system for the whole organization that would enable accurate forecasting, was far from being realized. As Clare said:

*They [the users] were not going to use it which made it difficult to obtain reporting about and to get insights into what was going on at the different customers.*

So, it took two years for management to realize that their method of implementation of ULTRA-CRM –high customization – was not working for Alpha Co. In 2004, the decision was taken to dispense with most of the customization and go back to the vanilla version. Although this was not, as Alan said, 'the best system in the world', it allowed data input by all users (company employees) in every department in the company, worldwide.

The above suggests that the customization stage may have been a necessary step for Alpha Co., which showed management that a balance was required between changing the system and changing organizational processes. As John –a project manager from the ULTRA-CRM implementation team –indicates: "this is our process and we must have it this way and only in hindsight we would say we could have customized less."

Our absorptive capacity lens view allows us to argue, in line with Cohen and Levinthal (1990), that the firm's capability to understand its needs in terms of how to manage processes, develops cumulatively. If we consider absorptive capacity as a dynamic process (Lane and Lubatkin, 1998; Lane, Salk, and Lyles, 2001; Meeus, Oerlemans, and Hage, 2001; Szulansky, 1996) we can see that the whole organization learned at both the individual and collective levels. For example, at the individual level Alan, the Sales Manager, and Nick, one of the company's General Managers, told us that they had learned lessons. The effect of forcing customization (against using the original software) was unpredictable. However, they had learned the delicacy involved in this decision and both now believe that they would be able to manage the tradeoff better in the future. At the collective level, the particular experience of customization has become part of the organizational memory (Moorman and Miner, 1992; Walsh and Ungson, 1991). For instance, current Alpha Co. employees not involved in the initial implementation of ULTRSA-CRM and the switch to the vanilla version of the software, know how to manage this tradeoff. For instance, John (who has only been working at Alpha Co. for a couple of years) told us that 'some parts of the package *have* to be customized while some others do not."

## USER ACCEPTANCE VS. THE BUSINESS PROCESS THAT MANAGERS WANT

The tradeoff between customization and configuration is linked to the tradeoff or balance between user oriented implementation and business oriented implementation. Introducing a system that is accepted by users is seen in the literature as critical to the success of ES implementation (Holland and Light, 1999; Markus et al., 2000; Nah et al., 2001; Nah et al., 2003; Parr et al., 1999; Rosario, 2000; Sumner, 2000). The "user perspective" includes support for users and managers and technical staff acceding, as much as possible, to user requests in their configuration and implementation of a CRM system. In contrast to the broad organizational level issues, users can have a significant input into the implementation of these systems through requests and queries submitted to the implementation team. Being responsive to user requests and configuring new systems to support users' business processes and work procedures is particularly important where senior management do not have hands on involvement in actual work procedures, as is the case with

CRM (Petersen, 1998) which involves several stakeholders with sometimes conflicting views and priorities (Kilker and Gay, 1998). Moreover, user acceptance is absolutely critical to the success of software projects, and user participation can help to achieve this (Davis and Olsen, 1985; Mumford and Weir, 1979; Mumford, 1983).

Implementing an ERP system to satisfy business requirements and improve efficiency is the priority for managers, who want the system to go live as quickly as possible. Involving users may lead to more effective implementation across the organization but also involves huge amounts of what some management consider to be "wasted time". This was confirmed by Alan, the Sales Department Manager in Alpha Co. Management often feels that it is a waste of valuable time to expend effort on promoting a new ERP, running user acceptance tests, and involving users in pre-implementation and implementation processes. Moreover, in large organizations with multiple different departments there are often political reasons why the implementation of an ERP may be perceived differently across organizational units (Umble, Haft, and,, Umble, 2003) so that involving users from different departments may lead to a stale-mate. The integration of an ERP system needs to be coupled with business integration, to produce business processes that are stream-lined across functions and departments although standardization of work practices across functional business areas is often difficult and often meets with resistance from stakeholder groups (Aladwani, 2002; Scott & Wagner, 2003).

Alpha Co. managed the pre-implementation and implementation phases of ULTRA-CRM without the involvement of all departments in the firm. Nick described how management's attempt to implement (and customize) the system for all departments was not successful:

*basically you would customize it for four or five different sales groups but they weren't really go-*

*ing to use it making it hard to do reporting and to get an insight into what was going on at the different customers ...*

Implementation of the CRM system started in the Sales Department because the thinking at that time was that the Sales people were the ones that "made the money," and therefore were most in need of an ERP system. Although some attempt was made to promote the new system in the Sales Department (e.g. the Sales managers provided information on the advantages of the new system) the sales staff were not involved in technical specifics, such as the type of interface that was required, the functionalities it would bring to facilitate the transfer of spreadsheet data to the CRM system, or the advantages of learning to use a new, different and more complicated system. Staff were told only that the new system would enable more effective forecasting - but were told nothing more.

In 2001 Nick was aware of management's objective in implementing ULTRA-CRM; he said that:

*The problem was that we went and implemented a tool for managers not end users. So the end users didn't use it, so the managers didn't benefit. So we ended up vacuuming out a bunch of baloney that we'd put in there to make it easier for both folks could use it.*

While senior management may be able to dictate that a particular functionality be implemented, this does not necessarily translate into company wide use, and there are many ways that users can resist a new system, or at least its use as intended (Bordreau and Robey, 2005) as was demonstrated at Alpha Co. after the initial implementation – nobody really used the system because it had been designed to support managers' needs but without a clear consideration of how users actually worked.

In 2007 and 2008, Alpha Co., based on what it had learned, spent a considerable amount of time running UAT across all departments, and finally in 2009 is experiencing positive results from its implementation of a CRM system. In 2009 Alpha Co. has introduced UAT and system tests for Value Added Resellers (VARs). The lessons learned are being applied along the whole supply chain. Alpha Co.'s management has accepted that is fundamental to involve all stakeholders. In an interview in November 2008, Claire explained that Alpha Co.'s management is focusing on Partnership Relationship Management (PRM):

*a lot of what we are doing around the PRM initiative, we are at the end of development and system testing and heading into user acceptance testing next month, but this time last year it was a lot of pie in the sky requirements and trying to understand how those would map out.*

We would argue that there is a tradeoff between step by step implementation involving users and 'big bang' implementation. Alpha Co.'s managers believed that the users (employees) could be constrained by a new system built by management but found it was impossible to make the system run effectively. In terms of the external users (such as the VARs), it is even more important to involve them. Alpha Co. has had to learn how to balance the conflicting interests of achieving user acceptance and introducing a new system without the necessary preparation. According to Dougherty (1992) the development of cross-functional absorptive capacity that allows all departments to communicate and collaborate over a common aim is very important. Communication and collaboration will be difficult since in different organizational units (and functions) there will be people with different backgrounds and thus different views (Dougherty. 1992). The co-existence and accommodation of disparate views is particularly important in ERP system implementation which promotes major organizational change and the institutionalization of a dominant perspective across the organization as a result of the software's integrated design (Wagner and Newell 2004). Learning how to accommodate these different needs occurred gradually in Alpha Co. to the point where the current development (VARs) is working with multiple user groups, including external partners, to negotiate a working system.

The trade-off described here, illustrates how many organizations when implementing an ES attempt to impose a single (typically managerial) vision and silence those who may dissent from this vision by not including them in decision-making. However, the inevitable existence of heterogeneous perspectives in an organization implies some skepticism about the ability to organize through common aims (Wagner and Newell, 2004). Fuller (1978) argues that it is important to consider the demands and requirements of all parties and negotiate. For Alpha Co. the negotiation phase, that is, the extension of the customization to all departments with the aim of progressive commitment from users, provided this lesson when it was found that nobody was using the system. They have subsequently learned that accommodation and comprise is necessary.

## ROI AND SHORT TERM BENEFITS VS. LONG TERM BENEFITS

Within this theme we highlight the different perspectives – short or long term – of rganizations implementing ERP systems. Many organizations focus initially on short term financial returns from ERP system implementation. Alpha Co. was no different, being convinced that a CRM system would bring short term tangible (financial) benefits so that management focused on ROI. More than two years after beginning the implementation of the package management was forced to acknowledge that a good post-implementation

process [of ULTRA-CRM] was more important than ROI. As Nick explained:

*We were talking about ROI and quality, and the head of marketing said, "Don't waste your time. We know it's going to help. It's going to be hard from a marketing ROI perspective, but it's only going to help them get their job done better. Let's just go do it."*

This lesson is consistent with the information systems literature which highlights the importance of considering an ERP system as an intangible asset that brings benefits in the long term (Hitt, Wu, and Zhou, 2002; Hitt, 2002; Nicolau, 2004). Moreover, the literature shows that ERP systems are associated with high levels of project failure (Robbins-Gioia, 2001). However, while 20% of information technology projects are shut down prior to installation (Cooke, Gelman, & Peterson 2001), 80% are implemented. This suggests that we should change our focus from short-term problems and opportunities from the implementation of an ERP system to understanding how organizations learn to exploit the functionality of these potentially powerful systems over the long term. Alpha Co.'s management came to understand what was important in ULTRA-CRM implementation. It can be difficult to convince senior management and board members of the importance of investing in an ERP system when the financial benefits will only accrue in the long term. Alpha Co. had to undergo a process of organizational learning in terms of the time required. It could be argued that a focus on ROI in the short term was necessary for Alpha Co. to consider embarking on the CRM system project. However, the company experienced errors and lessons from the series of learning cycles that were involved in its implementation, which created (accumulated) new knowledge at the individual (e.g. Nick) and organizational (e.g. Frank, who absorbed the knowledge from the organization) levels.

## ORGANIZATIONAL CAPABILITY TO RECOGNIZE NEW EXTERNAL KNOWLEDGE BY A CONSULTANT COMPANY

When Alpha Co. in 2001 decided to use ULTRA-CRM, the management chose to spend a considerable amount of money in a consultant company –Xcons –in order to be helped in the assessment and implementation process. We use this theme to investigate the capability of Alpha Co. to absorb new external knowledge by a consultant company. We focus on this story since we have observed that Alpha had difficulties in recognizing the value of the new external knowledge of Xcons. What we see is that Alpha in 2001 had not yet developed an organizational capability to both recognize and exploit new external knowledge.

When Alpha Co. decided to hire a consultant company Xcons was one of the most expensive but Alpha decided to go with the best one since it was the first time that Alpha was implementing an ERP. Xcons and Alpha worked together for more than a year: there were two teams, one from Xcons and one from Alpha. The aim was to work on the existent processes of Alpha and implement (both customizing and configuring) the new CRM. Alpha's team mirrored Xcons team and the aim of the mirroring was to transfer knowledge from Xcons to Alpha. Claire, a person that in 2001 was working for Xcons explained this:

*Yeah it [the Xcons team] was mirrored, they were joined at the hip working very closely together. We had a configuration lead and the team helped design and develop that and the three resources I mentioned from Alpha Co. helped develop that too, our config lead oversaw all of their work ... I was on the data side with conversions and the integration points and so I actually got to teach Nick those parts so he learned how to do the data points and helped out with the conversions and integration eventually assumed responsibility for*

*all that, so a lot of it was kind of ...coming on board, helping with the development / we were responsible for a lot of knowledge transfer and that was pretty routine for Xcons folks that as you know were coming towards the end of a project how you would transition that knowledge off to the customers resources, it wasn't very new to me but ...*

In trying to understand how the knowledge transfer worked we interviewed both Xcons and Alpha Co. employees and from the data analysis it emerged that the most important suggestion that Xcons gave to Alpha –to do very few customizations –wasn't followed by Alpha management. In fact –as we have explained before (see bullet point one in this section) Alpha started the implementation of the CRM with a lot of customization.

For sure Alpha didn't follow all recommendations from Xcons for political reasons –as we have argued before in this section –but at the same time we argue that the capability of an organization to acquire new knowledge is a capability that must be developed over time. Many scholars that wrote on absorptive capacity have studied the process of absorbing new knowledge from another organization (Dyer and Singh, 1998; Lane and Lubatkin, 1998; Lane, Salk, and Lyles 2001; Mowery, Oxley, and Silverman 1996). Particularly, Lane, Salk, and Lyles (2001) propose and test a model that points out the importance of trust between two firms in order to be able to absorb new external knowledge. Although their study focuses on firms in a competitive environment we argue that most of the problems of Alpha in accepting Xcons suggestions might depend on the level of trust. Again, this issue might be connected to the scarcity of experience of Alpha in managing a long term consultancy that, moreover, might have been sponsored by the management in order to make easier the absorption of knowledge by the whole firm.

## DISCUSSION

The Alpha Co. case study was helpful in understanding how organizations learn from their mistakes at both the individual and the firm level. The four stories describe episodes where decisions were made, errors emerged, and new decisions were made. The learning cycles are consistent with the double loop learning described by Dyer and Singh (1998), who put emphasis on motivation to propose a broad relational view of absorptive capacity, focusing on the "sociological interactions" and collaborative process between organizational units and individuals. Their idea of learning is in marked contrast with the single-loop learning process that is the firm's ability to value, assimilate, and commercially utilize new external knowledge (modifying actions) described by Cohen and Levinthal (1990), and they see absorptive capacity as an 'iterative process of exchange' (modifying assumptions). As the Alpha Co. case study has shown, the implementation of an ERP is in keeping with the idea of growth and emergence as opposed to design (Truex, Baskerville and Klein, 1999) where the implementation process will never be complete because organizations are constantly changing.

The absorptive model of Cohen and Levinthal can be used to highlight 1) the importance of knowledge accumulation, that enables organizations to recognize and exploit new knowledge and 2) the importance to consider absorptive capacity as a multilevel construct.

The importance of prior (accumulated) knowledge is highlighted in our case study when we describe the lessons learned. For instance the management at Alpha came to understand that there is no a best way to decide whether and how much to customize (theme 1 above); they moderated the "business view" and stopped overlooking the users acceptance issue (theme 2). Moreover, they moved from a short term approach to a long term approach (theme 3), and they recognized that they had to "learn how to learn" from Xcons (theme

1). In turn we evidence that absorptive capacity results from a prolonged process of investment and knowledge accumulation (Tsai, 2001) and it is path-dependent (Mowery and Oxely, 1996). Concluding with Cohen and Levinthal, "prior knowledge permits the assimilation and exploitation of new knowledge. Some portion of that prior knowledge should be very closely related to the new knowledge to facilitate assimilation [...] Accumulating absorptive capacity in one period will permit its more efficient accumulation in the next. By having already developed some absorptive capacity in a particular area, a firm may more readily accumulate what additional knowledge it needs in the subsequent periods in order to exploit any critical external knowledge that may become available" (1990: 135-136).

Our explorative case study has also highlighted the fundamental importance of studying absorptive capacity at multiple levels: we have observed that it is important to maintain an organizational memory of the lessons learned by both the individuals (seen as agents) and the organization (seen as the structure) in order to achieve a (dynamic) capability that allows the institution –the "organization" - to exploit past experiences (that is –knowledge) and build new knowledge. We have observed that the organizational memory helped them make better decisions based on past experiences and mistakes. This is consistent with previously published literature. For instance Moorman and Miner (1996) concluded that organizational memory is closely related to performance. In turn they posit that memory affects innovation by influencing the process by which firms interpret incoming information and act upon it. Similarly Tripsas and Gavetti (2000) observed that experience influences managerial cognition, which eventually determines a firm's ability to manage new external knowledge. Consequently, a firm's absorptive capacity to recognize new external knowledge is a path-dependent capability that is influenced by its past experiences that are internalized as organizational memory (Zahra and George, 2002). However, absorptive capacity doesn't reside in the firm alone, but is also a function of the personal absorptive capacity of its members, as well as the structure and processes of the organizational subunits to which they belong. According to Cohen and Levinthal "*an organization's absorptive capacity will depend on the absorptive capacities of its individual members*" (pg 131).

We have also highlighted that the ability to recognize new external knowledge (absorptive capacity) is a capability that is developed over the long term. This has emerged by studying the implementation phase of the Alpha Co. CRM. Our study has highlighted that in order to develop such capability the focus might usefully be turned from looking at the short-term problems and opportunities (e.g. focus on ROI) associated with an ES implementation project towards understanding how organizations learn to exploit the functionality of these potentially powerful systems over the long term. Our argument is consistent with prior literature e.g. Lane, Koka and Pathak (2006) highlight that absorptive capacity is developed over years and is critical to a firm's long term success. It is developed over years since it is treated as a dynamic capability (Eisenhardt and Martin, 2000; Leonard-Barton, 1992; Teece and Pisano, 1997) and is critical since it can enable competitive advantage, being unique for a firm (Petaraf, 1993; Penrose, 1957; Wernefelt, 1984).

Finally we have considered absorptive capacity at the interfirm level. The Alpha Co. case study underlines that new external knowledge is difficult to absorb and exploit from another firm, even if it comes from a consultant company that –by definition –has been hired to provide useful insights. While In the last decade scholars have focused on the interfirm exchange of knowledge using the absorptive capacity perspective (Lane and Lubatkin, 1998; Lane, Salk, and Lyles, 2001; Mowery et al., 1996; Parkhe, 1991), only a few studies have considered the knowledge exchange as a process between a firm and a consultant company (e.g.

Kirsch and King, 2005) and most studies focus on the antecedents and outcomes of the knowledge transfer, overlooking the processes that facilitate such transfer. We have tried to understand how the process of knowledge transfer between two firms takes place, when one is "acquiring" knowledge (Alpha co.) and the other is "giving" knowledge (Xcons). The difficulties that Alpha Co. experienced in the process of knowledge acquisition point out that it important for an organization to have the capability to absorb knowledge rather than simply having knowledge 'only' available. In fact, the process of knowledge transfer is for instance described in George and Zahra (2002) as a complex process that has, as the authors suggest, two general states: potential (the external knowledge that a firm could acquire and utilize) and realized (the external knowledge that a firm has acquired and utilized). The 'materialization' of new knowledge is, thus, neither immediate nor taken-for-granted. On the contrary, new knowledge is built through learning processes that, as we have presented, are double loop cycles.

## CONCLUSIONS

This book chapter contributes to the knowledge of ERP implementations presenting a case study (Alpha Co.) where the authors have observed a number of themes that represent learning cycles that occurred over nine years. This longitudinal study uses the lens of absorptive capacity to understand how Alpha has learned from its mistakes (knowledge accumulation). The literature contribution of this chapter is represented by a qualitative study that uses the absorptive capacity framework (that historically has been used with quantitative analysis) to look at the dynamic process of developing the capability to exploit a new ERP.

Further studies should focus more deeply on how the qualitative method can cover the research gaps in the quantitative literature of absorptive capacity that very often has been studied only in relation to R&D and operationalized with patents. We argue that studying the absorptive process (of new knowledge) and the knowledge transformation process with a case study can help to extend what we already know from the existing absorptive capacity literature, such as the fundamental importance of trial and error learning, and the impossibility to predict a best practice where there are tradeoffs to manage.

Moreover, we would like to encourage further research that focuses on the multilevel perspective of absorptive capacity. As we have seen in our case study, both the individual and the firm level of analysis were determinant in order to enable us to understand how an organization can learn to exploit and ERP like ULTRA-CRM.

Finally, we suggest that focusing on the team level (especially cross functional team) would represent a meaningful literature contribution on both the theoretical and the empirical perspectives of our study since 1) past literature on absorptive capacity has been almost silent on the team level and 2) in ERP implementations the teams play a determinant role in rolling up packages, developing software, implementing step-by-step modules in different organizational units, and talking to both the technical and business people.

## REFERENCES

Allison, G. T. (1971). Essence of Decision. Boston.

Alshawi, S., Themistocleous, M., & Almadani, R. (2004). Integrating diverse ERP Systems, A Case Study. *Journal of Enterprise Information Management*, *17*(6), 454–462. doi:10.1108/17410390410566742

Anderson, P. A. (1983). *Decision Making by objection and the Cuban Missile Crisis*. Boston: Little, Brown.

Argyris, C. (1999). *On Organizational Learning* (2nd ed.). Boston: Blackwell Publishing.

Argyris, C., & Schon, D. A. (1978). *Organizational Learning, A Theory of Action Perspective*. Reading, MA: Addison-Wesley Publishing Co.

Avison, D., & Fitzgerald, G. (1995). *Information Systems Development, Methodologies, Techniques and Tools* (2nd ed.). London: McGraw-Hill.

Bingi, P., Shama, M. K., & Godla, J. K. (2001). Critical Issues Affecting an ERP Implementation . In Myerson, J. M. (Ed.), *Enterprise Systems Integration*. San Francisco: Taylor & Francis.

Bogenrieder, I., & Nooteboom, B. (2004). Learning Groups, What type are there? A Theoretical Analysis and an Empirical Study in a Consultancy Firm. *Organization Studies*, *25*(2), 287–313. doi:10.1177/0170840604040045

Brehm, L., Heinzl, A., & Markus, M. L. (2001). Tailoring ERP Systems, A Spectrum of Choices and Their Implications. In *Proceedings of the Annual Hawaii International Conference on Information Systems*.

Brown, J. S., & Duguid, P. (1991). Organizational Learning and Communities of Practice, Toward a Unified View of Working, Learning, and Innovation. *Organization Science*, *2*(1), 40–57. doi:10.1287/orsc.2.1.40

Cohen, W. M. C., & Levinthal, D. A. (1990). Absorptive Capacity, A New Perspective on Learning and Innovation. *Administrative Science Quarterly*, *35*, 128–152. doi:10.2307/2393553

Cooper, R. B., & Zmud, R. W. (1990). Information Technology Implementation Research, A Technological Diffusion Approach. *Management Science*, *36*(2), 123–139. doi:10.1287/mnsc.36.2.123

Cortada, J. W. (1998). *Best Practices in Information Technology, How Corporations Get the Most Value form Exploiting Their Digital Investments*. Upper Saddle River, NJ: Prentice Hall.

Crossan, M., Lane, H., & White, R. E. (1999). An Organizational Learning Framework, From intuition to Institution. *Academy of Management Review*, *24*(3), 522–537. doi:10.2307/259140

Cyert, R. M., & March, J. G. (1963). *A Behavioral Theory of the Firm*. Englewood Cliffs, NJ: Prentice Hall.

Davenport, T. (1998). Putting the Enterprise into the Enterprise System. *Harvard Business Review*, *76*(4), 121–131.

Davenport, T. H. (2000). *Mission Critical, Realizing the Promise of Enterprise Systems*. Cambridge, MA: Harvard Business School Press.

Davis, G., & Olsen, M. (1995). *Management of Information Systems*. New York: McGraw-Hill.

Dearnley, P. A., & Mayhew, P. J. (1983). In favor of system prototypes and their integration into the system development life cycle. *The Computer Journal*, *26*(1). doi:10.1093/comjnl/26.1.36

Dyer, J. H., & Singh, H. (1998). The relational View, Cooperative Strategy and Sources of Interorganizational Competitive Advantage. *Academy of Management Review*, *23*, 660–679. doi:10.2307/259056

Eisenhardt, K. M. (1989). Building theories from case study research. *Academy of Management Review*, *14*(4), 532–550. doi:10.2307/258557

Eisenhardt, K. M. (1992). Making Fast Decision in High-Velocity Environments. *Academy of Management Journal*, *32*(2), 543–576.

Elbanna, A. R. (2006). The Validity of the Improvisation Argument in the Implementation of Rigid Technology. *The Case of ES Systems* . *Journal of Information Technology*, *21*, 165–175. doi:10.1057/palgrave.jit.2000069

Gefen, D. (2004). What Makes an ERP Implementation Relationship Worthwhile, Linking Trust Mechanisms and ERP Usefulness. *Journal of Management Information Systems*, *21*(1), 263–288.

Gibson, C. B. (2001). From Knowledge Accumulation to Accommodation. Cycles of Collective Cognition in Work Groups. *Journal of Organizational Behavior*, *22*(2), 121–134. doi:10.1002/job.84

Holland, C. R., & Light, B. (1999). A Critical Success Factor Model for ERP Implementation. *IEEE Software*, (May/June): 30–36. doi:10.1109/52.765784

Jacobs, F. R., & Weston, F. C. Jr. (2007). Enterprise Resource Planning (ERP), A Brief History. *Journal of Operations Management*, *25*, 357–363. doi:10.1016/j.jom.2006.11.005

Jones, M. (1999). Structuration Theory . In Currie, W. L., & Galliers, B. (Eds.), *Rethinking Management Information Systems*. New York: Oxford University Press.

Jones, M. C., Cline, M., & Ryan, S. (2006). Exploring Knowledge Sharing in ERP Implementation, An Organizational Culture Framework. *Decision Support Systems*, *41*(2), 411–434. doi:10.1016/j.dss.2004.06.017

Kilker, J., & Gay, G. (1998). The Social Construction of a Digital Library, A Case Study Examining Implication for Evaluation. *Information Technology and Library*, *17*(2), 60–70.

Kim, W. C., & Mauborgne, R. (1998). Procedural Justice, Strategic Decision Making, and the Knowledge Economy. *Strategic Management Journal*, *19*(4), 323–338. doi:10.1002/(SICI)1097-0266(199804)19:4<323::AID-SMJ976>3.0.CO;2-F

Lane, P. J., & Lubatkin, M. (1998). Relative absorptive capacity and interorganizational learning. *Strategic Management Journal, 19*, 461–477. doi:10.1002/(SICI)1097-0266(199805)19:5<461::AID-SMJ953>3.0.CO;2-L

Lane, P. J., Salk, J. E., & Lyles, M. A. (2001). Absorptive Capacity, Learning, and Performance in International Joint Ventures. *Strategic Management Journal, 22*, 1139–1161. doi:10.1002/smj.206

Lee, J., Siau, S., & Hong, S. (2003). Enterprise Integration with ERP and EAI. *Communications of the ACM, 46*(2), 54–60. doi:10.1145/606272.606273

Leonard-Burton, D. (1992). Core Capabilities and Core Rigidities, A paradox in Managing New Product Development. *Strategic Management Journal, 13*, 111–125. doi:10.1002/smj.4250131009

Levitt, B., & March, J. G. (1988). Organizational Learning. *Annual Review of Sociology, 14*, 319–340. doi:10.1146/annurev.so.14.080188.001535

Light, B. (1999). The maintenance implications of the customization of ERP software. *Journal of Software Maintenance and Evolution . Research and Practice, 13*(6), 415–429.

Luo, W., & Strong, D. M. (2004). A Framework for Evaluating ERP Implementation Choices. *IEEE Transactions on Engineering Management, 51*(3), 322–333. doi:10.1109/TEM.2004.830862

March, J. G. (1991). Exploration and Exploitation in Organizational Learning. *Organization Science, 2*(1), 71–87. doi:10.1287/orsc.2.1.71

Markus, M. L., Tanis, C., & Fenema, P. C. (2000). Multisite ERP implementation. *Communications of the ACM, 43*, 42–46. doi:10.1145/332051.332068

Meeus, M. T. H., Oerlemans, L. A. G., & Hage, J. (2001). Patterns of interactive learning in a high-tech region. *Organization Studies, 22*, 145–172. doi:10.1177/017084060102200106

Moorman, C., & Miner, A. S. (1998). Organizational Improvisation and Organizational Memory. *Academy of Management Review, 23*(4), 698–723. doi:10.2307/259058

Mowery, D. C., Oxley, J. E., & Silverman, B. S. (1996). Strategic Alliances and Interfirm Knowledge Transfer. *Strategic Management Journal, 17*, 77–91.

Mumford, E. (1983). Participative systems design, Practice and theory. *Journal of Occupational Psychology, 4*(1), 47–57.

Mumford, E., & Weir, D. (1979). *Computer systems in work design – the ETHICS method.* New York: Wiley.

Nutt, P. C. (1976). Models for Decision Making in Organizations and Some Contextual Variables Which Stipulate Optimal Use. *Academy of Management Review, 1*, 84–98. doi:10.2307/257489

Nutt, P. C. (1984). Types of Organizational Decision Processes. *Administrative Science Quarterly, 29*, 414–450. doi:10.2307/2393033

Pan, S. L., Newell, S., Huang, J. C., & Cheung, A. W. K. (2001). Knowledge Integration as a Key Problem in an ERP Implementation. In *Proceedings of the 22nd International Conference of Information Systems.*

Scapens, R. W. (1990). Researching management accounting practice, the role of case study methods. *The British Accounting Review, 22*(3), 259–281. doi:10.1016/0890-8389(90)90008-6

Scapens, R. W. (2004). Doing case study research . In Humphrey, C., & Lee, B. (Eds.), *The Real Life Guide to Accounting Research* (pp. 257–279). Oxford, UK: Elsevier. doi:10.1016/B978-008043972-3/50017-7

Srivardhana, T., & Pawlowski, S. D. (2007). ERP Systems as an Enabler of Sustained Business Process Innovation, A Knowledge-Based View. *The Journal of Strategic Information Systems, 16*(1), 51–69. doi:10.1016/j.jsis.2007.01.003

Stein, T. (1998, August 31). SAP Sued over R/3. *InformationWeek,* 134–135.

Teece, D. J., Pisano, G., & Shuen, A. (1997). Dynamic Capabilities and Strategic Management. *Strategic Management Journal, 18*(7), 509–533. doi:10.1002/(SICI)1097-0266(199708)18:7<509::AID-SMJ882>3.0.CO;2-Z

Truex, D., Baskerville, R., & Klein, H. (1999). Growing systems in emergent organizations. *Communications of the ACM, 42*(8), 117–123. doi:10.1145/310930.310984

Umble, E. J., Haft, R. R., & Umble, M. M. (2003). Enterprise Resource Planning, Implementation Procedures and Critical Success Factors. *European Journal of Operational Research, 146,* 241–257. doi:10.1016/S0377-2217(02)00547-7

Van de Bosch, F. A. J., Baaij, M. G., & Volberda, H. V. (2005). How Knowledge Accumulation has Changed Strategy Consulting. Strategic Option for Established Strategic Consulting Firms. *Strategic Change, 14*(1), 25–34. doi:10.1002/jsc.705

Walsh, J. P., & Ungson, G. R. (1991). Organizational Memory. *Academy of Management Review, 16*(1), 57–91. doi:10.2307/258607

Wenhong, L., & Strong, D. M. (2004). *A Framework For Evaluating ERP Implementation Choices.* Engineering Management –IEEE Transations.

Yin, R. (2003). *Case Study Research, Design and Methods* (3rd ed.). London: Sage.

## KEY TERMS AND DEFINITIONS

**Absorptive Capacity:** The capability to recognize, absorb, share, and exploit knowledge.

**Double Loop:** Represents a technique of learning. In other words actors benefit past experience to improve their knowledge.

**Iterative Process:** A process that develops cycles. It is referred to the learning process.

**Learning Process:** The process that occurs when actors, teams, organizations accumulate external knowledge. Learning process includes also the metabolization and the exploitation of such knowledge.

**Organizational Memory:** The memory that characterizes an organization leaving out of consideration the actors that is e.g. a capability which does not belongs to specific individuals or groups but belongs to the whole organization.

**Qualitative:** A research methodology and philosophy. Qualitative method is based on observing instead of measuring. Qualitative method privileges the subjective point of view of individuals and rejects positivistic approaches.

**Tradeoff:** An organizational dilemma. It occurs when making a choice emerges the need to balance between two alternatives which have both points of strength and points of weakness. Generally is impossible to build a best practice over a tradeoff since its management depends on a number of contingencies.

# Chapter 14
# Challenges in Enterprise Information Systems Implementation:
## An Empirical Study

**Ashim Raj Singla**
*Indian Institute of Foreign Trade, New Delhi, India*

## ABSTRACT

*Enterprise Information Systems are the most integrated information systems that cut across various organizations as well as various functional areas. Small and medium enterprises, competitor's behavior, business partner requirement are the identified and established dimensions that affect these systems. Further it has been observed that such enterprise wide software systems prove to be a failure either in the design or its implementation. A number of reasons contribute in the success or failure of such systems. Enterprise information systems inherently present unique risks due to tightly linked interdependencies of business processes, relational databases, and process reengineering, etc. Knowledge of such risks is important in design of system and program management as they contribute to success of overall system. In this chapter an attempt has been made to study the design and implementation risks factors for ERP systems in large scale manufacturing organizations. Based on the model used to study ERP risks and thus the findings, various recommendations have been put forward to suggest a strategy so as to mitigate and manage such risks.*

## INTRODUCTION

Enterprise Information systems are a corporate marvel, with a huge impact on both the business and information technology worlds. Organizations today have been talking about Enterprise Resource Solutions as a means of business innovation. They are designed to enhance competitiveness by upgrading an organization's ability to generate timely and accurate information throughout the enterprise and its supply chain. A successful Enterprise wide information system implementation can shorten production cycles, increases accuracy of demand for materials management & sourcing and leads to inventory reduction because of material management, etc. ERP is the first such enterprise wide product,

DOI: 10.4018/978-1-61520-625-4.ch014

Copyright © 2010, IGI Global. Copying or distributing in print or electronic forms without written permission of IGI Global is prohibited.

*Figure 1. Vendor sophistication: Number of vendors, vendor quality (source: Frost and Sullivan)*

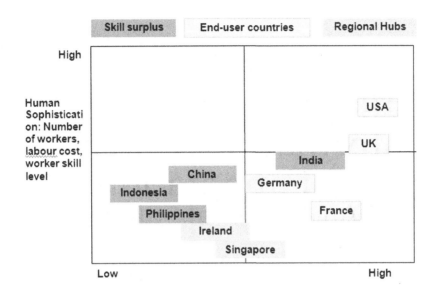

implementing client server concept and which has changed nature of jobs in all functional areas and provides one of the primary tool for reengineering. The ERP is being used for improving business productivity, streamlining business operations, reducing cost and improving efficiency worldwide. ERP systems act as integrators, bringing multiple systems together under one program and database. Further, CRM help in keeping a better track on customers thereby improving business processes. Whereas, a typical legacy IT systems are composed of multiple software products, each operating discretely, often resulting in conflicting information for an executive to reconcile when determining profitability status and growth strategies. With Sarbanes Oxley and other regulatory requirements, it is becoming increasingly difficult for utilities to operate or be compliant without full integration across the enterprise. Thus the adoption of ERP is going to increase.

Today, India has emerged as the fastest growing IT hub in the world with growth dominated by IT software and services such as Custom Application Development & Maintenance (CADM), System Integration, IT Consulting, Application Man-

agement, Infrastructure Management Services, Software testing, Service-oriented architecture and Web services.

## THE IT INTELLECTUAL ADVANTAGE FOR INDIAN SMES

India has always been considered as a strong IT destination due to its young tech-savvy English speaking population. When being rated on Human sophistication, India comes just below two nations which are US and UK while on vendor sophistication; we are almost equal to Germany and share way better than China. This is being depicted in the IT Intellectual advantage chart being shown above in figure 1. (Source: Frost & Sullivan, 2006).

Hence, the intellectual advantage is all there, but what India needs is that this knowledge should be passed to the grassroots. The challenging Indian mid-market needs an understanding of the advantages of technology as it helps them to integrate with large business supply chain for faster decision making and planned time management.

Enterprise applications usage in India began way back in the early 1990's when the large manufacturing enterprises started adopting ERP to streamline their processes through technology. Soon, the large enterprises from various verticals went into the bandwagon of adopting ERP, CRM and SCM solutions with the increasing complexities in their businesses. Presently, the Small and Medium Enterprises (SME's) are also adopting these enterprise applications in a big way with the increased growth, awareness and the need to streamline the business processes. This rising demand from the mid-market has attracted the focus of most ERP vendors and has made this segment a very competitive one in the Indian market. According to Frost & Sullivan, the Indian Enterprise Applications software license Market crossed the $100 million mark in 2007. With an expected overall 10-year CAGR of 16.77 percent, the market is estimated to reach $372.05 million in 2015.

Further, various other surveys on Indian mid-market Adoption of ERP indicate that:

- Small and Medium Enterprises have been slow at information technology adoption. Adoption of IT tools low in priority. Feeling is that the same money can be utilized to improve and expand business. Short term focus towards financial gains.
- Access Market International (AMI) study shows that only 3% of SMEs have a LAN at their office or factories, just 15% have internet connection, 4% have broadband and mere 1% have website.
- An IDC survey shows that 80% of large enterprises were aware of ERP and this was less than 35% in case of SMEs.

The result of such surveys indicates a slow growth of enterprise wide information systems in small and midsized organizations. So a study to identify challenges faced by such organizations in ERP systems implementation is highly important.

## Issues and Challenges in Enterprise Information Systems Implementation

Implementing an ERP system is a challenging endeavor as the implementation is complex and resource intensive and there are organizational, operational and cultural issues involved. According to Gray A. Langenwalter (2000), ERP implementation failure rate is from 40% to 60%, yet companies try to implement these systems because they are absolutely essential to responsive planning and communication. The competitive pressure unleashed by the process of globalization is driving implementation of ERP projects in increasingly large numbers, so an methodological framework for dealing with complex problem of evaluating ERP projects is required (AnandTeltumbde, 2000).

It has also been found that, unique risks in ERP design arises due to tightly linked interdependencies of business processes, relational databases and process reengineering (Dalal et al., 2004). Similarly, business risks drive from the models, artifacts and processes that are chosen and adopted as a part of implementation and are generated from the firm's portfolio of MAP's with respect to their internal consistency and their external match with business partners. Organizational risks derive from the environment – including personnel and organizational structure – in which the system is chosen and implemented (Holsapple et al., 2002).

According to Umble & Umble (2002), three main factors that can be held responsible for failure of ERP system are: poor planning or poor management; change in business goals during project; and lack of business management support. In another study, it has been found that companies spent large money in developing ERP systems that are not utilized. It is quite common for ERP project to finish late, cost more than predicted, unreliable and difficult to maintain. Moreover BPR also had a high failure rate with consultants estimating that as many as 70% of the BPR projects fails (Hammer

*Table 1. Challenges in enterprise information system implementation*

| Risk Factor | Discussions |
|---|---|
| Users involvement | Lack of full-time commitment of customers to project management and project activities. *MarySumner (2000)* |
| | Lack of sensitivity to user resistance is a risk. Avrahm Shtub (2001) |
| | Users are not adequately involved in ERP Design. *Daniel E.O'Leary (2002), Sally Wright and Arnold M. Wright (2002)* |
| Users training | Without adequate training, system can never be used properly, nor can it ever achieve the returns that were projected. Gibson Nicola et al (1999), *Daniel E. O'Leary (2002), Sally Wright and Arnold M. Wright (2002).* |
| Process reengineering (BPR) | Failure to redesign business processes. *MarySumner (2000)* |
| | Process Reengineering was required. *Sally Wright and Arnold M. Wright (2002)* |
| | If expert did not expect that process reengineering is required that would force us to question their expertise. *Ribbers Schoo (2002)* |
| | Employees feeling powerless due to downsizing, lack of critical information due to insufficient participation, may lead to BPR failure. *PERNILLE KRAEMMERAND, CHARLES MOLLER, HARRY BOER (2003)* |
| ERP lacked adequate control. | Inability to built bridges to legacy applications. *Teltumbde Anand (2000)* |
| | ERP system initially lacked adequate control *Umble & Umble (2002)* |
| | Control risk potential varies by mandatory nature of ERP subsystems. Risk is more aligned with the company's business operations. *Sally Wright and Arnold M. Wright (2002)* |
| System Design | Poorly designed, it did not adequately mirror required processes. *Daniel E. O'Leary (2002), Sally Wright and Arnold M. Wright (2002)* |
| | Failure to adhere to standardized specifications which the software supports. *MarySumner (2000)* |
| | Lack of integration. Avraham Shtub (2001) |
| | Every new versions changes processes; System increases variety and fragmentation of processes; Linking ERP to other system increases complexity. Ribbers Schoo (2002). |
| Vendor Performance | Potential problems arise with third party implementation partners. Vendors may be learning over the new version or deploy collage students on implementation. *Theodore Grossman and James Walsh (2004)* |
| | Vendors may over promise new features in new versions. Organizations should be highly skeptical of these promises because they often turn out to be worthless. *Theodore Grossman and James Walsh* (2004) |
| Infrastructure Design | Infrastructure design must be a collaborative effort between client and vendors. *Shivraj Shantanu (2000)* |
| | ERP systems are based on advanced technologies that require replacement of existing infrastructure. It is risky as it requires additional capital. *NIV AHITUV, SEEV NEUMANN and MOSHE ZVIRAN (2002)* |
| Implementation is poorly executed. | *Allen David (2002)* |
| | *Colette Rolland, Naveen Prakash (2001)* |
| System does not provide information needed. | System is not task-technology fit. *MarySumner (2000)* |
| | System designed did not provide information needed for the task. *Sally Wright and Arnold M. Wright (2002)* |
| Data conversion is poorly executed. | *Davis, Gorden B. (1986)* |
| | *Teltumbde Anand (2000)* |
| | Legacy data cannot always be converted for ERP systems. A group must be assigned responsibilities to evaluate the quality and completeness of legacy data. *Theodore Grossman and James Walsh (2004)* |
| Budget overrun. | *Ribbers Schoo (2002)* |
| Time overrun. | *Daniel E. O'Leary (2002)* |

*continued on following page*

*Table 1. continued*

| Risk Factor | Discussions |
|---|---|
| Skill Mix | Insufficient training and reskilling, insufficient internal expertise, lack of business and technology knowledge, failure to mix internal and external expertise effectively are risk factors. *MarySumner (2000)* |
| Management structure and strategy | Lack of top management support, Lack of proper management control structure, Lack of project champions and ineffective communications, etc. *Allen David (2002)* |
| Network capacity to allow proper access to ERP system. | Stress testing of network and system must be performed before going live. *Umble & Umble (2002)* |
| Security Risks | Some ERP subsystems (Payroll, supply-chain, financial) exhibit greater control and security risks than others. *Gibson Nichola et al (1999)* |
| | Failure to check unauthorized access to information *Sally Wright and Arnold M. Wright (2002)* |

and Champy, 1993). Hammer (1990) advocates that the power of modern technology should be used to radically design business processes to achieve dramatic improvements in their performance. From a software perspective ERP systems is complete. But from the business perspective it is found that software and business processes needs to be aligned, which involves a mixture of business process design and software configurations (Hamer, 1990). So a purely technical approach to ERP system design is insufficient.

According to David Allen, Thomas Kern (2002), a careful use of communication and change management procedures is required to handle the often business process reengineering impact of ERP systems which can alleviate some of the problems, but a more fundamental issue of concern is the cost feasibility of system integration, training and user licenses, system utilization, etc. needs to be checked. A design interface with a process plan is an essential part of the system integration process in ERP. By interfacing with a process plan module, a design interface module helps the sequence of individual operations needed for the step-by-step production of a finished product from raw materials (Hwa Gyoo Park).

Similar such contributions for identifying the challenges in enterprise information system implementation are made by various researchers. An attempt has been made to identify such challenges (see Table 1).

After summarizing the literature analysis given in table 1 and also based on the discussion with users of ERP, implementation consultants, academicians, etc. a list of risk factors in enterprise information systems implementation was prepared (see Table 2).

The knowledge of such risks factors is important in planning and conducting assurance engagements of the reliability of these complex computer systems. But it is also highly important to rank these risk factors in accordance to their importance. So, keeping in view this objective, a study with the objectives to identify and analyze risk factors in planning and design of ERP system was conducted. The study was conducted in two large manufacturing public sector organizations located in northern India. First organization specializes in R&D as well as manufacturing in telecommunication systems and various related equipments. It has developed its enterprise-wide product to streamline the whole system. On the other hand, the second organization is large tractor manufacturing unit and is controlling its own several subsidiary units. One of its subsidiaries is developing mini trucks. This organization is also using its self designed enterprise-wide product.

## Research Methodology Adopted

1. Secondary data for research was collected from related books, publication, annual

*Table 2. Risk factors in implementation of enterprise information system*

**Factor 1. General Risk factors**
    1. Users are not adequately involved in design.
    2. Users are not adequately trained to use the ERP system.
    3. Process reengineering is required.
    4. ERP system initially lacked adequate control.
    5. Poorly designed, it did not adequately mirror required processes.
    6. Implementation is poorly executed.
    7. System designed did not provide information needed to do the task.
    8. Data conversion is poorly executed.
    9. Difficulty in executing new processes.

**Factor 2. Risk factors on the basis of time, cost and other factors.**
    1. Budget overrun.
    2. Time overrun.
    3. Lack of benefits.
    4. System does not meet business plan criteria.

**Factor 3. Risk factors encountered while migrating to new system.**
    1. Time needed for implementation.
    2. Technical problems with new version.
    3. Bad estimates with migration partners.
    4. Cost involved.
    5. Quality of migration support.

**Factor 4. Risk factors from users involved in various phases of ERP system.**
    1. Inattention to work with the new system.
    2. Inadequate training or failure to follow procedures of new system.
    3. Not smart enough to understand the system advantages.
    4. Are lazy and want to continue working with traditional procedures.
    5. Overly perfectionist in their experience.
    6. Too difficult to learn and use in reasonable amount of time.
    7. Creating political problem with some users by changing political or work distribution in organization.
    8. Lack of internal expertise and skillset.
    9. Lack of ability to recruit and retain qualified ERP system developers.

**Factor 5. Risk factors in planning and Requirement analysis.**
    1. Lack of proper top management support.
    2. Lack of Champion and proper project management structure.
    3. Failure to redesign business processes.

**Factor 6. Risk factors in system design of ERP.**
    1. System is expensive.
    2. Increasing variety and fragmentation of processes.
    3. Choice of operating system may influence the knowledge and people required.
    4. Network capacity to allow proper access to ERP system.
    5. Every new versions changes processes.
    6. Linking ERP to other system increases complexity.

**Factor 7. Security issues**
    1. Too little effort goes into supporting effective use.
    2. System is not updated as business needs change.
    3. Failure to check unauthorized access to information.
    4. Unauthorized use of access codes and financial passwords.
    5. Theft by entering fraudulent transaction data.
    6. Theft by stealing or modifying data.

**Factor 8. Other risk factors.**
    1. Attempt in industry to steal business secrets.
    2. Extensive reliance on computer and internet connectivity.
    3. Large R&D effort as percentage of revenues.
    4. National / International media profile.
    5. Operator error while executing transaction.
    6. Software bugs or data errors

reports, and records of organization under study.

2. Primary data has been collected through questionnaire-cum-interview technique. For this purpose questionnaire was created on already established models and survey of literature. Questionnaire was first pre-tested on 20 managers from the actual sample to be interviewed for checking its reliability and content validity. Cronbach's alpha test was applied, where the value of coefficient was 0.87. Thus pre-tested & modified questionnaire was administered to all the sampled respondents. For developing design model, the managers in the EDP departments of each of the selected organizations were interviewed. Where as for the purpose of developing implementation model all the managers in the EDP departments along with an appropriate sample of the managers at the three levels of the management of each of the selected organizations were selected. The sample of the randomly selected managers was proportionate and statistically sound that represents the universe of managers of the selected organizations. 115 experienced respondents from both the companies who specialize in their related production skills and use of ERP system had participated in the study.

3. Data was collected on 5 point Likert scale depending on the relative importance of a factor. Finally the factor analysis is applied to analyze the data to arrive useful conclusions using SPSS package. Table 6 and 7 represents the rotated factor matrix, i.e. the final statistics, for risk factors in ERP implementation and risk factors in ERP design and planning. All the factor loadings that are greater than 0.45 (ignoring the sign) have been considered for further analysis. The 34 variables of these tables were then loaded on 8 factors (see table 3). In order to find out as to which of the above given

factors rank as the most satisfying/dissatisfying for ERP implementation, the factor wise average score (from 5 pt. Likert scale) was calculated. The satisfaction level of the factors on the basis of factor-wise average scores has been categorized as given below (see Table 4). The naming of the factors has been done on the basis of the size of the factor loadings for respective variables. Greater the factor loading, greater are the chances of the factor being named after these variables (see Table 3).

## RESULTS AND DISCUSSIONS

The thus collected data was subjected to various types of statistical methods to analyze the risk factors in ERP system design and implementation. Table 3 lists the score for each of the 5 risk factors in implementation and 3 risk factors in ERP system design. Table 4 gives the ranking of these implementation risk factors as calculated by factor analysis. The rotated component matrix of factor analysis for both the classes of implementation risk factors is given respectively in Table No. 6 and 7. An analysis of Table 3 reveals that many of these ERP implementation problems revolve around inadequate training, non involvement of users in the new system, project management issues, ineffective communication with users, implementation constraints, problems in process design and migration problems, etc. The analysis of table 4 reveals that project management issues (4.29) at various phases of ERP implementation is most important risk factor. It is important in accomplishing project objectives and aligning the whole system as per new implementation plan. It is also found that after the BPR is applied; jobs and responsibilities of users working in a particular system got changed which lead to political problems among employees. More over implementation of ERP creates fear in minds of the employees (users) of loosing their jobs; as the implementation of ERP

*Table 3. Average score of implementation risk factors as tested in both organizations (N=115)*

| Risk factors in ERP system Implementation. | | | | | | | |
|---|---|---|---|---|---|---|---|
| **Factor/ Rating** | **Issues** | **Frequency** | | | | | |
| | | **1** | **2** | **3** | **4** | **5** | **Avg** |
| Implementation Constraints (3.876) | Process reengineering is required. | 0 | 7 | 27 | 53 | 28 | 3.89 |
| | Budget overrun. | 0 | 1 | 12 | 43 | 59 | 4.39 |
| | Time overrun. | 0 | 6 | 18 | 52 | 39 | 4.08 |
| | Inattention to work with the new system. | 0 | 7 | 35 | 55 | 18 | 3.73 |
| | Not smart enough to understand the system advantages | 4 | 24 | 36 | 37 | 14 | 3.29 |
| After going live (3.4375) | Bad estimates with migration partners. | 1 | 32 | 50 | 26 | 6 | 3.03 |
| | Failure to check unauthorized access to information. | 0 | 7 | 53 | 35 | 20 | 3.59 |
| | Extensive reliance on computer and internet connectivity. | 1 | 26 | 53 | 23 | 12 | 3.17 |
| | Large R&D effort as percentage of revenues. | 0 | 1 | 35 | 47 | 32 | 3.96 |
| ERP Software (3.1325) | Too difficult to learn and use in reasonable amount of time | 0 | 37 | 46 | 25 | 5 | 2.95 |
| | Theft by entering fraudulent transaction data. | 0 | 21 | 66 | 22 | 6 | 3.11 |
| | Operator error while executing transaction. | 0 | 19 | 61 | 35 | 0 | 3.14 |
| | Software bugs or data errors | 2 | 13 | 49 | 47 | 4 | 3.33 |
| System Migration (3.25) | Data conversion is poorly executed. | 0 | 14 | 42 | 49 | 10 | 3.48 |
| | Difficulty in executing new processes. | 0 | 7 | 50 | 43 | 15 | 3.57 |
| | National / International media profile. | 8 | 32 | 61 | 14 | 0 | 2.70 |
| Project Management (4.29) | Users are not adequately trained to use the ERP system | 0 | 0 | 24 | 47 | 44 | 4.17 |
| | Implementation is poorly executed. | 0 | 5 | 14 | 58 | 38 | 4.12 |
| | Creating political problem with some users by changing political or work distribution in organization. | 0 | 1 | 15 | 36 | 63 | 4.40 |
| | Lack of internal expertise and skill set. | 0 | 0 | 15 | 30 | 70 | 4.48 |
| Risk factors in ERP system planning and design. | | | | | | | |
| System Design (3.35) | Users are not adequately involved in design. | 5 | 15 | 37 | 37 | 21 | 3.47 |
| | ERP system initially lacked adequate control. | 0 | 32 | 32 | 33 | 18 | 3.32 |
| | Poorly designed, it did not adequately mirror required processes. | 2 | 12 | 39 | 36 | 26 | 3.63 |
| | Technical problems with new version. | 4 | 3 | 23 | 58 | 27 | 3.88 |
| | Choice of operating system may influence the knowledge and people required. | 18 | 36 | 39 | 12 | 10 | 2.65 |
| | Extensive reliance on computer and internet connectivity. | 1 | 26 | 53 | 23 | 12 | 3.17 |
| Implementation team (3.76) | Lack of proper top management support. | 0 | 0 | 8 | 49 | 58 | 4.43 |
| | Lack of Champion and proper project management structure. | 0 | 7 | 34 | 44 | 30 | 3.84 |
| | Failure to redesign business processes. | 0 | 7 | 28 | 39 | 41 | 3.99 |
| | Network capacity to allow proper access to ERP system. | 1 | 52 | 35 | 24 | 3 | 2.79 |
| Business process design (3.76) | System does not meet business plan criteria. | 5 | 23 | 42 | 41 | 4 | 3.14 |
| | Increasing variety and fragmentation of processes | 0 | 4 | 4 | 54 | 53 | 4.36 |
| | Every new versions changes processes. | 0 | 22 | 25 | 47 | 21 | 3.58 |
| | Large R&D effort as percentage of revenues. | 0 | 1 | 35 | 47 | 32 | 3.96 |

*Table 4. Ranking of ERP system risk factors as tested in both organizations (N=115)*

| Implementation Risk Factors | | |
|---|---|---|
| **Risk Factors** | **Score** | **Ranking** |
| Project Management | 4.29 | 1 |
| Implementation constraints | 3.87 | 2 |
| Business Process design | 3.76 | 3 |
| Implementation team | 3.76 | 4 |
| After going live | 3.43 | 5 |
| System design | 3.35 | 6 |
| System migration | 3.25 | 7 |
| ERP Software | 3.13 | 8 |

system leads in downsizing the number of jobs required in different business processes. Similarly lack of experts; application specific knowledge; user experience and problem to recruit and retain good ERP specialists; also contribute to project risk. Followed by Project management issues are the risk factors arising due to implementation constraints (3.87), like budget overrun, time overrun and BPR, etc is ranked 2nd. Similarly the problems in business process design (3.76) and

*Table 5. Recommendations to reduce/control risks factors in ERP Projects*

| Risks | Strategies for ERP risk management |
|---|---|
| User involvement and training | - Communicating users about project strategy and objectives<br>- Classifying users on the basis of their experience & skill set and assigning them appropriate roles.<br>- Total user involvement and commitment.<br>- Effectual training strategy for different roles.<br>- Upgrading existing skillset to meet the requirements. |
| Project management | - Strategies for recruiting and retaining technical personnel<br>- Model based implementation strategy.<br>- Check on budget and time requirements at each stage of project.<br>- Attain top management commitment to redesign business processes<br>- Defining levels and hierarchies in organization for effective decision making. |
| Technology Implementation | - Strategy for migration and data conversion from existing legacy system to newly designed system.<br>- Maintain log of software bugs and transaction failures.<br>- Simple training strategy for even very complicated modules.<br>- Effective use of existing IT infrastructure |
| System Design | - Design should check process fragmentation.<br>- Strategy for migrating from existing software version to new version.<br>- Design should meet business plan criteria and adequately mirror required processes.<br>- Use Object- and component- oriented techniques in system design.<br>- COM/SOM/OMA/OMG object models can be used make object definition independent of programming language.<br>- System architecture should support partitioning of application on different computers. |
| Integration and Technology planning | - Carefully select operating system and network capacity keeping in mind the user requirement and transaction loads.<br>- Record of technical problems with new system.<br>- Client-Server / Distributed Network implementation based on object communication.<br>- Object communication can be implemented through CORBA or OLE. |

*Table 6. Rotated component matrix for risk factors in ERP system implementation as tested in both organizations. (N=115)*

| Issues | Component | | | | |
|---|---|---|---|---|---|
| | 1 | 2 | 3 | 4 | 5 |
| Users are not adequately trained to use the ERP system | .455 | .299 | -1.394E-02 | 3.412E-03 | .666 |
| Process reengineering is required. | .797 | .243 | 8.175E-02 | .170 | .178 |
| Implementation is poorly executed. | .464 | 4.914E-02 | .202 | .364 | .485 |
| Data conversion is poorly executed. | .269 | 4.749E-02 | .312 | .642 | .340 |
| Difficulty in executing new processes. | .101 | -1.597E-03 | .279 | .765 | .168 |
| Budget overrun. | .683 | -.121 | .280 | -3.843E-02 | .259 |
| Time overrun. | .763 | -.247 | .274 | .242 | .109 |
| Bad estimates with migration partners. | .272 | .589 | 6.407E-03 | .472 | .130 |
| Quality of migration support. | .449 | .454 | .411 | .173 | -4.345E-02 |
| Inattention to work with the new system. | .655 | .492 | .122 | 1.364E-02 | 3.242E-02 |
| Not smart enough to understand the system advantages. | .678 | .360 | .310 | .340 | 1.601E-02 |
| Too difficult to learn and use in reasonable amount of time. | .208 | .460 | .599 | .238 | -6.862E-02 |
| Creating political problem with some users by changing political or work distribution in organization. | -8.265E-03 | .273 | -.107 | .246 | .795 |
| Lack of internal expertise and skillset. | .222 | 1.028E-02 | .446 | 4.712E-02 | .658 |
| Failure to check unauthorized access to information. | -8.165E-02 | .688 | .243 | .120 | .334 |
| Theft by entering fraudulent transaction data. | 9.981E-02 | .437 | .500 | .382 | .122 |
| Extensive reliance on computer and internet connectivity. | 8.267E-02 | .750 | -.110 | .443 | 8.689E-02 |
| Large R&D effort as percentage of revenues. | 6.529E-02 | .759 | .286 | -.105 | .190 |
| National / International media profile. | 8.454E-02 | .324 | 3.378E-02 | .682 | -2.287E-02 |
| Operator error while executing transaction. | .221 | .283 | .808 | .164 | .122 |
| Software bugs or data errors | .304 | -4.219E-02 | .807 | .119 | 7.500E-02 |

system design (3.35) are ranked 3rd and 6th according to the study. In system design approach, less emphasis may be placed on the technical aspects of software development, but there is a need to balance the business process design, software configuration and project management aspects of ERP implementation with the overall strategy and structure of the organization. Project needs to be based on enterprise-wide design and we must define what is needed at the enterprise-wide level and then apply it to the business unit level. Similarly if a system design does not adequately mirror required processes, does not meet business plan and may also leads to increased variety and fragmentation of processes, than it becomes a potential risk factor. Risk factors in system design also include software factors like lack of discipline and standardization of code, developing wrong functions and wrong user interface, continuous stream of changes, lack of effective methodology and poor estimation which can lead to both cost and time overruns.

It is also found that lack of support at various management levels and problems in building a right implementation team (3.76) is ranked as 4th important risk factor. A improper manage-

*Table 7. Rotated component matrix for risk factors in ERP system design as tested in both organizations (N=115)*

| Issues | Component | | |
|---|---|---|---|
| | 1 | 2 | 3 |
| Users are not adequately involved in design. | .715 | -.184 | .431 |
| ERP system initially lacked adequate control. | .855 | .128 | .269 |
| Poorly designed, it did not adequately mirror required processes. | .798 | 3.250E-02 | 4.444E-02 |
| System does not meet business plan criteria. | .516 | .177 | .554 |
| Technical problems with new version. | .681 | -.106 | .565 |
| Lack of proper top management support. | .141 | .613 | .315 |
| Lack of Champion and proper project management structure. | -2.059E-03 | .875 | 6.089E-04 |
| Failure to redesign business processes. | -5.239E-03 | .883 | .135 |
| Increasing variety and fragmentation of processes | 7.265E-02 | .165 | .880 |
| Choice of operating system may influence the knowledge and people required. | .660 | .486 | -.170 |
| Network capacity to allow proper access to ERP system. | .424 | .648 | .255 |
| Every new versions changes processes. | 7.803E-02 | .457 | .636 |
| Extensive reliance on computer and internet connectivity. | .735 | .240 | 7.804E-02 |
| Large R&D effort as percentage of revenues. | .509 | .133 | .509 |

ment structure can lead to a decentralized system and thus created excessive duplication of effort. Further the presence of many people working at same level also is a reason of conflicts among their views and non resolution of problems. Similarly ERP implementation team must include right mix of people with functional & technical knowledge with best of the peoples available in the organization. Generally, it is very difficult to hire and retain good ERP professionals. Similarly in the After going live phase with new system (3.43), common problems include failure to check unauthorized access, extensive reliance on computer and internet connectivity, system migration (3.25), errors in data conversion and difficulty in executing new processes are the common risk factors.

According to the study, problems in the ERP software (3.13), is ranked lowest in the list. Some times there are few software bugs which can create transaction errors. Also it is quite possible that the software is too difficult to learn and use in reasonable amount of time.

Risk factors in terms of Inadequate technical infrastructure i.e. need for new hardware and software on the basis of application size (project scope, number of users), technical complexity and links to existing legacy system, etc. needs to be tackled.

## RECOMMENDATIONS

It emanates from the above discussions that ERP system links together an organizational strategy, structure and business processes with the IT systems. It is important to communicate what is happening, including the scope, objectives and activities of the ERP project. Similarly appropriate staffing and personnel shortfalls need to be checked carefully. In case of inadequate internal expertise, it is recommended that organization should hire consultants for technical and procedural challenges in design and implementation of specific application modules. Instead of large number of programmers with average skills, it would be better to have few business consultants those who have specialized expertise in their specific domains. Similarly, it is very important to create a perfect project management plan keeping in mind the project size & structure, skill set available, experience of the company, etc. to avoid high project cost and time overruns. The various strategies for mitigating as well as for managing ERP risks have been listed in Table 5.

To conclude, it may be emphasized that user involvement, user training, project management, technology implementation, system design, integration and technology planning are the key issues which are the critical risk factors in ERP design and implementation. A meticulous planning of these issues would surely help in smooth and successful implementation of ERP systems in any organization in general and in the selected organization in particular.

# REFERENCES

Ahituv, N., Neumann, S., Zviran, M. (2002). A system development methodology for ERP systems. *Journal of Computer Information Systems.*

Allen, D., Kern, T., & Havenhand, M. (2002). ERP Critical Success Factors: an exploration of the contextual factors in public sector institutions. In *Proceedings of 35th Annual Hawaii International Conference on System Sciences.*

Avraham, S. (2001). A framework for teaching and training in the ERP era. *International Journal of Production Research, 3*, 567–576.

Boynton, A. C., & Zmud, R. W. (1984). *An Assessment of Critical Success Factors. Sloan Management Review.* University of North Carolina.

Colette, R., & Naveen, P. (2001). Matching ERP system functionality to customer requirement. IEEE, 1090-705X.

Davis, G. B. (1986). An empirical study of the impact of user involvement on system usage and information satisfaction. *Communications of the ACM, 29*(3), 232–238. doi:10.1145/5666.5669

Franch, X., Illa, X., & Antoni, P. J. (2000). *Formalising ERP selection criteria.* Washington, DC: IEEE.

Gibson, N., Light, B., & Holland, C. P. (1999). Enterprise Resource Planning: A Business Approach to Systems Development. In *Proceedings of 32nd Hawaii International Conference on System Sciences.*

Goyal, D. P. (2000). *Management Information System Managerial Perspective.* New Delhi: Macmillan India Ltd.

Grossman, T., Walsh, J. (2004). Avoiding the pitfalls of ERP system implementation. *Information systems management.*

Hammer, M., & Champy, J. (1994). *Reengineering the Corporation.* London: Nicholas Brealy Publishing.

Hwa, G. P. (1999). Framework of Design interface module in ERP. In *1999 IEEE International Symposium on assembly and task planning.*

Kamna, M., & Goyal, D. P. (2001). Information Systems Effectiveness – An Integrated Approach. *IEEE Engineering and Management Conference (IEMC'01) Proceedings on Change Management and the New Industrial Revolution,* (pp. 189-194), Albany, NY.

Kraemmerand, P., Moller, C., & Boer, H. (2003). ERP implementation: an integrated process of radical change and continous learning. *Production Planning and Control, 14*(4), 38–348. doi:10.1080/0953728031000117959

Legare, T. L. (2002). The Role of Organizational Factors in Realizing ERP Benefits. *Information system management.*

O'Leary, D.E. (2002). Information system assurance for ERP systems: Unique Risk Considerations. *Journal of Information systems, 16,* 115-126.

Ribbers, S. (2002). Program management and complexity of ERP Implementation. *Engineering management Journal, 14*(2).

Saiu, K., & Messersmith, J. (2002). Enabling Technologies for E-Comm and ERP integration. *Quarterly Journal of Electronic Commerce, 3,* 43–52.

Scheer, W. & Habermann, F. (2000). Making ERP a success. *ACM, 43*(4).

Shivraj, S. (2000). Understanding user participation and involvement in ERP use. *Journal of Management Research, 1*(1).

Sumner, M. (2000). Risk factors in enterprise-wide/ERP projects. *Journal of Information Technology, 15,* 317–327. doi:10.1080/02683960010009079

Teltumbde, A. (2000). A framework for evaluating IS projects. *International Journal of Production Research, 38*(17).

Umble, E. J. & Umble, M.M. (2002). Avoiding ERP implementation Failure. *Industrial Management.*

Wright, S., & Wright, A. M. (2002). Information system assurance for Enterprise Resource planning systems: unique risk considerations. *Journal of Information Science, 16,* 99–113.

## APPENDIX

**Extraction Method:** Principal Component Analysis, **Rotation Method**: Varimax with Kaiser Normalization. Rotation converged in 14 iterations.

**Extraction Method**: Principal Component Analysis.**Rotation Method**: Varimax with Kaiser Normalization. Rotation converged in 8 iterations.

# Section 2
# Supply Chain Management (SCM) System using Information Technology (IT) and Mathematical Modeling

# Chapter 15

# Meta–Heuristic Approach to Solve Mixed Vehicle Routing Problem with Backhauls in Enterprise Information System of Service Industry

**S.P. Anbuudayasankar**
*Amrita School of Engineering, India*

**K. Ganesh**
*Global Business Services – Global Delivery, IBM India Private Limited, India*

**K.Mohandas**
*Amrita School of Engineering, India*

**Tzong-Ru Lee**
*National Chung Hsing University Taiwan, ROC*

## ABSTRACT

*This chapter presents the development of simulated annealing (SA) for a health care application which is modeled as Single Depot Vehicle routing problem called Mixed Vehicle Routing Problem with Backhauls (MVRPB), an extension of Vehicle Routing Problem with Backhauls (VRPB). This variant involves both delivery and pick-up customers and sequence of visiting the customers is mixed. The entire pick-up load should be taken back to depot. The latest rapid advancement of meta-heuristics has shown that it can be applied in practice if they are personified in packaged information technology (IT) solutions along with the combination of a Supply Chain Management (SCM) application integrated with an enterprise resource planning (ERP) resulted to this decision support tool. This chapter provides empirical proof in sustain of the hypothesis, that a population extension of SA with supportive transitions leads to a major increase of efficiency and solution quality for MVRPB if and only if the globally optimal solution is located close to the center of all local optimal solutions.*

DOI: 10.4018/978-1-61520-625-4.ch015

Copyright © 2010, IGI Global. Copying or distributing in print or electronic forms without written permission of IGI Global is prohibited.

## INTRODUCTION

Supply chain management (SCM) processes can be classified in to two major categories: planning and execution. While planning supply chain investigates the processes related to forecasting material requirements, planning for production and distribution, and so on where as execution in supply chain focuses on the actual implementation of the supply chain plan, comprising processes such as production and stock control, warehouse management, transportation, and delivery (Ballou, 1978; Lambert et al., 1998). Both planning and execution are widely considered due to its critical impact on customer service, cost effectiveness, and, thus, competitiveness in increasingly demanding global markets. At the same time equal importance is to be given to the service sectors like food distribution, medicine distribution, blood distribution, etc.

Modern information technology (IT) and the development in software applications facilitate solving the problems related to the supply chain processes at all three decisional levels of SCM namely, strategic, tactical and operational levels. In the recent days transportation planning at the operational level received wide attention due to its complexity of the problem and normally comprises of linear programming based models. Their functionality is mainly found in most ERP systems. The operational level applications utilise mostly heuristic and meta-heuristic algorithms.

Most of the Logistics Management problems have been largely addressed as Vehicle Routing Problem (VRP) particularly in the context of manufacturing industries (Laporte and Osman 1995). Modeling and analyzing the service sectors is equally important in the optimization point of view and the benefit of serving human life as well. Blood bank management is a vital, life-saving activity with some appealing characteristics as far as logistics is concerned.

In general blood will be procured in large quantity from blood donation camps. A Central Blood Bank (CBB) governs the procurement, processing, storage and distribution of blood. Regional Blood Banks (RBB) facilitates in the functions of CBB. Thus logistics of blood bank consists of blood procurement, processing, cross matching, storage, distribution, recycling, pricing, quality control and outdating (Pierskalla, 1974; Cohen et al., 1979; Pierskalla and Roach, 1972; Perry, 1996). This chapter considers routing of CBBs, RBBs and blood donation camps, where as pickup occurs in blood donation camps (fresh blood) and also in the RBBs (unused blood), to be transferred to another RBB so as to meet the demand. The sequence of visiting RBB and blood donation camps is mixed. This problem fit in to the variant of VRP called Mixed Vehicle Routing Problem with Backhauls (MVRPB).

The remainder of the chapter is organized as follows: The motivation of problem is explained in Section 2. The structure of blood bank supply chain is described in Section 3. The literature survey for blood bank logistics is detailed in Section 4. Detailed literature of VRPB and MVRPB is provided in Section 5. MVRPB is explained in Section 6. The lower bound of MVRPB is proposed in Section 7. Simulated Annealing for MVRPB is explained in Section 8. The computational results are detailed in Section 9. Section 10 concludes the chapter.

## MOTIVATION OF THE PROBLEM

In today's highly competitive and demanding environment, the pressure on both public and private organizations is to achieve a better way to deliver values to end customers. There has been a growing recognition that the two goals, cost reduction and customer service are achieved through logistics and SCM (Houlihan, 1988; New and Payne, 1995; New, 1997; and Hines *et al.*, 1998). Organizations have different strategies to manage various functions, based on their respective organizational circumstances. Though there are differences and changes in the strategies adopted by various organizations, major functions for any organization associated with SCM are procurement, forecasting demand, capacity planning, selecting vendors and customers, distribution, and inventory management.

This chapter is focused on the two issues, procurement and distribution management of SCM. To understand the relevance of SCM in government sectors, one must understand the difference between the objective of a government / public sector enterprise and that of a private sector enterprise. The objective of government / public sector enterprise is not maximization of profit solely, but also economic development of the nation (as a long term goal) and the welfare of the society; whereas a private sector enterprise is oriented towards the sole objective of maximization of profit (Gupta and Chandra, 2002). Although the objectives of the two exclusive categories of enterprises are entirely different, they share some features like the satisfaction of their respective consumers by providing them with the right product, in the right condition and at the right time, at the least cost by allocating limited resources (of the nation and/or enterprise) for this purpose. In the government sector (in India), the SCM paradigm that can be used by the public sector organizations involved in many areas, like fertilizer production industry, steel industry, food grain procurement and distributions, petroleum products, postal clearance and delivery system, import and export, banking and financial services and public health services. Out of which the public health service is the critical one. Hospitals, dispensaries and blood banks form the backbone of the health services offered by the government of India. The functioning of these organizations needs to be strengthened. Unavailability of essential drugs, blood and other medical supplies leads to crisis. So, the application of SCM for the procurement and distribution of the life saving medical drugs, blood and other medical items overcome this crisis and provide services in time for meeting social objectives and promotes welfare of the society at large.

## BACKGROUND OF BLOOD BANK LOGISTICS

A typical structure of a blood bank supply chain is shown in Figures 1 and 2 for a system with $p$ blood camps, $c$ CBBs and $r$ RBBs. The objective is to find the routes covering CBBs, RBBs and blood camps for blood distribution and collection (procurement) with a fleet of capacitated homogeneous vehicles.

*Figure 1.*

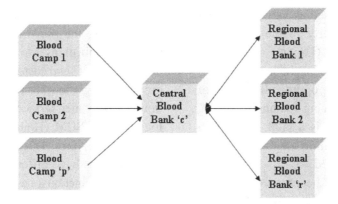

*Figure 2.*

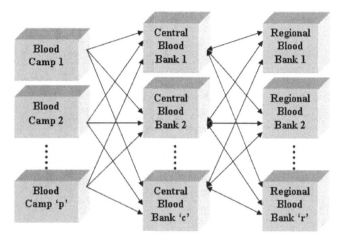

## Blood Collection and Distribution Problem

A distinctive blood bank has to make sure the availability of blood and should be able to deliver it as and when required, not only the quantity but the required blood group to the RBBs, which is highly uncertain. Though it represents the classical VRP, the practical state of affairs includes the complexity of mixed delivery and pickup of the vehicles along its route. Figure 3 represents the exact situation.

Blood camps (PP) will deliver blood to Central Blood Bank (C). We can categorize the Regional Blood Banks in two different ways. One is Regional Blood Bank with only Delivery (RD) and the other is RBB with only Pick-up (RP). From the RD, unused Blood will be taken from that node which will be delivered to C. So the flow of the vehicle is considered to be for both the purposes. Figure 3 represent the situation clearly which depict the lack of integration among the CBB, RBBs and blood camps.

The task is to find a route pattern from CBB to all RBBs for distribution and collection of blood and to all blood camps for collection of fresh blood. Typically, a vehicle can start from a CBB, distribute blood to the RBBs, and also

covers certain RBBs and blood camps in the middle of distribution to collect the blood. Figure 4 represent the route that covers both pickup and delivery nodes, where the CBB, RBBs and blood donation camps are integrated.

This problem can be represented as Mixed Vehicle Routing Problem with Backhauls (MVRPB). The assumption made here is that blood cannot be transferred from one RBB to another. All blood must either originate from or end up at the CBB.

## LITERATURE BACKGROUND FOR BLOOD BANK LOGISTICS

During the last 30 years, significant contributions have been made in addressing many blood management problems, especially the tactical and operational type at the hospital and regional level (Prastacos, 1984). These contributions include both interesting theoretical results and the successful implementation of the systems that was designed on the basis of these results.

A number of papers are available on the statistical analysis of demand and usage of blood in hospital and regional level, which is a vital input for blood distribution management (Elston and

*Figure 3.*

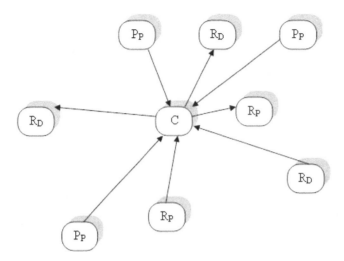

Pickrel, 1963; Rabinowitz and Valinsky 1970; and Brodheim and Prastacos, 1980). Ordering is one of the blood bank's most important policies which have an impact in distribution. The policy determines the frequency and the size of the orders placed by the inventory location (hospital) to the regional centers. Both analytical (Nahmias, 1977; Cohen, 1976; and Cosmetatos and Prastacos, 1981) and empirical research (Jennings, 1973; Brodheim et al. 1976 and Cohen and Pierskalla 1979) were attempted by several researchers. Collection and Distribution planning system involves targets for average daily collection (Prastacos and Brodheim, 1980), a forecasting system to predict the quantity of supply from different sources (Frankfurter et al., 1974), an information system (Prastacos and Brodheim, 1979 and Kendall, 1980) with an extensive data base and effective data base management and a routing and scheduling algorithm to schedule visits so as to achieve the desired targets. But only few papers addressed the issues of routing and scheduling algorithm. Pegels et al. (1975) developed an interactive planning and scheduling system for hospital level. Brodheim

*Figure 4.*

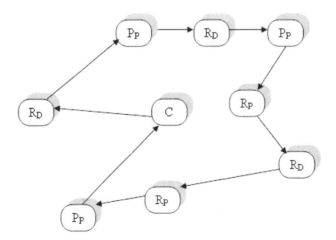

and Prastacos (1979) designed the decision support system namely Programmed Blood Distribution System (PBDS) focused mainly on the policy and inventory management issues. Prastacos (1981) devised the optimal policy by considering outdate and shortage costs for routing and scheduling systems. Federgruen et al. (1982) extended the same by considering location-dependent costs. Some of the recent literature on the routing variants for blood bank logistics include: Ganesh and Narendran (2005); Ganesh and Narendran (2007a); Ganesh and Narendran (2007b) and Ganesh and Narendran (2007c).

From this, it is evident that, there is a lot of scope in the research on routing and scheduling for blood bank distribution and collection systems.

## LITERATURE BACKGROUND FOR VRPB AND MVRPB

### Vehicle Routing Problem with Backhauls (VRPB)

For the classical VRPB, a number of exact and heuristic algorithms are available and its extensions have also been proposed considerably. Some recent research on VRPB is presented in this review.

The first constructive method for the classical VRPB was proposed by Deif and Bodin (1984) which is the extension of Clarke and Wright's (1964) savings algorithm. Goetschalckx and Jacobs-Blecha (1989) formulated the Vehicle Routing Problem with clustered Backhauls (VRPCB). They developed the heuristic method for the multi vehicle case in which the clustering as well as the routing part are solved by means of a space filling curve heuristic. Anily (1996) developed a lower bound on the optimal total cost and a heuristic solution for the VRPB.

Goetschalckx and Jacobs- Blecha (1993) used a clustering method in their second paper, which

is based on the generalized assignment approach proposed by Fisher and Jaikumar (1981) where the number of routes K that would be constructed in the heuristic was specified in advance. The line-haul customers and the backhaul customers are sorted according to their increasing distance from the depot and decreasing distance to the depot respectively. By solving the generalized assignment heuristics, both the customer sequences are divided into K clusters. After clustering both the customers separately, line-haul and backhaul routes are merged according to the best combination of connections that has the smallest distance, at the same time not allowing any backhaul customer before a line-haul customer is served.

Toth and Vigo (1999) proposed another two-phase method for the classical VRPB. They solved both symmetric and asymmetric VRPB problem using the cluster-first route-second heuristic approach.

Mingozzi et al. (1999) and Toth and Vigo (1997) approached VRPB with the exact methods. Mingozzi et al. (1999) formulated the VRPB as an integer programming problem and described a procedure that computes a valid lower bound to the optimal solution cost by combining different heuristic methods for solving the dual LP-relaxation of the exact formulation. Toth and Vigo (1997) described a new (0-1) integer programming formulation of the VRPB based upon a set-partitioning approach. They used a heuristic procedure to solve the dual LP-relaxation of the integer formulation to obtain a valid lower bound to the VRPB.

Wade and Salhi (2001) proposed an Ant System Algorithm for the VRPB. Ropke (2005) addressed the VRP with pickup and delivery and solved using Adaptive Large Neighborhood Search heuristic, Branch-and-Cut algorithm and Branch-and-price algorithms for the VRPB problems with time windows. Ropke and Pisinger (2006) improved their own version of the large neighborhood search heuristic (Ropke and Pisinger, 2004) to solve the

VRPB. Brandao (2006) presented a new tabu search algorithm which was able to match almost all the best published solutions and also found many new best solutions particularly for a large set of benchmark problems. In a nutshell Ropke and Pisinger (2006) and Brandao (2006) have proposed competing results for the benchmark data sets addressed so far. An extensive survey on VRPB and its sub classes is available in Ropke (2005) and Parragh et al. (2007).

Crispim and Brandao (2001) applied the reactive tabu search and Wassan (2007) proposed hybrid operation of reactive tabu search and adaptive memory programming to solve VRPB. For more heuristics and detailed explanations for the VRPB refer the book of Toth and Vigo (2002a).

## Mixed Vehicle Routing Problem with Backhauls (MVRPB)

Some of the recent works on MVRPB are presented in this review. The vehicle routing problem with mixed deliveries and pickups is a challenging extension to the vehicle routing problem that lately attracted growing attention in the literature (Wassan et al. 2008).

The first study for the MVRPB was presented by Deif and Bodin (1984). Casco et al. (1988) presented a load-based backhaul insertion algorithm which solves the mixed VRPB. A cluster-first route-second heuristic was adopted by Halse (1992) using a relaxed assignment problem and modified route improvement procedures. Mosheiov (1995) discussed an extension of the MVRPB, namely the pickup and delivery location problem in which the objective of the problem is the determination of the best location of the central depot. Mosheiov (1998) considered the multi vehicle case of the MVRPB in which the author proposed tour partitioning heuristics for solving the problem.

Salhi and Nagy (1999) investigated an extension to the insertion based heuristics which

is based on the idea of inserting more than one backhaul at a time in the MVRPB. Duhamel et al. (1997), Nanry and Barnes (2000) and Crispim and Brandão (2005) proposed tabu search heuristic to solve MVRPB.

Wade and Salhi (2002) proposed a new version of the MVRPB named as restricted VRPB (RVRPB) which aims at producing a practical compromise between the classical VRPB and the MVRPB. In this new type of the problem, mixed line-haul and backhaul customers are permitted but the position along the routes where the first backhaul may be served is restricted. The typical constraint of the problem prevents the inclusion of backhaul customers until a given percentage of the total line-haul load has been delivered. To solve this new backhaul they presented a heuristic where the user is asked to set a restriction percentage on the insertion of backhaul customers. Again Wade and Salhi (2003) proposed an ant system algorithm to find the set of routes with the least cost for the MVRPB.

Aringhieri et al. (2004) provided a graph model based on an Asymmetric Vehicle Routing formulation and for MVRPB. Ropke and Pisinger (2004) presented an improved version of the large neighborhood search heuristic proposed by Ropke (2003). They have proposed two data sets for the MVRPB. The first set is based on a relaxed version of Goetschalckx and Jacobs-Blecha (1989) problems which was already studied by Halse (1992) and Wade and Salhi (2003). Authors have constructed the other data set, which was proposed by Nagy and Salhi (2003), by transforming 14 well-known Capacited VRP (CVRP) instances into MVRPB instances. Three MVRPB instances were constructed from each CVRP instance, having 10%, 25% and 50% of the customers transformed to backhaul customers. They have applied the heuristics to the data sets proposed by Dethloff (2002), Salhi and Nagy (1999) and Nagy and Salhi (2003).

Tütüncü et al. (2009) presented a new visual

interactive approach for the classical VRP with backhauls and its extensions. The visual inter-active approach that is based on Greedy Randomised Adaptive Memory Programming Search (GRAMPS) is described.

Ganesh and Narendran (2007a) proposed a multi-constructive heuristic to solve a new variant of VRP with sequential delivery and pick-up. The proposed methodology can also be adapted to solve MVRPB. In their next paper Ganesh and Narendran (2007b) a multi-constructive heuristic is proposed to solve a new variant of VRP with sequential delivery, pick-up and time-windows. The proposed methodology can also be leveraged to solve MVRPB.

Gribkovskaia et al. (2008) developed classical construction and improvement heuristics, as well as a tabu search heuristic and tested on a number of instances derived from VRPLIB. Wassan et al. (2008) investigated two versions of the classical VRPB problems with a meta-heuristic approach based on reactive tabu search. They have designed the meta-heuristic initially for the simultaneous case and later solved the mixed case and suggested that the approach yields good results. Anbuu-dayasankar et al. (2008) proposed a two-phase solution methodology with the combination of clustering approach and Or-opt heuristic to solve MVRPB a case study of third party logistics service provider organization. Anbuudayasankar et al. (2009) proposed a Composite Genetic Algorithm for MVRPB.

From the study it is understood that the scope for the development of meta-heuristic methodology to solve MVRPB is wide.

## MIXED VEHICLE ROUTING PROBLEM WITH BACKHAULS

The classical *VRP* is concerned with a set of customers to be served by a set of vehicles housed at a depot or distribution centre located in the same geographical region. The objective of the problem is to devise a set of vehicle routes with minimum distance in such a way that all delivery points are served. The demands of the points assigned to each route do not exceed the capacity of the vehicle that serves the specified route. The objective is to minimise the total distance travelled by all the vehicles and in turn to minimise the overall distribution cost. While *VRP* has received much attention from researchers in the last four decades (Toth and Vigo, 2002), variants of this problem with more and more constraints have attracted the attention of scientific community of late.

One of the important extensions of the classical *VRP* is the *VRPB*. This addresses two types of customers called line-haul (delivery) and backhaul (pick-up). The critical assumption is that, on each route, all deliveries have to be made before any goods can be picked up so as to avoid rearranging the loads on the vehicle. The quantities to be delivered and picked up are fixed and known in advance and the vehicle fleet is assumed to be homogeneous (every vehicle is having the same capacity). An example for this type of problem is the distribution of mineral water from a producer to a retailer (line-haul) may be coupled with the collection of empty bottles from the retailer to the producer (backhaul). The feasible solution to the problem consists of a set of routes where all deliveries for each route are completed before any pickups are made and the vehicle capacity is not violated either by the line-haul or backhaul customers assigned to the route. The main objective of this problem is to find such a set of routes that minimises the total distance travelled.

The variant highlighted here is named as *MVRPB* which is an extension of classical variant *VRPB*. Here deliveries after pickups are allowed in which the line-haul and backhaul customers are mixed along the routes. The Objective and the constraints for the *MVRPB* are same as in the classical *VRPB* apart from the fact that backhauls can be served before all line-haul customers are served. More complications arise because of this fluctuating load. In the classical *VRPB* it is sufficient to check that the total delivery load and the total pickup load for each route do not separately exceed the maximum vehicle capacity. But in *MVRPB* it is not sufficient to check this alone as the load of the vehicle either decrease or increase at each customer depending on whether the customer has line-haul or backhaul load, respectively. So it is essential to check that the vehicle capacity should not exceed at any arc along the route. Once a backhaul customer is placed on a route in the classical *VRPB* then the route direction becomes fixed but this is not in the case of the *MVRPB* where direction may not necessarily be fixed by the inclusion of a backhaul customer. Hence, feasibility needs to be checked in both the directions.

*MVRPB* can be stated as follows: A set of *N* nodes with deterministic demands for delivery and pick-up services that have to be visited by a fleet of homogeneous vehicles in a pure mixed sequence, all of which originate and terminate at the same node (depot). The objective of *MVRPB* is to find optimal routes for an entire fleet of vehicles.

The following assumptions are made:

- all routes start and end at the node of origin, also known as depot
- each node in *N* is visited and served exactly once
- demand at any node shall never exceed the vehicle capacity *Q*
- all vehicles have the same capacity and are stationed at the node of origin
- split delivery is not permitted
- each vehicle makes exactly one trip
- all delivery quantities are loaded at the depot and all quantities picked up must be unloaded at the depot
- every route should start with a *pure delivery* node, then cover a mix of *delivery and pick-up* nodes to satisfy load feasibility.
- no route shall comprise *pick-up* nodes exclusively

With *VRP* itself being *NP*-hard (Aarts and Lenstra, 1997) and mixed sequence of delivery and pick-up being harder constraints, *MVRPB* is clearly *NP*-hard.

## LOWER BOUND FOR THE PROBLEM

Consider an optimal solution, which consists of partitions $(N_1, N_2, \ldots N_K)$ of the set of N nodes assigned to different vehicles (Mosheiov, 1994; Haimovich and Rinnooy Kan, 1985).

Notations

| | |
|---|---|
| L | Length of the optimal tour through the nodes in subset Nj. |
| Ri | Euclidean distance between the location of node i and CBB o. |
| $\overline{R}$ | Average Euclidean distance for all locations. |
| Z* | Cost corresponding to the optimal solution, and |
| $Z^H$ | Cost of tour obtained by for any given heuristic H. |

**Proposition 1:** A lower bound on the cost is

$$\frac{2}{3Q}\overline{R}N$$

A proof can be seen in Figure 5. The flow chart of the research methodology is explained in Figure 6.

## SIMULATED ANNEALING FOR MVRPB

The development of SA is initiated by the seminal work of Kirkpatrick (1983). The step-wise procedure of the proposed SA for MVRPB is explained below.

*Figure 5.*

Proof:

$$Z^* = \sum_{j=1}^{n} L\, N_j$$

$$\geq \sum_{j=1}^{n} 2 \max_{i \in N_j} R_i$$ → Since the farthest location in the set $N_j$ needs to be visited

$$\geq \sum_{j=1}^{n} \frac{2}{|N_j|} \sum_{i \in N_i} R_i$$ → Since no Euclidean distance in Nj is greater than the maximum

$$\geq \sum_{j=1}^{n} \frac{2}{3Q} \sum_{i \in N_i} R_i$$ → $|N_j|$ must be $\leq 3Q$ since Nj contains no more than Q pickup customers, no more than Q delivery customers and no more than Q pickup-delivery customers

$$= \frac{2}{3Q} \sum_{i \in N} R_i$$

$$= \frac{2}{3Q} \overline{R} N$$

*Figure 6.*

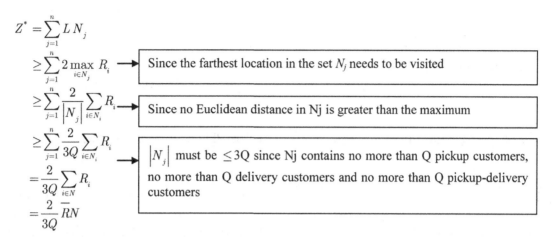

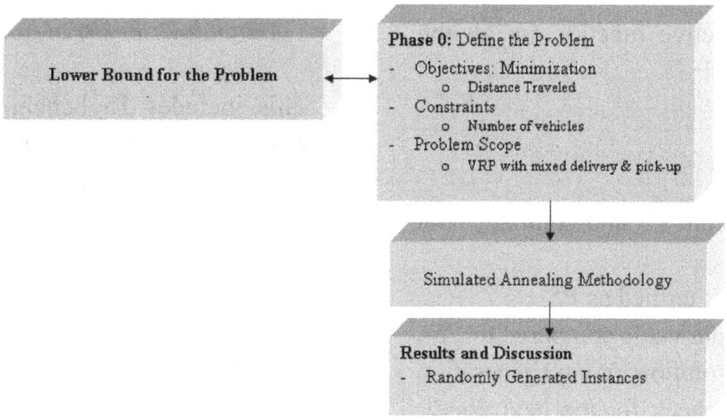

Step 0.

    Set the maximum number of generation (G)

Step 1.

    Initialize the Population Size (*PS*)

Step 2.

    Randomly generate the initial population (*IP*)

$IP = (P_1, P_{2,......}, P_{PS}) \in N$

    Where $N$ = Solution space

Step 3.

    Initialize the relation of neighbourhood

Step 4.

    Initialize the number of changeover

$C = m * PS$

Where m $\in$ {0.1}, a random number

**Step 5.**

Initialize the maximum temperature ($T_{max}$) and minimum temperature ($T_{min}$)

**Step 6.**

Initialize the cooling rate ($A$); Where A $\in$ *{0.1}*

**Step 7.**

Randomly select cooperator $P_o$

**Step 8.**

Calculate the objective function for all the solution in PS and for $P_o$

**Step 9.**

Choose the best from *PS* and compare with $P_o$.
The best from *PS* is termed as $PS_b$
If $P_o$ is the minimum value compared to $PS_b$, place the $P_o$ as initial solution for next generation for changeover, else check for the next condition.

**Step 10.**

Check for the following condition:
If Random(0,1) $\leq$ ($e^{(-D P_o)}$ / $T_{max}$)
Set $PS_b$ as initial solution for next generation for changeover.
Else, retain $P_o$ as solution for next generation for changeover.

**Step 11.**

Alter the maximum temperature for each solution as

$$T_{max} = A * T_{max}$$

After every iteration, increment G by 1

**Step 12.**

Stop, if G is reached. Else, go to Step 1.

## COMPUTATIONAL RESULTS

Computational results for MVRPB are detailed here. The proposed SA is programmed in C++ and executed on a 1.7 GHz Pentium IV. It has been tested on 15 benchmark data sets of *Anbuudayasankar et al.* (2009).

- *15 benchmark data-sets from Anbuudayasankar et al. (2009)*

This includes 15 benchmark data-sets are proposed by Anbuudayasankar *et al.* (2009). The node for the 15 data-sets ranges from 10 to 50 customers. The backhaul percentage for the data-sets is 50%, 66% and 80%, respectively. In order to evaluate the SA, we compute the Relative percentage Deviation (RD) for each solution. The RD of SA is defined as RD = ((($O^H$ – $O*$) / $O^H$) 100%) where $O^H$ is the objective value obtained by SA and $O*$ is the lower bound or best known solution of the variant. An average of the RD's is then calculated for the best solutions and presented in last row of each Table. Table 1 exhibit the outcome of SA for 15 benchmark data-sets from Anbuudayasankar *et al.* (2009).

## CONCLUSION

This chapter has developed a heuristic based on SA to solve MVRPB. The standard benchmark data-sets are chosen from the literature for comparison. In few cases, results show that SA is competitive in solving MVRPB. The advantages

*Table 1. Comparison of SA for MVRPB Benchmark Data-sets of Anbuudayasankar et al. (2009)*

| Name | Number of customers | Number of Backhauls | Number of Vehicles | Best Known Optimal Solution (BK) | SA Best Solution | RD from BK (%) |
|---|---|---|---|---|---|---|
| Data 1.1 | 10 | 25 | 2 | 83343 | 83343 | 0.00% |
| Data 1.2 | 15 | 16 | 3 | 88865 | 88865 | 0.00% |
| Data 1.3 | 25 | 10 | 4 | 109026 | 109026 | 0.00% |
| Data 2.1 | 10 | 38 | 2 | 112303 | 112303 | 0.00% |
| Data 2.2 | 15 | 25 | 3 | 118526 | 118526 | 0.00% |
| Data 2.3 | 25 | 15 | 4 | 132647 | 132647 | 0.00% |
| Data 3.1 | 10 | 25 | 2 | 119713 | 119713 | 0.00% |
| Data 3.2 | 15 | 16 | 3 | 136620 | 136620 | 0.00% |
| Data 3.3 | 25 | 10 | 4 | 165785 | 165785 | 0.00% |
| Data 4.1 | 35 | 38 | 5 | 162412 | 162412 | 0.00% |
| Data 4.2 | 50 | 25 | 6 | 198411 | 199382 | 0.49% |
| Data 5.1 | 35 | 15 | 5 | 222417 | 222417 | 0.00% |
| Data 5.2 | 50 | 50 | 6 | 202710 | 203458 | 0.37% |
| Data 6.1 | 35 | 33 | 5 | 220141 | 220141 | 0.00% |
| Data 6.2 | 50 | 20 | 6 | 286183 | 289623 | 1.20% |
| Average Relative Percentage Deviation (%) | | | | | | 0.14% |

Note: Negative Symbol Deviation indicates the better performance of SA

of the proposed heuristic include short time in finding the best solution for vehicle routing and scheduling and improved management of the distribution resources to enhance ERP. Combination of this technique with the advantage of new IT technologies perform better when compared to traditional management methods and enhances in better utilization of the distribution of resources, more effective processes, customer service level improvements, support of the supply chain operational decisions, a strategic and tactical decision support tool as well. The research limitations are the problem size and the number of data sets. This study perhaps will make a well-built groundwork for additional augmentation of relevance of meta-heuristic to solve MVRPB. SA can be enhanced using cooperative transitions. Time windows, heterogeneous capacitated vehicles and multiple objectives are the additional constraints for the future scope.

# REFERENCES

Anbuudayasankar, S.P., & Ganesh, K., Tzong-Ru Lee & Mohandas, K. (2009). COG: Composite Genetic Algorithm with Local Search Methods to Solve Mixed Vehicle Routing Problem with Backhauls – Application for Public Health Care System. *International Journal of Services and Operations Management*, *5*(5), 617–636. doi:10.1504/IJSOM.2009.025117

Anbuudayasankar, S. P., Ganesh, K., & Mohandas, K. (2008). CORE: a heuristic to solve vehicle routing problem with mixed delivery and pick-up. *ICFAI Journal of Supply Chain Management*, *5*(3), 7–18.

Anily, S. (1996). The vehicle-routing problem with delivery and back-haul options. *Naval Research Logistics*, *43*, 415–434. doi:10.1002/(SICI)1520-6750(199604)43:3<415::AID-NAV7>3.0.CO;2-C

Aringhieri, R., Bruglieri, M., Malucelli, F., & Nonato, M. (2004). An asymmetric vehicle routing problem arising in the collection and disposal of special waste. *Electronic Notes in Discrete Mathematics*, *17*(20), 41–47. doi:10.1016/j.endm.2004.03.011

Ballou, R. H. (1978). *Basic Logistics Management.* Englewood Cliffs, NJ: Prentice-Hall.

Brodheim, E., Hirsch, R., & Prastacos, G. (1976). Setting Inventory Levels for Hospital Blood Banks. *Transfusion*, *16*(1), 63–70.

Brodheim, E., & Prastacos, G. P. (1980). *Demand, usage and issuing of blood at hospital blood banks. Technical report.* Operations Research Laboratory, The New York Blood Center.

Cohen, M. A. (1976). Analysis of single critical number ordering policies for perishable inventories. *Operations Research*, *24*, 726–741. doi:10.1287/opre.24.4.726

Cohen, M. A., & Pierskalla, W. P. (1979). Target inventory levels for a hospital blood bank or a decentralized regional blood banking system. *Transfusion*, *19*(4), 444–454. doi:10.1046/j.1537-2995.1979.19479250182.x

Cohen, M. A., Pierskalla, W. P., Sassetti, R. J., & Consolo, J. (1979, September-October). An overview of a hierarchy of planning models for regional blood bank management, Administrative Report. *Transfusion*, *19*(5), 526–534. doi:10.1046/j.1537-2995.1979.19580059802.x

Cosmetatos, G., & Prastacos, G. P. (1981). *A perishable inventory system with fixed size periodic replenishments.* Working Paper 80-10-01, Department of Decision Sciences, the Wharton School, University of Pennsylvania.

Crispim, J., & Brandao, J. (2001). Reactive tabu search and variable neighbourhood descent applied to the vehicle routing problem with backhauls. In *MIC'2001 4th Metaheuristic International Conference, Porto, Portugal,* July 16–20.

Crispim, J., & Brandao, J. (2005). Metaheuristics applied to mixed and simultaneous extensions of vehicle routing problems with backhauls. *The Journal of the Operational Research Society*, *56*, 1296–1302. doi:10.1057/palgrave.jors.2601935

Deif, I., & Bodin, L. (1984). Extension of the Clarke and Wright algorithm for solving the vehicle routing problem with backhauling. In A. Kidder, (Ed.), *Proceedings of the Babson conference on software uses in transportation and logistic management,* Babson Park, (pp. 75–96).

Dethloff, J. (2002). Relation between vehicle routing problems: an insertion heuristic for the vehicle routing problem with simultaneous delivery and pick-up applied to the vehicle routing problem with backhauls. *The Journal of the Operational Research Society*, *53*(1), 115–118. doi:10.1057/palgrave/jors/2601263

Duhamel, C., Potvin, J. Y., & Rousseau, J. M. (1997). A tabu search heuristic for the vehicle routing problem with backhauls and time windows. *Transportation Science*, *31*, 49–59. doi:10.1287/trsc.31.1.49

Elston, R., & Pickrel, J. C. (1963). A statistical approach to ordering and usage policies for a hospital blood transfusion. *Transfusion*, *3*, 41–47. doi:10.1111/j.1537-2995.1963.tb04602.x

Federgruen, A., Prastacos, G. P., & Zipkin, P. (1982). *An allocation and distribution model for perishable products.* Research Working Paper 392A, Graduate School of Business, Columbia University, New York.

Fisher, M. L., & Jaikumar, L. N. (1981). A generalized assignment heuristic for the large scale vehicle routing. *Networks*, *11*, 109–124. doi:10.1002/net.3230110205

Frankfurter, G. M., Kendall, K. E., & Pegels, C. C. (1974). Management control of blood through a short-term supply-demand forecast system. *Management Science*, *21*, 444–452. doi:10.1287/mnsc.21.4.444

Ganesh, K., & Narendran, T. T. (2005). CLOSE: a heuristic to solve a precedence-constrained travelling salesman problem with delivery and pickup. *International Journal of Services and Operations Management, 1*(4), 320–343. doi:10.1504/IJSOM.2005.007496

Ganesh, K., & Narendran, T. T. (2007a). CLOVES: A cluster-and-search heuristic to solve the vehicle routing problem with delivery and pick-up. *European Journal of Operational Research, 178*(3), 699–717. doi:10.1016/j.ejor.2006.01.037

Ganesh, K., & Narendran, T. T. (2007b). CLASH: a heuristic to solve vehicle routing problems with delivery, pick-up and time windows. *International Journal of Services and Operations Management, 3*(4), 460–477. doi:10.1504/IJSOM.2007.013466

Ganesh, K., & Narendran, T. T. (2007c). TASTE: a two-phase heuristic to solve a routing problem with simultaneous delivery and pick-up. *International Journal of Advanced Manufacturing Technology, 37*(11-12), 1221–1231. doi:10.1007/s00170-007-1056-2

Goetschalckx, M., & Jacobs-Blecha, C. (1989). The vehicle routing problem with backhauls. *European Journal of Operational Research, 42*, 39–51. doi:10.1016/0377-2217(89)90057-X

Goetschalckx, M., & Jacobs-Blecha, C. (1993). *The vehicle routing problem with backhauls: properties and solution algorithms. Technical report.* Georgia Institute of Technology, School of Industrial and Systems Engineering.

Gupta, R.K. & Chandra, P. (2002). *Integrated Supply Chain Management in the Government Environment.* Technical papers and presentation, Mathematical Modelling and Simulation Division, National Informatics Center.

Haimovich, M., & Rinnooy Kan, A. H. G. (1985). Bounds and Heuristics for Capacitated Routing Problems. *Mathematics of Operations Research, 10*(4), 527–542. doi:10.1287/moor.10.4.527

Halse, K. (1992). *Modeling and solving complex vehicle routing problems.* PhD thesis, Institute of Mathematical Statistics and Operations Research (IMSOR), Technical University of Denmark.

Hines, P., Rich, N., Bicheno, J., Brunt, D., Taylor, D., Butterworth, C., & Sullivan, J. (1998). Value stream management. *International Journal of Logistics Management, 9*(1), 25–42. doi:10.1108/09574099810805726

Houlihan, J. B. (1988). International supply chains: a new approach. *Management Decision: Quarterly Review of Management Technology, 26*(3), 13–19. doi:10.1108/eb001493

Jennings, J. B. (1973). Blood bank inventory control. *Management Science, 19*, 637–645. doi:10.1287/mnsc.19.6.637

Kendall, K. E. (1980). Multiple objective planning for regional blood centers. *Long Range Planning, 13*(4), 88–94. doi:10.1016/0024-6301(80)90084-9

Kirkpatrick, S., Gelatt, C. D. Jr, & Vecchi, M. P. (1983). Optimization by Simulated Annealing. *Science, 220*, 671–680. doi:10.1126/science.220.4598.671

Lambert, D. M., Cooper, M. C., & Pagh, J. D. (1998). Supply chain management: implementation issues and research opportunities. *The International Journal of Logistics Management, 9*(2), 1–19. doi:10.1108/09574099810805807

Laporte, G., & Osman, I. H. (1995). Routing problems: a bibliography. *Annals of Operations Research, 61*, 227–262. doi:10.1007/BF02098290

Mingozzi, A., Giorgi, S., & Baldacci, R. (1999). An exact method for the vehicle routing problem with backhauls. *Transportation Science, 33*, 315–329. doi:10.1287/trsc.33.3.315

Moshciov, G. (1994). The traveling salesman problem with pickup and delivery. *European Journal of Operational Research, 79*, 299–310. doi:10.1016/0377-2217(94)90360-3

223

Mosheiov, G. (1995). The pick-up and delivery location problem on networks. *Networks, 26,* 243–251. doi:10.1002/net.3230260408

Mosheiov, G. (1998). Vehicle routing with pick-up and delivery: tour-partitioning heuristics. *Computers & Industrial Engineering, 34*(3), 669–684. doi:10.1016/S0360-8352(97)00275-1

Nagy, G., & Salhi, S. (2003). *Heuristic algorithms for single and multiple depot vehicle routing problems with pickups and deliveries.* Working Paper no. 42, Canterbury Business School.

Nahmias, S. (1977). Comparison between two dynamic perishable inventory models. *Operations Research, 25,* 168–172. doi:10.1287/opre.25.1.168

Nanry, W. P., & Barnes, J. W. (2000). Solving the pickup and delivery problem with time windows using reactive tabu search. *Transportation Research Part B: Methodological, 34*(2), 107–121. doi:10.1016/S0191-2615(99)00016-8

New, S. J. (1997). The scope of supply chain management research. *Supply Chain Management, 2*(1), 15–22. doi:10.1108/13598549710156321

New, S. J., & Payne, P. (1995). Research frameworks in logistics: three models, seven dinners and a survey. *International Journal of Physical Distribution and Logistics Management, 25*(10), 60–77. doi:10.1108/09600039510147663

Parragh, S. N., Doerner, K. F., & Hartl, R. F. (2007). A survey on pickup and delivery problems. *Part I: Transportation between customers and depot, Journal für Betriebswirtschaft . Institut für Betriebswirtschaftslehre, 72,* 1210.

Pegels, C. C., Seagle, J. P., Cumming, P. D., & Kendall, K. E. (1975). A computer based interactive planning system for scheduling blood collections. *Transfusion, 15*(4), 381–386. doi:10.1046/j.1537-2995.1975.15476034565.x

Perry, D. (1996, November-December). Analysis of a sampling control scheme for a perishable inventory system. *Operations Research, 47*(6), 966–973. doi:10.1287/opre.47.6.966

Pierskalla, W. P. (1974). *Regionalization of blood bank services. Project supported by the National Center for Health Services Research, OAHS.* DHHS.

Pierskalla, W. P., & Roach, C. (1972). Optimal issuing policies for perishable inventories. *Management Science, 18*(11), 603–614. doi:10.1287/mnsc.18.11.603

Prastacos, G. P. (1981). System analysis in regional blood management. In Mohr and Kluge, (pp. 110-131).

Prastacos, G. P. (1984). Blood inventory management: an overview of theory and practice. *Management Science, 30,* 777–800. doi:10.1287/mnsc.30.7.777

Prastacos, G. P., & Brodheim, E. (1979). Computer based regional blood distribution. *Computers & Operations Research, 6,* 69–77. doi:10.1016/0305-0548(79)90018-2

Prastacos, G. P., & Brodheim, E. (1980). PBDS: A decision support system for regional blood management. *Management Science, 26,* 451–463. doi:10.1287/mnsc.26.5.451

Rabinowitz, M., & Valinsky, D. (1970). *Hospital blood banking-An evaluation of inventory control policies.* Technical Report, Mt. Sinai School of Medicine, City University of New York.

Ropke, S. (2003). *A local Search heuristic for the pickup and delivery problem with time windows. Technical paper.* Copenhagen, Denmark: DIKU, University of Copenhagen.

Ropke, S. (2005) 'Heuristic and exact algorithms for vehicle routing problems', *Ph.D. thesis,* Department of Computer Science at the University of Copenhagen (DIKU), Denmark.

Ropke, S., & Pisinger, D. (2004). *A Unified Heuristic for a Large Class of Vehicle Routing Problems with Backhauls*. Technical Report no. 2004/14, ISSN: 0107-8283, University of Copenhagen, Denmark.

Ropke, S., & Pisinger, D. (2006). A unified heuristic for a large class of Vehicle Routing Problems with Backhauls. *European Journal of Operational Research, 171*(3), 750–775. doi:10.1016/j.ejor.2004.09.004

Salhi, S., & Nagy, G. (1999). A cluster insertion heuristic for single and multiple depot vehicle routing problems with backhauling. *The Journal of the Operational Research Society, 50,* 1034–1042.

Toth, P., & Vigo, D. (1997). An exact algorithm for the vehicle routing problem with backhauls. *Transportation Science, 31,* 372–285. doi:10.1287/trsc.31.4.372

Toth, P., & Vigo, D. (1999). A heuristic algorithm for the symmetric and asymmetric vehicle routing problem with backhauls. *European Journal of Operational Research, 113,* 528–543. doi:10.1016/S0377-2217(98)00086-1

Toth, P., & Vigo, D. (2002a). An Overview of Vehicle Routing Problems. In Toth, P., & Vigo, D. (Eds.), *The Vehicle Routing Problem* (pp. 1–26). Philadelphia: SIAM Monographs on Discrete Mathematics and Applications.

Toth, P., & Vigo, D. (2002b). VRP with backhauls . In Toth, P., & Vigo, D. (Eds.), *The Vehicle Routing Problem* (pp. 195–221). Philadelphia: SIAM Monographs on Discrete Mathematics and Applications.

Tütüncü, G. Y., Carreto, C. A. C., & Baker, B. M. (2009). A visual interactive approach to classical and mixed vehicle routing problems with backhauls. *Omega, 37*(1), 138–154. doi:10.1016/j.omega.2006.11.001

Wade, A., & Salhi, S. (2001). An ant system algorithm for the vehicle routing problem with backhauls. In *MIC'2001 - 4th Metaheursistic International Conference*.

Wade, A., & Salhi, S. (2003). An Ant System Algorithm for the mixed Vehicle Routing Problem with Backhauls . In *Metaheuristics: Computer Decision-Making* (pp. 699–719). Amsterdam: Kluwer Academic Publishers.

Wade, A. C., & Salhi, S. (2002). An investigation into a new class of vehicle routing problem with backhauls. *Omega, 30,* 479–487. doi:10.1016/S0305-0483(02)00056-7

Wassan, N. (2007). Reactive tabu adaptive memory programming search for the vehicle routing problem with backhauls. *The Journal of the Operational Research Society, 58,* 1630–1641. doi:10.1057/palgrave.jors.2602313

Wassan, N. A., Nagy, G., & Ahmadi, S. (2008). A heuristic method for the vehicle routing problem with mixed deliveries and pickups. *Journal of Scheduling, 11*(2), 149–161. doi:10.1007/s10951-008-0055-y

# Chapter 16
# Information Technology Enabled Vendor Managed Inventory in Modelling Supply Chain Issues:
## A Review

**Subramanian Nachiappan**
*Thiagarajar College of Engineering, Madurai, India*

**Natarajan Jawahar**
*Thiagarajar College of Engineering Madurai, India*

## ABSTRACT

*Supply chain is a network of firms interacting in a linear fashion to produce, sell and deliver a product or service to a predetermined market segment. It links all the chain partners within and across organization to work competitively by forming the partnerships together with the integration of business processes, technical and organizational aspects. The successful implementation of supply chain management depends on many soft issues (strategic/behavioural). The soft issues of supply chain models can be dealt through proper information sharing, communication and coordination between the stages of supply chain. Vendor managed inventory is a proven concept for successful collaborative and cooperative agreements in supply chain. This chapter reviews some of the soft issues in two-echelon supply chain models and proposes a classification schema. This chapter surveys the theoretical background and application of vendor managed inventory systems based on environment, operational issues and solution approaches. Hence it is concluded that the framework presented in this chapter would aid supply chain managers and researchers to further look into the soft issues while modeling supply chain with information technology enabled vendor managed inventory systems.*

DOI: 10.4018/978-1-61520-625-4.ch016

Copyright © 2010, IGI Global. Copying or distributing in print or electronic forms without written permission of IGI Global is prohibited.

*Figure 1. Model of SC process*

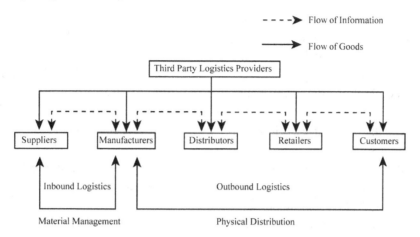

# \INTRODUCTION

Supply Chain (SC) is a network of firms interacting in a linear fashion to produce, sell and deliver a product or service to a predetermined market segment (Chopra and Meindl, 2001). Figure 1 shows the business model of SC process (Min and Zhou, 2002).

This arrangement is found in a wide-range of industries like Dupont, Exxon, General Motors, in pharmaceuticals like Pfizer and in carriers like Federal Express, UPS. This arrangement is also found with retailers like Wal-Mart, Home Depot, and Sears. SC links all the chain partners within and across organization to work together by forming the partnerships to make the whole supply chain competitive (Maloni and Benton, 1997). Organizations recognized that they could not excel at the necessary competitive dimensions at a level needed to gain a competitive advantage without the cooperation and input of both their suppliers and their customers. The ability to integrate the differing functional areas of an organization with its suppliers and partners was seen as a logical step to improve competitiveness (Greis and Kasarda 1997; Morash et al., 1997; Thomas and Griffin, 1996; Houlihan, 1988, Beamon, 1998; Melachrinoudis et al., 2000). This requires

integration of business processes, technical and organizational aspects. The concept of Supply Chain Management (SCM) emerged in the mid 1980s to meet this challenge of such integrations (Southard, 2001; Bowersox and Closs 1996). SCM is a recent evolution for such integration on the following grounds:

- *It speeds up the flow of information and materials through the whole process from the suppliers to the customers due to the advancements in information technology.*
- *It is also proven that supply chain partnerships lead to more technical innovation and better quality products.*
- *The concept that satisfies the essential customer attributes such as responsiveness, quality, flexibility, dependability and cost.*

However, the successful implementation of SCM depends on many soft issues (strategic/behavioural) such as organizational resistance to change, inter-functional conflicts, joint production planning, profit sharing, team oriented performance measures, channel power shift, information sharing, real time communication, inventory and technical compatibility (Min and Zhou 2002). Many of the above issues in SCM are conceptually addressed and lot of scope exists for improving the performance of SC with good modeling. This chapter reviews the role of Information Technology Enabled Vendor Managed Inventory in modeling the supply chain soft issues, proposes the classification schema and points out the scope for future research.

The rest of the chapter is organised as follows: Section 2 addresses the supply chain environment with different mode of operation and objectives considered ; Section 3 delineates the operational issues ; Section 4 reports the different solution approaches proposed by the researchers for the various models and issues ; Section 5 proposes a classification schema ; Sections 6 summarises the major contributions of various researchers and highlights the state of the art reviews in modeling soft issues; Finally, the last section 7 provides the concluding remarks along with future research directions.

## ENVIRONMENT

The Two-Echelon Supply chain, mode of operation and objectives considered by various researchers are reported in this section.

### Two-Echelon Supply chain

In the present internet / information technology arena, the stages in SC are becoming less and the manufacturers access the customer requirement through retailers. Dell computers have reoriented its strategy by reducing its down-stream stages and sells through its retail outlets in a particular region (Chopra, 2003). Procter and Gamble manages, monitors and replenishes its FMCG products in Wal-Mart stores (Clark and Croson, 1994). The success stories of these Giants have led the researchers to concentrate on two echelon supply chain (Cachon and Zipkin, 1999). The two-echelon can be considered sequentially between any two of these stages such as suppliers, manufacturers, dis-

tributors, wholesalers, retailers, and end-customer. There are three types of environments addressed in two-echelon SC and they are:

i.    Single vendor-single buyer (Banerjee, 1986; Goyal, 1997; Hill, 1997; Viswanathan, 1998; Bhattacharjee and Ramesh, 2000; Goyal and Nebebe, 2000; Hoque and Goyal, 2000; Dong and Xu, 2002; Lee and Chu, 2005),

ii.   Single vendor-multiple buyers (Lu 1995; Gavirneni, 2001 and Yao and Chiou 2004) and

iii.  Multiple vendors-multiple buyers (Cachon, 2001; Minner 2003; Sedarage et al., 1999; Ganeshan, 1999).

Single vendor-single buyer is considered as an idealistic one in dealing with bottleneck cases and the remaining two cases represent the most practical situations. Few examples for last two cases are: Tamilnadu Cooperative milk producers federation limited (AAVIN) Madurai, India (Single Vendor) selling its milk products to 423 commission agents (Multiple Buyers) in and around Madurai; Bharat Petroleum Corporation, Cochin, India (Single Vendor) distributing its petroleum products to 2500 sales points (Multiple Buyers) in southern part of India. Gold suppliers (Multiple Vendors) are selling gold through thousands of retailer's network (Multiple Buyers) and numerous grain suppliers (Multiple Vendors) supplying grains through thousands of retailers (Multiple Buyers). This chapter classifies the environment as two-echelon supply chain, multi-echelon, case studies, frame work, concepts and strategies.

### Mode of Operation

The soft issues of SC models can be dealt through proper information sharing, communication and coordination between the stages of SC. Examples of collaborative and cooperative agreements come in many forms and by many names, including Continuous Replenishment (CR), Vendor Managed Inventory (VMI), Collaborative Forecasting, Planning and Replenishment (CFPR) and Information Sharing Programs (ISP). The overall goal shared by all these programs is to reduce costs and to increase efficiency in the SC by sharing the information and/or by the transfer of decision rights (Mishra and Raghunathan, 2004; Fry, 2002; Ballou et al., 2000; Hammond, 1990). VMI is a proven concept for successful collaborative and cooperative agreements in SC. The core concept of VMI has been that the supplier monitors the customers' demand and inventory and replenishes that inventory as needed with no action on the part of the customer (Dong and Xu, 2002 ; Disney and Towill, 2002). Waller et al. (2001) noted that the main advantages of VMI were reduced costs and increased customer service levels to one or both of the participating members. VMI, however, has received very little attention in current operations' literature, particularly operations texts, but it has been widely recognized by industry leaders, such as Wal-Mart and the Campbell soup company for creating a competitive advantage. Franchise organizations have also made use of VMI to provide a higher level of operating efficiency (Williams, 2000). Cetinkaya and Lee (2000) noted that, with VMI, inventory carrying costs were generally reduced, as were stock out problems while the approach offered the ability to synchronise inventory and transportation decisions. VMI has differed from a fixed-order interval model or a fixed-order quantity model in that neither the time nor the quantity of replenishment was necessarily fixed. The supplier was responsible for managing the inventory at the customer's location, generally using information technology, and for sending the correct amount at the correct time (Burke, 1996; Parks and Popolillo, 1999). While research has been slowly increasing in the area of VMI, certain segments of business have appeared to be getting less attention than others (Latamore and Benton, 1999). The SC's of large retail and manufacturing organizations have been the foci of most of the research. Mabert and Venkataramanan (1998)

pointed out that little work had been carried out in applying SCM techniques to service sectors. The lack of research has been even more evident with regards to milk, agricultural and engineering services (Ross et al., 1998). *Therefore this chapter classifies the mode of operation as VMI (Information Technology enabled) and Non-VMI mode and reports the role of Information Technology enabled VMI in modeling soft issues of two-echelon SC.*

## Objective

The turnover and profit of an organisation depend on the price and demand of its products. The reasons for the non purchase of preferred commodities by customers are: 59% too expensive; 8% disliked appearance; 12% shelf life too short and 3% inconsistent quality (Tronstad, 1995). Most of the models on pricing focus on profit generation at single level (Rajan et al., 1992; Gallego and Vanryzin, 1994; Polatoglu, 1991; Desarbo et al., 1987). Manufacturers fix price to the wholesaler which is known as supply price, considering manufacturing and distribution costs. Wholesaler offers a price to the retailer based on money turnover / commission. The retailer sells at a price depending upon market conditions. Hence pricing is an essential component of a product which makes customer more sensitive. Rather, trial and error method is often followed in organizations which involve finding out customer demand and other influential parameters such as market share, economic conditions, manufacturing capacity, nature of the product, inventory costs, cyclic fluctuations in cost and demand and rapid deterioration of product. Pricing mechanism differs with nature of the product (perishable, storable, seasonal, etc.,), government regulations (duties, licensing, etc.) and type of market (monopoly, oligopoly etc.) (Klastorin, 2004). The conventional trial and error pricing mechanism may not yield fruitful solution to SC scenario, in which all the entities need to work together in order to meet the global competition (i.e., between supply chains) in the market for long term (Casati et al., 2001). Besides, revenue sharing is the concept in which total channel profit should be allocated among SC participants in different profit ratios (Giannoccaro and Pontrandolfo, 2004). The main focus of revenue sharing is to share the revenues/profits generated based on the assignments and responsibilities in order to avoid the conflict between SC partners (Maloni and Benton, 1997). Min and Zhou (2002) pointed out that profit sharing is believed as one of the major behavioural (soft) issues in strengthening the relationship between partners of SC to improve the performance. Gjerdrum et al. (2002) pointed out that fair optimized profit distribution between the partners would lead to better relationship and only this kind of distribution can be the genuine deal.

Members of SC addressed as partners, promote and adopt strategies to minimize cost or maximize turnover. The traditional objective of the supply chain is to minimize total supply chain cost to meet the given demand. Researchers argue that total cost minimization is an inappropriate and timid objective for the firm to pursue when it analyses its strategic and tactical supply chain plans (Shapiro, 2001; Gjerdrum et al., 2002). Instead maximization of net revenue could be considered as appropriate objective to supply chain. In the literature on Supply Chain Management (SCM), the net revenue is addressed as channel profit. This chapter classifies the objective of supply chain as profit maximisation, cost minimisation and performance improvement.

## OPERATIONAL ISSUES

Min and Zhou (2002) reported in his article that hard issues such as location/allocation, inventory control, production planning, transportation mode selection, and supplier selection with the commonly accepted value propositions such as cost minimization and profit maximization has

been dealt extensively by researchers and pointed out that scope exist only for soft issues (strategic/behavioural) such as organizational resistance to change, inter-functional conflicts, joint production planning, profit sharing, team oriented performance measures, channel power shift, information sharing, real time communication, inventory and technical compatibility. Hence, this chapter emphasises the role of VMI in soft issues.

## SOLUTION APPROACHES

Decision Support Systems (DSS) can be defined as an interactive computer based system that utilizes data and models for facilitating the decision makers in solving semi structured and unstructured problems. The role of DSS is to support a decision maker with the help of data and models while analyzing the problems. A DSS incorporate information from the organization's database into an analytical framework with the objective of easing and improving the decision making. DSS assist managers in decision making support rather than replace managerial judgment and improve effectiveness of decision making (Mohanty and Deshmukh, 2001). Structured decision admits automation of the situations; once an algorithm is checked out and implemented in the form of computer code, there is little scope for decision-maker to contribute. The semi-structure decision on the other hand needs continuous inputs from the decision maker by way of preferences, tradeoffs and value judgments that must be incorporated at different stages before the final result is produced by these systems. DSS concentrate on the insights into the system by providing what-if sensitivity questions. Many a times the decision maker prefers a satisfying solution assisted by a series of what-if questions. The key to success in SCM requires heavy emphasis on integration of activities, cooperation, coordination and information sharing throughout the entire supply chain, from suppliers to customers. To be able to respond to the challenge of integration, there is the need for sophisticated DSS, based on powerful mathematical models and solution techniques, together with the advances in information and communication technologies (Achabal et al., 2000; Talluri, 2000; Mentzer and Schuster, 1983). There is no doubt about the importance of quantitative models and computer based tools for decision making in today's business environment. This is especially true in the rapidly growing area of supply chain management. These computer-based logistics systems can make a significant impact in the decision process on the organizations. That's why the industry and the academia have become increasingly interested in DSS which is able to respond to the problems and issues posed by the changes in SCM and logistics (Lourenco, 2005).

Many well-known algorithmic advances in optimization have been made, but it turns out that most of them have not had the expected impact on the decisions for designing and optimizing supply chain related problems (Shapiro, 2001). For example, some optimization techniques are of little use because they are not well suited to solve complex real logistics problems in the short time, needed to make decisions. Also some techniques are highly problem-dependent and need high expertise. All the constraints of the problem may not be amenable to the mathematical articulation without such an articulation optimization may not be possible leaving the decision maker with no choice but to resort to his own experience. This adds difficulties in the implementations of optimization algorithms in the DSS which contradict the tendency to fast implementation in a rapid changing world. Alternatively for many of the problems, since the cost to find an optimal solution is so high, heuristic problem solving would suffice. Therefore, on the one hand there is the need for sophisticated logistics DSS to enable the organizations to respond quickly to new issues and problems faced on the SCM, and on the other hand there are advances in the area of heuristics that can provide an effective response to

complex problems. This provides a fertile ground for applications of these techniques to SCM and subsequently of the development of computer based systems to help logistics decisions. Well-designed heuristics packages can maintain their advantage over optimization packages in terms of computer resources required, a consideration unlikely to diminish in importance so long as the size and complexity of the models arising in practice continue to increase. This is true for many areas in the firm, but especially to SCM related problems.

A heuristic algorithm (often shortened to heuristic) is a solution method that does not guarantee an optimal solution, but, in general, has a good level of performance in terms of solution quality and convergence. To develop a heuristic for a particular problem, some problem-specific characteristics must be defined. The problem-specific may include the definition of a feasible solution, the neighbourhood of a solution, rules for changing solutions, and rules for setting certain parameters during the course of execution (Corne et al.,1999; Glover and Gkochenberger, 2001). In fact, some of the most popular commercial packages use heuristic methods or rules of thumb. Heuristic may be constructive (producing a single solution) or local search (starting from one or given random solutions and moving iteratively to other nearby solutions) or a combination (constructing one or more solutions and using them to start a local search).

The area of heuristic techniques has been the object of intensive studies in the last decades. Recent advances in heuristic technique include meta-heuristics, which gained widespread applications along with the computational power of the computer technology. A meta-heuristic is a framework for producing heuristics, such as Simulated Annealing (SAA), Genetic Algorithm (GA), Tabu Search (TS), Particle Swarm Optimisation (PSO), Ant Colony Optimisation (ACO), etc. (Yokota et al., 1996; Costa and Oliveira 2001; Wu, 2001). Meta-heuristics have many desirable features for becoming an excellent method: in general they are simple, easy to implement, robust and have been proven highly effective to solve hard problems. Even in their most simpler and basic implementation, the meta-heuristics have been able to effectively solve very hard and complex problems. There are several aspects which are worth enough to be mentioned. The most important one is the meta-heuristics modular nature that leads to short development times and updates, given a clear advantage over other techniques for industrial applications.

The other important aspect is that the amount of data involved in any optimization model for an integrated supply chain problem can be overwhelming. The complexity of the models for the SCM and the incapacity for solving in real time some of them by the traditional techniques force the use of the obvious techniques to reduce this complex issue by data aggregation (Simchi-Levi et al., 2000). Therefore, instead of aggregating data to be able to obtain a simple and solvable model, but which will not represent well the reality, researchers should consider the complex model by using an approximation algorithm. The scenario-based approaches can incorporate a meta-heuristic to obtain the best possible decision within a scenario. The combination of best characteristics of human decision-making and computerised model and algorithmic based systems into interactive and graphical design frameworks have proven to be very effective in SCM, since many supply chain problems are new, subject to rapid changes and moreover, there is no clear understanding of all of the issues involved. Taking into the above concerns, this chapter classifies the solution approaches into simulation, heuristics, meta-heuristics, decision support heuristics, application, mathematical model development and review.

## FRAMEWORK

Taxonomy for reviewing SCM research is very complex. While Caper et al. (2004) provided five different classification schemes for reviewing SCM literature with:

- Type of study
- SC environment
- SC activities
- Decision Making and degree of information sharing
- Product properties.

Ganeshan *et al.* (1999) reviewed the SCM research under the following three categories

- strategic
- tactical and
- operational

On the other hand, Chen and Paulraj (2004) developed theoretical framework for SCM research and classified them into four streams of research efforts as: Strategic purchasing, Supply management, Logistics integration, and Supply network coordination. It is understood from the above reviews that numerous elements/components exist in SCM and the taxonomy of the review is dependant on the nature of SCM research.

Based on the above guidelines, this chapter classifies the literature into three following categories for understanding the role of VMI in modeling supply chain soft issues:

- Environments
- Operational issues and
- Solution approaches.

Figure 2-5 provides the taxonomy adapted in this chapter.

*Figure 2. Classification of SCM*

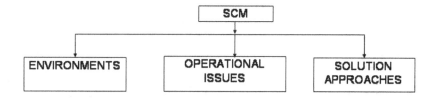

## SURVEY OF LITERATURE

The survey of literature is carried out with the above taxonomy. This section presents the details of research/study carried out with respect to application of Information Technology enabled VMI in different environments. Furthermore, details of survey is summarised in their chronological order (1960 -2005) in Table 1.

- Cachon and Fisher (1997) described how a continuous replenishment program (CRP) works in practice. More sophisticated inventory rules improve performance. Using CRP it was found that retailer inventories were reduced 66% without reducing service level. Cost of goods sold fell by 12% by adapting VMI.

- Holmstrom (1998) demonstrates the case study of VMI implementation and possibility to arrive at a simple and efficient solution in a standard systems environment. Implementation of vendor-managed inventory does not need complex technology but it needs the key of co-operation.

- Achabal *et al.* (2000) describe the market forecasting and inventory management components of a vendor managed inventory decision support system and how an apparel manufacturer and over 30 of this retail partners implemented this system. The decision support system helped the vendor and retailers arrive at jointly agreed upon customer service level and inventory turn over targets and discussed the insights for supply chain coordination.

- Waller *et al.* (2001) demonstrated the effect of VMI under varying demand and limited manufacturing capability. They emphasized the teamwork for VMI success and

*Figure 3. Classification of environment*

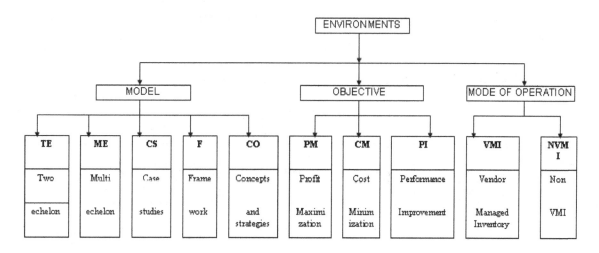

*Figure 4. Classification of operational issues*

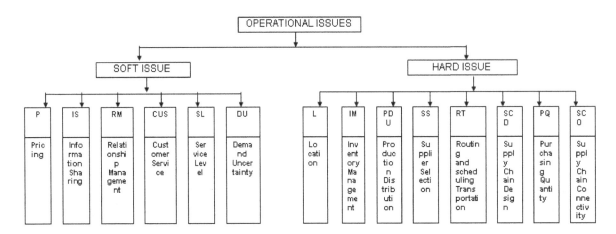

research methods to manage benefits sharing among members of the supply chain.

- Cachon (2001) studied the competitive and cooperative selection of inventory policies in a two-echelon supply chains with one supplier and N retailers facing stochastic demands. Found that optimal supply chain performance is obtained with Vendor Managed Inventory (VMI).

- Yu *et al.* (2001) examine the information-based supply-chain efforts that are often linked to VMI programs by considering a supplier serving multiple retailers located in a close proximity. This model can be extended to multiple suppliers with multiple retailers in different geographical locations

- Dong and Xu (2002) developed a VMI model for two echelon supply chain and

evaluated how VMI affects the channel profit. Authors compared their model with traditional business process. VMI model increases the channel profit while the traditional model does not pointed out the scope of forecasting in VMI

- Disney *et al.* (2003) investigated the performance of VMI mode of supply chain and traditional supply chain in transport operations and analysed the causes of Bull Whip Effect in two modes. VMI is found to respond better to volatile changes in demand (due to discounted ordering or price variations) than to traditional one.

- Disney and Towill (2003) compare the bullwhip effect caused in VMI mode of supply chain with those of a traditional "serial linked" supply chain they developed

*Figure 5. Classification of solution approaches*

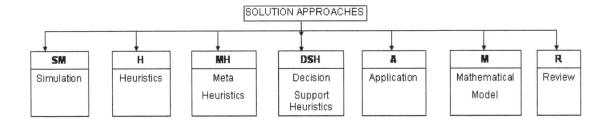

*Table 1. Summary of SCM and related literature*

| S.No | Author | Environments | | | Operational Issues | | Solution Approaches |
|---|---|---|---|---|---|---|---|
| | | Model | Objective | Mode of operation | Soft | Hard | |
| 1. | Clark and scarf (1960) | ME | CM | NVMI | - | PQ | M |
| 2. | Geoffrion and Graves (1974) | F | PI | NVMI | - | L | M |
| 3. | Glover *et al.*, (1979) | F | PI | NVMI | - | SCO | DSH |
| 4. | Cohen and Lee, (1988) | F | PI | NVMI | - | PD | M |
| 5. | Zinn and Levy (1988) | CO | PI | NVMI | - | IM | A |
| 6. | Bowersox and Morash (1989) | CO | PI | NVMI | - | SCO | A |
| 7. | Cohen and Lee (1989) | F | PI | NVMI | - | PDU | M |
| 8. | Towill (1992) | CO | PI | NVMI | DU | - | SM |
| 9. | Anupindi and Akella, (1993) | CO | CM | NVMI | - | IM | M |
| 10. | Lee and Billington (1993) | F | PI | NVMI | - | IM | DSH |
| 11. | Robinson *et al.*(1993) | TE | PI | NVMI | - | PDU | DSH |
| 12. | Srinivasan *et al.* (1994) | CO | PI | NVMI | - | SCO | A |
| 13. | Stenger (1994) | F | PI | NVMI | - | IM | A |
| 14. | Arntzen *et al.* (1995) | ME | PI | NVMI | - | SCD | M |
| 15. | Lee and Billington (1995) | CO | PI | NVMI | CUS | - | A |
| 16. | Lu (1995) | TE | CM | NVMI | - | IM | H |
| 17. | Anupindi and Bassok (1996) | CO | C | NVMI | IS | - | A |
| 18. | Bhaskaran (1996) | CO | PI | NVMI | - | IM | SM |
| 19. | Berry and Naim (1996) | CO | PI | NVMI | - | SCD | SM |
| 20. | Fisher and Raman (1996) | CO | CM | NVMI | - | IM | M |
| 21. | Hafeeza *et al.* (1996) | TE | PI | NVMI | - | IM | SM |
| 22. | Gentry (1996) | CS | PI | NVMI | RM | - | A |
| 23. | Tagaras and Lee (1996) | CO | PI | NVMI | - | SS | A |
| 24. | Satterfield and Robinson (1996) | F | CM | NVMI | - | SCD | A |
| 25. | Stenger (1996) | CO | PI | NVMI | - | IM | M |
| 26. | Thomas and Griffin (1996) | F | PI | NVMI | - | SCD | R |
| 27. | Ashayeri and Rongen (1997) | F | CM | NVMI | - | PDU | M |
| 28. | Cachon and Fisher (1997) | CO | PI | VMI | SL | - | A |
| 29. | Camm *et al.*, (1997) | F | PI | NVMI | - | L | M |
| 30. | Greis and Kasarda (1997) | CO | PI | NVMI | IS | - | A |
| 31. | Hill (1997) | TE | CM | NVMI | - | IM | M |
| 32. | Henig *et al.* (1997) | F | CM | NVMI | - | IM | M |
| 33. | Kruger (1997) | F | PI | NVMI | - | IM | SM |
| 34. | Lee *et al.* (1997) | CO | PI | NVMI | IS | - | M |

*continued on following page*

*Table 1. continued*

| S.No | Author | Environments | | | Operational Issues | | Solution Approaches |
|------|--------|-------|-----------|-----------------|------|------|-----------|
| | | **Model** | **Objective** | **Mode of operation** | **Soft** | **Hard** | |
| 35. | Lederer and Li (1997) | CS | PI | NVMI | CUS | - | A |
| 36. | Maloni and Benton (1997) | F | PI | NVMI | RM | SCD | R |
| 37. | Moinzadeh and Aggarwal (1997) | CS | CM | NVMI | - | IM | A |
| 38. | Viswanathan and Mathur (1997) | ME | CM | NVMI | - | IM | H |
| 39. | Gavireni *et al.* (1998) | CS | PI | NVMI | IS | - | A |
| 40. | Graves *et al.* (1998) | ME | PI | NVMI | - | IM | M |
| 41. | Holmstrom (1998) | CS | PI | VMI | RM | - | A |
| 42. | Carr and Smeltzer (1999) | CS | PI | NVMI | RM | - | A |
| 43. | Bylka (1999) | TE | PI | NVMI | - | PDU | M |
| 44. | Ganeshan (1999) | ME | CM | NVMI | - | IM | M |
| 45. | Min and Melachrinoudis (1999) | ME | PI | NVMI | - | SCO | M |
| 46. | Sedarage *et al.* (1999) | F | CM | NVMI | - | IM | M |
| 47. | Achabal *et al.* (2000) | CS | PI | VMI | CSL | IM | DSH |
| 48. | Andersson and Marklund (2000) | TE | CM | NVMI | - | IM | H |
| 49. | Ballou *et al.* (2000) | F | PI | NVMI | IS | - | A |
| 50. | Bhattacharjee and Ramesh (2000) | F | PM | NVMI | P | IM | H |
| 51. | Lamming (2000) | CS | C | NVMI | RM | - | A |
| 52. | Melachrinoudis and Min (2000) | F | PI | NVMI | - | L | M |
| 53. | Goyal (2000) | TE | PI | NVMI | - | IM | H |
| 54. | Goyal and Nebebe (2000) | TE | CM | NVMI | - | IM | H |
| 55. | Hoque and Goyal (2000) | TE | CM | NVMI | - | IM | H |
| 56. | Swamidass (2000) | CO | PI | NVMI | RM | IM | A |
| 57. | Waller *et al.* (2001) | CS | PI | VMI | RM | - | A |
| 58. | Cachon (2001) | T.E | P.I | VMI | - | IM | A |
| 59. | Gavirneni (2001) | TE | PI | NVMI | IS | - | A |
| 60. | Nozick and Turnquist (2001) | F | CM | NVMI | - | IM | M |
| 61. | Shapiro (2001) | CO | PI | NVMI | IS | - | A |
| 62. | Woo *et al.* (2001) | TE | CM | NVMI | - | IM | M |
| 63. | Yu *et al.* (2001) | TE | PI | VMI | IS | - | M |
| 64. | Dong and Xu (2002) | TE | PM | VMI | IS | - | M |
| 65. | Handfield and Bechtel (2002) | F | PI | NVMI | RM | - | M |
| 66. | Min and Zhou (2002) | F | PI | NVMI | P/IS/RM | - | R |

*continued on following page*

*Table 1. continued*

| S.No | Author | Environments | | | Operational Issues | | Solution Approaches |
|------|--------|-------|-----------|--------------------|------|------|------|
| | | Model | Objective | Mode of operation | Soft | Hard | |
| 67. | Yang and Wee (2002) | TE | CM | NVMI | - | IM | M |
| 68. | Abad (2003) | F | PI | NVMI | P | IM | M |
| 69. | Banerjee *et al.* (2003) | TE | PI | NVMI | - | RT | SM |
| 70. | Cheng and Koehler (2003) | CS | PI | NVMI | P | - | M |
| 71. | Chopra (2003) | F | PI | NVMI | - | SCD | A |
| 72. | Cousins and Spekman (2003) | CS | PI | NVMI | RM | - | A |
| 73. | Disney *et al.* (2003) | CS | PI | VMI | DU | - | SM |
| 74. | Disney and Towill (2003) | CO | PI | VMI | RM | - | SM |
| 75. | Jayaraman and Ross (2003) | ME | PI | NVMI | - | L | MH |
| 76. | Kaipia and Tanskanen (2003) | CS | PI | VMI | RM | - | A |
| 77. | Minner (2003) | TE | - | NVMI | - | - | R |
| 78. | Vickery *et al.* (2003) | CS | PI | NVMI | IS/CUS | - | A |
| 79. | Ahtiala (2004) | - | CM | NVMI | P | - | M |
| 80. | Ben-Daya and Hariga (2004) | TE | PI | NVMI | - | IM | H |
| 81. | Capar *et al.* (2004) | F | - | NVMI | - | - | R |
| 82. | Chen and Paulraj (2004) | F | - | NVMI | - | - | R |
| 83. | Choi *et al.* (2004) | TE | PI | VMI | SL | - | M |
| 84. | Gunasekaran and Ngai (2004) | F | C | NVMI | IS | - | R |
| 85. | Huang (2004) | TE | CM | NVMI | - | IM | H |
| 86. | Kuk (2004) | CS | PI | VMI | RM | - | A |
| 87. | Parlar and Weng (2004) | F | PI | NVMI | P | - | M |
| 88. | Teng, *et al.* (2004) | TE | PI | NVMI | P | IM | H |
| 89. | Yao and Chiou (2004) | TE | CM | NVMI | P | - | MH |
| 90. | Zhu and sarkis (2004) | CO | PI | NVMI | RM | - | M |
| 91. | Abad and Aggarwal (2005) | F | PI | NVMI | P | IM | M |
| 92. | Axsater (2005) | TE | CM | NVMI | - | IM | H |
| 93. | Banerjee (2005) | TE | PI | NVMI | P | IM | M |
| 94. | Bharadwaj and Matsuno (2006) | CO | PI | NVMI | CUS/RM | - | A |
| 95. | Benton and Maloni (2005) | CO | PI | NVMI | RM | - | R |
| 96. | Griffith *et al.* (2005) | CS | PI | NVMI | RM | - | A |
| 97. | Lancioni (2005) | CO | PI | NVMI | P | - | A |
| 98. | Lee and Chu (2005) | TE | PI | NVMI | - | IM | A |
| 99. | Li (2005) | CO | PI | NVMI | P | - | A |
| 100. | Lin (2005) | F | PM | NVMI | P | - | M |

*continued on following page*

*Table 1. continued*

| S.No | Author | Environments | | | Operational Issues | | Solution Approaches |
|---|---|---|---|---|---|---|---|
| | | Model | Objective | Mode of operation | Soft | Hard | |
| 101. | Lourenco (2005) | F | PI | NVMI | - | - | MH |
| 102. | Micheau (2005) | CS | PI | VMI | RM | - | A |
| 103. | Musalem and Dekker (2005) | CS | PI | NVMI | - | IM | SM |
| 104. | Netessine (2005) | CO | PI | NVMI | P | IM | M |
| 105. | Sucky (2005) | TE | CM | NVMI | RM | IM | M |
| 106. | Tang and Cheng (2005) | CO | PI | NVMI | P | L | M |
| 107. | Toni and Zamolo (2005) | CS | PI | VMI | - | IM | A |
| 108. | Torabi *et al.* (2005) | TE | CM | NVMI | - | IM | MH |
| 109. | Yoa *et al.* (2005) | TE | CM | VMI | - | IM | M |
| 110. | Yu *et al.* (2008) | TE | PM | VMI | IS,P, DU | - | H |
| 111. | Southard and. Swenseth (2008) | CS | PI | VMI | IS | IM | SM |
| 112. | Xu, K and Leung (2008) | TE | PM | VMI | DU, RM | IM | H |
| 113. | Wong *et al.* (2008) | TE | PI | VMI | IS,CS | - | SM |
| 114. | Yu *et al.* (2008a) | ME | PI | VMI | IS | - | SM |
| 115. | Gumus *et al* (2008) | TE | PI | VMI | IS | IM | SM |
| 116. | Michaelraj and Shahabudeen (2008) | TE | PM,CM | VMI | IS | IM | M |
| 117. | Al-Ameri *et al.* (2008) | ME | PM | VMI | IS | PQ | M |
| 118. | Yao and Dresner (2008) | TE | PI | VMI | IS, RM | PQ | M |
| 119. | Szmerekovsky and Zhang (2008) | TE | PI | VMI | IS | IM | M |
| 120. | Kwak *et al.* (2009) | TE | CM | VMI | DU | IM | SM |
| 121. | Soroor *et al.* (2009) | CD | PI | VMI | IS | - | A |

models for both conditions and simulated considering the sources of bull whip effect such as demand signal processing, rationing, gaming, order batching and price variations. Simulation results highlighted the elimination of two sources (rationing and gaming.) of bullwhip effect.

- Kaipia and Tanskanen (2003) propose a new process innovation, vendor managed category management with real case of grocery retailing industry. Outsourcing the management of non-core product categories enables retailers to make an effective and flexible move to an E-commerce environment.

- Choi *et al.* (2004) considered the decentralized two-party capacitated supply chain model for VMI implementation and demonstrated that the supplier's service level is in general insufficient for the manufacturer to warrant the desired service level at the customer end

- Kuk (2004) extended limits-to-value model to frame four research hypotheses related to the effects of organizational size, employee involvement, and logistics integration on the expected and perceived values of vendor-managed inventory (VMI) as implemented in the electronics industry. However, contrary to the notion that large organizations have more slack resources in technology adoption and implementation, VMI benefited small organizations most.

- Micheau (2005) described what led to the success of partnership between boeing and alcoa for a VMI program to succeed. There must be adaptation, flexibility and streamlining in both the organizations, electronic platforms help in communicating forecasts between parties quickly and in an orderly manner.

- Toni and Zamolo (2005) revealed that that vendor-managed inventory is also used very well in household electrical appliances sector. Taking Electrolux Italia as an example, the implementation of this technique is presented and analysed, highlighting the various processes involved (sales forecasting, capacity need forecasting, master planning, replenishment need calculation, dispatch planning, shipping), parameters (target stock, replenishment need, dispatch plan, assigned stock, etc.) needed to regulate vendor managed inventory. The chapter points out the benefits obtained following the implementation of this technique and presents based on the case the variables that define and characterize the conditions under which it can be applied.

- Yao *et al.* (2005) developed an analytical model that explores important supply chain parameters, which affects the cost savings to be realized from collaborative initiatives such as vendor-managed inventory (VMI). Results from the model show that benefits, in the form of inventory cost reductions, may be generated from integration depending upon the ratio of the order costs of the supplier to the buyer and the ratio of the carrying charges of the supplier to the buyer. Results also show that these benefits are disproportionally distributed between buyers and suppliers.

- Yu *et al.* (2008) discussed how a manufacturer and its retailers interact with each other in order to optimize their individual net profits by adjusting product marketing (advertising and pricing) and inventory policies in an information-asymmetric VMI. This problem is modeled as a Stackelberg game where the manufacturer is the leader and retailers are followers. An algorithm has been proposed to search the Stackelberg equilibrium. Authors addressed the following research questions under what circumstances the retailers and manufacturer should increase their advertising expenditures and/or reduce the retail prices and what actions should be taken if the prices of raw materials or their holding costs increase.

- Southard and. Swenseth (2008) provided empirical evidence that sufficient economic benefits could be achieved with the use of a technology-enabled vendor-managed inventory (VMI) system in a unique chain such that a firm could justify spending the money necessary to create the infrastructure to support it. Performance was measured in inventory costs, delivery costs and stockouts. The study found that VMI alternatives outperformed traditional delivery methods and that the use of such technology could be economically justified in many logistics problems dealing with variable demand patterns through the cost savings created.

- Xu, K and Leung (2008) focused on two-party VMI channel and proposes an analytical model for the partners in supply channel to determine the inventory policy with the objective of optimizing system net profit. The model explicitly incorporates issues from both the vendor and the retailer in order to derive a policy for mutual benefits. Proposed solution procedure, to illustrate the proposed model for various scenarios. Factors such as shelf-space-dependent demand, shelf-space capacity, demand pattern, logistics characteristics, and disparity between holding costs of the warehouse and the retail store are also investigated.

- Wong *et al.*(2008) detailed how a sales rebate contract helps achieve supply chain coordination which allows decentralized decisions of chain members to perform a centralized decision for the whole system. The proposed model demonstrates that the supplier gains more profit with competing retailers than without as competition among the retailers lowers the prices and thus stimulates demand.

- Yu *et al.* (2008a) showed how to analyze the intrinsic evolutionary mechanism of the VMI supply chains by applying the evolutionary game theories. results identify the conditions under which the VMI model is favorable over the traditional chain structure and shed lights on when and why collaboration is critical for a successful, long-term implementation of VMI.

- Gumus *et al*(2008) analyzed consignment inventory (CI) in supply chain under deterministic demand, and provided some general conditions under which CI creates benefits for the vendor, for the customer, and for the two parties together. They also considered similar issues for the combined use of CI and VMI.

- Michaelraj and Shahabudeen (2008) developed two models considering different demand and payment policies (unequal installments). Suggested optimal replenishment policies for the two models

- Al-Ameri *et al.* (2008) aims at designing a dynamic VMI system. The entire supply chain performance is optimized in terms of production planning at vendor's site, distribution strategy, and inventory management at manufacturer's site. Explored some of the complications involved in setting up such a system. The VMI system is modeled as a mixed-integer linear program (MILP) using discrete-time representation. Finally, a novel rolling horizon approach that simultaneously combines the aggregate and the detailed models is designed to solve the problem.

- Yao and Dresner (2008) extended the models in the literature Beyond "EDI: impact of continuous replenishment program (CRP) between a manufacturer and its retailers". Their analysis shows that Information sharing, Continuous replenishment program, and VMI bring varying benefits in terms of inventory cost savings to firms, and that the benefits are not consistently distributed between retailers and manufacturers.

- Szmerekovsky and Zhang (2008) studied the effect on manufacturers and retailers of attaching radio frequency identification (RFID) tags at the item level in a vendor managed inventory (VMI) system. Determined the optimal inventory policies in a centralized system and establish conditions under which the RFID system is preferable to the system without RFID. This initiative system has been implemented in the laboratory and has passed the evaluation processes successfully.

- Kwak *et al.* (2009) dealt with a VMI problem for managing a retailer's inventory under unstable customer demand situation. Developed a retrospective action-reward learning model, a kind of reinforcement learning techniques, which is faster in learning than conventional action-reward learning and more suitable to apply to the control domain where rewards for actions vary over time. A simulation based experiment has been carried out to to test the model.

• Soroor *et al.*(2009) devised an innovative model, based on the Intelligent Wireless Web services, for a typical mobile real-time supply chain coordination system which has been developed and tested in a real operational environment

Most of the papers address to two-echelon supply chain and others deal with concept, case study and framework. The concentration of the literature tends towards cost minimization and performance improvement with less attention to profit maximization. Soft issues have been dealt by few authors with minimum concentration towards pricing, Information sharing and revenue sharing. Few authors have addressed to VMI mode of operations, finally most of the VMI articles deal with case studies and implementation issues.

## State-of-the-Art

• It has been found out that with information technology enabled VMI, 66% of retailers' inventory has been reduced without reducing service level and cost of goods reduced by 12%.

• Most of the articles deal with concept and application of information technology enabled VMI with small consideration to mathematical modelling, parameter determination etc. Scope still exists for development of heuristics for VMI models

• Lot of scope for research exists in two-echelon SC under different environment conditions such as objective, mode of operation and various models.

• Channel profit maximization has to be considered explicitly instead of cost minimization

• The performance of supply chain can be improved by exploring soft issues

• Less number of articles have only addressed to pricing, to revenue share with information sharing

• Review reveals that obtaining optimal solutions to two echelon single vendor multiple buyers and two-echelon multiple vendors multiple buyer's problems are difficult to solve and there is a necessity to develop an efficient search algorithm to get near optimal solutions in the shortest time period.

• Decision support heuristics are required for the most normative models with different issues

## CONCLUDING REMARKS AND FUTURE RESEARCH DIRECTIONS

This chapter addressed the role of information technology enabled VMI in modeling soft issues of supply chain and found that few work on information technology enabled VMI has been applied to sectors such as milk, agricultural and engineering services. Hence it is concluded that the lot of potential exist to apply VMI in small and medium scale enterprises and in an unorganised sectors like agricultural to improve the organizational resistance to change, inter-functional conflicts, joint production planning, profit sharing, team oriented performance measures, channel power shift, information sharing, real time communication, inventory and technical compatibility. The classification schema and frame work presented would be highly useful to researchers for modeling soft issues of supply chain and would also aid SC managers to apply information technology enabled VMI to reap the major benefits in an unorganised sector. It is also noted that to achieve zero stock out information technology enabled VMI technique will be more useful and it also improves the performance of supply chain and the relationship between the partners. Furthermore, it is also identified that the inventory holding cost and order setup cost for vendor in all the models are assumed as sum of both holding cost and order setup cost, but in practice the inventory cost will be less. Therefore the vendor profit and channel profit would be more in real time. Future analysis can consider various combination of inventory holding and order setup cost to the above models and the insight of the problem could be studied. The distribution cost in most of cases varies parabolically depending upon the increase in quantity and mode of transportation. Since in VMI, the vendor has to monitor inventory and to replenish products as and when required, there will be exponential variation in distribution cost depending upon the increase in quantity and mode of transportation. Hence future research can represent distribution cost with respect to product and incorporate fixed transportation cost to depict the real cost of transportation. Most of papers assume reverse linear relationship between price-sales quantities. The impact on optimal operational parameters for various demand curves can be studied for other categories of product. VMI mode of operation assumes zero lead time and would not allow backlog and stock out. Researchers in future can accommodate these factors along with shortage cost for varying service levels while developing two-echelon models. Decision support heuristics could be extended for multi echelon models. Furthermore, it is also identified that the development of decision support heuristics can be extended to any kind of product. Development of knowledge managed systems for two-echelon information technology enabled VMI systems to determine operational parameters for maximum channel profit based on the experts experience and with the data available from the market. The soft issues such as organizational resistance to change, inter-functional conflicts, team oriented

performance measures and channel power shift have not been considered while modeling two-echelon SC. Hence future researchers may pay more attention to these issues.

## ACKNOWLEDGMENT

The authors thank the Management, the Principal, and the Head of Mechanical Engineering Department of Thiagarajar College of Engineering, Madurai, India and Nottingham University Business School, Nottingham, UK for providing necessary facilities to carry out this work. The authors specially thank AICTE, New Delhi for the career award grant ((AICTE CAYT 06-07 (F.No.1-51/FD/CA/(16.)/2006-07 dated: 12.12.06) titled (Development of Auction Based Mechanisms for Logistics and Supply Chain Management) and also thank Department of Science and Technology (SERC Division), New Delhi for the BOYSCAST fellowship to first author (SR/BY/E-09/06).

## REFERENCES

Abad, P. L. (2003). Optimal pricing and lot-sizing under conditions of perishability, finite production and partial backordering and lost sale. *European Journal of Operational Research, 144*, 677–685. doi:10.1016/S0377-2217(02)00159-5

Abad, P. L., & Aggarwal, V. (2005). Incorporating transport cost in the lot size and pricing decisions with downward sloping demand. *International Journal of Production Economics, 95*, 297–305. doi:10.1016/j.ijpe.2003.12.008

Achabal, D. D., Mcintyre, S. H., Smith, S. A., & Kalyanam, K. (2000). A Decision support system for VMI. *Journal of Retailing, 76*(4), 430–454. doi:10.1016/S0022-4359(00)00037-3

Ahtiala, P. (2004). The optimal pricing of computer software and other products with high switching costs. *International Review of Economics and Finance.* Available online, www.sciencedirect.com

Al-Ameri, T. A., Shah, N., & Papageorgiou, L. G. (2008). Optimization of vendor-managed inventory systems in a rolling horizon framework. *Computers & Industrial Engineering, 54,* 1019–1047. doi:10.1016/j.cie.2007.12.003

Andersson, J., & Marklund, J. (2000). Decentralized inventory control in a two-level distribution system. *European Journal of Operational Research, 127,* 483–506. doi:10.1016/S0377-2217(99)00332-X

Anupindi, R., & Akella, R. (1993). Diversification under supply chain uncertainty. *Management Science, 39,* 944–963. doi:10.1287/mnsc.39.8.944

Anupindi, R., & Bassok, R. (1996). Distribution Channels, Information Systems and Virtual Centralization. In *Proceedings of MSOM Conference,* (pp. 87-92).

Arntzen, B. C., Brown, G. G., Harrison, T. P., & Trafton, L. (1995). Global SCM at Digital Equipment Corporation. *Interfaces, 25,* 69–93. doi:10.1287/inte.25.1.69

Ashayeri, J., & Rongen, J. M. J. (1997). Central distribution in Europe: A multi-criteria approach to location selection. *The International Journal of Logistics Management, 9*(1), 97–106. doi:10.1108/09574099710805628

Axsater, S. (2005). A simple decision rule for decentralized two-echelon inventory control. *International Journal of Production Economics, 93–94,* 53–59. doi:10.1016/j.ijpe.2004.06.005

Ballou, R. H., Gilbert, S. M., & Mukherjee, A. (2000). New managerial challenges from supply chain opportunities. *Industrial Marketing Management, 29,* 7–18. doi:10.1016/S0019-8501(99)00107-8

Banerjee, A. (1986). A joint economic lot size model for purchaser and vendor. *Decision Sciences, 17,* 292–311. doi:10.1111/j.1540-5915.1986.tb00228.x

Banerjee, A. (2005). Concurrent pricing and lot sizing for make-to-order contract production. *International Journal of Production Economics, 94,* 89–195. doi:10.1016/j.ijpe.2004.06.017

Banerjee, A., Burton, J., & Banerjee, S. (2003). A simulation study of lateral shipments in single supplier, multiple buyers supply chain networks. *International Journal of Production Economics, 81–82,* 103–114. doi:10.1016/S0925-5273(02)00366-3

Beamon, B. M. (1998). Supply chain design and analysis: Models and methods. *International Journal of Production Economics, 55,* 281–294. doi:10.1016/S0925-5273(98)00079-6

Ben-Daya, M., & Harigab, M. (2004). Integrated single vendor single buyer model with stochastic demand and variable lead time. *International Journal of Production Economics, 92,* 75–80. doi:10.1016/j.ijpe.2003.09.012

Benton, W. C., & Maloni, M. (2005). The influence of power driven buyer/seller relationships on supply chain satisfaction. *Journal of Operations Management, 23,* 1–22. doi:10.1016/j.jom.2004.09.002

Berry, D., & Naim, M. M. (1996). Quantifying the relative improvements of redesign strategies in a PC supply chain. *International Journal of Production Economics,* (46-47): 181–196. doi:10.1016/0925-5273(95)00181-6

Bharadwaj, N., & Matsuno, K. (2006). Investigating the antecedents and outcomes of customer firm transaction cost savings in a supply chain relationship. *Journal of Business Research, 59*(1), 62–72. doi:10.1016/j.jbusres.2005.03.007

Bhaskaran, S. (1996). *Simulation Analysis of a Manufacturing Supply Chain*. Presented at Supply Chain Linkages Symposium, Indiana University.

Bhattacharjee, S., & Ramesh, R. (2000). A multi-period profit maximizing model for retail supply chain management: An integration of demand and supply side mechanism. *European Journal of Operational Research, 122*, 584–601. doi:10.1016/S0377-2217(99)00097-1

Bowersox, D. J., & Closs, D. J. (1996). *Logistics Management*. Hightstown, NJ: McGraw-Hill.

Bowersox, D. J., & Morash, E. A. (1989). The Integration of Marketing flows in Channels of Distribution. *European Journal of Marketing, 23*, 58–67. doi:10.1108/EUM0000000000546

Burke, M. (1996). Its Time for Vendor Managed Inventory. *Industrial Distribution*, 85-90.

Bylka, S. (1999). A dynamic model for the single-vendor, multi-buyer problem. *International Journal of Production Economics, 59*, 297–304. doi:10.1016/S0925-5273(98)00021-8

Cachon, G. P. (2001). Stock wars: Inventory competition in a two-echelon supply chain with multiple retailers. *Operations Research, 49*(5), 658–674. doi:10.1287/opre.49.5.658.10611

Cachon, G. P., & Fisher, M. L. (1997). Campbell Soup's Continuous Replenishment Program: Evaluation and Enhanced Inventory Decision Rules. *Production and Operations Management, 6*, 266–276.

Cachon, G. P., & Zipkin, P. H. (1999). Competitive and cooperative Inventory Policies in a two stage supply chain. *Management Science, 45*(7), 936–953. doi:10.1287/mnsc.45.7.936

Camm, J. D., Chorman, T., Dill, F., Evans, J., Sweeney, D., & Wegryn, G. (1997). Blending OR/MS Judgement, and GIS: Restructuring P&G's Supply Chain. *Interfaces, 27*, 128–142. doi:10.1287/inte.27.1.128

Capar, I., Ulengin, F., & Reisman, A. (2004). *A Taxonomy for Supply Chain Management Literature*. Retrieved from http://ssrn.com/abstract=531902

Carr, A. S., & Smeltzer, L. R. (1999). The relationship of strategic purchasing to supply chain management. *European Journal of Purchasing and Supply Management, 5*, 43–51. doi:10.1016/S0969-7012(98)00022-7

Casati, F., Dayal, U., & Shan, M-C. (2001). E Business Applications for Supply Chain Management: Challenges and Solutions. *IEEE Journal*, 1063-6382 / 01, 71-78.

Cetinkaya, S., & Lee, C. Y. (2000). Stock Replenishment and Shipment Scheduling For Vendor-Managed Inventory Systems. *Management Science, 46*(2), 217–232. doi:10.1287/mnsc.46.2.217.11923

Chen, I. J., & Paulraj, A. (2004). Understanding supply chain management: critical research and a theoretical framework. *International Journal of Production Research, 42*(1), 131–163. doi:10.1080/00207540310001602865

Cheng, H. K., & Koehler, J. (2003). Optimal pricing policies of web-enabled application services. *Decision Support Systems, 35*, 259–272. doi:10.1016/S0167-9236(02)00073-8

Choi, K. S., Dai, J. G., & Song, J. G. (2004). On Measuring Supplier Performance under Vendor-Managed-Inventory Programs in Capacitated Supply Chains. *Manufacturing and Service Operations Management, 6*(1), 53–72. doi:10.1287/msom.1030.0029

Chopra, S. (2003). Designing the Distribution Networks in a supply Chain. *Transportation Research Part E, Logistics and Transportation Review, 39,* 123–140. doi:10.1016/S1366-5545(02)00044-3

Chopra, S. & Meindl, P. (2001). *Supply Chain Management: Strategy, Planning and Operation.* New Dehli: Pearson Education Asia.

Clark, A., & Scarf, H. (1960). Optimal Policies for a Multi-Echelon Inventory Problem. *Management Science, 6,* 475–490. doi:10.1287/mnsc.6.4.475

Clark, T. H., & Croson, D. C. (1994). H.E. Butt Grocery Company: a leader in ECR implementation. *Harvard Business School Case, 9,* 195–125.

Cohen, M. A., & Lee, H. L. (1988). Strategic analysis of integrated production-distributed systems: models and methods. *Operations Research, 36*(2), 216–228. doi:10.1287/opre.36.2.216

Cohen, M. A., & Lee, H. L. (1989). Resource deployment analysis of global manufacturing and distribution networks. *Journal of Manufacturing and Operations Management, 2,* 81–104.

Corne, D., Dorigo, M., & Glover, F. (1999). *New Ideas in Optimisation.* New York: McGraw-Hill.

Costa, L., & Oliveira, P. (2001). Evolutionary algorithms approach to the solution of mixed integer nonlinear programming problems. *Computers & Chemical Engineering, 25,* 257–266. doi:10.1016/S0098-1354(00)00653-0

Cousins, P. D., & Spekman, R. (2003). Strategic supply and the management of inter-and intra-organisational relationships. *Journal of Purchasing and Supply Management, 9,* 19–29. doi:10.1016/S1478-4092(02)00036-5

Desarbo, W. S., Rao, V. R., Steckel, J. H., Wind, J., & Colombo, R. (1987). A Friction model for describing and forecasting price changes. *Journal of Marine Science, 6*(4), 299–319. doi:10.1287/mksc.6.4.299

Disney, S. M., Potter, A. T., & Gardner, B. M. (2003). The impact of vendor managed inventory on transport operations. *Transportation Research Part E, Logistics and Transportation Review, 39,* 363–380. doi:10.1016/S1366-5545(03)00014-0

Disney, S. M., & Towill, D. R. (2002). A procedure for optimization of the dynamic response of a Vendor Managed Inventory system. *Computers & Industrial Engineering, 43,* 27–58. doi:10.1016/S0360-8352(02)00061-X

Disney, S. M., & Towill, D. R. (2003). Vendor managed inventory and bull whip reduction in a two level supply chain. *International Journal of Operations & Production Management, 23*(6), 625–651. doi:10.1108/01443570310476654

Disney, S. M., & Towill, D. R. (2003). The effect of vendor managed inventory (VMI) dynamics on the Bullwhip Effect in supply chains. *International Journal of Production Economics, 85,* 199–215. doi:10.1016/S0925-5273(03)00110-5

Dong, Y., & Xu, K. (2002). A supply chain model of vendor managed inventory. *Transportation Research Part E, Logistics and Transportation Review, 38*(2), 75–95. doi:10.1016/S1366-5545(01)00014-X

Fisher, M. L., & Raman, A. (1996). Reducing the cost of demand uncertainty through accurate response to early sales. *Operations Research, 44,* 87–99. doi:10.1287/opre.44.1.87

Fry, M. J. (2002). *Collaborative and cooperative agreement in the supply chain.* Unpublished Ph.D. Thesis report, University of Michigan, Ann Arbor, MI.

Gallego, G., & Vanryzin, G. (1994). Optimal Dynamic Pricing of Inventories with Stochastic demand Over Finite Horizons. *Management Science, 40,* 999–1020. doi:10.1287/mnsc.40.8.999

Ganeshan, R. (1999). Managing supply chain inventories: A multiple retailer, one warehouse, multiple supplier model. *International Journal of Production Economics, 59,* 341–354. doi:10.1016/S0925-5273(98)00115-7

Ganeshan, R., Jack, E., Magazine, M. J., & Stephens, P. (1999). A Taxonomic Review of Supply Chain Management Research . In Tayur, S., Magazine, M., & Ganeshan, R. (Eds.), *Quantitative Models of Supply Chain Management* (pp. 841–878). Boston: Kluwer Academic Publishers.

Gavireni, S., Kapuscinski, R., & Tayur, S. (1998). Value of information in capacitated Supply Chains . In Magazine, M. J., Tayur, S., & Ganeshan, R. (Eds.), *Quantitative Models for Supply Chain Management.* Cambridge, UK: Kluwer.

Gavirneni, S. (2001). Benefits of cooperation in a production distribution environment. *European Journal of Operational Research, 130*(3), 612–622. doi:10.1016/S0377-2217(99)00423-3

Gentry, J. J. (1996). The role of carriers in buyer-supplier strategic partnerships: A supply chain management approach. *Journal of Business Logistics, 17,* 33–55.

Geoffrion, A. M., & Graves, G. W. (1974). Multi-Commodity Distribution Design by Benders Decomposition. *Management Science, 20,* 822–844. doi:10.1287/mnsc.20.5.822

Giannoccaro, I., & Pontrandolfo, P. (2004). Supply Chain Coordination by revenue sharing contracts. *International Journal of Production Economics, 89,* 131–139. doi:10.1016/S0925-5273(03)00047-1

Gjerdrum, J., Shah, N., & Papageorgiou, L. G. (2002). Fair Transfer Price and Inventory holding policies in Two Enterprise Supply Chains. *European Journal of Operational Research, 143,* 582–599. doi:10.1016/S0377-2217(01)00349-6

Glover, F., & Gkochenberger, G. (Eds.). (2001). *Handbook in Meta heuristics.* Amsterdam: Kluwer Academic Publishers.

Glover, F., Jones, G., Karney, D., & Klingman, D. & Mote. (1979). An integrated production, distribution, and inventory planning system. *Interfaces, 9*(5), 21–35. doi:10.1287/inte.9.5.21

Goyal, S. K. (1997). An integrated inventory model for a single supplier-single customer problem. *International Journal of Production Research, 15,* 107–111. doi:10.1080/00207547708943107

Goyal, S. K. (2000). On improving the single-vendor single-buyer integrated production inventory model with a generalized policy. *European Journal of Operational Research, 125,* 429–430. doi:10.1016/S0377-2217(99)00269-6

Goyal, S. K., & Nebebe, F. (2000). Determination of economic production- shipment policy for a single-vendor-single-buyer system. *European Journal of Operational Research, 121,* 175–178. doi:10.1016/S0377-2217(99)00013-2

Graves, S. C., Kletter, D. B., & William, H. B. (1998). A Dynamic Model for Requirements Planning with Application to Supply Chain Optimization. *Operations Research, 46*(3), 35–49. doi:10.1287/opre.46.3.S35

Greis, N. P., & Kasarda, J. D. (1997). Enterprise logistics in the information age. *California Management Review, 39,* 55–78.

Griffith, D.A., Harvey, M.G. & Lusch, R.F. (2005). Social exchange in supply chain relationships: The resulting benefits of procedural and distributive justice. *Journal of Operations management.*

Gumus, M., Jewkes, E. M., & Bookbinder, J. H. (2008). Impact of consignment inventory and vendor-managed inventory for a two-party supply chain. *International Journal of Production Economics, 113*, 502–517. doi:10.1016/j.ijpe.2007.10.019

Gunasekaran, A., & Ngai, E. W. T. (2004). Information systems in supply chain integration and management. *European Journal of Operational Research, 159*, 269–295. doi:10.1016/j.ejor.2003.08.016

Hafeeza, K., Griffiths, M., Griffiths, J., & Naim, M. M. (1996). Systems design of a two-echelon steel industry supply chain. *International Journal of Production Economics, 45*, 121–130. doi:10.1016/0925-5273(96)00052-7

Hammond, J. H. (1990). Quick response in the apparel industry. Harvard Business School Note N9-690-038, Cambridge, MA.

Handfield, R. B., & Bechtel, C. (2002). The role of trust and relationship structure in improving supply chain responsiveness. *Industrial Marketing Management, 31*, 367–382. doi:10.1016/S0019-8501(01)00169-9

Henig, M., Gerchak, Y., Ernst, R., & Pike, D. (1997). An Inventory Model Embedded in Designing a Supply Contract. *Management Science, 43*, 184–197. doi:10.1287/mnsc.43.2.184

Hill, R. M. (1997). The single-vendor single-buyer integrated production-inventory model with a generalised policy. *European Journal of Operational Research, 97*, 493–499. doi:10.1016/S0377-2217(96)00267-6

Holmstrom, J. (1998). Business process innovation in the supply chain – a case study of implementing vendor managed inventory. *European Journal of Purchasing and Supply Management, 4*, 127–131. doi:10.1016/S0969-7012(97)00028-2

Hoque, M. A., & Goyal, S. K. (2000). An optimal policy for a single-vendor single-buyer integrated production-inventory system with capacity constraint of the transport equipment. *International Journal of Production Economics, 65*, 305–315. doi:10.1016/S0925-5273(99)00082-1

Houlihan, J. B. (1988). International Supply Chain Management: A New approach. *Management Decision, 26*(3), 13–19. doi:10.1108/eb001493

Huang, C.-K. (2004). An optimal policy for a single-vendor single-buyer integrated production–inventory problem with process unreliability consideration. *International Journal of Production Economics, 91*, 91–98. doi:10.1016/S0925-5273(03)00220-2

Jayaraman, V., & Ross, A. (2003). A simulated annealing methodology to distribution network design and management. *European Journal of Operational Research, 144*, 629–645. doi:10.1016/S0377-2217(02)00153-4

Kaipia, R., & Tanskanen, K. (2003). Vendor managed category management—an outsourcing solution in retailing. *Journal of Purchasing and Supply Management, 9*, 165–175. doi:10.1016/S1478-4092(03)00009-8

Klastorin, T. (2004). New Product Introduction: Timing, Design, and Pricing. *Manufacturing and Service Operations Management, 6*(4), 302–320. doi:10.1287/msom.1040.0050

Kruger, G. A. (1997). The Supply Chain Approach to Planning and Procurement Management. Hewlett-Packard Journal, 28-38.

Kuk, G. (2004). Effectiveness of vendor-managed inventory in the electronics industry: determinants and outcomes. *Information & Management, 41*, 645–654. doi:10.1016/j.im.2003.08.002

Kwak, C., Choi, J. S., Kim, C. O., & Kwon, I. (2009). Situation reactive approach to Vendor Managed Inventory problem. *Expert Systems with Applications.* .doi:10.1016/j.eswa.2008.12.018

Lamming, R. (2000). Japanese Supply Chain Relationships in Recession. *Long Range Planning, 33,* 757–778. doi:10.1016/S0024-6301(00)00086-8

Lancioni, R. A. (2005). A strategic approach to industrial product pricing: The pricing plan. *Industrial Marketing Management, 34,* 177–183. doi:10.1016/j.indmarman.2004.07.015

Latamore & Benton, G. (1999). The farm business unit customers, Customers, Suppliers Drawing Closer through VMI. *APICS: The Performance Advantage, 12*(7), 22-25.

Lederer, P. J., & Li, L. (1997). Pricing, Production, Scheduling and Delivery-Time Competition. *Operations Research, 45,* 407–420. doi:10.1287/opre.45.3.407

Lee, C. C., & Chu, W. H. J. (2005). Who should control inventory in a supply chain. *European Journal of Operational Research, 164*(1), 158–172. doi:10.1016/j.ejor.2003.11.009

Lee, H. L., & Billington, C. (1993). Material management in decentralized supply chains. *Operations Research, 41,* 835–847. doi:10.1287/opre.41.5.835

Lee, H. L., & Billington, C. (1995). The evolution of supply chain management models and practice at Hewlett-Packard. *Interfaces, 25,* 42–63. doi:10.1287/inte.25.5.42

Lee, H. L., Padmanabhan, V., & Whang, S. (1997). Information Distortion in a Supply Chain: The Bullwhip Effect. *Management Science, 43,* 546–558. doi:10.1287/mnsc.43.4.546

Li, M. Z. F. (2005). Pricing non-storable perishable goods by using a purchase restriction: General optimality results. *European Journal of Operational Research, 161,* 838–853. doi:10.1016/j.ejor.2003.06.033

Lin, K. Y. (2005). Dynamic pricing with real-time demand learning. *European Journal of Operational Research.*

Lourenco, H. R. (2005). Logistics Management: an opportunity for Metaheuristics . In Rego, C., & Alidaee, B. (Eds.), *Metaheuristics Optimization via Memory and Evolution* (pp. 329–356). Kluwer Academic Publishers.

Lu, L. (1995). A one-vendor multi-buyer integrated inventory model. *European Journal of Operational Research, 81*(2), 312–323. doi:10.1016/0377-2217(93)E0253-T

Mabert, V. A., & Venkataramanan, M. A. (1998). Special Research Focus on Supply Chain Linkages: Challenges for Design and Management in the 21st Century. *Decision Sciences, 29*(3), 537–552. doi:10.1111/j.1540-5915.1998.tb01353.x

Maloni, M. J., & Benton, W. C. (1997). Supply Chain Partnership: Opportunities for Operations Research. *European Journal of Operational Research, 101,* 419–429. doi:10.1016/S0377-2217(97)00118-5

Melachrinoudis, E., & Min, H. (2000). The dynamic relocation and phase-out of a hybrid, two-echelon plant/warehousing facility: A multiple objective approach. *European Journal of Operational Research, 123*(1), 1–15. doi:10.1016/S0377-2217(99)00166-6

Melachrinoudis, E., Min, H., & Messac, A. (2000). The relocation of a manufacturing/distribution facility from supply chain perspectives: A physical programming approach. *Multi-Criteria Applications, 10,* 15–39.

Mentzer, J. T., & Schuster, A. D. (1983). Computer modelling in logistics: Existing models and future outlook. *Journal of Business Logistics, 3*(2), 1–55.

Michaelraj, L. A., & Shahabudeen, P. (2008). Replenishment policies for sustainable business development in a continuous credit based vendor managed inventory distribution system. *Computers & Industrial Engineering.* doi:.doi:10.1016/j.cie.2008.05.014

Micheau, V. A. (2005). How Boeing and Alcoa Implemented A Successful Vendor Managed Inventory Program. *The Journal of Business Forecasting, 24*(1), 17–19.

Min, H., & Melachrinoudis, E. (1999). The relocation of a hybrid manufacturing/distribution facility from supply chain perspectives: A case study. *Omega, 27*(1), 75–85. doi:10.1016/S0305-0483(98)00036-X

Min, H., & Zhou, G. (2002). Supply chain modelling: past, present and future. *Computers & Industrial Engineering, 43*, 231–249. doi:10.1016/S0360-8352(02)00066-9

Minner, S. (2003). Multiple-supplier inventory models in supply chain management: A review. *International Journal of Production Economics, 81-82*, 265–279. doi:10.1016/S0925-5273(02)00288-8

Mishra, B. K., & Raghunathan, S. (2004). Retailer vs. Vendor Managed Inventory and Brand Competition. *Management Science, 50*(4), 445–457. doi:10.1287/mnsc.1030.0174

Mohanty, R.P. & Deshmukh, S.G. (2001). *Essentials of Supply Chain Management.* New Delhi, India: Phoenix publishing house Pvt., Ltd.

Moinzadeh, K., & Aggarwal, P. K. (1997). An information Based Multi-Echelon Inventory System with Emergent Orders. *Operations Research, 45*, 694–701. doi:10.1287/opre.45.5.694

Morash, E. A., Droge, C., & Vickery, S. (1997). Boundary-spanning interfaces between logistics, production, marketing and new product development. *International Journal of Physical Distribution and Logistics Management, 27*, 350–369. doi:10.1108/09600039710175921

Musalem, E. P., & Dekker, R. (2005). Controlling inventories in a supply chain: A case study. *International Journal of Production Economics, 93-94*, 179–188. doi:10.1016/j.ijpe.2004.06.016

Netessine, S. (2005). Dynamic pricing of inventory/capacity with infrequent price changes. *European Journal of Operational Research, 174*(1), 553–580. doi:10.1016/j.ejor.2004.12.015

Nozick, L. K., & Turnquist, M. A. (2001). Inventory, transportation, service quality and the location of distribution centers. *European Journal of Operational Research, 129*, 362–371. doi:10.1016/S0377-2217(00)00234-4

Parks, L., & Popolillo, M. C. (1999). Co-Managed Inventory is focus of Vendor/ Retailer Pilot. *Drug Store News, 27*, 71.

Parlar, M. & Weng, Z. K. (2004). Coordinating pricing and production decisions in the presence of price competition. *European Journal of Operational Research.*

Polatoglu, L. H. (1991). Optimal order quantity and pricing decisions in single period inventory systems. *International Journal of Production Economics, 23*, 175–185. doi:10.1016/0925-5273(91)90060-7

Rajan, A., Rakesh, A., & Steinberg, R. (1992). Dynamic pricing and ordering decisions by a monopolist. *Management Science, 38*, 240–262. doi:10.1287/mnsc.38.2.240

Robinson, E. P., Gao, L., & Muggenborg, S. D. (1993). Designing an integrated distribution system at DowBrands, inc. *Interfaces, 23*, 107–117. doi:10.1287/inte.23.3.107

Ross, A., Venkataramanan, M. A., & Ernstberger, K. (1998). Reconfiguring the supply network using current performance data. *Decision Sciences, 29*(3), 707–728. doi:10.1111/j.1540-5915.1998.tb01360.x

Satterfield, R., & Robinson, E. P. (1996). *Designing Distribution Systems to Support Vendor Strategies in Supply Chain Management*. Presented at Supply Chain Linkages Symposium, Indian University.

Sedarage, D., Fujiwara, O., & Luong, H. T. (1999). Determining optimal order splitting and reorder level for N-supplier inventory systems. *European Journal of Operational Research, 116*, 389–404. doi:10.1016/S0377-2217(98)00179-9

Shapiro, J. F. (2001). *Modeling the supply chain*. Pacific Grove, CA: Wadsworth Group.

Simchi-Levi, D., Kaminsky, P., & Simchi-Levi, E. (2000). *Designing and Managing the Supply Chain*. New York: McGraw-Hill.

Soroor, J., Tarokh, M. J., & Shemshadi, A. (2009). Initiating a state of the art system for real-time supply chain coordination. *European Journal of Operational Research, 196*, 635–650. doi:10.1016/j.ejor.2008.03.008

Southard, P. B. (2001). *Extending VMI into alternate supply chains: A simulation Analysis of cost and service levels*. Unpublished Ph.D. Thesis report, Faculty of graduate college at university of Nebraska.

Southard, P. B., & Swenseth, S. R. (2008). Evaluating vendor-managed inventory (VMI) in non-traditional environments using simulation. *International Journal of Production Economics, 116*, 275–287. doi:10.1016/j.ijpe.2008.09.007

Srinivasan, K., Kekre, B., & Mukhopadhyay, T. (1994). Impact of electronic data interchange technology on JIT shipments. *Management Science, 40*, 1291–1304. doi:10.1287/mnsc.40.10.1291

Stenger, A. J. (1994). Distribution Resource Planning. In Roberson, Capacino & Howe, (Eds.) the Logistics Handbook. New York: Free Press.

Stenger, A. J. (1996). Reducing inventories in a multi-echelon manufacturing firm: A case study. *International Journal of Production Economics, 45*, 239–249. doi:10.1016/0925-5273(94)00146-4

Sucky, E. (2005). Inventory management in supply chains: A bargaining problem. *International Journal of Production Economics, 93-94*, 253–262. doi:10.1016/j.ijpe.2004.06.025

Swamidass, P. M. (2000). *Encyclopedia of production and manufacturing management*. Boston: Kluwer Academic Publishers. doi:10.1007/1-4020-0612-8

Szmerekovsky, J. G., & Zhang, J. (2008). Coordination and adoption of item-level RFID with vendor managed inventory. *International Journal of Production Economics, 114*, 388–398. doi:10.1016/j.ijpe.2008.03.002

Tagaras, G., & Lee, H. L. (1996). Economic models for vendor evaluation with quality cost analysis. *Management Science, 42*, 1531–1543. doi:10.1287/mnsc.42.11.1531

Talluri, S. (2000). An IT/IS acquisition and justification model for supply chain management. *International Journal of Physical Distribution and Logistics Management, 30*(3/4), 221–237. doi:10.1108/09600030010325984

Tang, Q. C., & Cheng, H. K. (2005). Optimal location and pricing of Web services intermediary. *Decision Support Systems, 40*, 129–141. doi:10.1016/j.dss.2004.04.007

Teng, J., Chang, C., & Goyal, S. K. (2004). Optimal pricing and ordering policy under permissible delay in payments. *International Journal of Production Economics, 97*, 121–129. doi:10.1016/j.ijpe.2004.04.010

Thomas, D. J., & Griffin, P. M. (1996). Coordinated supply chain management. *European Journal of Operational Research, 94*(1), 1–15. doi:10.1016/0377-2217(96)00098-7

Toni, A. F. D., & Zamolo, E. (2005). From a traditional replenishment system to vendor-managed inventory: A case study from the household electrical appliances sector. *International Journal of Production Economics, 96*, 63–79. doi:10.1016/j.ijpe.2004.03.003

Torabi, S.A., Ghomi, S.M.T.F. & Karimi, B. (2005). A hybrid genetic algorithm for the finite horizon economic lot and delivery scheduling in supply chains. *European Journal of Operational Research.*

Towill, D. R., Naim, N. M., & Wikner, J. (1992). Industrial Dynamics Simulation Models in the Design of Supply Chains. *International Journal of Physical Distribution & Logistics Management, 22*, 3–13. doi:10.1108/09600039210016995

Tronstad, R. (1995). Pricing. *Journal of Market Analysis and Pricing*, 39-45.

Tyan, J., & Wee, H. M. (2003). Vendor Managed Inventory: a survey of the Taiwanese grocery industry. *Journal of Purchasing and Supply Management, 9*(1), 11–18. doi:10.1016/S0969-7012(02)00032-1

Vickery, S. K., Jayaram, J., Droge, C., & Calantone, R. (2003). The effects of an integrative supply chain strategy on customer service and financial performance: an analysis of direct versus indirect relationships. *Journal of Operations Management, 21*, 523–539. doi:10.1016/j.jom.2003.02.002

Viswanathan, S. (1998). Optimal strategy for the integrated vendor-buyer inventory model. *European Journal of Operational Research, 105*(1), 38–42. doi:10.1016/S0377-2217(97)00032-5

Viswanathan, S., & Mathur, K. (1997). Integrating Routing and Inventory Decisions in One-Warehouse Multi-Retailer, Multi-Product Distribution Systems. *Management Science, 43*, 294–312. doi:10.1287/mnsc.43.3.294

Waller, M., Johnson, M. E., & Davis, T. (2001). Vendor managed inventory in the retail supply chain. *Journal of Business Logistics, 20*(1), 183–203.

Williams, M. K. (2000). Making Consignment and Vendor Managed Inventory work for you. *Hospital Materiel Management Quarterly, 21*(4), 59–63.

Wong, W. K., Qi, J., & Leung, S. Y. S. (2008). Coordinating supply chains with sales rebate contracts and vendor- managed inventory. *International Journal of Production Economics*. doi:. doi:10.1016/j.ijpe.2008.07.025

Woo, Y. Y., Hsu, S. L., & Wu, S. (2001). An integrated inventory model for a single vendor and multiple buyers with ordering cost reduction. *International Journal of Production Economics, 73*, 203–215. doi:10.1016/S0925-5273(00)00178-X

Wu, D. J. (2001). Software agents for knowledge management: coordination in multi-agent supply chains and auctions. *Expert Systems with Applications, 20*, 51–64. doi:10.1016/S0957-4174(00)00048-8

Xu, K., & Leung, M. T. (2008). Stocking policy in a two-party vendor managed channel with space restrictions. *International Journal of Production Economics*. doi:.doi:10.1016/j.ijpe.2008.11.003

Yang, P. C., & Wee, H. M. (2002). A single-vendor and multiple-buyers production–inventory policy for a deteriorating item. *European Journal of Operational Research, 143*, 570–581. doi:10.1016/S0377-2217(01)00345-9

Yao, M. J., & Chiou, C. C. (2004). On a replenishment coordination model in an integrated supply chain with one vendor and multiple buyers. *European Journal of Operational Research, 159*, 406–419. doi:10.1016/j.ejor.2003.08.024

Yao, Y., & Dresner, M. (2008). The inventory value of information sharing, continuous replenishment, and vendor-managed inventory. *Transportation Research Part E, Logistics and Transportation Review*, *44*, 361–378. doi:10.1016/j.tre.2006.12.001

Yao, Y., Evers, P.T. & Dresner, M.B. (2005). Supply chain integration in vendor-managed inventory. *Decision Support Systems*.

Yokota, T., Gen, M., & Li, Y. X. (1996). Genetic Algorithm for non linear mixed integer programming problems and its applications. *Computers & Industrial Engineering*, *30*(4), 905–917. doi:10.1016/0360-8352(96)00041-1

Yu, H., Zeng, A. Z., & Zhao, L. (2008a). Analyzing the evolutionary stability of the vendor-managed inventory supply chains. *Computers & Industrial Engineering*. doi:.doi:10.1016/j.cie.2008.05.016

Yu, Y., Huang, G. Q., & Liang, L. (2008). Stackelberg Game-Theoretic Model for Optimizing advertising, pricing and Inventory Policies in Vendor Managed Inventory (VMI) Production supply chains. *Computers & Industrial Engineering*. doi:.doi:10.1016/j.cie.2008.12.003

Yu, Z., Yan, H., & Cheng, T. C. E. (2001). Benefits of information sharing with supply chain partnerships. *Industrial Management & Data Systems*, *101*(3), 114–119. doi:10.1108/02635570110386625

Zhu, Q., & Sarkis, J. (2004). Relationships between operational practices and performance among early adopters of green supply chain management practices in Chinese manufacturing enterprises. *Journal of Operations Management*, *22*, 265–289. doi:10.1016/j.jom.2004.01.005

Zinn, W., & Levy, M. (1988). Speculative Inventory Management: A Total Channel Perspective. *International Journal of Physical Distribution & Materials Management*, *18*, 34–39.

# Chapter 17
# Two-Way Substitutable Inventory System with N-Policy

**N. Anbazhagan**
*Alagappa University Karaikudi, India*

## ABSTRACT

*This article presents a two commodity stochastic inventory system under continuous review. The maximum storage capacity for the i-th item is fixed as $S_i$ (i = 1, 2). It is assumed that demand for the i-the commodity is of unit size and demand time points form Poisson distribution with parameter $\lambda_i$, i = 1, 2. The reorder level is fixed as $s_i$ for the i-th commodity (i = 1, 2) and the ordering policy is to place order for $Q_i (= S_i - s_i)$ items for the i-th commodity (i = 1, 2) when both the inventory levels are less than or equal to their respective reorder levels. The lead time is assumed to be exponential. The two commodities are assumed to be substitutable. That is, if the inventory level of one commodity reaches zero, then any demand for this commodity will be satisfied by the item of the other commodity. If no substitute is available, then this demand is backlogged up to a certain level $N_i$, (i = 1, 2) for the i-th commodity. Whenever the inventory level reaches $N_i$, (i = 1, 2), an order for $N_i$ items is replenished instantaneously. For this model, the limiting probability distribution for the joint inventory levels is computed. Various operational characteristics and expression for long run total expected cost rate are derived.*

## INTRODUCTION

In many practical multi-item inventory systems concentrated the coordination of replenishment orders for group of items. Now a days it is very much applicable to run a successful Business and Industries. These systems unlike those dealing with single commodity involve more complexities in the reordering procedures. The modelling of multi-item

DOI: 10.4018/978-1-61520-625-4.ch017

inventory system under joint replenishment has been receiving considerable attention for the past three decades.

In continuous review inventory systems, (Ballintfy, 1964) and (Silver, 1974) have considered a coordinated reordering policy which is represented by the triplet $(S, c, s)$, where the three parameters $S_i, c_i$ and $s_i$ are specified for each item $i$ with $s_i < c_i < S_i$, under the unit sized Poisson demand and constant lead time. In this policy, if the level of i-th com-

Copyright © 2010, IGI Global. Copying or distributing in print or electronic forms without written permission of IGI Global is prohibited.

modity at any time is below $s_i$, an order is placed for $S_i - s_i$ items and at the same time, any other item $j(\neq i)$ with available inventory at or below its can-order level $c_j$, an order is placed so as to bring its level back to its maximum capacity $S_j$. Subsequently many articles have appeared with models involving the above policy and another article of interest is due to (Federgruen, Groenevelt and Tijms, 1984), which deals with the general case of compound Poisson demands and non-zero lead times. A review of inventory models under joint replenishment is provided by (Goyal and Satir, 1989).

(Kalpakam and Arivarignan, 1993) have introduced $(s, S)$ policy with a single reorder level $s$ defined in terms of the total number of items in the stock. This policy avoids separate ordering for each commodity and hence a single processing of orders for both commodities has some advantages in situation where in procurement is made from the same supplies, items are produced on the same machine, or items have to be supplied by the same transport facility.

(Krishnamoorthy, Iqbal Basha and Lakshmy, 1994) have considered a two commodity continuous review inventory system without lead time. In their model, each demand is for one unit of first commodity or one unit of second commodity or one unit of each commodity 1 and 2, with prefixed probabilities. (Krishnamoorthy and Varghese, 1994) have considered a two commodity inventory problem without lead time and with Markov shift in demand for the type of commodity namely "commodity-1", "commodity-2" or "both commodity", using the direct Markov renewal theoretical results. And also for the same problem, (Sivasamy and Pandiyan, 1998) had derived various results by the application of filtering technique.

(Anbazhagan and Arivarignan, 2000) have considered a two commodity inventory system with Poisson demands and a joint reorder policy which placed fixed ordering quantities for both commodities whenever both inventory levels are less than or equal to their respective reorder levels.

(Anbazhagan and Arivarignan, 2001) have analyzed models with a joint ordering policy which places orders for both commodities whenever the total net inventory level drops to a prefixed level $s$.

(Anbazhagan and Arivarignan, 2004) have analysed models with individual and joint ordering policy. For the individual reorder policy, the reorder level for $i$-th commodity is fixed as $r_i$ and whenever the inventory level of $i$-th commodity falls on $r_i$ an order for $P_i (= S_i - r_i)$ items is placed for that commodity irrespective of the inventory level of the other commodity. A joint reorder policy is used with prefixed reorder levels $s$ and order for $Q_x^1 (S_1 - x)$ and $Q_y^2 (S_2 - y)$ items is placed for both commodities by cancelling the previous orders, whenever both commodities have their inventory level drops to a reorder level $s$, ( $x + y = s$ ).

In this paper the demand points for each commodity form independent Poisson processes and the lead times initiated by joint reorder policy are assumed to be independent and distributed as negative exponential. The two commodities are assumed to be substitutable. That is, if the inventory level of one commodity reaches zero, then any demand for this commodity will be satisfied by the item of the other commodity. If no substitute is available, then this demand is backlogged. The backlog is allowed upto the level $N_i$, $(i = 1, 2)$ for the $i$-th commodity. Whenever the inventory level reaches $N_i$, $(i = 1, 2)$, an order for $N_i$ items are placed which is replenished instantaneously. The limiting probability distribution of the joint inventory level is derived. Various measures of system performance in the steady state are also obtained.

## MODEL DESCRIPTION

Consider a two commodity stochastic inventory system with the maximum capacity $S_i$ units for $i$-th commodity $(i = 1, 2)$. The demand for $i$-th commodity is of unit size and the time points of demand occurrences form independent Poisson processes each with parameter $\lambda_i$, ($i = 1, 2$). The reorder level for the $i$-th commodity is fixed at $s_i$, ($1 \le s_i \le S_i$) and ordering quantity for $i$-th commodity is $Q_i (= S_i - s_i > s_i + N_i)$ items when both inventory levels are less than or equal to their respective reorder levels. The requirement $S_i - s_i > s_i + N_i$, ensures that after a replenishment the inventory levels of both commodities will be always above the respective reorder levels. Otherwise it may not be possible to place reorder which leads to perpetual shortage. That is, if $L_i(t)$ represents inventory level of $i$-th commodity at time $t$, then a reorder is made when $L_1(t) \le s_1$ and $L_2(t) \le s_2$. The lead time is assumed to be distributed as negative exponential with parameter $\mu (> 0)$. The two commodities are assumed to be substitutable. That is, if the inventory level of one commodity reaches zero, then any demand for this commodity will be satisfied by the item of the other commodity. If no substitute is available, then this demand is backlogged. The backlog is allowed up to the level $N_i$, ($i = 1, 2$) for the $i$-th commodity. Whenever the inventory level reaches $N_i$, ($i = 1, 2$), an order for $N_i$ items are placed which is replenished instantaneously.

## Notations

**0**: zero matrix

$1'_N$ : $(1, 1, \cdots, 1)_{1 \times N}$

$I_N$ : an identity matrix of order $N$

$\delta_{ij}$ : Kronecker delta.

$$\sum_{k=i}^{j} a^k = \begin{cases} a^i + a^{i+1} + \cdots + a^j, & if \; i < j \\ 0, & otherwise \end{cases}$$

$\left[A\right]_{ij}$ : $(i, j)$ − th element of the matrix $A$.

$$H(x) = \begin{cases} 1 & if \; x \ge 0 \\ 0 & if \; x < 0 \end{cases}$$

## ANALYSIS

The stochastic process $\{L_1(t), L_2(t)), t \ge 0\}$ has the state space $E = E_1 \cup E_2 \cup E_3$, where

$$E_1 = \{(i, j) \mid i = 1, 2 \cdots, S_1, j = 0, 1, \cdots, S_2\},$$

$$E_2 = \{(i, j) \mid i = 0, j = -(N_2 - 1), -(N_2 - 2), \cdots, 0, 1, \cdots, S_2\},$$

and

$$E_3 = \{(i, j) \mid i = -(N_1 - 1), -(N_1 - 2), \cdots, -1, j = -(N_2 - 1), -(N_2 - 2), \cdots, -1, 0\}.$$

From the assumptions made on demand and on replenishment processes, it follows that

$\{L_1(t), L_2(t)), t \ge 0\}$ is a Markov process. To determine the infinitesimal generator $\tilde{A} = ((a((i, j), (k, l))))$, $(i, j), (k, l) \in E$, of this process.

**Theorem 1:** The infinitesimal generator of this Markov process is given by,

$$a((i,j),(k,l)) = \begin{cases} \lambda_1, & k = i-1, & l = j, \\ & i = 1, 2, \cdots, S_1, & j = 1, \cdots, S_2 \\ \lambda_1, & k = i-1, & l = j, \\ & i = 0, -1, \cdots, -(N_1-2), & j = 0, -1, \cdots, -(N_2-1) \\ \lambda_1, & k = i+N_1-1, & l = j, \\ & i = -(N_1-1), & j = 0, -1, \cdots, -(N_2-1) \\ \lambda_1+\lambda_2, & k = i-1, & l = j, \\ & i = 1, 2, \cdots, S_1, & j = 0 \\ \lambda_1+\lambda_2, & k = i, & l = j-1, \\ & i = 0, & j = 1, \cdots, S_2 \\ \lambda_2, & k = i, & l = j-1, \\ & i = 1, 2, \cdots, S_1, & j = 1, 2, \cdots, S_2 \\ \lambda_2, & k = i, & l = j-1, \\ & i = 0, -1, \cdots, -(N_1-1), & j = 0, -1, \cdots, -(N_2-2) \\ \lambda_2, & k = i, & l = j+N_2-1, \\ & i = 0, -1, \cdots, -(N_1-1), & j = -(N_2-1) \\ -(\lambda_1+\lambda_2), & k = i, & l = j, \\ & i = s_1+1, \cdots, S_1, & j = 0, 1, \cdots, S_2 \\ -(\lambda_1+\lambda_2), & k = i, & l = j, \\ & i = 0, 1, \cdots, s_1, & j = s_2+1, \cdots, S_2 \\ -(\lambda_1+\lambda_2+\mu), & k = i, & l = j, \\ & i = 1, 2, \cdots, s_1, & j = 0, 1, \cdots, s_2 \\ -(\lambda_1+\lambda_2+\mu), & k = i, & l = j, \\ & i = 0, & j = -(N_2-1), \cdots, s_2 \\ -(\lambda_1+\lambda_2+\mu), & k = i, & l = j, \\ & i = -(N_1-1), \cdots, -1, & j = -(N_2-1), \cdots, 0 \\ \mu, & k = i+Q_1, & l = j+Q_2, \\ & i = 1, \cdots, s_1, & j = 0, 1, \cdots, s_2 \\ \mu, & k = i+Q_1, & l = j+Q_2, \\ & i = 0, & j = -(N_2-1), \cdots, s_2 \\ \mu, & k = i+Q_1, & l = j+Q_2, \end{cases}$$

Proof:

The infinitesimal generator $a((i,j),(k,l))$ of this process can be obtained using the following arguments:

(i) Let $i > 0$ and $j > 0$.

  (a) A demand takes the inventory level $(i,j)$ to $(i-1,j)$ with intensity $\lambda_1$ the demand being for the first commodity or to $(i, j-1)$ with intensity $\lambda_2$ the demand being for the second commodity.

  (b) The level $(i,0)$, and $(0,j)$ respectively, is taken to $(i-1,0)$, and $(0, j-1)$ due to both the way of substitutable with intensity $\lambda_1 + \lambda_2$.

(ii) For $i = 0, -1, \cdots, -(N_1 - 2)$ and $j = 0, -1, \cdots, -(N_2 - 2)$.

  (a) A demand takes the inventory level $(i,j)$ to $(i-1,j)$ with intensity $\lambda_1$ the demand being for the first commodity or to $(i, j-1)$ with intensity $\lambda_2$ the demand being for the second commodity.

  (b) From a state $(i, -(N_2 - 1))$, a demand for second commodity take the inventory level to $(i, -N_2)$ and due to instantaneous replenishment by the emergency purchase for the second commodity alone take the inventory level to $(i, 0)$. Similarly from a state $(-(N_1 - 1), j)$, a demand for first commodity take the inventory level to $(-N_1, j)$ and due to instantaneous replenishment by the emergency purchase for the first commodity alone take the inventory level to $(0, j)$.

(iii) From a state $(i, j)$, $(\leq (s_1, s_2))$, a replenishment by the delivery of orders for both commodities takes the inventory level to $(i + Q_1, j + Q_2)$ with intensity of transition $\mu$.

(iv) We observe that no transition other than the above is possible except $(i,j) \neq (k,l)$.

(v) Finally the value of $a((i,j),(i,j))$ is obtained by

$$a((i,j),(i,j)) = -\sum_{k}\sum_{\substack{l \\ (k,l)\neq(i,j)}} a((i,j),(k,l))$$

Hence we get the infinitesimal generator $a((i,j),(k,l))$.

The infinitesimal generator $\tilde{A}$ can be conveniently expressed as a block partitioned matrix:

$$\tilde{A} = ((A_{ij})),$$

where

$$A_{ij} = \begin{cases} A_3 & j = i, \, i = -(N_1 - 1), -(N_1 - 2), \ldots, -1 \\ A_2 & j = i, \, i = 0 \\ A_1 & j = i, \, i = 1, 2, \ldots, s_1 \\ A & j = i, \, i = s_1 + 1, s_1 + 2, \ldots, S_1 \\ B_4 & j = i + N_1 - 1, i = -(N_1 - 1) \\ B_3 & j = i - 1, \, i = -(N_1 - 2), \ldots, -1 \\ B_2 & j = i - 1, \, i = 0 \\ B_1 & j = i - 1, \, i = 1 \\ B & j = i - 1, \, i = 2, 3, \ldots, S_1 \\ C_2 & j = i + Q_1, i = -(N_1 - 1), -(N_1 - 2), \ldots, -1 \\ C_1 & j = i + Q_1, i = 0, \\ C & j = i + Q_1, i = 1, 2, \ldots, s_1, \\ 0 & Otherwise. \end{cases}$$

$$[C_2]_{pq} = \begin{cases} \mu, & q = p + Q_2, \quad p = -(N_2 - 1), -(N_2 - 2), \ldots, -1, 0, \\ 0, & otherwise \end{cases}$$

$$[C_1]_{pq} = \begin{cases} \mu, & q = p + Q_2, \quad p = -(N_2 - 1), \ldots, 0, \ldots, s_2 \\ 0, & otherwise \end{cases}$$

$$[C]_{pq} = \begin{cases} \mu, & q = p + Q_2, \quad p = 0, 1, \ldots, s_2 \\ 0, & otherwise \end{cases}$$

$$[B_4]_{pq} = \begin{cases} \lambda_1, & q = p, & p = -(N_2 - 1), -(N_2 - 2), \ldots, -1, 0, \\ 0, & otherwise \end{cases}$$

$$[A]_{pq} = \begin{cases} \lambda_2, & q = p - 1, & p = 1, 2, \ldots, S_2, \\ -(\lambda_1 + \lambda_2), & q = p, & p = 0, 1, \ldots, S_2, \\ 0, & otherwise \end{cases}$$

$$[B_3]_{pq} = \begin{cases} \lambda_1, & q = p, & p = -(N_2 - 1), -(N_2 - 2), \ldots, -1, 0, \\ 0, & otherwise \end{cases}$$

$$[B_2]_{pq} = \begin{cases} \lambda_1, & q = p, & p = -(N_2 - 1), -(N_2 - 2), \ldots, -1, 0, \\ 0, & otherwise \end{cases}$$

$$[B_1]_{pq} = \begin{cases} \lambda_1, & q = p, & p = 1, 2, \ldots, S_2, \\ \lambda_1 + \lambda_2, & q = p, & p = 0, \\ 0, & otherwise \end{cases}$$

$$[B]_{pq} = \begin{cases} \lambda_1, & q = p, & p = 1, 2, \ldots, S_2, \\ \lambda_1 + \lambda_2, & q = p, & p = 0, \\ 0, & otherwise \end{cases}$$

It may be noted that the matrices $A$, $A_1$, $B$ and $C$ are of size $(S_2 + 1) \times (S_2 + 1)$, $A_3$ and $B_3$ are of size $N_2 \times N_2$, $C_1$ is of size $(S_2 + N_2) \times (S_2 + 1)$ $C_2$ is of size $N_2 \times (S_2 + 1)$, $B_4$ is of size $N_2 \times (S_2 + N_2)$, $B_2$ is of size $(S_2 + N_2) \times N_2$, $B_1$ is of size $(S_2 + 1) \times (S_2 + N_2)$, $A_2$ is of size $(S_2 + N_2) \times (S_2 + N_2)$.

$$[A_3]_{pq} = \begin{cases} \lambda_2, & q = p - 1, & p = -(N_2 - 2), \ldots, -1, 0, \\ \lambda_2, & q = p + N_2 - 1, & p = -(N_2 - 1) \\ -(\lambda_1 + \lambda_2 + \mu), & q = p, & p = -(N_2 - 1), \ldots, -1, 0, \\ 0, & otherwise \end{cases}$$

It can be seen from the structure of $\tilde{A}$ that the homogeneous Markov process $\{L_1(t), L_2(t)), t \geq 0\}$ on the finite state space $E$ is irreducible. Hence the limiting distribution

$$\Phi = \left( \varphi^{(S_1)}, \varphi^{(S_1 - 1)}, \cdots, \varphi^{(0)}, \cdots, \varphi^{-(N_1 - 1)} \right)$$

with

$$\phi^{(m)} = \begin{cases} \left( \phi^{(m, S_2)}, \phi^{(m, S_2 - 1)}, \cdots, \phi^{(m, 1)}, \phi^{(m, 0)} \right), & m = 1, 2, \cdots, S_1 \\ \left( \phi^{(m, S_2)}, \phi^{(m, S_2 - 1)}, \cdots, \phi^{(m, -(N_2 - 1))} \right), & m = 0 \\ \left( \phi^{(m, -(N_2 - 1))}, \phi^{(m, -(N_2 - 2))}, \cdots, \phi^{(m, 0)} \right), & m = -(N_1 - 1), \cdots, -1 \end{cases}$$

$$[A_2]_{pq} = \begin{cases} \lambda_1 + \lambda_2, & q = p - 1, & p = 1, 2, \ldots, S_2, \\ \lambda_2, & q = p - 1, & p = -(N_2 - 2), \ldots, -1, 0, \\ \lambda_2, & q = p + N_2 - 1, & p = -(N_2 - 1) \\ -(\lambda_1 + \lambda_2 + \mu), & q = p, & p = -(N_2 - 1), \ldots, s_2 \\ -(\lambda_1 + \lambda_2), & q = p, & p = s_2 + 1, \ldots, S_2 \\ 0, & otherwise \end{cases}$$

where $\varphi^{(i,j)}$ denotes the steady state probability for the state $(i, j)$ of the inventory level process, exists and is given by

$$[A_1]_{pq} = \begin{cases} \lambda_2, & q = p - 1, & p = 1, 2, \ldots, S_2, \\ -(\lambda_1 + \lambda_2), & q = p, & p = s_2 + 1, \ldots, S_2, \\ -(\lambda_1 + \lambda_2 + \mu), & q = p, & p = 0, 1, \ldots, s_2, \\ 0, & otherwise \end{cases}$$

$$\Phi \tilde{A} = 0 \quad and \sum_{(i,j) \in E} \sum \varphi^{(i,j)} = 1. \tag{1}$$

**Theorem 2:** The steady state probability $\Phi$ is given by

$$\phi^{(i)} = \phi^{(S_1)} \theta_i, \quad i = -(N_1 - 1), \cdots, 0, 1, \cdots, S_1$$

where

$$\theta_i = \begin{cases} -\theta_{i+1}B_3A_3^{-1} & i=-(N_1-1),\cdots,-3,-2 \\[2mm] -\theta_{i+1}B_2A_3^{-1} & i=-1 \\[2mm] -(\theta_{i+1}B_1+\theta_{-N_1+1}B_4)A_2^{-1} & i=0 \\[2mm] -\theta_{i+1}BA_1^{-1} & i=1,2,\cdots,s_1 \\[2mm] -\theta_{i+1}BA^{-1} & i=s_1+1\cdots,Q_1-N_1 \\[2mm] -(\theta_{i+1}B+\theta_{i-Q_1}C_2)A^{-1} & i=Q_1-N_1+1,\cdots,Q_1-1 \\[2mm] I & i=Q_1 \\[2mm] -(\theta_{i+1}B+\theta_{i-Q_1}C)A^{-1} & i=Q_1+1,\cdots,S_1-1 \\[2mm] -\theta_{i-Q_1}CA^{-1} & i=S_1 \end{cases}$$

The value of $\varphi^{(Q_1)}$ can be obtained from the relation $\sum\sum_{(i,j)\in E}\varphi^{(i,j)}=1$, as

$$\varphi^{(Q_1)}=\left(I+\sum_{\substack{i=-(N_1-1)\\i\neq Q_1}}^{S_1}\theta_i\right)^{-1}$$

Proof:
The first equation of (1) yields the following set of equations:

$$\varphi^{(i)}A_3+\varphi^{(i+1)}B_3=0, \quad i=-(N_2-1),-(N_2-2),\cdots,-2,$$
$$\varphi^{(i)}A_3+\varphi^{(i+1)}B_2=0, \quad i=-1,$$
$$\varphi^{(i)}A_2+\varphi^{(i+1)}B_1+\varphi^{(-(N_1-1))}B_4=0, \quad i=0,$$
$$\varphi^{(i)}A_1+\varphi^{(i+1)}B=0, \quad i=1,2,\cdots,s_1,$$
$$\varphi^{(i)}A+\varphi^{(i+1)}B=0, \quad i=s_1+1,\cdots,Q_1-N_1$$
$$\varphi^{(i)}A+\varphi^{(i+1)}B+\varphi^{(i-Q_1)}C_2=0, \quad i=Q_1-N_1+1,\cdots,Q_1-1,$$
$$\varphi^{(i)}A+\varphi^{(i+1)}B+\varphi^{(i-Q_1)}C_1=0, \quad i=Q_1$$

$$\varphi^{(i)}A+\varphi^{(i+1)}B+\varphi^{(i-Q_1)}C=0, \quad i=Q_1+1,\cdots,S_1-1$$

and $\varphi^{(S_1)}A+\varphi^{(s_1)}C=0.$

Solving the above set of equations we get the required result.

## SYSTEM PERFORMANCE MEASURES

In this section we derive some measures of system performance in the steady state under consideration.

### Expected Reorder Rate

Let $R$ denote the mean joint reorder rate for both the commodity in the steady state which is given by,

$$R=\sum_{j=0}^{s_2}(\lambda_1+\delta_{0j}\lambda_2)\varphi^{(s_1+1,j)}+\sum_{i=0}^{s_1}(\delta_{i0}\lambda_1+\lambda_2)\varphi^{(i,s_2+1)}$$

Let $R_1$ denote the mean individual reorder rate for first commodity in the steady state which is given by,

$$R_1=\sum_{j=-(N_2-1)}^{0}\lambda_1\varphi^{(-(N_1-1,j))}$$

Let $R_2$ denote the mean individual reorder rate for second commodity in the steady state which is given by,

$$R_2=\sum_{i=-(N_1-1)}^{0}\lambda_2\varphi^{(i,-(N_2-1))}$$

### Mean Backlogging

Let $B_1$ denote the mean backlogging of the first commodity in the steady state then we have

*Table 1.*

| |
|---|
| $h_1$: the inventory carrying cost per item per unit time of first commodity. |
| $h_2$: the inventory carrying cost per item per unit time of second commodity. |
| $c_s$: setup cost per joint order. |
| $c_{s1}$: setup cost per order for first commodity. |
| $c_{s2}$: setup cost per order for second commodity. |
| $c_{b1}$: backlog cost per unit item of the first commodity. |
| $c_{b2}$: backlog cost per unit item of the second commodity. |

$$B_1 = \sum_{i=-(N_1-1)}^{-1} \sum_{i=-(N_2-1)}^{0} |i| \, \varphi^{(i,j)}$$

Let $B_2$ denote the mean backlogging of the second commodity in the steady state then we have

$$B_2 = \sum_{j=-(N_2-1)}^{-1} \sum_{i=-(N_1-1)}^{0} |j| \, \varphi^{(i,j)}$$

### Expected Inventory Level

Let $I_1$ denote the expected inventory level of the first commodity in the steady state which is given by

$$I_1 = \sum_{i=1}^{S_1} i \left( \sum_{j=0}^{S_2} \varphi^{(i,j)} \right)$$

Let $I_2$ denote the expected inventory level of the second commodity in the steady state. Then we have

$$I_2 = \sum_{j=1}^{S_2} j \left( \sum_{i=0}^{S_1} \varphi^{(i,j)} \right)$$

### Total Expected Cost Rate

To compute the total expected cost rate, the following costs are considered.

The long run total expected cost rate is given by

$$TC(S_1, s_1, N_1, S_2, s_2, N_2)$$
$$= h_1 I_1 + h_2 I_2 + c_s R + c_{s1} R_1 + c_{s2} R_2 + c_{b1} B_1 + c_{b2} B_2$$

## CONCLUSION

In this chapter we have described a two commodity substitutable inventory system with partial backlogging. This model is most suitable to two different items which are substitutable and may be extended to the case of renewal demand and perishable items. We have derived the joint probability distribution of the inventory levels in the steady state. We have also derived the stationary measures of system performances.

## REFERENCES

Anbazhagan, N., & Arivarignan, G. (2000). Two-Commodity Continuous Review Inventory system with Coordinated Reorder Policy. *International Journal of Information and Management Sciences*, *11*(3), 19–30.

Ballintify, J. L. (1964). On a basic class of inventory problems. *Management Science*, *10*, 287–297. doi:10.1287/mnsc.10.2.287

Federgruen, A., Groenvelt, H., & Tijms, H. C. (1984). Coordinated replenishment in a multi-item inventory system with compound Poisson demands. *Management Science, 30,* 344–357. doi:10.1287/mnsc.30.3.344

Goyal, S. K., & Satir, T. (1989). Joint replenishment inventory control: Deterministic and stochastic models. *European Journal of Operational Research, 38,* 2–13. doi:10.1016/0377-2217(89)90463-3

Kalpakam, S., & Arivarignan, G. (1993). A coordinated multicommodity (s,S) inventory system. *Mathematical and Computer Modelling, 18,* 69–73. doi:10.1016/0895-7177(93)90206-E

Krishnamoorthy, A., Iqbal Basha, R., & Lakshmy, B. (1994). Analysis of two commodity problem. *International Journal of Information and Management Sciences, 5*(1), 55–72.

Krishnamoorthy, A., & Varghese, T. V. (1994). A two commodity inventory problem. *Information and Management Sciences, 5*(3), 127–138.

Silver, E. A. (1974). A control system of coordinated inventory replenishment. *International Journal of Production Research, 12,* 647–671. doi:10.1080/00207547408919583

Sivasamy, R., & Pandiyan, P. (1998). A two commodity Inventory Model Under $(s_k, S_k)$ Policy. *International Journal of Information and Management Sciences, 9*(3), 19–34.

Yadavalli, V. S. S., Anbazhagan, N., & Arivarignan, G. (2004). A Two-Commodity Continuous Review Inventory System with Lost Sales. *Stochastic Analysis and Applications, 22,* 479–497. doi:10.1081/SAP-120028606

# Chapter 18
# A Fuzzy AHP Model for 3PL Selection in Lead Logistics Provider Scenarios

**Rajbir Singh Bhatti**
*Indian Institute of Technology Roorkee, India*

**Pradeep Kumar**
*Indian Institute of Technology Roorkee, India*

**Dinesh Kumar**
*Indian Institute of Technology Roorkee, India*

## ABSTRACT

*Selection of service providers in the global supply chains of today has been recognized as having a very important effect on the competitiveness of the entire supply chain. It results in achieving high quality end results (products and/or services), at reasonable cost coupled with high customer satisfaction. This article discusses the use of Fuzzy Analytic Hierarchy Process (FAHP) to effectively manage the qualitative and quantitative decision factors which are involved in the selection of providers of 3PL services under Lead Logistics Provider (LLP) environments of today. Lead logistics providers (LLP) are increasingly being banked upon to integrate the best of 3PL service providers and allow for synchronized and optimized operations. In the asset free environments of today, many a times, the LLP uses the services of the 3PL and hence the issue of reliably choosing them assumes increasingly greater significance. The fuzzy-AHP has been adequately demonstrated in literature to be an effective tool which can be used to factor-in the fuzziness of data. Triangular Fuzzy Numbers (TFN) have been deployed to make over the linguistic comparisons of criteria, sub-criteria and the alternatives. The FAHP based model formulated in this chapter is applied to a case study in the Indian context using data from three leading LSPs with significant operating leverages in the province of Uttrakhand (India). The proposed model can provide the guidelines and directions for the decision makers to effectively select their global service providers in the present day competitive logistics markets.*

DOI: 10.4018/978-1-61520-625-4.ch018

Copyright © 2010, IGI Global. Copying or distributing in print or electronic forms without written permission of IGI Global is prohibited.

## INTRODUCTION

In the present day environments of global competition, the modern logistics business organizations pay a special attention to the identification and selection among alternative sources. Traditionally, business organizations have tried to meet demand targets by a specific focus on bigger inventories and faster (and better) transportation modes. The emerging need of the day is to achieve increased levels of system design, logistics process management, data collection and storage analysis (Shen Shaoji, 2000). Companies are outsourcing their entire set of "non-core competency works" to organizations that have adequately well demonstrated and established professional excellence in those areas – logistics or otherwise. They are being asked to assess, design and execute/run integrated end-to-end supply chain solutions. Initially, outsourcing was at play in specific areas to specific players - the widely known third party logistics (3PL) concept. But, an increasing number of 3PLs led to a chaos of another kind. The scope for a 3PL provider was (and continues to be) immense. Many 3PLs failed at their own business transformation. The international 3PLs failed to provide domestic services and vice-versa. The shippers focused only on cost reduction, all the while ignoring their requirements for those specific services which they needed. Hence, it was in the resulting service vacuum created by 3PLs that the concept of Lead Logistics Provider (LLP) emerged. The LLP is essentially a 3PL with advantages of scale and other abilities which allow it to act as the "Lead" 3PL. It serves as a single point of contact as regards the organization and all the 3PLs it has hired. The LLP integrates and serves to co-ordinate the activities of the other 3PLs and hence emerges as a sort of Fourth Party service provider – though not really a 4PL in the sense we normally know 4PLs. The term 4PL or Fourth Party Logistics is a trademark of Accenture (formerly called the Anderson Consulting). The LLP builds on the foundations of 3PL and additionally delivers a comprehensive supply chain solution with integrated skills aimed at an optimally leveraged supply chain. The LLP is a BPO provider whose sole edge over the 3PL is his ability to bring value and a re-engineered attitudinal approach to the customer and his needs. The LLP manages other 3PLs while maintaining the shippers' perspective in the long term. The basic purpose of this evolution (LLP) is to infuse a maximized overall benefit to the end user/the customer. The Lead Logistics Provider (LLP) is a supply chain integrator who assembles and manages the resources, capabilities and technology of its own organization with those of complementary service provider to deliver a comprehensive supply chain solution (Xu Jianxin, 2002). The LLP thrives by leveraging the competencies of the 3PLs and the business process managers to deliver a comprehensive and integrated supply chain solution through a centralized point of contact.

The selection of 3PLs is a very important multi-criterion decision making issue. The globalization of the firm's operations signifies the establishment of long-term business relationship with often unfamiliar and unproven international partners. The selection of global 3PLs is a rather complicated task fraught with risks. Selection of 3PLs is one of the most important aspects that firms must incorporate into their strategic processes. As organizations become more and more dependent on service providers, the direct and indirect consequences of poor decision making in selecting the 3PL extensions will become more and more important and critical as well. Frequently changing the 3PLs is also not a very feasible scenario given the current globally competitive markets. The focus of the present work is to derive and develop, through fuzzy analytical modeling techniques, the selection of 3PLs by the LLP rather than by the shipper.

In the present article, we have initially identified the critical criteria associated with the process. The selection of decision variables is basically based on the knowledge and information gathered from the group of experts and the past researches available in the respective areas. The overall objective of the selection process is to identify the high potential 3PL which can stand on the LLP firm's specific decision criteria. The LLP analyses each 3PL's ability to meet its needs of integration in a systematic, transparent and IT supported method so that there is chain-wide confidence. This may not be easy to convert its needs into useful criteria because needs are often expressed as a general qualitative concepts while criteria should be quantitatively evaluated. This problem has been attempted for solution using the Fuzzy Analytic Hierarchy Process (FAHP) approach. The linguistic preferences are changed into the triangular fuzzy numbers for the pairwise comparison scale. Many conflicting criteria should be analyzed with precision. The 3PL selection is a vehicle that can be used to increase the efficiency of the entire supply chain. The rest of this paper is organized as: The immediately next section discusses the findings of previous researches available in this area. Thereafter, the article dwells upon the discussion about the basics of AHP and the Fuzzy set theory. The different decision criteria and sub-criteria considered in selecting the best 3PL are discussed in the ensuing portion. This is followed by a section on the Fuzzy Analytic Hierarchy Process (FAHP).In the penultimate section there is a discussion on a case study illustration of the proposed FAHP approach. The last section presents the conclusion and provides future research direction in this area.

## AN OVERVIEW OF RELEVANT LITERATURE

A vast spectrum of literature is available on aspects relating to 3PL vendor selection. All of that is focused on choices to be made by the organization / shipper. Of the many aspects which might affect the choice of a 3PL vendor, like the quality of service offered, timelines etc. different

choices and priorities are thrown up by different users. Hence, the need for developing a systematic and universally acceptable 3PL vendor selection process mechanism. In this paper fuzzy-AHP is used to tackle the problem because of the ability of fuzzy sets to resemble with the human-decision nature. Earliest work in fuzzy AHP appeared in Van laarhoven and Pedrycz (1983). Many OTHER authors have also suggested the application of AHP (Wang & Chin, 2009; Wang, Chin, & Leung, 2009; Tang & Xie, 2008; Sevkli, Koh, Zaim, Demirbag, & Tatoglu, 2008; Ozan, 2008; Nachiappan & Ramanathan, 2008; Chan, Kumar, Tiwari, Lau, & Choy, 2008; Kaur & Mahanti, 2008; Levary, 2008; Narasimahn,1983; Nydick RL,1992; Partovi FY,1990; Barbarosoglu, G., & Yazgac, T., 1997) approach for vendor selection problems. Weber et al. (1991, 1993) reviewed and classified various articles related to vendor selection and discussed the impact of just-in-time (JIT) manufacturing strategy on it. They used Dickson's (1996) 23 criteria and indicated that net price, delivery and quality were discussed in 80, 59 and 54% of the 74 articles, respectively. Newer studies focus on EAHP/GRAP (Zou & Yuan, 2009). AHP also helps in prioritizing the criterion under consideration. Chan et. al, (2008) have proposed a fuzzy AHP model for global supplier selection. Since the selection problem is complex and vague (at times), fuzzifying the hitherto discreet issues is proposed to help take care of the finer points in the minds of the decision maker. Since AHP fails to tackle the inter-dependencies of the variables, some studies have proposed the use of analytical network process (ANP) as well (Kaur & Mahanti, 2008). Some recent studies have focused on risk issues in selecting foreign suppliers (Levary, 2008). The selection of the global supplier or partner is much different from the domestic one and it involves much complexity in terms of the selection of the different effective criteria (Min 1994). Choy and Lee (2002) used the case based reasoning approach for intelligent supplier selection to enhance the performance of the selection as compared to traditional approaches. Liu and Hai (2005) proposed voting analytic hierarchy process, which allows the purchasing manager to generate non-inferior purchasing options and systematically analysis the inherent trade-offs among the relevant criteria. Cakravastia and Takahashi (2004) proposed a multi-objective model to support the process of supplier selection and negotiation that considers the effect of these decisions on the manufacturing plan. The model also takes into account several theoretical concepts in the negotiation process, concession force, resistance force and effective alternatives.

Data Envelopment Analysis approach has also been used to compare 3PLs of China. Attempts have also been made to use the benefits of both the DEA and the AHP in 3PL selection (Zhang et. al, 2006). Handfield, et. al (2002) have used AHP for supplier assessment by considering environmental criteria. They have used the help of a case study to show the supremacy of the method. Özdağoğlu, A., & Ozdağoğlu, G. (2007), have presented a detailed and comprehensive comparison of AHP and fuzzy AHP for multi-criteria decision making processes with linguistic evaluations. Similarly, fuzzy AHP has been used also for selection of plant location issues (Kaboli, Shahanaghi, & Niroomand, 2007). Numerous other works have been carried out in this direction with a focus on supplier selection using fuzzy AHP and incorporating the concepts of fuzzy set theory (Ayağ & Özdemir, 2006; Bohui, 2007; Boran, Genç, Kurt, & Akay, 2009; Lee, 2009; Liu & Wang, 2009; Nejati, Nejati, & Shafaei, 2009; Pi & Low, 2006; Zhongwei & Jianzhong, 2008).

## ESSENTIALS OF FUZZY SET THEORY AND AHP

This paper aims to discuss the fuzzy-AHP approach to tackle the problem of 3PL choice by leading LLPs of this region. Fuzzy-AHP is basically the combination of the two concepts: fuzzy set theory

and the AHP. The fuzzy set theory resembles human reasoning in its use of approximate information and uncertainty to generate decisions. It has the advantage of mathematically represent uncertainty and vagueness to provide formalized tool for dealing with the imprecision intrinsic to many problems.

## Analytic Hierarchy Process (AHP)

AHP (Saaty 1980) is a well-known multi-criterion decision making technique. It is a useful, simple and systematic approach. In this approach first a hierarchy is developed from more general (upper levels) criterion to the particular (bottom levels) or from the uncertain or uncontrollable to the more certain or controllable one. The hierarchy of the decision variables is the subject of a pairwise comparison of the AHP. In the traditional AHP, the pairwise comparison is made using a nine-point scale (1-9) which converts the human preferences between available alternatives as equally, moderately, strongly, very strongly or extremely preferred. Thus the AHP uses only absolute scale numbers for judgments and for their resulting priorities. Even though the discrete scale of AHP has the advantages of simplicity and ease of use, it is not sufficient to take in account the uncertainty associated with the mapping of one's perception to a number. In spite of its popularity and simplicity in concept, this method is often criticized for its inability to adequately handle the inherent uncertainty and imprecision associated with the mapping of the decision-maker's perception to exact numbers. In the traditional formulation of the AHP, human's judgments are represented as exact (or crisp, according to the fuzzy logic terminology) numbers. However, in many practical cases the human preference model is uncertain and decision-makers might be reluctant or unable to assign exact numerical values to the comparison judgments. Since some of the evaluation criteria are subjective and qualitative in nature, it is very difficult for the decision-maker to express the

*Figure 1. A triangular fuzzy number, N~*

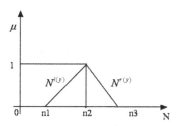

preferences using exact numerical values and to provide exact pairwise comparison judgments. The traditional AHP cannot straightforwardly be applied to solving uncertain decision-making problems. In order to eliminate this limitation, in the next section we discuss the fuzzy set theory, which is capable for tackling the uncertainty and imprecision of service evaluation process. It is more desirable for decision makers to use interval or fuzzy evaluations to handle the vagueness of the data involved in multi-criterion decision making problems.

## Fuzzy Set Theory

Fuzzy set theory has proven advantages within vague, imprecise and uncertain contexts and it resembles human reasoning in its use of approximate information and uncertainty to generate decisions. It was specially designed to mathematically represent uncertainty and vagueness and provide formalized tools for dealing with the imprecision intrinsic to many decision problems. Fuzzy set theory implements classes and grouping of data with boundaries that are not sharply defined (i.e. fuzzy). Fuzzy set theory includes the fuzzy logic, fuzzy arithmetic, fuzzy mathematical programming, fuzzy graph theory and fuzzy data analysis, usually the term fuzzy logic is used to describe all of these. The major contribution of fuzzy set theory is its capability of representing vague data.

A fuzzy set is characterized by a membership function, which assigns to each object a grade of membership ranging between 0 and 1. In this set the general terms such as 'large', 'medium' and 'small' each will be used to capture a range of numerical values. A fuzzy set is represented by putting a tilde '~' on a letter. If n1, n2 and n3, respectively, denote the smallest possible value, the most promising value and the largest possible value that describe a fuzzy event then the triangular fuzzy number (TFN) can be denoted as a triplet

(n1, n2, n3). A fuzzy number N expresses the meaning of 'about N'. A TFN N is shown in Figure 1.

**Definition**: The membership function of a TFN which associated with a real number in the interval [0,1] can be defined as:

$$\mu_N(x) = \begin{cases} \{(x - n_1)/(n_2 - n_1)\}; x \in [n_1, n_2] \\ \{(n_3 - x)/(n_3 - n_2)\}; x \in [n_2, n_3] \\ 0.....otherwise \end{cases} \quad (1)$$

A fuzzy number is also represented by the corresponding left and right representation of each degree of membership:

$$N = (N^{l(y)}, N^{r(y)})$$
$$= (n_1 + (n_2 - n_1)y, n_3 + (n_3 - n_2)y), \ y \in [0,1] \quad (2)$$

Here l(y) and r(y) are the left and rght side representation of a fuzzy number.

Fuzzy numbers are naturally easy to deploy in the expression of the decision maker's assessment of the qualitative situations.

## METHODOLOGY

In this paper fuzzy-AHP methodology has been discussed. Basically fuzzy-AHP is the fuzzy modified form of AHP. It has the ability to extract the merits of both approaches to efficiently and effectively tackle the multi-attribute decision making problems like 3PL selection. The AHP is one of the extensively used multi-criterion deci-sion making methods but it has been generally criticized because of the use of a discrete scale of one to nine which cannot handle the uncertainty and ambiguity present in deciding the priorities of different attributes. The relative importance of different decision criteria involves a high degree of subjective judgment and individual preferences. The linguistic assessment of human feelings and judgments are vague and it is not reasonable to represent it in terms of precise numbers. It feels more confident to give interval judgments than fixed value judgment. To improve the AHP method, this paper discusses a fuzzy modified AHP approach using triangular fuzzy numbers to represent decision makers' comparison judg-ments and fuzzy synthetic extent analysis method to decide the final priority of different decision criteria. In particular, the approach developed can adequately handle the inherent uncertainty and imprecision of the human decision making process and provide the flexibility and robustness needed for the decision maker to understand the decision problem. These merits of the approach developed would facilitate its use in real situations for making effective decisions.

Based on this first the weight vectors of alter-natives, sub-criteria and criteria are decided. As a result, the final priority weights of the alternative global suppliers are decided based on the different weights of criteria and sub-criteria. The highest priority would be given to the supplier with high-est weight.

## Calculation of Priority Weights

If the object set is given as $P=\{p_1,p_2,....p_n\}$ and the objective set is proposed as $R =\{r_1,r_2,...r_m\}$, then as per extent analysis each object is taken and the analysis is performed for all $O_i$. The value of fuzzy synthetic extent analysis wrt the $i^{th}$ object is proposed as:

$$F_i = \sum_{j=1}^{m} N_{oi}^{\ j} \otimes \left[\sum_{i=1}^{n}\sum_{j=1}^{m} N_{oi}^{\ j}\right]^{-1} \quad (3)$$

A fuzzy addition of m extent analysis values yields the value of $\sum_{j=1}^{m} N_{oi}^{\ j}$ .

$$\sum_{j=1}^{m} N_{oi}^{\ j} = \left(\sum_{j=1}^{m} N_{1j}, \sum_{j=1}^{m} N_{2j} \sum_{j=1}^{m} N_{3j}\right) \quad (4)$$

At the same time, the value of $\left[\sum_{i=1}^{n}\sum_{j=1}^{m} N_{oi}^{\ j}\right]^{-1}$

is obtained by doing a fuzzy addition operation of $N_{oi}^{j}$ (j=1,2,3,...m) such that

$$\sum_{i=1}^{n}\sum_{j=1}^{m} N_{oi}^{\ j} = \left(\sum_{j=1}^{m} N_{1j}, \sum_{j=1}^{m} N_{2j} \sum_{j=1}^{m} N_{3j}\right) \quad (5)$$

$\left[\sum_{i=1}^{n}\sum_{j=1}^{m} N_{oi}^{\ j}\right]^{-1}$ is calculated by solving the

inverse of the above equation(5), as given below:

$$\left[\sum_{i=1}^{n}\sum_{j=1}^{m} N_{oi}^{\ j}\right]^{-1} = \left(1 / \sum_{i=1}^{n} N_{3i}, 1 / \sum_{i=1}^{n} N_{2i}, 1 / \sum_{i=1}^{n} N_{1i}\right)$$
$$(6)$$

Here, the degree of possibility of $N_1=(n_{11},n_{12},n_{13})$ $\geq N_2(n_{21},n_{22},n_{23})$ is given as:

$$V(N_1 \geq N_2) = \sup_{x\geq y}\left[\min\left(m_{N1}(x), m_{N2}(y)\right)\right]$$
$$(7)$$

Such that a pair (x,y) exists where, x≥y and $\mu_{N1}(x) = \mu_{N2}(y) = 1$ and V(N1≥N2)=1. Given that N1 andN2 are convex fuzzy numbers, so V(N1≥N2)=1 if $n_{11} \geq n_{21}$. And also

$$V(N_2 \geq N_1) = hgt\left[N_1 \bigcap N_2\right] = \mu_{N1}(d) \quad (8)$$

In the above, d is the ordinate of the highest intersection point D between $\mu_{N1}$ and $\mu_{N2}$. In cases where $N_1 = (n_{11}, n_{12}, n_{13})$ and $N_2(n_{21}, n_{22}, n_{23})$, the ordinate of D is calculated as

$$V(N_2 \geq N_1) = hgt \left[ N_1 \bigcap N_2 \right]$$
$$= \left( n_{11} - n_{23} \right) / \left[ \left( n_{22} - n_{23} \right) - \left( n_2 - n_{11} \right) \right]$$
(9)

The degree of possibility of a (convex) fuzzy number to be greater than k other (convex) fuzzy numbers is defined as:

$$V(N \geq N_1, N_2, \ldots \ldots N_k) = \min V(N \geq N_i) \quad (10)$$

$$\text{If } m(P_i) = \min V(F_i \geq F_k) \quad (11)$$

The weight is given as

$$W_p = (m(P_1), m(P_2), m(P_3), \ldots \ldots m(P_n))^T \quad (12)$$

Normalization of the above value of $W_p$ we get:

$$W = (h(P_1), h(P_1), h(P_1), \ldots h(P_1),)^T \quad (13)$$

## IDENTIFICATION OF DECISION CRITERION

Dickson (1966), provided a set of twenty three criterions (Table1) which form the backbone of almost all vendor selection efforts. His list had factors like price, performance history, technical capability, delivery, financial position, quality and warranties. The study was based in a questionnaire sent to 273 purchasing agents and managers selected from the membership list of the National Association of Purchasing Managers. The list included purchasing agents and managers from the United States and Canada. A total of 170 (62.3%) responses were received. Table 1 summarizes the findings of Dickson's study regarding the importance of the 23 criteria for vendor selection (Weber.

C.A. et al., 1991). Some other subsequent studies have identified additional number of criteria that can be applied to select a 3PL vendor.

As part of the present work, an extensive survey of the LLPs operating in Uttrakhand province in India was carried out. Sample questionnaires were prepared and discussed with five decision makers .(DM) from the academia. Thereafter, these were revised and finally administered to the LLPs who are providing lead logistics services in the province.

While personal interviews were held with some local LLP operators, the questionnaire was also sent by email to other LLPs in India. Response rate was 27 percent (approximately). The criteria that emerged were also used to derive an ISM (Interpretive Structural Modeling) model also, so that the relative position of the parameters, in terms of their being driven or being drivers, can also be established. The underlying aim of the survey was to establish the factors/parameters at play when LLPs have to select the 3PLs, as also to establish the relative ranking of these parameters amongst themselves.

The factors in Table2 were considered to be the pertinent criterion (from survey results) and were deployed to arrive at an appropriate FAHP based model for selecting the 3PL service provider in a LLP scenario. It is a study using the nine point scale proposed by Saaty (1994). These are an extension of the works of Zhang et al. (2004), who have used a limited scope. Herein, the scope has been extended to global LLP environments. Hence there is a shift in parametric considerations Scale of Operations (SOPS) is measured on a Likert scale and assessed by the decision makers (DM) based on their knowledge and understanding of the 3PL. Operational Boundaries (OPBR) refers to the areas where the 3PL has been operating. The 3PLs with maximum global operating spread were rated 5 while local players were rated 1. Global Market Ranking (GMR) is a DM assessed score which is reflective of the perceived market rank of the 3PL, as a global player in the 3PL industry. Local Market ranking (LMR) is a simi-

*Table 1. Dickson's vendor selection criteria*

| Rank | Factor | Mean Rating | Evaluation |
|------|--------|-------------|------------|
| 1 | Quality | 3.508 | Extreme importance |
| 2 | Delivery | 3.417 | |
| 3 | Performance history | 2.998 | |
| 4 | Warranties and claim policies | 2.849 | |
| 5 | Production facilities and capacity | 2.775 | Considerable importance |
| 6 | Price | 2.758 | |
| 7 | Technical capability | 2.545 | |
| 8 | Financial position | 2.514 | |
| 9 | Procedural compliance | 2.488 | |
| 10 | Communication system | 2.426 | |
| 11 | Reputation and position in industry | 2.412 | |
| 12 | Desire for business | 2.256 | |
| 13 | Management and organization | 2.216 | |
| 14 | Operating controls | 2.211 | |
| 15 | Repair service | 2.187 | Average importance |
| 16 | Attitude | 2.120 | |
| 17 | Impression | 2.054 | |
| 18 | Packaging ability | 2.009 | |
| 19 | Labor relations record | 2.003 | |
| 20 | Geographical location | 1.872 | |
| 21 | Amount of past business | 1.597 | |
| 22 | Training aids | 1.537 | |
| 23 | Reciprocal arrangements | 0.610 | Slight importance |

lar construct which is indicative of the trust and respect commanded by the 3PL in the context of Indian operations. Logistics technology (LTEC) represents a Likert rating provided by the DM indicating the technological advancement of the 3PL (for instance the use of RFID etc). Logistics apparatus (LAPP) represents the strength of the 3PL in terms of its assets. Maintenance Cost (MCOST) is a figure in Indian rupees which we obtained from the 3PLs. It is intended to use the preventive and corrective maintenance costs incurred by the 3PL as an indicator of the strength of their logistic systems. Throughput capabilities (THUCAP) are the ability of the 3PL to move a given logistics bulk in a short span of time. Article

of Trade Wastage (AOTW) is a percentage which indicates the ability of the 3PL to deliver supplies with minimum in-transit loss of material, in terms of its quality and quantity. IT based abilities have come out as the new mantra for LLPs and 4PLs. Those 3PLs which have better IT enabled networks and electronic data interfaces are been increasingly seen as preferred partners in the logistics business. This is probably on account of the transparency and trust which these technologies weave into the entire chain. Very recently, we have seen people using social networking sites like Facebook and Twitter to constantly update their clients of the status of the in-transit material. These are being actively linked to GPS enabled devices (including

*Figure 2. Third Party Logistics' Service Provider Selection Model*

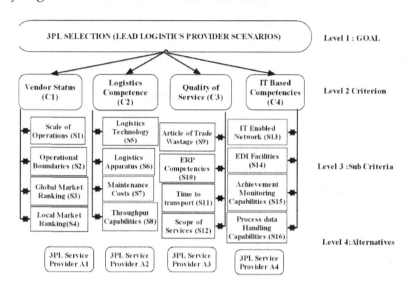

*Table 2. The sub-criteria for assessment.*

| Serial No. | Sub Criterion | Unit / Scale |
|---|---|---|
| **Vendor Status (VS)** | | |
| 1 | Scale of Operations (SOPS) | Likert Scale |
| 2 | Operational Boundaries(OPBR) | Likert Scale |
| 3 | Global Market Ranking(GMR) | Likert Scale |
| 4 | Local Market ranking(LMR) | Likert Scale |
| **Logistics Competence (LC)** | | |
| 5 | Logistics technology(LTEC) | Likert Scale |
| 6 | Logistics apparatus(LAPP) | Likert Scale |
| 7 | Maintenance Cost(MCOST) | Thousand Rupees |
| 8 | Throughput capabilities(THUCAP) | Tonnes |
| **Quality of Service(QS)** | | |
| 9 | Article of Trade Wastage(AOTW) | Percentage |
| 10 | ERP Competence(ERCAP) | Likert Scale |
| 11 | Time to transport(TTT) | Likert Scale |
| 12 | Scope of Services(SOS) | Likert Scale |
| **IT Based Competencies(ITCOM)** | | |
| 13 | IT Enabled Network(ITNET) | Likert Scale |
| 14 | EDI Facilities(EDIFAC) | Likert Scale |
| 15 | Achievement Monitoring Capabilities(AMCAP) | Likert Scale |
| 16 | Processed Data Handling Capabilities(PDHCAP) | Likert Scale |

mobile phones) via Google Maps, to locate seamlessly, the exact current locations of the bulk. All these ideas add value and lend the much needed confidence in the shipper and the LLP, both.

## Why Fuzzy-AHP?

In the traditional formulation of the AHP, human's judgements are represented as exact (or crisp, according to the fuzzy logic terminology) numbers. In many practical cases the human preference model is uncertain and decision makers might be reluctant or unable to assign exact numerical values to the comparison judgments. Since some of the evaluation criteria are subjective and qualitative in nature, it is very difficult for the decision maker to express the preferences using exact numerical values and to provide exact pairwise comparison judgments. In place of the exact number for the comparison, triangular fuzzy numbers are used in fuzzy-AHP to transform the linguistic preferences into the quantitative form for comparison. The triangular fuzzy numbers helps in tacking the problems encountered in the AHP. Fuzzy-AHP methodology discussed in this paper has the ability to effectively handle the vague and imprecise information involves in the multi-attribute decision making problems. The conventional AHP is mainly used in nearly well structured decision applications and its rankings are not precise, whereas the fuzzy-AHP is more effective and precise to handle the uncertain and conflicting decision criteria. The Fuzzy-AHP with extent analysis is simple and easy to implement to prioritize customer requirements as compared with the conventional AHP (Kwong and Bai 2003). This can improve the imprecise ranking of customer requirements inherited from studies based on the conventional AHP. The simplicity, ease of use, flexibility and its ability to handle complex and ill structured problems have led to its popularity as a multi-attribute decision making tool. The mathematical programming model applied to supplier selection always encounters problems including qualitative criteria that are very important in the decision making, especially for supplier partnership policies (Ghodsypour and O'Brien 1998). Therefore fuzzy extended approach is applied in this paper, since it is a more efficient approach in treating the fuzziness of data involved in analyzing the qualitative factors than other methods such as weighting or mathematical programming models.

## Illustrative Case

In this global environment, manufacturers with limited resources want to spend as much time and effort as possible in evaluating the potential suppliers for their critical parts that have relative importance in making the final products. The problem of a LLP organization has been taken in account in this section to discuss the numerical illustration of the fuzzy-AHP. The company wants to take into account all the possible important criteria which are affecting the behavior and performance of the 3PL. A long discussion on every criterion, attribute and alternative 3PLs has been conducted and based on intensive discussion, four prime criteria are identified. The discussion has been further prolonged to decide the sixteen sub-criteria and four potential 3PLs.

The computational procedure for calculating the priority weights of the different decision variables and finally deciding the best 3PL using the fuzzy-AHP technique can be summarized as follows:

Construct the fuzzy comparison matrices of criteria with respect to the goal with the help of the questionnaire form. Determine the fuzzy synthetic extent value with respect to the each criterion with the help of the equations discussed. Determine the degree of possibility of the superiority of each fuzzy synthetic extent value with respect to each other. Decide the minimum degree of possibility of the superiority of each criterion over another. Determine the weight vectors of the criteria with the help of minimum degree of possibility of superiority of each criterion. Normalize this weight vectors and determine the final weight of the decision criteria with respect to the goal. Repeat this process to decide the final weight of all the sub-criteria with respect to their specific criteria. Similarly decide the priority of the decision alternatives with respect to the sub-attributes. Multiply the priority weights of the decision alternatives with the sub-criteria and decide the priority of the alternatives with respect to the main criteria. Multiply the priority weights of the decision alternatives with the priority weight of criteria and decide the final priority of the decision alternatives with respect to the primary goal. Decide the best global supplier with the highest priority weight. The numerical analysis of deciding the weight vectors of the criteria with respect to goal is discussed as follows: First the fuzzy comparison matrix of the criteria is constructed by the pairwise comparison of the different criterion relevant to the overall objective, which is shown in table 3. The fuzzy synthetic extent value with respect to each criterion is calculated by using equation (9).

## Sample Calculations

The values of fuzzy extent w.r.t. the four different criteria are F1, F2,F3 and F4 and they are computed as

$F1 = (\ 6.50\ 7.50\ 8.75\ ) \otimes (\ 0.06\ 0.05\ 0.04\ ) = (\ 0.27\ 0.39\ 0.56\ )$

$F2 = (\ 3.67\ 5.25\ 7.00\ ) \otimes (\ 0.06\ 0.05\ 0.04\ ) = (\ 0.15\ 0.28\ 0.45\ )$

$F3 = (\ 2.50\ 3.29\ 4.33\ ) \otimes (\ 0.06\ 0.05\ 0.04\ ) = (\ 0.11\ 0.17\ 0.28\ )$

$F4 = (\ 2.94\ 2.97\ 3.67\ ) \otimes (\ 0.06\ 0.05\ 0.04\ ) = (\ 0.12\ 0.16\ 0.23\ )$

Since n11 >= n21, therefore,

$V(F1 >= F2) = 1$

Similarly,

$V(F1 >= F3) = 1$; $V(F1 >= F4) = 1$; $V(F4 >= F3) = 1$; $V(F2 >= F3) = 1$ ; $V(F3 >= F4) = 1$; ; $V(F2 >= F4) = 1$

Also,

$V(F2 >= F1) = 0.60$
$V(F3 >= F1) = 0.02$
$V(F3 >= F2) = 1.38$
$V(F4 >= F1) = 1.45$
$V(F4 >= F2) = 0.40$

Hence, we get the following values for the minimum degrees of possibility:

$m(C1) = 1.00$
$m(C2) = 0.60$
$m(C2) = 0.02$
$m(C2) = 0.40$

After normalizing, these values turn into 0.50, 0.30,0.01 and 0.20 respectively. Hence,

*Table 3. Fuzzy comparison matrix of criteria with respect to overall objectives*

| Goal | C1 | | | C2 | | | C3 | | | C4 | | | Normalized Weight |
|------|------|------|------|------|------|------|------|------|------|------|------|------|-------------------|
| | n1 | n2 | n3 | n1 | n2 | n3 | n1 | n2 | n3 | n1 | n2 | n3 | |
| C1 | 1.00 | 1.00 | 1.00 | 1.50 | 2.00 | 3.00 | 2.50 | 3.00 | 3.50 | 1.50 | 2.00 | 2.50 | 0.61 |
| C2 | 0.33 | 0.50 | 0.67 | 1.00 | 1.00 | 1.00 | 1.50 | 2.00 | 2.50 | 1.50 | 2.00 | 2.50 | 0.33 |
| C3 | 0.29 | 0.33 | 0.40 | 0.40 | 0.50 | 0.67 | 1.00 | 1.00 | 1.00 | 1.50 | 2.00 | 2.50 | 0.04 |
| C4 | 0.40 | 0.50 | 0.67 | 0.40 | 0.50 | 0.67 | 0.40 | 0.50 | 0.67 | 1.00 | 1.00 | 1.00 | 0.02 |

W=(0.50, 0.30,0.01,0.20)$^T$

The complete result is also given in table 3.

Now the different sub-criteria are compared under each of the criterion separately by following the same procedure as discussed above. Whenever the value of $(n_{11} - n_{23}) > 0$, the elements of the matrix must be take normalized and then do the same process to find the weight vector of each attribute. The fuzzy comparison matrices of sub-criteria and the weight vectors of each sub-criterion are shown in tables 4-7.

Similarly the fuzzy evaluation matrices of decision alternatives and corresponding weight vector of each alternative with respect to corresponding sub-criteria are also calculated but to make the paper concise only comparison matrices with respect to sub-criteria S1 and S2 are shown in the paper in tables 8 and 9.

Other comparison matrices of decision alternatives with respect to sub-criteria S3 to S19 can easily be formed as similar to the S1 and S2. The priority weights of suppliers with respect to the each criterion are given by adding the weights per supplier multiplied by weights of the corresponding sub-criteria. The results are shown in tables 10-13.

Finally the priority weights of each supplier can be calculated by weights per supplier multiplied by weights of the corresponding criterion. The

*Table 4. Fuzzy comparison matrix of sub-criteria with respect to C1*

| C1 | S1 | | | S2 | | | S3 | | | S4 | | | Normalized Weight |
|----|----|----|----|----|----|----|----|----|----|----|----|----|----|
| | n1 | n2 | n3 | n1 | n2 | n3 | n1 | n2 | n3 | n1 | n2 | n3 | |
| S1 | 1.00 | 1.00 | 1.00 | 1.50 | 2.00 | 2.50 | 2.50 | 2.51 | 3.50 | 1.50 | 2.00 | 2.50 | 0.51 |
| S2 | 0.40 | 0.50 | 0.67 | 1.00 | 1.00 | 1.00 | 1.00 | 2.00 | 2.50 | 1.00 | 1.00 | 1.00 | 0.14 |
| S3 | 0.29 | 0.40 | 0.40 | 0.40 | 0.50 | 1.00 | 1.00 | 1.00 | 1.00 | 0.66 | 1.50 | 2.00 | 0.02 |
| S4 | 0.40 | 0.50 | 0.67 | 1.00 | 1.00 | 1.00 | 0.50 | 0.67 | 1.52 | 1.00 | 1.00 | 1.00 | 0.33 |

*Table 5. Fuzzy comparison matrix of sub-criteria with respect to C2*

| C2 | S5 | | | S6 | | | S7 | | | S8 | | | Normalized Weight |
|----|----|----|----|----|----|----|----|----|----|----|----|----|----|
| | n1 | n2 | n3 | n1 | n2 | n3 | n1 | n2 | n3 | n1 | n2 | n3 | |
| S5 | 1.00 | 1.00 | 1.00 | 1.00 | 2.00 | 2.50 | 2.50 | 2.51 | 3.50 | 1.50 | 2.00 | 2.25 | 0.50 |
| S6 | 0.40 | 0.50 | 1.00 | 1.00 | 1.00 | 1.00 | 1.50 | 2.00 | 2.50 | 1.00 | 1.00 | 1.00 | 0.19 |
| S7 | 0.29 | 0.40 | 0.40 | 0.40 | 0.50 | 0.67 | 1.00 | 1.00 | 1.00 | 0.66 | 1.50 | 2.00 | 0.01 |
| S8 | 0.44 | 0.50 | 0.67 | 1.00 | 1.00 | 1.00 | 0.50 | 0.67 | 1.52 | 1.00 | 1.00 | 1.00 | 0.30 |

*Table 6. Fuzzy comparison matrix of sub-criteria with respect to C3*

| C3 | S9 | | | S10 | | | S11 | | | S12 | | | Normalized Weight |
|----|----|----|----|----|----|----|----|----|----|----|----|----|----|
| | n1 | n2 | n3 | n1 | n2 | n3 | n1 | n2 | n3 | n1 | n2 | n3 | |
| S9 | 1.00 | 1.00 | 1.00 | 1.00 | 1.50 | 2.50 | 2.50 | 2.51 | 3.50 | 1.50 | 2.00 | 2.50 | 0.52 |
| S10 | 0.40 | 0.67 | 1.00 | 1.00 | 1.00 | 1.00 | 1.00 | 1.50 | 2.00 | 1.00 | 1.50 | 1.00 | 0.17 |
| S11 | 0.29 | 0.40 | 0.40 | 0.50 | 0.67 | 1.00 | 1.00 | 1.00 | 1.00 | 1.00 | 1.50 | 2.00 | 0.06 |
| S12 | 0.40 | 0.50 | 0.67 | 1.00 | 0.67 | 1.00 | 0.50 | 0.67 | 1.00 | 1.00 | 1.00 | 1.00 | 0.25 |

highest score of the supplier gives the idea about the best 3PL. The results are shown in table 14.

According to the final score the alternative supplier A1 is the most preferred 3PL and A4 is the alternative 3PL. Through the illustration of the fuzzy-AHP model, it is found that the problem can be solved in a structural and timely manner.

*Table 7. Fuzzy comparison matrix of sub-criteria with respect to C4*

| C4 | S13 | | | S14 | | | S15 | | | S16 | | | Normalized Weight |
|-----|------|------|------|------|------|------|------|------|------|------|------|------|-----|
| | n1 | n2 | n3 | n1 | n2 | n3 | n1 | n2 | n3 | n1 | n2 | n3 | |
| S13 | 1.00 | 1.00 | 1.00 | 1.00 | 1.50 | 2.00 | 2.00 | 2.50 | 3.50 | 1.00 | 1.50 | 2.00 | 0.42 |
| S14 | 0.50 | 0.67 | 1.00 | 1.00 | 1.00 | 1.00 | 1.00 | 1.25 | 1.50 | 1.00 | 1.25 | 1.00 | 0.16 |
| S15 | 0.29 | 0.40 | 0.50 | 0.67 | 0.80 | 1.00 | 1.00 | 1.00 | 1.00 | 1.00 | 1.50 | 2.00 | 0.14 |
| S16 | 0.50 | 0.67 | 1.00 | 1.00 | 0.80 | 1.00 | 0.50 | 0.67 | 1.00 | 1.00 | 1.00 | 1.00 | 0.28 |

*Table 8. Fuzzy comparison matrix of alternatives with respect to S1*

| S1 | A1 | | | A2 | | | A3 | | | A4 | | | Normalized Weight |
|-----|------|------|------|------|------|------|------|------|------|------|------|------|-----|
| | n1 | n2 | n3 | n1 | n2 | n3 | n1 | n2 | n3 | n1 | n2 | n3 | |
| A1 | 1.00 | 1.00 | 1.00 | 1.00 | 1.50 | 2.00 | 2.00 | 2.50 | 3.50 | 1.00 | 1.25 | 2.00 | 0.41 |
| A2 | 0.50 | 0.67 | 1.00 | 1.00 | 1.00 | 1.00 | 1.00 | 1.25 | 1.50 | 1.00 | 1.25 | 1.00 | 0.16 |
| A3 | 0.29 | 0.40 | 0.50 | 0.67 | 0.80 | 1.00 | 1.00 | 1.00 | 1.00 | 1.00 | 1.50 | 2.00 | 0.14 |
| A4 | 0.50 | 0.80 | 1.00 | 1.00 | 0.80 | 1.00 | 0.50 | 0.67 | 1.00 | 1.00 | 1.00 | 1.00 | 0.28 |

*Table 9. Fuzzy comparison matrix of alternatives with respect to S2*

| S2 | A1 | | | A2 | | | A3 | | | A4 | | | Normalized Weight |
|-----|------|------|------|------|------|------|------|------|------|------|------|------|-----|
| | n1 | n2 | n3 | n1 | n2 | n3 | n1 | n2 | n3 | n1 | n2 | n3 | |
| A1 | 1.00 | 1.00 | 1.00 | 1.00 | 1.00 | 1.50 | 2.00 | 2.50 | 3.00 | 1.50 | 2.00 | 2.25 | 0.52 |
| A2 | 0.67 | 1.00 | 1.00 | 1.00 | 1.00 | 1.00 | 1.00 | 1.50 | 1.75 | 1.00 | 1.25 | 1.00 | 0.18 |
| A3 | 0.33 | 0.40 | 0.50 | 0.57 | 0.67 | 1.00 | 1.00 | 1.00 | 1.00 | 1.00 | 1.50 | 2.00 | 0.09 |
| A4 | 0.44 | 0.50 | 0.67 | 1.00 | 0.80 | 1.00 | 0.50 | 0.67 | 1.00 | 1.00 | 1.00 | 1.00 | 0.21 |

*Table 10. Summary Merger of Priority Weights vis-à-vis C1*

| Weights → | 0.51 | 0.14 | 0.02 | 0.33 | Alternate Priority Weights |
|-----------|------|------|------|------|-----|
| Alternatives ↓ | S1 | S2 | S3 | S4 | |
| A1 | 0.41 | 0.52 | 0.63 | 0.51 | 0.46 |
| A2 | 0.16 | 0.18 | 0.29 | 0.12 | 0.15 |
| A3 | 0.14 | 0.09 | 0.07 | 0.11 | 0.12 |
| A4 | 0.28 | 0.21 | 0.02 | 0.26 | 0.26 |

*Table 11. Summary Merger of Priority Weights vis-à-vis C2*

| Weights → | 0.50 | 0.19 | 0.01 | 0.30 | Alternate Priority Weights |
|---|---|---|---|---|---|
| Alternatives ↓ | S5 | s6 | S7 | S8 | |
| A1 | 0.50 | 0.56 | 0.51 | 0.51 | 0.52 |
| A2 | 0.15 | 0.29 | 0.21 | 0.19 | 0.19 |
| A3 | 0.09 | 0.02 | 0.09 | 0.10 | 0.08 |
| A4 | 0.25 | 0.13 | 0.19 | 0.20 | 0.21 |

*Table 12. Summary merger of priority weights vis-à-vis C3*

| Weights → | 0.52 | 0.17 | 0.06 | 0.25 | Alternate Priority Weights |
|---|---|---|---|---|---|
| Alternatives ↓ | S9 | S10 | S11 | S12 | |
| A1 | 0.50 | 0.49 | 0.57 | 0.46 | 0.49 |
| A2 | 0.16 | 0.17 | 0.08 | 0.13 | 0.15 |
| A3 | 0.24 | 0.07 | 0.15 | 0.13 | 0.18 |
| A4 | 0.10 | 0.27 | 0.20 | 0.29 | 0.18 |

*Table 13. Summary merger of priority weights vis-à-vis C4*

| Weights → | 0.42 | 0.16 | 0.14 | 0.28 | Alternate Priority Weights |
|---|---|---|---|---|---|
| Alternatives ↓ | S13 | S14 | S15 | S16 | |
| A1 | 0.49 | 0.43 | 0.39 | 0.50 | 0.47 |
| A2 | 0.14 | 0.30 | 0.20 | 0.30 | 0.22 |
| A3 | 0.09 | 0.10 | 0.17 | 0.01 | 0.08 |
| A4 | 0.28 | 0.17 | 0.24 | 0.20 | 0.23 |

*Table 14. Summary merger of priority weights vis-à-vis overall goal*

| Weights → | 0.61 | 0.33 | 0.04 | 0.02 | Alternate Priority Weights |
|---|---|---|---|---|---|
| Alternatives ↓ | C1 | C2 | C3 | C4 | |
| A1 | 0.46 | 0.52 | 0.49 | 0.47 | **0.48** |
| A2 | 0.15 | 0.19 | 0.15 | 0.22 | 0.17 |
| A3 | 0.12 | 0.08 | 0.18 | 0.08 | 0.11 |
| A4 | 0.26 | 0.21 | 0.18 | 0.23 | 0.24 |

## CONCLUSION AND FUTURE RESEARCH

In supply chain, manufacture-supplier collaboration is typically a difficult and important link which can control the channel of distribution. The good coordination and information exchange with the suppliers may be very helpful in deciding the performance of the 3PL firm. Efficient 3PL is always important for the LLP firm because the failure of its coordination results in excessive delays, and ultimately leads to poor customer services. In this paper a fuzzy modified AHP (fuzzy-AHP) approach is used to select the best 3PL. The main criteria and sub-criteria are decided considering the current business scenario and experience of the experts in the respective fields. The large number of criteria and sub-criteria show that the selection of 3PLs is not an easy task. We have tried to take most of the important deciding factors which can affect the supply from global sourcing. The fuzzy-AHP model discussed in this paper is proved to be simple, less time taking and having less computational expense. The use of fuzzy AHP does not involve cumbersome mathematical operation and so it is easy to handle the multi-attribute decision making problems like the present case. It has the ability to capture the vagueness of human thinking style and effectively solve multi-attribute decision making problems. The illustrative example shows the thoughtfulness, flexibility and efficiency of the proposed model to directly tap the subjectivity and preferences of the decision makers. The paper attempts successfully to identify the possible threats on 3PL selection process and tried to analysis it using fuzzy extended AHP approach.

## REFERENCES

Ayağ, Z., & Özdemir, R. (2006). A Fuzzy AHP Approach to Evaluating Machine Tool Alternatives. *Journal of Intelligent Manufacturing, 17*(2), 179–190. doi:10.1007/s10845-005-6635-1

Barbarosoglu, G., & Yazgac, T. (1997). An application of the analytic hierarchy process to the supplier selection problem. *Production and Inventory Management Journal, 38*(1), 14–21.

Boer, L., Wegen, L., & Telgen, J. (1998). Outranking method in support of supplier selection. *European Journal of Operational Research, 4*, 109–118.

Bohui, P. (2007). *Multi-criteria Supplier Evaluation Using Fuzzy AHP.* Paper presented at the International Conference on Mechatronics and Automation (ICMA).

Boran, F. E., Genç, S., Kurt, M., & Akay, D. (2009). A multi-criteria intuitionistic fuzzy group decision making for supplier selection with TOPSIS method. *Expert Systems with Applications, 36*(8), 11363–11368. doi:10.1016/j.eswa.2009.03.039

Cakravastia, A., & Takahashi, K. (2004). Integrated model for supplier selection and negotiation in a make-to-order environment. *International Journal of Production Research, 42*(21), 4457–4474. doi:10.1080/00207540410001727622

Chan, F. T. S., Kumar, N., Tiwari, M. K., Lau, H. C. W., & Choy, K. L. (2008). Global supplier selection: a fuzzy-AHP approach. *International Journal of Production Research, 46*(14), 3825–3857. doi:10.1080/00207540600787200

Choy, K. L., & Lee, W. B. (2002). On the development of a case based supplier management tool for multinational manufacturers. *Measuring Business Excellence, 6*(1), 15–22. doi:10.1108/13683040210420501

Dickson, G. W. (1966). An analysis of vendor selection systems and decisions. *Journal of purchasing, 2*(1), 5-17.

Dickson, G. W. (1996). An analysis of vendor selection systems and decisions. *J. Purchasing, 2*(1), 5–17.

Ghodsypour, S.H. & O'brien, C. (1998). A decision support system for supplier selection using an integrated analytic hierarchy process and linear programming. *International Journal of Production Economics, 56-57*, 119–212. doi:10.1016/S0925-5273(97)00009-1

Handfield, R., Walton, S. V., Sroufe, R., & Melnyk, S. A. (2002). Applying environmental criteria to supplier assessment: a study in the application of the analytical hierarchy process. *European Journal of Operational Research, 141*(1), 70–87. doi:10.1016/S0377-2217(01)00261-2

Kaboli, A. A. M.B., Shahanaghi, K., & Niroomand, I. (2007, Oct. 7-10). *A new method for plant location selection problem: A fuzzy-AHP approach.* Paper presented at the IEEE International Conference on Systems, Man and Cybernetics.

Kaur, P., & Mahanti, N. C. (2008). A Fuzzy ANP-Based Approach for Selecting ERP Vendors. *International Journal of Soft Computing, 3*(I), 24–32.

Kwong, C. K., & Bai, H. (2003). Determining the importance weights for the customer requirements in QFD using a fuzzy AHP with an extent analysis approach. *IIE Transactions, 35*(7), 619–626. doi:10.1080/07408170304355

Lee, A. H. I. (2009). A fuzzy supplier selection model with the consideration of benefits, opportunities, costs and risks. *Expert Systems with Applications, 36*(2, Part 2), 2879–2893. doi:10.1016/j.eswa.2008.01.045

Levary, R. R. (2008). Using the analytic hierarchy process to rank foreign suppliers based on supply risks. *Computers & Industrial Engineering, 55*, 535–542. doi:10.1016/j.cie.2008.01.010

Liu, H.-T., & Wang, W.-K. (2009). An integrated fuzzy approach for provider evaluation and selection in third-party logistics. *Expert Systems with Applications, 36*(3, Part 1), 4387–4398. doi:10.1016/j.eswa.2008.05.030

Min, H. (1994). International supplier selection: a multi-attribute utility approach. *Int. J. Phys Distribution Logistics Manage., 24*(5), 24–33. doi:10.1108/09600039410064008

Nachiappan, S., & Ramanathan, R. (2008). *Robust decision making using Data Envelopment Analytic Hierarchy Process.* Paper presented at the 7th WSEAS Int. Conf. on Artificial Intelligence, Knowledge Engineering And Data Bases (AIKED'08)

Narasimhan, R. (1983). An analytical approach to supplier selection. *Journal of Purchasing and materials Management, 19*(4), 27-32.

Nejati, M., Nejati, M., & Shafaei, A. (2009). Ranking airlines' service quality factors using a fuzzy approach: study of the Iranian society. *International Journal of Quality & Reliability Management, 26*(3), 247–260. doi:10.1108/02656710910936726

Nydick, R. L., & Hill, R. P. (1992). Using the Analytic Hierarchy Process to Structure the Supplier Selection Procedure. *International Journal of Purchasing and Materials Management, 28*(2), 31–36.

Ozan, C. (2008). On the order of the preference intensities in fuzzy AHP. *Computers & Industrial Engineering, 54*(4), 993–1005. doi:10.1016/j.cie.2007.11.010

Özdağoğlu, A. & Ozdağoğlu, G. (2007). Comparison of AHP and Fuzzy AHP for the Multicriteria Decision Making Processes with Linguistic Evaluations. *İstanbul Ticaret Üniversitesi Fen Bilimleri Dergisi, 6*(11), 65-85.

Partovi, F. Y., Burton, J., & Banerjee, A. (1990). Application of analytical hierarchy process in operations management. *International Journal of Operations & Production Management, 10*(3), 5–19. doi:10.1108/01443579010134945

Pi, W.-N., & Low, C. (2006). Supplier evaluation and selection via Taguchi loss functions and an AHP. *International Journal of Advanced Manufacturing Technology*, *27*(5), 625–630. doi:10.1007/s00170-004-2227-z

Saaty, T. L. (1980). *The analytic hierarchy process*. New York: McGraw-Hill.

Saaty, T. L., & Vargas, L. G. (1994). *Decision making in economic, political, social, and technological environments with the analytic hierarchy process*. Pittsburgh, PA: RWS Publications.

Sevkli, M., Koh, S. C. L., Zaim, S., Demirbag, M., & Tatoglu, E. (2008). Hybrid analytical hierarchy process model for supplier selection. *Industrial Management & Data Systems*, *108*(1), 21. doi:10.1108/02635570810844124

Shen, S. (2000). The Report of Analysis of the Supply and Demand Status of Chinese Logistics Market. *Logistics Management*, *2*(1), 3–14.

Tang, Q., & Xie, F. (2008). *A Holistic Approach for Selecting third Party Logistcs Providers in Fourth Party Logistics*. Paper presented at the Seventh International Conference on Machine Learning and Cybernetics, China.

Van laarhoven, P.J.M. & Pedrycz, W. (1983). A fuzzy extension of Saaty's priority theory. *Fuzzy Sets and Systems, 11*, 229-241.

Wang, Y.-M., & Chin, K.-S. (2009). A new data envelopment analysis method for priority determination and group decision making in the analytic hierarchy process. *European Journal of Operational Research, 195*, 239–251. doi:10.1016/j.ejor.2008.01.049

Wang, Y.-M., Chin, K.-S., & Leung, J. P.-F. (2009). A note on the application of the data envelopment analytic hierarchy process for supplier selection. *International Journal of Production Research, 47*(11), 3121–3138. doi:10.1080/00207540701805653

Weber, C., Current, J. R., & Benton, W. C. (1991). Vendor selection criteria and methods. *European Journal of Operational Research, 50*(1), 2–18. doi:10.1016/0377-2217(91)90033-R

Xu, J. (2002). New Pattern of Supply Chain Management—the Fourth Distribution Channel. *Policy-making Reference, 15*(1), 11–15.

Zhang, H., Li, X., & Liu, W. (2006). An AHP/DEA Methodology for 3PL Vendor Selection in 4PL. [Berlin: Springer-Verlag.]. *Lecture Notes in Computer Science, 3865*, 646–655. doi:10.1007/11686699_65

Zhang, H., Li, X., Liu, W., Li, B., & Zhang, Z. (2004). *An application of the AHP in 3PL vendor selection of a 4PL system*. Paper presented at the IEEE International conference on Systems, Man and Cybernetics.

Zhongwei, Z., & Jianzhong, X. (2008). *Research of the Application of Fuzzy AHP in Supplier Evaluation and Selection*. Paper presented at the 4th International Conference on Wireless Communications, Networking and Mobile Computing, (WiCOM '08).

Zou, P., & Yuan, Y.-N. (2009). Supplier selection based on EAHP/GRAP. *Xitong Gongcheng Lilun Yu Shijian/System Engineering. Theory into Practice, 29*(3), 69–75.

# Chapter 19
# Achieving Alignment in Production and Logistics Operations in Three Echelon Supply Chain Network Through New Heuristic Optimizer

**Rajeshwar S. Kadadevaramath**
*Siddaganga Institute of Technology, India*

**Jason C.H. Chen**
*Gonzaga University, USA*

**Mohanasundaram K.M**
*Karpagam College of Engineering, India*

## ABSTRACT

*During the past decade, great studies have been made in the development of standardized tools for supply chain modeling and network optimization Network optimization is the most basic type of modeling that can be performed with tools which helps to identity optimum paths or flow of goods in supply chain network. In this case, the network is defined by the flow of finished goods from origin to destination. Network modeling becomes more complex as the dimensions and scope of the supply chain expand Uncertainties in the supply chain usually increase the variance of profit or cost to the company, increasing the likely hood of decreased profit i.e. increase in total supply chain cost. Demand uncertainty and constraints posed by the every echelon are important factors to be considered in the supply chain design operations. This chapter specifically deals with the modeling and optimization of a three echelon supply chain network architecture using new Particle Swarm Optimization algorithm.*

DOI: 10.4018/978-1-61520-625-4.ch019

Copyright © 2010, IGI Global. Copying or distributing in print or electronic forms without written permission of IGI Global is prohibited.

## INTRODUCTION

The supply chain is made up of all the activities required to deliver products to the customer, from designing product to receiving orders, procuring materials, marketing, manufacturing, logistics, customer service, receiving payment and so on. Anyone, anything, anywhere that influences a product's time-to-market, price, quality, information exchange or delivery, among other activities, is part of the supply chain. The old way of delivering product was to develop relatively inaccurate projections of demand, then manufacture the product and fill up warehouses with finished goods. The old ways are fading fast as management across all industries has come to accept that collaboration with customers and suppliers in the planning and replenishment process can and must be made to work very effectively. As customers and suppliers band together in mutually beneficial partnerships, the need for getter supply chain management processes and systems are more evident and becomes a very high business priority. For many companies, it has become clear that a supply chain that flows information and material best can be a significant differentiator, the competitive winner. All the way to the boardroom, improving supply chain management is getting lots of attention because forward-thinking management knows it is the best strategy to increase and maintain market share, reduce costs, minimize inventories and, of course, improve profits. In many industries, market share will be won and lost based on supply chain performance. With the stakes so high, there is a frenzy of activity along the supply chain front. Executive managers are assessing how their companies do business, especially in supply chain activities. They often find dysfunctional sets of policies, processes, systems and measurements. And these exist at all points in the supply chain, including business partners. The former vague image of a company of silos is very apparent and, most importantly, a new clarity of needs and goals emerges for supply chain management.

There is a need to transform from dysfunctional and unsynchronized decision making—which results in disintegrated and very costly supply activities—to a supply chain that performs in such a way that it is one of the company's competitive advantages.

Effectively integrating the information and material flows within the demand and supply process is what supply chain management is all about. In most companies, however, two major and very interdependent issues must be simultaneously addressed. The first deals with delivering products with customer-acceptable quality, with very short lead times, at a customer-acceptable cost—while keeping inventories throughout the supply chain at a minimum. The second issue, which tends to be less understood and accepted, is the need for high-quality, relevant and timely information that is provided when it needs to be known. For any customers and manufacturers, business processes and support systems will not measure up to the task of quickly providing planning and execution information from the marketplace to production and on to vendors so that the customer's objectives are consistently met. The fact is, most information supplied is excessive, often late and frequently inaccurate. Regardless of your industry and customer base, more effective supply chain management will be a prerequisite to your future success. In fact, effective supply chain management must become an integral part of your competitive and survival strategy.

Supply chain decisions are broadly classified into strategic, tactical, and operational. Supply Chain Management (SCM) research based on these three categories, and addressed the SCM research with operational perspective in terms of four operational problem areas, namely, Inventory Management and control, Production Planning and Scheduling, Information Sharing, Coordination, Monitoring, and Operation Tools. Some of the important objectives of SCM are inventory management, procurement, production scheduling and storage and distribution management operations accounts for significant fraction of the value of the product. Also, inventory stored at different points of the supply chain has a different impact on the cost and performance. Therefore some of the critical important issue is to coordinate various activities efficiently in the whole supply chain network from demand planning to procurement, manufacturing, and distribution of products.

These firms have asked questions such as:

- How many plants? Where to be located?
- How much capacity of each plant?
- What products to be produced in each plant?
- What demand regions should each plant serve?
- Which vendors to serve each plant?
- Which parts should be supplied from each vendor?

Hence, In recent years, optimization algorithms have received wide attention by the research community as well as the industry. Many real word supply chain issues are optimization problems and are NP hard and combinatorial in nature. Over the years, modern heuristics such as Tabu Search (TS), Genetic Algorithms (GA) and Ant Colony Optimization (ACO) algorithms are being used to solve the real world problems. These metaheuristics has significantly increased the ability to find good quality solutions to these problems in a reasonable time.

Particle Swarm Optimization algorithm (PSO) is a relatively new evolutionary computational approach in modern heuristics for optimization. Like the other evolutionary computing techniques such as Genetic Algorithms, PSO is a population based search algorithm and is initialized with a population of random solutions, called particles. Unlike the other evolutionary techniques, each particle in the PSO is also associated with a velocity. Particles fly through the search space with a specified velocity which is dynamically adjusted according to their historical behaviors.

PSO algorithm was first proposed by Kennedy and Eberhart (1995) for continuous function optimization. Since its introduction, PSO has attracted a lot of researchers around the world. This paper illustrates an attempt to design and analyze Multi Echelon Supply Chain Networks using PSO algorithms.

The reminder of this chapter is arranged as follows. Section 2 provides brief review of related literature in supply chain management, optimization algorithms used in supply chain. In section 3, we present the supply chain configuration optimization model. Section 4 introduces the solution algorithm for the problem considered. Section 5 illustrates the input data for the model and results and discussions. This paper is concluded in section 6 by summarizing some main findings and insight gained in this research.

## BACKGROUND

A large amount of literature on supply management places great emphasis on integration of different components of the chain. Finding the right strategy that is optimal across the entire supply chain is a huge challenge (Quinn,2000.,.Simchi-Levi.et al, 2001). An emerging principle for the management of supply chains is that a supply chain perspective provides the opportunity for significant savings in inventories from the better coordination and proper scheduling purchasing, production and distribution of goods across the supply chain network. As described by Hicks,(1999) supply chains can be defined as "...real world systems that transform raw materials and resources into end products that are consumed by customers. Supply chains encompass a series of steps that add value through time, place, and material transformation. Each manufacturer or distributor has some subset of the supply chain that it must manage and run profitably and efficiently to survive and grow." From the above definition it is comprehensible that there are many independent entities in a supply chain each of which try to maximize their own inherent objective functions (or interests) in business transactions. One of the earliest works in supply chain configuration design area was initiated in 1974 by Geoffrion and Graves(1974). They described the mixed integer programming model for determination of distribution facility locations and a solution technique based on Bender's decomposition. As recent researcher Truong and Azadivar(1974) rightly mention, supply chain problems are complex and difficult to solve. The reasons could be the number of entities in the supply chain (length), the lead times at each node (Cakravastia, et al, 2002), inventory management (Giannoccaro and Pontrandolfo, 2002), logistics (Lummus, et al 2001), to mention a few. Most of the research in this area is based on the classic work of Clark and Scarf (1960,1962) more recent discussion of two echelon models may be found in Diks et al(1996) and Houtum et al (1996). Willims (1981) presents heuristics algorithms for scheduling production and distribution operations in an assembly supply chain network and also he developed a dynamic programming algorithm for simultaneous determining the production and distribution batch sizes at each node within a supply chain network. Ishii et al. (1988) developed deterministic model for determining the base stock levels and lead times associated with the lowest cost solutions for an integrated supply chain on a finite horizon. Cohen and Lee (1989), present a deterministic mixed integer, nonlinear mathematical programming model, based on economic order quantity techniques. Cohen and Moon(1990) extend Cohen and Lee (1989) by developing a constrained optimization model, called PILOT, to investigate the effects of various parameter on supply chain cost and consider the additional problem of determining which manufacturing facilities and distribution centers should be open. Lee and Billington (1993) developed a supply chain model operating under a periodic review base stock system at Hewlett Packard, and employed a search heuristic to find the optimal

inventory levels across the supply chain.

Supply chain concepts aim at coordinating the procurement of raw material, production and the distribution of final products to customers to form a single integrated process. The positive impact of optimizing the supply chain (SC) is continuously reported in the literature. Companies such as Dow Brands Inc (Robinson and Muggenborg 1993), Libbey-Owens-Ford (Martin et al 1993), General Motors (Blumenfeld, et al 1987) and Digital Equipment Corporation(Arntzen et al.1995) achieved substantial cost savings through the optimization of the supply chain. Recent review papers on the supply chain design problem include Beamon (1998), Slats et al (1995) and Thomas and Griffin (1996). Von and Nyhuis(2007) author says that Despite spending considerable effort on the design and operation of production planning and control systems, manufacturing companies experience logistic performance deficits. Frequently, these are due to inconsistencies between the logistic objectives the companies set themselves and the planning and control actions they take to achieve the objectives. He suggests, that the qualitative influence models that identify these interdependencies within individual logistic processes and across process boundaries. Hans et al (2007), outlines an innovative approach to this problem, which is based on the application of artificial neural networks for the iterative design process of a production line was initiated by a customer request, which classifies the layout as stable or unstable. In case of stable layouts, the performance and cost values are visualized with operating figures. Nyhuis et al (2007) illustrates the Fundamentals concepts to considered in designing the production and logistics operations in supply chain network. Klaus et al (2007) states that to improve flexible production process and in order to ensure a suitable process strategy a simulation-tool was being developed and it comprises a geometric-kinematic process simulation and a finite elements simulation. Heinz et.al (2007) their article presents a newly developed method in which the design of the cooling ducts can be systematically optimized by using a test tool . Reimund et al (2007) introduces, Virtual Reality (VR) competence components can be described for a competence-cell-based networking approach. Concerning the competence-cell-based description, a differentiation is made between the VR business object model, VR activity model, VR method model and the model of non-personal VR resources. Their intended objective was to perform VR services within the networked value-added chain and thus to increase the efficiency of value-added processes.

Most of the reviews agree on the benefits of integrating the various echelons of the supply chain. Being aware that this leads to very complex decision problems, they emphasize the need for good analytical models and efficient solution methods to help decision-making.

The Particle Swarm Optimization (PSO) method is a member of the wide category of Swarm Intelligence methods (Kennedy and Eberhart 2001) for solving GO problems. It was originally proposed by J. Kennedy as a simulation of social behavior, and it was initially introduced as an optimization method in 1995 (Eberhart and Kennedy 1995). PSO is related with Artificial Life, and specifically to swarming theories, and also with EC(Evolutionary Computation), especially ES (Evolutionary Strategy) and GA (Genetic Algorithm). PSO can be easily implemented and it is computationally in expensive, since its memory and CPU speed requirements are low. Moreover, it does not require gradient information of the objective function under consideration, but only its values, and it uses only primitive mathematical operators. PSO has been proved to be an efficient method for many GO problems and in some cases it does not suffer the difficulties encountered by other EC techniques (Eberhart and Kennedy1995) .Velocity updates in PSO, can also be clamped with a user defined maximum velocity ($V_{max}$), which would prevent them from exploding, thereby causing premature

convergence. Some of the first applications of PSO were to train Neural Networks (NNs). Results have shown that PSO is better than GA .PSO is easy to implement and has been successfully applied to solve a wide range of optimization problems such as continuous nonlinear and discrete optimization problems.(Kennedy and Eberhart 1995), (Eberhart and Shi, 1998).

## Motivation for the Study

It is observed that, in practice, a supply chain is likely to be much more complex and several challenging problems associated with integrated supply chain configuration design optimization.

It is understood from the literature review that little work has been done on modelling, analysis and quantitative measurement of performance of Multi Echelon Supply Chain Networks and also it is found that very little work has been done on general supply chain network catering to small and medium scale industries. In practice, a supply chain is likely to be much more complex as there may be a considerable mesh or network of supply chain partners. Hence, this literature review on supply chain network has motivated to carry out, some studies on optimization of three echelon, network configurations. Therefore, the aim of supply chain configuration optimization is to find the best or the near best alternative configuration with which the supply chain can achieve a high-level performance. In order to achieve high performance, supply chain functions must operate in an integrated and coordinated manner. The following, Several challenging problems associated with integrated supply chain design are tackled:

(1) Coordinating the supply chain business processes, specifically in the area of supply chain workflows;

(2) Analyzing the performance of an integrated supply chain network so that optimization techniques can be employed to improve Profit, customer service and reduce the total

supply chain operating cost, average inventory cost; and

(3) Evaluating the dynamic supply chain networks and to obtain a comprehensive understanding of decision-making issues related to supply network configurations.

These problems are most representative in the supply chain theory's research and applications.

In recent years, extensive study has been done in understanding social psychology of fish schools, birds flock and bug swarms. It has been observed that social behavior does play a very crucial role in the survival of species and its adoption to the changing environment. PSO originates from social psychology as a simulation of socio-cognitive process to try to model abstract concepts of swarm intelligence that have the several advantages like, easy to describe, simple to implement, few parameters to adjust, uses relatively small populations, needs a relatively small number of functions evaluations to converge and is fast.

From the literature survey, indicates that the PSO algorithm is found to be quite powerful by various researchers to find the minimum of a numerical function on a continuous definition domain (Clerc and Kennedy, 2002) and very little research has been carried out to implement PSO algorithm in a discrete combinatorial optimization problem such as flow shop scheduling . No literature is found till date, application of the PSO algorithms in solving multi echelon supply chain network optimization problems.

Several challenging problems associated with integrated supply chain design are:

- How to model and coordinate the supply chain business processes, specifically in the area of supply chain workflows;
- How to analyze the performance of an integrated supply chain network so that optimization techniques can be employed to improve customer service and reduce total

supply chain operating cost, Improve the profit of the organization and GMROI

XL solver and Lingo commercial packages are costly and can handle only small number of variables and are time consuming. Hence in recent years, **The** above challenges are addressed and there has been a great interest in developing optimization algorithms for solving combinatorial optimization problems .Accurate models of the real world problems most of such problems are often multi-modal and non- differentiable in respect of their objective function and decision variables. Meta heuristics used to solve a wide variety of such optimization problems and they do not require gradient information. This is mainly due to the increasing computational speed of computers, which enables the use of meta-heuristics .Various meta-heuristics are have already been proposed in the literature, such as the Genetic Algorithm, Simulated Annealing, Tabu Search. PSO was first introduced to optimize various continuous non linear functions by Kennedy and Eberhart (1995).Of late, PSO algorithm has been applied to well-known benchmark functions and shown successfully optimize a wide range of continuous and discrete functions. The PSO algorithm is found to be the quite powerful by various researchers to find minimum of a numerical function. (see Clerc and Kennedy (2002).

In summary, this brief literature review has motivated us in following distinctive ways. First to develop a integer linear programming model to streamline operations and improve scheduling process with objective function is formulated to minimize total operating cost of supply chain to absorb unexpected demand and subjected to five types of constraints. Second, we are the first to use new optimizer, particle swarm optimization (PSO), for procurement, production and distribution in multi echelon supply chain optimization

## MATHEMATICAL MODELING

This section discusses the objective and the mathematical formulation of three echelon supply chain network model.

### Objective of Study

This paper specifically deals with the modeling and optimization of a three stage multi echelon supply chain network architecture using the new Particle Swarm Optimization algorithms. Total Supply Chain operating Cost (TSCC) of the supply chain network is considered as a performance indicator.

The objective of supply chain management is to minimize total supply chain cost to meet given demand in the market.

This total cost may be comprised of a number of terms including

- Raw material and other acquisition costs
- In-bound transportation costs
- Direct and indirect manufacturing costs
- Direct and indirect distribution center costs
- Inventory holding costs
- Inter-facility transportation costs
- Out-bound transportation costs.

Supply chain network architecture consists of many stages or echelons . In this research, the supply chain architecture consists of three echelons (stages) i.e. vendors, manufacturing plants, and retailers in order of their contributions to the chain. Each supply chain echelon has a set of control parameters that affects the performance of other components. This work considers a constrained objective problem formulation for a pull based supply chain architecture and proposes the PSO algorithms for solving the constraint optimization problem. The performance of the each echelon will be optimized simultaneously at tactical level

planning. It optimizes material flows throughout the supply chain, gives the optimal procurement, production and distribution scheduling plans.

### Problem Description

This problem attempts to capture the dynamics of a single product being manufactured out of three different components. There are three vendors, two manufacturing plants, and six retailer zones as shown in figure 1.Where all the vendors can supply all the plants with the components. In a more general formulation of this problem the three different components can be supplied by any of the three vendors. These components can be shipped to any of the two plants where the product is made. Then the product made out of them is being shipped to retailer zones based on the demand at that retailer zone.

### Model Assumptions

- Problem is tactical or snap shot pull based problem
- A single product flows through the supply chain network
- A product is made up of three components
- Distribution centers face random customer demand and demand distribution is assumed to be uniform
- Quantity of goods at every installation takes integer values
- Linear holding cost rates exists only for manufacturing plants in the supply chain
- Shortages are not permitted (no shortage cost)
- Transportation costs are directly proportional to the quantity shipped
- Manufacturing costs are directly proportional to the quantity of products produced.
- All installations have finite capacity

*Figure 1. supply chain network configuration*

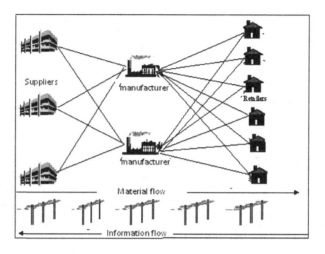

## Notations for Variables

Indices used in the model are represented in the table 1 and there are three kinds of variables used in this formulation;

## The Mathematical Model

This sub section develops a mathematical model to quantify the relationship between all the decision variables involved in supply chain network and supply chain decisions in terms of total supply chain operating cost (TSCC) as the performance indicator. The problem of optimizing the supply chain configuration can be summarized in the following mathematical model. Table 1 explains all the symbols used in the above definition. The objective function, the total supply chain operating cost, consists of four parts: supplier cost of material supplied, Supplier Transportation Cost, Total Manufacturing Cost and Plant Transportation Cost.ie equations 3.1 to 3.4. The constraints 3.9 to 3.12 depicts the plant capacity, vendor capacity for raw material, demand constraints of retailers and finally the inventory balancing constraints at plants.

1. Total Vendors Cost

$$SC = \sum_c \sum_v (CS_{c,v} * X_{c,v,p}) \qquad (3.1)$$

2. Total Suppliers Transportation Cost

$$STC = \sum_c \sum_v \sum_p (X_{c,v,p} * STC_{c,v,p}) \qquad (3.2)$$

3. Total Manufacturing Cost

$$TMC = \sum_p \{ (MC_p)*(\sum_r Y_{p,r})\} + \{\sum_p (IC_p * \sum_c I_{c,p}\} \qquad (3.3)$$

4. Total Plant Transportation Cost

$$PTC = \sum_p \sum_r (Y_{p,r} * PTC_r) \qquad (3.4)$$

5. Total Transportation Cost

$$TTC = STC + PTC \qquad (3.5)$$

6. Total supply chain Operating Cost

$$(TSCC) = SC + TMC + TTC \qquad (3.6)$$

7. $\text{Profit} = \sum_r (D_r * SP_r) - TOC \qquad (3.7)$

*Table 1. Nomenclature used in the supply chain model*

| INDICES | DEFINITIONS |
|---|---|
| C | Number of Components (c=1,2…C) |
| V | Number of Vendors (v=1,2…V) |
| P | Number of Plants (p=1,2…P) |
| R | Number of Retailer zones (r=1,2….R) |
| **PARAMETRS** | |
| $L_{c,v}$ | Capacity of vendor 'v' for component 'c' |
| $CS_{c,v}$ | Cost of making a component 'c' by vendor 'v' |
| $STC_{c,v,p}$ | Transportation cost of a component 'c' from vendor 'v' to plant 'p'/unit |
| $U_p$ | Capacity of plant 'p' |
| $MC_p$ | Manufacturing cost of plant 'p'/unit |
| $IC_p$ | Inventory carrying cost at plant 'p'/unit/period |
| $I_{c,p}$ | Inventory (qty) of components 'c' at plant 'p' |
| $PTC_{p,r}$ | Plant transportation cost from plant 'p' to Retailer zone 'r |
| $D_r$ | Demand at Retailer zone 'r |
| $SP_r$ | Selling price at Retailer zone 'r'/unit |
| **DECISION VARIABLES** | |
| $X_{c,v,p}$ | Amount of component shipped 'c' from vendor 'v' to plant 'p' |
| $Y_{p,r}$ | Amount of product shipped from plant 'p' to Retailer Zone 'r' |
| **TSCC** | **Total supply chain operating cost** |

(note: Equation 3.7 considers the profit supply chain as it is the total revenue generated at all the retailers minus the total supply chain operating cost)

## Objective Function

**Minimize** TSCC = SC + TMC + TTC     (3.8)

Subject to following supply chain constraints:

$$U_p \geq \sum_r Y_{p,r} \qquad \forall \quad p \quad (3.9)$$

$$L(c,v) \geq \sum_p X_{c,v,p} \qquad \forall \quad c,v \quad (3.10)$$

$$\sum_d Y_{p,r} \geq D_r \qquad \forall \ r \qquad (3.11)$$

$$\sum X_{c,v,p} \geq \sum_r Y_{p,r} \forall c, p \qquad (3.12)$$

All the decision variables should integers and non negative.

## METHODOLOGY

This section discusses the introduction, solution algorithm, parameters of the new optimizer, particle swarm optimization.

### Introduction to Particle Swarm Optimization

Particle swarm optimization (PSO) is a form of swarm intelligence. (Kennedy and Eberhart 2001). Imagine a swarm of insects or a school of fish. If one sees a desirable path to go (e.g., for food, protection, etc.) the rest of the swarm will be able to follow quickly even if they are on the opposite side of the swarm. On the other hand, in order to facilitate felicitous exploration of the search space, typically one wants each particle to have a certain level of "craziness" or randomness in their movement, so that the movement of the swarm has a certain explorative capability: the swarm should be influenced by the rest of the swarm but also should independently explore to a certain extent.

## Particle Swarm Optimization Algorithm

The Particle Swarm Optimization (PSO) algorithm has become increasingly popular in the last few years, mainly in numerical optimization tasks . However, PSO, like other evolutionary algorithms, lacks an explicit mechanism to incorporate constraints. Remarkably, there has been little work related to the incorporation of constraints into the PSO algorithm, despite the fact that most real-world applications have constraints.

PSO learned from the scenario and used it to solve the optimization problems (Kennedy, and Eberhart, 1995) . PSO is initialized with a group of random particles (solutions) and then searches for optima by updating generations. In every iteration, each particle is updated by following two "best" values. The first one is the best solution (fitness) it has achieved so far. (The fitness value is also stored.) This value is called pbest. Another "best" value that is tracked by the particle swarm optimizer is the best value, obtained so far by any particle in the population. This best value is a global best and called gbest.

After finding the two best values, the particle updates its velocity and positions with following equation (a) and (b).

Equations Used in PSO are [27]:

1.    Equation for Updating Particle Velocity:

$V[t+1] = [V[t] + \{c1 \; rand() \; (pbest[t] - present[t])\} + \{c2 \; rand()(gbest[t] - present[t])\}]$    (a)

2.    Equation for Updating Particle Position:

$present[t+1] = present[t] + v[t+1]$    (b)

Where,

$V[]$ is the particle velocity,
present [] is the current particle (solution).
pbest[] and gbest[] are defined as stated before.
rand () is a random number between (0,1).
c1, c2 are learning factors.

## PSO and Constrained Optimization

Most engineering problems are constrained problems. However, the basic PSO is only defined for unconstrained problems. One way to allow the PSO to optimize constrained problems is by adding a penalty function to the original fitness function. In this paper, a constant penalty function is added to the original fitness function for each particle with violated constraints (Kalyanmoy Deb,2003).

## General Structure of Optimization of Three Stage Multi-Echelon Supply Chain Network Architecture Using Pso Algorithm

Following are the general procedural steps involved in the optimization of three stage multi echelon supply chain network architecture using PSO algorithm.

*Figure 2. The pseudo code of the procedure*

```
function CPSO Algorithm
Begin
    For Each particle
        1. Initialize
        2. Compute fitness value
        3. p_best=fitness value
    EndFor
    Do
        4. Choose the particle with the
           best fitness value in the population.
           Call it g_best
        For each particle
            If the fitness value is better than
            p_best then
                5. p_best=fitness value
            EndIF
            6. Perform the flight
            7. Update fitness value
        EndFor
    While Stopping condition not satisfied
End.
```

*Table 2.*

| Step 1: | Initializing the particle position $\{X_{kd}, d = 1,2,...D\}$ <br> Where 'k' denotes the number of particles, 'D' denotes maximum number of dimensions within the minimum and maximum limits for each dimension. |
|---|---|
| Step 2: | Initialize the particle velocity $\{v_{kd}, d=1,2,......D\}$ <br> Where 'k' denotes the number of particles, 'D' denotes maximum number of dimensions within the minimum and maximum limits for each dimension. |
| Step 3: | Calculate the maximum velocity of the particles <br> $v_{max}$ =0.5 * Upper bound of the components dimensions. |
| Step 4: | If $v_{kd}^{new} > v_{max}$ <br> set $v_{kd}^{new} = v_{max}$ for all 'k' and 'd'. |
| Step 5: | Evaluate $Z\{X_{kd}\}$ (function value for all particles). |
| Step 6: | Initialize/ Update $\{P_{kd}\}$ (best point of the particle, ie particle best)and $\{G_d\}$(global best). |
| Step 7: | Calculate new velocity $v_{kd}^{new}$ is the PSO velocity equations. <br> $v_{kd} > v_{max}$ <br> set $v_{kd} = v_{max}$ for all 'k' as 'd'. |
| Step 8: | Updated position of the particle <br> $X_{kd}^{new} = v_{kd}^{new} + X_{kd}$ |
| Step 9: | If terminate condition is not met then go back to step5 <br> Else go to step 10. |
| Step10: | Print $\{G_d\}$ or Z $\{G_d\}$ <br> Stop |

*Table 3. Particle representation in PSO algorithm for three stage SCN configuration*

| Component 1 from V1,V2,V3 | | | | | | Component 2 from V1,V2,V3 | | | | | | Component 3 from V1,V2,V3 | | | | | | Products from P1 to All DCs | | | | | | Products from P2 to All DCs | | | | | |
|---|---|---|---|---|---|---|---|---|---|---|---|---|---|---|---|---|---|---|---|---|---|---|---|---|---|---|---|---|---|
| $x_{111}$ | $x_{112}$ | $x_{121}$ | $x_{122}$ | $x_{131}$ | $x_{132}$ | $x_{211}$ | $x_{212}$ | $x_{221}$ | $x_{222}$ | $x_{231}$ | $x_{232}$ | $x_{311}$ | $x_{312}$ | $x_{321}$ | $x_{322}$ | $x_{331}$ | $x_{332}$ | $Y_{11}$ | $Y_{12}$ | $Y_{13}$ | $Y_{14}$ | $Y_{15}$ | $Y_{16}$ | $Y_{21}$ | $Y_{22}$ | $Y_{23}$ | $Y_{24}$ | $Y_{25}$ | $Y_{26}$ |
| 137 | 47 | 75 | 72 | 73 | 65 | 115 | 19 | 56 | 82 | 114 | 83 | 126 | 160 | 42 | 20 | 118 | 4 | 39 | 68 | 32 | 29 | 55 | 62 | 43 | 30 | 23 | 28 | 34 | 26 |

*Table 4. Swarm representation in PSO algorithm for three stage SCN configuration*

| Representation of swarm size = 5 particles (Decision variables) | | | | | | | | | | | | | | | | | | | | | | | | | | | | | | |
|---|---|---|---|---|---|---|---|---|---|---|---|---|---|---|---|---|---|---|---|---|---|---|---|---|---|---|---|---|---|---|
| Particle | $x_{111}$ | $x_{112}$ | $x_{121}$ | $x_{122}$ | $x_{131}$ | $x_{132}$ | $x_{211}$ | $x_{212}$ | $x_{221}$ | $x_{222}$ | $x_{231}$ | $x_{232}$ | $x_{311}$ | $x_{312}$ | $x_{321}$ | $x_{322}$ | $x_{331}$ | $x_{332}$ | $Y_{11}$ | $Y_{12}$ | $Y_{13}$ | $Y_{14}$ | $Y_{15}$ | $Y_{16}$ | $Y_{21}$ | $Y_{22}$ | $Y_{23}$ | $Y_{24}$ | $Y_{25}$ | $Y_{26}$ |
| 1 | 137 | 47 | 75 | 72 | 73 | 65 | 115 | 19 | 56 | 82 | 114 | 83 | 126 | 160 | 42 | 20 | 118 | 4 | 39 | 68 | 32 | 29 | 55 | 62 | 43 | 30 | 23 | 28 | 34 | 26 |
| 2 | 149 | 30 | 61 | 68 | 88 | 90 | 109 | 24 | 98 | 128 | 91 | 37 | 142 | 39 | 60 | 27 | 99 | 123 | 60 | 36 | 31 | 58 | 63 | 50 | 36 | 25 | 29 | 23 | 29 | 46 |
| 3 | 111 | 58 | 85 | 48 | 74 | 90 | 71 | 31 | 65 | 150 | 138 | 14 | 108 | 20 | 22 | 122 | 140 | 53 | 40 | 51 | 26 | 39 | 39 | 75 | 48 | 19 | 28 | 43 | 37 | 20 |
| 4 | 60 | 83 | 30 | 13 | 244 | 28 | 39 | 56 | 222 | 34 | 83 | 47 | 214 | 40 | 26 | 71 | 93 | 13 | 48 | 26 | 92 | 93 | 42 | 32 | 20 | 34 | 4 | 0 | 13 | 50 |
| 5 | 124 | 23 | 70 | 74 | 44 | 108 | 116 | 13 | 56 | 34 | 66 | 158 | 59 | 78 | 28 | 108 | 151 | 20 | 33 | 60 | 24 | 35 | 31 | 55 | 32 | 19 | 39 | 63 | 25 | 27 |

*Table 5. Decision variables and their lower and upper bounds for SCS*

| S No | Decision Variable | Lower Bound (quantity) | Upper Bound (quantity) |
|---|---|---|---|
| 1 | $X_{111}$ | 0 | 200 |
| 2 | $X_{112}$ | 0 | 200 |
| 3 | $X_{121}$ | 0 | 300 |
| 4 | $X_{122}$ | 0 | 300 |
| 5 | $X_{131}$ | 0 | 300 |
| 6 | $X_{132}$ | 0 | 300 |
| 7 | $X_{211}$ | 0 | 150 |
| 8 | $X_{212}$ | 0 | 150 |
| 9 | $X_{221}$ | 0 | 400 |
| 10 | $X_{222}$ | 0 | 400 |
| 11 | $X_{231}$ | 0 | 250 |
| 12 | $X_{232}$ | 0 | 250 |
| 13 | $X_{311}$ | 0 | 400 |
| 14 | $X_{312}$ | 0 | 400 |
| 15 | $X_{321}$ | 0 | 150 |
| 16 | $X_{322}$ | 0 | 150 |
| 17 | $X_{331}$ | 0 | 250 |
| 18 | $X_{332}$ | 0 | 250 |
| 19 | $Y_{11}$ | 0 | 400 |
| 20 | $Y_{12}$ | 0 | 400 |
| 21 | $Y_{13}$ | 0 | 400 |
| 22 | $Y_{14}$ | 0 | 400 |
| 23 | $Y_{15}$ | 0 | 400 |
| 24 | $Y_{16}$ | 0 | 400 |
| 25 | $Y_{21}$ | 0 | 300 |
| 26 | $Y_{22}$ | 0 | 300 |
| 27 | $Y_{23}$ | 0 | 300 |
| 28 | $Y_{24}$ | 0 | 300 |
| 29 | $Y_{25}$ | 0 | 300 |
| 30 | $Y_{26}$ | 0 | 300 |

## Generation of Initial Particles in the Proposed PSO Algorithms

Generate K (Swarm Size) solutions $\{X_{kd}, d = 1,2....,D\}$, $(k = 1,2....,5)$, as follows:

Set $X_{kd} = LL_d + (UL_d - LL_d) \times U(0,1)$, for $d = 1,2,...., D$.

where $LL_d$ and $UL_d$ denotes the minimum and maximum limits on value of $X_{kd}$ with respect to dimension space d, and U (0,1) denotes the uniformly distributed random number in the range (0,1). Initial particle and swarm size for PSO algorithm is shown in Table 3 & 4. Table 5 depicts Decision variables and their lower and upper bounds for SCS.

## Generation of Initial Velocities in the Proposed PSO Algorithms

Generate K (Swarm Size) solutions $\{v_{kd}, d = 1, 2...., D\}$, $(k = 1, 2...., 5)$, as follows:

Set $v_{kd} = LL_d + (UL_d - LL_d) \times U(0,1)$, for $d = 1, 2, ...., D$.

where $LL_d$ and $UL_d$ denotes the minimum and maximum limits on value of $X_{kd}$ with respect to dimension space d, and $U(0,1)$ denotes the uniformly distributed random number in the range $(0,1)$.

## Optimization of Three Stage Multi echelon Supply Chain Architecture Using Genetic Algorithm (GA)

Genetic Algorithms are stochastic search method inspired from the metaphor of natural biological evolution and was introduced by John Holland (1975). These algorithms operate on a population of potential solutions applying the principle of survival of the fittest to produce better approximations to a solution. The initial population is randomly generated over the search space. At each generation, operators borrowed from natural genetics such as selection, recombination, cross over and mutation, etc. are applied to the individuals from the population. By applying genetic operators these individuals are evolved. Following sections explains the GA operators used in this study.

## Selection

The selection function chooses parents for the next generation based on their scaled values from the fitness scaling function. Stochastic uniform lays out a line in which each parent corresponds to a section of the line of length proportional to its expectation. The algorithm moves along the line in steps of equal size, one step for each parent. At each step, the algorithm allocates a parent from the section it lands on. The first step is a uniform random number less than the step size. Remainder assigns parents deterministically from the integer part of each individual's scaled value and then uses roulette selection on the remaining fractional part. Roulette simulates a roulette wheel with the area of each segment proportional to its expectation. The algorithm then uses a random number to select one of the sections with a probability equal to its area. Tournament selects each parent by choosing individuals at random, the number of which you can specify by Tournament size, and then choosing the best individual out of that set to be a parent.

## Crossover

Crossover combines two individuals, or parents, to form a new individual, or child, for the next generation. Scattered creates a random binary vector. It then selects the genes where the vector is a 1 from the first parent, and the genes where the vector is a 0 from the second parent, and combines the genes to form the child. For example, consider the first 12 genes of chromosome 1 and 2 of length of 30 genes of three echelon SCN configuration to explain the working principle.

p1 = [137 47 75 72 73 65 115 19 56 82 114 83]
p2 = [149 30 61 68 88 90 109 24 98 128 91 87]
Random crossover vector = [1 1 0 0 1 0 0 0 1 1 0 0]
child = [137 47 61 68 73 90 109 24 56 82 91 87]

Single point cross over chooses a random integer n between 1 and Number of variables, and selects the vector entries numbered less than or equal to n from the first parent, selects genes numbered greater than n from the second parent, and concatenates these entries to form the child. For example, consider the first 12 genes of chromosome 1 and 2 of length of 30 genes of three echelon SCN configuration.

*Table 6. Parameter setting for PSO*

| S.No. | Parameter | Notation | Value |
|-------|-----------|----------|-------|
| 1 | Particle size | K | 5 |
| 2 | Learning factor | $c_1$ | 2 |
| 3 | Learning factor | $c_2$ | 1.45 |
| 4 | Initial inertia weight | $w_{min}$ | 0.2 |
| 5 | starting iteration number | iter | 0 |
| 6 | Maximum number of iterations | $iter_{max}$ | 2000 |
| 7 | Coefficient for best results | n | 1.2 |
| 8 | Coefficient for best results | m | $-2.5*10-4$ |
| 9 | Penalty parameter | $R_m$ | 0.01 |
| 10 | Penalty multiplication factor | f | 10 |

p1 = [137 47 75 72 73 65 115 19 56 82 114 83]
p2 = [149 30 61 68 88 90 109 24 98 128 91 87]
Random crossover point = 5
child = [137 47 75 72 73 90 109 24 98 128 91 87]

Two point cross over selects two random integers m and n between 1 and Number of variables. The algorithm selects genes numbered less than or equal to m from the first parent, selects genes numbered from m+1 to n from the second parent, and selects genes numbered greater than n from the first parent. The algorithm then concatenates these genes to form a single gene. For example,

p1 = [137 47 75 72 73 65 115 19 56 82 114 83]
p2 = [149 30 61 68 88 90 109 24 98 128 91 87]
Random crossover point = 3, 7
Child = [137 47 75 68 88 90 109 19 56 82 114 83]

## Mutation

Mutation functions make small random changes in the individuals in the population, which provide genetic diversity and enable the Genetic Algorithm to search a broader space.

## Programming Language

Coding is done in c-programming language.

## PSO & GA ALGORITHM RESULTS AND DISCUSSIONS

This section discusses the experimental design for the performance analysis of GA and PSO. Finally the results of the PSO algorithms were compared with the results of the genetic algorithm.

NOTE: XL Solver or Lingo produces better quality solutions with limited number of variables i.e. cannot handle large number variables (complex jobs or NP-hard problems)and is time consuming where as meta heuristic evolutionary algorithms are used and compared as they produce approximate solutions for complex problems with less time.

## Experimental Design

To evaluate the performance measure the supply chain settings called SCS-I is used in this computational study. PSO algorithms were used to optimize the SCS-I with an objective of minimizing total supply chain cost(TSCC). We have

*Table 7. Parameter setting for GA*

| S.No | Parameter | Notation | Value |
|------|-----------|----------|-------|
| 1 | Population size | N | 20 |
| 2 | Maximum number of iterations | $iter_{max}$ | 500 |
| 3 | Cross over probability | Cr | 0.8 |
| 4 | Mutation probability | Mr | 0.01 |
| 5 | Selection method: Tournament | Tour | - |
| 6 | Cross over: two point method | - | - |

*Table 8. Capacity (quantity) of vendor 'j' for component 'i' for SCS-I*

| | Component 1 | Component 2 | Component 3 |
|------|-------------|-------------|-------------|
| Vendor 1 | 200 | 150 | 400 |
| Vendor 2 | 300 | 400 | 150 |
| Vendor 3 | 300 | 250 | 250 |

considered twenty demand scenarios for each Supply chain settings. These supply chain test settings consists of different raw material costs, capacities, transportation costs, inventory holding cost, distribution costs and selling prices. Different supply chain settings are used to check the robustness of the proposed algorithms in terms of their consistent and good performance across supply chain network.

The performance of PSO algorithm are analyzed by considering the customer demand as uniformly distributed in the range [50,100] for Supply

*Table 9. Cost of making a component 'c' by vendor 'v' in Rs. for SCS-I*

| | Component 1 | Component 2 | Component 3 |
|------|-------------|-------------|-------------|
| Vendor 1 | 300 | 115 | 90 |
| Vendor 2 | 320 | 120 | 85 |
| Vendor 3 | 290 | 125 | 75 |

*Table 10. Transportation cost of a component 1 from vendor 'v' to plant 'p'/unit for SCS-I*

| | Plant 1 | Plant 2 |
|------|---------|---------|
| Vendor 1 | 10 | 13 |
| Vendor 2 | 15 | 17 |
| Vendor 3 | 12 | 15 |

*Table 11. Transportation cost of a component 2 from vendor 'v' to plant 'p'/unit for SCS-I*

| | Plant 1 | Plant 2 |
|------|---------|---------|
| Vendor 1 | 6 | 7 |
| Vendor 2 | 4 | 6 |
| Vendor 3 | 5 | 7 |

*Table 12. Transportation cost of a component 3 from vendor 'v' to plant 'p'/unit for SCS-I*

|  | Plant 1 | Plant 2 |
|---|---|---|
| Vendor 1 | 3 | 4 |
| Vendor 2 | 5 | 6 |
| Vendor 3 | 6 | 4 |

*Table 13. Data related to plants for SCS-I*

|  | Plant 1 | Plant 2 |
|---|---|---|
| Capacity of plant 'p' | 400 | 300 |
| Labor cost of plant 'p'/unit | 100 | 110 |
| Manufacturing cost of plant 'p'/unit | 1800 | 1900 |
| Inventory cost of plant 'p'/unit | 50 | 45 |

chain setting-I. Customer demand is sampled from a uniform distribution because, given the minimum and maximum values that a random variable can take, the variance is maximum when the random variable follows the uniform distribution.

The proposed algorithm is coded in the C Language and are implemented on the Intel centrino dual core processor running @1.86 GHz with 1 GB of RAM. The algorithms were allowed to run only once. Fifteen replications are considered to report the results. Taillard random number generator (1993) is used to generate the uniformly distributed random numbers.

## Parameters Settings for GA and the PSO Variants

Pilot studies have been conducted in this research work to arrive at the best values of parameters for GA and PSO algorithm. Parameter values used in the PSO algorithm such as Swarm size 'n', learning parameters $c_1$ and $c_2$, inertia weight 'w' and initial and incremental penalty parameters, etc are shown in Table 6 Similarly, for GA also, pilot study was performed with respect to different methods of selection, cross over and mutations. Parameter used in the GA is set and are shown in Table 7.

*Table 14. Plant transportation cost (Rs/unit) for SCS-I*

|  | D C 1 | DC 2 | DC 3 | DC4 | DC 5 | DC 6 |
|---|---|---|---|---|---|---|
| Plant 1 | 7 | 12 | 15 | 17 | 18 | 20 |
| Plant 2 | 12 | 10 | 11 | 13 | 15 | 17 |

*Table 15. Selling price at Distribution Center for SCS-I*

|  | D C 1 | DC 2 | DC 3 | DC4 | DC 5 | DC 6 |
|---|---|---|---|---|---|---|
| Selling price at Distribution center 'SP'/unit in Rs. | 3500 | 3400 | 3700 | 3800 | 4000 | 3600 |

*Table 16. Selling price at Distribution Center for SCS-I*

| Scenario | Demand U(50, 100) | | | | | |
|---|---|---|---|---|---|---|
| | R1 | R2 | R3 | R4 | R5 | R6 |
| 1 | 83 | 98 | 55 | 57 | 89 | 90 |
| 2 | 96 | 61 | 60 | 81 | 92 | 96 |
| 3 | 88 | 70 | 54 | 82 | 76 | 95 |
| 4 | 68 | 60 | 95 | 93 | 55 | 82 |
| 5 | 64 | 79 | 63 | 98 | 56 | 82 |
| 6 | 61 | 95 | 56 | 89 | 75 | 77 |
| 7 | 82 | 89 | 90 | 71 | 56 | 82 |
| 8 | 62 | 74 | 63 | 59 | 98 | 73 |
| 9 | 73 | 86 | 65 | 78 | 78 | 58 |
| 10 | 81 | 76 | 69 | 66 | 69 | 58 |
| 11 | 86 | 58 | 93 | 53 | 61 | 72 |
| 12 | 96 | 95 | 67 | 51 | 74 | 55 |
| 13 | 91 | 76 | 72 | 69 | 91 | 73 |
| 14 | 90 | 64 | 54 | 89 | 79 | 54 |
| 15 | 80 | 72 | 61 | 85 | 71 | 96 |
| 16 | 91 | 66 | 64 | 69 | 54 | 56 |
| 17 | 72 | 85 | 53 | 77 | 57 | 63 |
| 18 | 60 | 100 | 68 | 58 | 62 | 52 |
| 19 | 82 | 67 | 58 | 56 | 72 | 57 |
| 20 | 81 | 81 | 95 | 63 | 81 | 54 |

## Input Data for the Supply Chain Model

This sub section illustrates the input data related to vendors, manufactures and distribution centers for the analysis of three echelon supply chain network.

The input data of the SCS-I are exhibited in the Tables 8 to 16 . The data information of all the vendors about their capacities for each component, the cost of components, and the transportation costs for all the components are represented in Tables 8 to 12 for SCS-I. The manufacturing plant capacity, labor cost of manufacturing a product, manufacturing cost of product and inventory carrying cost of each plant for SCS-I is shown in

Table 13 . Plant transportation cost of product to all dealers and Selling price of product at different dealers are listed in Tables 14 and 15 for SCS-I . Table 16 Shows 20 random U(50,100) demand scenarios.

To evaluate best performing algorithm for the SCS-I, the mean relative percentage error or increase in the objective function value is evaluated by the following procedure:

Let, H1 best –heuristic solution of GA
H2 best –heuristic solution of PSO

We calculate the relative percentage error or increase (REP) in the objective function value yielded by heuristic approach 'i' as follows:

*Table 17. Performance evaluation -best TSCC value and relative percentage increase in TSCC of three echelon SCN yielded by PSO and GA for SCS-I*

| SR | Best TSCC of each scenarios | | Relative % increase in Best TSCC value | |
|---|---|---|---|---|
| | GA | PSO | GA | PSO |
| 1 | 1345621 | 1166627 | 15.34 | 0 |
| 2 | 1363457 | 1209032 | 12.77 | 0 |
| 3 | 1247364 | 1155789 | 7.923 | 0 |
| 4 | 1293452 | 1123155 | 15.16 | 0 |
| 5 | 1247645 | 1100947 | 13.32 | 0 |
| 6 | 1309467 | 1127205 | 16.17 | 0 |
| 7 | 1283567 | 1171024 | 9.867 | 0 |
| 8 | 1235464 | 1068508 | 15.63 | 0 |
| 9 | 1278654 | 1087377 | 17.59 | 0 |
| 10 | 1222345 | 1043365 | 17.32 | 0 |
| 11 | 1238746 | 1055309 | 17.38 | 0 |
| 12 | 1273245 | 1092194 | 16.58 | 0 |
| 13 | 1292435 | 1174379 | 10.05 | 0 |
| 14 | 1278655 | 1068645 | 19.65 | 0 |
| 15 | 1286467 | 1159934 | 10.91 | 0 |
| 16 | 1164533 | 997122 | 16.79 | 0 |
| 17 | 1199857 | 1010813 | 18.7 | 0 |
| 18 | 1155436 | 995907 | 16.02 | 0 |
| 19 | 1074353 | 974146 | 10.29 | 0 |
| 20 | 1293245 | 1132332 | 14.21 | 0 |

Note: SR - Simulation Run
GA - Genetic Algorithm
PSO - Non-Linear Inertia Weight Particle Swarm Optimization Algorithm
TSCC - Total Supply Chain operating Cost

$REP_i = [H_i - \min (H_k, k=1,2,\ldots,5)] \times 100 / (\min (H_k, k=1,2,\ldots,5))$     (3.27)

To evaluate the best performing algorithm, by using above equation the best relative percentage increase in TSCC is calculated and is shown in Table 17. It is seen from the outperformed matrix Table 18 for best value of TSCC . PSO algorithm perform very well and produces better quality solutions when compared with GA.

*Table 18. Performance evaluation-matrix of outperforming Best TSCC instances of solution methodologies yielded by PSO variant and GA for SCS-I*

| | GA | PSO |
|---|---|---|
| GA | ----- | 0 |
| PSO | 20 | ------- |

*Table 19. Performance evaluation-Average iterations & Average Computational effort of all algorithms*

| Scen'o | GA | | PSO | | |
|---|---|---|---|---|---|
| | Iter's | Time in sec | Iter's | Iter's | Time in sec |
| 1 | 1234 | 134 | 908 | 197 | 17 |
| 2 | 1324 | 145 | 1424 | 198 | 21 |
| 3 | 1242 | 112 | 1103 | 194 | 21 |
| 4 | 1232 | 132 | 1334 | 182 | 20 |
| 5 | 1063 | 122 | 1191 | 186 | 22 |
| 6 | 1122 | 144 | 1262 | 191 | 20 |
| 7 | 1543 | 133 | 1467 | 194 | 19 |
| 8 | 976 | 90 | 892 | 191 | 18 |
| 9 | 1243 | 111 | 1111 | 208 | 17 |
| 10 | 1176 | 87 | 911 | 205 | 19 |
| 11 | 1287 | 99 | 1046 | 197 | 20 |
| 12 | 987 | 87 | 889 | 195 | 19 |
| 13 | 1153 | 121 | 1017 | 197 | 21 |
| 14 | 1234 | 87 | 1130 | 212 | 18 |
| 15 | 1343 | 87 | 1238 | 205 | 17 |
| 16 | 876 | 78 | 745 | 200 | 20 |
| 17 | 1023 | 89 | 754 | 193 | 18 |
| 18 | 986 | 76 | 732 | 178 | 17 |
| 19 | 894 | 65 | 666 | 207 | 19 |
| 20 | 1124 | 121 | 1217 | 205 | 18 |

An another important key determinant of measure of effectiveness to evaluate the performance of the solution procedure is the computational effort required by an algorithm, which is expressed in terms of the number of iterations and time in seconds that an algorithm has enumerated to converge to the near optimal solutions of TSCC. This computational effort for each seed in obtaining feasible solution (TSCC) for all scenarios for various solution methodologies of PSO tabulated. The average Computational effort involved in obtaining feasible solution (TSCC) for all scenarios

*Table 20. Various optimal supply chain cost components of scenario 1 of SCS-I obtained by PSO Algorithm*

| Revenue | TSCC | Profit | TMSC | TMC | TDC |
|---|---|---|---|---|---|
| 1716600 | 1166627 | 549973 | 240250 | 908490 | 17887 |

*Table 21. Optimal procurement of component 1 from vendors for production for scenario 1 of SCS-I obtained by PSO algorithm*

|  | Plant1 | Plant2 |
|---|---|---|
| Vendor1 | 137 | 06 |
| Vendor2 | 143 | 48 |
| Vendor3 | 64 | 73 |

*Table 22. Optimal procurement of component 2 from vendors for production for scenario 1 of SCS-I obtained by PSO algorithm*

|  | Plant1 | Plant2 |
|---|---|---|
| Vendor1 | 107 | 19 |
| Vendor2 | 42 | 81 |
| Vendor3 | 197 | 27 |

for various solution methodologies of PSO and their relative performance analysis are evaluated and compared in Table 19. It is evident from figure that, PSO took very less computational time in evaluation of feasible solutions in comparison with GA, i.e. the these algorithms gave fairly good solutions with the reasonable computational effort. Whereas PSO took very computational time in evaluation of feasible solutions in comparison with GA and also it outperformed and produced better quality solutions in comparison with all solution

methodologies used in this research work. The better results are due to the novel solution construction procedure implemented to generate a new particle on the basis of non linear inertia weight variation of dynamic adaptation in PSO algorithm.

A sample of near best optimal supply chain cost components, optimal procurement of component 1, component 2, component 3 from vendor 1, vendor 2, vendor 3, and optimal product manufacturing and distribution from plant1 and plant 2 to all six distribution Centers to satisfy the demand, obtained

*Table 23. Optimal procurement of component 3 from vendors for production for scenario 1 of SCS-I obtained by PSO algorithm*

|  | Plant1 | Plant2 |
|---|---|---|
| Vendor1 | 155 | 30 |
| Vendor2 | 20 | 95 |
| Vendor3 | 169 | 02 |

*Table 24. Optimal product manufacturing and distribution from plants to all distribution centers for scenario 1 of SCS-I obtained by PSO algorithm*

|  | D C 1 | DC 2 | DC 3 | DC4 | DC 5 | DC 6 |
|---|---|---|---|---|---|---|
| Plant 1 | 59 | 66 | 44 | 47 | 42 | 85 |
| Plant 2 | 24 | 32 | 11 | 10 | 47 | 03 |

*Figure 3. Penalty term v/s number of constraints satisfied*

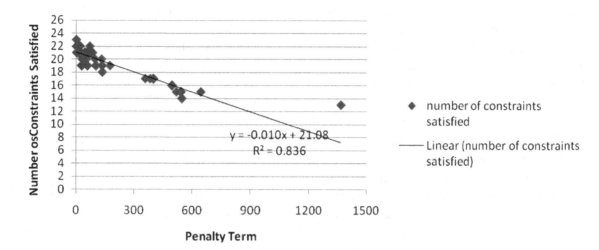

by best solution algorithm PSO for scenario 1 of SCS-I is listed in Tables 16 to 20 respectively.

## Effect of Penalty Parameter

The effect of penalty parameter on the number of constraints of model satisfied and the penalty term is analyzed and is show in the figure 3 and figure 4. In complex problems like this supply chain model, it is difficult to find a feasible point.

In interior penalty approach for violating constraints the initial point should be a feasible point. Hence, we cannot use interior penalty method for this model. Hence, exterior penalty approach is used for violating the constraints for this supply chain model.

In exterior penalty method the penalty parameter is updated every time by multiplying with a constant term. The constant term chosen for solving this model is 10. The increase in penalty

*Figure 4. Penalty parameter v/s penalty term*

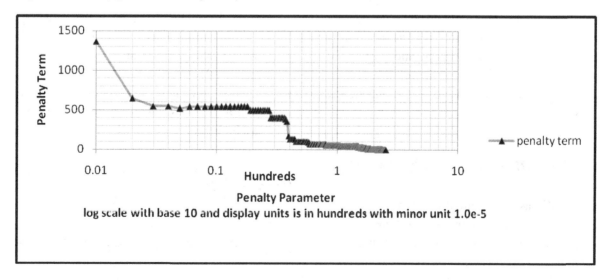

parameter slowly reduces the constraint violation. Which implies the constraints satisfied will be increased with the increase in penalty term.

Penalty functions have been a part of the literature on constrained optimization for decades. Three degrees of penalty functions exist: barrier methods in which no infeasible solution is considered, partial penalty functions in which a penalty is applied near the feasibility boundary, and global penalty functions which are applied throughout the infeasible region. In the area of combinatorial optimization, the popular Lagrangian relaxation method is a variation on the same theme: temporarily relax the problem's most difficult constraints, using a modified objective function to avoid straying too far from the feasible region.

It can be difficult to find a penalty function which is an effective and efficient surrogate for the missing constraints. The effort required to tune the penalty function to a given problem instance or repeatedly calculate it during search may negate any gains in eventual solution quality. Much of the difficulty arises because the optimal solution will frequently lie on the boundary of the feasible region. Many of the solutions most similar to the genotype of the optimum solution will be infeasible. Therefore, restricting the search to only feasible solutions or imposing very severe penalties makes it difficult to find the schemata that will drive the population toward the optimum as shown in the research. Conversely, if the penalty is not severe enough, then too large a region is searched and much of the search time will be used to explore regions far from the feasible region. Then, the search will tend to search outside the feasible region.

## FUTURE RESEARCH DIRECTIONS

- PSO has been applied successfully to many continuous optimization problems, but their applications to discrete optimization problems are few. Future research may be conducted to further investigate the applications of discrete PSO to other supply chain and scheduling problems.
- We can include other performance indicators to measure the effectiveness of a supply chain network.
- We may even try to use the Supply Chain Operations Reference (SCOR) Model as a guide line to analyze the supply chain performance
- The model can also be more sophisticated in a way to better reflect the real situations in real world industrial practices. Hence the model can be further improved to capture the real life situations.
- Further effort is needed to investigate, how to incorporate factors such as other stochastic models and bull whip effect in to the model
- The future work can be directed towards developing multi objective PSO algorithms for obtain real Pareto front for continuous and discrete optimization problems.
- A hybrid particle swarm optimizer with mass extinction, which has been suggested to be an important mechanism for evolutionary progress in biological world, is presented to enhance the capacity in reaching optimal solution. The testing results of three benchmark functions that typically used in evolutionary optimization research indicate this method improves the performance effectively.
- Finally, the new intelligent tools like Neural network and fuzzy logic concepts are included.

## CONCLUSION

The present work in this chapter considered the mathematical modeling of three echelon supply chain network and application of variants of Particle Swarm Optimization algorithm for the best alignment of procurement, production and distribution in three echelon supply chain network in order to optimize TSCC in supply chain network optimization for the first time. The model was mathematically represented considering the capacity, inventory balancing and demand constraints at various stages of the supply chain. The mathematical model was solved using PSO algorithm with handling constraints by exterior penalty method. Finally supply chain network was analyzed and optimized the component and products distribution with near optimal total cost of the supply chain. Then the results were compared with Genetic algorithm. Results indicates that the PSO algorithm has generated better quality solutions to the combinatorial complex supply chain network architecture problem considered in this study. The better performance of the above solution methodology is due to the novel solution construction procedure implemented in the algorithm.

# REFERENCES

Arntzen, B. C., Brown, C. G., Harrison, T. P., & Trafton, L. L. (1995). Global supply chain management at Digital Equipment Corporation. *Interfaces*, *25*, 69–93. doi:10.1287/inte.25.1.69

Beamon, B. M. (1998). Supply chain design and analysis: Models and methods. *International Journal of Production Economics*, *55*, 281–294. doi:10.1016/S0925-5273(98)00079-6

Blumenfeld, D. E., Burns, L. D., Daganzo, C. F., Frick, M. C., & Hall, R. W. (1987). Reducing logistics costs At General Motors. *Interfaces*, *17*, 26–47. doi:10.1287/inte.17.1.26

Cakravastia, A., Toha, I. S., & Nakamura, N. (2002). A two-stage model for the design of supply chain Networks. *International Journal of Production Economics*, *80*, 231–248. doi:10.1016/S0925-5273(02)00260-8

Clark, A. J., & Scarf, H. (1960). Optimal Policies For A Multi echelon Inventory Problem. *Management Science*, *6*(4), 475–490. doi:10.1287/mnsc.6.4.475

Clark, A. J., & Scarf, H. (1962). Approximate Solutions To A Simple Multi-Echelon Inventory Problem . In Arros, K. J., Karlin, S., & Scarf, H. (Eds.), *Studies In Applied Probability And Management Science* (pp. 88–110). Stanford, CA: Stanford University Press.

Cohen, M. A., & Lee, H. L. (1989). Resource Deployment Analysis Of Global Manufacturing And Distribution Networks. *Journal Of Manufacturing And Operations Management*, *2*, 81–104.

Cohen, M. A., & Moon, S. (1990). Impact, Of Production Scale Economies, Manufacturing Complexities And Transpiration Costs On Supply Chain Facility Networks. *Journal Of Manufacturing And Operations Management*, *3*, 269–292.

Diks, E. B., De Kok, A. G., & Lagodimos, A. G. (1996). Multi-Echelon Systems: A Service Measure Perspective. *European Journal of Operational Research*, *95*, 241–263. doi:10.1016/S0377-2217(96)00120-8

Eberhart, R. C., & Kennedy, J. (1995). A New Optimizer Using Particle Swarm Theory. In *Proceedings Sixth Symposium on Micro Machine and Human Science*, (pp. 39–43). Piscataway, NJ: IEEE Service Center.

Eberhart, R. C., & Shi, Y. (1998). Comparison between genetic algorithms and Particle Swarm Optimization . In Porto, V. W., Saravanan, N., Waagen, D., & Eiben, A. E. (Eds.), *Evolutionary Programming* (*Vol. 7*, pp. 611–616). Berlin: Springer. doi:10.1007/BFb0040812

Geoffrion, A., & Graves, G. (1974). *Multicommodity Distribution System Design By Benders Decomposition*. Management Science.

Giannoccaro, I., & Pontrandolfo, P. (2002). Inventory Management In Supply Chains: A Reinforcement Learning Approach. *International Journal of Production Economics, 78*, 153–161. doi:10.1016/S0925-5273(00)00156-0

Hicks, D. A. (1999). Four-Step Methodology For Using Simulation And Optimization Technologies In Strategic Supply Chain Planning. In *Proceedings Of The 1999 Winter Simulation Conference*, (Vol. 2, pp.1215-1220).

Ishii, K., Takahashi, K., & Muramatsu, R. (1988). Integrated Production, Inventory And Distribution Systems. *International Journal of Production Research, 26*(3), 473–482. doi:10.1080/00207548808947877

Kalyanmoy, D. (2003). *Optimization For Engineering Design* (3rd ed., pp. 153–160). New Delhi, India: Prentice-Hall Of India Pvt Ltd.

Kennedy, J., & Eberhart, R. C. (1995). Particle Swarm Optimization. In *Proceedings IEEE International Conference on Neural Networks,* IV, (pp. 1942–1948). Piscataway, NJ: IEEE Service Center.

Kennedy, J., & Eberhart, R. C. (2001). *Swarm Intelligence*. San Francisco: Morgan Kaufmann Publishers.

Lee, H. L., & Billington, C. (1993). Material Management In Decentralized Supply Chains. *Operations Research, 41*, 835–847. doi:10.1287/opre.41.5.835

Lummus, R. R., Krumwiede, D. W., & Vokurka, R. J. (2001). The Relationship Of Logistics To Supply Chain Management: Developing A Common Industry Definition. *Industrial Management & Data Systems, 101*(8-9), 426–431. doi:10.1108/02635570110406730

Martin, C. H., Dent, D. C., & Eckhart, J. C. (1993). Integrated production distribution and inventory planning at Libbey-Owens-Ford. *Interfaces, 23*, 68–78. doi:10.1287/inte.23.3.68

Neugebauer, R., Weidlich, D., & Riegel, J. (2007). Approach to describing virtual reality competence components for services in production networks. *Journal of Production Engineering Research and Development, 1*, 291–296. doi:10.1007/s11740-007-0044-6

Nyhuis, P., & Wiendahl, H.-P. (2007). *Fundamentals of production logistics*. Berlin: Springer.

Quinn, F.J. (2000). The Master Of Design: An Interview With David Simchi-Levi. *Supply Chain Management Review,* (pp. 74-80).

Robinson, E. P. Jr, Gao, L. L., & Muggenborg, S. D. (1993). Designing an integrated distribution System at dowbrands. *Interfaces, 23*, 107–117. doi:10.1287/inte.23.3.107

Simchi-Levi, D., Kaminsky, D., & Simchi-Levi, E. (2001). *Designing And Managing The Supply Chain: Concepts, Stretegies And Case Studies*. Melbourne, Australia: Irwin/Mcgraw-Hill.

Slats, P. A., Bhola, B., Evers, J. M., & Dijkhuizen, G. (1995). Logistic Chain Modeling: An invited review. *European Journal of Operational Research, 87*, 1–20. doi:10.1016/0377-2217(94)00354-F

Steinbeiss, H., So, H., Michelitsch, T., & Hoffmann, H. (2007). Method for optimizing the cooling design of hot stamping tools. *Journal of Production Engineering Research and Development, 1*(2), 149–156. doi:10.1007/s11740-007-0010-3

Thomas, D. J., & Griffin, P. M. (1996). Coordinated supply chain management: An invited review. *European Journal of Operational Research, 94*, 1–15. doi:10.1016/0377-2217(96)00098-7

Tönshoff, H. K., Reinsch, S., & Dreyer, J. (2007). Soft-computing algorithms as a tool for the planning of cyclically interlinked production lines. *Journal of Production Engineering Research and Development*, *1*(1).

Truong, T. H., & Azadivar, F. (1974). Simulation Based Optimization for Supply Chain Configuration Design. In *Proceedings of the 2003 Winter Simulation Conference*, (pp. 1268-1275).

Van Houtum, G. J., Indefurth, K., & Zijm, W. H. M. (1996). Material Coordination In Stochastic Mutli- Echelon Systems. *European Journal of Operational Research*, *95*, 1–23. doi:10.1016/0377-2217(96)00080-X

Von Cieminski, G., & Nyhuis, P. (2007). Modeling and analyzing logistic inter-dependencies in industrial-enterprise logistics. *Journal of Production Engineering Research and Development*, *1*(3).

Weinert, K., Blum, H., Jansen, T., & Rademacher, A. (2007, June). Simulation based optimization of the NC-shape grinding process with toroid grinding wheels. *Journal of Production Engineering Research and Development*, *1*(3), 245–252. doi:10.1007/s11740-007-0042-8

Williams, J. F. (1981). Heuristic Techniques For Simultaneous Scheduling Of Production In Multi- Echelon Structures: Theory And Empirical Comparisons. *Management Science*, *27*(3), 336–352. doi:10.1287/mnsc.27.3.336

# Chapter 20
# Achieving Supply Chain Management (SCM):
## Customer Relationship Management (CRM) Synergy Through Information and Communication Technology (ICT) Infrastructure in Knowledge Economy

**Ashutosh Mohan**
*Banaras Hindu University (BHU), India*

**Shikha Lal**
*Banaras Hindu University (BHU), India*

## ABSTRACT

*Information and communication technology infrastructure has changed modern business practice. The ever-changing information and communication technology infrastructure of organizations' is opening new vista, which has not only bundles of opportunities to encash but also tremendous obstacles as survival threats. The concern about organizational competitiveness and development is closely linked to notions of the information sensitive society and global knowledge based economies. The business organizations under global knowledge economy can emerge and grow rapidly by formulating and adopting the innovative business practices. Information's impact is easily seen—it substitutes for inventory, speeds product design and delivery, drives process reengineering, and acts as a coordinating mechanism, helping different members of the supply chain work together effectively. While the potential of information sharing is widely promoted, relatively few companies have fully harnessed its capability to enhance competitive performance. The chapter tries to provide insight into how information and communication technology can be leveraged for supply chain value creation and make it possible to achieve synergy with customer relationship management.*

DOI: 10.4018/978-1-61520-625-4.ch020

Copyright © 2010, IGI Global. Copying or distributing in print or electronic forms without written permission of IGI Global is prohibited.

## INTRODUCTION

The third wave of industrial transformation is more precisely known as the digital age and/or knowledge economy are terms used to describe a new era of significant changes, just like the second wave of turning an agricultural society to an industrial economy. The knowledge economy is fueled by the rampant development of Information and Communication Technology (ICT) infrastructure that not only facilitates data processing and information usage but also application of acquired knowledge. The advancements of information and communication technology turn into many new developments of scientific knowledge and discoveries began to take place such as new manufacturing or distribution technology, alternative energy, fuel source and biotechnology etc. Advancement in the digital arena not only includes integration of information technology and communication technology, but also virtual reality, artificial intelligence, robotics, and organic light-emitting diode etc., just to name a few. Knowledge management is one of the major driving forces of organizational change and value creation since the early 1990. As with any evolving managerial concept, knowledge management has ineradicably and increasingly become more and more complex. There is always possible convergence of related concepts that directly or indirectly connect with knowledge management, such topics include various business processes and concepts (such as supply chain management, customer relationship management etc.), intellectual capital, organizational learning and various learning theories, intangible assets, social network, neural network, market or competitive intelligence, competitive strategy, change management, corporate culture, creativity and innovation, information technologies (such as artificial intelligence application, decision support system, and expert system), and, not to forget the most important dimension of organizational performance management. Although the knowledge economy is still in its formative years, it promises to advance human understanding and knowledge in depth and widespread. Advancement of human knowledge may lead to improved problem-solving skills, decision-making skills, analytical, conceptual and strategic thinking skills, human intelligence in terms of Intelligence Quotient (IQ), Emotional Quotient (EQ) and Spiritual Quotient (SQ), inter-personal communication skills etc. While organizations continue to upgrade from their intensive data processing operations to information-based operations to knowledge-based business operations, which clearly depicts the need to understand knowledge management. The need to integrate major functions across the entire supply chain and not just within the enterprise would also begin to surface. The major functions within the supply chain include *Supply Chain Management (SCM)*, Product Development Management (PDM), Enterprises Resource Planning (ERP), *Customer Relationship Management (CRM)* and Retail Network Management (RNM).

For an enterprise that already manages its customers as its core business, customer relationship management is its core competency, and, most likely, also its competitive advantage. Customer relationship management system was born out of necessity, i.e., from sales transactions (such as call centers) and customer complaint handling. Only when marketing and customer orientation concepts began to take hold of the organization, customer relationship management begin to emphasize customer value added and customized services and customer relationship building. There are three levels of customer relationship management that progress in sophistication with each level up. Firstly, they are transaction-based data processing customer services; secondly, informed decision based customized services, and thirdly, knowledge-based customer and value driven relationship management. In order for an enterprise to achieve the third level of customer relationship management sophistication by upgrading its core competency and competitiveness, knowledge management must be introduced into the organization as a strategic change. To accomplish that effect to its full potential, the key lies in the strategic intent of the enterprise must be explored. The enterprise must therefore identify the intermediate and ultimate goal of developing its sustainable competitive advantage and core competency. Here, we must accept that customer service is the focal point of the business strategy for the enterprise. In recent years, supply chain management has attracted renewed interest by the development of advanced information and communication technology technologies including world wide web/internet, e-commerce, Electronic Data Interchange (EDI), Supply Chain Operations Reference (SCOR) models, Enterprise Resource Planning (ERP) systems, Radio Frequency Identification (RFID) and mobile technology. The availability of timely information enables the various stages of supply chain participants to be better integrated/coordinated to implement a new, cost effective and dynamic supply chain operation so as to deal with small-lot, high-variety production and also to manufacture and supply customized items in single units at a cost effective and efficient manner (Lyon *et al.,* 2006). The use of *information and communication technology* infrastructure can enable rapid research, access and retrieval of information to support collaboration and communication between supply chains collaborates (Wong, 2005). In a global environment, supply chain strategy needs a tight integration of the upstream supplier of parts, midstream manufacturer, assembler of components, and the downstream distributors of finished goods (Chen *etal.,* 2003). Hence, there is an increased emphasis on electronic collaboration facilitated by an internet and web-based system. Such a system has enhanced cooperation, coordination of various decisions, sharing of resources, and has added value to products and improved partners' profitability (Cheng *etal.,* 2006). That is why, information and communication technology infrastructure of organization is raising the issue of achieving supply chain and customer relation-

ship synergy while addressing the challenge of being competitive at market place under global knowledge economy.

## Concept of Global Knowledge Economy & Management

Knowledge plays a major role in development of the system and takes place at all levels from the individual, through to the organization, on to inter-organizational knowledge sharing, institutional and cross-institutional knowledge to the whole system – known as knowledge economy. As all human economic activity depends upon knowledge, so in trivial sense, all economies are *'knowledge economies'*. However, because knowledge cannot be possessed in the way, for example, gold can, it can be appropriated by anyone capable of using it and these are mainly a means for securing some economic return to invention rather than keeping knowledge confidential. Cooke (2002) identified three key issues related with knowledge economies as:

- Knowledge ages and is superseded by new knowledge that ideally requires what Johnson (1992) calls 'creative forgetting', namely, the stowing away of redundant knowledge and the learning of new.
- The kind of knowledge that is frequently high value now a day is scientific including social scientific. So called 'Scientific management' was practiced at Ford plant in the first quarter of last century, ultimately proving fatal to craft-based production or ultimately to mass customization methods in car industry. This clearly indicates that economies of scope means variety could outweigh those of economies of scale, i.e., volume.
- Knowledge economies are not defined in terms of their use of scientific and technological knowledge, including their willingness to update knowledge and creative

forget old knowledge through learning. Rather, knowledge economies are characterized by exploitation of new knowledge in order to create knowledge that is more new.

For example, the discovery of the genetic code structure allows sampling or the recombination of DNA to produce therapeutic products for healthcare or food product application, while the decoding of the human genome both creates opportunities for value creation and opens up the need to discover the biochemistry of proteins, giving rise to the new knowledge field of proteomics. To the extent genomics and proteomics give rise to superior tests or drugs to those presently available at comparable cost, knowledge is acting on knowledge itself to enhance productivity.

According to Archibugi *etal.* (1999), uncertainty, unequal access to information, dynamic economies of scale and other difficulties which economists normally present as a phenomenon of marginal importance are gradually becoming the rule rather than the exceptions under the phenomenon of global knowledge economy.

Underlying the move towards an increasingly *knowledge economy* are giving rise to two phenomenons as discussed by Lundvall (1999) as:

- It reflects intensified and increasingly global competition, which makes it more difficult for firms in high-income countries to survive simply by producing traditional products with old-fashioned strategies and processes by using semi-skilled or unskilled workers.
- The second phenomenon is related with dramatic advances in information and communication technology through which drastically reducing the price of data and simple information. At the same time, as its diffusion gives rise to an increase in demand for new skills and qualifications as well as formulation of

strategies and realignment or restructuring of various functions and processes of the organization.

Introduction of knowledge management into an organization is a key strategic issue and thus requires a proper strategic plan. The plan should involve not only the supply chain management and customer relationship management function but also other supporting functions and processes. Adopting knowledge management also requires a strategic review of the organization's business model to deduce its effects and challenges of implementation. Viewing knowledge management just on an operational level would not be sufficient as it involves issues of change management, corporate culture, effective leadership, and competency development, all of which would have major impact on the business model and competitiveness of the organization.

The objectives of knowledge management are:

- to avoid re-inventing of the wheel in organizations or reduce duplication of knowledge-based activities, which basically depicts the intent of full knowledge utilization
- to facilitate continuous innovation that can be capitalized and
- to increase people competencies and thus organizational competencies that would eventually lead to greater competitiveness.

Knowledge management program can facilitate knowledge transfer or knowledge flow within, as well as between supply chain partners. Continuous knowledge creation and application on product and service development and/or operational process development creates greater value and competitiveness whether they are introduced as incremental creativity or disruptive creativity. New knowledge created, shared, and applied within the business operations would also build organizational intellectual capital, i.e., human capital, structural capital, and relationship capital through the development of competencies of the people in the organization. Human resource management would play a major role in competency development such as job rotation, job enrichment, e-training/e-learning, cross-functional projects, experimentation, leadership development, and team building activities etc. Collective individual competencies can be organized and converted into structural capital and relationship capital creating greater financial value and competitiveness. Due to the strategic nature of the relationships, organization must have a performance monitoring system to ensure continuous improvements throughout the supply chain.

## Evolution of Supply Chain Management and Customer Relationship Management

In last 10 years, the term *Supply Chain Management (SCM)* got the prominence (Cooper, Ellram, Gardner & Hanks, 1997). This concept is getting popularity with fast pace due to trends in global sourcing, an emphasis on time, quality and cost based competition and their cumulative contribution towards greater environmental uncertainty. Some authors treat supply chain management in operational terms involving the flow of materials and products (Tyndall *etal.*, 1998), others view it as a management philosophy (Ellram & Cooper, 1990) and still other view, it in terms of a management process (LaLonde, 1997). *Supply chain management* has evolved through different phases of management practices. The earliest part of this was traced with Materials Management function after 1850 with the introduction and development of railroads. Traditionally, materials management was responsible for various aspects related to material flow within an organization. The next period was witness of Physical Distribution Management. At that time, it was playing a key role in creating and maintaining brand loyalty and market share

of company. The real difference between the materials management era and physical distribution era was that under later phase the importance of transportation, as well as packaging increased significantly so that finished goods are delivered to customers without any damage in transit. During World War – II, problems involving the movement of huge quantities of supply, made the operations of logistics as a distinct technical field for smooth operations of firm. Even after World War – II, organizations could not enjoy the smooth flow of resources with their physical distribution system and it forced them to adopt cost saving practices with full utilization of resources. These developments gave rise to Logistics management. Therefore, logistics management involves forecasting the future requirements, arranging and managing the flow of raw materials, components, manufactured parts and packaged products. Rapid spread of information with information and communication technology enabled services gave rise to concept of unified world as a global village. Under these circumstances, organizations could not encash the opportunities existing throughout the world by its own efforts. They need partners to pool the efforts and expertise of others to derive the benefits of the same. According to Sardana and Sahay (1999), supply chain management extends the scope to link external partners like suppliers, vendors, distributors and customers and advocates managing relationship, information and material flow across enterprises borders. Further, Galasso and Thierry (2008) pointed that supply chain management emphasizes the necessity to establish cooperative processes that rationalize or integrate the forecasting and management of demand, reconcile the order, book processes and mitigate risks.

In the new business era, *supply chain management* is considered as a medium for achieving short-term economic benefits and gaining long-term competitive advantages. Supply chain management can be considered as an aggregation of approaches and efforts supporting the efficient consolidation of producers, suppliers and distributors, in effect a co-ordination of the value chain so that products are produced and distributed in the right quantity, having the right quality, at the right rime and at the right place ultimately to achieve consumer satisfaction. Current advances in information and communication technology (ICT) have revolutionized supply chain management to make it a mechanism that enables diverse and geographically disperse companies to create alliances to meet a new form of Internet-oriented consumer demand. These alliances represent advanced and dynamically changing networks that aim to become competitive by focusing their resources on bringing elements of e-business to specific market segments. In other words, the focus of supply chain management has shifted from the engineering and improvement of individual functional processes to the co-ordination of the activities of a dynamic supply chain network.

The development of marketing as a field of study and practice is undergoing a re-conceptualization in its orientation from transaction to relationship (Webster, 1992). The emphasis on relationship as opposed to transaction-based exchanges is very likely to redefine the domain of marketing (Sheth, Gardner & Garrett, 1988). Relationship marketing attempts to involve and integrate customers, suppliers and other infra - structural partners into a firm's developmental and marketing activities (Mckenna, 1991: Shani & Chalasani, 1991). Such involvement results in close interactive relationship with suppliers, customer or other value – chain partners of the firm that is why interactive relationship between marketing actors are inherently compared with the arm's length relationship implied under the transactional orientation (Parvatiyar, Sheth & Whittington, 1992).

The first *customer relationship management* development stage is a non-information technology assisted stage. Organizations belonging to this stage have a very limited or not at all use of information technology as far as the management of customer relationships is concerned. However, the organizations use customer related knowledge management instruments and have some type of a mostly manual customer satisfaction and customer complain data, which clearly indicate organizations' positive attitude and orientation towards defensive relationship marketing.

The second customer relationship management development stage is the information technology assisted customer relationship management, predominately a manual process that uses information technology to enhance the organization-customer relationship and analyze customer-related data. Customer data is primarily collected manually but recorded and analyzed by information technology tools and techniques such as spreadsheets, database systems and statistical packages. Organizations belonging to same stage are expected even today to have some Internet presence and manage customer satisfaction and complaint behavior optimally.

The third customer relationship management development stage is the information and communication technology-automated customer relationship management, which emphasizes customer interaction by using a number of technologies, such as the Internet and telephone/computer integration. Acquisition of customer profiles, tracking of customer purchase patterns and trends and interactive service provisions have been made possible by the advances in information and communication technology. Organizations belonging to third stage are having active Web presence, engage in e-commerce and have implemented Enterprises Resource Planning (ERP) and operational customer relationship management systems aimed at business processes optimization and sales force automation. Processing of customer requests, orders, and management of customer accounts are expected to be timely and accurate and generally at a high level of efficiency.

The fourth customer relationship management development stage is the integrated customer relationship management, leading to customer personalization and high level of service and customer satisfaction. Fourth stage, companies employ sophisticated customer relationship management information systems providing highly integrated back-office, front office and Internet functions. These integrated customer relationship management software systems should be flexible enough to adapt to changing customer needs over the product's life cycle and analytical in order to dynamically monitor consumer preferences. Personalization software includes a number of analysis technologies such as data warehousing and mining, collaborative filtering and rules engines. Supply chain optimization and analytic functions are also expected at this stage using Web-enabled decision support software systems. The fourth stage will essentially require sharing of information not only across the supply chain partners so that customer-centric knowledge could be available to every decision maker inside the organization and partners of the organization but also sharing of relevant business information with customers and business partners aiming at overall customer satisfaction, processes efficiency and cost minimization.

## EVOLUTION OF INFORMATION AND COMMUNICATION TECHNOLOGY (ICT) TOOLS AND TECHNIQUES IN GLOBAL KNOWLEDGE ORGANIZATIONS

As discussed earlier information plays a crucial and dominant role under global knowledge economy, that is why, it serves as the glue between the supply chain and customer relationship and facilitate the other processes, departments and organizations to work together so as to build an integrated, coordinated functioning of an organization. *Information and Communication Technology (ICT)* tools and techniques consist of the hardware and software used throughout the organization to gather and analyze information. Over a period, information and communication technology tools

and techniques have evolved from just a support function to an essential tool of decision-making process, which can be categorized in five phases shown in Figure 1.

### Phase – I

Under the first phase of evolution of information and communication technology tools and techniques, it was used to automate routine, repetitive and operational functions. The purpose of information and communication technology was to replace clerical system so that organization could get benefits of clerical and administrative savings of time and cost.

### Phase – II

Under this phase, information and communication technology tools and techniques became a little more sophisticated and focus was shifted towards the efficient and effective use of assets to enhance profitability. Some of the processes of organization, which were smoothened with the use of information and communication technology, were cash management, sales analysis, resource scheduling, inventory management etc.

The first two phases of information and communication technology evolution were targeted towards cost reduction and productivity enhancement exercises. Second phase helped organizations to integrate and coordinate various functions of the same. These efforts moved organizations towards the price war at marketplace.

### Phase – III

This phase witnessed the development of various communication networks and easy availability of technology at reduced price. These developments helped organizations to work more closely as a single entity and re–define / re–design the business processes to enhance productivity with profitability. Development of communication

*Figure 1. Evolution of IT in organization*

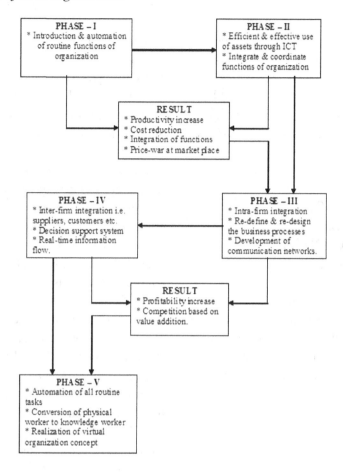

networks made easy the task of data storage and its retrieval. Some of the popular applications were Just In Time (JIT), Enterprises Resource Planning (ERP), On-line shopping, payment systems through credit cards etc.

## Phase – IV

This phase of information and communication technology evolution is witnessing the out-of-box thinking of an organization. Information and communication technology tools and techniques are helping organizations to be connected with their suppliers, distributors, customers, i.e., inter–firm coordination and integration of the same. With the flow of real – time information, information and communication technology gives a big boost to

the real – time decision making with higher level of accuracy.

The last two phases of information and communication technology evolution helped organizations to focus on their core – competency and pooling the strengths of other to add value in its offerings. This exercise leads to competition at market place based on value addition for customers.

## Phase – V

The customer expectations are ever increasing. This new paradigms will throw challenges for an organization. Technology will ensure the automation of all routine task of organization. Intelligent human brains will be free to focus on strategies to serve customer better and better, i.e., transition of physical worker into knowledge worker. The new organizational structure will be much more fluid, which will lead towards virtual organization concept. It means the rigid hierarchies of today will give way to virtual teams formed by individuals with complementary skills and get connected through IT innovations to deliver higher and higher values to customer.

## NEED FOR SUPPLY CHAIN MANAGEMENT AND CUSTOMER RELATIONSHIP MANAGEMENT SYNERGY

The shift in decision criteria coupled with heightened awareness of the customer under global *knowledge economy* will throw new challenges towards organization. Brown and Gulycz (2002) identify the reasons associated with difficulty to manage customer relationship profitably:

- Increasingly informed customers have more choice and are less loyal to their suppliers.
- New distribution channels and communication media mean that the customer interaction mix is more complex, difficult to integrate and potentially expensive.
- Delivery channels are increasingly complex.
- Numerous powerful technology enablers are now available but are expensive to implement, and historic returns are uncertain.
- Marketplaces and exchanges threaten to bring manufacturer closer to their customer, i.e., process of dis-intermediation.

Consumer likes to move towards those organizations, which have been able to decrease response and delivery lead times and costs associated with it. The changes in expectation of consumers forced a shift in the attitude and working of organization and its managers, who now accept the need for close integration and partnership with complementary entities and most importantly with customers. Under the new global knowledge economy age, Indian market is forcing companies to segment customers not only on traditional lines of demography and behavioral aspects but also based on decision criteria. Some new segment parameters could be product and brand awareness, risk-taking propensity, value awareness and its delivery process, technology sensitivity, information orientation and relationship efforts.

Stevens (1989) stated that the objective of managing the supply chain is to synchronize the requirements of customers with the flow of materials from suppliers in order to affect a balance between what are often seen as conflicting goals of high customer service, low inventory management and low unit cost. Ellram & Cooper (1990) define *supply chain management* as an integrative philosophy to manage the total flow of a distribution channel from supplier to ultimate user.

Whereas Sheth and Parvatiyar (2000) defined customer relationship management as the ongoing process of engaging in cooperative and collaborative activities and programmes with immediate and end-user customers to create or enhance the mutual economic value at reduced cost. Gartner group, a reputed research organization defines customer relationship management as follows: It is a business strategy, the outcomes of which optimize profitability, revenue and customer satisfaction by organizing around customer segments, fostering customer-satisfying behaviors and implementing customer centric process.

The objective of customer relationship management is to build long-term relationship for retaining the customers and prospective customers, whereas, supply chain management tries to improve the efficiency of procurement, production and distribution process by taking a holistic view of entire chain's operations across internal and external customers. The ultimate aim of both is to generate value for customers as well as organization. If a customer perceives positive value with the use of product/service then it means organization will get benefits in terms of cost advantages by retaining old customers, easy adoption of new products, word-of-mouth (WoM) by customers etc. With the increase importance of long-term relationships, trust, commitment, cooperation and information sharing in supply chain management, the management of customer interface can greatly affect customer satisfaction and loyalty. As a result, it is likely to influence the levels of trust and openness for information exchange process, which is crucial for supply chain processes and greatly facilitated by the tools and techniques of information technology.

*Supply chain management* is emerging into consumer driven value chain management, which in addition to pursuing efficiency improvements, recognizes the importance of consumer needs and attempts to capture the subtleties of consumer value as source of differentiation and supply chain competitiveness (Christopher, 2005). According to Hau L. Lee (2001), managing demand for the total value maximization of the enterprises and the supply chains is the "competitive battleground" of the twenty-first century. The mentioned studies are revealing the importance of customer driven supply chain management to gain competitive advantage. Similarly, Langerak and Verhoef (2003) highlighted the importance of customer relationship management concept as the customer relationship management concept is embedded in organization's strategy so that executives will be able to take into account the complexities that exist in business environment and introduce policies that allow organizations to co-evolve, i.e., either the organization is evolving alongside the competitor organizations or in tandem with the partner organizations.

The literature related with the proposed research is limited. The available studies are primarily concentrating on multifaceted relationship issues in supply chain, i.e., buyer – supplier relationships in various organizational sectors. Few studies are also concentrating towards analyzing the impact of supply chain relationship on organizational performance matrices. Vickery *etal.* (2003) indicated that supply chain integration incorporating both 'supplier partnering' and 'closer customer relationships' was directly related to customer service, and that the relationship between supply chain integration and financial performance was mediated by customer service. The advent of supply chain collaboration creates the need, at the intercompany level, to pay special attention to the understanding of collaboration in order to prepare chain members to create collaborative efforts successfully (Lambert *etal.*, 2004).

There are few indicative studies highlighted the importance of supply chain management and customer relationship management synergy as J. Woods *etal.* (2002) under Gartner Research emphasized that if organizations pursue supply chain management and customer relationship management separately, it can result in missed opportunities and poor performance. According to McCluskey *etal.* (2006), a customer relationship does not end with delivery of the product or service because that is just the beginning. Further, they introduced the concept of Service Life Cycle Management, which is the process of combining supply chain management, customer relationship management and product life cycle management to meet individual customer's ongoing needs after the initial sales and delivery. Based on the findings of an extensive global study of nearly 250 major consumer businesses and their executive team in 28 countries, the Deloitte Research (2006) concludes that 'consumer businesses that have integrated their customer relationship management and supply chain management capabilities have dramatically and measurably outperformed their competition in virtually every critical financial and operating category i.e. two to five times more likely to achieve superior performance in sales, market share, customer service and other key measures.'

The applicability of *supply chain management* and *customer relationship management* synergy in retail sector is analyzed by Tierney (2003) for the success of 7-Eleven, Japan, whose stock prices kept rising despite Japan's recession for the past ten years due to its demand led management, which led it to intensify sales patterns and customer preferences and to match those by re-engineering its category management and store product layouts, resulting in increased sales and profits.

The concept of supply chain management, customer relationship management and synergy of both are catching the attention of Indian organizations. The applicability of supply chain management and customer relationship management synergy in Indian organization is still in fancy stage that is why the availability of supply chain management and customer relationship management synergy literature in Indian context is limited or missing.

## SUPPLY CHAIN MANAGEMENT: CUSTOMER RELATIONSHIP MANAGEMENT SYNERGY IN KNOWLEDGE ECONOMY

According to Harry *etal.* (2007), knowledge can contribute substantially to an intangible 'strategic resource' in the supply chain and customer relationship *synergy* in the *knowledge economy*. Information is used when making decisions about inventory, transportation and facilities within a supply chain as well as in formulating and implementing the strategies for customer service in global knowledge economic organizations.

Stone, Woodcock and Wilson (1996) suggest that in future, customers will increasingly seek to manage the relationship themselves; using new technologies and those companies need to prepare themselves for this world. Sisodia and Wolfe (2000) identify that the use of technology changes both scale and scope economies of relationship marketing. Even though, it is possible

to perform customer relationship management at small scale without using the information and communication technology. However, information and communication technology becomes essential for performing customer relationship management practices on large-scale i.e. global economy. Organizations can serve large number of customers with small transaction volumes of the same. Besides the scale economies, information and communication technology has enabled information and communication technology tools and techniques. Scale and scope economic of relationship marketing is not confounded with customers only. This concept helps the relationship marketing efforts with outside partners of organizations e.g. suppliers, vendors etc. For example, the Internet/intranet can facilitate connections between the focal firms, suppliers, dealers and customers.

Sisodia and Wolfe (2000) identify the drivers of technology-enabled relationship marketing as shown in figure 2. In broad terms, the intelligent use of information technology in relationship marketing will lead to a close customer focus with respect for customer's time and intelligence.

Under Indian context, Marico Industries rollout its Midas – MI Net supply chain initiative with three basic objectives – to ensure real – time connectivity with distributors, to create a control room for management to focus on sales productivity and to function as a kind of virtual sales office for the field force.

Information and communication technology systems facilitate the functioning of *customer relationship management* up to great extent, nevertheless, information and communication technology systems play a pre–dominant role in every stage of the supply chain as inventory, warehousing, transportation, manufacturing, suppliers and distributors management etc., by enabling companies to gather, analyze and extract information.

A growing body of research has focused on the relationship between information and communica-

*Figure 2. Drivers of technology enabled relationship marketing (source: Sisodia & Wolfe, 2000)*

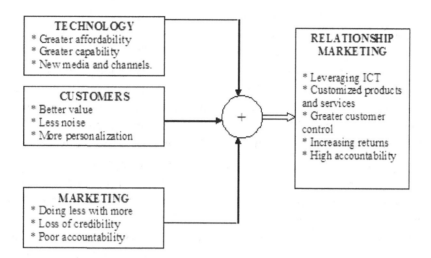

tion technology and supply chain management. Experts have sought to emphasize the critical role of information and communication technology in supply chain management application (Andel, 1997, Barnes, 1997), explore different kinds of information and communication technology applications in supply chain management and have documented successful implementation of information and communication technology in the supply chain management context (Wenston,1997). Evolution of information and communication technology applications in the supply chain started with the Legacy systems, which were characterized as narrow in scope, operational in nature and worked as stand-alone functions. Later on, Enterprises Resource Planning (ERP) system came into limelight. This operational information and communication technology system gathers information from across all of a company's functions. These systems are good at monitoring transactions but lack the analytical capabilities to determine what transactions ought to happen. At present, analytical systems are gaining an edge over previous systems. Analytical systems are more focused on planning and decision making activities. They analyze the information supplied

to them by legacy or ERP system so that to take correct decisions. For example: ERP system may provide demand history, inventory levels and supplier lead times, on the basis of these information, analytical application will determine the profitable level of inventory. Some of the analytical application systems are Advance Planning & Scheduling (APS), Transportation Planning System (TPS), Demand Management System (DMS), Customer Relationship Management (CRM), Sales Force Automation (SFA), Inventory Management System (IMS), Manufacturing Execution System (MES), Warehouse Management System (WMS), and Supply Chain Management (SCM) etc.

Implementation of information and communication technology driven *supply chain management* initiative brings multiple process changes in both suppliers and customers. Changed processes lead to integrated information, coordinated workflow and synchronized planning. Information and communication technology driven supply chain management initiatives bring in coordinated workflow, which simplifies the complexity of procurement, order processing and financial flow. Besides, integrated processes among supply chain partners have a positive impact on product development and ability to deal with volatile demand resulting from frequent changes in competition, technology and regulations. Coordination in business processes among supply chain partners improves the buyer-supplier relation, as changed processes will bring reduced variability and uncertainty in information possessed by both parties. Extensive inter-organizational information sharing trim downs information asymmetry and likelihood of opportunistic moves at the expense of other party such as Electronic Data Interchange (EDI) works as inter-organizational system allowing business partners to exchange structured business information. Electronic data interchange has been reported to yield reduction in transaction cost, higher information quality, increased operational efficiency, better customer service and improved inter-firm relations.

The impact of information and communication technology tools and techniques on the management of relationships in the supply chain consists in measuring the impact of the deployment of inter-organizational information systems over different variables such as

**Quality of Relations:**Larson and Kulchitsky (2000) demonstrated that while EDI increases the integration across supply chain, it does not affect the feeling of cooperation between the parties. Whipple and Daugherty (2002) confirm that the deployment of EDI or other IT tools is not a guarantee of integration but that integration depends on the quality of information exchanged. It is also the sum of the information provided and shared by each of the partners that improves the satisfaction perceived by alliance. The quality of relations depends on the accuracy of the information exchanged among purchasers, suppliers, focal firm, customers etc. at the right time.

**Cooperation and Coordination:**Bowersox and Daugherty (1995) believe that the development of broader external relations is a tendency resulting from opportunities provided by information technology in coordinating inter-organizational activities. IT tools and techniques favour cooperative relations although collaboration is first based on human interactions that IT may support but cannot replace.

**Commitment – Trust:** The use of EDI contributes to the improvement of purchaser-vendor relations through the commitment developed by each party when system is implemented. A greater frequency in electronic communication and exchanges of information is associated with greater commitment. Trust between parties increases thereafter through the sharing of information and the reduction of poorly processed orders.

**Balance of Power and Control within the Supply Chain:** The presence of information and communication technology tools and techniques may change the balance of power between the chain partners, in particular by making the information and product flow independent. While product follow a traditional path as manufacturer – intermediary – retailer, EDI allows for a flat information structure, in which the manufacturer is the single coordination point within the entire chain. Researches indicate that technologies first benefit the leader of the supply chain i.e. focal firm, establishing or reinforcing its dominance over its partners. The use of EDI technology may reduce the negotiating power of a distributor by allowing the manufacturer to collect more information and therefore achieve greater flexibility.

The efficient and effective knowledge management can yield benefits, which include supply chain planning (Apostolou et al, 1999; Chandra et al, 2001), improved buyer and supplier relationships (Bates and Slack, 1998; Beecham and Cordey-Hayes, 1998), collaboration/coordination (Lin et al, 2002), improved supplier sourcing and new product development (Hansen, 2002; Vries and Brijder, 2000; Griffin and Hauser, 1996), smoother project development (Kumaraswamy *etal.*, 2005), improved manufacturing process design (Samaddar and Kadiyala, 2006), better tender selection and greater customer satisfaction (Gilsby and Holden, 2005). Christensen et al. (2005) examine the relationship between knowledge management strategy and the application of down-stream oriented supply chain and knowledge related to customers. Further, the research work of Christensen et al. (2005) provides evidence that organizations must increase their capability of managing the supply chain and customer knowledge resources in order to succeed in a knowledge economy. Few cases studies of commercial organizations that are applying knowledge management initiatives in the areas of supply chain management and customer relationship management are summarized below:

1.  IBM, the world's largest IT providers, is doing business in over 140 countries. To enable business partners to provide excellent service with IBM, software, namely PartnerInfo, has been developed. It provides business partners with the information and knowledge they need to service their customers. Business partners can beneficially use more than a million documents and thousands of applications. PartnerInfo provides business partners with a single pathway to vital information, business programs and shared projects with IBM and other business partners. Through using the PartnerInfo, business partners can access the most up-to-date and accurate information and knowledge. Knowledge facilitates the product development stage and shortens the time spent for management communication. By doing this, product life cycles are significantly reduced thereby meeting the fast changing demand requirements of customers (Vries and Brijder, 2000).

2.  Toyota's consulting team shares valuable knowledge with suppliers, helps make changes, and allows the value of the benefits to remain with the supplier for some time before Toyota begins sharing them in the form of lower prices for components (Dyer and Nobeoka, 2000).

3.  General Motors (GM) consultants walk into supplier plants, analyze what changes are needed in operations, recommend the changes to the plant, and then immediately ask for a price decrease, leaving the plant to figure out how to implement the change in a timely manner (Dyer and Nobeoka, 2000).

4.  Dell coordinates information sharing, incentive alignment and collective learning to focus on direct selling and build-to-order. Direct selling allows Dell to have a better understanding about customer needs and wants. This knowledge can be used to improve the accuracy of demand forecasts. The sharing of this knowledge about build-to-order, visibility of demand information, inventory speed, and supplier and customer relationships results in Dell and its suppliers reaping mutual benefits, such as customer satisfaction, profitability and high-market shares (Govindarajan and Gupat, 2001; Holweg and Pil, 2004).

## CREATING VALUE THROUGH SUPPLY CHAIN MANAGEMENT–CUSTOMER RELATIONSHIP MANAGEMENT SYNERGY IN KNOWLEDGE ECONOMY

Higher levels of responsiveness to the changes in customer demands, a cost effective production scheme for a small volume of product, as well as fast and reliable distribution methods are the key success factors for the organization under global knowledge economy. To achieve the same, multiple independent supply chain members may take joint decisions on production and logistics for large parts of their collective supply chain work (Akkermans et al, 2004). It requires both information and knowledge flow for supporting decision-making (Choi and Hong, 2002). With the knowledge flow, there is also knowledge creation (e.g. new product development, innovative process improvements, technology development) and knowledge transfer between organizations (Samaddar and Kadiyala,

2006). Supply chain management and customer relationship management under knowledge economy is becoming an integral part of every organization whether large or small ones. The benefits derived by opting information and communication technology driven supply chain management – customer relationship management *synergy* under global knowledge economy can be categorized as:

## Value for Organization

The job of strategic planning and scheduling and its implementation becomes easy for organizations under information technology driven *supply chain management* and *customer relationship management* synergy as:

- Improved ability to produce plans that meets management objectives.
- Significant cost reduction in a short period.
- Improved cash flow or quick Return on Investment.
- Increased productivity and asset utilization.
- Better capacity planning, which results as increased productivity.
- Increased on time procurement and delivery, which in turn enhance the reliability.
- Technology enabled supply chain management and customer relationship management synergy will lead to higher levels of marketing effectiveness in terms of anticipation of customer's need, increased level of automated transactions and ability to time effective distribution along with advertising and promos.
- Increased competitiveness and enhanced reputation of organization due to adherence with Available-to-Promise (ATP).
- Better communication and coordination within and outside the organization.
- Improved Customer/distributor and vendor relationships.

- Wired and Wireless technologies efforts will give rise to virtual office for sales force, which enable them to direct access to product and company information.
- Overall increased profits and higher shareholder value.

## Value for Customers

Entire philosophy information technology driven supply chain management and customer relationship management synergy revolves around the customer, so customers will get the maximum benefits whenever organizations opt for the same as:

- Easy retrieval and dissemination of product/service and organization related information i.e. easy to place the customized orders.
- Able to track the progress of order.
- Availing the product/service according to decided available-to-promise norms.
- Achieving 'value' for money spent.
- Quick trouble shooting through timely feedback and corrective actions.

## CONCLUSION

The information and communication technology driven supply chain management and customer relationship management synergy should feature such a degree of organization that no other competitors is able to provide the same services more flexible, faster and efficiently under ever changing global knowledge economy. Based on the literature review, case studies and theory development, it is concluded that information and communication technology infrastructure development is really worthwhile and really successful investment that enables organizations in achieving supply chain and customer relationship management synergy. An ideal synergy of supply chain management and customer relationship management backed by information and communication technology infrastructure gives an organization's employees, suppliers, customers and other stakeholder easy access to the information they need to do their job effectively, ability to analyze and easily share the information with others in knowledge economy. It facilitates scrutinizing every aspect of organization's operations to find new revenue or squeeze out additional cost savings by supplying decision support information. Therefore, only those organizations, which opted for planned information and communication infrastructure, will garner net optimum profits by having the required resources available at the lowest price and on time, i.e., not more – that would be wasteful or not less – that would delay processes. Either of these two is undesired under global knowledge economy.

## REFERENCES

Akkermans, H., Bogerd, P., & Doremalen, J. V. (2004). Travail, Transparency and Trust: A Case Study of Computer Supported Collaborative Supply Chain Planning in High-tech Electronics. *European Journal of Operational Research, 153*(2), 445–456. doi:10.1016/S0377-2217(03)00164-4

Andel, T. (1997). Information Supply Chain: Set and Get Your Goal. *Journal of transportation and Distribution, 8*(2).

Apostolou, D., Sakkas, N., & Mentzae, G. (1999). Knowledge Networking in Supply Chains: A Case Study in the Wood/Furniture Sector. *Information-Knowledge-System Management, 1*(3/4), 267–281.

Archibugi, D., Howells, J., & Michie, J. (1999). *Innovation Policy in a Global Economy*. Cambridge, UK: Cambridge University Press. doi:10.1017/CBO9780511599088

Barnes, C. R. (1997). Lowering Cost through Distribution network Planning. *Industrial Management (Des Plaines), 39*(5).

Bates, H., & Slack, N. (1998). What Happen When the Supply Chain Manages You? A Knowledge-based Response. *European Journal of Purchasing & Supply Management, 4*(1), 63–72. doi:10.1016/S0969-7012(98)00008-2

Beecham, M. A., & Cordey-Hayes, M. (1998). Partnering and Knowledge Transfer in the UK Motor Industry. *Technovation, 18*(3), 191–205. doi:10.1016/S0166-4972(97)00113-2

Bowersox, D. J., & Daugherty, P. J. (1995). Logistics Paradigms: The Impact of Information Technology. *Journal of Business Logistics, 16*(1), 65–81.

Brown, S. A., & Gulycz, M. (2002). *Performance Driven CRM* (pp. 7–23). New York: John Wiley & Sons.

Chandra, C., Kumar, S., & Smirnov, A. V. (2001). E-management of Scalable Supply Chains: Conceptual Modeling and Information Technologies Framework. *Human Systems Management, 20*(2), 83–94.

Chen, R. S., Lu, K. Y., Yu, S. C., Tzeng, H. W., & Chang, C. C. (2003). A Case Study in the Design of BTO Shop Floor Control System. *Information & Management, 41*(1), 25–37. doi:10.1016/S0378-7206(03)00003-X

Cheng, E. W. L., Love, P. E. T., Standing, C., & Gharavi, H. (2006). Intention to e-Collaborate: Approach Propagation of Research Propositions. *Industrial Management & Data Systems, 106*(1), 139–152. doi:10.1108/02635570610641031

Choi, T. Y., & Hong, V. (2002). Unveiling the Structure of Supply Networks: Case Studies in Honda, Acura and Daimler-Chrysler. *Journal of Operations Management, 20*(5), 4439–4493. doi:10.1016/S0272-6963(02)00025-6

Christensen, W. J., Germain, R., & Birou, L. (2005). Build. to-order and Just-in-time as Predictors of Applied Supply Chain Knowledge and Market Performance. *Journal of Operations Management, 23*(5), 470–481. doi:10.1016/j.jom.2004.10.007

Christopher, M. (2005). *Logistics and Supply Chain Management: Creating Value Adding Networks.* Upper Saddle River, NJ: Pearson publications.

Cooke, P. (2002). *Knowledge Economies: Clusters, Learning and Cooperative Advantage.* New York: Routledge.

Cooper, M. C., Ellram, L. M., Gardner, J. T., & Hanks, A. M. (1997). Meshing Multiple Alliances. *Journal of Business Logistics, 18*(1), 67–89.

Deloitte Research. (2006). Consumer Business Digital Loyalty Networks: Increasing Shareholder's Value through Customer Loyalty and Network Efficiency. *Deloitte Research,* 1.

Dyer, J. H., & Nobeoka, K. (2000). Creating and Managing a High-Performance Knowledge-Sharing Network: The Toyota Case. *Strategic Management, 21*(3), 345–367. doi:10.1002/(SICI)1097-0266(200003)21:3<345::AID-SMJ96>3.0.CO;2-N

Ellram, L. M., & Cooper, M. C. (1990). Supply Chain Management Partnership and the Shipper – Third Party Relationship. *International Journal of Logistics Management, 4*(1), 1–12. doi:10.1108/09574099310804911

Galasso, F. & Thierry, C. (2008). Design of Cooperative Processes in a Customer – Supplier Relationship: An Approach Based on Simulation and Decision. *Engineering Application of Artificial Intelligence.* doi: 10.1016/j.engappai.2008.10.008

Gilsby, M., & Holden, N. (2005). Apply Knowledge Management Concepts to the Supply Chain: How a Danish Firm Achieved a Remarkable Breakthrough in Japan. *The Academy of Management Executive, 19*(2), 85–89.

Govindarajan, V., & Gupat, A. K. (2001). Strategic Innovation: A Conceptual Road-map. *Business Horizons, 44*(4), 3–12. doi:10.1016/S0007-6813(01)80041-0

Griffin, A., & Hauscr, J. (1996). Integrating R&D and Marketing: A Review and Analysis of the Literature. *Journal of Product Innovation Management, 13*(1), 137–151.

Hansen, M. T. (2002). Knowledge Networks: Explaining Effective Sharing in Multiunit Companies. *Organization Science, 13*(3), 232–249. doi:10.1287/orsc.13.3.232.2771

Harry, K.H., & Chow, K.L., Choy, & Lee, W.B. (2007). Knowledge Management Approach in Build-to-order Supply Chains. *Industrial Management & Data Systems, 107*(6), 882–919. doi:10.1108/02635570710758770

Holweg, M., & Pil, F. K. (2004). *The Second Centumy — Reconnecting Customer and Value Chain Through Built-to-Order.* Cambridge, MA: MIT Press.

Johnson, B. (1992). Institutional Learning. In Lundvall, B. (Ed.), *National Systems of Innovation: Towards a Theory of Innovation and Interactive Learning.* London: Pinter.

Kumaraswamy, M. M., Palaneeswaran, E., Rahman, M. M., Ugwu, O., & Ng, T. S. (2005). Synergising R&D Initiatives for Enhancing Management Support Systems. *Automation in Construction, 15*(6), 681–692. doi:10.1016/j.autcon.2005.10.001

La Londe, B. J. (1997). Supply Chain Management: Myth or Reality? *Supply Chain Management Review, 1*(Spring), 6–7.

Lambert, D. M., Knemeyer, A. M., & Gardner, J. T. (2004). Supply Chain Partnerships: Model Validation and Implementation. *Journal of Business Logistics*, *25*(2), 21–42.

Langerak, F., & Verhoef, P. C. (2003). Strategically Embedding CRM. *Business Strategy Review*, *14*(4), 73–80. doi:10.1111/j..2003.00289.x

Larson, P. D., & Kulchitsky, J. D. (2000). The Use and Impact of Communication in Purchasing and Supply Management. *Journal of Supply Chain Management*, *36*(3), 29–39. doi:10.1111/j.1745-493X.2000.tb00249.x

Lee, H. L. (2001). Ultimate Enterprise Value Creation Using Demand Based Management. Stanford Global Supply Chain Forum, (September), 1.

Lin, C., Hung, H. C., & Wu, J. Y. (2002). A Knowledge Management Architecture in Collaborative Supply Chain. *Journal of Computer Information Systems*, *42*(5), 83–94.

Lundvall, B.-A. (1999). Technology policy in the Learning economy . In Archibugi, D., Howells, J., & Michie, J. (Eds.), *Innovation Policy in a Global Economy*. New York: Cambridge University Press. doi:10.1017/CBO9780511599088.004

Lyon, A., Coronado, A., & Michaelides, Z. (2006). The Relationship Between Proximate Supply and Build-to-order Capability. *Industrial Management & Data Systems*, *106*(8), 1095–1111. doi:10.1108/02635570610710773

McCluskey, M., Bijesse, J., & Higgs, L. (2006, August). Service Life Cycle Management. *AMR Research*, *1*, 3.

McKenna, R. (1991). *Relationship Marketing: Successful Strategies for the Age of the Customer*. Reading, MA: Addison-Wesley.

Mohan, A. (2006). *A Critical Analysis of Supply Chain Management Practices in Indian Fast moving Consumer Goods Industry*. Doctoral Dissertation Report submitted at Faculty of Management Studies (FMS), University of Delhi, Delhi, India.

Parvatiyar, A., Sheth, J. N., & Whittington, F. B. (1992). *Paradigm Shift in Interfirm Marketing Relationships: Emerging Research Issue*. Working Paper No. CRM 92-101, Emory University, Center for Relationship Marketing, Atlanta, GA.

Samaddar, S., & Kadiyala, S. S. (2006). An Analysis of Inter-organizational Resource Sharing Decisions in Collaborative Knowledge Creation. *European Journal of Operational Research*, *170*(1), 192–210. doi:10.1016/j.ejor.2004.06.024

Sardana, G. D., & Sahay, B. S. (1999). Strategic Supply Chain Management: A Case Study of Business Transformation . In Sahay, B. S. (Ed.), *Supply Chain Management for Global Competitiveness* (pp. 25–46). New Dehli, India: MacMillan India Ltd.

Shani, D., & Chalasani, S. (1992). Exploiting Niches using Relationship Marketing. *Journal of Consumer Marketing*, *9*(3), 33–42. doi:10.1108/07363769210035215

Sheth, J. N., Gardner, D. M., & Garrett, D. E. (1988). *Marketing Theory: Evolution and Evaluation*. New York: John Wiley.

Sheth, J. N., & Parvatiyar, A. (2000). The Domain and Conceptual Foundation of Relationship Marketing . In Sheth, J. N., & Parvatiyar, A. (Eds.), *Handbook of Relationship Marketing* (pp. 1–38). London: Sage Publication Inc.

Sisodia, R. S., & Wolfe, D. B. (2000). Information Technology: Its Role in Building, Maintaining & Enhancing Relationships . In Sheth, J. N., & Parvatiyar, A. (Eds.), *Handbook of Relationship Marketing* (pp. 523–563). London: Sage Publication Inc.

Stevens, G. C. (1989). Integrating the Supply Chain. *International Journal of Physical Distribution and Materials Management, 19*(8), 3–8.

Stone, M., Woodcock, N., & Wilson, M. (1996). Managing the Change from Marketing Planning to Customer Relationship Management. *Long Range Planning, 29,* 675–683. doi:10.1016/0024-6301(96)00061-1

Tierney, S. (2003). Tune Up for Super Efficient Supply Chain with A Traingle. *Journal of Logistic Management, 11*(2), 45–56.

Tyndall, G., Gopal, C., Partsch, W., & Kamauff, J. (1998). *Supercharging Supply Chains: New Ways to Increase Value through Global Operational Excellence*. New York: John Wiley & Sons.

Vickery, S. K., Jayram, J., Droge, C., & Calantone, R. (2003). The Efffects of An Integrative Supply Chain Strategy on Customer Service and Financial Performance: An Analysis of Direct Vs. Indirect Relationships. *Journal of Operations Management, 21*(5), 523–539. doi:10.1016/j.jom.2003.02.002

Vries, E. J., & Brijder, H. G. (2000). Knowledge Management in Hybrid Supply Channels: A Case Knowledge study. *International Journal of Technology Management, 20*(8), 569–587. doi:10.1504/IJTM.2000.002882

Webster, F. E. Jr. (1992). The Changing Role of Marketing in the Corporation. *Journal of Marketing, 56*(4), 1–17. doi:10.2307/1251983

Wenston, R. (1997). Domino's Supply Chain Overhaul to Save Dough. *Computerworld, 31,* 50.

Whipple, J. M., Frankel, R., & Daugherty, P. J. (2002). Information Support for Alliances: Performance Implications. *Journal of Business Logistics, 23*(2), 67–82.

Wong, K. Y. (2005). Critical Success Factors for Implementing Knowledge Management in Small and Medium Enterprises. *Industrial Management & Data Systems, 105*(3), 261–279. doi:10.1108/02635570510590101

Woods, J., Peterson, W.K. & Jimenez, M. (2002, October). *Demand Chain Management Synchronizes CRM & SCM*. Gartner Research.

# Chapter 21
# Benefits of Information Technology Implementations for Supply Chain Management:
## An Explorative Study of Progressive Indian Companies

**Prashant R. Nair**
*Amrita University, Coimbatore, India*

## ABSTRACT

*The usage of Information Technology (IT) in organizations across the supply chain has become a determinant of competitive advantage for many corporations. This chapter focuses on the usage of IT tools for Supply Chain Management (SCM). It also highlights the contribution of IT in helping restructure the entire distribution set-up to achieve higher service levels, lower inventory, and lower supply chain costs. An overview and tangible benefits of the existing IT tools, which are widely deployed, is provided with focus on existing configuration considerations, available applications, and deployments in India. The role of existing communication technologies in making IT an enabler of SCM, is highlighted by addressing a range of different point and enterprise solutions in a variety of supply chain settings. Critical IT demonstrations and implementations in SCM are discussed. Fundamental changes have occurred in today's global economy. These changes alter the relationship that we have with our customers, our suppliers, our business partners, and our colleagues. Reflection on the evolving and emerging IT trends like software agents, RFID, web services, virtual supply chains, electronic commerce, and decision support systems, further highlights the importance of IT in the context of increasingly global competition. The rapid adoption of the Internet for communication with all stakeholders, seems to reflect the potential of the new-age communication media. It has also been observed that several progressive Indian companies are extensively using emerging tools like virtual supply chains, web services, RFID, and electronic commerce to shore up their supply chain operations. However, adoption of tools like software agents and decision support systems for supply chain integration by Indian companies, is limited.*

DOI: 10.4018/978-1-61520-625-4.ch021

Copyright © 2010, IGI Global. Copying or distributing in print or electronic forms without written permission of IGI Global is prohibited.

## INTRODUCTION TO SUPPLY CHAIN MANAGEMENT

Supply Chain Management (SCM) is the management of a network of interconnected businesses involved in the ultimate provision of product and service packages required by end customers (Harland, 1996). This term was coined by Keith Oliver, a Booz Allen Hamilton executive, in 1982.

SCM spans all movement and storage of raw materials, work-in-process inventory, and finished goods from point-of-origin to point-of-consumption (supply chain). It also encompasses the planning and management of all activities involved in sourcing, procurement, conversion, and logistics management activities. Importantly, it also includes coordination and collaboration with channel partners, which can be suppliers, intermediaries, third-party service providers, and customers. In essence, supply chain management integrates supply and demand management within and across companies. More recently, the loosely coupled, self-organizing network of businesses that cooperates to provide product and service offerings, has been called the extended enterprise (Ross, 2006).

Supply chain management must address the following problems:

- **Distribution Network Configuration:** Number, location, and network missions of suppliers, production facilities, distribution centers, warehouses, cross-docks, and customers.
- **Distribution Strategy:** Including questions of operating control (centralized, decentralized or shared); delivery scheme (e.g., direct shipment, pool point shipping, Cross docking, Direct Store Delivery (DSD), closed loop shipping); mode of transportation (e.g., motor carrier, including truckload, parcel; railroad; ocean freight; airfreight); replenishment strategy (e.g., pull, push or hybrid); and transportation control (e.g., owner-operated, private carrier, common carrier, contract carrier, or third party logistics (3PL)).

Supply chain execution is the management and coordination of the movement of material, information, and funds across the supply chain. This movement is bi-directional. The basic elements of the supply chain are:

- Information: Integration of processes through the supply chain to share valuable information, including demand signals, forecasts, inventory, transportation, and potential collaboration
- Inventory Management: Quantity and location of inventory including raw materials, work-in-progress (WIP), and finished goods
- Cash Flow: Arranging the payment terms and the methodologies for fund flow across entities within the supply chain.

Recent development in information technologies enables organizations to avail information easily in their premises. These technologies are helpful to effectively coordinate various supply chain activities. The cost of information is

*Figure 1. Integrated supply chain model*

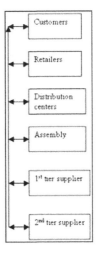

decreased due to the increasing rate of technologies. In the integrated supply chain model (Fig.1), bi-directional arrow reflects the accommodation of reverse material and information feedback flows. The manager also needs to understand that information technology is more than just computers. It also includes computer data recognition equipment, communication technologies, factory automation, hardware, and services.

## INFORMATION TECHNOLOGY AS AN ENABLER OF SUPPLY CHAIN MANAGEMENT

Prior to the 1980s, information flow between functional areas within an organization and between supply chain member partners, were paper-based. This paper-based transaction and communication is slow. During this period, information was often overlooked as a critical competitive resource, because its value to supply chain members was not clearly understood. IT infrastructure capabilities provide a competitive positioning of business initiatives like cycle-time reduction and implementation of redesigned cross-functional processes.

Three factors have strongly impacted this change in the importance of information. First, satisfying or rather pleasing customers has become something of a corporate obsession. Serving the customer in the best, most efficient, and effective manner has become critical. Second, information is a crucial factor in the managers' abilities to reduce inventory and human resource requirement to a competitive level. Information flow plays a crucial role in strategic planning.

Information sharing between partners in the supply chain is also critical and these integration attempts are accompanied by IT initiatives. Such IT initiatives include:

- use of bar-coding in logistics systems;
- use of EDI to communicate between branches;
- use of material requirements planning;

- enterprise Solutions like ERP; and
- Internet and web services for communication between partners.

Early studies on the impact of Electronic Data Interchange (EDI) on Just-in-Time (JIT) shipments in the automobile industry showed significant earnings with lowered shipment errors (Srinivasan, 1994).

In the seven principles of SCM, Anderson (1996) pointed out that it is necessary to develop a supply chain-wide technology strategy that supports multiple levels of decision-making and gives a clear view of the flow of products, services, and information. For this, an IT system should integrate capabilities of three essential kinds.

For the short term, the system must be able to handle day-to-day transactions and electronic commerce across the supply chain and thus help align supply and demand by sharing information on orders and daily scheduling. From a mid-term perspective, the system must facilitate planning and decision-making; supporting the demand & shipment planning and master production scheduling needed to allocate resources efficiently. To add long-term value, the system must enable strategic analysis by providing tools such as an integrated network model, which synthesizes data for use in high-level "what-if" scenario planning, to help managers evaluate plants, distribution centers, suppliers, and third-party service alternatives.

The functional roles of IT in SCM have been outlined as follows (Auramo, 2005):

## OBJECTIVES AND BENEFITS OF INFORMATION TECHNOLOGY IN SUPPLY CHAIN MANAGEMENT

The objectives of IT in SCM are (Simchi-Levi, 2003):

- providing information availability and visibility;
- enabling a single point of contact for data;

*Figure. 2. Functional Roles of IT in SCM*

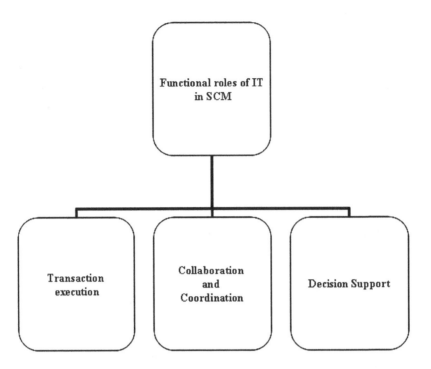

- allowing decisions based on total supply chain information; and
- enabling collaboration with partners.

IT in SCM enables great opportunities, ranging from direct operational benefits to the creation of strategic advantage. It changes industry structures and even the rules of competition. IT is key in supporting companies creating strategic advantage by enabling centralized strategic-planning with day-to-day centralized operations. In fact, supply chain management tends to become more market-oriented because of IT usage.

Cisco reported savings of $500 million by restructuring its internal operations and integrating processes with suppliers and customers with the help of web-based tools (Berger, 2009). Wal-Mart and Proctor & Gamble (P&G) have successfully demonstrated how information sharing can be utilized for mutual advantage. Through sound

information technologies, Wal-Mart shares point of sale information from its many retail outlets directly with P&G and other major suppliers (Anderson, 1996).

Celestica, one of the world's largest electronic manufacturing services companies, has applied a web-based IT tool to regulate its global supply base (Shore, 2001). IT has helped Celestica to improve its responsiveness to customers, thus helping its customer, Dell to maintain its delivery promise to end-users.

## CHALLENGES IN IMPLEMENTING INFORMATION TECHNOLOGY IN SUPPLY CHAIN MANAGEMENT

Any company that has undertaken the mission of implementing an integrated supply chain management strategy with the use of IT tools, knows that one of the greatest challenges that it faces is the significant change in internal culture that is required to make the supply chain redesign successful. It is not an easy thing to re-condition people to accept change, especially in organizations, where a certain mindset has prevailed for many years. However difficult it may be to accomplish, change can be implemented successfully when directed by a strong and knowledgeable leader, who understands the tools available for achieving positive change, as well as their role in initiating and sustaining these changes.

Integrating new applications with existing and legacy systems could also pose problems. Incompatible systems at buyer and vendor facilities are another management challenge to tackle. Sharing of data with diverse stakeholders like suppliers and customers, filtering, and mining data generated and thereby finding "business" value of the data are other issues.

Disconnected enterprise systems create data redundancy, errors and can lead to costly business inefficiencies. Poor coordination between enterprise systems leads to flawed production plans, increased supply chain pressure, and poor customer service. Lack of visibility of orders, schedules, and shipments can lead to costly administrative decision-making processes.

According to Macleod (1994), supply chain managers increasingly want to automate all of the supply chain, from forecasting to distribution, and to link every element of the chain. More and more companies want an integrated solution to enable them to see the entire supply chain at once. For instance, they want to know that if they drill down to forecast, they can see the demand history, which is a combination of data that has come from sales order processing, inventory management, and the warehousing system.

According to Van Oldenborgh (1994), the ability to reduce human intervention along the entire length of the supply chain can help dramatically in cutting logistics costs and boosting customer satisfaction. Unfortunately, for many midsize

companies in these times of economic recession, such clarity in global distribution remains largely restricted to major multinationals with deep pockets and volumes large enough to justify the hefty initial investment in IT, which can run into millions of dollars.

Towill (1997) states that "to survive, let alone win, a company must be part of one or more supply chains producing world class performance." Hence, companies need to work together and optimize the complete pipeline by establishing a seamless supply chain to maximize their market share. Significant and radical improvements in individual business performance can be realized only with the support of this holistic chain concept. Process manufacturers and IT system vendors are working to develop a filter to sift through the barrage of data from process control systems to move important information to higher level IT systems.

## EXISTING INFORMATION TECHNOLOGY TOOLS AND APPLICATIONS IN SUPPLY CHAIN MANAGEMENT

### Electronic Data Interchange (EDI)

Introduced in the 1970s and popularized in the 1980s, Electronic Data Interchange (EDI) technology has been widely used by firms in supply chains to facilitate transactions and information exchanges. EDI is defined as computer-to-computer exchange of structured data for automatic processing. EDI is used by supply chain partners to exchange essential information necessary for the effective running of their businesses. These structural links are usually set up between organizations that have a long-term trading relationship. For example, some multiple retailers will supply electronic point of sale (EPOS) data directly to suppliers, which in turn triggers replenishment of the item sold. Therefore, the consequence of this type of strong link is that those suppliers will be able to build a historical sales pattern, which will assist their own demand forecasting activities. EDI also provides timely and accurate information about customers' sales. Moreover, it is utilized for sending invoices, bills of lading, confirmation of dispatch, shipping details, and any information between supply chain partners (Rushton, 2000). The benefits of EDI are quick process to information, better customer service, reduced paper work, increased productivity, improved tracing and expediting, cost efficiency, and improved billing. With EDI, supply chain partners can overcome the distortions and exaggeration in supply and demand information by improving technologies to facilitate real time-sharing of actual demand and supply information.

## Bar coding and Scanner

Bar Codes are the representation of a number or code in a form suitable for reading by machines (Rushton, 2000). Bar codes are widely used throughout the supply chain to identify and track goods at all stages in the process. Bar codes are a series of different width lines that may be presented in a horizontal order, called ladder orientation, or a vertical order, called picket fence orientation. For example, goods received in a warehouse may be identified by the warehouse management system and added to stock held in the warehouse. When put away, the bar code is used to associate the storage location with the bar-coded stock, and on dispatch, the stock record is amended. The use of bar codes can speed up operations significantly. On the other hand, the problems can occur if bar codes are defaced or the labels fall off in transit. Bar code scanners are most visible in the checkout counters of supermarkets and hypermarkets. The bar code specifies the name of the product and its manufacturer. Bar codes are also used for tracking of moving items such as components in PC assembly operations and automobiles in assembly plants. In 1983, with bar codes printed on most

goods, Wal-Mart introduced checkout scanners in all its stores. These scanners updated inventory numbers for individual items at point of sale and enabled headquarters to easily aggregate sales and inventory data at its centralized IT department. Later in 1987, a satellite communications network installation linked all the stores with the headquarters with real-time inventory data (Johnson, 2002).

## Enterprise Resource Planning (ERP) Systems

Enterprise Resource Planning (ERP) systems are enterprise-wide information systems used for automating all activities and functions of a business. These transaction-based information systems are integrated across the whole business. ERP systems facilitate data capture for the whole business into a single computer package, which provides a single source for all key business information activities, such as customer orders, inventory, and financials. Many companies now view ERP systems from vendors like Baan, SAP, and People Soft as the core of their IT infrastructure. ERP systems have become enterprise-wide transaction processing tools, which capture the data and reduce the manual activities and tasks, which are normally associated with processing financial, inventory, and customer order information. ERP systems achieve a high level of integration by utilizing a single data model, developing a common understanding of what the shared data represents and establishing a set of rules for accessing data. In addition to the huge costs that are involved in procuring an ERP application, installation of such systems will entail widespread change within the organization. It will have implications in terms of Business Process Re-engineering (BPR), changes in organizational structure, people, and change management. Many companies have benefited from using this system while some have experienced severe problems with their application. Generally, they also require a lot of customization and training for each user.

## Warehouse Management Systems

Warehouse management systems are systems that control all the traditional activities of warehouse operations. Areas covered usually include receipt of goods, allocation or recording of storage locations, replenishment of picking locations, production of picking instructions or lists, order picking, order assembly, and stock rotation. Some systems are used in conjunction with radio frequency (RF) communication equipment. This equipment can be mounted on forklift trucks. The warehouse management system communicates with the RF system and directs the activities of the warehouse staff (Thongchattu, 2007). For example, when picking, it will provide the tasks for the operative to carry out. Once the task is complete, the operative updates the system and is directed to the next task. This has the advantage of updating the stock holding in real-time. There are highly sophisticated systems that control the operations of fully automated warehouses. This may include automated storage and retrieval systems, automated guided vehicles, and other devices that are relatively common in today's modern warehouse such as conveyors, carousels, and sortation systems. A number of computer models have now been developed to assist in the planning of warehouse design and configuration. These are generally very sophisticated 3D simulation models that provide a graphic, moving illustration on the computer screen of the layout of the warehouse.

## Transportation Management Systems

Transportation Management Systems provide more visibility into shipments and orders. Scheduling issues are also addressed on time. Multiple transportation options can be explored as a result of earlier visibility into the supply chain. Timely communication and status reports can also be obtained. By having control on its supply chain, businesses can make efficient routing decisions.

An example of such a system is developed by Target Corporation and NTE. Initially, Target was making transportation requests manually for inbound shipments (Thongchattu, 2007). There was limited visibility for shipments and as a result of this, there were more number of less-than-truckloads, which was not cost-effective. Implementation of the new system resulted in Target vendors submitting the relevant freight information electronically with increased speed and efficiency. The new system resulted in improved cost controls, better labor planning and reduced administrative overheads.

## Inventory Management Systems

During the mid to late 1990s, retailers began implementing modern inventory management systems, made possible in large part by advances in computer technology. The systems work in a circular process, from purchase tracking to inventory monitoring to re-ordering and back around again. Retailers such as Target, Lowe's and Best Buy stock tens of thousands of items from all over the world. Wal-Mart alone stocks items made in more than 70 countries, according to its corporate website. It is estimated that at any given time, the Arkansas-based retailer manages an average of $32 billion in inventory. With those kinds of numbers, having an effective, efficient inventory control system, or inventory management system, is imperative. Wal-Mart's system helps it maintain its signature 'everyday low prices' by telling store managers about the products that are selling and those, which are taking up shelf and warehouse space. Inventory management systems are the rule for such enterprises, but smaller businesses and vendors use them, too. The systems ensure customers always have enough of what they want and balance that goal against a retailer's financial need to maintain as little stock as possible. Factors such as quicker production cycles, a proliferation of products, and multi-national production contracts make them a necessity. Modern inventory management systems must have the ability to track sales and available inventory, communicate with suppliers in near real-time and receive and incorporate other data, such as seasonal demand (Crosby, 2009).

## SUPPLY CHAIN MANAGEMENT IN INDIA: SUCCESSFUL DEMONSTRATIONS OF INFORMATION TECHNOLOGY USAGE IN INDIAN COMPANIES

### Tanishq

One of the largest Indian business conglomerates in India, TATA through its group company, TITAN industries, wanted to open a new line of jewellery, under the brand name, Tanishq in 1996. The supply chain of Tanishq consisted of raw material suppliers, manufacturing divisions, carry and forward agents (CFA), and retail stores or boutiques. It was necessary to connect and integrate 69 boutiques and 32 CFAs of the new jewellery chain. A web-based IT solution, "Gold Mine" was used to connect factory with the boutiques and CFA. The system offered visibility on the status of orders placed by boutiques and production was synchronized with an internal ERP system. Sales information flowing in from the boutique gave managers full track of the effectiveness of their marketing programmes, category-wise and price band-wise. Bulletin boards and online discussion forums further added to the application. Today Tanishq is the largest branded jeweler in India with a market share of around 25% (Kannabiran, 2005).

### ITC's e-Choupal: Landmark in Rural Deployment

ITC Limited is one of the premier and diversified conglomerates in India. From a traditional tobacco and cigarette producer, it has grown into a group of companies with interests in hotels, agriculture, information technology, and fast-moving consumer goods (FMCGs). ITC initiated its e-Choupal a few years back with a focus to streamline its dealings with Indian farmers. This is one of the mega projects in rural India. It has covered more than 40,000 villages in ten states, including Uttar Pradesh, Madhya Pradesh, Andhra Pradesh, Maharashtra, Rajasthan, and Karnataka.

With the initial launch in June 2000, e-Choupal has become one of the largest initiatives in rural India. Today, the services through this system serve more than 50,000 villages through over 7,000 kiosks in various states. The initiative was launched with a view to providing instant access to real-time information in regional languages for crop cultivation, as well as empowering farmers with decision-making ability. A web-based initiative of ITC's international business division, e-Choupal is one of the leading programs that offer the farmers with the necessary information and services for the enhancement of farm productivity and improvement of farm-gate price realization, as well as reduction in transactional costs. e-Choupal offers farmers access to the latest local and global information on weather, scientific farming practices and market prices at the village itself through the Web portal - all in Hindi.

ITC plans to operate such kiosks so that they can create an electronic stock exchange for the marketing of agricultural commodities through the use of ICT. The agri-business division of ITC has implemented e-Choupal project in order to tackle the most pressing demands of the agriculture sector in India. The solution provided under this project serves farmers through several essential modes, as well as addresses their basic needs. Through the e-Choupal portals, farmers can access the latest local and global information on weather, scientific farming practices, and market prices at the village level. It also facilitates the supply of high quality farm inputs as well as purchases of produce at the farmers' doorstep. This IT-backed business solution includes a computer, stationed at a farmer's house, and is linked to the Internet via VSAT connection. This single point of communication serves an average of more than 500 farmers within a radius of 5 km. Each e-Chaupal comes with an expenditure of nearly US $ 3000 with a maintenance cost of somewhere between US $ 100 and US $ 200 annually. However, the host farmer- sanchalak incurs some operating expense and gets substantial benefits from all e-Choupal transactions. From an IT perspective, the solution is one of the landmarks in the rural segment having created an IT-based integrated supply chain for the company also. The web-driven project offers scalability and effectiveness of communication mechanism, as well as real-time information and facilitates collaboration between various parties for the full spectrum of farmer needs (Abbas, 2009).

## BPCL

In 2001, Bharat Petroleum Corporation Limited (BPCL), a leading player in the Indian petroleum industry, successfully implemented an Enterprise Resource Planning (ERP) solution. Implementation began in April 2000 after the company decided to integrate all its activities through the ERP package SAP R/3 BPCL divided its IT initiatives into a three-pronged strategy, wherein it planned to create a communication network within the organization, create a basic information network for the entire corporation, and process transactions with customers all over the country. The strategy was devised after the company divided the organization into six Strategic Business Units (SBU) and conducted a detailed evaluation of the company as a whole. The organization was restructured to help focus on specific customer segments and address their individual needs. SAP R/3 helped BPCL to successfully launch its e-business initiatives, the first of which was to allow its customers to track the status of their orders online. This not only allowed the company to retain existing customers, but also helped in attracting new customers.

According to company sources, BPCL's biggest advantage from the ERP implementation was regarding the management of inventory. Before ERP implementation, the company's practice of monthly inventory reviews frequently led to time lag in processing orders (ERP Implementation at BPCL, 2009).

## Mahindra and Mahindra

Mahindra & Mahindra started its IT initiatives in 1995 with the launch of a dedicated network across 8 manufacturing locations, 33 area offices and 4 branch offices. In June 1996, M&M launched its website mahindraworld.com, which was one of the first corporate websites in India. In 2000, M&M extended the Intranet to three websites dedicated to suppliers and dealers of the automotive and farm equipment sectors. In the same year, it started Customer Relationship Management (CRM) and SCM initiatives, which helped in analyzing customer buying behavior and product development with the help of data mining tools. In 2003, these initiatives played an important part in M&M's farm equipment division winning Japan's prestigious Deming award (Dutta, 2009).

## Larsen and Toubro

Larsen and Toubro (L&T) is one of the largest engineering companies in India. Its largest division, ECC handles turnkey industrial and infrastructure projects in civil, mechanical, electrical, and instrumentation engineering. L&T also offers large turnkey construction services. Headquartered in Chennai and with more than 50 years of experience and expertise, ECC commanded a leadership position in the industry. ECC structured itself into seven regions in order to handle the complexity in terms of stage of completion, size of project, and the geo-political situation. Each region catered to the demand of specialized construction services in that region and had its own materials department.

The materials department of ECC also got itself ISO-9002 certified; indicating the level of importance, it gave to the management of its suppliers. ECC adopted a sound and efficient supply chain management strategy in order to keep the supply chain costs to the minimum. Its quality policies emphasized minimum landed costs, transparent practices, and optimum inventory levels. One constant challenge that ECC faced was in integrating and collaborating its supply chain participants. The root cause of this challenge was the construction industry itself. The project sites being spread out at various locations and the large supplier base made it difficult for ECC to minimize its supply chain cost. In order to handle the complex challenge of implementing an effective supply chain management system in the company, L&T ECC opted to implement a web-based SCM solution built on Microsoft technologies - SQL Server 2000 and Windows 2000 Server in early 2000. The system worked on an online order and offline delivery strategy. The company could now streamline its entire vendor network. ECC also arranged a proper training program for its vendors in order to familiarize them with the functioning of the system (Supply Chain Management in L&T ECC Division, 2009).

## Hindustan Unilever

Hindustan Unilever Limited (HUL) is India's largest Fast Moving Consumer Goods (FMCG) company, touching the lives of two out of three Indians with over 20 distinct categories in home & personal care products, and foods & beverages. HUL's brands like Lifebuoy, Lux, Surf Excel, Rin, Wheel, Fair & Lovely, Ponds, Sunsilk, Pepsodent, Close-up, Lakme, Brooke Bond, Kissan, Knorr-Annapurna, and Kwality Walls are household names across the country and span many categories - soaps, detergents, personal products, tea, coffee, branded staples, ice cream, and culinary products. They are manufactured over 40 factories across India. The operations involve over 2,000 suppliers and associates. HUL's distribution network, comprising about 4,000 redistribution stockists, covering 6.3 million retail outlets reaching the entire urban population, and about 250 million rural consumers. Hindustan Unilever distribution covers over 1 million retail outlets across India directly and its products are available in over 6.3 million outlets in India, i.e. nearly 80% of the retail outlets in India. HUL, in its endeavor to move from the existing push-based planning system to a pull-based system, wanted to develop a SCM solution that would ensure informed decisions are made during procurement, manufacturing, replenishment, and distribution. Specifically, the distribution operation was suffering because of high margin of errors. This problem was compounded by increasing instances of out-of-stock inventory, which led to demand-supply mismatches. HUL wanted a solution that could provide visibility across its entire value chain.

An IT-powered system has been implemented to supply stocks to redistribution stockists on a continuous replenishment basis. The objective is to catalyze HUL's growth by ensuring that the right product is available at the right place in right quantities, in the most cost-effective manner. For this, stockists have been connected with the company through an Internet-based network, called RSNet, for online interaction on orders, dispatches, information sharing, and monitoring. RS Net covers about 80% of the company's turnover. Today, the sales system gets to know every day what HUL stockists have sold to almost a million outlets across the country. RS Net is part of Project Leap, HUL's end-to-end supply chain, which also includes a back-end system connecting suppliers, all company sites, and stretching right up to stockists. The IT solution for SCM has improved HUL's proactive planning capability, manufacturing, and distribution efficiency, which has in turn helped the company ensure a more responsive and dynamic system of distribution. It has enabled the company gain visibility across its supply chain, reduce distribution lead-time and minimize cost incurred on its supply chain. Availability of stock has increased considerably from 65 per cent to 90 per cent. HUL has also been able to distribute its stocks more equitably with marked decline in mal-distribution from 19 per cent to 6 per cent of its total volume transported. Manual intervention has come down from 40 per cent to sub-zero levels. Direct dispatches from factories to wholesaler network have increased. Hindustan Unilever, which once pioneered distribution in India, is today using IT to reinvent distribution - creating new channels, and redefining the way current channels are serviced. In the process, it is converging product availability, with brand communication and brand experience. Although, HUL was using the ERP solution, "MFG/ PRO," its parent, Unilever is presently implementing SAP ERP package across all geographies (Supply Chain Management Solution for Hindustan Lever: Case Study, 2009).

## Pantaloon

Pantaloon, one of India's largest retail apparel giants, uses the SAP retail solution in a bid to use IT for supply chain management. The solution supports product development, sourcing, procurement, collaboration, and communication between supply chain partners. The solution also supports handling the logistics of moving finished goods from the source to stores i.e. transportation and warehouse management systems (Pantaloons - Information Technology in the Supply Chain: Case Study, 2009).

## EDI Implementations in India

The EDI network involves the ministry of commerce, customs, airlines, ports, directorate general of foreign trade, banks, regional licensing authorities, and other organizations. The major EDI users in India presently are governmental departments of commerce and customs, port trusts, shipping agents, couriers, custom house agents, educational institutes, importers/exporters, ministry of transport etc. There are two approaches to implementing EDI. Many large organizations acquire or build their own proprietary systems, often in association with their business partners. The other approach is to work with a VAN (value added network) provider like VSNL and NIC, which provides EDI transaction services, security, document interchange assistance, standard message formats, communication protocols, and communication parameters for EDI (Report of the CEFACT Rapporteur for Asia, 2009).

## Key ERP Implementations in India

All the key players in the ERP global market are practically present in India. This includes SAP with their flagship product R/3, Baan Company with their Baan IV product, Oracle with their Oracle Applications and the world-class ERP product, Marshall from the rising Indian star Ramco Systems. The other major players in the global ERP Market, namely, PeopleSoft has entered the Indian market only very recently. Yet another leading product MFG/ PRO from QAD has been present for a while with its major two customers being Hindustan Unilever and Godrej. SAP has been exceptionally successful in India with nearly two-thirds of the Indian market share. The major industrial houses Tata, Reliance, Essar, Mahindra, and Kirloskar have embraced SAP. Baan has been very successful in major manufacturing companies such as TVS. Oracle has been a playing a dominant role in the telecom centre with a stronghold among all cellular phone companies. Ramco Marshall has a good client base among the process industry in the south and a few public sector undertakings (Sadagopan, 2009).

*Figure 3. RFID reader and tag communication flow diagram.*

## EMERGING AND NEW INFORMATION TECHNOLOGY TOOLS FOR SUPPLY CHAIN MANAGEMENT

### Radio Frequency Identification (RFID)

RFID technology is fast replacing bar code in various supply chain operations like inventory tracking and management. The advantage that RFID has over the bar code is that it can uniquely identify the specific object such as when items are produced, which lot does the item belong to, and when will the items expire. In bar coding, the reading device scans a printed label with optical laser or imaging technology. However, in RFID, the reading device scans a tag by using radio frequency signals. The need to minimize operating costs and employed assets has resulted in the adoption of radio frequency technology to track inventories within a supply chain down to the item level, thus reducing channel volume and enhancing forecasting and planning capabilities (D'Avanzo, 2004). In this system, data is transmitted by a portable device, called a tag, which is read by an RFID reader and processed according to the needs of a particular application. The data transmitted by the tag may provide identification or location information, or specifics about the product tagged, such as price, color, date of purchase, etc. (RFID Systems, 2009).

Reno GmbH, one of Europe's largest shoe companies, operating more than 700 stores in 15 countries, plans to embed wireless RFID chips in shoes sold at stores across the continent. Reno has been using RFID technology to track product shipments from its factories to its stores for several years but has not yet used the technology to track individual products inside each store. For individual product tracking, wafer-thin RFID chips are being designed for shoes from Reno's Asian production facilities. By integrating RFID tags into its shoes, Reno aims to curb theft of boxed products, products on display, and the shoes customers try on inside the stores (Schneider, 2003). Schiff Nutrition International, a midsize company based in Salt Lake City, is a maker of vitamins and nutritional supplements. Schiff is in the process of deployment of the RFID technology in order to continue doing business with Wal-Mart. In 2003, Wal-Mart began setting deadlines for suppliers to start using RFID tags on their shipments (Krotov, 2008).

## Software Agents

A software agent is a software system that has attributes of intelligence, autonomy, perception or acting on behalf of a user. Agents can behave autonomously or proactively. The intelligence of an agent refers to its ability of performing tasks or actions using relevant information gathered as part of different problem-solving techniques such as influencing, reasoning and application specific knowledge. One category of agents, monitoring and surveillance agents are being used to observe and report on equipment, usually computer systems. These agents can also keep track of company inventory levels, observe competitors' prices and relay them back to the company, watch stock manipulation by insider trading and rumors, etc. Along with data mining agents, agent-based solutions are being considered for applications in SCM. For example, NASA's Jet Propulsion Laboratory has an agent that monitors inventory, planning, and scheduling equipment ordering to keep costs down, as well as food storage facilities. These agents usually monitor complex computer networks that can keep track of the configuration of each computer connected to the network. Air Liquide America LP, a producer of liquefied industrial gases, reduced its production and distribution costs using agents. Merck and Co, a leading research-driven pharmaceutical company used agents to help it find more efficient ways to distribute anti-HIV drugs. Proctor and Gamble used agents to transform its supply chain network into a network of software agents, whose behaviors are programmed through rules (Cobzaru, 2003).

## Decision Support Systems

Decision Support Systems (DSS) are a specific class of computerized information systems that supports business and organizational decision-making activities. A properly designed DSS is an interactive software-based system intended to help decision-makers compile useful information from raw data, documents, personal knowledge, and/or business models to identify and solve problems and make decisions. Typical information that a decision support application might gather and present would be an inventory of all current information assets (including legacy and relational data sources, data warehouses, and data marts) or comparative sales figures between one week and the next week. In SCM, there is always a likelihood of having disagreements among parties for a certain decision-making process. This phenomenon gets worse, when the business environment becomes more competitive and turbulent. Accordingly, decision support systems have been used in various areas like logistics, inventory management, facility design, sales analysis etc for negotiation among supply chain partners. Baan, a leading ERP vendor unveiled an application, Baan Enterprise Decision Manager for aiding corporate decision-making. Major retailers like Wal-Mart, Sara Lee, and Roebuck have increasingly started using Collaborative Forecasting and Replenishment (CFAR), which uses DSS for jointly developing forecasts. GAF Materials Corp, the largest manufacturer of asphalt-based roofing materials in the US, uses a freight-management DSS (Lee, 1999).

## Web Services

Web services are application interfaces accessible via Internet standards that use XML and that employ at least one of the following standards: Simple Object Access Protocol (SOAP), Web Services Description Language (WSDL) or Universal Description, Discovery and Integration (UDDI). These standards, and the next-generation standards that are being built on them, are defining the way that forward-thinking enterprises manage lightweight integration tasks. To fulfill orders, the retailer has to manage stock levels in warehouses (Coronado, 2006) . For stock re-ordering and replenishment, manual means have been usually employed. All this could be automated using web services as shown

*Figure 4. Web services architecture*

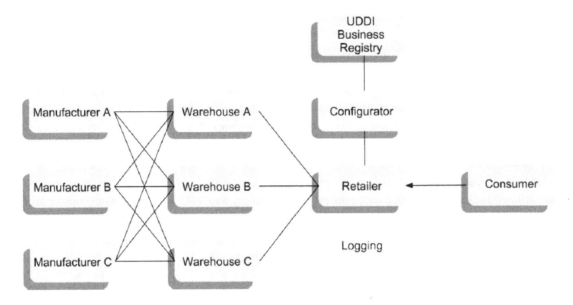

in example (figure 4).

In the example shown in Figure 4, there is one retailer, one logging facility, three warehouses, three manufacturers, and one configurator, and thus a total of nine web services, which are all integrated using the Universal Description, Discovery And Integration (UDDI) protocol. UDDI creates a standard interoperable platform that enables companies and applications to dynamically use web services over the Internet. UDDI is a cross-industry effort driven by major platform and software providers, as well as marketplace operators and e-business leaders (Universal Description, Discovery and Integration, 2009).

## Electronic Commerce

Electronic commerce refers to the wide range of tools and techniques utilized to conduct business in a paperless environment. Electronic commerce therefore includes electronic data interchange, e-mail, electronic fund transfers, electronic publishing, image processing, electronic bulletin boards, and shared databases. Companies are able to automate the process of moving documents electronically between suppliers and customers. This system provides access to customers all over the world and thus eliminates geographical limitations. Some of the e-commerce applications in the B2C (Business to Consumer) and B2B (Business-to-Business) space, include e-Tailing (using the Internet for selling goods and services over the Internet, examples are companies such as Amazon and e-bay); e-Procurement (using the Internet for purchase of goods and services which are not directly used in the main business of a company like a car manufacturer procuring stationery for its employees), and e-Auctions (Sites on the web, which run conventional auctions). There are two types of e-Auctions: those that are carried out in real-time, where participants log in to an auction site using a browser at a specified time and bid for an article until the highest price is reached and no other bids are forthcoming. The other type of site and the most common, is where an item is offered for sale and a date advertised after which no more bids are accepted.

## Electronic Supply Chains

Electronic Supply Chains (ESC) refers to those supply chains that are electronically facilitated between or among participating firms. Also called virtual supply chains, these are realized in two forms, EDI-based or Internet-based. EDI generally connects firms through proprietary Value Added Networks (VAN), whereas the Internet generally connects firms through open networks, which use standard protocols. The ESC links trading partners to allow them to buy, sell and move products, costs, the introduction of the Internet has brought about opportunities that allow firms to transact with other enterprises electronically. Amazon is one such example. The virtual supply chain also envisages use of Internet-based applications to transact and exchange information like product and inventory information with their downstream or upstream trading partners. Supply chain initiatives like Collaborative Planning, Forecasting and Replenishment (CPFR), Vendor Managed Inventory (VMI), Efficient Customer Response (ECR) and quick response have been increasingly facilitated in the new e-supply chain paradigm. Information sharing among suppliers, manufacturers, distributors, and retailers are greatly improved. American-On-Line and lastminute.com have achieved innovative results using ESCs (Gunasekharan, 2004).

## Collaborative Product Commerce

Collaborative product commerce (CPC) is a set of tools that allows companies to manage product information and share that information with suppliers and partners through the web. CPC tools typically combine information management, version-control, configuration management, workflow-management, and collaborative tools. CPC helps a company's development strategy to become three-dimensional. This is by facilitating the collaborative development of products, processes, and supply chain strategies such as

Build-to-Order (BTO) (Turner, 2001). In the future, CPC is expected to co-ordinate and control virtually all supply, design, manufacturing, and customer-relationship processes. Collaborative Product Commerce (CPC) embraces the product design, development, and introduction processes as well as the associated management of product data and requires a coalition of internal and external constituencies. The benefits of developing robust CPC capabilities can be compelling. They typically come in the form of integration of design processes and supply chains, increased revenue and margin, lower operating costs, better customer response, JIT processes, and higher quality improvement. Figure 5 shows components of a typical CPC solution (True, 2002).

## IMPLEMENTATIONS OF EMERGING INFORMATION TECHNOLOGY TOOLS IN INDIAN COMPANIES

Several progressive Indian companies are extensively adopting emerging IT tools like RFID, web services, electronic commerce, and virtual supply chains to shore up their supply chain operations. Leading Indian IT service providers like Tata Consultancy Services, Infosys, and Wipro are developing RFID-based solutions for supply chain management in sectors like manufacturing, retail, telecom, government, hospitals, and educational facilities like libraries. These solution providers are also developing web services based packages to facilitate virtual supply chains, EDI, e-Tailing, and e-Procurement. Retail giants like Pantaloon, ITC, Wills Lifestyle, Madura Garments, Big Bazaar, and Total Mall have already implemented RFID at their retail outlets for product tracking and warehouse management. Automobile major, Mahindra and Mahindra is another early adopter, using RFID for scheduling and logistics management (Nallayam, 2009). The manufacturing giant, Ashok Leyland, is using RFID for plant assembly operations. Even small players have started to use

*Figure 5. CPC architecture*

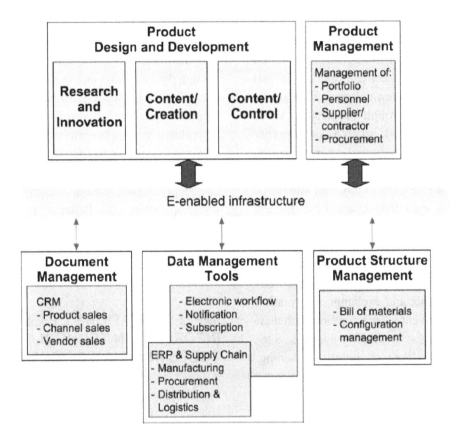

RFID for their supply chain integration. Sabare International, a home furnishings textiles exporter, headquartered in the small south Indian town of Karur, has deployed RFID tags to reduce its operating costs. As a result of this deployment, production efficiency at their plants has improved by over 5 percent (Giridhar, 2009).

The total RFID market (including tags, readers, software and services) has been growing exponentially over the last decade. Today it is around US $ 5.5 billion and the forecast is that it may touch US $ 25 billion by 2015 of which a large chunk will come from emerging economies like China and India. This acceleration will be facilitated by rapid declines in the RFID tag prices and extensive use in various applications. One estimate suggests that the RFID tag market will by

several billion tags today to tens of trillions of tags by 2015 (RFID market to reach $7.26Bn, 2009). Forecasts also project over 1.3 million jobs will be directly created by RFID technology by 2015 (RFID Workforce: Mining the RFID Technology Gold Rush, 2009).

The electronic business market has also grown by leaps and bounds with the present market space being estimated at almost US $ 1.8 billion (Ashish, 2009) with several players like Indian railways, skumars.com, e-bay, and all leading banks and financial institutions like ICICI, HDFC, IDBI etc.

Several large manufacturers in India are also architecting virtual supply chains. Maruti-Suzuki, the largest car manufacturer in India, which has more than 200 vendors and suppliers, has connected to all vendors using web services and high-bandwidth networking. Vendors are linked through this Internet-based supply chain, which maintains online information regarding order status and delivery instructions. These have substantially helped in reducing both inventory levels and lead times required for the supply of various components (Harikanth, 2009).

However, deployment of tools like DSS and software agents for supply chain management in Indian companies is limited. A few IT service companies like PTC and Rolta are offering CPC solutions for manufacturing companies, which are mainly used for computer-integrated design and manufacturing. Usage of DSS and software agents for SCM are at the research or experimental stages. Indian companies must rapidly adopt these technologies for SCM and derive potential benefits.

## ITC Wills Lifestyle – An RFID Success Story

Wills Lifestyle is an apparel company owned by the diversified ITC group. The chain of Wills Lifestyle stores offers a complete fashion wardrobe comprising 'Wills Classic' formal wear, 'Wills Sport' relaxed wear, and 'Wills Clublife' evening wear, along with accessories for both men and women. Wills Lifestyle is also rated as among the top five luxury brands in India.

In December 2006, Wills Lifestyle added a technology enabler, RFID to their showrooms and warehouses. Deployed across 7 retail showrooms and 2 warehouses, the project reaped wide-ranging benefits to internal business users as well as consumers. RFID proved its mettle in terms of speeding up of existing processes, reducing the time-to-market, efficient material handling, and accuracy of books versus physical stock. During the bar-code era, each piece of garment was individually scanned and lots of manpower was involved, also at the end of the day accuracy of stocks received/dispatched at the warehouse was a key concern. With RFID in place, the time taken to receive 1 carton (about

30 to 35 garments) was reduced from about 5 to 8 minutes to about 20 to 30 seconds. With the usage of RFID tunnels, the output per person increased from 300 to 400 pieces per day to about 2000 to 3000 pieces per day. Reduced scanning time enabled faster receiving and dispatch of merchandize, thereby reducing the time to market. Thus, an extra 10 to 15 day window was available leading to increased contribution to the business by over 2 percent. Owing to increased inventory velocity in the supply chain, the merchandize lies for a lesser time in the warehouse, thereby eliminating the need for additional warehouse space. Earlier, about 20% of the non-saleable returns from the stores were attributed to the reason of mishandling at the warehouse. With the project in action, since the physical handling at the warehouse is reduced, the percentage of non-saleable garments has reduced considerably. With unique identity of each tag, and faster reconciliation, the magnitude of manual errors was also greatly reduced.

Every garment was also getting about seven days earlier to the store. With some garments getting as much as an extra 10 to 15 day window, ITC lifestyle retailing has seen a 2 percent growth in sales. In addition, the percentage of manual errors has been reduced greatly because each tag has a unique identity and reconciliation is more accurate. Assuming a 0.1 percent error rate across three lakh products every month, the company estimates saving worth US $ 120,000 a year (Goswami, 2009).

## Mahindra and Mahindra – RFID Usage for SCM in Manufacturing sector

Mahindra & Mahindra (M&M) is India's largest farm equipment company and the largest manufacturer of tractors in India with sustained market leadership of over 20 years. Mahindra is also the first tractor company in the world to win the Deming Prize. All of M&M's plants have been certified for ISO 9001, QS-9000, and ISO 14001.

Inventory accuracy, shrinkage control, controlling delays in vendor shipments, and minimizing dud production schedules were of critical importance to M&M in their drive to improve supply chain efficiencies. The need to maintain accurate information and avoidance of human errors were the factors that drove M&M to look for real-time data capture solutions. SkandSoft Technologies Private Limited, an upcoming IT service provider, was chosen to provide an user-friendly, single-window solution to this complex challenge. SkandSoft, after a comprehensive study of M&M's existing inbound supply chain, developed an RFID-based SCM solution. The RFID solution was in tune with the evolving specifications of RFID hardware and systems. It was also integrated with the legacy SAP MM and APO modules of M&M. The business results after deploying this solution were complete reduction in manpower involved in physical count check and stock verification. Picking and docking personnel saved 32% of their time. The company achieved near-zero shrinkage of the items covered and 14% reduction in costs by FIFO compliance in storage (Success stories: Mahindra and Mahindra, 2009).

## FedEx India Virtual Supply Chain

Blue Dart Express, is India's premier integrated air express carrier and logistic-services provider. Blue dart is also the Indian global service participant of Federal Express (FedEx), the world's leading air express transportation company. Using web services, Blue dart has evolved an e-strategy to integrate all partners and customers with its e-shipping tools. All 14 of the company's warehouses are connected to this system. All customers can track their shipments through single or multiple waybills online. This solution is also ported to an e-mail or mobile response system. Customers can register and gain access entire waybill tracking data, which are available for 45 days online. This web-enabled solution with additional features like e-logistics, e-fulfillment, inventory control etc, has also been integrated to the ERP system, "COSMATH," which has been indigenously de-

veloped by the company (Federal Express India supply chain, 2009).

## CONCLUSION

Industry trends like globalization, outsourcing, customization, time to market, and pricing pressure have compelled enterprises to adopt efficient and effective supply chain management technologies, practices, and policies. Customers' expectations are also increasing and companies are prone to more and more uncertain environments in the face of increasing competition. To survive in these times, companies will find that their conventional supply chain integration will have to be expanded beyond their boundaries so as to integrate all stakeholders. Adoption of IT tools is vital for such efforts.

This chapter discusses the role of IT as an enabler in supply chain management and also highlights the vast benefits to companies with a comprehensive IT strategy. An overview and deployment of the present alignments of widely deployed IT tools like EDI, ERP, bar codes, inventory management, transportation management, and warehouse management systems is provided. Successful IT implementations of SCM of progressive Indian companies are also described. The basic elements of emerging and new age tools like RFID, software agents, decision support systems, web services, electronic commerce, and virtual supply chains are reviewed. Rapid advances in Internet technology have changed the way companies do business. Enterprises must harness the power of these emerging information technology tools for supply chain integration and collaboration. While it has been observed that usage of tools like RFID, web services, electronic commerce, and IT solutions to facilitate virtual supply chains, has been on the rise, Indian companies are yet to tap the vast potential of the application of software agents and decision support systems in supply chain management.

# REFERENCES

Abbas, M. (2009). *ITC's e-Choupal: Landmark in rural deployment*. Retrieved April 15, 2009, from http://www.cxotoday.com/India/Case_Study/ITCs_e-Choupal_Landmark_in_Rural_Deployment/551-99474-1004.html.

Anderson, D. L. Britt., F. E., & Favre, D. J. (1997). The seven principles of supply chain management. Supply Chain Management Review, (Spring), 31-41.

Ashish, D. (2009). E-commerce in India. *Pluggedin*. Retrieved April 20, 2009, from http://www.pluggd.in/india/ecommerce-in-india-irctc-contribution-3961/

Auramo, J., Kauremaa, J., & Tanskanen, K. (2005). Benefits of IT in supply chain management: An explorative study of progressive companies. *International Journal of Physical Distribution and Logistics Management*, *35*(2), 82–90. doi:10.1108/09600030510590282

Berger, A. (2009). *Five steps to an eSynchronized Supply Chain*. Retrieved April 27, 2009, from www.accenture.com/NR/rdonlyres/18099CFB-1D5F-4FA7-BBC4-862EC465123D/0/esynchronized_supply_chain_pov_ref.pdf

Cobzaru, M. (2003). *Agent-based Supply Chain Management System*. Unpublished doctoral dissertation, University of Calgary, Calgary, Canada.

Coronado, A. E., Lyons, A. C., Michaelides, Z., & Kehoe, D. F. (2006). Automotive supply chain models and technologies: A review of some latest developments. *Journal of Enterprise Information Management*, *19*(5), 551–562. doi:10.1108/17410390610703675

Crosby, T. (2009). *How Inventory Management Systems Work*. Retrieved May 4, 2009, from http://communication.howstuffworks.com/how-inventory-management-systems-work.htm

D'Avanzo, R., Starr, E., & Lewinski, H. V. (2004). Supply chain and the bottom line: A critical link. *Outlook: Accenture*, *1*, 39–45.

Description, U. *Discovery and Integration*. (2009). Retrieved May 12, 2009, from http://uddi.xml.org/

Dutta, S., & Kumar, A. (2009). Mahindra & Mahindra's E-Business Initiatives. *ECCH Case Collection*. Retrieved May 12, 2009, from from http://www.asiacase.com/ecatalog/NO_FILTERS/page-ERP-602916.html

ERP Implementation at BPCL. *Case Study*. (2009). Retrieved May 2, 2009, from http://www.icmrindia.org/casestudies/catalogue/IT%20and%20Systems/ITSY005.htm

*Federal Express India supply chain*. (2009). Retrieved May 15, 2009, from http://www.scribd.com/doc/2165098/Supply-Chain-Management-at-Fedex-India

Giridhar, C. (2009). India tests RFID waters. *Electronic Busines*. Retrieved May 18, 2009, from http://www.edn.com/article/CA6388858.html

Goswami, K. (2009). RFID Speeds Up Wills Lifestyle Business. *Real CIO World*. Retrieved May 18, 2009, from http://www.cio.in/case-study/rfid-speeds-wills-lifestyle-business

Gunasekharan, A., & Ngai, E. W. T. (2004). Virtual Supply Chain Management. *Production Planning and Control*, *15*(6), 584–595. doi:10.1080/09537280412331283955

Haag, S., Cummings, M., & Philips, A. (2006). *Management Information Systems for the Information Age*. New York: McGraw Hill.

Harikanth, S. (2009). Maruti Value Chain. *OP Papers.com*. Retrieved May 20, 2009, from http://www.oppapers.com/essays/Maruti-Value-Chain/167129

Harland, C. M. (1996). Supply chain management: relationships, chains, and networks. *British Journal of Management, 7,* 63–80. doi:10.1111/j.1467-8551.1996.tb00148.x

Johnson, A. H. (2002 September 30). Wal-Mart put intelligence in its inventory and recognized the value of sharing data. *Computerworld.*

Kannabiran, G., & Bhaumik, S. (2005). Corporate Turnaround through effective supply chain management: The case of a leading jewellery manufacturer in India. *Supply Chain Management, 10*(5), 340. doi:10.1108/13598540510624160

Krotov, V., & Junglas, I. (2008). RFID as a disruptive innovation. *Journal of Theoretical and Applied Electronic Commerce Research, 3*(2), 44–59. doi:10.4067/S0718-18762008000100005

Lee, C., Lee, K. C., & Han, J. H. (1999). *A Web-based Decision Support System for Logistics Decision-Making.* Paper presented at the meeting of the Academy of Information and Management Sciences, Myrtle Beach, SC.

Macleod, M. (1994, June). What's new in supply chain software? *Purchasing & Supply Management,* (pp. 22-25).

Nallayam, R. (2009). RFID Reality Check. *Channelworld.in.* Retrieved May 16, 2009, from http://www.channelworld.in/specialreports/index.jsp/artId=5013515

Pantaloons - Information Technology in the Supply Chain. Case Study. (2009). *ECCH Case Collection.* Retrieved April 16, 2009, from http://www.icmrindia.org/casestudies/catalogue/Supply%20chain%20Management/CLSCM002.htm

Report of the CEFACT Rapporteur for Asia. (2009). Retrieved April 19, 2009, from http://www.unece.org/trade/untdid/download/99cp3.rtf

RFID market to reach $7.26Bn in 2008. (2009). *IDTechEx.* Retrieved May 27, 2009, from www.idtechex.com/products/en/articles/00000169.asp

*RFIDSystems.* (2009). Retrieved May 10, 2009, from http://epic.org/privacy/rfid

Ross, J. (2006). *Enterprise Architecture As Strategy: Creating a Foundation for Business Execution.* Cambridge, UK: Harvard Business School Press.

Rushton, A., Oxley, J., & Croucher, P. (2000). *The Handbook of Logistics and Distribution Management.* Glasgow, UK: Bell & Bain Ltd.

Sadagopan, S. (2009). Freqently asked questions on ERP in India. *ERP Study centre, IIM-B.* Retrieved April 17, 2009, from http://www.iiitb.ac.in/ss/erp-faq/main4pg1.htm

Sammon, D., & Hanley, P. (2007). Case Study: Becoming a 100 per cent e-corporation: benefits of pursuing an e-supply chain strategy. *Supply Chain Management, 12*(4), 297–303. doi:10.1108/13598540710759817

Schneider, M. (2003). *Radio Frequency Identification (RFID) Technology and its Applications in the Commercial Construction Industry.* Unpublished doctoral dissertation, University of Kentucky, Lexington, KY.

Shore, B. (2001). Information sharing in global supply chains. *Journal of Global Information Technology Management, 4*(3), 27–46.

Simchi-levi, D., Kaminsky, P., & Simchi-levi, E. (2003). *Managing The Supply Chain: The Definitive Guide For The Business Professional.* New York: Irwin /Mc Graw Hill.

Srinivasan, K., Kekre, S., & Mukhopadhyay, T. (1994). Impact of Electronic Data Interchange Technology on JIT Shipments. *Management Science, 40*(10), 1291–1304. doi:10.1287/mnsc.40.10.1291

*Success stories: Mahindra and Mahindra.* (2009). Retrieved May 17, 2009, from http://www.skandsoft.com/successstories.html#1

Supply Chain Management in L&T ECC Division. (2009). *ECCH Case Collection.* Retrieved April 29, 2009, from http://www.icmrindia.org/casestudies/catalogue/Operations/OPER045.htm

Supply Chain Management Solution for Hindustan Lever. *Case Study.* (2009). Retrieved May 3, 2009, from http://fmcg-marketing.blogspot.com/2007/10/supply-chain-management-solution-for.html

Thongchattu, C., & Buranajarukorn, P. (2007). *The Utilisation of e-Tools of Information Technology Towards Thorough Supply Chain Management.* Paper presented at the Naresuan University Research Conference, Thailand.

Towill, D. (1997). The seamless supply chain - the predator's strategic advantage. *International Journal of Technology Management, 13*(1), 37–56. doi:10.1504/IJTM.1997.001649

True, M., & Izzi, C. (2002). Collaborative product commerce: creating value across the enterprise . *Ascet, 4,* 27–35.

Van Oldenborgh, M. (1994). Distribution superhighway. *International Business, 7*(6), 80–84.

Workforce, R. F. I. D. Mining the RFID Technology Gold Rush. (2009). *RFID Tribe.* Retrieved May 27, 2009, from www.rfidtribe.com/news-05-05-11.html

# Chapter 22
# Mathematical Modeling of Supply Chain Management Systems

**C. Elango**
*Cardamom Planters' Association College, India*

**N. Anbazhagan**
*Alagappa University, India*

## ABSTRACT

*Supply Chain Management (SCM) is the practice of coordinating the flow of goods, services, information and finances as they move from raw materials to parts supplier to manufacturer to wholesaler to retailer to consumer. Different supply chains have been designed for a variety of firms and this chapter discusses some issues in this regard. This chapter attempts to find why we require different supply chain for different companies. In this chapter we discuss the role of stochastic models in supply chain management system, and also discuss other mathematical models for SCM.*

## INTRODUCTION

Our growing global economy has caused a dramatic shift in inventory management in recent years. Now, as never before, the inventory of many manufacturers is scattered throughout the world. Even the inventory of an individual product may be dispersed globally.

Most of the MNCs implemented an ERP strategy to solve production and inventory management problems arise in the industry. Hindustan Oil Corporation (HOC) is an example from Inidia on ERP based system management. The (ERP) selection was

based on the data and process integration that can be provided by the ERP package, rich functionality are features of the ERP, product support and services. Indian presence of ERP vendor and recommendations by leading management consultants, track a record of the vendor company in India and abroad. This is basis for supply chain managemnet system. The major modules which facilitated the supply Chain efficiency include demand planning (forecasting accuracy), data warehouse(reduce maldistribution and lost sales), vendor management of inventory (to improve response time).

A manufacturer's inventory may be stored initially at the point or points of manufacture (one echelon of the inventory system), then at national

DOI: 10.4018/978-1-61520-625-4.ch022

Copyright © 2010, IGI Global. Copying or distributing in print or electronic forms without written permission of IGI Global is prohibited.

or regional warehouses (a second echelon) then at field distribution centers (a third echelon), and so on, thus each stage at which inventory is held in progression through a multistage inventory system is called multi-echelon inventory system. In the case of a fully integrated corporation that both manufactures its products and sells them at the retail level, its echelons will extend all the way to its retail outlets.

Some co-ordination is needed between the inventories of any particular or the different echelons. Since the inventory at each echelon(except the last one)is used to replenish the inventory at the next echelon as needed, the inventory level currently needed at an echelon is affected by how soon replenishment will be needed at the various locations for the next echelon.

The analysis of multi-echelon inventory system is a major challenge. However, considerable innovative research (tracing back to the middle of the 20th century) has been conducted to develop tractable multi-echelon inventory models. With the growing prominence of multi-echelon inventory systems, this undoubtedly will continue to be an active area of research.

Another key concept that has emerged in the global economy is that of supply chain management. This concept pushes the management of multi-echelon inventory system one step further by also considering what need to happen to bring a product into inventory system in the first place. However, as with inventory management, the main purpose still is to win the competitive battle against other companies in bringing the product to the customers as promptly as possible.

A supply chain is a network of facilities that procure raw materials, transform them into intermediate goods and then final products, and finally deliver the products to customers through a distribution system that includes (probably multi-echelon) inventory system. Thus Supply Chain consists of all parties involved directely in fulfilling a customer request. The supply chain includes manufacturers, suppliers, transporters, warehouses, retailers and customers themselves. Whithin each organization such as manufacturers the Supply Chain includes all functions involved in receiving and filling the customer request. These functions includes but are not limited to new product developmnet marketing, operations, distribution, finance and customer service.

A supply chain spans procurement, manufacturing, and distribution. Since inventories are needed at all these stages, effective inventory management is one key element in managing supply chain. To fill orders efficiently, it is necessary to understand the linkages and inter-relationship of all the key elements of supply chain. Therefore, integrated management of the supply chain has become a key success factor for some of today's leading companies.

The Hewlett-Packard was one of the early pioneers in using operation research to help implement effective supply chain management throughout the corporation. Wal-Mart, Dell computers are other major players in the field of Supply Chain Management Systems

A typical supply chain may have variety of stages. The different stages of SC (Supply Chain) are:

- Customers
- Retailers
- Wholesalers/ Distributors
- Manufacturers
- Compnents/ Raw material suppliers

## THE OBJECTIVE OF A SUPPLY CHAIN

The objective of every supply chain is to maximize the overall value generated. The value a supply chain generate is the difference between what the final product worth and the effort the supply chain expends in filling the customer request.

In most of the Commercial Supply chains the value will be strongly correlated with the supply chain profitability which is computed as the difference the revenue generated from the customer and the overall cost across the supply chain. All flows of information, products or funds generate costs within the supply chain.

## DECISION PROCESS IN SCM

**Supply chain decision phases** are categorized based on frequency with which they are made and the time frame they take into account. Three major decision phases involved are:

1. Supply Chain Strategy or Design
2. Supply Chain Planning
3. Supply Chain Operation

### Supply Chain Strategy or Design

During this phase, a company decides how to structure the supply chain over the next several years. It decides the company's SC configuration and allocation of resources. This also includes the location and capacities of warehouse and production. Consequently, when companies make these decisions, they may take into account uncertainty in anticipated market conditions over the next few years.

### Supply Chain Planning

For decisions made during this phase, the time frame considered is a quarter to a year. With the fixed SC configuration the planning phase starts with forecasting of demand for the next few years in different markets. As a result of the planning phase the companies define a set of operating policies that govern short term operations.

### Supply Chain Operation

The time horizon here is weekly or daily. During this phase companies make decisions regarding individual customer orders. At the operational level, supply chain configuration is fixed and planning polices are already defined. The goal of supply chain operations is to handle incoming customer's orders in the best possisble manner. Because operational decisions are being made in the short term (minutes, hours or days) there is less uncertinty about demand information.

The design, planning and operation of a supply chain have a strong impact on overall profitability and success.

## PROCESS VIEW OF A SUPPLY CHAIN

As per definition **Supply Chain** is a sequences of processes and flows that takes place within and between different stages and combine to fill a cutomer need for a product. There are two different ways to view the processes performed in a Supply Chain:

- Cycle View
- Push/Pull View

### Cycle View of Supply Chain

The processes in the supply chain are divided into a series of cycles, each performed at the interface between two successive stages of the supply chain.

Given the five stages of supply chain (supplier, manufacturer, Distributor, Retailer and Customer), all supply chain processes can be broken into the following four process cycles:

- Customer order cycle
- Replenishment cycle
- Manufacturing cycle
- Procurement cycle

Each cycle occurs at the interface between two successive stages of the supply chain.

*Table 1.*

| SRM | ISCM | CRM |
|---|---|---|
| *Source | * Strategic planning | *Market |
| *Negotiate | * Demand planning | *Sell |
| *Supply collaborations | * Field service | |

## Push/ Pull View of Supply Chain

The processes in a supply chain are viewed in two different ways, depending on whether they are executed in response to a customer order or in anticipation of customer orders. Pull processes are initiated by customer order whereas Push processes are initiated and performed in anticipation of customer orders.

## SUPPLY CHAIN MACRO PROCESSES IN A FIRM

All supply chain processes in a firm can be classified into the following three Macro processes:

1.  Customer Relationship Management(CRM)

    All processes that focus on the interface between the firm and its customers.

2.  Internal Supply chain Management(ISCM)

    All processes that are internal to the firm.

3.  Supplier Relationship Management(SRM)

    All processes that focus on the interface between the firm and its suppliers.

## SUPPLY CHAIN PERFORMENCES- STARTEGIC FIT

A company's competetive strategy defines the set of customer needs that it it seeks to satisfy through its products and services. A lack of strategic fit between the competetive and supply chain strategy can result in the supply chain taking actions that are not consistent with customer needs.This leads to a reduction in supply chain surplus and decreasing supply chain profitability. Strategic fit requires that all functions and stages in the supply target the same goal, one that is consistent with customer needs.

## SUPPLY CHAIN DRIVERS AND OBSTACLES

In this section we introduce the four major drivers-facilities, inventory, transportation, and information- that determine the performance of any supply chain. We discuss how these basic drivers of supply chain are used in design, planning and operation process. Some of the obstacles option faced by SC managers in maintaining supply chain.

## Drivers of Supply Chain Performance

The strategic fit discussed earlier requires that a company achieve balance between responsiveness and efficiency in its supply chain that best meets the needs of the company's competetive strategy. To understand how a company can improve supply chain performance in terms of responsiveness and efficiency, we must examine the four drivers of supply chain performance: facilities, inventory, transportation and information. These drivers not only determine the supply chain's performance in terms of responsivenes and efficiency, they also determine whether strategic fit is achieved across the supply chain. Next we define each driver and discuss it's impact on the performance of the supplychain.

- Facilities
- Inventory
- Transportation
- Information

## Facilities

Facilities are the places in the supply chain network, where product is stored, assembled or fabricated. Two major types of facilities are production sites and storage sites. The location and capacity of the facilities have direct impact on the supply chain's performance.

## Inventory

Inventory in supply chain means all raw materials, work in process, and finished goods within a supply chain. Inventory is an important supply chain driver because changing inventory policies can dramatically alter the supply chain's efficiency and responsiveness. The trade of between efficiency and responsiveness is essential in all supply chains.

## Transportation

Transportation entails moving inventory from point to point in a supply chain. Transportation can take the form of many combinations of modes and routes, each with its performance characteristics. Transportation choices have large impact on suppy chain responsiveness and efficiency.

## Information

Information consists of data and analysis concerning facilities, inventory, transportation and customers throughout the supply chain. Information is potentially the biggest driver of performance in the supply chain as it directly affects each of the other drivers. Information presents management with the opportunity to make supply chains more responsive and efficient.

## INVENTORY CONTROL IN SUPPLY CHAIN

To aid in supply chain management, multi-echelon inventory models now are likely to include echelons that incorporate the early part of the supply chain as well as the echelons for the distribution of the finished product. Thus the first echelon might be the inventory of raw materials or components that eventually will be used to produce the product. A second echelon could be the inventory of sub assemblies into the final product. This might then lead into the echelons for the distribution of the finished product, starting with storage at the point or points of manufacture, then at national or regional warehouses, then at field distribution centers, and so on.

The usual objective for a multi-echelon inventory model is to coordinate the inventories at the various echelons so as to minimize the total cost associated with the entire multi-echelon inventory system. This is a natural objective for a fully integrated corporation that operates this entire system. It might also be a suitable objective when certain echelons are managed by either the suppliers or the customers of the company. The reason is that a key concept of supply chain management is that a company should strive to develop an informal partnership relation with its suppliers and customers that enables them jointly to maximize their total profit. This often leads to developing mutually beneficial supply chain contracts that

*Figure 1. A serial two-echelon inventory system*

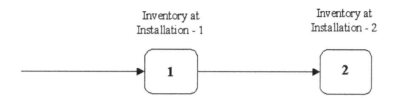

enable reducing the total cost of operating a jointly managed multi-echelon inventory system.

The analysis of multi-echelon inventory models tends to be considerably more complicated than those for single-facility inventory models.

## Basic Structures

### A Serial Two-Echelon System

The simplest possible multi-echelon inventory system is one where there are only two echelons and only a single installation at each echelon. The fig(1)depicts such system, where the inventory at installation 1 is used to periodically replenish the inventory at installation 2.

### A Serial Multi-Echelon System

A serial system with more than two echelons is known as multi-echelon system. Figure 2 depicts this kind of system, where installation 1 has its inventory replenished periodically, then the inventory at installation 1 is used to replenish the inventory at installation 2 periodically, then installation 2 does the same for installation 3, and so on down to the final installation(installation N)

## Extended Structures

### Distribution System

The two models presented previously in this section represent serial inventory system. Many real multi-echelon inventory system are more complicated than this. An installation might have multiple immediate successors, such as when a

*Figure 2. A serial multi-echelon inventory system*

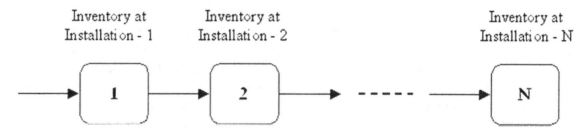

*Figure 3. A typical distribution inventory system*

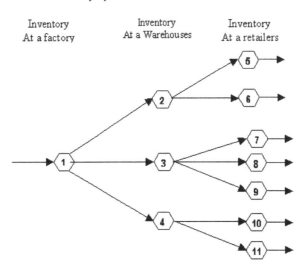

factory supplies multiple warehouses or when a warehouse supplies multiple retailers, such an inventory system is called distribution system. Figure (3) shows a typical distribution inventory system for a particular product.

## Assembly System

Another common generalization of a serial multi-echelon inventory system arises when some installations have multiple predecessor, such as when a sub assembly plant receives its components from multiple suppliers or when a factory receives its sub assemblies from multiple subassembly plants. Such an inventory system is called an assembly system. Figure(4) shows the typical assembly inventory system.

Supply Chain exists in both service and manufacturing organizations, although the complexity of the chain may vary greatly from industry to industry and firm to firm. A force to describe and explain **Supply Chain Management(SCM)** have recently lead to a vast scale research and writing in this field.

SCM is now seen as a governing element in strategy and effective way of creating value for customers. However there is still a lack of possessive information that explain the SCM concept. A very simple example for simple Supply Chain for a single product is a network in which raw material is procured form vendor, transformed into finished goods in a single step and then transported to distribution centers and ultimately customers. Realistic Supply Chain have multiple end products with shared component facilities and capacities. A flow of materials is not always along an arborecent network, various modes of transportation may be considered. As a result SCM is typically viewed to lie between fully vertically integrated firms where the entire material flow is owned by a single firm, and those where each channel members operates independently. Therefore coordination between various operators in the chain is an important factor for its effective management. An effective SCM may be compared with a well- balanced and well-practiced **relay team**. The relationship are the strongest between players who directly pass the portion but the entire team needs to make a coordination effort to win the race.

The major focus of research in SCM is on operational decisions such as inventory control and distribution management in **Supply Chain**.

*Figure 4. Typical assembly inventory system*

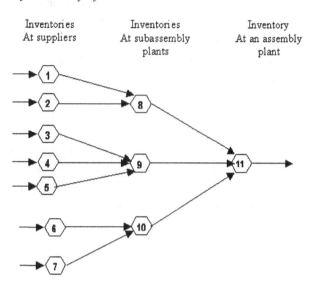

The motivation of present research lies with real life serially connected locations and the need of optimal policies for its efficient maintenance. Even though the numbers of models analyzed within the preview of Supply Chain are limited, The flow of goods through the Supply Chain which are both perishable and non-perishable are studied. Most of the models assume Poisson demand and exponential lead times. Even though this simplifies the positioning of events (demands, placement of orders, replenishments), the deterministic demand at the retailer node is not more realistic. Since the demand is highly fluctuating and its position can be considered as a random process, so in most of the works considered Supply Chain with random type demands and lead times only. There are two types of inventory control policies adopted by researchers in the SCM modeling. First one is an *installation based policy* and in which each location maintains its own inventory and follows different policy in conjunction with its general objective of the SCM. The second type of policy namely, *echelon based policy* consider a whole structure of the SC as a one unit and optimiza-

tion is done for each echelon inventory (The $j^{th}$ echelon inventory consist of the inventory at location j, together with the inventories at each of the location $i > j$). This policy is also termed as **nested policy** and also proved that the nested policy dominates [ see Paul Zipkin (2000)] all non-nested policies.

## The Evolution of Supply Chain Management(Literature Review)

Generally supply chain models has been designed on the basis of inputs and objectives of the study. There are four different kinds of models designed so far

i.   Deterministic analytical models
ii.  Stochastic analytical models
iii. Economic models
iv.  Simulation models

## Deterministic Analytical Models:

Assembly supply chain is the basic structure, based on which model designed as deterministic analytic models are designed. Williams (1981) presents seven heuristics algorithms for scheduling production and distribution operations in an assembly supply chain network. The performance of each heuristic is compared using a wide range of empirical experiments. The objective of the heuristic is to minimize the average cost per period over an infinite horizon. Williams(1983) developed a dynamic programming algorithm for simultaneously determining the production and distribution batch sizes.

Cohen and Lee(1989) present a deterministic, mixed integer, non-linear mathematical programming model, based on economic order quantity (EOQ) techniques, to develop 'global resource deployment policy'. Cohen and Moon (1990) extend Cohen and Lee (1989) by developing a constrained optimization model, called PILOT. The objective function of the PILOT is a cost function consisting of fixed and variable production and transportation costs, subject to supply-capacity assignment, demand and raw material requirement constraints. Newhart, et. al. (1993) design an optimal supply chain using a two phase approach. The first phase is a combination of mathematical program and heuristic model. The second phase is a spread-sheet based inventory model which determines the minimum safety stock required. They considered four facility location alternatives for the placement of various facilities with in the supply chain and decision process is implemented to select minimum inventory investment facility from the alternatives. Arntzen, et. al(1995) develop a mixed integer programming model, called GSCM(Global Supply Chain Model) that can accommodate multiple products, facilities, stages(echelons), time periods and transportation models. GCSM is a black box type model which requires (1) bills of materials (2) demand volumes (3) costs and taxes and(4) activity day requirements as input. The output comprises

(a) The number and location of distribution centers

(b) The customer-distribution center assignment

(c) The number of echelons (amount of vertical integration)

(d) The product-plant assignment .

Voudouris(1996) develops a mathematical model designed to improve efficiency and responsiveness in a supply chain. This model maximizes system flexibility, using the difference between capacities and utilization of the two prime resources namely *inventory* and *activities*. Inventory resources are directly proportional to inventory on hand and activity resources are computed by the resources required to maintain material flow. For this mathematical model inputs are:(i) product-based resource consumption data, (ii) bill-of-material information and the outputs are:(a) a production, shipping, and delivery schedule for each product and (b) target inventory levels for each product.

## Stochastic Analytical Models

Stochastic modeling in SCM is an active research area started around 1985. In real life supply chain in any business involves random phenomena in terms of demand, supply and material flow.

The first work in this direction was initiated by Cohen and Lee(1988). They develop a stochastic model for establishing a material requirement policy(MRP) for all materials for every stage in the supply chain production system. The authors use four different cost based sub models.

(a) Material control

Input: Lead times, fill rates, bill of materials, cost data and production requirements.

Output: Material ordering quantities, reorder intervals and estimated response times.

(b)   Production control

Input: Material response times.
Output: Production lot sizes and lead times for each product

(c)   Finished goods stock

Input: Cost data, fill rate, production lead times and demand data.
Output: Economic order size and quantity for each product.

(d)   Distribution

Input: Transportation time requirements, demand data, cost data, network data and fill rate objectives.
Output: Inventory ordering policy for each distribution facility.

Each of these sub-models is based on a minimum cost objective. In the final computational step, an approximate optimal ordering policies using a mathematical programming which minimizes the total sum of the costs for each of the four sub-models.

Lee and Billington (1993) develop a heuristic stochastic model for managing material flows on site-by-site basis. Given a material ordering policy, the model tries to determine the service level for each product at each facility or for a given service level at each facility the material ordering policy is determined.

Lee, et. al.(1995) develop a stochastic periodic review, order-up-to inventory model to develop a procedure for process localization in the supply chain for **Hewlett-Packard**. The authors propose an approach to operational and delivery process that consider differences in languages, environment and governments. They came with optimal solutions with low cost and highest customer service levels.

Pyke and Cohen (1993) develop a mathematical programming model for an integrated supply chain using stochastic sub-models to calculate the values of the included random variables. They consider a three level supply chain, consisting of one product, one manufacturing facility, one warehousing facility and one retailer. The model studies the optimization principles to minimize the total cost subject to a service level constraint and holds the setup times, processing times and replenishment lead times constant.

The same author extend their work (1993 and 1994) by including more complicated production network. They again consider an integrated supply chain with one manufacturing facility, one warehouse and one retailer but multiple product types, Approximate economic reorder interval, replenishment batch sizes and the order-up-to product levels for a particular supply chain network. Tzafestas and Kapsiotis(1994) utilize a deterministic mathematical programming approach to optimize a supply chain, then use simulation techniques to analyze a numerical example of their optimization model. In this work the author perform the optimization under three different scenarios.

1.   Manufacturing facility optimization: Under this scenario, the objective is to minimize the total cost incurred by the manufacturing facility only, the costs experienced by other facility is ignored.

2.   Global supply chain optimization: This scenario assumes a cooperative relationship among all stages of the supply chain and therefore minimize the total operational cost of the chain as a whole.

3.   Decentralized optimization: This scenario optimizes each of the supply chain components individually and thus minimizes the cost experienced by each level.

Towill and Del Vecchio(1994) consider the application of filter theory and simulation to the study of supply chains. In this research, the authors compare filter characteristics of supply chains to analyze various supply chain responses to randomness in the demand pattern. These responses are then compared using simulation, in order to specify the minimum safety stock requirements that achieve a particular desired service level. Lee and Feitzinger(1995) develop a analytical model to analyze product configuration for postponement, assuming stochastic product demands. The authors assume a manufacturing process with I number of production steps that may be performed at a factory or one of the M number of distribution centers. The problem is to determine a step number P such that steps 1 through P will be performed at the factory and steps (P+1) to I will be performed at the DCs. The authors solve this problem by calculating an expected cost for the various product configuration, as a sum of inventory, freight, customs, setup, and processing costs. The optimal value of P is the one that minimizes the sum of these costs.

Finally Lee, et. al. (1997) develop stochastic mathematical model describing the 'Bull-whip effect', which is defined as the phenomenon in which the variance of the buyer demand becomes increasingly amplified and distorted at each echelon upwards throughout the supply chain. That is the actual variance and magnitude of the orders at each echelon is increasingly higher than the variance and magnitude of the sales, and that this phenomenon propagates upstream with in the chain. In this research, the authors develop stochastic analytical models describing the four causes of the Bull-whip effect and show how these causes contribute to the effect.

## Economic Models

Christy and Grout (1994) develop an economic, game-theoretic framework for modeling the buyer-supplier relationship in a supply chain. The basis of this work is a 2x2 supply chain 'relationship matrix', which may be used to identify conditions under which each type of relationship is desired. These conditions range from high to low process specificity, and from high to low product specificity. Thus, the relative risks assumed by the buyer and the supplier are captured within the matrix. For example if the process specificity is low, then the supplier assumes the risk. For each of the four quadrants, the authors go on to assign appropriate techniques for modeling the buyer-supplier relationship.

## Simulation Model

Towill(1991) and Towill, et. al. (1992) use simulation techniques to evaluate the effects of various supply chain strategies on demand amplification. The strategies investigated are as follows.

1. Eliminating the distribution echelon of the supply chain, by including the distribution function in the manufacturing echelon.
2. Integrating the flow of information throughout the supply chain.
3. Implementing the Just-In-Time (JIT) inventory policy to reduce time delays.
4. Improving the movement of intermediate products and materials by modifying the order quantity procedures.
5. Modifying the parameters of the existing order quantity procedures. The objective of the simulation model is to determine which strategies are the most effective in smoothing the variations in the demand pattern. The Just-in-time strategy and the echelon removal strategy were observed to be the most effective in smoothing demand variations.

Wikner, et. al. (1991) examine five supply chain improvement strategies, then implement these strategies on a three-stage reference supply chain model. The five strategies are

1. Fine-tuning the existing decision rules.
2. Reducing the delays at and within each stage of the supply chain .
3. Eliminating the distribution stage from the supply chain.
4. Improving the decision rules at each stage of the supply chain.
5. Integrating the flow of information, and separating demands into a 'real' orders, which are true market demands, and 'cover' orders, which are orders that bolster safety stocks.

Their reference model includes a single factory, distribution facilities and retailers. The implementation of each of the five different strategies is carried out using simulation, the results of which are then used to determine the effects of the various strategies on minimizing demand fluctuations. The authors conclude that the most effective improvement strategy is strategy (5), improving the flow of information at all levels throughout the chain, and separating orders.

Most of the articles in the literature deal with two types of inventory policies.

i. Installation based
ii. Echelon based, in serial, assembly, tree and general - connected SC.

A new viable inventory policy, which is neither installation based nor echelon based, but have the characteristics of both of them is need of the hour.

## CONCLUSION

Although current research in multi-echelon inventory based supply chain inventory problems show considerable promise in reduce inventories with increased customer service the studies have several notable limitations. First, these studies largely ignore the production side of the supply chain. They concentrate on finished good stockpile and policies are given to manage them effectively. Second, even on the distribution side, almost all published results assumed an arborescence structure, i.e. each site receives resupply from only one higher level site but can distribute to several lower levels. Third the researchers are largely focussed on inventory system only, but in logistic-system theory, the transportation and inventory are the primary components of the order fulfillment process in terms of cost and service levels. Fourth, most of the models under inventory theoretic paradigm are very restrictive in nature in terms of known forms of demand (Poisson and Compound Poisson) or lead time or both, often quite contrary to the real situation.

## REFERENCES

Arntzen, B. C., Brown, G. G., Harrison, T. P., & Trafton, L. L. (1995). Global Supply Chain Management at Digital Equipment Corporation. *Interfaces*, *25*, 69–93. doi:10.1287/inte.25.1.69

Axaster, S. (1993a). Exact and approximate evaluation of batch-ordering policies for two level inventory systems. *Operations Research*, *41*, 777–785. doi:10.1287/opre.41.4.777

Beamon, B. M. (1998). Supply Chain Design and Analysis: Models and Methods. *International Journal of Production Economics*, *55*(3), 281–294. doi:10.1016/S0925-5273(98)00079-6

Bovet, D. M., & Frentzel, D. G. (1999). The ValueNet: connecting for Profitable Growth. Supply Chain Management Review, (Fall), 96-104.

Cavinato, J. (2002). What is Your Supply Chain Type. *Supply chain management . RE:view*, (May-June): 60–80.

Christy, D. P., & Grout, J. R. (1994). Safeguarding Supply Chain Relationships. *International Journal of Production Economics, 36*, 233–242. doi:10.1016/0925-5273(94)00024-7

Clark, A. J., & Scarf, H. (1960). Optimal Policies for a Multi-Echelon Inventory Problem. *Management Science, 6*(4), 475–490. doi:10.1287/mnsc.6.4.475

Cohen, M. A., & Lee, H. L. (1988). Strategic Analysis of Integrated Production-Distribution Systems: Models and Methods. *Operations Research, 36*(2), 216–228. doi:10.1287/opre.36.2.216

Cohen, M. A., & Lee, H. L. (1989). Resource Deployment Analysis of Global Manufacturing and Distribution Networks. *Journal of Manufacturing and Operations Management, 2*, 81–104.

Cohen, M. A., & Moon, S. (1990). Impact of Production Scale Economies, Manufacturing Complexity, and Transportation Costs on Supply Chain Facility Networks. *Journal of Manufacturing and Operations Management, 3*, 269–292.

Elango, C. (2001). *A continuous review perishable inventory system at service facilities*. Unpublished Ph. D., Thesis, Madurai Kamaraj University, Madurai.

Elango, C. & Arivarignan, G. (2001). A lost sales inventory system with multiple reorder levels Engineering Simulation, *23*, 74 - 81.

Federgruen, A. (1993). Centralized planning models for multi echelon inventory system under uncertainty . In Graves, S. C. (Eds.), *Handbooks in ORMS* (*Vol. 4*, pp. 133–173). Amsterdam: North-Holland.

Hadley, G., & Whitin, T. M. (1963). *Analysis of inventory systems*. Englewood Cliff, NJ: Prentice-Hall.

Lee, H. L., & Billington, C. (1993). Material Management in Decentralized Supply Chains. *Operations Research, 41*(5), 831–847. doi:10.1287/opre.41.5.835

Lee, H. L., & Feitzinger, E. (1995). Product Configuration and Postponement for Supply Chain Efficiency. In *Institute of Industrial Engineers, Fourth Industrial Engineering Research Conference Proceedings*, (pp. 43-48).

Lee, H. L., Padmanabhan, V., & Whang, S. (1997). Information Distortion in a Supply Chain. *The Bullwhip Effect* . *Management Science, 43*(4), 546–558. doi:10.1287/mnsc.43.4.546

Marien, E. J. (2000). The four Supply Chain Enablers. Supply Chain Management Review, (March- April), 60- 68.

Masters, J. M. (1993). Determination of Near Optimal stock levels for multi-echelon distribution inventories. *Journal of business logistics, 14*(2), 165-195.

Newhart, D. D., Stott, K. L., & Vasko, F. J. (1993). Consolidating Product Sizes to Minimize Inventory Levels for a Multi-Stage Production and Distribution Systems. *The Journal of the Operational Research Society, 44*(7), 637–644.

Peterson, R., & Silver, E. A. (1979). *Decision systems for inventory management and production*. New York: John Wiley and Sons.

Pyke, D. F., & Cohen, M. A. (1993). Performance Characteristics Stochastic Integrated Production-Distribution System. *European Journal of Operational Research, 68*(1), 23–48. doi:10.1016/0377-2217(93)90075-X

Pyke, D. F., & Cohen, M. A. (1994). Multi-Product Integrated Production-Distribution Systems. *European Journal of Operational Research, 74*(1), 18–49. doi:10.1016/0377-2217(94)90201-1

Raafat, F. (1991). A survey of literature on continuously deteriorating inventory models. *The Journal of the Operational Research Society*, *42*, 27–37.

Ross, S. M. (2000). *Introduction to probability models*. Singapore: Harcourt Asia PTE Ltd.

Schwarz, L. B. (1981). Introduction in: Studies in Managemnet Sciences: *Vol. 16. Multi-Level production/inventory control systems* (pp. 163–193). Amsterdam: North Holland.

Shapiro, R. D. (1984). Get Leverage from Logistics. *Harvard Business Review*, (May- June): 199–127.

Silver, E. A. (1974). A control system for coordinated inventory replenishment. *International Journal of Production Research*, *12*, 647–671. doi:10.1080/00207547408919583

Silver, E. A. (1981). Operations research in inventory management: A review and critique. *Operations Research*, *29*, 628–645. doi:10.1287/opre.29.4.628

Towill, D. R. (1991). Supply Chain Dynamics. *International Journal of Computer Integrated Manufacturing*, *4*(4), 197–208. doi:10.1080/09511929108944496

Towill, D. R., & Del Vecchio, A. (1994). The Application of Filter Theory to the Study of Supply Chain Dynamics. *Production Planning and Control*, *5*(1), 82–96. doi:10.1080/09537289408919474

Towill, D. R., Naim, M. M., & Wikner, J. (1992). Industrial Dynamics Simulation Models in the Design of Supply Chains. *International Journal of Physical Distribution and Logistics Management*, *22*(5), 3–13. doi:10.1108/09600039210016995

Tzafestas, S., & Kapsiotis, G. (1994). Coordinated Control of Manufacturing/Supply Chains Using Multi-Level Techniques. *Computer Integrated Manufacturing Systems*, *7*(3), 206–212. doi:10.1016/0951-5240(94)90039-6

Voudouris, V. T. (1996). Mathematical Programming Techniques to Debottleneck the Supply Chain of Fine Chemical Industries. *Computers & Chemical Engineering*, *20*, S1269–S1274. doi:10.1016/0098-1354(96)00219-0

Whitin, T. M. (1953). *The theory of inventory management*. Princeton, NJ: Princeton University press.

Wikner, J., Towill, D. R., & Naim, M. (1991). Smoothing Supply Chain Dynamics. *International Journal of Production Economics*, *22*(3), 231–248. doi:10.1016/0925-5273(91)90099-F

Williams, J. F. (1981). Heuristic Techniques for Simultaneous Scheduling of Production and Distribution in Multi-Echelon Structures: Theory and Empirical Comparisons. *Management Science*, *27*(3), 336–352. doi:10.1287/mnsc.27.3.336

Williams, J. F. (1983). A Hybrid Algorithm for Simultaneous Scheduling of Production and Distribution in Multi-Echelon Structures. *Management Science*, *29*(1), 77–92. doi:10.1287/mnsc.29.1.77

Zipkin, P. H. (2000). *Foundations of Inventory Management*. Boston: McGraw Hill.

# Chapter 23
# Stochastic Modeling of Supply Chain Management Systems

**C. Elango**
*Cardomam Planters' Association College, India*

## ABSTRACT

*Logistics is that part of the supply chain process that plans, implements, and controls the efficient, effective flow and storage of goods, services, and related information from the point-of-origin to the point-of-consumption in order to meet customers' requirements. Supply Chain Management (SCM) is the practice of coordinating the flow of goods, services, information and finances as they move from raw materials to parts supplier to manufacturer to wholesaler to retailer to consumer. This chapter introduces the concept of Supply Chain Management System(SCMS). Two stochastic modeling problems are discussed in this chapter. Poisson demand process with (s,S) installation policy at retailer nodes are assumed to simplify the study. The system performance measures are computed with reference to specific cost structure. The total average annual variable cost is taken as optimization criterion. Numerical examples are provided to illustrate the problem.*

## INTRODUCTION

Our growing global economy has caused a dramatic shift in inventory management in recent years. Now, as never before, the inventory of many manufacturers is scattered throughout the world. Even the inventory of an individual product may be dispersed globally.

A manufacturer's inventory may be stored initially at the point or points of manufacture (one echelon of the inventory system), then at national or regional warehouse (a second echelon) then at field distribution centers (a third echelon), and so on, thus, each stage at which inventory held in progression through a multistage inventory system is called multi-echelon inventory system. In the case of a fully integrated corporation that both manufactures its products and

DOI: 10.4018/978-1-61520-625-4.ch023

Copyright © 2010, IGI Global. Copying or distributing in print or electronic forms without written permission of IGI Global is prohibited.

sells them at the retail level, its echelons will extend all the way to its retail outlets.

Some co-ordination is needed between the inventories of any particular point at the different echelons. Since the inventory at each echelon(except the last one)is used to replenish the inventory at the next echelon as needed, the inventory level currently needed at an echelon is affected by how soon replenishment will be needed at the various locations for the next echelon.

The analysis of multi-echelon inventory system is a major challenge. However, considerable innovative research (tracing back to the middle of the 20th century) has been conducted to develop tractable multi-echelon inventory models. With the growing prominence of multi-echelon inventory systems, this undoubtedly will continue to be an active area of research.

Another key concept that has emerged in the global economy is that of supply chain management. This concept pushes the management of multi-echelon inventory system one step further by also considering what need to happen to bring a product into inventory system in the first place. However, as with inventory management, the main purpose still is to win the competitive battle against other companies in bringing the product to the customers as promptly as possible.

## SUPPLY CHAIN

A **supply chain** is a network of facilities that procure raw materials, transform them into intermediate goods and then final products, and finally deliver the products to customers through a distribution system that includes as (probably multi-echelon) inventory system. Thus, a supply chain spans procurement, manufacturing, and distribution. Since inventories are needed at all these stages, effective inventory management is one key element in managing supply chain. To fill orders efficiently, it is necessary to understand the linkages and inter-relationship of all the key elements of supply chain. Therefore, integrated management of the supply chain has become a key success factor for some of today's leading companies. The Hewlett-Packard was one of the early pioneers in using operation research to help implement effective supply chain management throughout the corporation.

To aid in supply chain management, multi-echelon inventory, models now are likely to include echelons that incorporate the early part of the supply chain as well as the echelons for the distribution of the finished product. Thus the first echelon might be the inventory of raw materials or components that eventually will be used to produce the product. A second echelon could be the inventory of sub assemblies into the final product. This might then lead into the echelons for the distribution of the finished product, starting with storage at the point or points of manufacture, then at national or regional warehouses, then at field distribution centers, and so on.

The usual objective for a multi-echelon inventory model is to coordinate the inventories at the various echelons so as to minimize the total cost associated with the entire multi-echelon inventory system. This is a natural objective for a fully integrated corporation that operates this entire system. It might also be a suitable objective when certain echelons are managed by either the suppliers or the customers of the company. The reason is that a key concept of supply chain management is that a company should strive to develop an informal partnership relation with its suppliers and customers that enables them jointly to maximize their total profit. This often leads to developing mutually beneficial supply chain contracts that enable reducing the total cost of operating a jointly managed multi-echelon inventory system.

The analysis of multi-echelon inventory models tends to be considerably more complicated than those for single-facility inventory models. Supply Chain is a network of facilities and distribution options that performs the functions of procurement of materials, transformation of these materials into intermediate and finished products and the distribution of these finished products to customers. Supply Chain exists in both service and manufacturing organizations, although the complexity of the chain may vary greatly from industry to industry and firm to firm. A force to describe and explain Supply Chain Management(SCM) have recently lead to a vast scale research and writing in this field.

SCM is now seen as a governing element in strategy and effective way of creating value for customers. However there is still a lack of possessive information that explain the SCM concept. A very simple example for simple Supply Chain for a single product is a network in which raw material is procured form vendor, transformed into finished goods in a single step and then transported to distribution centers and ultimately customers. Realistic Supply Chain have multiple end products with shared component facilities and capacities. A flow of materials is not always along an arborecent network, various modes of transportation may be considered. As a result SCM is typically viewed to lie between fully vertically integrated firms where the entire material flow is owned by a single firm, and those where each channel members operates independently . Therefore coordination between various operators in the chain is an important factor for its effective management. An effective SCM may be compared with a well- balanced and well-practiced relay team . The relationship are the strongest between players who directly pass the portion but the entire team needs to make a coordination effort to win the race.

The major focus of our research is on operational decisions such as inventory control and distribution management in Supply Chain. The motivation of our research lies with real life serially connected locations and the need of optimal policies for its efficient maintenance. Even though the numbers of models analyzed with in the preview of Supply Chain are limited, we studied the flow of goods through the Supply Chain which

are both perishable and non-perishable. Most of our models assume Poisson demand and exponential lead times. Even though this simplifies the positioning of events (demands, placement of orders, replenishments). The deterministic demand at the retailer node is not more realistic. Since the demand is highly fluctuating and its position can be consider as a random process, so throughout the thesis we consider Supply Chain with random type demands and lead times only. There are two types of inventory control policies adopted by researchers in the SCM, modeling. First one is an installation based policy and in which each location maintains its own inventory and follows different policy in conjunction with its general objective of the SCM. The second type of policy namely echelon based policy consider a whole structure of the SC as a one unit and optimization is done for each echelon inventory (The j th echelon inventory consist of the inventory at location j, together with the inventories at each of the location i $>$ j). This policy is also termed as **nested policy** and also proved that the nested policy dominates all non-nested policies.

## The Evolution of Supply Chain Management

Generally supply chain models has been designed on the basis of inputs and objectives of the study. There are four different kinds of models designed so far

i.  Deterministic analytical models
ii.  Stochastic analytical models
iii.  Economic models
iv.  Simulation models

## Scope of this Article

Throughout this article we tried new policy almost equivalent to one-for-one policy in a specific sense. The order quantity $Q$ at the lowest level (retailer node) will act as a fundamental quantity of ordering in the upward location. This policy has the character of both installation and echelon based policy which triggers re-orders in the upward direction in turn flow of goods in the downward directions.

In this article we discuss a model in which a single product is supplied from warehouse to retailer who adopts $(s, S)$ policy for maintaining inventory of his own. The demand at retailer node follows a Poisson distribution with mean $\lambda(> 0)$. Supply to the retailer in packets of $Q = (S - s)$ items is administrate with exponential lead time having parameter $\mu(> 0)$. We assume that the supplier (ware house) acts as a distribution center which adopts $(0, M)$ policy where $M = nQ, Q = S - s, n \in N$. The replenishment of items in terms of pockets (from source) at distribution center is instantaneous from an abundant source(manufacturing unit). In our model the maximum inventory levels M and S are fixed and reorder level s vary such that $S - s = Q$ and $M = nQ, n = 1, 2, \ldots [\dfrac{M}{Q}]$ where $[x]$ denotes the integral part of the real number x. The optimal value of $s^*$, $Q^*$ and $n^*$ are obtained.

According to the above definition the *on hand inventory levels* over time at both nodes follow random processes. This tandem supply structure is studied for the flow of both perishable and non-perishable goods. The steady state probabilities and the system performance measures are obtained explicitly. The cost function is computed for both the models. By using numerical searching algorithms the optimal reorder points are obtained for various input parameters. Sensitivity analysis are discussed for various cost parameters such as holding cost, setup cost etc. The above said model is extended for the case in which item are of perishable nature.

# NON-PERISHABLE INVENTORY SYSTEM I

## Introduction

A supply chain may be defined as an integrated process wherein a number of various business entities (suppliers, distributors and retailers) work together in an effort to (1) acquire raw materials (2) process them and then produce valuable products and (3)transport these final product to retailers. The process and delivery of goods through this network needs efficient communication and transportation system. The supply chain is traditionally characterized by a forward flow of materials and products and backward flow of information. Within manufacturing research, the supply chain concept grow largely out of two-stage multi-echelon inventory models, and it is important to note that considerable research in this area is based on the classic work of Clark and Scarf (1960). A complete review on this development were recorded by Federgruen(1993). Recent developments in two-echelon models may be found in Axaster.S(1993a). Continuous review Perishable inventory with instantaneous replenishment was considered by Kalpakam, S and Arivarignan, G(1988).

We consider a simple supply chain that is modeled as a single warehouse and multiple retailer system handling a single product. In order to avoid the complexity, at the same time without loss of generality, we assumed identical demand pattern at each node. This restricts our study to design and analyze a tandem network of inventory, which is a building block in the whole supply chain system. The rest of the article is organized as follows. The model formulation for inventory control of item in supply chain is described in subsection 2. Subsection 3, 4 and 5 describes the transient and steady state analysis. Subsection 6 deals with the operating characteristics of the system and subsection 7, the cost analysis for the operation. In subsection 8, some numerical examples are given.

## The Model Description

The inventory control system in supply chain considered in this section is defined as follows. A product is supplied from warehouse to retailer who adopts $(s, S)$ policy. The demand at retailer node follows a Poisson process with parameter $\lambda(> 0)$ . Supply to the retailer in packets of $Q = (S - s)$ items is administrate with exponential lead time having parameter $\mu(> 0)$ . We assume that the supplier (warehouse) acts as a distribution center which adopts $(0, M)$ policy where $M = nQ, Q = S - s, n \in N$ .Eventhough the replenishment of items in terms of packets (from source) at distribution center is instantaneous from an abundant source(manufacturing unit). We assume that the transit time between DC and retailer nodes are negligible. In our model the maximum inventory levels M and S are fixed and reorder level s vary such that $S - s = Q$ and

$$M = nQ, n = 1, 2, ... [\frac{M}{Q}]$$ where $[x]$ denotes the integral part of the real number x. According to the above definition the *on hand inventory levels* at both nodes are random processes.

Notations:

- $f_\alpha^*$ = Laplace transform of any arbitrary function f(t) or matrix A(t) for real $\alpha > 0$ .
- $N^0 = \{0, 1, 2, ...\}$.
- $e' = (1, 1, 1...1)$.
- $Q = S - s$.
- $E = \{(j, q) \, / \, j = 0, 1, 2..., S; q = Q, 2Q, ..., nQ\}$

## Analysis

Let $I_0(t)$ and $I_1(t)$ denote the *on hand inventory level* at retailer node and warehouse (distribution node) respectively at time t . From the assumptions on the input and output process, define $I(t) = (I_0(t), I_1(t))$ then we have

$$\{I(t) : t \geq 0\} = \{(I_0(t), I_1(t)) : t \geq 0\}.$$

is a Markov process with state space E.

Theorem 1:The vector process $\{I(t) : t \geq 0\}$ where $I(t) = (I_0(t), I_1(t))$ for $t \geq 0$ is a continuous time Markov Chain with state space $E = \{(j, q) \, / \, j = 0, 1, 2..., S; q = Q, 2Q, ..., nQ\}$.

Proof:The stochastic process $\{I(t) : t \geq 0\}$ has a discrete state space with order relation $' \leq'$ that $(j, q) \leq (k, r)$ if and only if $j \leq k$ and $q \leq r$ . To prove that $\{I(t) : t \geq 0\}$ is a Markov chain, first we do a transformation for state space E to S such that $(j, q) \rightarrow j + q \in S$ .

Now we may realize that $\{I(t) : t \geq 0\}$ is a stochastic process with discrete state space $S = \{Q, Q + 1, ..., Q + S, ...., nQ + S\}$ . The joint distribution of random variables $\{I(t_1), I(t_2), ..., I(t_n)\}$ and $\{I(t_1 + \tau), I(t_2 + \tau), ..., I(t_n + \tau)\}$ with $\tau > 0$ an arbitrary real number are equal.In particular the conditional probability

$$Pr\{I_n = k \, / \, I_{n-1} = j, I_{n-2} = i, ..... I_0 = 1\} = Pr\{I_n = k \, / \, I_{n-1} = j\}$$

due to the single step transition of states in E.Hence $\{I(t) : t \geq 0\}$ is a continuous time Markov Chain.

Remark:*Since S is finite and all its states are recurrent non-null, S is an irreducible state space. Hence $\{I(t) : t \geq 0\}$ is an ergodic process. Hence* the limiting distribution exists and is posses on E independent of the initial state.

The infinitesimal generator of this process $A = (a(j, q : k, r))_{(j,q),(k,r) \in E}$ can be obtained using the following arguments.

- The arrival of a demand makes a transition in the Markov Process from (j,q) to (j-1,q) with intensity of transition $\lambda$ .
- Replenishment of inventory at retailer node makes a transition from (j,nQ) to (j+Q,

(n-1)Q) with rate of transition $\mu(>0)$.

Hence entities of $A$ are given by

$$
a(j,q:k,r) = \begin{cases}
\lambda & \begin{aligned} &j = S, S-1,...1. \\ &q = nQ, (n-1)Q,...Q. \\ &k = j-1; r = q. \end{aligned} \\
-\lambda & \begin{aligned} &j = S, S-1,...s+1. \\ &q = nQ, (n-1)Q,...Q. \\ &k = j; r = q. \end{aligned} \\
-(\lambda+\mu) & \begin{aligned} &j = s, s-1,...1. \\ &q = nQ, (n-1)Q,...Q. \\ &k = j; r = q. \end{aligned} \\
\mu & \begin{aligned} &j = s, s-1,...0 \\ &q = Q; k = S, S-1,...Q; r = nQ \end{aligned} \\
\mu & \begin{aligned} &j = s, s-1,...0 \\ &q = nQ, (n-1)Q,...2Q \\ &k = S, S-1,...Q \\ &r = (n-1)Q, (n-2)Q,...Q \end{aligned} \\
-\mu & \begin{aligned} &j = 0; q = nQ, (n-1)Q,...Q. \\ &k = j; r = q \end{aligned} \\
0 & \text{otherwise.}
\end{cases}
$$

The infinitesimal generator $A$ is given by

$$
A = \begin{pmatrix}
-\lambda & \lambda & & & & & & \\
& -\lambda & \lambda & & & & & \\
\vdots & \vdots & \vdots & & & & & \\
& & & -(\lambda+\mu) & \lambda & \mu & & \\
& & & & -(\lambda+\mu) & \lambda & \mu & \\
\cdots & \cdots & & & & & & \cdots \\
\cdots & \cdots & & & & & & \cdots \\
& & \mu & & & -(\lambda+\mu) & \lambda & \\
& & & \mu & & & & -\mu
\end{pmatrix}
$$

## Transient Analysis

Define the transition probability function

$$
P_{j,q}(k,r:t) = Pr\left\{(I_0(t), I_1(t)) = (k,r) \mid (I_0(0), I_1(0)) = (j,q)\right\}
$$

The corresponding transient matrix function is given by

$$
P(t) = \left(P_{j,q}(k,r:t)\right)_{(j,q)(k,r)\in E}
$$

which satisfies the Kolmogorov- forward equation

$$
P'(t) = P(t)A
$$

where $A$ is the infinitesimal generator.

From the above equation, together with initial condition $P(0) = I$, the solution can be expressed in the form

$$
P(t) = P(0)e^{At} = e^{At}
$$

where the matrix expansion in power series form is

$$
e^{At} = I + \sum_{n=1}^{\infty} \frac{A^n t^n}{n!}
$$

**case(i):** suppose that the eigen values of $A$ are all distinct. Then from the spectral theorem of matrices, we have

$$
A = HDH^{-1}
$$

where $H$ is the non-singular (formed with the right eigen vectors of A) and $D$ is the diagonal matrix having its diagonal elements the eigen values of A. Now $0$ is an eigen value of $A$ and if $d_i \neq 0, i = 1, 2, ..., m$ are the distinct eigen values then

$$D = \begin{pmatrix} 0 & 0 & . & . & . & . & 0 \\ 0 & d_1 & 0 & . & . & . & 0 \\ \cdots & \cdots & & & & & \cdots \\ \cdots & \cdots & & & & & \cdots \\ 0 & & & & d_{m-1} & & 0 \\ 0 & . & . & . & . & . & d_m \end{pmatrix}.$$

We then have

$$D^n = \begin{pmatrix} 0 & 0 & . & . & . & . & 0 \\ 0 & (d_1)^n & 0 & . & . & . & 0 \\ \cdots & \cdots & & & & & \cdots \\ \cdots & \cdots & & & & & \cdots \\ 0 & & & & (d_{m-1})^n & & 0 \\ 0 & & . & . & . & . & (d_m)^n \end{pmatrix}$$

and

$$A^n = HD^nH^{-1}$$

Using $A^n$ in $P(t)$ we have the explicit solution of $P(t)$ as $P(t) = He^{Dt}H^{-1}$ where

$$e^{Dt} = \begin{pmatrix} 1 & 0 & . & . & . & . & 0 \\ 0 & e^{d_1 t} & 0 & . & . & . & 0 \\ \cdots & \cdots & & & & & \cdots \\ \cdots & \cdots & & & & & \cdots \\ 0 & & & & e^{d_{m-1} t} & & 0 \\ 0 & & . & . & . & . & e^{d_m t} \end{pmatrix}$$

case(ii): Suppose the eigen values of $A$ are all not distinct, we can find a canonical representation as $A = SZS^{-1}$. From this the transition matrix $P(t)$ can be obtained in a modified form. (Medhi, J[?]).

For the input $S = 6, s = 2, Q = 4, M = 12 = nQ$, the transient state probabilities are obtained as follows.

## Steady State Analysis

The structure of the infinitesimal generator $A$ reveals that the state space $E$ of the Markov Chain $\{I(t) : t \geq 0\}$, is finite and irreducible. Let the limiting distribution of the *inventory level* process be defined by

$$\nu_j^q = \lim_{t \to \infty} Pr\{(I_0(t), I_1(t)) = (j, q)\}_{(j,q) \in E}$$

(Cinlar).

Let $\nu = (\nu^{nQ}, \nu^{(n-1)Q}, \ldots \nu^Q)$ denote the steady state probability distribution where $\nu^q = (\nu_s^q, \nu_{s-1}^q, \ldots, \nu_0^q)$ for the system under consideration. For each (j, q), $\nu_j^q$ can be obtained by solving the matrix equation $\nu A = 0$ together with the normalizing condition

$$\sum_{j,q} \nu_j^q = 1.$$

Assuming $\nu_Q^Q = a$ we obtain the steady state probabilities,

$$\nu_Q^q = a \quad \text{for} \quad \nu_Q^q = a \quad q = Q, 2Q, \ldots, nQ \quad \text{for} \quad q = Q, 2Q, \ldots, nQ$$

$$\nu_j^q = a\left(\frac{\lambda}{\lambda + \mu}\right)^{s-j+1} \quad \text{for} \quad \nu_j^q = a\left(\frac{\lambda}{\lambda + \mu}\right)^{s-j+1}$$

$$j = Q-1, Q-2, \ldots 1; q = Q, 2Q, \ldots, nQ \quad \text{for} \quad j = Q-1, Q-2, \ldots 1; q = Q, 2Q, \ldots, nQ$$

$$\nu_0^q = a\frac{\lambda}{\mu}\left(\frac{\lambda}{\lambda + \mu}\right)^s \qquad \nu_0^q = a\frac{\lambda}{\mu}\left(\frac{\lambda}{\lambda + \mu}\right)^s$$
$$\text{for}$$
$$q = Q, 2Q, \ldots, nQ. \quad \text{for} \quad q = Q, 2Q, \ldots, nQ.$$

$$\nu_j^q = a \frac{\mu}{\lambda} \sum_{i=1}^{S-j+1} \left( \frac{\lambda}{\lambda + \mu} \right)^i \quad \text{for}$$

$$\nu_j^q = a \frac{\mu}{\lambda} \sum_{i=1}^{S-j+1} \left( \frac{\lambda}{\lambda + \mu} \right)^i$$

$$j = Q+1, ..., S; q = Q, 2Q, ..., nQ \quad \text{for}$$

$$j = Q+1, ..., S; q = Q, 2Q, ..., nQ$$

where $a = \dfrac{1}{n(1+T)}$ in turn,

$$T = \sum_{j=1}^{Q-1} \left( \frac{\lambda}{\lambda + \mu} \right)^{s-j+1} + \frac{\lambda}{\mu} \left( \frac{\lambda}{\lambda + \mu} \right)^s + \frac{\mu}{\lambda} \sum_{j=Q+1}^{S} \sum_{i=1}^{S-j+1} \left( \frac{\lambda}{\lambda + \mu} \right)^i.$$

## Operating Characteristics

### Reorder Rate

Consider the event $r_i$ of reorders at node i(i=0,1). Observe that $r_0$ - event occur whenever the inventory level at retailer node reaches $s$ whereas the $r_1$ -event occurs whenever the inventory level at DC reaches 0. The mean reorder rate at retailer node is given by

$$\beta_0 = \lambda \sum_{q=Q}^{nQ} \nu_{s+1}^q$$

The reorder rate at the DC is given by

$$\beta_1 = \mu \sum_{j=0}^{s} \nu_j^q.$$

### Mean Inventory Level

Let $\overline{I_i}$ denote the mean inventory level in the steady state at node i (i=0,1). Thus,

$$\overline{I_0} = \sum_{q=Q}^{nQ} \left( \sum_{j=0}^{S} j . \nu_j^q \right)$$

and

$$\overline{I_1} = \sum_{j=0}^{S} \left( \sum_{q=Q}^{nQ} q . \nu_j^q \right)$$

## Shortage Rate

Shortage occur only at retailer node and the shortage rate is given by

$$\alpha_0 = \lambda \sum_{q=Q}^{nQ} \nu_0^q.$$

## Cost Analysis

In this section we discuss the problem of minimizing the steady state expected cost rate under the following cost structure. $k_0$ and $k_1$ are setup costs, $h_0$ and $h_1$ are holding cost per unit item per unit time at retailer, distributor nodes respectively. The long run expected cost rate C(s,Q) is given by

$$C(s,Q) = h_0 \overline{I_0} + h_1 \overline{I_1} + k_0 \beta_0 + k_1 \beta_1 + \alpha_0 g$$

where $h_i$ is the holding cost per unit item per unit time at node i, $k_i$ is the setup cost for node i (i=0,1)and g is the shortage cost per unit shortage . Although we have not proved analytically the convexity of the cost function $C(s,Q)$, our experience with considerable number of numerical examples indicates that $C(s,Q)$ for fixed $Q$ to be convex in $s$. In some cases it turned out to be an increasing function of $s$. Hence we adopted the numerical search procedure to determine the optimal values $s*$ and $Q*$, consequently we obtain optimal $n^* = [\frac{M}{Q^*}]$. Sensitivity analysis of the optimal values by varying the different cost parameters is presented below.

## Numerical Example

In this section we discuss the problem of minimizing the steady state expected cost rate under the following cost structure. We assume $k_1 \geq k_0$, since the setup cost which includes the freight charges could be higher for the larger size order(packets) compared to that of the small one initiated at retailer nodes. Regarding the holding cost $h_1 \leq h_0$, since the holding cost at distribution node is less than that of the retailer node as the rental charge may be high at retailer node. The results we obtained in the steady state case may be illustrated through the following numerical examples. The expected cost rate $C(s,Q)$ for different reorder levels are shown in Tables 1, 2 and 3. We have considered values of parameters for three different cases as shown below.

(i)   $S = 6$,   $M = 12$,   $\lambda = 0.4$,   $\mu = 0.5$
    $h_0 = 0.5$,   $h_1 = 0.3$,   $k_0 = 5$,   $k_1 = 10$,
    $g = 0.5$

(ii)   $S = 6$, $M = 12$,   $\lambda = 0.6$,   $\mu = 0.7$,
    $h_0 = 1$,   $h_1 = 0.8$,   $k_0 = 10$,   $k_1 = 15$,
    $g = 0.4$

(iii)   $S = 10$,   $M = 20$,   $\lambda = 0.5$,   $\mu = 0.7$,
    $h_0 = 0.5$,   $h_1 = 0.2$,   $k_0 = 5$,   $k_1 = 10$,
    $g = 0.3$

For each of the inventory capacity S, the optimal reorder level and optimal cost are indicated by the symbol '*'. We observe that the optimal reorder level is S-1, that is one-for-one order policy is optimal.

For a fixed capacity S = 6,M = 12,and other parameters $\lambda = 0.5$, $\mu = 0.6$ (varying g, $h_0$, $h_1$, $k_0$ and $k_1$ only)the long-run costs are given in tables 3.4, 3.5 and 3.6. The first entry in each cell gives optimal cost rate and the second and third entries are $s^*$ and $Q^*$ respectively.

Figure 4 presents a numerical study to exhibit the sensitivity of optimal values to variation in $g$

(penalty cost) and $h_0$. The optimal cost rate does not change with $g$ but it increases with $h_0$. Here optimal $s^*$ and $Q^*$ are not disturbed.

Figure 5 shows the effect of varying $h_0$ and $h_1$ on the optimal values. Optimal cost rate increases monotonically with increase in $h_0$ and $h_1$, but the $s^*$ and $Q^*$ are not affected.

Figure 6 indicates the effect of varying $k_0$ and $k_1$ on the optimal cost rate. The example shows no deviation in $s^*$ and $Q^*$, but the optimal cost rate increases with both $k_0$ and $h_0$.

Figure 7 indicates the effect of varying the cost parameters $h_0$ and $h_1$ on the optimal cost rate. The optimal cost rate increases with both $k_0$ and $h_0$ at the same time s* and Q* remains constant. The reorder level $s^* = 0$, whenever $k_0 \geq 28h_0$.

In Figure 8, the cost rate is varying(increasing) with that of $k_1$ and $h_1$. The reorder level s* = 0 whenever $k_1 \geq 100h_1$.

## PERISHABLE INVENTORY SYSTEM II

## Model Description

A perishable inventory control system in supply chain considered in this section. A perishable product is supplied from warehouse to retailer who adopts $(s, S)$ policy for maintaining inventory of his own. The life time of each item supplied is exponentially distributed with parameter $\gamma(> 0)$. It is assumed that the items in stock perishes only at the time of handling them at a retailer node. The demand at retailer node follows a Poisson processes with parameter $\lambda(> 0)$. Assume that the maximum inventory level at retailer node S is (fixed). Supply to the retailer in packets of $Q = S - s$ items is administrate with exponential lead time having parameter $\mu(> 0)$. We assume that the supplier(ware house)acts as a distribution center which adopts $(0, M)$ policy where M is fixed quantity. The

*Figure 1.*

| s | Q | C(s,Q) |
|---|---|---|
| 0 | 6 | 4.91 |
| 2 | 4 | 5.06 |
| 3 | 3 | 5.22 |
| 4 | 2 | 4.89 |
| 5* | 1 | 4.15* |

*Figure 2.*

| s | Q | C(s,Q) |
|---|---|---|
| 0 | 6 | 11.66 |
| 2 | 4 | 12.22 |
| 3 | 3 | 12.45 |
| 4 | 2 | 11.59 |
| 5* | 1 | 9.81* |

replenishment of items in terms of packets (from source) at distribution center is instantaneous and hence the optimal reorder level is 0. In our model the maximum inventory levels M and S are fixed and reorder level s vary such that $S - s = Q$ and

$M = nQ + \varepsilon, 0 \leq \varepsilon < Q, n = 1, 2, ... [\frac{M}{Q}]$ where $[x]$ denotes the integral part of the real number x. The cost components of the inventory control system are assumed as follows. There are fixed ordering costs $k_1$ associated with each order initiated from warehouse to source and $k_0$ that of from retailer to warehouse(distribution) regardless of the order size. The holding cost $h_1$ per unit of item per unit time at warehouse and the holding cost $h_0$ per unit of item per unit time at retailer node are considered. As the demands during stock-out

period are lost, we assume a penalty cost $g$ per unit item is incurred at retailer node. According to the above definition the *on hand inventory levels* over time at both nodes are random processes. We fix the following notations for the forthcoming analysis part of our model.

Notations:

- $f_\alpha^*$ = Laplace transform of any arbitrary function f(t) or matrix A(t) for real $\alpha > 0$.
- $N^0 = \{0, 1, 2, ...\}$.
- $e' = (1, 1, 1...1)$.
- $Q = S - s$.
- $E = \{(j, q) / j = 0, 1, 2..., S; q = Q, 2Q, ..., nQ\}$
- $\sum_{k=0}^{j} = \begin{cases} a_0 + a_1 + + a_j & if\ j \geq 0 \\ 0 & if\ j < 0. \end{cases}$

*Figure 3.*

| s | Q | C(s,Q) |
|---|---|---|
| 0 | 10 | 7.15 |
| 5 | 5 | 6.87 |
| 6 | 4 | 6.80 |
| 8 | 2 | 5.89 |
| 9* | 1 | 5.19* |

*Figure 4. Sensitivity analysis: $k_0 = 5$, $k_1 = 10$, $h_1 = 0.3$*

| h0 / g | 0.1 | 0.2 | 0.3 | 0.4 | 0.5 |
|--------|-----|-----|-----|-----|-----|
| 0.2 | 3.302, 5,1 | 3.302, 5,1 | 3.302, 5,1 | 3.302, 5,1 | 3.302, 5,1 |
| 0.4 | 3.945, 5, 1 | 3.945, 5, 1 | 3.945, 5, 1 | 3.945, 5, 1 | 3.945, 5, 1 |
| 0.6 | 4.587, 5, 1 | 4.587, 5, 1 | 4.587, 5, 1 | 4.587, 5, 1 | 4.587, 5, 1 |
| 0.8 | 5.229, 5, 1 | 5.229, 5, 1 | 5.229, 5, 1 | 5.229, 5, 1 | 5.229, 5, 1 |
| 1.0 | 5.872, 5, 1 | 5.872, 5, 1 | 5.872, 5, 1 | 5.872, 5, 1 | 5.872, 5, 1 |

*Figure 5. Sensitivty analysis: $k_0 = 5$, $k_1 = 10$, $g = 0.3$*

| h0 / h1 | 0.1 | 0.2 | 0.3 | 0.4 | 0.5 |
|---------|-----|-----|-----|-----|-----|
| 0.6 | 3.287, 5, 1 | 3.937, 5, 1 | 4.587, 5, 1 | 5.237, 5, 1 | 5.887, 5, 1 |
| 0.7 | 3.608, 5, 1 | 4.258, 5, 1 | 4.908, 5, 1 | 5.558, 5, 1 | 6.208, 5, 1 |
| 0.8 | 3.929, 5, 1 | 4.579, 5, 1 | 5.229, 5, 1 | 5.879, 5, 1 | 6.529, 5, 1 |
| 0.9 | 4.250, 5, 1 | 4.900, 5, 1 | 5.550, 5, 1 | 6.200, 5, 1 | 6.850, 5, 1 |
| 1.0 | 4.571, 5, 1 | 5.221, 5, 1 | 5.871, 5, 1 | 6.521, 5, 1 | 7.171, 5, 1 |

- $$\prod_{k=1}^{j} = \begin{cases} a_1.a_2..a_j & if\ j \geq 1 \\ 1 & if\ j < 1. \end{cases}$$

- $[X]_{pq} = (p,q)^{th}$ element of the matrix $(X)$ where $p,q = S, S-1,...,1,0.$

## Analysis

Let $I_1(t)$ and $I_0(t)$ denote the *on hand inventory level* at warehouse (distribution node) and retailer node at time $t^+$. From the assumptions on the input and output process

$$\{I(t) : t \geq 0\} = \{(I_0(t), I_1(t)) : t \geq 0\}$$

*Figure 6. Sensitivity analysis: $h_0 = 0.5$, $h_1 = 0.3$, $g = 0.3$*

| k0 / k1 | 30 | 35 | 40 | 45 | 50 |
|---------|-----|-----|-----|-----|-----|
| 5 | 5.042, 0, 6 | 5.070, 0, 6 | 5.099, 0, 6 | 5.127, 0, 6 | 5.156, 0, 6 |
| 10 | 5.099, 0, 6 | 5.127, 0, 6 | 5.156, 0, 6 | 5.184, 0, 6 | 5.213, 0, 6 |
| 15 | 5.156, 0, 6 | 5.184, 0, 6 | 5.213, 0, 6 | 5.241, 0, 6 | 5.270, 0, 6 |
| 20 | 5.213, 0, 6 | 5.241, 0, 6 | 5.270, 0, 6 | 5.298, 0, 6 | 5.326, 0, 6 |
| 25 | 5.270, 0, 6 | 5.298, 0, 6 | 5.326, 0, 6 | 5.355, 0, 6 | 5.383, 0, 6 |

*Figure 7. Sensitivity analysis: $k_1 = 30$, $h_1 = 0.5$, $g = 0.3$*

| k0 / h0 | 0.6 | 0.7 | 0.8 | 0.9 | 1.0 |
|---------|-----|-----|-----|-----|-----|
| 5 | 6.782, 5, 1 | 7.103, 5, 1 | 7.424, 5, 1 | 7.745, 5, 1 | 8.066, 5, 1 |
| 10 | 7.044, 5, 1 | 7.365, 5, 1 | 7.686, 5, 1 | 8.008, 5, 1 | 8.329, 5, 1 |
| 15 | 7.306, 5, 1 | 7.628, 5, 1 | 7.949, 5, 1 | 8.270, 5, 1 | 8.591, 5, 1 |
| 20 | 7.435, 0, 6 | 7.852, 0, 6 | 8.211, 5, 1 | 8.532, 5, 1 | 8.853, 5, 1 |
| 25 | 7.492, 0, 6 | 7.914, 0, 6 | 8.337, 0, 6 | 8.759, 0, 6 | 9.116, 5, 1 |

*Figure 8. Sensitivity analysis: $k_0 = 5$, $h_0 = 0.6$, $g = 0.3$*

| k1 / h1 | 0.1 | 0.2 | 0.3 | 0.4 | 0.5 |
|---|---|---|---|---|---|
| 10 | 3.287, 5, 1 | 3.937, 5, 1 | 4.587, 5, 1 | 5.237, 5, 1 | 5.887, 5, 1 |
| 15 | 3.511, 5, 1 | 4.161, 5, 1 | 4.811, 5, 1 | 5.461, 5, 1 | 6.111, 5, 1 |
| 20 | 3.608, 0, 6 | 4.384, 5, 1 | 5.034, 5, 1 | 5.684, 5, 1 | 6.334, 5, 1 |
| 25 | 3.636, 0, 6 | 4.536, 0, 6 | 5.258, 5, 1 | 5.908, 5, 1 | 6.558, 5, 1 |
| 30 | 3.664, 0, 6 | 4.564, 0, 6 | 5.464, 0, 6 | 6.132, 5, 1 | 6.782, 5, 1 |

with state space E is a Markov process. The infinitesimal generator of this process $A = (a(j, q : k, r))_{(j,q),(k,r) \in E}$ can be obtained using the following arguments.

- The arrival of a demand (or) perish of an item makes a transition in the Markov

Process from (j,q) to (j-1,q) with intensity of transition $\lambda$ or $\gamma(> 0)$.

- Replenishment of inventory at retailer node makes a transition from (j,nQ) to

(j+Q,(n-1)Q) with rate of transition $\mu(> 0)$. Hence entities of $A$ are given by

$$
a(j,q:k,r) = \begin{cases}
\lambda + j\gamma & \begin{aligned}&j = S, S-1,...1.\\ &q = nQ, (n-1)Q,...Q.\\ &k = j-1; r = q.\end{aligned} \\
-(\lambda + j\gamma) & \begin{aligned}&j = S, S-1,...s+1.\\ &q = nQ, (n-1)Q,...Q.\\ &k = j; r = q.\end{aligned} \\
-(\lambda + j\gamma + \mu) & \begin{aligned}&j = s, s-1,...1.\\ &q = nQ, (n-1)Q,...Q.\\ &k = j; r = q.\end{aligned} \\
\mu & \begin{aligned}&j = s, s-1,...0\\ &q = Q; k = S, S-1,...Q; r = nQ\end{aligned} \\
\mu & \begin{aligned}&j = s, s-1,...0\\ &q = nQ, (n-1)Q,...2Q\\ &k = S, S-1,...Q\\ &r = (n-1)Q, (n-2)Q,...Q\end{aligned} \\
-\mu & \begin{aligned}&j = 0; q = nQ, (n-1)Q,...Q.\\ &k = j; r = q\end{aligned} \\
0 & \text{otherwise}
\end{cases}
$$

The infinitesimal generator $A$ can be written in terms of sub matrices $A_{jk}$, namely $A = ((A_{jk}))$ where

$$
A_{jk} = \begin{cases}
D & j = k \\
M & k = j+1; j = 1, 2...n-1. \\
M & j = n; k = 1. \\
0 & \text{otherwise}
\end{cases}
$$

with

$$
[D]_{pq} = \begin{cases}
\lambda + i\gamma & p = q+1; i, p = S, S-1,...,1. \\
-(\lambda + i\gamma) & p = q; i, p = S, S-1,...,s+1. \\
-(\lambda + i\gamma + \mu) & p = q; i, p = s, s-1,...,1. \\
-\mu & p = q; p = 0; \\
0 & \text{otherwise}.
\end{cases}
$$

$$
[M]_{pq} = \begin{cases}
\mu & q = p+Q; p = s, s-1,...,0. \\
0 & \text{otherwise}.
\end{cases}
$$

Now the infinitesimal generator of $\{I(t) : t \geq 0\}$ is of the form

$$
A = \begin{pmatrix}
D & M & 0 & 0\cdots & \cdots & 0 \\
0 & D & M & 0\cdots & \cdots & 0 \\
\vdots & \vdots & \vdots & \vdots & \vdots & \vdots \\
0 & \cdots & \cdots & \cdots & D & M \\
M & 0 & \cdots & \cdots & \cdots & D
\end{pmatrix}
$$

## Transient Analysis

Define the transition probability function

$$P_{j,q}(k, r : t) = Pr\left\{(I_0(t), I_1(t)) = (k, r) \mid (I_0(0), I_1(0)) = (j, q)\right\}$$

The corresponding transient matrix function is given by

$$P(t) = (P_{j,q}(k, r : t))_{(j,q)(k,r)\in E}$$

which satisfies the Kolmogorov- forward equation

$$P'(t) = P(t)A$$

where $A$ is the infinitesimal generator.

From the above equation, together with initial condition $P(0) = I$, the solution can be expressed in the form

$$P(t) = P(0)e^{At} = e^{At}$$

where the matrix expansion in power series form is

$$e^{At} = I + \sum_{n=1}^{\infty} \frac{A^n t^n}{n!}$$

(For solution procedure, see Appendix - A)

## Steady State Analysis

The structure of the infinitesimal generator $A$ reveals that the state space $E$ of the Markov process $\{I(t) : t \geq 0\}$, is finite and irreducible. Let the limiting distribution of the *inventory level* process be defined by

$$\nu_j^q = \lim_{t \to \infty} Pr\{(I_0(t), I_1(t)) = (j, q)\}_{(j,q)\in E},$$

where $\nu_j^q$ is the steady state probability for the system for $(j, q) \in E$ (Cinlar). Let $\nu = (\nu^{nQ}, \nu^{(n-1)Q}, ...\nu^Q)$ denote the steady state probability distribution where $\nu^q = (\nu_s^q, \nu_{s-1}^q, ..., \nu_0^q)$ for the system under consideration. For each (j, q), $\nu_j^q$ can be obtained by solving the matrix equation $\nu A = 0$ together with normalizing condition

$$\sum_{j,q} \nu_j^q = 1.$$

Assuming $\nu_0^q = a$ we get

$$\nu_j^q = \frac{a\mu \prod_{k=1}^{j-1}(\lambda + \mu + k\gamma)}{\prod_{k=1}^{j}(\lambda + k\gamma)}$$

for $q = Q, 2Q, ..., nQ; \quad j = 1, 2, ..., (s + 1).$

$$\nu_j^q = \left(\frac{a\mu}{\lambda + j\gamma}\right)\left[\prod_{k=1}^{s}(\lambda + \mu + k\gamma)\prod_{k=s+1}^{Q}(\lambda + k\gamma) - \sum_{k=0}^{j-S+1}\left(\frac{\mu}{\lambda + \mu}\right)^k\right]$$

for $q = Q, 2Q, ..., nQ; \quad j = s + 2, s + 3..., S$

where $a = \left[n(1 + T)\right]^{-1}$, with

$$T = \sum_{j=1}^{s+1}\left(\frac{\mu \prod_{k=1}^{j-1}(\lambda + \mu + k\gamma)}{\prod_{k=1}^{j}(\lambda + k\gamma)}\right) + $$

$$\sum_{j=s+2}^{S}\left(\frac{\mu}{\lambda + j\gamma}\right)\left[\prod_{k=1}^{s}(\lambda + \mu + k\gamma)\prod_{k=s+1}^{Q}(\lambda + k\gamma) - \sum_{k=0}^{j-S+1}\left(\frac{\mu}{\lambda + \gamma}\right)^k\right].$$

## Operating Characteristics

### Reorder Rate

Let $r_i$ denote the occurrence of the reorder event at node $i(i = 0, 1)$. Observe that $r_0$ - event occur whenever the inventory level reaches s, whereas the $r_1$ -event occurs at the DC, whenever the inventory level reaches 0. The mean reorder rate $\beta_0$ at retailer node is given by

$$\beta_0 = \lambda \sum_{q=Q}^{nQ} \nu_{s+1}^q + \gamma \sum_{q=Q}^{nQ} \nu_{s+1}^q.$$

The reorder rate $\beta_1$ at the DC is

$$\beta_1 = \mu \sum_{j=0}^{s} \nu_j^q.$$

### Mean Inventory Level

Let $\overline{I}_i$ denote the mean inventory level in the steady state at node i (i=0,1). Thus,

$$\overline{I}_0 = \sum_{q=Q}^{nQ} \sum_{j=0}^{s} j.\nu_j^q$$

and

$$\overline{I}_1 = \sum_{j=0}^{s} \sum_{q=Q}^{nQ} q.\nu_j^q$$

### Shortage rate

Shortage occur only at retailer node and the shortage rate is given by

$$\alpha_0 = \lambda \sum_{q=Q}^{nQ} \nu_0^q.$$

*Figure 9.* $S = 6$, $M = 12$, $\lambda = 0.4$, $\mu = 0.5$, $\gamma = 0.3$, $h0 = 0.5$, $h1 = 0.3$, $k0 = 5$, $k1 = 10$, $g = 0.5$.

| s | Q | C(s,Q) |
|---|---|--------|
| 2 | 4 | 5.1895 |
| 3 | 3 | 4.9393 |
| 4 | 2 | 4.1541 |
| 5* | 1 | 2.9184* |

*Figure 10.* $S = 6$, $M = 12$, $\lambda = 0.5$, $\mu = 0.6$, $\gamma = 0.4$, $h0 = 0.8$, $h1 = 0.4$, $k0 = 6$, $k1 = 12$, $g = 0.6$.

| s | Q | C(s,Q) |
|---|---|--------|
| 2 | 4 | 7.4234 |
| 3 | 3 | 7.0081 |
| 4 | 2 | 5.7911 |
| 5* | 1 | 4.0150* |

## Cost Analysis

In this section we analyze the cost structure for the proposed model by considering the minimization of the steady state total expected cost per unit time. The long run expected cost rate C(s,Q) is given by

$$C(s,Q) = h_0 \overline{I_0} + h_1 \overline{I_1} + k_0 \beta_0 + k_1 \beta_1 + \alpha_0 g$$

where $h_i$ is the holding cost at node i, $k_i$ is the setup cost for node i (i=0,1)and g is the shortage cost for unit shortage .

For considerably large number of cases the function C(s, Q) revealed a convex structure for the different values of s(or Q). Hence we adopted a numerical search procedure to obtain the optimal value s* for each maximum inventory capacity S. Sensitivity analysis of the optimal values by varying different parameters is presented in the next section.

## Numerical Examples

In this section we discuss the problem of minimizing the steady state expected cost rate under the following cost structure. We assume $k_1 \geq k_0$, since the setup cost which includes the freight charges could be higher for the larger size order(packets) compared to that of the small one initiated at retailer nodes. Regarding the holding cost $h_1 \leq h_0$, since the holding cost at distribution node is less than that of the retailer node as the rental charge may be high at retailer node. The results we obtained in the steady state case may be illustrated through the following numerical examples.

## REFERENCES

Arrow, K. J., Harris, T., & Marschak, T. (1951). Optimal inventory policy. *Econometrica, 19*(3), 250–272. doi:10.2307/1906813

Axaster, S. (1993). Exact and approximate evaluation of batch-ordering policies for two level inventory systems. *Operations Research, 41*, 777–785. doi:10.1287/opre.41.4.777

Beamon, B. M. (1998). Supply Chain Design and Analysis: Models and Methods. *International Journal of Production Economics, 55*(3), 281–294. doi:10.1016/S0925-5273(98)00079-6

Cinlar, E. (1975). *Introduction to stochastic processes.* Englewood Cliff, NJ: Prentice-Hall.

Clark, A. J., & Scarf, H. (1960). Optimal Policies for a Multi-Echelon Inventory Problem. *Management Science, 6*(4), 475–490. doi:10.1287/mnsc.6.4.475

Elango, C. (2001). *A continuous review perishable inventory system at service facilities.* Unpublished Ph. D., Thesis, Madurai Kamaraj University, Madurai.

Elango, C., & Arivarignan, G. (2003). A continuous review perishable inventory systems with poisson demand and partial backlogging . In Balakrishnan, N. (Eds.), *Statistical Methods and Practice: Recent Advances.* New Delhi, India: Narosa Publishing House.

Federgruen, A., & Zipkin, P. (1993). An efficient algorithm for computing optimal policies. *Operations Research, 32*, 1268–1285. doi:10.1287/opre.32.6.1268

Feller, W. (1965). *An introduction to probability theory and its applications (Vol. I).* New York: John Wiley and Sons, Inc.

Hadley, G., & Whitin, T. M. (1963). *Analysis of inventory systems.* Englewood Cliff, NJ: Prentice-Hall.

Kalpakam, S., & Arivarignan, G. (1984). Semi-Markov models in inventory systems. *Journal of Mathematical and Physical Sciences, 5,* S1–S17.

Karlin, S., & Taylor, H. M. (1975). *A first course in stochastic processes* (2nd ed.). New York: Academic press.

Lee, H. L., & Billington, C. (1993). Material Management in Decentralized Supply Chains. *Operations Research, 41*(5), 831–847. doi:10.1287/opre.41.5.835

Lee, H. L., Padmanabhan, V., & Whang, S. (1997). Information Distortion in a Supply Chain. *The Bullwhip Effect . Management Science, 43*(4), 546–558. doi:10.1287/mnsc.43.4.546

Nahmias, S. (1982). Perishable inventory theory: A review. *Operations Research, 30,* 680–708. doi:10.1287/opre.30.4.680

Raafat, F. (1991). A survey of literature on continuously deteriorating inventory models. *The Journal of the Operational Research Society, 42,* 27–37.

Schultz, C. R. (1990). On the Optimality of the (S-1, S) Policy. *Novel Research Logistics, 37,* 715–723. doi:10.1002/1520-6750(199010)37:5<715::AID-NAV3220370510>3.0.CO;2-U

Sivazlian, B. D. (1974). A continuous review $(S, s)$ inventory system with arbitrary inter-arrival distribution between unit demands. *Operations Research, 22,* 65–71. doi:10.1287/opre.22.1.65

Svoronos, A., & Zipkin, P. (1991). Evaluation of One-for-One Replenishment Policies for Multi-echelon Inventory Systems. *Management Science, 37*(1), 68–83. doi:10.1287/mnsc.37.1.68

Yadavalli, V. S. S., Van Schoor Cde, W., Strashein, J. J., & Udayabaskaran, S. (2004). A single product perishing inventory model with demand interaction. *ORiON, 20*(2), 109–124.

Zipkin, P. H. (1991). *Foundations of Inventory Management.*

# Compilation of References

Abad, P. L. (2003). Optimal pricing and lot-sizing under conditions of perishability, finite production and partial backordering and lost sale. *European Journal of Operational Research, 144,* 677–685. doi:10.1016/S0377-2217(02)00159-5

Abad, P. L., & Aggarwal, V. (2005). Incorporating transport cost in the lot size and pricing decisions with downward sloping demand. *International Journal of Production Economics, 95,* 297–305. doi:10.1016/j.ijpe.2003.12.008

Abbas, M. (2009). *ITC's e-Choupal: Landmark in rural deployment.* Retrieved April 15, 2009, from http://www.cxotoday.com/India/Case_Study/ITCs_e-Choupal_Landmark_in_Rural_Deployment/551-99474-1004.html.

Achabal, D. D., Mcintyre, S. H., Smith, S. A., & Kalyanam, K. (2000). A Decision support system for VMI. *Journal of Retailing, 76*(4), 430–454. doi:10.1016/S0022-4359(00)00037-3

Adam, F., & O'Doherty, P. (2000). Lessons from enterprise resource planning implementations in Ireland – towards smaller and shorter ERP projects. *Journal of Information Technology, 15*(4), 305–317. doi:10.1080/02683960010008953

Agrawal, R., Imielinski, T., & Swami, A. (1993). Mining associations between sets of items in massive databases. In *Proceedings of the ACM SIGMOID International Conference on Management of Data*, Washington D.C., (pp. 207-216).

Ahtiala, P. (2004). The optimal pricing of computer software and other products with high switching costs. *International Review of Economics and Finance.* Available online, www.sciencedirect.com

Aishayeb, M., & Li, W. (2003). An empirical validation of object-oriented metrics in two different iterative processes. *IEEE Transactions on Software Engineering, 29*(11).

Akkermans, H., Bogerd, P., & Doremalen, J. V. (2004). Travail, Transparency and Trust: A Case Study of Computer Supported Collaborative Supply Chain Planning in High-tech Electronics. *European Journal of Operational Research, 153*(2), 445–456. doi:10.1016/S0377-2217(03)00164-4

Aladwani, A. M. (2001). Change management strategies for successful ERP implementation. *Business Process Management Journal, 7*(3), 266–275. doi:10.1108/14637150110392764

Al-Ameri, T. A., Shah, N., & Papageorgiou, L. G. (2008). Optimization of vendor-managed inventory systems in a rolling horizon framework. *Computers & Industrial Engineering, 54,* 1019–1047. doi:10.1016/j.cie.2007.12.003

Albus, J. S., & Meystel, A. M. (2001). *Engineering of Mind – An Introduction to the Science of Intelligent Systems.* New York: John Wiley & Sons Inc.

Alexander, E. (1995). *How Organizations Act Together: Interorganizational Coordination.* Amsterdam: Gordon & Breach.

Copyright © 2010, IGI Global, distributing in print or electronic forms without written permission of IGI Global is prohibited.

Alexis, L. (2005). *Enterprise resource planning*. New Delhi, India: Tata McGraw-Hill.

Aljazeera. (2005). *Tsunami slowed time* [Online]. Retrieved April 2008, from http://english.aljazeera.net/NR/exeres/A46E0B05-1DC7-4852-83A1-5B6C1D9521E3.htm

Alleman, G. B. (2002). Agile Project Management Methods for ERP: How to Apply Agile Processes to Complex COTS Projects and Live to Tell About It. In Extreme Programming and Agile Methods: XP/Agile Universe 2002 (LNCS 2418, pp. 70–88). Berlin: Springer Verlag.

Alleman, G. B. (2002). *Architecture–Centered ERP Systems in the Manufacturing Domain*. USA: Nivot.

Allen, D., Kern, T., & Havenhand, M. (2002). ERP Critical Success Factors: an exploration of the contextual factors in public sector institutions. In *Proceedings of 35th Annual Hawaii International Conference on System Sciences*.

Allison, G. T. (1971). Essence of Decision. Boston.

Al-Mashari, M., Al-Mudimigh, A., & Zairi, M. (2003). Enterprise resource planning: a taxonomy of critical factors. *European Journal of Operational Research, 146*, 352–364. doi:10.1016/S0377-2217(02)00554-4

Al-Mashari, M., Ghani, S. K., & Al-Rashid, W. (2006). A study of the Critical Success Factors of ERP implementation in developing countries. *International Journal of Internet & Enterprise Management, 4*(1), 1–1.

Alsène, É. (2007). ERP systems and the coordination of the enterprise. *Business Process Management Journal, 13*(3), 417–432. doi:10.1108/14637150710752326

Alshawi, S., Themistocleous, M., & Almadani, R. (2004). Integrating diverse ERP Systems, A Case Study. *Journal of Enterprise Information Management, 17*(6), 454–462. doi:10.1108/17410390410566742

Alstyne, M. (1997). The state of network organizations: A survey in three frameworks. *Journal of Organizational Computing, 7*(3), 83–151. doi:10.1207/s15327744joce0702&3_2

Ambler, S. (2002). *Agile Modeling: Effective Practices for Extreme Programming and the Unified Process*. New York: Wiley.

Ambler, S. (2008). When IT Gets Cultural: Data Management and Agile Development. *IEEE IT Professional, 10*(6), 11–14. doi:10.1109/MITP.2008.135

Anbazhagan, N., & Arivarignan, G. (2000). Two-Commodity Continuous Review Inventory system with Coordinated Reorder Policy. *International Journal of Information and Management Sciences, 11*(3), 19–30.

Anbuudayasankar, S. P., Ganesh, K., & Mohandas, K. (2008). CORE: a heuristic to solve vehicle routing problem with mixed delivery and pick-up. *ICFAI Journal of Supply Chain Management, 5*(3), 7–18.

Anbuudayasankar, S.P., & Ganesh, K., Tzong-Ru Lee & Mohandas, K. (2009). COG: Composite Genetic Algorithm with Local Search Methods to Solve Mixed Vehicle Routing Problem with Backhauls – Application for Public Health Care System. *International Journal of Services and Operations Management, 5*(5), 617–636. doi:10.1504/IJSOM.2009.025117

Andel, T. (1997). Information Supply Chain: Set and Get Your Goal. *Journal of transportation and Distribution, 8*(2).

Anderson, D. L. Britt., F. E., & Favre, D. J. (1997). The seven principles of supply chain management. Supply Chain Management Review, (Spring), 31-41.

Anderson, P. A. (1983). *Decision Making by objection and the Cuban Missile Crisis*. Boston: Little, Brown.

Andersson, J., & Marklund, J. (2000). Decentralized inventory control in a two-level distribution system. *European Journal of Operational Research, 127*, 483–506. doi:10.1016/S0377-2217(99)00332-X

Anily, S. (1996). The vehicle-routing problem with delivery and back-haul options. *Naval Research Logistics, 43*, 415–434. doi:10.1002/(SICI)1520-6750(199604)43:3<415::AID-NAV7>3.0.CO;2-C

Anupindi, R., & Akella, R. (1993). Diversification under supply chain uncertainty. *Management Science, 39*, 944–963. doi:10.1287/mnsc.39.8.944

Anupindi, R., & Bassok, R. (1996). Distribution Channels, Information Systems and Virtual Centralization. In *Proceedings of MSOM Conference*, (pp. 87-92).

Apostolou, D., Sakkas, N., & Mentzae, G. (1999). Knowledge Networking in Supply Chains: A Case Study in the Wood/Furniture Sector. *Information-Knowledge-System Management, 1*(3/4), 267–281.

Applegate, L. M., McFarlan, F. W., & McKenney, J. L. (1999). *Corporate Information Systems Management: Text and Cases* (5th ed.). New York: McGraw-Hill.

Appuswamy, R. (2000). Implementation issues in ERP. In *I$^{st}$ Intl. Conference on Systems Thinking in Management.*

Archibugi, D., Howells, J., & Michie, J. (1999). *Innovation Policy in a Global Economy.* Cambridge, UK: Cambridge University Press. doi:10.1017/CBO9780511599088

Argyris, C. (1999). *On Organizational Learning* (2nd ed.). Boston: Blackwell Publishing.

Argyris, C., & Schon, D. A. (1978). *Organizational Learning, A Theory of Action Perspective.* Reading, MA: Addison-Wesley Publishing Co.

Aringhieri, R., Bruglieri, M., Malucelli, F., & Nonato, M. (2004). An asymmetric vehicle routing problem arising in the collection and disposal of special waste. *Electronic Notes in Discrete Mathematics, 17*(20), 41–47. doi:10.1016/j.endm.2004.03.011

Arntzen, B. C., Brown, C. G., Harrison, T. P., & Trafton, L. L. (1995). Global supply chain management at Digital Equipment Corporation. *Interfaces, 25*, 69–93. doi:10.1287/inte.25.1.69

Arrow, K. J., Harris, T., & Marschak, T. (1951). Optimal inventory policy. *Econometrica, 19*(3), 250–272. doi:10.2307/1906813

Arthur, L. J. (1997). Quantum improvement in software system quality. *Communications of the ACM, 40*(6), 47–52.

Ashayeri, J., & Rongen, J. M. J. (1997). Central distribution in Europe: A multi-criteria approach to location selection. *The International Journal of Logistics Management, 9*(1), 97–106. doi:10.1108/09574099710805628

Ashish, D. (2009). E-commerce in India. *Pluggedin.* Retrieved April 20, 2009, from http://www.pluggd.in/india/ecommerce-in-india-irctc-contribution-3961/

Askenäs, L., & Westelius, A. (2000). Five roles of an information system: a social constructionist approach to analyzing the use of ERP systems. In *Proceedings of 21st International Conference on Information Systems.* Brisbane, Australia: Association for Information Systems.

Auf der Heide, E. (2004). *Disaster response: Principles of preparation and coordination.* Retrieved March 2008 from http://orgmail2.coe-dmha.org/dr/pdf/Disaster-Response.pdf

Auramo, J., Kauremaa, J., & Tanskanen, K. (2005). Benefits of IT in supply chain management: An explorative study of progressive companies. *International Journal of Physical Distribution and Logistics Management, 35*(2), 82–90. doi:10.1108/09600030510590282

Avison, D., & Fitzgerald, G. (1995). *Information Systems Development, Methodologies, Techniques and Tools* (2nd ed.). London: McGraw-Hill.

Avraham, S. (2001). A framework for teaching and training in the ERP era. *International Journal of Production Research, 3*, 567–576.

Axaster, S. (1993). Exact and approximate evaluation of batch-ordering policies for two level inventory systems. *Operations Research, 41*, 777–785. doi:10.1287/opre.41.4.777

Axsater, S. (2005). A simple decision rule for decentralized two-echelon inventory control. *International Journal of Production Economics, 93–94*, 53–59. doi:10.1016/j.ijpe.2004.06.005

Ayağ, Z., & Özdemir, R. (2006). A Fuzzy AHP Approach to Evaluating Machine Tool Alternatives. *Journal of Intelligent Manufacturing, 17*(2), 179–190. doi:10.1007/s10845-005-6635-1

Azadeh, A., Ghaderi, S. F., & Sohrabkhani, S. (2007). Forecasting electrical consumption by integration of Neural Network, time series and ANOVA. *Applied Mathematics and Computation*, *186*, 1753–1761. doi:10.1016/j. amc.2006.08.094

Babiak, K. M. (2009). Criteria of Effectiveness in Multiple Cross-sectoral Interorganizational Relationships. *Evaluation and Program Planning*, *32*(1), 1–12. doi:10.1016/j. evalprogplan.2008.09.004

Babu, T. K. S., & Dalal, S. S. (2006). ERP Implementation Issues in SMEs: 'Microsoft Great Plains' Implementation in a BPO Organization. *South Asian Journal of Management, 13*(1, Jan.-Mar.), 61-75.

Bain, S. (2008). *Emergent Design: The Evolutionary Nature of Professional Software Development*. Reading, MA: Addison-Wesley.

Bajwa, D. S., Garcia, J. E., & Mooney, T. (2004). An integrative Framework for the Assimilation of Enterprise Resource Planning Systems: Phases, Antecedents and Outcomes. *Journal of Computer Information Systems*, *44*(3), 81–90.

Baldwin, S. (1999). *ERPs Second Wave: Maximizing the Value of ERP-Enabled Processes*. Retrieved May 4, 2008 from http://www.ctiforum.com/technology/CRM/ wp01/download/erp2w.pdf

Ballintify, J. L. (1964). On a basic class of inventory problems. *Management Science*, *10*, 287–297. doi:10.1287/ mnsc.10.2.287

Ballou, R. H. (1978). *Basic Logistics Management*. Englewood Cliffs, NJ: Prentice-Hall.

Ballou, R. H., Gilbert, S. M., & Mukherjee, A. (2000). New managerial challenges from supply chain opportunities. *Industrial Marketing Management*, *29*, 7–18. doi:10.1016/S0019-8501(99)00107-8

Bancroft, N., Seip, H., & Sprengel, A. (1998). *Implementing SAP R/3: How to introduce a large system into a large organization*. Greenwich, CT: Manning Publishing Company.

Banerjee, A. (1986). A joint economic lot size model for purchaser and vendor. *Decision Sciences*, *17*, 292–311. doi:10.1111/j.1540-5915.1986.tb00228.x

Banerjee, A. (2005). Concurrent pricing and lot sizing for make-to-order contract production. *International Journal of Production Economics*, *94*, 89–195. doi:10.1016/j. ijpe.2004.06.017

Banerjee, A., Burton, J., & Banerjee, S. (2003). A simulation study of lateral shipments in single supplier, multiple buyers supply chain networks. *International Journal of Production Economics*, *81–82*, 103–114. doi:10.1016/ S0925-5273(02)00366-3

Barbarosoglu, G., & Yazgac, T. (1997). An application of the analytic hierarchy process to the supplier selection problem. *Production and Inventory Management Journal*, *38*(1), 14–21.

Barnes, C. R. (1997). Lowering Cost through Distribution network Planning. *Industrial Management (Des Plaines)*, *39*(5).

Bates, H., & Slack, N. (1998). What Happen When the Supply Chain Manages You? A Knowledge-based Response. *European Journal of Purchasing & Supply Management*, *4*(1), 63–72. doi:10.1016/S0969-7012(98)00008-2

Beamon, B. M. (1998). Supply Chain Design and Analysis: Models and Methods. *International Journal of Production Economics*, *55*(3), 281–294. doi:10.1016/ S0925-5273(98)00079-6

Beck, K. (1999). Embracing changes with extreme programming. *Computer*, Embracing change with extreme programming, 70–77. doi:10.1109/2.796139

Beck, K. (1999). *Extreme Programming Explained: Embrace Change*. Reading, MA: Addison-Wesley.

Beck, K. (2007). *Implementation Patterns*. Reading, MA: Addison-Wesley.

Beck, K., & Andres, C. (2004). *Extreme Programming Explained: Embrace Change* (2nd ed.). Reading, MA: Addison-Wesley.

Beck, K., & Fowler, M. (2000). *Planning Extreme Programming*. Reading, MA: Addison-Wesley.

Beck, K., et al. (2001). *Manifesto for Agile Software Development*. Retrieved February 10, 2009, from http://agilemanifesto.org

Beecham, M. A., & Cordey-Hayes, M. (1998). Partnering and Knowledge Transfer in the UK Motor Industry. *Technovation*, *18*(3), 191–205. doi:10.1016/S0166-4972(97)00113-2

Ben-Daya, M., & Harigab, M. (2004). Integrated single vendor single buyer model with stochastic demand and variable lead time. *International Journal of Production Economics*, *92*, 75–80. doi:10.1016/j.ijpe.2003.09.012

Bendoly, E., & Jacobs, F. R. (2004). ERP architectural/operational alignment for order-processing performance. *International Journal of Operations & Production Management*, *24*(1), 99–117. doi:10.1108/01443570410511013

Benton, W. C., & Maloni, M. (2005). The influence of power driven buyer/seller relationships on supply chain satisfaction. *Journal of Operations Management*, *23*, 1–22. doi:10.1016/j.jom.2004.09.002

Berger, A. (2009). *Five steps to an eSynchronized Supply Chain*. Retrieved April 27, 2009, from www.accenture.com/NR/rdonlyres/18099CFB-1D5F-4FA7-BBC4-862EC465123D/0/esynchronized_supply_chain_pov_ref.pdf

Berry, D., & Naim, M. M. (1996). Quantifying the relative improvements of redesign strategies in a PC supply chain. *International Journal of Production Economics*, (46-47): 181–196. doi:10.1016/0925-5273(95)00181-6

Berson, A. smith, S. & Thearling, K. (2000). Building Data Mining Applications for CRM. New Dehli, India: Tata McGraw Hill.

Bharadwaj, N., & Matsuno, K. (2006). Investigating the antecedents and outcomes of customer firm transaction cost savings in a supply chain relationship. *Journal of Business Research*, *59*(1), 62–72. doi:10.1016/j.jbusres.2005.03.007

Bhaskaran, S. (1996). *Simulation Analysis of a Manufacturing Supply Chain*. Presented at Supply Chain Linkages Symposium, Indiana University.

Bhattacharjee, S., & Ramesh, R. (2000). A multi-period profit maximizing model for retail supply chain management: An integration of demand and supply side mechanism. *European Journal of Operational Research*, *122*, 584–601. doi:10.1016/S0377-2217(99)00097-1

Bingi, P., Shama, M. K., & Godla, J. K. (2001). Critical Issues Affecting an ERP Implementation. In Myerson, J. M. (Ed.), *Enterprise Systems Integration*. San Francisco: Taylor & Francis.

Biscarri, F., Monedero, I., León, C., Guerrero, J. I., Biscarri, J., & Millán, R. (2008, June). A data mining method based on the variability of the customer consumption: A special application on electric utility companies. In *Proceedings of the Tenth International Conference on Enterprise Information Systems, Volume Artificial Intelligence and Decision Support System (AIDSS)* (pp. 370-374). Barcelona, Spain.

Blackstone, J. H., Jr., & Cox, J. F. (2005). APICS Dictionary, (11th ed., pp. 38). Chicago: APICS: The Association for Operations Management.

Blumenfeld, D. E., Burns, L. D., Daganzo, C. F., Frick, M. C., & Hall, R. W. (1987). Reducing logistics costs At General Motors. *Interfaces*, *17*, 26–47. doi:10.1287/inte.17.1.26

Bock, G. W., Kwan, S. K., Flores, E., Latumahina, D., Cheng, H., & Lam, C. V. (2009). Integrating ERP Systems in a Decentralized Company: A Case Study. *Journal of Information Technology Cases and Research*, *11*(1).

Boehm, B. (1981). *Software Engineering Economics*. Upper Saddle River, NJ: Prentice-Hall.

Boer, L., Wegen, L., & Telgen, J. (1998). Outranking method in support of supplier selection. *European Journal of Operational Research*, *4*, 109–118.

Bogenrieder, I., & Nooteboom, B. (2004). Learning Groups, What type are there? A Theoretical Analysis and an Empirical Study in a Consultancy Firm. *Organization Studies, 25*(2), 287–313. doi:10.1177/0170840604040045

Bohui, P. (2007). *Multi-criteria Supplier Evaluation Using Fuzzy AHP.* Paper presented at the International Conference on Mechatronics and Automation (ICMA).

Booch, G. (1999). *The unified modeling language user guide*. Reading, MA: Addison Wesley.

Booch, G., Rumbaugh, J., & Jacobson, I. (1999). *The unified modeling language user guide*. Reading, MA: Addison Wesley.

Boran, F. E., Genç, S., Kurt, M., & Akay, D. (2009). A multi-criteria intuitionistic fuzzy group decision making for supplier selection with TOPSIS method. *Expert Systems with Applications, 36*(8), 11363–11368. doi:10.1016/j.eswa.2009.03.039

Botta-Genoulaz, V., Millet, P. A., & Grabot, B. (2006). A survey on the recent research literature on ERP systems. *Computers in Industry, 56*(6), 510–522. doi:10.1016/j.compind.2005.02.004

Bovet, D. M., & Frentzel, D. G. (1999). The ValueNet: connecting for Profitable Growth. Supply Chain Management Review, (Fall), 96-104.

Bowersox, D. J., & Closs, D. J. (1996). *Logistics Management*. Hightstown, NJ: McGraw-Hill.

Bowersox, D. J., & Daugherty, P. J. (1995). Logistics Paradigms: The Impact of Information Technology. *Journal of Business Logistics, 16*(1), 65–81.

Bowersox, D. J., & Morash, E. A. (1989). The Integration of Marketing flows in Channels of Distribution. *European Journal of Marketing, 23*, 58–67. doi:10.1108/EUM0000000000546

Boynton, A. C., & Zmud, R. W. (1984). *An Assessment of Critical Success Factors. Sloan Management Review*. University of North Carolina.

Branquinho, J. (Ed.). (2001). *The Foundations of Cognitive Science*. Oxford, UK: Clarendon Press.

Brass, D. J., Galaskiewicz, J., Greve, H. R., & Wenpin, T. (2004). Taking stock of networks and organizations: a multilevel perspective. *Academy of Management Journal, 47*(6), 795–817.

Brehm, L., Heinzl, A., & Markus, M. L. (2001). Tailoring ERP Systems: A Spectrum of Choices and their Implications. In *Proceedings of the 34th Hawaii International Conference on System Sciences.*

Brodheim, E., & Prastacos, G. P. (1980). *Demand, usage and issuing of blood at hospital blood banks. Technical report*. Operations Research Laboratory, The New York Blood Center.

Brodheim, E., Hirsch, R., & Prastacos, G. (1976). Setting Inventory Levels for Hospital Blood Banks. *Transfusion, 16*(1), 63–70.

Brooks, F. P. (1995). *The Mythical Man-Month*. Reading, MA: Addison-Wesley.

Brown, A. W. & Wallnau, K. C. (1998). *The Current state of CBSE.*

Brown, C. V., & Vessey, I. (2003). Managing the next wave of enterprise systems – leveraging lessons from ERP. *MIS Quarterly Executive, 2*(1), 65–77.

Brown, J. S., & Duguid, P. (1991). Organizational Learning and Communities of Practice, Toward a Unified View of Working, Learning, and Innovation. *Organization Science, 2*(1), 40–57. doi:10.1287/orsc.2.1.40

Brown, S. A., & Gulycz, M. (2002). *Performance Driven CRM* (pp. 7–23). New York: John Wiley & Sons.

Brown, W. A., Conallen, J., & Tropeano, D. (2005). Practical insights into MDA: Lessons from the design and use of an MDA toolkit . In Beydeda, S., Book, M., & Gryhn, V. (Eds.), *Model-driven software development* (pp. 403–432). New York: Springer. doi:10.1007/3-540-28554-7_18

Brynjolfsson, E., & Hitt, L. (1996). Paradox lost? Firm-level evidence on the returns to information systems. *Management Science, 42*(4), 541–558. doi:10.1287/mnsc.42.4.541

Brynjolfsson, E., & Hitt, L. (2000). Beyond computation: Information technology, organizational transformation and business performance. *The Journal of Economic Perspectives, 14*(4), 23–48.

Bulka, A. (2001). *Relationship Manager Pattern*. Retrieved January 31, 2009 from http://www.atug.com/andypatterns/rm.htm

Burke, M. (1996). Its Time for Vendor Managed Inventory. *Industrial Distribution*, 85-90.

Burns, O. M., Turnipseed, D., & Riggs, W. E. (1991). Critical success factors in manufacturing resource planning implementation. *International Journal of Operations & Production Management, 11*(4), 5–19. doi:10.1108/01443579110136221

Bylka, S. (1999). A dynamic model for the single-vendor, multi-buyer problem. *International Journal of Production Economics, 59*, 297–304. doi:10.1016/S0925-5273(98)00021-8

Cabral, J., Pinto, J. O. P., Gontijo, E., & Filho, J. Reis (2004, October). Fraud Detection In Electrical Energy Consumers Using Rough Sets. In *IEEE International Conference on System, Man and Cybernetics,* (Vol. 4, pp. 3625-3629).

Cabral, J., Pinto, J., Linares, K., & Pinto, A. (in press). Methodology for fraud detection using rough sets. *IEEE International Conference on Granular Computing.*

Cachon, G. P. (2001). Stock wars: Inventory competition in a two-echelon supply chain with multiple retailers. *Operations Research, 49*(5), 658–674. doi:10.1287/opre.49.5.658.10611

Cachon, G. P., & Fisher, M. L. (1997). Campbell Soup's Continuous Replenishment Program: Evaluation and Enhanced Inventory Decision Rules. *Production and Operations Management, 6*, 266–276.

Cachon, G. P., & Zipkin, P. H. (1999). Competitive and cooperative Inventory Policies in a two stage supply chain. *Management Science, 45*(7), 936–953. doi:10.1287/mnsc.45.7.936

Cäker, M. (2008). Intertwined coordination mechanisms in interorganizational relationships with dominated suppliers. *Management Accounting Research, 19*(3), 231–251. doi:10.1016/j.mar.2008.06.003

Cakravastia, A., & Takahashi, K. (2004). Integrated model for supplier selection and negotiation in a make-to-order environment. *International Journal of Production Research, 42*(21), 4457–4474. doi:10.1080/00207540410001727622

Cakravastia, A., Toha, I. S., & Nakamura, N. (2002). A two-stage model for the design of supply chain Networks. *International Journal of Production Economics, 80*, 231–248. doi:10.1016/S0925-5273(02)00260-8

Camm, J. D., Chorman, T., Dill, F., Evans, J., Sweeney, D., & Wegryn, G. (1997). Blending OR/MS Judgement, and GIS: Restructuring P&G's Supply Chain. *Interfaces, 27*, 128–142. doi:10.1287/inte.27.1.128

Capar, I., Ulengin, F., & Reisman, A. (2004). *A Taxonomy for Supply Chain Management Literature*. Retrieved from http://ssrn.com/abstract=531902

Carmel, E., & Sawyer, S. (1998). Packaged software development teams: what makes them different? *Information Technology & People, 11*(1), 7–19. doi:10.1108/09593849810204503

Carr, A. S., & Smeltzer, L. R. (1999). The relationship of strategic purchasing to supply chain management. *European Journal of Purchasing and Supply Management, 5*, 43–51. doi:10.1016/S0969-7012(98)00022-7

Carvalho, R. A., & Monnerat, R. M. (2007). ERP5: Designing for Maximum Adaptability. In G. Wilson & A. Oram, (Org.), Beautiful Code: Leading Programmers Explain How They Think, (pp. 339-351). Sebastopol, CA: O'Reilly Media.

Carvalho, R. A., & Monnerat, R. M. (2008). Development Support Tools for Enterprise Resource Planning. *IT Professional, 10*, 39–45. doi:10.1109/MITP.2008.100

Carvalho, R. A., Campos, R., & Monnerat, R. M. (2009). ERP System Implementation from the Ground up: The ERP5 Development Process and Tools . In Ramachandran, M., & Carvalho, R. A. (Eds.), Org.), *Handbook of Research on Software Engineering and Productivity Technologies: Implications of Globalisation*. Hershey, PA: IGI Global.

Casati, F., Dayal, U., & Shan, M-C. (2001). E Business Applications for Supply Chain Management: Challenges and Solutions. *IEEE Journal*, 1063-6382 / 01, 71-78.

Cavinato, J. (2002). What is Your Supply Chain Type. *Supply chain management . RE:view*, (May-June): 60–80.

Cetinkaya, S., & Lee, C. Y. (2000). Stock Replenishment and Shipment Scheduling For Vendor-Managed Inventory Systems. *Management Science, 46*(2), 217–232. doi:10.1287/mnsc.46.2.217.11923

Champy, J. (2008). *X-Engineering the Corporation: the Next Frontier of Business Performance*. New York: Warner Books.

Chan, F. T. S., Kumar, N., Tiwari, M. K., Lau, H. C. W., & Choy, K. L. (2008). Global supplier selection: a fuzzy-AHP approach. *International Journal of Production Research, 46*(14), 3825–3857. doi:10.1080/00207540600787200

Chandra, C., Kumar, S., & Smirnov, A. V. (2001). E-management of Scalable Supply Chains: Conceptual Modeling and Information Technologies Framework. *Human Systems Management, 20*(2), 83–94.

Cheesman, J., & Daniels, J. (2000). *UML Components*. Reading, MA: Addison Wesley.

Chen, C. C., Chuck, C. H., & Yang, S. C. (2009, February). Managing ERP Implementation Failure: A Project Management Perspective. *IEEE Transactions on Engineering Management, 98*(2), 189–203.

Chen, I. J., & Paulraj, A. (2004). Understanding supply chain management: critical research and a theoretical framework. *International Journal of Production Research, 42*(1), 131–163. doi:10.1080/0020754031000160 2865

Chen, R. S., Lu, K. Y., Yu, S. C., Tzeng, H. W., & Chang, C. C. (2003). A Case Study in the Design of BTO Shop Floor Control System. *Information & Management, 41*(1), 25–37. doi:10.1016/S0378-7206(03)00003-X

Cheng, E. W. L., Love, P. E. T., Standing, C., & Gharavi, H. (2006). Intention to e-Collaborate: Approach Propagation of Research Propositions. *Indus-trial Management & Data Systems, 106*(1), 139–152. doi:10.1108/02635570610641031

Cheng, H. K., & Koehler, J. (2003). Optimal pricing policies of web-enabled application services. *Decision Support Systems, 35*, 259–272. doi:10.1016/S0167-9236(02)00073-8

Chidamber, S. R., & Kemerer, C. F. (1994). A metrics suite for object-oriented design. *IEEE Transactions on Software Engineering, 20*(6). doi:10.1109/32.295895

Cho, Y., Im, I., Fjermestad, J., & Hiltz, R. (2002). An analysis of online customer complaints: Implications for Web complaint management. In *Proceedings of the 35th Hawaii International Conference on System Sciences*, Big Island, Hawaii.

Choi, K. S., Dai, J. G., & Song, J. G. (2004). On Measuring Supplier Performance under Vendor-Managed-Inventory Programs in Capacitated Supply Chains. *Manufacturing and Service Operations Management, 6*(1), 53–72. doi:10.1287/msom.1030.0029

Choi, T. Y., & Hong, V. (2002). Unveiling the Structure of Supply Networks: Case Studies in Honda, Acura and Daimler-Chrysler. *Journal of Operations Management, 20*(5), 4439–4493. doi:10.1016/S0272-6963(02)00025-6

Chopra, S. & Meindl, P. (2001). *Supply Chain Management: Strategy, Planning and Operation*. New Dehli: Pearson Education Asia.

Chopra, S. (2003). Designing the Distribution Networks in a supply Chain. *Transportation Research Part E, Logistics and Transportation Review, 39*, 123–140. doi:10.1016/S1366-5545(02)00044-3

Choy, K. L., & Lee, W. B. (2002). On the development of a case based supplier management tool for multinational manufacturers. *Measuring Business Excellence, 6*(1), 15–22. doi:10.1108/13683040210420501

Christensen, W. J., Germain, R., & Birou, L. (2005). Build-to-order and Just-in-time as Predictors of Applied Supply Chain Knowledge and Market Performance. *Journal of Operations Management, 23*(5), 470–481. doi:10.1016/j.jom.2004.10.007

Christiansen, P. E., Kotzab, H., & Mikkola, J. H. (2007). Coordination and sharing logistics information in league supply chains . *International Journal of Procurement Management, 1*(1-2), 79–96. doi:10.1504/IJPM.2007.015356

Christiansson, B., & Jacobsson, L. (1999). Component-Based Software Development Life Cycles. Karlstad University, Institution for Information technology, Sweden.

Christopher, M. (2005). *Logistics and Supply Chain Management: Creating Value Adding Networks.* Upper Saddle River, NJ: Pearson publications.

Christoplos, I., Mitchell, J. & Liljelund, A. (2001). Re-framing Risk: The Changing Context of Disaster Mitigation and Preparedness, September 2001. *Disasters journal, 25* (3) 185.

Christy, D. P., & Grout, J. R. (1994). Safeguarding Supply Chain Relationships. *International Journal of Production Economics, 36*, 233–242. doi:10.1016/0925-5273(94)00024-7

Cinlar, E. (1975). *Introduction to stochastic processes.* Englewood Cliff, NJ: Prentice-Hall.

Clark, A. J., & Scarf, H. (1960). Optimal Policies For A Multi echelon Inventory Problem. *Management Science, 6*(4), 475–490. doi:10.1287/mnsc.6.4.475

Clark, A. J., & Scarf, H. (1962). Approximate Solutions To A Simple Multi-Echelon Inventory Problem . In Arros, K. J., Karlin, S., & Scarf, H. (Eds.), *Studies In Applied Probability And Management Science* (pp. 88–110). Stanford, CA: Stanford University Press.

Clark, A., & Scarf, H. (1960). Optimal Policies for a Multi-Echelon Inventory Problem. *Management Science, 6*, 475–490. doi:10.1287/mnsc.6.4.475

Clark, T. H., & Croson, D. C. (1994). H.E. Butt Grocery Company: a leader in ECR implementation. *Harvard Business School Case, 9*, 195–125.

Clemmons, S., & Simon, S. J. (2001). Control and coordination in global ERP configuration. *Business Process Management Journal, 7*(3), 205–215. doi:10.1108/14637150110392665

Cobzaru, M. (2003). *Agent-based Supply Chain Management System.* Unpublished doctoral dissertation, University of Calgary, Calgary, Canada.

Cohen, H., & Lefebvre, C. (Eds.). (2005). *Handbook of Categorization in Cognitive Science.* Amsterdam: Elsevier.

Cohen, M. A. (1976). Analysis of single critical number ordering policies for perishable inventories. *Operations Research, 24*, 726–741. doi:10.1287/opre.24.4.726

Cohen, M. A., & Lee, H. L. (1988). Strategic analysis of integrated production-distributed systems: models and methods. *Operations Research, 36*(2), 216–228. doi:10.1287/opre.36.2.216

Cohen, M. A., & Lee, H. L. (1989). Resource deployment analysis of global manufacturing and distribution networks. *Journal of Manufacturing and Operations Management, 2*, 81–104.

Cohen, M. A., & Moon, S. (1990). Impact of Production Scale Economies, Manufacturing Complexity, and Transportation Costs on Supply Chain Facility Networks. *Journal of Manufacturing and Operations Management, 3*, 269–292.

Cohen, M. A., & Pierskalla, W. P. (1979). Target inventory levels for a hospital blood bank or a decentralized regional blood banking system. *Transfusion, 19*(4), 444–454. doi:10.1046/j.1537-2995.1979.19479250182.x

Cohen, M. A., Pierskalla, W. P., Sassetti, R. J., & Consolo, J. (1979, September-October). An overview of a hierarchy of planning models for regional blood bank management, Administrative Report. *Transfusion, 19*(5), 526–534. doi:10.1046/j.1537-2995.1979.19580059802.x

Cohen, W. M. C., & Levinthal, D. A. (1990). Absorptive Capacity, A New Perspective on Learning and Innovation. *Administrative Science Quarterly, 35*, 128–152. doi:10.2307/2393553

Colette, R., & Naveen, P. (2001). Matching ERP system functionality to customer requirement. IEEE, 1090-705X.

Cooke, P. (2002). *Knowledge Economies: Clusters, Learning and Cooperative Advantage.* New York: Routledge.

Cooper, M. C., Ellram, L. M., Gardner, J. T., & Hanks, A. M. (1997). Meshing Multiple Alliances. *Journal of Business Logistics, 18*(1), 67–89.

Cooper, R. B., & Zmud, R. W. (1990). Information Technology Implementation Research, A Technological Diffusion Approach. *Management Science, 36*(2), 123–139. doi:10.1287/mnsc.36.2.123

Corne, D., Dorigo, M., & Glover, F. (1999). *New Ideas in Optimisation.* New York: McGraw-Hill.

Coronado, A. E., Lyons, A. C., Michaelides, Z., & Kehoe, D. F. (2006). Automotive supply chain models and technologies: A review of some latest developments. *Journal of Enterprise Information Management, 19*(5), 551–562. doi:10.1108/17410390610703675

Cortada, J. W. (1998). *Best Practices in Information Technology, How Corporations Get the Most Value form Exploiting Their Digital Investments.* Upper Saddle River, NJ: Prentice Hall.

Cosmetatos, G., & Prastacos, G. P. (1981). *A perishable inventory system with fixed size periodic replenishments.* Working Paper 80-10-01, Department of Decision Sciences, the Wharton School, University of Pennsylvania.

Costa, L., & Oliveira, P. (2001). Evolutionary algorithms approach to the solution of mixed integer nonlinear programming problems. *Computers & Chemical Engineering, 25*, 257–266. doi:10.1016/S0098-1354(00)00653-0

Cousins, P. D., & Spekman, R. (2003). Strategic supply and the management of inter-and intra-organisational relationships. *Journal of Purchasing and Supply Management, 9*, 19–29. doi:10.1016/S1478-4092(02)00036-5

Crispim, J., & Brandao, J. (2001). Reactive tabu search and variable neighbourhood descent applied to the vehicle routing problem with backhauls. In *MIC'2001 4th Metaheuristic International Conference, Porto, Portugal,* July 16–20.

Crispim, J., & Brandao, J. (2005). Metaheuristics applied to mixed and simultaneous extensions of vehicle routing problems with backhauls. *The Journal of the Operational Research Society, 56*, 1296–1302. doi:10.1057/palgrave.jors.2601935

Crispin, L. (2006). Driving Software Quality: How Test-Driven Impacts Software Quality. *IEEE Software, 23*(6), 70–71. doi:10.1109/MS.2006.157

Crosby, T. (2009). *How Inventory Management Systems Work.* Retrieved May 4, 2009, from http://communication.howstuffworks.com/how-inventory-management-systems-work.htm

Crossan, M., Lane, H., & White, R. E. (1999). An Organizational Learning Framework, From intuition to Institution. *Academy of Management Review, 24*(3), 522–537. doi:10.2307/259140

Currion, P., Chamindra, S., & Bartel, V. (2007). Open source software for disaster management evaluating how the Sahana disaster information system coordinates disparate institutional and technical resources in the wake of the Indian Ocean tsunami. *Communications of the ACM, 50*(3).

Cyert, R. M., & March, J. G. (1963). *A Behavioral Theory of the Firm.* Englewood Cliffs, NJ: Prentice Hall.

D'Avanzo, R., Starr, E., & Lewinski, H. V. (2004). Supply chain and the bottom line: A critical link. *Outlook: Accenture, 1*, 39–45.

D'Souza & Wills. (1999). *Objects, components and frameworks with UML.* Reading, MA: Addison Wesley.

Danese, P., Romano, P., & Vinelli, A. (2004). Managing business processes across supply chain networks: the role of coordination mechanisms. *Journal of Purchasing and Supply Management, 10*, 165–177. doi:10.1016/j.pursup.2004.11.002

Daneva, M. (2004). ERP requirements engineering practice: lessons learnt. *IEEE Software, 21*(2), 26–33. doi:10.1109/MS.2004.1270758

Daneva, M., & Wieringa, R. J. (2006). A requirements engineering framework for cross-organizational ERP systems. *Springer Requirement Engineering Journal, 11*(3), 194–204.

Daniel, E. M., & White, A. (2005). The future of inter-organizational system linkages: findings of an international delphi study. *European Journal of Information Systems, 14*(2), 188–203. doi:10.1057/palgrave.ejis.3000529

Daskalaki, S., Kopanas, I., Goudara, M., & Avouris, N. (2003). Data Mining for decision support on customer insolvency in telecommunications business. *European Journal of Operational Research, 145*, 239–255. doi:10.1016/S0377-2217(02)00532-5

Davenport, T. (2005). The Coming Commodization of PROCESSES. *Harvard Business Review, 83*(6), 100–108.

Davenport, T. H. (1998, July-August). Putting the enterprise into the enterprise system. *Harvard Business Review, 76*(4), 121–131.

Davenport, T. H. (2000). *Mission Critical, Realizing the Promise of Enterprise Systems.* Cambridge, MA: Harvard Business School Press.

Davis, G. B. (1986). An empirical study of the impact of user involvement on system usage and information satisfaction. *Communications of the ACM, 29*(3), 232–238. doi:10.1145/5666.5669

Davis, G., & Olsen, M. (1995). *Management of Information Systems.* New York: McGraw-Hill.

Davis, K. H., & Aiken, P. H. (2000). Data reverse engineering: A historical survey. In *Proceedings of the Seventh Working Conference on Reverse Engineering (WCRE'00)*, 1095-1350, IEEE.

Dawson, J., & Jonathan, O. (2008). Critical success factors in the chartering phase: a case study of an ERP implementation. *International Journal of Enterprise Information, 14*(3).

de Seán, B., Fynes, B., & Marshall, D. (2005). Strategic technology adoption: extending ERP across the supply chain. *Journal of Enterprise Information Management, 18*(4), 427–440. doi:10.1108/17410390510609581

Dearnley, P. A., & Mayhew, P. J. (1983). In favor of system prototypes and their integration into the system development life cycle. *The Computer Journal, 26*(1). doi:10.1093/comjnl/26.1.36

Deif, I., & Bodin, L. (1984). Extension of the Clarke and Wright algorithm for solving the vehicle routing problem with backhauling. In A. Kidder, (Ed.), *Proceedings of the Babson conference on software uses in transportation and logistic management*, Babson Park, (pp. 75–96).

Deloitte Research. (2006). Consumer Business Digital Loyalty Networks: Increasing Shareholder's Value through Customer Loyalty and Network Efficiency. *Deloitte Research,* 1.

Desarbo, W. S., Rao, V. R., Steckel, J. H., Wind, J., & Colombo, R. (1987). A Friction model for describing and forecasting price changes. *Journal of Marine Science, 6*(4), 299–319. doi:10.1287/mksc.6.4.299

Description, U. *Discovery and Integration.* (2009). Retrieved May 12, 2009, from http://uddi.xml.org/

Dethloff, J. (2002). Relation between vehicle routing problems: an insertion heuristic for the vehicle routing problem with simultaneous delivery and pick-up applied to the vehicle routing problem with backhauls. *The Journal of the Operational Research Society, 53*(1), 115–118. doi:10.1057/palgrave/jors/2601263

Dickson, G. W. (1966). An analysis of vendor selection systems and decisions. *Journal of purchasing, 2*(1), 5-17.

Diks, E. B., De Kok, A. G., & Lagodimos, A. G. (1996). Multi-Echelon Systems: A Service Measure Perspective. *European Journal of Operational Research, 95*, 241–263. doi:10.1016/S0377-2217(96)00120-8

Disney, S. M., & Towill, D. R. (2002). A procedure for optimization of the dynamic response of a Vendor Managed Inventory system. *Computers & Industrial Engineering, 43*, 27–58. doi:10.1016/S0360-8352(02)00061-X

Disney, S. M., & Towill, D. R. (2003). The effect of vendor managed inventory (VMI) dynamics on the Bullwhip Effect in supply chains. *International Journal of Production Economics, 85*, 199–215. doi:10.1016/S0925-5273(03)00110-5

Disney, S. M., & Towill, D. R. (2003). Vendor managed inventory and bull whip reduction in a two level supply chain. *International Journal of Operations & Production Management, 23*(6), 625–651. doi:10.1108/01443570310476654

Disney, S. M., Potter, A. T., & Gardner, B. M. (2003). The impact of vendor managed inventory on transport operations. *Transportation Research Part E, Logistics and Transportation Review, 39*, 363–380. doi:10.1016/S1366-5545(03)00014-0

Dong, Y., & Xu, K. (2002). A supply chain model of vendor managed inventory. *Transportation Research Part E, Logistics and Transportation Review, 38*(2), 75–95. doi:10.1016/S1366-5545(01)00014-X

Drabek, T. (1990). *Emergency Management: Strategies for Maintaining Organizational Integrity.* New York: Springer-Verlag.

Dugerdil, P., & Gaillard, G. (2006). Model-driven ERP implementation. In *Proceedings of the 2nd international workshop on model-driven enterprise information systems.*

Duhamel, C., Potvin, J. Y., & Rousseau, J. M. (1997). A tabu search heuristic for the vehicle routing problem with backhauls and time windows. *Transportation Science, 31*, 49–59. doi:10.1287/trsc.31.1.49

Dumbrava, S., Panescu, D., & Costin, M. (2005). A Three-tier Software Architecture for Manufacturing Activity Control in ERP Concept. *International Conference on Computer Systems and Technologies - CompSysTech'05.*

Dunne, A. J. (2008). The impact of an organization's collaborative capacity on its ability to engage its supply chain partners. *British Food Journal, 11*(4-5), 361–375. doi:10.1108/00070700810868906

Dunsmore, H. E. (1984). Software metrics: an overview of an evolving methodology. *Information Processing & Management, 20*, 183–192. doi:10.1016/0306-4573(84)90048-7

Dutta, S., & Kumar, A. (2009). Mahindra & Mahindra's E-Business Initiatives. *ECCH Case Collection.* Retrieved May 12, 2009, from from http://www.asiacase.com/ecatalog/NO_FILTERS/page-ERP-602916.html

Duvall, P. (2007). *Continuous Integration: Improving Software Quality and Reducing Risk.* Reading, MA: Addison-Wesley.

Dyer, J. H., & Nobeoka, K. (2000). Creating and Managing a High-Performance Knowledge-Sharing Network: The Toyota Case. *Strategic Management, 21*(3), 345–367. doi:10.1002/(SICI)1097-0266(200003)21:3<345::AID-SMJ96>3.0.CO;2-N

Dyer, J. H., & Singh, H. (1998). The relational View, Cooperative Strategy and Sources of Interorganizational Competitive Advantage. *Academy of Management Review, 23*, 660–679. doi:10.2307/259056

EAI-Enterprise. (2009). *EAI-Enterprise Application Integration – Solutions from iWay software.* Retrieved April 2009, from http://www.iwaysoftware.com/eai-enterprise-application-integration.html

Eberhart, R. C., & Kennedy, J. (1995). A New Optimizer Using Particle Swarm Theory. In *Proceedings Sixth Symposium on Micro Machine and Human Science,* (pp. 39–43). Piscataway, NJ: IEEE Service Center.

Eberhart, R. C., & Shi, Y. (1998). Comparison between genetic algorithms and Particle Swarm Optimization. In Porto, V. W., Saravanan, N., Waagen, D., & Eiben, A. E. (Eds.), *Evolutionary Programming* (Vol. 7, pp. 611–616). Berlin: Springer. doi:10.1007/BFb0040812

Ehie, I. C., & Madsen, M. (2005). Identifying critical issues in enterprise resource planning (ERP) implementation. *Computers in Industry, 56*(6), 545–557. doi:10.1016/j.compind.2005.02.006

Eisenhardt, K. M. (1989). Building theories from case study research. *Academy of Management Review, 14*(4), 532–550. doi:10.2307/258557

Eisenhardt, K. M. (1992). Making Fast Decision in High-Velocity Environments. *Academy of Management Journal, 32*(2), 543–576.

Elango, C. & Arivarignan, G. (2001). A lost sales inventory system with multiple reorder levels Engineering Simulation, *23*, 74 - 81.

Elango, C. (2001). *A continuous review perishable inventory system at service facilities*. Unpublished Ph. D., Thesis, Madurai Kamaraj University, Madurai.

Elango, C., & Arivarignan, G. (2003). A continuous review perishable inventory systems with poisson demand and partial backlogging . In Balakrishnan, N. (Eds.), *Statistical Methods and Practice: Recent Advances*. New Delhi, India: Narosa Publishing House.

Elbanna, A. R. (2006). The Validity of the Improvisation Argument in the Implementation of Rigid Technology. *The Case of ES Systems .Journal of Information Technology, 21*, 165–175. doi:10.1057/palgrave.jit.2000069

Ellram, L. M., & Cooper, M. C. (1990). Supply Chain Management Partnership and the Shipper – Third Party Relationship. *International Journal of Logistics Management, 4*(1), 1–12. doi:10.1108/09574099310804911

Elston, R., & Pickrel, J. C. (1963). A statistical approach to ordering and usage policies for a hospital blood transfusion. *Transfusion, 3*, 41–47. doi:10.1111/j.1537-2995.1963.tb04602.x

Enterprise Application. (2009). *Enterprise application integration techniques*. Retrieved April 2009, from http://www.cs.ucl.ac.uk/staff/ucacwxe/lectures/3C05-02-03/aswe21-essay.pdf

Enterprise. (2009). *Enterprise resource planning*. Retrieved March 2009, from http://moneyterms.co.uk/erp/

Ericsson, E. H., & Penker, M. (2000). Business modeling with UML business patterns at work. Needham, MA: OMGPress.

ERP Implementation at BPCL. *Case Study.* (2009). Retrieved May 2, 2009, from http://www.icmrindia.org/casestudies/catalogue/IT%20and%20Systems/ITSY005.htm

Esteves, J., & Bohorquez, V. (2007). An updated ERP systems annotated bibliography: 2001-2005. *Communications of AIS, 19*, 386–446.

Esteves, J., & Pastor, J. (2000).*Towards the unification of critical success factors for ERP implementations.* Paper presented at 10th Annual BIT Conference.

Evans, E. (2004). *Domain-Driven Design: Tackling Complexity in the Heart of Software*. Reading, MA: Addison-Wesley.

Fayyad, U. M., Piatetsky-Shapiro, G., Smyth, P., & Uthurusamy, R. (1966).*Advances in Knowledge Discovery and Data mining*. Cambridge, UK: A AAI/MIT Press.

*Federal Express India supply chain.* (2009). Retrieved May 15, 2009, from http://www.scribd.com/doc/2165098/Supply-Chain-Management-at-Fedex-India

Federgruen, A. (1993). Centralized planning models for multi echelon inventory system under uncertainty . In Graves, S. C. (Eds.), *Handbooks in ORMS* (*Vol. 4*, pp. 133–173). Amsterdam: North-Holland.

Federgruen, A., & Zipkin, P. (1993). An efficient algorithm for computing optimal policies. *Operations Research, 32*, 1268–1285. doi:10.1287/opre.32.6.1268

Federgruen, A., Groenvelt, H., & Tijms, H. C. (1984). Coordinated replenishment in a multi-item inventory system with compound Poisson demands. *Management Science, 30*, 344–357. doi:10.1287/mnsc.30.3.344

Federgruen, A., Prastacos, G. P., & Zipkin, P. (1982). *An allocation and distribution model for perishable products*. Research Working Paper 392A, Graduate School of Business, Columbia University, New York.

Feller, W. (1965). *An introduction to probability theory and its applications* (*Vol. I*). New York: John Wiley and Sons, Inc.

Fenton, N. E., & Pfleeger, S. L. (2003). *Software Metrics-A rigorous and Practical approach*. New York: Thomson Publisher.

Finney, S., & Corbett, M. (2007). ERP implementation: a compilation and analysis of critical success factors. *Business Process Management Journal, 13*(3), 329–347. doi:10.1108/14637150710752272

Fisher, M. L., & Jaikumar, L. N. (1981). A generalized assignment heuristic for the large scale vehicle routing. *Networks, 11*, 109–124. doi:10.1002/net.3230110205

Fisher, M. L., & Raman, A. (1996). Reducing the cost of demand uncertainty through accurate response to early sales. *Operations Research, 44*, 87–99. doi:10.1287/opre.44.1.87

Fjermestad, J., & Romano, N. C. Jr. (2006). *Electronic Customer Relationship Management (Advances in Management Information Systems)*. New Dehli, India: Prentice-Hall.

Fowler, M. (2005). *The New Methodology*. Retrieved January 28, 2009 from http://martinfowler.com/articles/newMethodology.html

Fowler, M. (2006). *Continuous Integration*. Retrieved February 8, 2009 from http://martinfowler.com/articles/continuousIntegration.html

Fowler, M. (2008). *AgileVersusLean*. 2008. Retrieved January 12, 2009 from http://martinfowler.com/bliki/AgileVersusLean.html

Franch, X., Illa, X., & Antoni, P. J. (2000). *Formalising ERP selection criteria*. Washington, DC: IEEE.

Frankel, D. S. (2003). *Model driven architecture applying MDA to enterprise computing*. New York: Wiley Publishing Inc. OMG Press.

Frankfurter, G. M., Kendall, K. E., & Pegels, C. C. (1974). Management control of blood through a short-term supply-demand forecast system. *Management Science, 21*, 444–452. doi:10.1287/mnsc.21.4.444

Frédéric, A., & O'Doherty, P. (2000). Lessons from enterprise resource planning implementations in Ireland – towards smaller and shorter ERP projects. *Journal of Information Technology - Regular Paper, 15*(4), 305-317.

Fry, M. J. (2002). *Collaborative and cooperative agreement in the supply chain*. Unpublished Ph.D. Thesis report, University of Michigan, Ann Arbor, MI.

Fulcher, C., Prato, T., Vance, S., Zhou, Y., & Barnett, C. (1995). *Flood impact decision support system for St.* Retrieved March 2008 from http://gis.esri.com/library/userconf/proc95/to150/p118.html

Furomo, K., & Melcher, A. (2006). The importance of social structure in implementing ERP systems: A case study using adaptive structuration theory. *Journal of Information Technology Cases and Research, 8*(2), 39–39.

Gable, G. G., Sedera, D., & Chan, T. (2003). Enterprise Systems Success: A measurement model. In *Proceedings of the 24th International Conference on Information Systems,* (pp.576-576).

Gaiser, T. (1997). Conducting online focus groups: A methodological discussion. *Social Science Computer Review, 15*(2), 135–144. doi:10.1177/089443939701500202

Galasso, F. & Thierry, C. (2008). Design of Cooperative Processes in a Customer – Supplier Relationship: An Approach Based on Simulation and Decision. *Engineering Application of Artificial Intelligence*. doi: 10.1016/j.engappai.2008.10.008

Gallego, G., & Vanryzin, G. (1994). Optimal Dynamic Pricing of Inventories with Stochastic demand Over Finite Horizons. *Management Science, 40*, 999–1020. doi:10.1287/mnsc.40.8.999

Galván, J. R., Elices, A., Muñoz, A., Czernichow, T., & Sanz-Bobi, M. A. (1998, November). System For Detection Of Abnormalities and Fraud In Customer Consumption. In *12th Conference on the Electric Power Supply Industry*, Pattaya, Thailand.

Gamma, E. (1995). *Design Patterns: Elements of Reusable Object-Oriented Software*. Reading, MA: Addison-Wesley.

Ganesh, K., & Narendran, T. T. (2005). CLOSE: a heuristic to solve a precedence-constrained travelling salesman problem with delivery and pickup. *International Journal of Services and Operations Management, 1*(4), 320–343. doi:10.1504/IJSOM.2005.007496

Ganesh, K., & Narendran, T. T. (2007a). CLOVES: A cluster-and-search heuristic to solve the vehicle routing problem with delivery and pick-up. *European Journal of Operational Research, 178*(3), 699–717. doi:10.1016/j.ejor.2006.01.037

Ganesh, K., & Narendran, T. T. (2007b). CLASH: a heuristic to solve vehicle routing problems with delivery, pick-up and time windows. *International Journal of Services and Operations Management, 3*(4), 460–477. doi:10.1504/IJSOM.2007.013466

Ganesh, K., & Narendran, T. T. (2007c). TASTE: a two-phase heuristic to solve a routing problem with simultaneous delivery and pick-up. *International Journal of Advanced Manufacturing Technology, 37*(11-12), 1221–1231. doi:10.1007/s00170-007-1056-2

Ganeshan, R. (1999). Managing supply chain inventories: A multiple retailer, one warehouse, multiple supplier model. *International Journal of Production Economics, 59*, 341–354. doi:10.1016/S0925-5273(98)00115-7

Ganeshan, R., Jack, E., Magazine, M. J., & Stephens, P. (1999). A Taxonomic Review of Supply Chain Management Research . In Tayur, S., Magazine, M., & Ganeshan, R. (Eds.), *Quantitative Models of Supply Chain Management* (pp. 841–878). Boston: Kluwer Academic Publishers.

Gargeya, V. B., & Brady, C. (2005).Success and failure factors of adopting SAP in ERP system implementation. *Business Process Management Journal, Research paper, 11*(5), 501-516.

Gasevic, D., Djuric, D., & Devedzic, D. (2006). *Model driven architecture and ontology development*. Berlin: Springer.

Gattiker, T. F. (2007). Enterprise resource planning systems and the manufacturing-marketing interface: an information-processing theory view. *International*

*Journal of Production Research, 45*(13), 2895–2917. doi:10.1080/00207540600690511

Gavireni, S., Kapuscinski, R., & Tayur, S. (1998). Value of information in capacitated Supply Chains . In Magazine, M. J., Tayur, S., & Ganeshan, R. (Eds.), *Quantitative Models for Supply Chain Management*. Cambridge, UK: Kluwer.

Gavirneni, S. (2001). Benefits of cooperation in a production distribution environment. *European Journal of Operational Research, 130*(3), 612–622. doi:10.1016/S0377-2217(99)00423-3

Gavrilas, M., Ciutea, I., & Tanasa, C. (2001, June). Medium-term load forecasting with artificial neural network models. *CIRED2001, Conference Publication No. 482.*

Gefen, D. (2004). What makes an ERP implementation relationship worthwhile: Linking trust mechanisms and ERP usefulness. *Journal of Management Information Systems, 21*(1), 263–288.

Gentry, J. J. (1996). The role of carriers in buyer-supplier strategic partnerships: A supply chain management approach. *Journal of Business Logistics, 17*, 33–55.

Geoffrion, A. M., & Graves, G. W. (1974). Multi-Commodity Distribution Design by Benders Decomposition. *Management Science, 20*, 822–844. doi:10.1287/mnsc.20.5.822

Gerrard, P. (2007). Test methods and tools for ERP implementations. *Testing: Academic and Industrial Conference Practice and Research Techniques – MUTATION*, 40-46.

Ghodsypour, S.H. & O'brien, C. (1998). A decision support system for supplier selection using an integrated analytic hierarchy process and linear programming. *International Journal of Production Economics, 56-57*, 119–212. doi:10.1016/S0925-5273(97)00009-1

Giannoccaro, I., & Pontrandolfo, P. (2002). Inventory Management In Supply Chains: A Reinforcement Learning Approach. *International Journal of Production Economics, 78*, 153–161. doi:10.1016/S0925-5273(00)00156-0

Giannoccaro, I., & Pontrandolfo, P. (2004). Supply Chain Coordination by revenue sharing contracts. *International Journal of Production Economics*, *89*, 131–139. doi:10.1016/S0925-5273(03)00047-1

Gibson, C. B. (2001). From Knowledge Accumulation to Accommodation. Cycles of Collective Cognition in Work Groups. *Journal of Organizational Behavior*, *22*(2), 121–134. doi:10.1002/job.84

Gibson, N., Light, B., & Holland, C. P. (1999). Enterprise Resource Planning: A Business Approach to Systems Development. In *Proceedings of 32nd Hawaii International Conference on System Sciences*.

Gilsby, M., & Holden, N. (2005). Apply Knowledge Management Concepts to the Supply Chain: How a Danish Firm Achieved a Remarkable Breakthrough in Japan. *The Academy of Management Executive*, *19*(2), 85–89.

Giridhar, C. (2009). India tests RFID waters. *Electronic Busines.* Retrieved May 18, 2009, from http://www.edn.com/article/CA6388858.html

Gjerdrum, J., Shah, N., & Papageorgiou, L. G. (2002). Fair Transfer Price and Inventory holding policies in Two Enterprise Supply Chains. *European Journal of Operational Research*, *143*, 582–599. doi:10.1016/S0377-2217(01)00349-6

Glass, R. L. (1998). Enterprise Resource Planning—Breakthrough and/or term problems. *The Data Base for Advances in Information Systems*, *29*(2), 14–16.

Glover, F., & Gkochenberger, G. (Eds.). (2001). *Handbook in Meta heuristics*. Amsterdam: Kluwer Academic Publishers.

Glover, F., Jones, G., Karney, D., & Klingman, D. & Mote. (1979). An integrated production, distribution, and inventory planning system. *Interfaces*, *9*(5), 21–35. doi:10.1287/inte.9.5.21

Goetschalckx, M., & Jacobs-Blecha, C. (1989). The vehicle routing problem with backhauls. *European Journal of Operational Research*, *42*, 39–51. doi:10.1016/0377-2217(89)90057-X

Goetschalckx, M., & Jacobs-Blecha, C. (1993). *The vehicle routing problem with backhauls: properties and solution algorithms. Technical report.* Georgia Institute of Technology, School of Industrial and Systems Engineering.

Goodhue, D. L., Wixom, B. H., & Watson, H. J. (2002). Realizing business benefits through CRM: Hitting the right target the right way. *MIS Quarterly Executive*, *1*(2), 79–94.

Gorton, I., Thurman, D., & Thomson, J. (2003). Next generation application integration challenges and new approaches. In *Proceedings of 27th Annual International Computer Software and Applications Conference (COMPSAC)*, 585-590, IEEE.

Gosain, S., Zoonky, L., & Yongbeom, K. (2005). The nanagement of cross-functional inter-dependencies in ERP implementations: Emergent coordination patterns. *European Journal of Information Systems*, *14*(4), 371–387. doi:10.1057/palgrave.ejis.3000549

Goswami, K. (2009). RFID Speeds Up Wills Lifestyle Business. *Real CIO World*. Retrieved May 18, 2009, from http://www.cio.in/case-study/rfid-speeds-wills-lifestyle-business

Govindarajan, V., & Gupat, A. K. (2001). Strategic Innovation: A Conceptual Road-map. *Business Horizons*, *44*(4), 3–12. doi:10.1016/S0007-6813(01)80041-0

Goyal, D. P. (2000). *Management Information System Managerial Perspective*. New Delhi: Macmillan India Ltd.

Goyal, S. K. (1997). An integrated inventory model for a single supplier-single customer problem. *International Journal of Production Research*, *15*, 107–111. doi:10.1080/00207547708943107

Goyal, S. K. (2000). On improving the single-vendor single-buyer integrated production inventory model with a generalized policy. *European Journal of Operational Research*, *125*, 429–430. doi:10.1016/S0377-2217(99)00269-6

Goyal, S. K., & Nebebe, F. (2000). Determination of economic production- shipment policy for a single-vendor-single-buyer system. *European Journal of Operational Research, 121,* 175–178. doi:10.1016/S0377-2217(99)00013-2

Goyal, S. K., & Satir, T. (1989). Joint replenishment inventory control: Deterministic and stochastic models. *European Journal of Operational Research, 38,* 2–13. doi:10.1016/0377-2217(89)90463-3

Grady, R., & Caswell, D. (1999). *Software Metrics: Establishing a Company-wide program.* Upper Saddle River, NJ: Prentice Hall.

Graves, S. C., Kletter, D. B., & William, H. B. (1998). A Dynamic Model for Requirements Planning with Application to Supply Chain Optimization. *Operations Research, 46*(3), 35–49. doi:10.1287/opre.46.3.S35

Greis, N. P., & Kasarda, J. D. (1997). Enterprise logistics in the information age. *California Management Review, 39,* 55–78.

Griffin, A., & Hauscr, J. (1996). Integrating R&D and Marketing: A Review and Analysis of the Literature. *Journal of Product Innovation Management, 13*(1), 137–151.

Griffith, D.A., Harvey, M.G. & Lusch, R.F. (2005). Social exchange in supply chain relationships: The resulting benefits of procedural and distributive justice. *Journal of Operations management.*

Grossman, T., & Walsh, J. (2004). Avoiding the pitfalls of ERP system Implementation. *Information Systems Management, 21*(2, Spring), 38-42.

Grudin, J. (1991). Interactive Systems: Bridging the Gaps Between Developers and Users. *Computer, 24*(4), 59–69. doi:10.1109/2.76263

Guide, M. D. A. *V1.0.1.* (n.d.). Retrieved 2003, from Object Management Group Web site http://www.omg.org

Gulati, R., & Oldroyd, J. (2005). The quest for customer focus. *Harvard Business Review, 83*(4), 92–101.

Gulati, R., Nohria, N., & Zaheer, A. (2000). Strategic networks. *American Journal of Sociology, 104*(5), 203–215.

Gumus, M., Jewkes, E. M., & Bookbinder, J. H. (2008). Impact of consignment inventory and vendor-managed inventory for a two-party supply chain. *International Journal of Production Economics, 113,* 502–517. doi:10.1016/j.ijpe.2007.10.019

Gunasekaran, A., & Ngai, E. W. T. (2004). Information systems in supply chain integration and management. *European Journal of Operational Research, 159,* 269–295. doi:10.1016/j.ejor.2003.08.016

Gunasekharan, A., & Ngai, E. W. T. (2004). Virtual Supply Chain Management. *Production Planning and Control, 15*(6), 584–595. doi:10.1080/09537280412331283955

Gupta, R.K. & Chandra, P. (2002). *Integrated Supply Chain Management in the Government Environment.* Technical papers and presentation, Mathematical Modelling and Simulation Division, National Informatics Center.

Haag, S., Cummings, M., & Philips, A. (2006). *Management Information Systems for the Information Age.* New York: McGraw Hill.

Hadley, G., & Whitin, T. M. (1963). *Analysis of inventory systems.* Englewood Cliff, NJ: Prentice-Hall.

Hafeeza, K., Griffiths, M., Griffiths, J., & Naim, M. M. (1996). Systems design of a two-echelon steel industry supply chain. *International Journal of Production Economics, 45,* 121–130. doi:10.1016/0925-5273(96)00052-7

Haimovich, M., & Rinnooy Kan, A. H. G. (1985). Bounds and Heuristics for Capacitated Routing Problems. *Mathematics of Operations Research, 10*(4), 527–542. doi:10.1287/moor.10.4.527

Halse, K. (1992). *Modeling and solving complex vehicle routing problems.* PhD thesis, Institute of Mathematical Statistics and Operations Research (IMSOR), Technical University of Denmark.

Hammer, M., & Champy, J. (1994). *Reengineering the Corporation*. London: Nicholas Brealy Publishing.

Hammond, J. H. (1990). Quick response in the apparel industry. Harvard Business School Note N9-690-038, Cambridge, MA.

Hand, J. D. (2001). Prospecting for gems in credit card data. *IMA Journal of Management Mathematics, 12*, 172–200. doi:10.1093/imaman/12.2.173

Handfield, R. B., & Bechtel, C. (2002). The role of trust and relationship structure in improving supply chain responsiveness. *Industrial Marketing Management, 31*, 367–382. doi:10.1016/S0019-8501(01)00169-9

Handfield, R., Walton, S. V., Sroufe, R., & Melnyk, S. A. (2002). Applying environmental criteria to supplier assessment: a study in the application of the analytical hierarchy process. *European Journal of Operational Research, 141*(1), 70–87. doi:10.1016/S0377-2217(01)00261-2

Hansen, M. T. (2002). Knowledge Networks: Explaining Effective Sharing in Multiunit Companies. *Organization Science, 13*(3), 232–249. doi:10.1287/orsc.13.3.232.2771

Harikanth, S. (2009). Maruti Value Chain. *OP Papers. com.* Retrieved May 20, 2009, from http://www.oppapers. com/essays/Maruti-Value-Chain/167129

Harland, C. M. (1996). Supply chain management: relationships, chains, and networks. *British Journal of Management, 7*, 63–80. doi:10.1111/j.1467-8551.1996. tb00148.x

Harry, K.H., & Chow, K.L., Choy, & Lee, W.B. (2007). Knowledge Management Approach in Build-to-order Supply Chains. *Industrial Management & Data Systems, 107*(6), 882–919. doi:10.1108/02635570710758770

Hasselbring, W. (2000). Information system integration. *Communications of the ACM, 43*(6), 33–38. doi:10.1145/336460.336472

Hawking, P., Stein, A., & Foster, S. (2004). Revisiting ERP Systems: Benefit Realization. In *Proceedings of the 37th Hawaii International Conference on System Sciences.* Edwards, H.M. & Humphries, L. P. (2005).

Change Management of People & Technology in an ERP Implementation. *Journal of Cases on Information Technology, 7*(4, Oct-Dec), 144-160.

Henig, M., Gerchak, Y., Ernst, R., & Pike, D. (1997). An Inventory Model Embedded in Designing a Supply Contract. *Management Science, 43*, 184–197. doi:10.1287/mnsc.43.2.184

Hicks, D. A. (1999). Four-Step Methodology For Using Simulation And Optimization Technologies In Strategic Supply Chain Planning. In *Proceedings Of The 1999 Winter Simulation Conference*, (Vol. 2, pp.1215-1220).

Hill, R. M. (1997). The single-vendor single-buyer integrated production-inventory model with a generalised policy. *European Journal of Operational Research, 97*, 493–499. doi:10.1016/S0377-2217(96)00267-6

Hillman, T. W., Hillary, A., & Brown, W. (2002). Extending the value of ERP. *Industrial Management & Data Systems, 102*(1).

Hines, P., Rich, N., Bicheno, J., Brunt, D., Taylor, D., Butterworth, C., & Sullivan, J. (1998). Value stream management. *International Journal of Logistics Management, 9*(1), 25–42. doi:10.1108/09574099810805726

Hitt, L. M., Wu, D. J., & Zhou, X. (2002). Investment in Enterprise Resource Planning: Business Impact and Productivity Measures. *Journal of Management Information Systems, 19*(1), 71–98.

Hobbs, B. F., Helman, U., Jitprapaikulsarn, S., Konda, S., & Maratukulam, D. (1998). Artificial neural networks for short-term energy forecasting: accuracy and economic value. *Neurocomputing, 23*, 71–84. doi:10.1016/S0925-2312(98)00072-1

Holland, C. P. (2003). Introduction to international examples of large scale systems: Theory and practice. *Communications of the Association for Information Systems, 11*(19).

Holland, C. P., & Light, B. (1999, May/June). A Critical success factor model for ERP implementation. *IEEE Software, 1999*, 30–36. doi:10.1109/52.765784

Holland, C. P., Shaw, D. R., & Kawalek, P. (2005). BP's multi-enterprise asset management system. *Information and Software Technology, 47*(15), 999–1007. doi:10.1016/j.infsof.2005.09.006

Holland, C., Light, B., & Gibson, N. (1999). *A critical success factors model for enterprise resource planning implementation*. Paper presented at 7th European Conference on Information Systems ECIS.

Holmstrom, J. (1998). Business process innovation in the supply chain – a case study of implementing vendor managed inventory. *European Journal of Purchasing and Supply Management, 4*, 127–131. doi:10.1016/S0969-7012(97)00028-2

Holweg, M., & Pil, F. K. (2004). *The Second Centumy — Reconnecting Customer and Value Chain Through Built-to-Order*. Cambridge, MA: MIT Press.

Hoque, M. A., & Goyal, S. K. (2000). An optimal policy for a single-vendor single-buyer integrated production-inventory system with capacity constraint of the transport equipment. *International Journal of Production Economics, 65*, 305–315. doi:10.1016/S0925-5273(99)00082-1

Houlihan, J. B. (1988). International supply chains: a new approach. *Management Decision: Quarterly Review of Management Technology, 26*(3), 13–19. doi:10.1108/eb001493

*How systems will be built*. (n.d.). Retrieved 2009, from Object Management Group Web site http://omg.org

How the future. (2009). *How the future of the EAI Market?* Retrieved March 2009, from http://toostep.com/idea/how-the-future-of-the-eai-market

Hsu, L. L., Robert, S. Q., & Weng, Y. (2008). Understanding the critical factors effect user satisfaction and impact of *ERP* through innovation of diffusion theory. *International Journal of Technology Management, 43*(1-3), 30–47. doi:10.1504/IJTM.2008.019405

http://portal.acm.org http://ieeexplore.ieee.org

Huang, C.-K. (2004). An optimal policy for a single-vendor single-buyer integrated production–inventory problem with process unreliability consideration. *International Journal of Production Economics, 91*, 91–98. doi:10.1016/S0925-5273(03)00220-2

Huang, S., Hung, Y. H., Chen, H., & Ku, C. (2004).Transplanting the best practice for implementation of an ERP System: A structured inductive study of an international company. *The Journal of Computer Information Systems, 44*(4, Summer), 101-110.

Huang, Z., & Palvia, P. (2001). ERP implementation issues in advanced and developing countries. *Business Process Management Journal, 7*(3), 276–285. doi:10.1108/14637150110392773

Humphrey, W. (1989). *Managing the software process*. Reading, MA: Addison-Wesley.

Hwa, G. P. (1999). Framework of Design interface module in ERP. In *1999 IEEE International Symposium on assembly and task planning*.

IFRCRCS. (2004). International Federation of Red Cross and Red Crescent Societies. *World Disasters Report* [Online]. Available April 2008 from http://www.ifrc.org/publicat/wdr2004/chapter8.asp

Inmon, W. (2000). A brief history of integration. *eAI Journal*. Retrieved from www.eaijournal.com/applicationintegration/BriefHistory.asp

Inmon, W. H. (1996). *Building the Data Warehouse*. New York: John Wiley and Sons.

Ioannou, G., & Papadoyiannis, C. (2004). Theory of constraints-based methodology for effective ERP implementations. *International Journal of Production Research, 42*(23), 4927–4954. doi:10.1080/00207540410001721718

Ishii, K., Takahashi, K., & Muramatsu, R. (1988). Integrated Production, Inventory And Distribution Systems. *International Journal of Production Research, 26*(3), 473–482. doi:10.1080/00207548808947877

Jacobs, F. R., & Weston, F. C. (2007). Enterprise resource planning (ERP): A Brief History. *Journal of Operations Management, 25*(2), 357–363. doi:10.1016/j.jom.2006.11.005

Jayaraman, V., & Ross, A. (2003). A simulated annealing methodology to distribution network design and management. *European Journal of Operational Research, 144,* 629–645. doi:10.1016/S0377-2217(02)00153-4

Jeffries, R. (2000). *Extreme Programming Installed.* Reading, MA: Addison-Wesley.

Jennings, J. B. (1973). Blood bank inventory control. *Management Science, 19,* 637–645. doi:10.1287/mnsc.19.6.637

Johansson, B., & Carvalho, R. A. (2009). Management of Requirements in ERP development: A Comparison between Proprietary and Open Source ERP. In SAC conference 2009, Hawaii.

Johnson, A. H. (2002 September 30). Wal-Mart put intelligence in its inventory and recognized the value of sharing data. *Computerworld.*

Johnson, B. (1992). Institutional Learning . In Lundvall, B. (Ed.), *National Systems of Innovation: Towards a Theory of Innovation and Interactive Learning.* London: Pinter.

Johnson, J. (2002). *ROI, It's Your Job.* Published Keynote on the 3rd International Conference on Extreme Programming, Alghero, Italy.

Johnson, N., Uba, O. G., McGuire, M., Milheizler, J., Schneider, P., & Whitney, M. (1997). Fire flood, quake, wind! GIS to the rescue: how new mapping systems are being used to cope with natural disasters. *Planning, 63*(7).

Johnston, J. K., & Brown, A. W. (2005). Model-driven development approach to creating service-oriented solutions . In Beydeda, S., Book, M., & Gyhn, V. (Eds.), *Model-driven software development.* New York: Springer.

Johnston, S. (2004). Rational UML profile for business modeling. *IBM developerworks.* Retrieved from http://www.ibm.com/developerworks/rational/library/5167.html.

Jones, M. (1999). Structuration Theory . In Currie, W. L., & Galliers, B. (Eds.), *Rethinking Management Information Systems.* New York: Oxford University Press.

Jones, M. C., Cline, M., & Ryan, S. (2006). Exploring Knowledge Sharing in ERP Implementation, An Organizational Culture Framework. *Decision Support Systems, 41*(2), 411–434. doi:10.1016/j.dss.2004.06.017

Kaboli, A. A. M.B., Shahanaghi, K., & Niroomand, I. (2007, Oct. 7-10). *A new method for plant location selection problem: A fuzzy-AHP approach.* Paper presented at the IEEE International Conference on Systems, Man and Cybernetics.

Kaipia, R., & Tanskanen, K. (2003). Vendor managed category management—an outsourcing solution in retailing. *Journal of Purchasing and Supply Management, 9,* 165–175. doi:10.1016/S1478-4092(03)00009-8

Kalpakam, S., & Arivarignan, G. (1984). Semi-Markov models in inventory systems. *Journal of Mathematical and Physical Sciences, 5,* S1–S17.

Kalpakam, S., & Arivarignan, G. (1993). A coordinated multicommodity (s,S) inventory system. *Mathematical and Computer Modelling, 18,* 69–73. doi:10.1016/0895-7177(93)90206-E

Kalyanmoy, D. (2003). *Optimization For Engineering Design* (3rd ed., pp. 153–160). New Delhi, India: Prentice-Hall Of India Pvt Ltd.

Kamna, M., & Goyal, D. P. (2001). Information Systems Effectiveness – An Integrated Approach. *IEEE Engineering and Management Conference (IEMC'01) Proceedings on Change Management and the New Industrial Revolution,* (pp. 189-194), Albany, NY.

Kannabiran, G., & Bhaumik, S. (2005). Corporate Turnaround through effective supply chain management: The case of a leading jewellery manufacturer in India. *Supply Chain Management, 10*(5), 340. doi:10.1108/13598540510624160

Kaplan, L. G. (1996). *Emergency and Disaster Planning Manual. New York: McGraw-Hill, & Emergency Planning, Perspective on Britain.* London: James & James.

Karakanian, M. (1999). Choosing an ERP implementation strategy Year 2000. *The Practitioner, 2*(7), 1–6.

Karlin, S., & Taylor, H. M. (1975). *A first course in stochastic processes* (2nd ed.). New York: Academic press.

Kaur, P., & Mahanti, N. C. (2008). A Fuzzy ANP-Based Approach for Selecting ERP Vendors. *International Journal of Soft Computing, 3*(1), 24–32.

Kawalek, P., Warboys, B. C., & Greenwood, R. M. (1999). The case for an explicit coordination layer in modern business information systems architectures. *IEE Software, 146*(3), 160–166. doi:10.1049/ip-sen:19990615

Keen, P. W., Ballance, C., Chan, S., & Schrump, S. (2000). *Electronic Commerce relationships: Trust by Design.* Upper Saddle River, NJ: Prentice Hall.

Kelly, S., & Holland, C. P. (2002). The ERP systems development approach to achieving an adaptive enterprise: the impact of enterprise process modelling tools . In Henderson, P. (Ed.), *Systems engineering for business process change* (pp. 241–252). London: Springer.

Kendall, K. E. (1980). Multiple objective planning for regional blood centers. *Long Range Planning, 13*(4), 88–94. doi:10.1016/0024-6301(80)90084-9

Kennedy Carter Inc. (n.d.). Retrieved 2009, from Kennedy Carter Web site http://www.kc.com

Kennedy, J., & Eberhart, R. C. (1995). Particle Swarm Optimization. In *Proceedings IEEE International Conference on Neural Networks, IV*, (pp. 1942–1948). Piscataway, NJ: IEEE Service Center.

Kennedy, J., & Eberhart, R. C. (2001). *Swarm Intelligence.* San Francisco: Morgan Kaufmann Publishers.

Kilker, J., & Gay, G. (1998). The Social Construction of a Digital Library, A Case Study Examining Implication for Evaluation. *Information Technology and Library, 17*(2), 60–70.

Kim, B.-O., & Lockwood, D. (2001). A component-based design approach to ERP design in a distributed object environment. In IACIS 01.

Kim, W. C., & Mauborgne, R. (1998). Procedural Justice, Strategic Decision Making, and the Knowledge Economy. *Strategic Management Journal, 19*(4), 323–338.

doi:10.1002/(SICI)1097-0266(199804)19:4<323::AID-SMJ976>3.0.CO;2-F

Kim, Y., Lee, Z., & Gosain, S. (2005). Impediments to successful ERP implementation process. *Business Process Management Journal, 11*(2), 158–170. doi:10.1108/14637150510591156

Kimball, R., & Ross, M. (2002). *The Data Warehouse Toolkit: The Complete Guide to Dimensional Modeling* (2nd ed.). New York: John Wiley & Sons Computer Publishing.

Kirchmer, M. (1999). *Business Process Oriented Implementation of Standard Software: How to Achieve Competitive Advantage Efficiently and Effectively* (2nd ed.). Berlin: Springer.

Kirkpatrick, S., Gelatt, C. D. Jr, & Vecchi, M. P. (1983). Optimization by Simulated Annealing. *Science, 220*, 671–680. doi:10.1126/science.220.4598.671

Kitchenham, B. A., Huges, R. T., & Linkman, S. G. (2002). Modeling software measurement data. *IEEE Transactions on Software Engineering, 27*(9), 788–804. doi:10.1109/32.950316

Kivits, J. (2005). Online interviewing and the research relationship . In Hine, C. (Ed.), *Virtual methods: issues in social research on the internet* (pp. 35–49). Oxford, UK: Berg Publishers.

Klastorin, T. (2004). New Product Introduction: Timing, Design, and Pricing. *Manufacturing and Service Operations Management, 6*(4), 302–320. doi:10.1287/msom.1040.0050

Kleppe, A., Warmer, J., & Blast, W. (2003). *MDA explained the model driven architecture: Practice and promise.* Reading, MA: Addison Wesley.

Kniberg, H. (2007). *Scrum and XP from the Trenches: How We Do Scrum.* Retrieved December 28, 2008 from http://www.crisp.se/henrik.kniberg/ScrumAndXpFromTheTrenches.pdf

Knolmayer, G., Mertens, P., & Zeier, A. (2001). *Supply chain management based on SAP systems.* Berlin: Springer.

Koh, C., Soh, C., & Markus, M. L. (2000). A Process Theory Approach to Analyzing ERP Implementation and Impacts: The Case of Revel Asia. *Journal of Information Technology Cases and Research, 2*(1).

Koskela, L. (2007). *Test-Driven: TDD and Acceptance TDD for Java Developers*. Manning.

Kotter, J. P. (2005). Leading Change: Why transformation efforts fail. *Harvard Business Review*, (March-April): 59.

Kou, Y., Lu, C., Sinvongwattana, S., & Huang, Y. (2004). Survey of Fraud Detection Techniques. In *Proceedings of the 2004 IEEE Intenational Conference on Networking, Sensing & Control,* (pp. 21-23), Taipei, Taiwan.

Kraemmerand, P., Møller, C., & Boer, H. (2003). ERP Implementation: an integrated process of radical change and continuous learning. *Production Planning and Control, 14*(4), 338–349. doi:10.1080/0953728031000117959

Krishnamoorthy, A., & Varghese, T. V. (1994). A two commodity inventory problem. *Information and Management Sciences, 5*(3), 127–138.

Krishnamoorthy, A., Iqbal Basha, R., & Lakshmy, B. (1994). Analysis of two commodity problem. *International Journal of Information and Management Sciences, 5*(1), 55–72.

Krishnan, M. S., & Kellner, M. I. (1999). Measuring process consistency: Implications for reducing software defects. *IEEE Transactions on Software Engineering, 25*(6), 800–815. doi:10.1109/32.824401

Krotov, V., & Junglas, I. (2008). RFID as a disruptive innovation. *Journal of Theoretical and Applied Electronic Commerce Research, 3*(2), 44–59. doi:10.4067/S0718-18762008000100005

Krueger, R. A., & Casey, M. A. (2008). *Focus groups: A practical guide for applied research*. Thousand Oaks, CA: Sage.

Kruger, G. A. (1997). The Supply Chain Approach to Planning and Procurement Management. Hewlett-Packard Journal, 28-38.

Kuk, G. (2004). Effectiveness of vendor-managed inventory in the electronics industry: determinants and outcomes. *Information & Management, 41*, 645–654. doi:10.1016/j.im.2003.08.002

Kumar, S., & Mota, K. (2009). *Enterprise application integration*. Retrieved March 2009, from http://www.roseindia.net/eai/enterpriseapplicationintegration.shtml

Kumaraswamy, M. M., Palaneeswaran, E., Rahman, M. M., Ugwu, O., & Ng, T. S. (2005). Synergising R&D Initiatives for Enhancing Management Support Systems. *Automation in Construction, 15*(6), 681–692. doi:10.1016/j.autcon.2005.10.001

Kwak, C., Choi, J. S., Kim, C. O., & Kwon, I. (2009). Situation reactive approach to Vendor Managed Inventory problem. *Expert Systems with Applications*. .doi:10.1016/j.eswa.2008.12.018

Kwong, C. K., & Bai, H. (2003). Determining the importance weights for the customer requirements in QFD using a fuzzy AHP with an extent analysis approach. *IIE Transactions, 35*(7), 619–626. doi:10.1080/07408170304355

La Londe, B. J. (1997). Supply Chain Management: Myth or Reality? *Supply Chain Management Review, 1*(Spring), 6–7.

Lambert, D. M., Cooper, M. C., & Pagh, J. D. (1998). Supply chain management: implementation issues and research opportunities. *The International Journal of Logistics Management, 9*(2), 1–19. doi:10.1108/09574099810805807

Lambert, D. M., Knemeyer, A. M., & Gardner, J. T. (2004). Supply Chain Partnerships: Model Validation and Implementation. *Journal of Business Logistics, 25*(2), 21–42.

Lamming, R. (2000). Japanese Supply Chain Relationships in Recession. *Long Range Planning, 33*, 757–778. doi:10.1016/S0024-6301(00)00086-8

Lan, W. H., Eric, T. G. W., & Hung, J. P. (2005). Understanding misalignment and cascading change of ERP implementation: a stage view of process analysis. *European Journal of Information Systems, 14*(01 Dec), 324-334

Lancioni, R. A. (2005). A strategic approach to industrial product pricing: The pricing plan. *Industrial Marketing Management*, *34*, 177–183. doi:10.1016/j.indmarman.2004.07.015

Lane, P. J., & Lubatkin, M. (1998). Relative absorptive capacity and interorganizational learning. *Strategic Management Journal*, *19*, 461–477. doi:10.1002/(SICI)1097-0266(199805)19:5<461::AID-SMJ953>3.0.CO;2-L

Lane, P. J., Salk, J. E., & Lyles, M. A. (2001). Absorptive Capacity, Learning, and Performance in International Joint Ventures. *Strategic Management Journal*, *22*, 1139–1161. doi:10.1002/smj.206

Langerak, F., & Verhoef, P. C. (2003). Strategically Embedding CRM. *Business Strategy Review*, *14*(4), 73–80. doi:10.1111/j..2003.00289.x

Laporte, G., & Osman, I. H. (1995). Routing problems: a bibliography. *Annals of Operations Research*, *61*, 227–262. doi:10.1007/BF02098290

Larson, P. D., & Kulchitsky, J. D. (2000). The Use and Impact of Communication in Purchasing and Supply Management. *Journal of Supply Chain Management*, *36*(3), 29–39. doi:10.1111/j.1745-493X.2000.tb00249.x

Latamore & Benton, G. (1999). The farm business unit customers, Customers, Suppliers Drawing Closer through VMI. *APICS: The Performance Advantage*, *12*(7), 22-25.

Lau, H. C. W., Cheng, E. N. M., Lee, C. K. M., & Ho, G. T. S. (2008). A fuzzy logic approach to forecast energy consumption change in a manufacturing system. *Expert Systems with Applications*, *34*, 1813–1824. doi:10.1016/j.eswa.2007.02.015

Laudon, K. C., & Laudon, J. P. (2003). *Management information systems* (8th ed.). Upper Saddle River, NJ: Pearson Education Publications.

Lavell, A. (1999). *Natural and Technological Disasters, Capacity Building and Human Resource Development for Disaster Management*, [Online]. Retrieved April 2008 from http://www.desenredando.org/public/articulos/1999/ntd/ntd1999_mar-1-2002.pdf

Lederer, P. J., & Li, L. (1997). Pricing, Production, Scheduling and Delivery-Time Competition. *Operations Research*, *45*, 407–420. doi:10.1287/opre.45.3.407

Lee, A. H. I. (2009). A fuzzy supplier selection model with the consideration of benefits, opportunities, costs and risks. *Expert Systems with Applications*, *36*(2, Part 2), 2879–2893. doi:10.1016/j.eswa.2008.01.045

Lee, C. C., & Chu, W. H. J. (2005). Who should control inventory in a supply chain. *European Journal of Operational Research*, *164*(1), 158–172. doi:10.1016/j.ejor.2003.11.009

Lee, C., Lee, K. C., & Han, J. H. (1999). *A Web-based Decision Support System for Logistics Decision-Making*. Paper presented at the meeting of the Academy of Information and Management Sciences, Myrtle Beach, SC.

Lee, H. L. (2001). Ultimate Enterprise Value Creation Using Demand Based Management. Stanford Global Supply Chain Forum, (September), 1.

Lee, H. L., & Billington, C. (1993). Material management in decentralized supply chains. *Operations Research*, *41*, 835–847. doi:10.1287/opre.41.5.835

Lee, H. L., & Billington, C. (1995). The evolution of supply chain management models and practice at Hewlett-Packard. *Interfaces*, *25*, 42–63. doi:10.1287/inte.25.5.42

Lee, H. L., & Feitzinger, E. (1995). Product Configuration and Postponement for Supply Chain Efficiency. In *Institute of Industrial Engineers, Fourth Industrial Engineering Research Conference Proceedings*, (pp. 43-48).

Lee, H. L., Padmanabhan, V., & Whang, S. (1997). Information Distortion in a Supply Chain. *The Bullwhip Effect. Management Science*, *43*(4), 546–558. doi:10.1287/mnsc.43.4.546

Lee, J., Siau, K., & Hong, S. (2003). Enterprise integration with ERP and EAI. *Communications of the ACM*, *46*(2), 54–60. doi:10.1145/606272.606273

Leonard-Burton, D. (1992). Core Capabilities and Core Rigidities, A paradox in Managing New Product Development. *Strategic Management Journal, 13*, 111–125. doi:10.1002/smj.4250131009

Levary, R. R. (2008). Using the analytic hierarchy process to rank foreign suppliers based on supply risks. *Computers & Industrial Engineering, 55*, 535–542. doi:10.1016/j.cie.2008.01.010

Levine, D. M., Berenson, M., & Stephan, D. (1999). *Statistics for managers*. Upper Saddle River, NJ: Prentice Hall.

Levitt, B., & March, J. G. (1988). Organizational Learning. *Annual Review of Sociology, 14*, 319–340. doi:10.1146/annurev.so.14.080188.001535

Li, M. Z. F. (2005). Pricing non-storable perishable goods by using a purchase restriction: General optimality results. *European Journal of Operational Research, 161*, 838–853. doi:10.1016/j.ejor.2003.06.033

Light, B. (1999). The maintenance implications of the customization of ERP software. *Journal of Software Maintenance and Evolution . Research and Practice, 13*(6), 415–429.

Lin, C., Hung, H. C., & Wu, J. Y. (2002). A Knowledge Management Architecture in Collaborative Supply Chain. *Journal of Computer Information Systems, 42*(5), 83–94.

Lin, K. Y. (2005). Dynamic pricing with real-time demand learning. *European Journal of Operational Research*.

Linthicum, D. (1999). *Enterprise Application Integration*. Reading, MA: Addison-Wesley Publications.

Linthicum, D. (2001). *B2B application integration*. Reading, MA: Addison-Wesley Publication.

Liu, H.-T., & Wang, W.-K. (2009). An integrated fuzzy approach for provider evaluation and selection in third-party logistics. *Expert Systems with Applications, 36*(3, Part 1), 4387–4398. doi:10.1016/j.eswa.2008.05.030

Loh, T. C., & Koh, S. C. L. (2004). Critical elements for a successful enterprise resource planning implementation in small-and medium-sized enterprises. *International Journal of Production Research, 42*(17), 3433–3455. doi:10.1080/00207540410001671679

Lorenzoni, G., & Lipparini, A. (1999). The leveraging of interfirm relationships as a distinctive organizational capability: a longitudinal study. *Strategic Management Journal, 20*(4), 317–338. doi:10.1002/(SICI)1097-0266(199904)20:4<317::AID-SMJ28>3.0.CO;2-3

Lourenco, H. R. (2005). Logistics Management: an opportunity for Metaheuristics . In Rego, C., & Alidaee, B. (Eds.), *Metaheuristics Optimization via Memory and Evolution* (pp. 329–356). Kluwer Academic Publishers.

Lu, J. (n.d.). *Predicting Customer churn in the Telecommunications industry – An application of survival Analysis Modeling using SAS*. Overland Park, KS . *Sprint Communication. (2005)... Marketing Intelligence & Planning, 18*, 19–23.

Lu, L. (1995). A one-vendor multi-buyer integrated inventory model. *European Journal of Operational Research, 81*(2), 312–323. doi:10.1016/0377-2217(93)E0253-T

Lucus, H. C. (n.d.). Implementation: The Key to Successful Information Systems. *Columbia Management, 11*(4), 191–198.

Lummus, R. R., Krumwiede, D. W., & Vokurka, R. J. (2001). The Relationship Of Logistics To Supply Chain Management: Developing A Common Industry Definition. *Industrial Management & Data Systems, 101*(8-9), 426–431. doi:10.1108/02635570110406730

Lundvall, B.-A. (1999). Technology policy in the Learning economy . In Archibugi, D., Howells, J., & Michie, J. (Eds.), *Innovation Policy in a Global Economy*. New York: Cambridge University Press. doi:10.1017/CBO9780511599088.004

Luo, W., & Strong, D. M. (2004). A Framework for Evaluating ERP Implementation Choices. *IEEE Transactions on Engineering Management, 51*(3), 322–333. doi:10.1109/TEM.2004.830862

Lyon, A., Coronado, A., & Michaelides, Z. (2006). The Relationship Between Proximate Supply and Build-to-order Capability. *Industrial Management & Data Systems, 106*(8), 1095–1111. doi:10.1108/02635570610710773

Mabert, V. A., & Venkataramanan, M. A. (1998). Special Research Focus on Supply Chain Linkages: Challenges for Design and Management in the 21st Century. *Decision Sciences*, *29*(3), 537–552. doi:10.1111/j.1540-5915.1998. tb01353.x

Macleod, M. (1994, June). What's new in supply chain software? *Purchasing & Supply Management*, (pp. 22-25).

Malm, B. (2001). Component-based ERP systems. Master thesis, Mid Sweden University, Sundsvall, Sweden.

Malone, T., & Crowston, K. (1994). The interdisciplinary study of coordination. *ACM Computing Surveys*, *26*(1), 87–119. doi:10.1145/174666.174668

Maloni, M. J., & Benton, W. C. (1997). Supply Chain Partnership: Opportunities for Operations Research. *European Journal of Operational Research*, *101*, 419–429. doi:10.1016/S0377-2217(97)00118-5

March, J. G. (1991). Exploration and Exploitation in Organizational Learning. *Organization Science*, *2*(1), 71–87. doi:10.1287/orsc.2.1.71

Marcotte, F., Grabot, B., & Affonso, R. (2008). Cooperation models for supply chain management. *International Journal of Logistics Systems and Management*, *5*(1-2), 123–153.

Marien, E. J. (2000). The four Supply Chain Enablers. Supply Chain Management Review, (March- April), 60- 68.

Markus, M. L., & Tanis, C. (2000). The enterprise systems experience: from adoption to success . In Zmud, R. W. (Ed.), *Framing the domains of IT research: Glimpsing the future through the past* (pp. 173–207). Cincinnati, OH: Pinnaflex Educational Resources Inc.

Markus, M. L., Axline, S., Petrie, D., & Tanis, S. C. (2000). Learning from adopters' experiences with ERP: problems encountered and success achieved. *Journal of Information Technology*, *15*(4), 245–265. doi:10.1080/02683960010008944

Markus, M. L., Tanis, C., & Fenema, P. C. (2000). Multi-site ERP implementation. *Communications of the ACM*, *43*, 42–46. doi:10.1145/332051.332068

Martin, C. H., Dent, D. C., & Eckhart, J. C. (1993). Integrated production distribution and inventory planning at Libbey-Owens-Ford. *Interfaces*, *23*, 68–78. doi:10.1287/inte.23.3.68

Martin, R. (1999). *Iterative and Incremental Development*. Retrieved February 1, 2009 from http://www.objectmentor.com/resources/ articles/IIDII.pdf

Martin, R. (2008). *Clean Code: A Handbook of Agile Software Craftsmanship*. Upper Saddle River, NJ: Prentice-Hall.

Masters, J. M. (1993). Determination of Near Optimal stock levels for multi-echelon distribution inventories. *Journal of business logistics, 14*(2), 165-195.

McCluskey, M., Bijesse, J., & Higgs, L. (2006, August). Service Life Cycle Management. *AMR Research, 1*, 3.

McKenna, R. (1991). *Relationship Marketing: Successful Strategies for the Age of the Customer*. Reading, MA: Addison-Wesley.

McNeile, A., & Simons, N. (2003). MDA the visison with the hole. *White Paper, Metamaxim Ltd.* Retrieved from http://www.metamaxim.com.

McNeile, A., & Simons, N. (2004). Methods of behaviour modelling a comentary on behaviour modelling techniques for MDA. *White Paper, Metamaxim Ltd.* Retrieved from http://www.metamaxim.com

Medvidovic, N. (2002). On the role of middleware in architecture-based software development. In *Proceedings of the 14th International Conference on Software Engineering and Knowledge Engineering (SEKE)*, 299-306, New York, ACM Press.

Meeus, M. T. H., Oerlemans, L. A. G., & Hage, J. (2001). Patterns of interactive learning in a high-tech region. *Organization Studies*, *22*, 145–172. doi:10.1177/017084060102200106

Melachrinoudis, E., & Min, H. (2000). The dynamic relocation and phase-out of a hybrid, two-echelon plant/warehousing facility: A multiple objective approach. *European Journal of Operational Research*, *123*(1), 1–15. doi:10.1016/S0377-2217(99)00166-6

Melachrinoudis, E., Min, H., & Messac, A. (2000). The relocation of a manufacturing/distribution facility from supply chain perspectives: A physical programming approach. *Multi-Criteria Applications, 10*, 15–39.

Mellor, S. J., & Balcer, M. J. (2002). *Executable UML, a foundation for model driven architecture.* Reading, MA: Addison Wesley.

Mentzer, J. T., & Schuster, A. D. (1983). Computer modelling in logistics: Existing models and future outlook. *Journal of Business Logistics, 3*(2), 1–55.

Meszaros, G., & Aston, J. (2007). Agile ERP: "You don't know what you've got 'till it's gone!" In *Proceedings of the Agile 2007 Conference* (pp. 143-149). Washington, DC.

Metaxiotis, K., Zafeiropoulos, I., Nikolinakou, K., & Psarras, J. (2005). *Goal directed project management methodology for the support of ERP implementation and optimal adaptation.*

Meyer, B. (1988). *Object-oriented software construction.* Englewood Cliffs, NJ: Prentice Hall.

Meyer, B. (1992). *Eiffel: The language.* Upper Saddle River, NJ: Prentice Hall. (n.d.). Retrieved 2003, from MDA Guide V1.0.1 Web site: http://www.omg.org

Michael, J. Berry, A. & Linoff, G. (2000). Mastering Data Mining- The Art and Science of Customer Relationship Management. India: Wiley Computer Publishing.

Michaelraj, L. A., & Shahabudeen, P. (2008). Replenishment policies for sustainable business development in a continuous credit based vendor managed inventory distribution system. *Computers & Industrial Engineering.* doi:.doi:10.1016/j.cie.2008.05.014

Micheau, V. A. (2005). How Boeing and Alcoa Implemented A Successful Vendor Managed Inventory Program. *The Journal of Business Forecasting, 24*(1), 17–19.

Miller, S. (1998). *ASAP Implementation at the Speed of Business: Implementation at the Speed of Business Computing.* New York: Mcgraw-Hill.

Min, H. (1994). International supplier selection: a multi-attribute utility approach. *Int. J. Phys Distribution Logistics Manage., 24*(5), 24–33. doi:10.1108/09600039410064008

Min, H., & Melachrinoudis, E. (1999). The relocation of a hybrid manufacturing/distribution facility from supply chain perspectives: A case study. *Omega, 27*(1), 75–85. doi:10.1016/S0305-0483(98)00036-X

Min, H., & Zhou, G. (2002). Supply chain modelling: past, present and future. *Computers & Industrial Engineering, 43*, 231–249. doi:10.1016/S0360-8352(02)00066-9

Mingozzi, A., Giorgi, S., & Baldacci, R. (1999). An exact method for the vehicle routing problem with backhauls. *Transportation Science, 33*, 315–329. doi:10.1287/trsc.33.3.315

Minner, S. (2003). Multiple-supplier inventory models in supply chain management: A review. *International Journal of Production Economics, 81-82*, 265–279. doi:10.1016/S0925-5273(02)00288-8

Mishra, B. K., & Raghunathan, S. (2004). Retailer vs. Vendor Managed Inventory and Brand Competition. *Management Science, 50*(4), 445–457. doi:10.1287/mnsc.1030.0174

Mohan, A. (2006). *A Critical Analysis of Supply Chain Management Practices in Indian Fast moving Consumer Goods Industry.* Doctoral Dissertation Report submitted at Faculty of Management Studies (FMS), University of Delhi, Delhi, India.

Mohanty, R.P. & Deshmukh, S.G. (2001). *Essentials of Supply Chain Management.* New Delhi, India: Phoenix publishing house Pvt., Ltd.

Moinzadeh, K., & Aggarwal, P. K. (1997). An information Based Multi-Echelon Inventory System with Emergent Orders. *Operations Research, 45*, 694–701. doi:10.1287/opre.45.5.694

Molla, A., & Bhalla, A. (2006). Business transformation through ERP: Case of an Asian company. *Journal of Information Technology Cases and Research, 8*(1), 34–34.

Monnerat, R. M., Carvalho, R. A., & Campos, R. (2008). Enterprise Systems Modeling: the ERP5 Development Process. In *Proceedings of the XXIII ACM Simposium on Applied Computing.* v. II. (pp. 1062-1068). New York: ACM.

Moorman, C., & Miner, A. S. (1998). Organizational Improvisation and Organizational Memory. *Academy of Management Review, 23*(4), 698–723. doi:10.2307/259058

Morash, E. A., Droge, C., & Vickery, S. (1997). Boundary-spanning interfaces between logistics, production, marketing and new product development. *International Journal of Physical Distribution and Logistics Management, 27*, 350–369. doi:10.1108/09600039710175921

Morgan, D. L. (1997). Focus Group as Qualitative Research Method, (2nd Ed., Qualitative Research Method Series, Vol. 16). Thousand Oaks, CA: Sage.

Morton, N. A., & Hu, Q. (2008). Implications of the fit between organizational structure and ERP: A structural contingency theory perspective. *International Journal of Information Management, 28*(5), 391–402. doi:10.1016/j.ijinfomgt.2008.01.008

Mosawil, A. A., Zhao, L., & Macaulay, L. (2006). A model driven architecture for enterprise application integration. In *Proceedings of the 39th Hawaii International Conference on System sciences.*

Mosheiov, G. (1994). The traveling salesman problem with pickup and delivery. *European Journal of Operational Research, 79*, 299–310. doi:10.1016/0377-2217(94)90360-3

Mosheiov, G. (1995). The pick-up and delivery location problem on networks. *Networks, 26*, 243–251. doi:10.1002/net.3230260408

Mosheiov, G. (1998). Vehicle routing with pick-up and delivery: tour-partitioning heuristics. *Computers & Industrial Engineering, 34*(3), 669–684. doi:10.1016/S0360-8352(97)00275-1

Mowery, D. C., Oxley, J. E., & Silverman, B. S. (1996). Strategic Alliances and Interfirm Knowledge Transfer. *Strategic Management Journal, 17*, 77–91.

Mumford, E. (1983). Participative systems design, Practice and theory. *Journal of Occupational Psychology, 4*(1), 47–57.

Mumford, E., & Weir, D. (1979). *Computer systems in work design – the ETHICS method.* New York: Wiley.

Musalem, E. P., & Dekker, R. (2005). Controlling inventories in a supply chain: A case study. *International Journal of Production Economics, 93-94*, 179–188. doi:10.1016/j.ijpe.2004.06.016

mVerville, J., & Halingten, A. (2001). Decision Process for Acquiring Complex ERP Solutions: The Case of ITCom. *Journal of Information Technology Cases and Research, 3*(2).

Nachiappan, S., & Ramanathan, R. (2008). *Robust decision making using Data Envelopment Analytic Hierarchy Process.* Paper presented at the 7th WSEAS Int. Conf. on Artificial Intelligence, Knowledge Engineering And Data Bases (AIKED'08)

Nagy, G., & Salhi, S. (2003). *Heuristic algorithms for single and multiple depot vehicle routing problems with pickups and deliveries.* Working Paper no. 42, Canterbury Business School.

Nah, F. F., Islam, Z., & Tan, M. (2007). Empirical Assessment of Factors Influencing Success of Enterprise Resource Planning Implementations. *Journal of Database Management, 18*(4), 26–50.

Nah, F. F., Lau, J. L., & Kuang, J. (2001). Critical factors for successful implementation of enterprise systems. *Business Process Management Journal, 7*(3), 285–296. doi:10.1108/14637150110392782

Nah, F. F., Zuckweiler, K. M., & Lau, J. L. (2000). ERP Implementation - CIOs Perceptions of CSFs. *International Journal of Human-Computer Interaction, 16*(1), 5–22.

Nahmias, S. (1977). Comparison between two dynamic perishable inventory models. *Operations Research, 25*, 168–172. doi:10.1287/opre.25.1.168

Nahmias, S. (1982). Perishable inventory theory: A review. *Operations Research, 30*, 680–708. doi:10.1287/opre.30.4.680

Nallayam, R. (2009). RFID Reality Check. *Channelworld. in*. Retrieved May 16, 2009, from http://www.channel-world.in/specialreports/index.jsp/artId=5013515

Nanry, W. P., & Barnes, J. W. (2000). Solving the pickup and delivery problem with time windows using reactive tabu search. *Transportation Research Part B: Methodological, 34*(2), 107–121. doi:10.1016/S0191-2615(99)00016-8

Narasimhan, R. (1983). An analytical approach to supplier selection. *Journal of Purchasing and materials Management, 19*(4), 27-32.

Narayanan, V. G., & Ananth, R. (2004). Aligning incentives in supply chains. *Harvard Business Review, 82*(11), 94–102.

Nassambeni, G. (1998). Network structures and coordination mechanisms: A taxonomy. *International Journal of Operations & Production Management, 18*(6), 538–554. doi:10.1108/01443579810209539

Nejati, M., Nejati, M., & Shafaei, A. (2009). Ranking airlines' service quality factors using a fuzzy approach: study of the Iranian society. *International Journal of Quality & Reliability Management, 26*(3), 247–260. doi:10.1108/02656710910936726

Netessine, S. (2005). Dynamic pricing of inventory/capacity with infrequent price changes. *European Journal of Operational Research, 174*(1), 553–580. doi:10.1016/j.ejor.2004.12.015

Neugebauer, R., Weidlich, D., & Riegel, J. (2007). Approach to describing virtual reality competence components for services in production networks. *Journal of Production Engineering Research and Development, 1*, 291–296. doi:10.1007/s11740-007-0044-6

New, S. J. (1997). The scope of supply chain management research. *Supply Chain Management, 2*(1), 15–22. doi:10.1108/13598549710156321

New, S. J., & Payne, P. (1995). Research frameworks in logistics: three models, seven dinners and a survey. *International Journal of Physical Distribution and Logistics Management, 25*(10), 60–77. doi:10.1108/09600039510147663

Newhart, D. D., Stott, K. L., & Vasko, F. J. (1993). Consolidating Product Sizes to Minimize Inventory Levels for a Multi-Stage Production and Distribution Systems. *The Journal of the Operational Research Society, 44*(7), 637–644.

Nicolaou, A. I. (2008). Research issues on the use of ERP in inter-organizational relationships. *International Journal of Accounting Information Systems, 9*(4), 216–226. doi:10.1016/j.accinf.2008.09.003

Nozick, L. K., & Turnquist, M. A. (2001). Inventory, transportation, service quality and the location of distribution centers. *European Journal of Operational Research, 129*, 362–371. doi:10.1016/S0377-2217(00)00234-4

Nutt, P. C. (1976). Models for Decision Making in Organizations and Some Contextual Variables Which Stipulate Optimal Use. *Academy of Management Review, 1*, 84–98. doi:10.2307/257489

Nutt, P. C. (1984). Types of Organizational Decision Processes. *Administrative Science Quarterly, 29*, 414–450. doi:10.2307/2393033

Nydick, R. L., & Hill, R. P. (1992). Using the Analytic Hierarchy Process to Structure the Supplier Selection Procedure. *International Journal of Purchasing and Materials Management, 28*(2), 31–36.

Nyhuis, P., & Wiendahl, H.-P. (2007). *Fundamentals of production logistics*. Berlin: Springer.

O'Leary, D. (2000). *Enterprise Resource Planning Systems: Systems, Life Cycle, Electronic Commerce, and Risk* (1st ed.). Cambridge, UK: Cambridge University Press.

O'Leary, D.E. (2002). Information system assurance for ERP systems: Unique Risk Considerations. *Journal of Information systems, 16*, 115-126.

*Object management group* [OMG]. (2009). Retrieved from http://omg.org

*Object Management Group*. (n.d.). Retrieved 2009, from Object Management Group Web site: http://omg.org

Ogiela, L. (2009). UBIAS Systems for the Cognitive Interpretation and Analysis of Medical Images. *Opto-Electronics Review*, 17(2), 17.

Ogiela, L., Tadeusiewicz, R., & Ogiela, M. R. (2007). Cognitive Informatics In Automatic Pattern Understanding. In D. Zhang, Y. Wang, & W. Kinsner, (eds.), *Proceedings of the Sixth IEEE International Conference on Cognitive Informatics, ICCI 2007*, Lake Tahoe, CA, (pp. 79-84).

Ogiela, L., Tadeusiewicz, R., & Ogiela, M. R. (2008). Cognitive techniques in medical information systems. *Computers in Biology and Medicine*, 38, 502–507. doi:10.1016/j.compbiomed.2008.01.017

Ogiela, M. R., Tadeusiewicz, R., & Ogiela, L. (2006). Image languages in intelligent radiological palm diagnostics. *Pattern Recognition*, 39, 2157–2165. doi:10.1016/j.patcog.2006.03.014

*OMG Model driven architecture: How systems will be built*. (2009). Retrieved from http://omg.org

OMG/MDA. (2009). *How systems will be built*. Retrieved 2009, from Object Management Group Web site http://omg.org

Orgad, S. (2005). From online to offline and back: Moving from online to offline relationships with research informants . In Hine, C. (Ed.), *Virtual methods: Issues in social research on the internet* (pp. 51–65). Oxford, UK: Berg Publishers.

Oscar, P., & Juan Carlos Molina. (2007). *Model-driven architecture in practice*. Germany:

Osterle, H., Fleisch, E., & Alt, R. (2001). *Business Networking: Shaping Collaboration Between Enterprises* (pp. 7–54). Berlin: Springer.

Ozan, C. (2008). On the order of the preference intensities in fuzzy AHP. *Computers & Industrial Engineering*, 54(4), 993–1005. doi:10.1016/j.cie.2007.11.010

Özdağoğlu, A. & Ozdağoğlu, G. (2007). Comparison of AHP and Fuzzy AHP for the Multicriteria Decision Making Processes with Linguistic Evaluations.

*İstanbul Ticaret Üniversitesi Fen Bilimleri Dergisi*, 6(11), 65-85.

Padmakumari, K., Mohandas, K. P., & Thiruvengadam, S. (1999). Long term distribution demand forecasting using neuro fuzzy computations. *Electrical Power and Energy Systems*, 21, 315–322. doi:10.1016/S0142-0615(98)00056-8

Pan, S. L., Newell, S., Huang, J. C., & Cheung, A. W. K. (2001). Knowledge Integration as a Key Problem in an ERP Implementation. In *Proceedings of the 22nd International Conference of Information Systems*.

Pantaloons - Information Technology in the Supply Chain. Case Study. (2009). *ECCH Case Collection*. Retrieved April 16, 2009, from http://www.icmrindia.org/casestudies/catalogue/Supply%20chain%20Management/CLSCM002.htm

Papajorgji, P., & Pardalos, P. M. (2006). *Software engineering techniques applied to agricultural systems an object-oriented and UML approach*. New York: Springer.

Papajorgji, P., & Shatar, T. (2004). Using the unified modeling language to develop soil water-balance and irrigation-scheduling models. *Environmental Modelling & Software*, 19, 451–459. doi:10.1016/S1364-8152(03)00160-9

Papajorgji, P., Clark, R., & Jallas, E. (2009). The Model driven architecture approach: A framework for developing complex agricultural Systems. In P. Papajorgji & P. M. Pardalos (Eds.), Advances in modeling agricultural systems. New York: Springer. (Springer Optimization and Its Applications).

Parks, L., & Popolillo, M. C. (1999). Co-Managed Inventory is focus of Vendor/ Retailer Pilot. *Drug Store News*, 27, 71.

Parlar, M. & Weng, Z. K. (2004). Coordinating pricing and production decisions in the presence of price competition. *European Journal of Operational Research*.

Parr, A., & Shanks, G. (2000). A model of ERP project implementation. *Journal of Information Technology*, 15(4), 289-303. doi:10.1080/02683960010009051

Parr, A., Shanks, G., & Darke, P. (1999). Identification of necessary factors for successful implementation of ERP systems. New Information Technologies in Organizational Processes – Field Studies and Theoretical Reflections on the Future of Work, (pp. 99-119). Kingston-upon-Thames, UK: Kluwer Academic Publishers.

Parragh, S. N., Doerner, K. F., & Hartl, R. F. (2007). A survey on pickup and delivery problems. *Part I: Transportation between customers and depot, Journal für Betriebswirtschaft . Institut für Betriebswirtschaftslehre, 72,* 1210.

Parthasarathy, S., & Anbazhagan, N. (2007). Evaluating ERP Implementation Choices using AHP. *International Journal of Enterprise Information Systems, 3*(3), 52–65.

Parthasarathy, S., & Ramachandran, M. (2008). Requirements Engineering Method and Maturity Model for ERP Projects. [IJEIS]. *International Journal of Enterprise Information Systems, 4*(1), 1–14.

Partovi, F. Y., Burton, J., & Banerjee, A. (1990). Application of analytical hierarchy process in operations management. *International Journal of Operations & Production Management, 10*(3), 5–19. doi:10.1108/01443579010134945

Parvatiyar, A., Sheth, J. N., & Whittington, F. B. (1992). *Paradigm Shift in Interfirm Marketing Relationships: Emerging Research Issue.* Working Paper No. CRM 92-101, Emory University, Center for Relationship Marketing, Atlanta, GA.

Pastor, O., & Molina, J. C. (2007). *Model-driven architecture in practice.* Germany: Springer Verlag.

Pegels, C. C., Seagle, J. P., Cumming, P. D., & Kendall, K. E. (1975). A computer based interactive planning system for scheduling blood collections. *Transfusion, 15*(4), 381–386. doi:10.1046/j.1537-2995.1975.15476034565.x

Peppard, J., & Ward, J. (2005). Unlocking sustained business value from IT investments. *California Management Review, 48*(1), 52–70.

Perry, D. (1996, November-December). Analysis of a sampling control scheme for a perishable inventory system. *Operations Research, 47*(6), 966–973. doi:10.1287/opre.47.6.966

Peterson, R., & Silver, E. A. (1979). *Decision systems for inventory management and production.* New York: John Wiley and Sons.

Pi, W.-N., & Low, C. (2006). Supplier evaluation and selection via Taguchi loss functions and an AHP. *International Journal of Advanced Manufacturing Technology, 27*(5), 625–630. doi:10.1007/s00170-004-2227-z

Pierskalla, W. P. (1974). *Regionalization of blood bank services. Project supported by the National Center for Health Services Research, OAHS.* DHHS.

Pierskalla, W. P., & Roach, C. (1972). Optimal issuing policies for perishable inventories. *Management Science, 18*(11), 603–614. doi:10.1287/mnsc.18.11.603

Plant, R., & Willcocks, L. (2007).critical success factors in international ERP implementations: a case research approach. *Journal of Computer Information Systems, 47*(3, Spring), 60-70.

Polatoglu, L. H. (1991). Optimal order quantity and pricing decisions in single period inventory systems. *International Journal of Production Economics, 23,* 175–185. doi:10.1016/0925-5273(91)90060-7

Polson, J. (2008). *Why you should use SAP ERP System.* Retrieved December 2008, from www.planetarticle.net

Poppendieck, M., & Poppendieck, T. (2003). *Lean Software Development: An Agile Toolkit.* Addison-Wesley.

Prasad, B., Sharma, M. K., & Godla, J. K. (1999). Critical issues affecting an ERP implementation. *Information Systems Management, 16*(3).

Prastacos, G. P. (1981). System analysis in regional blood management. In Mohr and Kluge, (pp. 110-131).

Prastacos, G. P. (1984). Blood inventory management: an overview of theory and practice. *Management Science, 30,* 777–800. doi:10.1287/mnsc.30.7.777

Prastacos, G. P., & Brodheim, E. (1979). Computer based regional blood distribution. *Computers & Operations Research, 6*, 69–77. doi:10.1016/0305-0548(79)90018-2

Prastacos, G. P., & Brodheim, E. (1980). PBDS: A decision support system for regional blood management. *Management Science, 26*, 451–463. doi:10.1287/mnsc.26.5.451

Pressman, S. (2001). *Software engineering-A practioner's approach*. New Dehli, India: Tata McGraw-Hill.

Pyke, D. F., & Cohen, M. A. (1993). Performance Characteristics Stochastic Integrated Production-Distribution System. *European Journal of Operational Research, 68*(1), 23–48. doi:10.1016/0377-2217(93)90075-X

Pyke, D. F., & Cohen, M. A. (1994). Multi-Product Integrated Production-Distribution Systems. *European Journal of Operational Research, 74*(1), 18–49. doi:10.1016/0377-2217(94)90201-1

Quality, E. A. I. (2003). *EAI quality assurance a service oriented architecture*. Zetta Works. Retrieved March 2009, from http://hosteddocs.ittoolbox.com/ER102904.pdf

Quinn, F.J. (2000). The Master Of Design: An Interview With David Simchi-Levi. *Supply Chain Management Review*, (pp. 74-80).

Raafat, F. (1991). A survey of literature on continuously deteriorating inventory models. *The Journal of the Operational Research Society, 42*, 27–37.

Rabinowitz, M., & Valinsky, D. (1970). *Hospital blood banking-An evaluation of inventory control policies*. Technical Report, Mt. Sinai School of Medicine, City University of New York.

Rajan, A., Rakesh, A., & Steinberg, R. (1992). Dynamic pricing and ordering decisions by a monopolist. *Management Science, 38*, 240–262. doi:10.1287/mnsc.38.2.240

Ramachandran, M. (2008). *Software components: guidelines and applications*. New York: Nova Publishers.

Raman, S. (1998). Lean Software Development: Is It Feasible? In *Proceedings of the 17th Digital Avionics Systems Conference* (pp 13-18). Washington, DC: IEEE.

Ramasubbu, N., Kompalli, P., & Krishnan, M. S. (2005). Leveraging global resources: A process maturity model for managing distributed development. *IEEE Software, 22*(3), 80–86. doi:10.1109/MS.2005.69

Reeves, J. (1992). What Is Software Design? In *C++ Journal, Fall 1992*. Retrieved January 10, 2009 from http://www.developerdotstar.com/mag/articles/reeves_design.html

Reisberg, D. (2001). *Cognition, Exploring the science of the mind*. New York: W.W. Norton & Company, Inc.

Report of the CEFACT Rapporteur for Asia. (2009). Retrieved April 19, 2009, from http://www.unece.org/trade/untdid/download/99cp3.rtf

RFID market to reach $7.26Bn in 2008. (2009). *IDTechEx*. Retrieved May 27, 2009, from www.idtechex.com/products/en/articles/00000169.asp

*RFIDSystems*. (2009). Retrieved May 10, 2009, from http://epic.org/privacy/rfid

Ribbers, S. (2002). Program management and complexity of ERP Implementation. *Engineering management Journal, 14*(2).

Robey, D., Ross, J. W., & Boudreau, M. C. (2002). Learning to implement enterprise systems: An exploratory study of the dialectics of change. *Journal of Management Information Systems, 19*(1).

Robinson, E. P., Gao, L., & Muggenborg, S. D. (1993). Designing an integrated distribution system at DowBrands, inc. *Interfaces, 23*, 107–117. doi:10.1287/inte.23.3.107

Rohde, J. (2005). *Conquering the challenge of global SAP implementations: SAP roll-out strategy & best practices*. Greenwood Village, CO: CIBER Inc.

Rolland, C., & Prakash, N. (2000). Bridging the gap between organizatonal needs and ERP functionality . *Requirements Engineering, 5*, 180–193. doi:10.1007/PL00010350

Ropke, S. (2003). *A local Search heuristic for the pickup and delivery problem with time windows. Technical paper*. Copenhagen, Denmark: DIKU, University of Copenhagen.

Ropke, S. (2005) 'Heuristic and exact algorithms for vehicle routing problems', *Ph.D. thesis,* Department of Computer Science at the University of Copenhagen (DIKU), Denmark.

Ropke, S., & Pisinger, D. (2004). *A Unified Heuristic for a Large Class of Vehicle Routing Problems with Backhauls.* Technical Report no. 2004/14, ISSN: 0107-8283, University of Copenhagen, Denmark.

Ropke, S., & Pisinger, D. (2006). A unified heuristic for a large class of Vehicle Routing Problems with Backhauls. *European Journal of Operational Research, 171*(3), 750–775. doi:10.1016/j.ejor.2004.09.004

Rose, J., & Kraemmergaard, P. (2006). ERP systems and technological discourse shift: Managing the implementation journey. *International Journal of Accounting Information Systems, 7*(3), 217–237. doi:10.1016/j.accinf.2006.06.003

Ross, A., Venkataramanan, M. A., & Ernstberger, K. (1998). Reconfiguring the supply network using current performance data. *Decision Sciences, 29*(3), 707–728. doi:10.1111/j.1540-5915.1998.tb01360.x

Ross, J. (2006). *Enterprise Architecture As Strategy: Creating a Foundation for Business Execution.* Cambridge, UK: Harvard Business School Press.

Ross, S. M. (2000). *Introduction to probability models.* Singapore: Harcourt Asia PTE Ltd.

Ruh, W., Maginnis, F., & Brown, W. (2000). *Enterprise Application Integration.* New York: John Wiley &Sons Inc., Publications.

Rushton, A., Oxley, J., & Croucher, P. (2000). *The Handbook of Logistics and Distribution Management.* Glasgow, UK: Bell & Bain Ltd.

Rutkowski, L. (2008). *Computational Intelligence, Methods and Techniques.* Berlin: Springer Verlag-Heidelberg.

Saaty, T. L. (1980). *The analytic hierarchy process.* New York: McGraw-Hill.

Saaty, T. L., & Vargas, L. G. (1994). *Decision making in economic, political, social, and technological environ-ments with the analytic hierarchy process.* Pittsburgh, PA: RWS Publications.

Sadagopan, S. (2009). Freqently asked questions on ERP in India. *ERP Study centre, IIM-B.* Retrieved April 17, 2009, from http://www.iiitb.ac.in/ss/erp-faq/main4pg1.htm

Saiu, K., & Messersmith, J. (2002). Enabling Technologies for E-Comm and ERP integration. *Quarterly Journal of Electronic Commerce, 3,* 43–52.

Salhi, S., & Nagy, G. (1999). A cluster insertion heuristic for single and multiple depot vehicle routing problems with backhauling. *The Journal of the Operational Research Society, 50,* 1034–1042.

Saliola, F., & Zanfei, A. (2009). Multinational firms, global value chains and the organization of knowledge transfer. *Research Policy, 38*(2), 369–381. doi:10.1016/j.respol.2008.11.003

Samaddar, S., & Kadiyala, S. S. (2006). An Analysis of Inter-organizational Resource Sharing Decisions in Collaborative Knowledge Creation. *European Journal of Operational Research, 170*(1), 192–210. doi:10.1016/j.ejor.2004.06.024

Sambamurthy, V., & Kirsch, L. J. (2000). An integrative framework of the information systems development process. *Decision Sciences, 31*(2), 391–411. doi:10.1111/j.1540-5915.2000.tb01628.x

Sammon, D., & Hanley, P. (2007). Case Study: Becoming a 100 per cent e-corporation: benefits of pursuing an e-supply chain strategy. *Supply Chain Management, 12*(4), 297–303. doi:10.1108/13598540710759817

Sankar, C. S., Raju, P. K., Nair, A., Patton, D., & Bleidung, N. (2005). Enterprise Information Systems and Engineering Design at Briggs & Stratton: K11 Engine Development. *Journal of Information Technology Cases and Research, 7*(1).

Sardana, G. D., & Sahay, B. S. (1999). Strategic Supply Chain Management: A Case Study of Business Transformation. In Sahay, B. S. (Ed.), *Supply Chain Management for Global Competitiveness* (pp. 25–46). New Dehli, India: MacMillan India Ltd.

Satterfield, R., & Robinson, E. P. (1996). *Designing Distribution Systems to Support Vendor Strategies in Supply Chain Management*. Presented at Supply Chain Linkages Symposium, Indian University.

Sauer, L. D., Clay, R. L., & Armstrong, R. (2000). Meta-component architecture for software interoperability. In *Proceedings of International Conference on Software Methods and Tools (SMT)*, 75-84, IEEE.

Sawah, S. E., Tharwat, A. A. E. F., & Rasmy M. H.(2008). A quantitative model to predict the Egyptian ERP Implementation success index. *Business Process Management Journal, 14*(3, June), 288-306.

Sawer, P., Sommerville, I., & Viller, S. (1999). Capturing the benefits of requirements engineering. *IEEE Software, 16*(2), 78–85. doi:10.1109/52.754057

Scapens, R. W. (1990). Researching management accounting practice, the role of case study methods. *The British Accounting Review, 22*(3), 259–281. doi:10.1016/0890-8389(90)90008-6

Scapens, R. W. (2004). Doing case study research . In Humphrey, C., & Lee, B. (Eds.), *The Real Life Guide to Accounting Research* (pp. 257–279). Oxford, UK: Elsevier. doi:10.1016/B978-008043972-3/50017-7

Scheer, W. & Habermann, F. (2000). Making ERP a success. *ACM, 43*(4).

Schneider, M. (2003). *Radio Frequency Identification (RFID) Technology and its Applications in the Commercial Construction Industry.* Unpublished doctoral dissertation, University of Kentucky, Lexington, KY.

Schultz, C. R. (1990). On the Optimality of the (S-1, S) Policy. *Novel Research Logistics, 37*, 715–723. doi:10.1002/1520-6750(199010)37:5<715::AID-NAV3220370510>3.0.CO;2-U

Schwaber, K. (2004). *Agile Project Management with Scrum*. Redmond, WA: Microsoft Press.

Schwarz, L. B. (1981). Introduction in: Studies in Managemnet Sciences: *Vol. 16. Multi-Level production / inventory control systems* (pp. 163–193). Amsterdam: North Holland.

Sedarage, D., Fujiwara, O., & Luong, H. T. (1999). Determining optimal order splitting and reorder level for N-supplier inventory systems. *European Journal of Operational Research, 116*, 389–404. doi:10.1016/S0377-2217(98)00179-9

Senger, E., Gronover, S., & Riempp, G. (2002). Customer Web interaction: Fundamentals and decision tree. In *Proceedings of the Eighth Americas Conference on Information Systems (AMCIS)*, (pp.1966-76). Dallas: AmCIS. *SPSS for Windows, Rel. 15.0.0.* (2006). Chicago: SPSS Inc.

Seradex. (2009). *Lean Manufacturing: Seradex ERP Solutions*. Retrieved February 5, 2009 from http://www.seradex.com/ERP/Lean_Manufacturing_ERP.php

Sevkli, M., Koh, S. C. L., Zaim, S., Demirbag, M., & Tatoglu, E. (2008). Hybrid analytical hierarchy process model for supplier selection. *Industrial Management & Data Systems, 108*(1), 21. doi:10.1108/02635570810844124

Sewal, S. J. (2003). *Executive justification for adopting model driven architecture*. Retrieved from http://omg.org/mda/presentations.html

Shakouri, H., Nadimi, R., & Ghaderi, F. (2008). A hybrid TSK-FR model to study short-term variations of electricity demand versus the temperature changes. *Expert Systems with Applications*. doi:.doi:10.1016/j.eswa.2007.12.058

Shaluf, I. M. (2007). Disaster types, University of Zawia, Libya. *Disaster Prevention and Management, 16*(5), 704–717. doi:10.1108/09653560710837019

Shang, S., & Seddon, P. B. (2002). Assessing and managing the benefits of enterprise systems: the business manager's perspective. *Information Systems Journal, 12*, 271–299. doi:10.1046/j.1365-2575.2002.00132.x

Shani, D., & Chalasani, S. (1992). Exploiting Niches using Relationship Marketing. *Journal of Consumer Marketing, 9*(3), 33–42. doi:10.1108/07363769210035215

Shanks, G., Sheldon, P. B., & Wilcocks, L. P. (2003). *Effectiveness*. Cambridge, UK: Cambridge University Press.

Shapiro, J. F. (2001). *Modeling the supply chain*. Pacific Grove, CA: Wadsworth Group.

Shapiro, R. D. (1984). Get Leverage from Logistics. *Harvard Business Review*, (May- June): 199–127.

Sharma & Goyal. (1994). *Mathematical statistics*. Meerut, India: Krishna Prakashan Mandir.

Sharma, R., Palvia, P., & Salam, A. F. (2002). ERP Selection at Custom Fabrics. *Journal of Information Technology Cases and Research, 4*(2).

Shaw, R. (2006). Indian Ocean tsunami and aftermath Need for environment-disaster synergy. *Disaster Prevention and Management, 15*(1), 5–20. doi:10.1108/09653560610654202

Shehab, E. M., Sharp, M. W., Supramaniam, L., & Spedding, T. A. (2004). Enterprise resource planning: An integrative review. *Business Process Management Journal, 10*(4), 359–386. doi:10.1108/14637150410548056

Shen, H., Wall, B., Zaremba, M., Chen, Y., & Browne, J. (2004). Integration of Business Modeling Methods for Enterprise Information System Analysis and User Requirements Gathering. *Computers in Industry, 54*(3), 307–323. doi:10.1016/j.compind.2003.07.009

Shen, S. (2000). The Report of Analysis of the Supply and Demand Status of Chinese Logistics Market. *Logistics Management, 2*(1), 3–14.

Sheth, J. N., & Parvatiyar, A. (2000). The Domain and Conceptual Foundation of Relationship Marketing . In Sheth, J. N., & Parvatiyar, A. (Eds.), *Handbook of Relationship Marketing* (pp. 1–38). London: Sage Publication Inc.

Sheth, J. N., Gardner, D. M., & Garrett, D. E. (1988). *Marketing Theory: Evolution and Evaluation*. New York: John Wiley.

Shivraj, S. (2000). Understanding user participation and involvement in ERP use. *Journal of Management Research, 1*(1).

Shore, B. (2001). Information sharing in global supply chains. *Journal of Global Information Technology Management, 4*(3), 27–46.

Shore, J. (2005). *Continuous Integration is an Attitude, Not a Tool*. Retrieved December 30, 2008 from http://jamesshore.com/Blog/Continuous-Integration-is-an-Attitude.html

Siau, K. (2004). Enterprise resource planning (ERP) implementation methodologies. *Journal of Database Management, 15*(1, Jan-Mar).

Sieber, T., Keng, S., Fiona, N., & Sieber, M. (2000). SAP Implementation at the University of Nebraska. *Journal of Information Technology Cases and Research, 2*(1).

Silver, E. A. (1974). A control system of coordinated inventory replenishment. *International Journal of Production Research, 12*, 647–671. doi:10.1080/00207547408919583

Silver, E. A. (1981). Operations research in inventory management: A review and critique. *Operations Research, 29*, 628–645. doi:10.1287/opre.29.4.628

Simatupang, T. M., Sandroto, I. V., & Lubis, S. B. H. (2004). Supply chain coordination in a fashion firm. *International Journal of Supply Chain Management, 9*(3), 256–268. doi:10.1108/13598540410544953

Simatupang, T. M., Wright, A. C., & Sridharan, R. (2002). The knowledge of coordination for supply chain integration. *Business Process Management Journal, 8*(3), 289–308. doi:10.1108/14637150210428989

Simchi-Levi, D., Kaminsky, D., & Simchi-Levi, E. (2001). *Designing And Managing The Supply Chain: Concepts, Stretegies And Case Studies*. Melbourne, Australia: Irwin/Mcgraw-Hill.

Simchi-Levi, D., Kaminsky, P., & Simchi-Levi, E. (2000). *Designing and Managing the Supply Chain*. New York: McGraw-Hill.

Simchi-levi, D., Kaminsky, P., & Simchi-levi, E. (2003). *Managing The Supply Chain: The Definitive Guide For The Business Professional*. New York: Irwin /Mc Graw Hill.

Sisodia, R. S., & Wolfe, D. B. (2000). Information Technology: Its Role in Building, Maintaining & Enhancing Relationships . In Sheth, J. N., & Parvatiyar, A. (Eds.),

*Handbook of Relationship Marketing* (pp. 523–563). London: Sage Publication Inc.

Sivasamy, R., & Pandiyan, P. (1998). A two commodity Inventory Model Under Policy. *International Journal of Information and Management Sciences, 9*(3), 19–34.

Sivazlian, B. D. (1974). A continuous review inventory system with arbitrary inter-arrival distribution between unit demands. *Operations Research, 22,* 65–71. doi:10.1287/opre.22.1.65

Slats, P. A., Bhola, B., Evers, J. M., & Dijkhuizen, G. (1995). Logistic Chain Modeling: An invited review. *European Journal of Operational Research, 87,* 1–20. doi:10.1016/0377-2217(94)00354-F

Sleeper, S. Z. (2004). *AMR Analysts Discuss Role-Based ERP Interfaces - The User-Friendly Enterprise*. Retrieved December 20, 2008 from http://www.sapdesignguild.org/editions/edition8/print_amr.asp

Smets-Solanes, J., & Carvalho, R. A. (2002). An Abstract Model for An Open Source ERP System: The ERP5 Proposal. In *Proceedings of the VIII International Conference on Industrial Engineering and Operations Management,* Curitiba, Brazil.

Smets-Solanes, J.-P., & Carvalho, R. A. (2003). ERP5: A Next-Generation, Open-Source ERP Architecture. *IEEE IT Professional, 5*(4), 38–44. doi:10.1109/MITP.2003.1216231

Smith-Doerr, L., & Powell, W. W. (2005). Networl and economic life . In Smelser, N., & Swedberg, R. (Eds.), *The Handbook of Economic Sociology* (pp. 379–402). Princeton, NJ: Princeton University Press.

Snider, B., Silveira, G. J. C., & Balakrishnan, J. (2009). ERP implementation at SMEs: analysis of five Canadian cases. *International Journal of Operations & Production Management, 29*(1/2), 4–29. doi:10.1108/01443570910925343

Soh, C., Kien, S. S., & Tay-Yap, J. (2000). Cultural fits and misfits: Is ERP a universal solution? *Communications of the ACM, 43*(4), 47–51. doi:10.1145/332051.332070

Soh, C., Sia, S. K., Boh, W. F., & Tang, M. (2003). Misalignments in ERP implementations: A dialectic perspective. *International Journal of Human-Computer Interaction, 16*(1), 81–100. doi:10.1207/S15327590IJHC1601_6

Soh, C., Sia, S. K., Boh, W. F., & Tang, M. (2003). Misalignments in ERP Implementation: A Dialectic Perspective. *International Journal of Human-Computer Interaction, 16*(1, May), 81-100.

Somers, T., & Nelson, K. (2001).The impact of critical success factors across the stages of enterprise resource planning implementations, In *Proceedings of the 34th Hawaii International Conference on System Sciences HICSS.*

Sommerville, I., & Sawyer, P. (1998). *Requirements engineering: A good practice guide.* London: Wiley.

Soroor, J., Tarokh, M. J., & Shemshadi, A. (2009). Initiating a state of the art system for real-time supply chain coordination. *European Journal of Operational Research, 196,* 635–650. doi:10.1016/j.ejor.2008.03.008

Southard, P. B. (2001). *Extending VMI into alternate supply chains: A simulation Analysis of cost and service levels.* Unpublished Ph.D. Thesis report, Faculty of graduate college at university of Nebraska.

Southard, P. B., & Swenseth, S. R. (2008). Evaluating vendor-managed inventory (VMI) in non-traditional environments using simulation. *International Journal of Production Economics, 116,* 275–287. doi:10.1016/j.ijpe.2008.09.007

Srinivasan, K., Kekre, B., & Mukhopadhyay, T. (1994). Impact of electronic data interchange technology on JIT shipments. *Management Science, 40,* 1291–1304. doi:10.1287/mnsc.40.10.1291

Srinivasan, K., Kekre, S., & Mukhopadhyay, T. (1994). Impact of Electronic Data Interchange Technology on JIT Shipments. *Management Science, 40*(10), 1291–1304. doi:10.1287/mnsc.40.10.1291

Srivardhana, T., & Pawlowski, S. D. (2007). ERP Systems as an Enabler of Sustained Business Process Innovation, A Knowledge-Based View. *The Journal of*

*Strategic Information Systems, 16*(1), 51–69. doi:10.1016/j.jsis.2007.01.003

Stedman, C. (1999). Failed ERP Gamble haunts Hershey. *Computerworld, 1*(Nov).

Stein T. (1999). Making ERP add up. *Information Week*, May 24, 59-59.

Stein, T. (1998, August 31). SAP Sued over R/3. *InformationWeek*, 134–135.

Stein, T. (1999, May 24). Making ERP add up. *Information Week*, 59.

Steinbeiss, H., So, H., Michelitsch, T., & Hoffmann, H. (2007). Method for optimizing the cooling design of hot stamping tools. *Journal of Production Engineering Research and Development, 1*(2), 149–156. doi:10.1007/s11740-007-0010-3

Stenger, A. J. (1994). Distribution Resource Planning. In Roberson, Capacino & Howe, (Eds.) the Logistics Handbook. New York: Free Press.

Stenger, A. J. (1996). Reducing inventories in a multi-echelon manufacturing firm: A case study. *International Journal of Production Economics, 45*, 239–249. doi:10.1016/0925-5273(94)00146-4

Stensurd, E., & Myrtveit, I. (2003, May). Identifying high performance ERP projects. *IEEE Transactions on Software Engineering, 29*(5).

Stevens, G. C. (1989). Integrating the Supply Chain. *International Journal of Physical Distribution and Materials Management, 19*(8), 3–8.

Stone, M., Woodcock, N., & Wilson, M. (1996). Managing the Change from Marketing Planning to Customer Relationship Management. *Long Range Planning, 29*, 675–683. doi:10.1016/0024-6301(96)00061-1

Stonebraker, M., & Hellerstein, J. M. (2001). Content integration for E-Business. *SIGMOD Record, 30*(2), 552–560. doi:10.1145/376284.375739

Strong, D. M., & Volkoff, O. (2004). *A Roadmap for Enterprise System Implementation*. Washington, DC: IEEE Computer Society.

*Success stories: Mahindra and Mahindra*. (2009). Retrieved May 17, 2009, from http://www.skandsoft.com/successstories.html#1

Sucky, E. (2005). Inventory management in supply chains: A bargaining problem. *International Journal of Production Economics, 93-94*, 253–262. doi:10.1016/j.ijpe.2004.06.025

Sumner, M. (2000). Risk factors in enterprise-wide/ERP projects. *Journal of Information Technology, 15*(4), 317–327. doi:10.1080/02683960010009079

Sumner, M. (2000). Risk factors in enterprise-wide/ERP projects. *Journal of Information Technology, 15*, 317–327. doi:10.1080/02683960010009079

Sumner, M. (2004). *Enterprise Resource Planning*. Upper Saddle River, NJ: Prentice Hall.

Sun, A.Y.T., Yazdani, A., & Overend, J. D. (2005). Achievement assessment for enterprise resource planning (ERP) system implementations based on critical success factors (CSFs). *International Journal of Production Economics, 98*(2, Nov), 189-203.

Supply Chain Management in L&T ECC Division. (2009). *ECCH Case Collection*. Retrieved April 29, 2009, from http://www.icmrindia.org/casestudies/catalogue/Operations/OPER045.htm

Supply Chain Management Solution for Hindustan Lever. *Case Study*. (2009). Retrieved May 3, 2009, from http://fmcg-marketing.blogspot.com/2007/10/supply-chain-management-solution-for.html

Sutton, J. M. (1996). Lean Software for the Lean Aircraft. In *Proceedings of the 15th Digital Avionics Systems Conference* (pp. 49-54). Washington, DC: IEEE.

Svoronos, A., & Zipkin, P. (1991). Evaluation of One-for-One Replenishment Policies for Multiechelon Inventory Systems. *Management Science, 37*(1), 68–83. doi:10.1287/mnsc.37.1.68

Swamidass, P. M. (2000). *Encyclopedia of production and manufacturing management*. Boston: Kluwer Academic Publishers. doi:10.1007/1-4020-0612-8

Szkuta, B. R., Sanabria, L. A., & Dillon, T. S. (1999, August). Electricity Price Short-Term Forecasting using artificial neural networks. *IEEE Transactions on Power Systems, 14*(3). doi:10.1109/59.780895

Szmerekovsky, J. G., & Zhang, J. (2008). Coordination and adoption of item-level RFID with vendor managed inventory. *International Journal of Production Economics, 114*, 388–398. doi:10.1016/j.ijpe.2008.03.002

Szyperski, C. (1998). *Component Software*. Reading, MA: Addison Wesley.

Tadeusiewicz, R., & Ogiela, L. (2008). Selected Cognitive Categorization Systems. *LNAI, 5097*, 1127–1136.

Tadeusiewicz, R., & Ogiela, M. R. (2003). Artificial intelligence techniques in retrieval of visual data semantic information. *LNAI, 2663*, 18–27.

Tadeusiewicz, R., Ogiela, L., & Ogiela, M. R. (2008). The automatic understanding approach to systems analysis and design. *International Journal of Information Management, 28*, 38–48. doi:10.1016/j.ijinfomgt.2007.03.005

Tadeusiewicz, R., Ogiela, M., & Ogiela, L. (2007). A New Approach to the Computer Support of Strategic Decision Making in Enterprises by Means of a New Class of Understanding Based Management Support Systems. In *IEEE Proceedings 6th International Conference CI-SIM'07 – Computer Information Systems and Industrial Management Applications,* Ełk, Poland, (pp. 9-13).

Tagaras, G., & Lee, H. L. (1996). Economic models for vendor evaluation with quality cost analysis. *Management Science, 42*, 1531–1543. doi:10.1287/mnsc.42.11.1531

Talluri, S. (2000). An IT/IS acquisition and justification model for supply chain management. *International Journal of Physical Distribution and Logistics Management, 30*(3/4), 221–237. doi:10.1108/09600030010325984

Tanaka, E. (1995). Theoretical aspects of syntactic pattern recognition . *Pattern Recognition, 28*, 1053–1061. doi:10.1016/0031-3203(94)00182-L

Tang, Q. C., & Cheng, H. K. (2005). Optimal location and pricing of Web services intermediary. *Decision Support Systems, 40*, 129–141. doi:10.1016/j.dss.2004.04.007

Tang, Q., & Xie, F. (2008). *A Holistic Approach for Selecting third Party Logistcs Providers in Fourth Party Logistics.* Paper presented at the Seventh International Conference on Machine Learning and Cybernetics, China.

Teece, D. J., Pisano, G., & Shuen, A. (1997). Dynamic Capabilities and Strategic Management. *Strategic Management Journal, 18*(7), 509–533. doi:10.1002/(SICI)1097-0266(199708)18:7<509::AID-SMJ882>3.0.CO;2-Z

Teltumbde, A. (2000). A framework for evaluating IS projects. *International Journal of Production Research, 38*(17). Legare, T. L. (2002). The Role of Organizational Factors in Realizing ERP Benefits. *Information system management.*

Teng, J., Chang, C., & Goyal, S. K. (2004). Optimal pricing and ordering policy under permissible delay in payments. *International Journal of Production Economics, 97*, 121–129. doi:10.1016/j.ijpe.2004.04.010

Thomas, D. J., & Griffin, P. M. (1996). Coordinated supply chain management: An invited review. *European Journal of Operational Research, 94*, 1–15. doi:10.1016/0377-2217(96)00098-7

Thomas, L. J. (2002). *ERP et progiciel de gestion integres*. Paris: Dunod.

Thongchattu, C., & Buranajarukorn, P. (2007). *The Utilisation of e-Tools of Information Technology Towards Thorough Supply Chain Management.* Paper presented at the Naresuan University Research Conference, Thailand.

Thought works. (2008). Thought works: *Recession news Cios can use, adding value in uncertain Times – the Agile and lean Advantage.* Retrieved June 2008.

Tierney, S. (2003). Tune Up for Super Efficient Supply Chain with A Traingle. *Journal of Logistic Management, 11*(2), 45–56.

Toni, A. F. D., & Zamolo, E. (2005). From a traditional replenishment system to vendor-managed inventory: A case study from the household electrical appliances sector. *International Journal of Production Economics, 96*, 63–79. doi:10.1016/j.ijpe.2004.03.003

Tönshoff, H. K., Reinsch, S., & Dreyer, J. (2007). Soft-computing algorithms as a tool for the planning of cyclically interlinked production lines. *Journal of Production Engineering Research and Development, 1*(1).

Torabi, S.A., Ghomi, S.M.T.F. & Karimi, B. (2005). A hybrid genetic algorithm for the finite horizon economic lot and delivery scheduling in supply chains. *European Journal of Operational Research.*

Toth, P., & Vigo, D. (1997). An exact algorithm for the vehicle routing problem with backhauls. *Transportation Science, 31*, 372–285. doi:10.1287/trsc.31.4.372

Toth, P., & Vigo, D. (1999). A heuristic algorithm for the symmetric and asymmetric vehicle routing problem with backhauls. *European Journal of Operational Research, 113*, 528–543. doi:10.1016/S0377-2217(98)00086-1

Toth, P., & Vigo, D. (2002a). An Overview of Vehicle Routing Problems . In Toth, P., & Vigo, D. (Eds.), *The Vehicle Routing Problem* (pp. 1–26). Philadelphia: SIAM Monographs on Discrete Mathematics and Applications.

Toth, P., & Vigo, D. (2002b). VRP with backhauls . In Toth, P., & Vigo, D. (Eds.), *The Vehicle Routing Problem* (pp. 195–221). Philadelphia: SIAM Monographs on Discrete Mathematics and Applications.

Towill, D. (1997). The seamless supply chain - the predator's strategic advantage. *International Journal of Technology Management, 13*(1), 37–56. doi:10.1504/IJTM.1997.001649

Towill, D. R. (1991). Supply Chain Dynamics. *International Journal of Computer Integrated Manufacturing, 4*(4), 197–208. doi:10.1080/09511929108944496

Towill, D. R., & Del Vecchio, A. (1994). The Application of Filter Theory to the Study of Supply Chain Dynamics. *Production Planning and Control, 5*(1), 82–96. doi:10.1080/09537289408919474

Towill, D. R., Naim, M. M., & Wikner, J. (1992). Industrial Dynamics Simulation Models in the Design of Supply Chains. *International Journal of Physical Distribution and Logistics Management, 22*(5), 3–13. doi:10.1108/09600039210016995

Tronstad, R. (1995). Pricing. *Journal of Market Analysis and Pricing*, 39-45.

True, M., & Izzi, C. (2002). Collaborative product commerce: creating value across the enterprise . *Ascet, 4*, 27–35.

Truex, D., Baskerville, R., & Klein, H. (1999). Growing systems in emergent organizations. *Communications of the ACM, 42*(8), 117–123. doi:10.1145/310930.310984

Truong, T. H., & Azadivar, F. (1974). Simulation Based Optimization for Supply Chain Configuration Design. In *Proceedings of the 2003 Winter Simulation Conference,* (pp. 1268-1275).

Tsunami Evaluation Coalition. (2006). *Joint Evaluation of the International Response to the Indian Ocean Tsunami.* Tsunami Evaluation Coalition.

Tütüncü, G. Y., Carreto, C. A. C., & Baker, B. M. (2009). A visual interactive approach to classical and mixed vehicle routing problems with backhauls. *Omega, 37*(1), 138–154. doi:10.1016/j.omega.2006.11.001

Tyan, J., & Wee, H. M. (2003). Vendor Managed Inventory: a survey of the Taiwanese grocery industry. *Journal of Purchasing and Supply Management, 9*(1), 11–18. doi:10.1016/S0969-7012(02)00032-1

Tyndall, G., Gopal, C., Partsch, W., & Kamauff, J. (1998). *Supercharging Supply Chains: New Ways to Increase Value through Global Operational Excellence.* New York: John Wiley & Sons.

Tzafestas, S., & Kapsiotis, G. (1994). Coordinated Control of Manufacturing/Supply Chains Using Multi-Level Techniques. *Computer Integrated Manufacturing Systems, 7*(3), 206–212. doi:10.1016/0951-5240(94)90039-6

Ahituv, N., Neumann, S., Zviran, M. (2002). A system development methodology for ERP systems. *Journal of Computer Information Systems.* Grossman, T., Walsh, J. (2004). Avoiding the pitfalls of ERP system implementation. *Information systems management.*

Umble, E. J., & Umble, M. M. (2002). Avoiding ERP Implementation Failure. *Industrial Management (Des Plaines)*, *44*(1), 25–34.

Umble, E. J., Haft, R. R., & Umble, M. M. (2003). Enterprise Resource Planning, Implementation Procedures and Critical Success Factors. *European Journal of Operational Research*, *146*, 241–257. doi:10.1016/S0377-2217(02)00547-7

UML. (2009). *UML™ for EAI*. Retrieved April 2009, from http://www.omg.org/docs/ad/01-09-17.pdf

Van de Bosch, F. A. J., Baaij, M. G., & Volberda, H. V. (2005). How Knowledge Accumulation has Changed Strategy Consulting. Strategic Option for Established Strategic Consulting Firms. *Strategic Change*, *14*(1), 25–34. doi:10.1002/jsc.705

van der Putten, P. (1999). *Sentient Machine Research*. CMG Academy.

van Everdingen, Y., van Hillergersberg, J., & Waarts, J. (2000). ERP adoption bu european midsize companies. *Communications of the ACM*, *43*(4), 27–31. doi:10.1145/332051.332064

Van Houtum, G. J., Indefurth, K., & Zijm, W. H. M. (1996). Material Coordination In Stochastic Mutli- Echelon Systems. *European Journal of Operational Research*, *95*, 1–23. doi:10.1016/0377-2217(96)00080-X

Van laarhoven, P.J.M. & Pedrycz, W. (1983). A fuzzy extension of Saaty's priority theory. *Fuzzy Sets and Systems, 11*, 229-241.

Van Oldenborgh, M. (1994). Distribution superhighway. *International Business*, *7*(6), 80–84.

Vengayil, P. (2009). *Quality assurance in EAI projects*. Wipro Technologies. Retrieved March 2009, from http://hosteddocs.ittoolbox.com/PV111805.pdf

Venkatesan, R., & Kumar, V. (2004). A customer lifetime value framework for customer selection and resource allocations strategy. *Journal of Marketing*, *68*(4), 106–125. doi:10.1509/jmkg.68.4.106.42728

Vernadat, F. B. (2002). Enterprise Modeling and Integration (EMI): Current Status and Research Perspectives. *Annual Reviews in Control*, *26*, 15–25. doi:10.1016/S1367-5788(02)80006-2

Vickery, S. K., Jayaram, J., Droge, C., & Calantone, R. (2003). The effects of an integrative supply chain strategy on customer service and financial performance: an analysis of direct versus indirect relationships. *Journal of Operations Management*, *21*, 523–539. doi:10.1016/j.jom.2003.02.002

*Visual Enterprise*. (2009). Retrieved 2009, from http://intelliun.com

Viswanathan, S. (1998). Optimal strategy for the integrated vendor-buyer inventory model. *European Journal of Operational Research*, *105*(1), 38–42. doi:10.1016/S0377-2217(97)00032-5

Viswanathan, S., & Mathur, K. (1997). Integrating Routing and Inventory Decisions in One-Warehouse Multi-Retailer, Multi-Product Distribution Systems. *Management Science*, *43*, 294–312. doi:10.1287/mnsc.43.3.294

Von Cieminski, G., & Nyhuis, P. (2007). Modeling and analyzing logistic inter-dependencies in industrial-enterprise logistics. *Journal of Production Engineering Research and Development*, *1*(3).

Voudouris, V. T. (1996). Mathematical Programming Techniques to Debottleneck the Supply Chain of Fine Chemical Industries. *Computers & Chemical Engineering*, *20*, S1269–S1274. doi:10.1016/0098-1354(96)00219-0

Vries, E. J., & Brijder, H. G. (2000). Knowledge Management in Hybrid Supply Channels: A Case Knowledge study. *International Journal of Technology Management*, *20*(8), 569–587. doi:10.1504/IJTM.2000.002882

Vujasinovic, M., Marjanovic, Z., & Bussler, C. (2006). Data level application integration. [*BPM workshops*, Springer Verlag Berlin Heidelberg.]. *LNCS*, *3812*, 390–395.

Wade, A. C., & Salhi, S. (2002). An investigation into a new class of vehicle routing problem with backhauls. *Omega*, *30*, 479–487. doi:10.1016/S0305-0483(02)00056-7

Wade, A., & Salhi, S. (2001). An ant system algorithm for the vehicle routing problem with backhauls. In *MIC'2001 - 4th Metaheursistic International Conference*.

Wade, A., & Salhi, S. (2003). An Ant System Algorithm for the mixed Vehicle Routing Problem with Backhauls . In *Metaheuristics: Computer Decision-Making* (pp. 699–719). Amsterdam: Kluwer Academic Publishers.

Wallace, T. F., & Kremzer, M. H. (2001). *ERP: Making It Happen: The Implementers' Guide to Success with Enterprise Resource Planning* (3rd ed.). New York: Wiley.

Waller, M., Johnson, M. E., & Davis, T. (2001). Vendor managed inventory in the retail supply chain. *Journal of Business Logistics, 20*(1), 183–203.

Walsh, J. P., & Ungson, G. R. (1991). Organizational Memory. *Academy of Management Review, 16*(1), 57–91. doi:10.2307/258607

Wang, Y. (2003). On Cognitive Informatics. *Brain and Mind: A Transdisciplinary Journal of Neuroscience and Neurophilosophy, 4*(2), 151-167.

Wang, Y. (2007). The Cognitive Processes of Formal Inferences. *International Journal of Cognitive Informatics and Natural Intelligence, 1*(4), 75–86.

Wang, Y.-M., & Chin, K.-S. (2009). A new data envelopment analysis method for priority determination and group decision making in the analytic hierarchy process. *European Journal of Operational Research, 195*, 239–251. doi:10.1016/j.ejor.2008.01.049

Wang, Y.-M., Chin, K.-S., & Leung, J. P.-F. (2009). A note on the application of the data envelopment analytic hierarchy process for supplier selection. *International Journal of Production Research, 47*(11), 3121–3138. doi:10.1080/00207540701805653

Warmer, J., & Kleppe, A. (1999). *The object constraint language precise modeling with UML*. Reading, MA: Addison Wesley.

Wassan, N. (2007). Reactive tabu adaptive memory programming search for the vehicle routing problem with backhauls. *The Journal of the Operational Re-*

*search Society, 58*, 1630–1641. doi:10.1057/palgrave.jors.2602313

Wassan, N. A., Nagy, G., & Ahmadi, S. (2008). A heuristic method for the vehicle routing problem with mixed deliveries and pickups. *Journal of Scheduling, 11*(2), 149–161. doi:10.1007/s10951-008-0055-y

Weber, C., Current, J. R., & Benton, W. C. (1991). Vendor selection criteria and methods. *European Journal of Operational Research, 50*(1), 2–18. doi:10.1016/0377-2217(91)90033-R

Webster, F. E. Jr. (1992). The Changing Role of Marketing in the Corporation. *Journal of Marketing, 56*(4), 1–17. doi:10.2307/1251983

Wei, H., Wang, E. T. G., & Ju, P. (2005). Understanding misalignment and cascading change of ERP implementation: a stage view of process analysis. *European Journal of Information Systems, 14*(01 Dec), 224-334.

Weinert, K., Blum, H., Jansen, T., & Rademacher, A. (2007, June). Simulation based optimization of the NC-shape grinding process with toroid grinding wheels. *Journal of Production Engineering Research and Development, 1*(3), 245–252. doi:10.1007/s11740-007-0042-8

Wenhong, L., & Strong, D. M. (2004). *A Framework For Evaluating ERP Implementation Choices*. Engineering Management –IEEE Transactions.

Wenston, R. (1997). Domino's Supply Chain Overhaul to Save Dough. *Computerworld, 31*, 50.

Wheeler, R., & Aitken, S. (2000). Multiple Algorithms for Fraud Detection. *Review Knowledge-Based Systems, 13*, 93–99. doi:10.1016/S0950-7051(00)00050-2

Whipple, J. M., Frankel, R., & Daugherty, P. J. (2002). Information Support for Alliances: Performance Implications. *Journal of Business Logistics, 23*(2), 67–82.

Whitin, T. M. (1953). *The theory of inventory management*. Princeton, NJ: Princeton University press.

Wier, B., Hunton, J., & Hassab-Elnaby, H. R. (2007). Enterprise Resource Planning Systems and Non-Financial Performance Incentives: The Joint Impact on

Corporate Performance. *International Journal of Accounting Information Systems, 8*, 165–190. doi:10.1016/j.accinf.2007.05.001

Wikner, J., Towill, D. R., & Naim, M. (1991). Smoothing Supply Chain Dynamics. *International Journal of Production Economics, 22*(3), 231–248. doi:10.1016/0925-5273(91)90099-F

Williams, J. F. (1981). Heuristic Techniques For Simultaneous Scheduling Of Production In Multi-Echelon Structures: Theory And Empirical Comparisons. *Management Science, 27*(3), 336–352. doi:10.1287/mnsc.27.3.336

Williams, J. F. (1983). A Hybrid Algorithm for Simultaneous Scheduling of Production and Distribution in Multi-Echelon Structures. *Management Science, 29*(1), 77–92. doi:10.1287/mnsc.29.1.77

Williams, M. K. (2000). Making Consignment and Vendor Managed Inventory work for you. *Hospital Materiel Management Quarterly, 21*(4), 59–63.

Witten, I. H. & Eibe, F. (1999). *Data Mining: Practical Machine Learning Tools and Techniques with Java Implementations.*

Wong, K. Y. (2005). Critical Success Factors for Implementing Knowledge Management in Small and Medium Enterprises. *Industrial Management & Data Systems, 105*(3), 261–279. doi:10.1108/02635570510590101

Wong, W. K., Qi, J., & Leung, S. Y. S. (2008). Coordinating supply chains with sales rebate contracts and vendor-managed inventory. *International Journal of Production Economics.* doi:.doi:10.1016/j.ijpe.2008.07.025

Woo, Y. Y., Hsu, S. L., & Wu, S. (2001). An integrated inventory model for a single vendor and multiple buyers with ordering cost reduction. *International Journal of Production Economics, 73*, 203–215. doi:10.1016/S0925-5273(00)00178-X

Woods, J., Peterson, W.K. & Jimenez, M. (2002, October). *Demand Chain Management Synchronizes CRM & SCM.* Gartner Research.

Workforce, R. F. I. D. Mining the RFID Technology Gold Rush. (2009). *RFID Tribe.* Retrieved May 27, 2009, from www.rfidtribe.com/news-05-05-11.html

Wright, S., & Wright, A. M. (2002). Information system assurance for Enterprise Resource planning systems: unique risk considerations. *Journal of Information Science, 16*, 99–113.

Wu, D. J. (2001). Software agents for knowledge management: coordination in multi-agent supply chains and auctions. *Expert Systems with Applications, 20*, 51–64. doi:10.1016/S0957-4174(00)00048-8

www.proquest.com http://ernesto.emeraldinsight.com

Wylie, L. (1990). A Vision of the Next-Generation MRP II. *Scenario,* S-300-339.

Xu, J. (2002). New Pattern of Supply Chain Management—the Fourth Distribution Channel. *Policy-making Reference, 15*(1), 11–15.

Xu, K., & Leung, M. T. (2008). Stocking policy in a two-party vendor managed channel with space restrictions. *International Journal of Production Economics.* doi:. doi:10.1016/j.ijpe.2008.11.003

Xu, L., & Beamon, B. (2006). Supply chain coordination and cooperation mechanisms: An attribute-based approach. *Journal of Supply Chain Management, 42*(1), 4–12. doi:10.1111/j.1745-493X.2006.04201002.x

Yadavalli, V. S. S., Anbazhagan, N., & Arivarignan, G. (2004). A Two-Commodity Continuous Review Inventory System with Lost Sales. *Stochastic Analysis and Applications, 22*, 479–497. doi:10.1081/SAP-120028606

Yadavalli, V. S. S., Van Schoor Cde, W., Strashein, J. J., & Udayabaskaran, S. (2004). A single product perishing inventory model with demand interaction. *ORiON, 20*(2), 109–124.

Yakovlev, I. V., & Anderson, M. L. (2001). Lessons from an ERP Implementation. IT Professional Magazine, 3(4, Jul/Aug), 24-30.

Yang, P. C., & Wee, H. M. (2002). A single-vendor and multiple-buyers production–inventory policy for a deteriorating item. *European Journal of Operational Research, 143*, 570–581. doi:10.1016/S0377-2217(01)00345-9

Yao, M. J., & Chiou, C. C. (2004). On a replenishment coordination model in an integrated supply chain with one vendor and multiple buyers. *European Journal of Operational Research, 159*, 406–419. doi:10.1016/j.ejor.2003.08.024

Yao, Y., & Dresner, M. (2008). The inventory value of information sharing, continuous replenishment, and vendor-managed inventory. *Transportation Research Part E, Logistics and Transportation Review, 44*, 361–378. doi:10.1016/j.tre.2006.12.001

Yao, Y., Evers, P.T. & Dresner, M.B. (2005). Supply chain integration in vendor-managed inventory. *Decision Support Systems*.

Yin, R. (2003). *Case Study Research, Design and Methods* (3rd ed.). London: Sage.

Yokota, T., Gen, M., & Li, Y. X. (1996). Genetic Algorithm for non linear mixed integer programming problems and its applications. *Computers & Industrial Engineering, 30*(4), 905–917. doi:10.1016/0360-8352(96)00041-1

Yongbeom, K., Lee, Z., & Gosain, S. (2005). Impediments to successful ERP implementation process. *Business Process Management Journal, 11*(2), 158–170. doi:10.1108/14637150510591156

Young, P., Chaki, N., & Berzins, V. & Luqi. (2003). Evaluation of middleware architectures in achieving system interoperability. In *Proceedings of 14th IEEE International Workshop on Rapid Systems Prototyping*, 108-116, IEEE.

Yu, C. (2005). Causes influencing the effectiveness of the post-implementation ERP system. *Industrial Management + Data Systems, 105*(1/2), 115-131.

Yu, H., Zeng, A. Z., & Zhao, L. (2008a). Analyzing the evolutionary stability of the vendor-managed inventory supply chains. *Computers & Industrial Engineering*. doi:.doi:10.1016/j.cie.2008.05.016

Yu, Y., Huang, G. Q., & Liang, L. (2008). Stackelberg Game-Theoretic Model for Optimizing advertising, pricing and Inventory Policies in Vendor Managed Inventory (VMI) Production supply chains. *Computers & Industrial Engineering*. doi:.doi:10.1016/j.cie.2008.12.003

Yu, Z., Yan, H., & Cheng, T. C. E. (2001). Benefits of information sharing with supply chain partnerships. *Industrial Management & Data Systems, 101*(3), 114–119. doi:10.1108/02635570110386625

Zhang, H., Li, X., & Liu, W. (2006). An AHP/DEA Methodology for 3PL Vendor Selection in 4PL. [Berlin: Springer-Verlag.]. *Lecture Notes in Computer Science, 3865*, 646–655. doi:10.1007/11686699_65

Zhang, H., Li, X., Liu, W., Li, B., & Zhang, Z. (2004). *An application of the AHP in 3PL vendor selection of a 4PL system.* Paper presented at the IEEE International conference on Systems, Man and Cybernetics.

Zhongwei, Z., & Jianzhong, X. (2008). *Research of the Application of Fuzzy AHP in Supplier Evaluation and Selection.* Paper presented at the 4th International Conference on Wireless Communications, Networking and Mobile Computing, (WiCOM '08).

Zhu, J., Tian, Z., T., Li, Sun, W., & al, e. (2004). Model driven business process integration and management. A case study with bank sinoPac regional platform. *IBM Journal of Research and development*.

Zhu, Q., & Sarkis, J. (2004). Relationships between operational practices and performance among early adopters of green supply chain management practices in Chinese manufacturing enterprises. *Journal of Operations Management, 22*, 265–289. doi:10.1016/j.jom.2004.01.005

Zineldin, M. (2000). Beyond relationship marketing: Technologicalship marketing.

Zinn, W., & Levy, M. (1988). Speculative Inventory Management: A Total Channel Perspective. *International Journal of Physical Distribution & Materials Management, 18*, 34–39.

Zipkin, P. H. (1991). *Foundations of Inventory Management*.

Zipkin, P. H. (2000). *Foundations of Inventory Management*. Boston: McGraw Hill.

Zou, P., & Yuan, Y.-N. (2009). Supplier selection based on EAHP/GRAP. *Xitong Gongcheng Lilun Yu Shijian/System Engineering . Theory into Practice, 29*(3), 69–75.

# About the Contributors

**S. Parthasarathy**, Head, Department of Computer Applications, Thiagarajar College of Engineering, Madurai, India is a B.Sc., (Mathematics), M.C.A. (Master of Computer Applications), M.Phil., (Computer Science), P.G.D.B.A. (Business Administration), P.G.D.P.M. (Planning and Project Management) professional. He holds a Ph.D., in Computer Applications from Anna University, Chennai, India. A habitual rank holder, he has been teaching at the post-graduate level since 2002. He has published research papers in peer reviewed international journals, national and international conferences. He has authored several chapters in the refereed edited books of IGI, USA. He has written a textbook "Enterprise Resource Planning (ERP) – A Managerial and Technical Perspective", published by The New Age International Publishers (P), Ltd., New Delhi, India, in the year 2007. He is the Principal Investigator for the research project "Requirements Management in COTS Software Projects" funded by the University Grants Commission, New Delhi, India. His current research interests include enterprise information systems, enterprise resource planning and software engineering. He can be reached at spcse@tce.edu and parthatce@gmail.com.

\*\*\*

**N. Anbazhagan** is currently Reader in Alagappa University, Karaikudi, India. He received his M. Phil and Ph.D in Mathematics from Madurai Kamaraj University, Madurai, India and M.Sc in Mathematics from Cardamom Planters Association College, Bodinayakanur, India. He has received Young Scientist Award (2004) from DST, New Delhi, India, Young Scientist Fellowship (2005) from TNSCST, Chennai, India and Career Award for Young Teachers(2005) from AICTE, India. He has successfully completed one research project, funded by DST, India. His research interests include Stochastic modeling, Optimization Techniques, Inventory and Queueing Systems. He has published the research articles in several journals, including Stochastic analysis and applications, APJOR and ORiON.

**S.P. Anbuudayasankar** belongs to the Faculty of Mechanical Engineering Department at Amrita School of Engineering, Amrita University. He holds a Bachelor's degree in Mechanical Engineering, a Master's degree in Industrial Engineering and a Management degree in Production. He is currently pursuing the doctoral research in the area of Combinatorial Optimization Problems. His research interests include multi-objective optimization and supply chain location and allocation problems. He has published several papers in national and international Journals and Conferences.

Copyright © 2010, IGI Global, distributing in print or electronic forms without written permission of IGI Global is prohibited.

**S. R. Balasundaram** earned a doctorate in Computer Applications from National Institute of Technology, Tiruchirappalli, India in 2008 with an M.C.A. from P.S.G.College of Technology, Coimbatore, India. Working since 1987 in the Department of Computer Applications, NIT, Trichy. Research interest includes E-Learning/Web Based Learning; Pervasive Computing; Mobile Data Management. Has more than 20 publications in refereed International Conferences and Journals. Currently working as Assistant Professor.

**Rajbir Singh Bhatti**, is an Asst. Professor at the SBS Government College of Engg & Technology in Ferozepur,(Punjab),India, and is pursuing Ph.D at the Indian Institute of Technology Roorkee. He has a B.E. in Industrial Engg. from Thapar Institute of Engg & Technology, Patiala, and has a M.Tech. in Industrial engineering from NIT Jalandhar(Punjab). He has 10 years of teaching experience at graduate level and one year in industry. His areas of interest include Industrial Engineering, Quality Engineering, Production & Operations Management, Quality Standards, Total Quality Management (TQM) and Supply Chain Management (SCM). He has been a quality consultant prior to his present assignment and has vast experience in quality certifications. He is the corresponding author and can be reached at rajbirbhatti@gmail.com.

**Félix Biscarri** received the B.Sc. degree in electronic physics and the Ph.D. degree in computer science from the University of Seville, Seville, Spain, in 1991 and 2001 respectively. He is currently a Coordinating Professor of Power Electronic with the Polytechnic University School of Seville. His research areas include electricity markets, electrical customer classification and fraud detection in the power electric industry.

**Jesús Biscarri** received the B.Sc. and the Ph.D. degrees in electronic physics from the University of Seville, Seville, Spain, in 1982 and 2001 respectively. He has been working in Endesa since 1985 at IT, Measure and Non Technical Losses Control Areas. Currently he is also collaborating as Associate Professor at the Polytechnic University School of Seville.

**Rogerio Atem de Carvalho** holds Doctoral and Master degrees in Production Engineering, and a Bachelor degree in Computer Science. He is a teacher and researcher with Fluminense Federal Institute (IFF) and State University of North Fluminense (UENF), Campos, Brazil. He is also a consultant for Brazilian and foreign companies, and a project leader for enterprise systems development initiatives of the Brazilian Federal Government. He was awarded in 2006 by IFIP for his research on Free/Open Source Enterprise Information Systems (EIS), and is a member of the IFIP's Working Group on EIS (IFIP TC8 WG8.9). His research interests also include Project Management and Decision Support Systems.

**Jason C. H. Chen** received Ph.D. in Business Administration with the areas of Management Information Systems in the year 1985 from Management Science and Computer Science department , The University of Texas USA. . He is currently working as Professor and Coordinator of the Management Information Systems, Gonzaga University, Spokane. He has published books and many research papers in International / National journals. He is presently acting as guest editor and Editorial member for many International Journals. his research area include e-commerce, e-and DSS business models.

**Maya Daneva** is an assistant professor with the Information Systems department at the University of Twente, the Netherlands, where she leads a research program on ERP Requirements-based project estimation. Maya serves as the empirical research liaison to the Dutch IT industry and the Dutch Function Point User Group (NESMA). Prior to this, Maya spent 9 years as a business process analyst in the Architecture Group of TELUS, Canada's second largest telecommunication company in Toronto, where she consulted on ERP requirement engineering processes and their evaluation as well as on ERP-supported coordination models and business process design. Maya authored more than 70 research and experience papers.

**C. Elango**, Reader in Mathematical Sciences, Cardamom Planters' Association College, has earned his B.Sc degree from Scott Christian College, Nagarkovil and M.Sc degree form ANJA College Sivakasi. He obtained Ph.D in School of Mathamatical sciences, Madurai Kamaraj University, Madurai and he is an active researcher in Stochastic modeling and supply chain Management Systems. He has published more than 15 research articles in reputed journels. He is a regular member of Institute for operations and researchs and management science (INFORMS), USA.

**K. Ganesh** is currently working as Assistant Consultant in Manufacturing Industry Solutions Unit at Tata Consultancy Services, Limited, Mumbai. He holds a Bachelor's degree in Mechanical and Production Engineering, a Master's degree in Industrial Engineering and a Doctorate from IIT Madras. His research interests lie in the application of meta-heuristics and decision-making tools to logistics management. He has published several papers in leading research journals such as the European Journal of Operational Research and International Journal of Advanced Manufacturing Technology.

**Juan Ignacio Guerrero** received the B.Sc. degree in Computer Science from the University of Seville, Seville, Spain, in 2006. He is currently an Assistant Professor and he is pursuing the Ph.D. degree at the Electronic Technology Department of the University of Seville. His research areas include artificial intelligence, neural networks, expert systems and data mining focus on Utilities System Management.

**Manoj Kumar Jha**, a Gold Medallist from XLRI has been associated with Enterprise Resource Systems for over a decade. In different roles, he has experienced the ERP adoption from various perspectives and the present article is his attempt to share his experiences. Apart from being involved in full life cycle ERP implementation projects, he has also worked on Business Process Transformation projects for large multinational organizations primarily in the area of HCM. Apart from contributing to successes of organizations in HCM areas. Manoj is also interested in Supply Chain Management, Project Management, Theory of Constraints and Rural Marketing.

**Björn Johansson** holds a Doctoral and a Licentiate degree in Information Systems Development from the Department of Management & Engineering at Linköping University and a Bachelor degree in Business Informatics from Jönköping International Business School. He defended his doctoral thesis "Deciding on Sourcing Option for Hosting of Software Applications in Organisations" in 2007. Currently he works at the Center for Applied ICT at Copenhagen Business School, within the 3gERP project (http://www.3gERP.org). He is a member of the IFIP Working Group on Diffusion, Adoption and Implementation of Information and Communication Technologies (IFIP TC8 WG8.6), the IFIP Working Group on Enterprise Information Systems (IFIP TC8 WG8.9) and the research networks: VITS Work practice development, IT usage, Coordination and Cooperation and KiO Knowledge in Organizations.

**Rajeshwar. S. Kadadevaramath** received M.E Degree in Production Management in 1991 from Karnataka University Dharwar (India) and PhD Degree in supply chain management in the year 1991 from Anna University Chennai (India) . He is currently working as Professor in the Department of Industrial Engineering and Management , Siddaganga Institute of Technology, Tumkur (India).He has published totally fifteen research papers in International / National journals, and presented forty papers in International and National Conferences. He is acting as a referee for International Journals of Revenue Management (IJRM), International Journal Business and Systems Research (IJBSR), International Journal of Artificial Systems Technology & Applications (IJASTA Presently, he is the Editorial member for International Journal of Revenue Management and International Journal of Business and Systems Research ( Inderscience Publications) from India.

**Anurag Keshan** is currently working as an Consultant at IBM India. He is currently posted in Sweden on a field project. Mr Anurag Keshan has completed his Bachelor's degree in engineering from Manipal Institute of Technology. His email id is : anuragkeshan@gmail.com

**Dinesh Kumar** is a Professor at the IIT Roorkee in the department of Mechanical and Industrial Engineering. He obtained his B.Sc- Hons, degree in Mechanical Engg. in 1980 from Punjab University, Chandigarh. He completed his master's degree in Mechanical Engineering University of Roorkee in 1984. It was in 1991, that Dr Dinesh Kumar completed his PhD in Mechanical engineering from the University of Roorkee. He has about 125 publications to his credit and his areas of interest are supply chains, reliability engineering and maintenance engineering.

**Pradeep Kumar** is Professor and Head of the Department of Mechanical & Industrial Engineering, IIT Roorkee (India). He is also a Joint Professor at the Department of Management Studies at IIT Roorkee. During 1996, he was a visiting Assistant Professor in the department of Industrial and Manufacturing System Engineering, West Virginia University, U.S.A. He has also served the Department of Industrial and Manufacturing Engineering, Wayne State University, U.S.A. as a Research Associate during 1998-1999. He has contributed more than 300 research papers in industrial engineering, supply chains and advanced manufacturing. His other research interests include Industrial Engineering, Quality Engineering: Robust Design Methodologies, Reliability Engineering, Project Management, Production & Operations Management, Total Quality Management (TQM), Supply Chain Management (SCM), Multi-Characteristics Optimization, Advanced Manufacturing Processes and Metal Casting. He has supervised 15 Ph.D. theses while 7 Ph. D theses are in progress. He is also offering consultancy in the areas of his interest to the industry.

**Sanjay Kumar** is currently working as Associate Professor of Operations Management & Information Systems, at XLRI School of Management, Jamshedpur, India. Dr Kumar is a renowned researcher and expert in the field of ERP systems. He was named amongst the top 30 researchers in the world (2006) in the field of ERP systems by SAP Germany. He is a part of a select global 'Think Tank', chosen by SAP to guide it's search for new technologies at the cutting edge of research for the year 2006. In year 2008, his research project titled "Effect of subcontractor relationship 'closeness' on MES integration requirements for shop floor visibility in distributed manufacturing" won the "First SAP Research and Innovation Award, India" and was awarded a project funding of Rs 1.1 million. He also held various technical and administrative positions in organizations such as Eicher Goodearth Ltd, LML Ltd and Premier Data Products P. Ltd, (where he was working as the Managing Director). He often serves as a Consultant/ advisor for various public sector and private firms. He holds a PhD in Industrial and Management Engineering from Indian Institute of Technology, Kanpur, India, M. Tech in Manufacturing Science from Indian Institute of Technology, Kanpur, India and a B. E. (Mechanical Engineering) from Indian Institute of Technology, Roorkee, India. His email id is : Professor.skumar@gmail.com

**Shikha Lal** did her masters in Business Administration from Ghan Shyam Binani Academy of Management Sciences, UP Technical University, Lucknow. She did her B.Sc. from Purvanchal University and currently working as a Research Scholar at Faculty of Management Studies (FMS), Banaras Hindu University (BHU), Varanasi. Her doctoral research work is based on the Customer Relationship Management (CRM) practices in Indian retail sector.

**Carlos León** received the B.Sc. degree in electronic physics in 1991 and the Ph.D. degree in computer science in 1995, both from the University of Seville, Seville, Spain. He is a professor of Electronic Engineering at the University of Seville since 1991 and currently CIO of the University of Seville. His research areas include knowledge based systems and computational intelligence focus on Utilities System Management. He is a Member of the IEEE Power Engineering Society.

**Rodrigo Soares Manhães** holds a Master degree in Operations Research and Computational Intelligence. He is a associated researcher with Fluminense Federal Institute, system developer on North Fluminense State University, agile development practitioner and has been teaching undergraduate courses for the last five years. He is author of articles on decision support systems and software development.

**Marco Marabelli** works as a research assistant at CeTIF (Research Center on Technology, Innovation, and Finance) and is a PhD student in Management at Cattolica University of Milan. His research focuses on organizational learning, knowledge management, and innovation. His research method is qualitative and he focuses on ERP implementation and usage to dig deeper into the process of appropriation of IS by users. He also studies how such process is created to understand the behavioral dynamics that allow organizations to develop learning cycles, in a multilevel perspective. He also focuses on how (acquired) knowledge is disseminated within organizations and how to deal with knowledge stickiness. Finally he studies organizational ambidexterity and he focuses on cultural and informal practices which help organizations managing both exploratory and exploitative innovation. Marco Marabelli is reviewer for AOM, ECIS, and ICIS and participates to these conferences as attendant, presenter, and session chair. His teaching activities include organizational theories and ARE management courses.

**Souvik Mazumdar** is currently pursuing his MBA degree from Tata Institute of Social Sciences, Mumbai, India. Mr Mazumdar has completed his Bachelor's degree in engineering from Manipal Institute of Technology. His email id is : souvik.cv.use@gmail.com

**Rocío Millán** received the B.Sc. degree and the Ph.D. degree in Economics and Business Administration in 1985 and 1996 respectively, both from the University of Seville, Spain. She worked as professor of Economic Theory and Finance in this University for more than 10 years and is working for Endesa as Metering Control Deputy Director. Her research areas include public deficit, energy futures markets and NTL's detection in electricity companies.

**Ashutosh Mohan** did his masters in Business Administration from Faculty of Management Studies (FMS), Banaras Hindu University, Varanasi in 2000 with top honors. He worked as Senior Research Fellow at Faculty of Management Studies (FMS), University of Delhi, for three years after clearing the UGC-JRF examination and received Doctorate Degree. He is a recipient of AICTE's Career Award for Young Teachers (CAYT) and has one Major Project funded by ICSSR, New Delhi. He has published nearly six papers in referred journals and presented more than 18 research papers at various international and national forums including the paper presentation in prestigious IPSERA conference at University of San Diego, USA. He is also a recipient of CAPS Fellowship, University of Arizona, USA. He is serving as Member of Editorial Board from India (one out of two members from India) of esteemed journal titled as Journal of Supply Chain Management, USA. He conducted and / or served as resource person at various forums such as MDP of GAIL & Apollo Hospital, AICTE – QIP Programmes, TSM, FMS-DU, IIT-D, UGC-Refresher and Orientation Courses etc. He coordinated One National Conference, Two Executive Development Programmes (EDP) and Two Quality Improvement Programmes sponsored by AICTE. He worked as faculty at Centre for Management Studies, Jamia Millia Islamia, New Delhi for two years. Presently, he has been in teaching, research and consultancy as Asstt. Professor at Faculty of Management Studies (FMS), Banaras Hindu University (BHU), Varanasi, and is currently focusing on the Supply Chain Management (SCM) practices and its collaboration with Customer Relationship Management (CRM) in Retailing and SMEs.

**K. M. Mohanasudaram** received his bachelor degree in mechanical engineering from Madras University, Chennai, India in 1982 and Master of Engineering, degree and PhD from Bharathiar University Coimbatore, India in 1986 and in1997 respectively. His research interests include simulation of manufacturing systems, industrial engineering and supply chain management. He has coordinated/ organized National and International conferences. He has published many technical papers in various international and national journals conferences.

**K Mohandas** is Professor and Chairman of Mechanical Engineering Department at Amrita School of Engineering, Amrita University. He holds a Bachelor's degree in Mechanical Engineering, a Master's degree in Maintenance Engineering and Management and a Doctorate from IIT Madras. His research interests lie in Reliability Engineering and Optimization. He has published papers in leading research journals such as Reliability Engineering and System Safety and Microelectronics and reliability

**Íñigo Monedero** received the B.Sc. and Ph.D. degrees in computer science from the University of Seville, Seville, Spain, in 1994 and 2004 respectively. He joined the Automatics and Robotics Department for two years and he is currently professor from the Electronic Technology Department of the University of Seville since 1998. His research areas include artificial intelligence, expert systems and data mining in the power electricity industry.

**Subramanian Nachiappan** is an Associate Professor in Mechanical Engineering at the Thiagarajar College of Engineering, Madurai, India. He was a visiting scholar at Nottingham university business school, He has two years of industrial experience and Ten years of teaching experience. He has published more than 60 technical papers in refereed journals and conferences and is connected with three research and development projects funded by AICTE / DRDO. He has coordinated training programmes in Supply chain management and CAD/CAM modeling software. He has won a BOYSCAST Fellow Award, Career Award for young teachers, Young Scientist Fellowship Award, best paper award and prizes for his academic achievements. His research has appeared in Industrial Marketing Management, European Journal of Operational Research, International Journal of Production Research, Journal of Advanced Manufacturing Systems, International Journal of Industrial and Systems Engineering, International Journal of Logistics System Management and International Journal of Service and Operations Management. He is in the editorial board of internal journal of integrated supply management and serves as a reviewer in numerous top tier reputed production and operations management journals. His research interests are performance measurement, supply chain operations, modeling and analysis of manufacturing systems.

**Prashant R. Nair** is presently working as Vice-Chairman of Information Technology at Amrita University, Coimbatore. He has 10 years of experience in teaching, training, consultancy, research, and academic administration. He was a rank holder from the third batch of Amrita School of Business. He has also taught at academic programs in USA and Europe, having been a visiting faculty at University of California, San Diego, and Sofia University. He has over 10 publications in leading journals and conferences like "Indian Management," "University News", "D-Lib", "National Convention of Computer Engineers", "Asia Pacific Telecom" etc. He is currently holding the positions of Honorary Secretary of Institution of Electronics and Telecommunication Engineers (IETE), Tamil Nadu region and Joint Secretary of Computer Society of India (CSI), Coimbatore Chapter. He has been on the program committee of the World Congress of Computer Science, Computer Engineering and Applied Science since 2007.

**Jawahar Natarajan** received his B.E. (Hons) degree in Mechanical Engineering from Madras University, M.E. Degree with distinction in Production Engineering from Annamalai University and completed his Ph.D. in Bharathiar University. He was employed in TI Diamond Chain Ltd., Madras from 1982 to 1983 and NLC Ltd, Neyveli from 1983 to 1989. Since 1989 he is working in the department of mechanical engineering of Thiagarajar College of Engineering, Madurai and currently holds the post of Professor & Head. He has published 41 papers in refereed journals and 120 technical articles in conferences, and completed four research projects. He is a reviewer for many journals including IEEE (ASE), IJPR, IJRP, EJOR, IJAR and JIMO. He has coordinated CNC Programming and SCM programmes. He is a Fellow Member in IE (India), ISME, IIPE, ISTE and ORSI. Six scholars have obtained Ph.D. under his guidance and currently working in Logistics, SCM, Optimization and Evolutionary Computation.

**Sue Newell** is the Cammarata Professor of Management, Bentley University, US and a part-time Professor of Information Management at Warwick University, UK. She has a BSc and PhD from Cardiff University, UK. Sue is currently the PhD Director at Bentley. Sue's research focuses on understanding the relationships between innovation, knowledge and organisational networking (ikon) - primarily from an organisational theory perspective. She was one of the founding members of ikon, a research centre based at Warwick University. She has been involved in many of the ikon projects and has recently completed a project titled 'The evolution of biomedical knowledge: interactive innovation in the UK and US'. She is also involved in research which focuses on exploring the implementation and use of packaged information systems, for example to support distributed project work or health records. Her research emphasises a critical, practice-based understanding of the social aspects of innovation, change, knowledge management and inter-firm networked relations. Sue has published over 80 journal articles in the areas of organization studies, management and information systems, as well as numerous books and book chapters.

**Lidia Ogiela** is a computer scientist, mathematician, and economist. She received Master of Science in mathematics from the Pedagogical University in Krakow, and Master of Business Administration in management and marketing from AGH University of Science and Technology in Krakow, both in 2000. In 2005 she was awarded the title of Doctor of Computer Science and Engineering at the Faculty of Electrical, Automatic Control, Computer Science and Electronic Engineering of the AGH University of Science and Technology, for her thesis and research on cognitive analysis techniques and its application in intelligent information systems. She is an author a few dozen of scientific international publications on information systems, cognitive analysis techniques, biomedical engineering, and computational intelligence methods. She is a member of few prestigious international scientific societies as: SIAM – Society for Industrial and Applied Mathematics, as well as SPIE – The International Society for Optical Engineering. Currently she is at the associate professor position, and works in Management Faculty at the AGH University of Science and Technology.

**Marek R. Ogiela** D.Sc, Ph.D., works in Bio-Cybernetics laboratory at the AGH University of Science and Technology in Krakow. In 1992 graduated from the Mathematics and Physics Department at the Jagiellonian University. In 1996 for his honours doctoral thesis on syntactic methods of analysis and image recognition he was awarded the title of Doctor of Control Engineering and Robotics at the Faculty of Electrical, Automatic Control, Computer Science and Electronic Engineering of the AGH University of Science and Technology. In 2001 he was awarded the title of Doctor Habilitated in Computer Science for his research on medical image automatic analysis and understanding. In 2005 he received a professor title in technical sciences. Member of numerous world scientific associations as well as of the Forecast Committee 'Poland 2000 Plus' of the Polish Academy of Science and member of Interdisciplinary Scientific Committee of the Polish Academy of Arts and Sciences (Bio cybernetics and Biomedical Engineering Section). Author of more than 150 scientific international publications on pattern recognition and image understanding, artificial intelligence, IT systems and biocybernetics. Author of recognised monographs in the field of cryptography and IT techniques; author of an innovative approach to cognitive medical image analysis. For his achievements in these fields he was awarded many prestigious scientific honors, including Prof. Takliński´s award (twice) and the first winner of Prof. Engel`s award, nominated in the category Science to the Silver Nike award in 2003. Reviewer of world scientific periodicals.

**Petraq J. Papajorgji** is a Research Scientist at the Center for Applied Optimization at the Industrial and Systems Engineering department, University of Florida , Gainesville, Fl USA. His area of expertise is modeling methodologies with a focus on the Model Driven Architecture (MDA). He is author of a number of scientific papers and of two books on software engineering. Dr. Petraq Papajorgji is editor-in-chief of the International Journal of Agricultural and Environmental Information Systems.

**Panos M. Pardalos** is a Distinguished Professor and Director of the Center for Applied Optimization at the Industrial and Systems Engineering department, University of Florida , Gainesville, Fl USA. His area of expertise is optimization. Professor Pardalos is author and editor of a long list of books and is editor-in-chief, associate editor and member of advisory board of 27 scientific internationally known journals.

**Muthu Ramachandran** is currently a principal lecturer in the Faculty of Innovation North: Information and Technology, Leeds Metropolitan University, Leeds, UK. Previously he spent nearly eight years in industrial research (Philips Research Labs and Volantis Systems Ltd, Surrey, UK) where he worked on software architecture, reuse, and testing. Prior to that he was teaching at Liverpool John Moores University and received his PhD was from Lancaster University. His first career started as a research scientist from India Space Research Labs where he worked on real time systems development projects. Ramachandran has widely published articles on journals, chapters, and conferences on various advanced topics on software engineering and education. He did his masters degrees from Indian Institute of Technology, Madras and from Madurai Kamaraj University, Madurai, India. Muthu is also a member of various professional organizations and computer societies: IEEE, ACM, BCS, HEA.

**B. Ramadoss** earned a doctorate in Applied Mathematics from IIT Bombay in 1983 and was awarded an M.Tech. in CSE from IIT Delhi in 1995. Having more than 24 years of teaching and research experience at National Institute of Technology, Tiruchirappalli, India. Was on a teaching assignment with Sharjah College, Sharjah, UAE during 1997-2000. Research interest includes Software Testing; Multimedia Database; Web based Learning. Has more than 25 publications in refereed International Journals and Conferences. Awarded Best Teacher in Computer Applications at NIT, Trichy during 2006-2007. Currently working as Professor.

**Al-Marri Salem** is currently full time PhD student and doing his research in Information Management at Leeds Metropolitan University, Leeds, UK. His area of research is "A Critical Role of Information Technology / Information System Managers in the Significant Company in case of Natural Disasters in Qatar". He graduated in MSc Information System from University of Hertfordshire 2004. He attended many conferences, and attended seminars in Research philosophy and methods that was a part of his degree at the University of Hertfordshire. Al-Marri has widely published articles on disaster management issues, and attended conferences on various advanced topics on Information Technology and disaster management. Mr. Al-Marri has been working for eight years for the H.E. Minister of Education Office in Qatar with his recent designation being a Director.

**Ashim Singla** is a PhD and MCA from Punjabi University, Patiala. Presently, Dr Singla is working as Assistant Professor with Indian Institute of Foreign Trade, New Delhi. He has also worked with Institute of Management Technology (IMT) Ghaziabad, Punjab Comm. Ltd, Mohali, and Networld Solutions, Chandigarh, India. His area of interest includes ERP, Databases, Web Technology and Programming languages. His research comprises of articles on ERP systems, published in a variety of national /international journals. He has also attended several National/ International conferences on IT systems and executed several key IT projects like: Order tracking system, portal for online shopping business model, Network Management System (NMS) for Department of Telecom (DoT) and eLearning solution.

**Ryszard Tadeusiewicz,** Studied at the Electrical Engineering Department of the University of Mining and Metallurgy in Krakow (Poland) from which he graduated (with honors) in 1971. Additionally, after receiving his degree in Automatic Control Engineering, he studied at the Faculty of Medicine at the Medical Academy, as well as undertook studies in the field of mathematical and computer methods in economics. He has written and published over 600 scientific papers, which were published in prestigious Polish and foreign scientific journals as well as numerous conference presentations - both national and international. Prof. Tadeusiewicz wrote over 70 scientific monographs and books, among them are highly popular textbooks (which had many reprints). He was supervisor of 56 doctoral thesis and reviewer of more than 200 doctoral thesis. Polish scientists elected him to be President of IEEE Computational Intelligence Society – Polish Chapter, and members of Polish Academy of Science elected him to be member of this Academy.

**M. Vignesh** is working as a lecturer in the Department of Management Studies, The American College, Madurai and handling papers as Information Technology for Managerial Decisions, datamining and CRM, E-Business and Operations Management. He is a post graduate in Agriculture from Tamilnadu Agricultural University and later on he completed his Masters degree in Business Administration and also a holder of post graduate diploma in Bioinformatics. After gaining experience in industry atmosphere, he turned out as an academician. He presented papers in National and International Conference. His area of interests includes trends in E-business, cyber entrepreneurship and novel aspects as grid computing and cloud computing.

# Index

Copyright © 2010, IGI Global, distributing in print or electronic forms without written permission of IGI Global is prohibited.

## N

## V